AMERICAN FOREIGN POLICY & PROCESS

AMERICAN FOREIGN POLICY & PROCESS

THIRD EDITION

James M. McCormick
Iowa State University

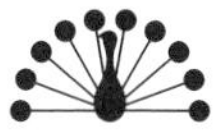

F. E. Peacock Publishers, Inc.
Itasca, Illinois

Cover and part openers:

J. Patton/H. Armstrong Roberts

Photo credits:

Page	
5	UPI/Corbis-Bettmann
37	Archive Photos
71	Archive Photos
109	UPI/Corbis-Bettmann
151	Reuters/Corbis-Bettmann
215	Reuters/Gary Hershorn/Archive Photos
275	Reuters/Corinne Dufka/Archive Photos
321	Reuters/Corbis-Bettmann
373	Reuters/Archive Photos
423	Corbis-Bettmann
471	Reuters/Corbis-Bettmann
521	Wide World Photos
573	Reuters/Rick Wilking/Archive Photos

Library of Congress Catalog Card No. 97-66352
ISBN 0-87581-410-7
Printing 10 9 8 7 6 5 4 3 2 1
Year 03 02 01 00 99 98

CONTENTS

CHRONOLOGIES, DOCUMENTS AND DOCUMENT SUMMARIES, FIGURES, MAPS, AND TABLES

CHRONOLOGIES

DOCUMENTS AND DOCUMENT SUMMARIES

FIGURES

MAPS

TABLES

PREFACE

The third edition of *American Foreign Policy and Process* is revised and updated, covering policy and process developments through the Clinton administration. The book is intended to serve as a comprehensive text for the first course in U.S. foreign policy and as a supplemental text in a global politics or comparative foreign policy course where American actions are analyzed. In addition, it remains appropriate as a ready reference for the first graduate course in the study of American foreign policy or the foreign policy process.

Values and beliefs remain as the basic organizing theme for the text because policy actions are always taken within a value context. Yet, this emphasis on values and beliefs is not necessarily done in a way to promote a particular point of view. Instead, the intent is to portray how values and beliefs toward foreign affairs have changed over the course of the history of the Republic and how U.S. foreign policy has thus changed from its earliest years through the end of the Cold War and beyond.

To accomplish this end, the text is once again divided into three parts. Part 1, which consists of six chapters, focuses upon the values and beliefs that have shaped policy historically (Chapter 1), during the height of American globalism and the Cold War years (Chapters 2 and 3), during the immediate post-Vietnam years of Nixon, Ford, and Carter (Chapter 4), during the Reagan-Bush years (Chapter 5), and during the Clinton administration (Chapter 6). In each of these chapters, we discuss a wide variety of foreign policy actions that illustrate the various values and beliefs of the particular period and administration. Part 2, which also consists of six chapters, examines in some detail the policy-making process and how various institutions and groups—the president (Chapter 7), the Congress (Chapter 8), the key bureaucracies (Chapters 9 and 10), political parties and interest groups (Chapter 11), and the media and public opinion (Chapter 12)—compete to promote their own values and beliefs in American policy abroad. At this juncture, too, we provide essential information on how foreign policy decisions are made, and we assess the relative importance of these institutions and groups in that process. Part 3, a concluding chapter, discusses alternate views of what values and beliefs may shape American foreign policy as we approach the twenty-first century.

Those familiar with the second edition will immediately recognize some changes. First, each chapter has been revised and fully updated to reflect important changes in both U.S. policy and in the policy-making process. Second, while the total number of chapters has remained the same at thirteen, several chapters have been restructured and a new separate chapter on the Clinton administration has been added. Chapters 2 and 3, for example, now contain some new research on American actions throughout the Cold War and on the role of the Korean War in particular. Chapter 4 continues to contrast the approaches adopted by the Nixon and Carter administrations in the post-Vietnam era, but Chapter 5 now combines the Reagan and Bush administrations and illustrates the similarities and differences in approach of these two presidencies. Chapter 6 on the Clinton administration is entirely new and discusses how that administration has sought to adopt a different approach to the post–Cold War world than did its predecessors, including actions in the second term. Chapters 7 and 8 update and include the latest research on the role of the president and the role of Congress through the Clinton presidency. Chapters 9 and 10 once again discuss the bureaucracies across two chapters, but the economic bureaucracies have been expanded and their role discussed in greater detail. Chapters 11 and 12 are separate treatments of political parties and interest groups on the one hand and media and public opinion on the other. The most significant addition here is an entire new section on the media and its impact on the foreign policy process.

Third, this edition also incorporates the use of a number of tables, figures, and maps to portray more fully the story of American foreign policy and the process of policy formulation. Chronologies of major events, including new ones on Somalia, Haiti, and Bosnia, and summaries of key documents, including the NAFTA, GATT, and START II pacts, remain an important feature to provide greater detail to the discussion and to enable students to gain a greater understanding of these important foreign policy events. Finally, and perhaps most importantly, greater attention was added to make the writing "reader friendly" by providing the most up-to-date policy examples and through greater use of headings throughout the text.

In the course of undertaking these substantial revisions, I have incurred a number of debts to many individuals and institutions. I am now happy to have the opportunity to acknowledge my thanks to several of them publicly. First of all, colleagues at a variety of institutions offered their comments and suggestions for improving the book from the second edition: Lawrence LeBlanc of Marquette University, James M. Lindsay of the University of Iowa, Priscilla L. Southwell of the University of Oregon, Donald Sylvan of Ohio State University, and several anonymous instructors from the Air Force ROTC program who generously (and accurately) critiqued the second edition. I am particularly indebted to James M. Lindsay for his careful reading of the revised manuscript, his detailed suggestions for changing it, and his numerous suggestions for structural and stylistic improvements. His efforts saved me from several inaccuracies and helped to improve the final product. Thanks, too, to Eugene R. Wittkopf of Louisiana State University for allowing me to use some recent data on U.S. foreign policy and for his good advice on completing this revision, and to Ole R. Holsti of Duke University and James Meernik of the University of North Texas for permission to use their data. An author's stubbornness, of course, precluded me from incorporating all of the suggestions of these good critics, but I can assure them that the comments were given careful consideration.

Second, colleagues in the Department of Political Science at Iowa State University provided moral support from time to time. I particularly want to thank Young Kihl, Jorgen Rasmussen, and Jerry Shakeshaft for their suggestions over several particular puzzles that arose in doing the revisions. Beverly Christensen and Josh Johanningmeier generously afforded me various forms of clerical and research assistance during the course of doing these revisions, for which I am most thankful. Once again, too, I am delighted to thank the staff of the William Robert Parks and Ellen Sorge Parks Library at Iowa State University. They were superb in assisting me in obtaining numerous idiosyncratic pieces of information on American foreign policy. Finally, too, I am grateful to officials at various executive branch agencies who answered my peculiar inquiries, both graciously and often expeditiously.

Third, my students in the first course in U.S. foreign policy at Iowa State University and in a senior seminar on foreign policy institutions have been especially helpful to me since the last edition. They have graciously endured virtually all of the arguments presented here; they have gently challenged and questioned many of them; and they have often suggested important research that ought to be done! From that process, they have unwittingly contributed to making this a better text. I am delighted to acknowledge their contribution.

Fourth, I had the good fortune of working with an excellent copyeditor during the production stage of the book. John Beasley carefully perused the manuscript for potential inaccuracies, cheerfully brought to my attention several passages that needed clarification or correction, and gently suggested the need for more headings at various locations. For such attention to detail on my behalf, I am indeed grateful. Kim Vander Steen, cheerfully and with great skill, carried out the production of the book, even as I made change after change in the proofs. For such assistance, I am most appreciative. I especially must acknowledge the assistance and encouragement provided by Dick Welna, associate publisher at F. E. Peacock Publishers, Inc. Slow as I was to complete this revision, he never lost faith. Indeed, he was a constant source of encouragement when the revisions seemed so daunting. For that I am most grateful. Finally, and as always, the support of Ted Peacock is greatly appreciated. As I noted in earlier editions, and which warrants repeating once again, from my first association with Peacock Publishers, I sensed the commitment to its authors and to quality publishing. Happily, I can report that those commitments were meaningful and remain wholly intact.

All of these individuals and institutions (and others whom I may have inadvertently omitted) deserve my sincere thanks. As always, though, final responsibility for the book rests with me, and any errors of fact and interpretation are mine alone.

I

VALUES AND POLICIES IN AMERICAN FOREIGN AFFAIRS

In Part I of *American Foreign Policy and Process*, we survey the beliefs and values that have been the basis of America's foreign policy actions. While we provide the reader with an overview of the beliefs that have shaped American foreign policy throughout its history, we place special emphasis on the post–World War II period—the era of greatest American global involvement. Values and beliefs have been chosen as the basic organizing scheme because policy actions are always taken within such a value context. The beginning analyst who can appreciate how belief systems influence policy choices will be in a good position to understand the foreign policy actions of a nation.

But values and beliefs cannot be understood in isolation; their importance is useful only within the context of actual foreign policy behavior. Thus, as an aid in appreciating how beliefs and attitudes have shaped American policy, we provide a narrative of foreign policy actions that reflect the underlying belief system during various periods of U.S. diplomatic history. It is our hope that through illustrations of both beliefs and actions, the reader will come away better able to interpret the foreign policy of the United States.

To accomplish these ends, Part I is divided into six chapters. In Chapter 1, we begin our analysis by discussing the effects of two important traditions on American foreign policy: the commitment to isolationism and the reliance on moral principles as important foreign policy guides. These traditions are reviewed to illustrate how they affected American international behavior throughout the first 150 years of the nation and how they continue to influence American policy to the present day. In Chapter 2, we focus on the development of American globalism in the immediate post–World War II years and how America's beliefs about the world changed sharply. We discuss in detail the emergence of the Cold War and the military, economic, and political dimensions of the new U.S. foreign policy doctrine—the global containment of communism. This doctrine both represented a dramatic departure from America's isolationist past, since it called for universal action on the part of the United States, and reflected substantial continuity as well, since it sought to be grounded in moral principle. In Chapter 3, we continue this discussion of America's emerging globalism by describing the new set of values and beliefs—the Cold War consensus—that came to dominate America's thinking about its role in the world from the late 1940s to the mid-1960s. This consensus produced a discernible set of foreign policy responses by the United States, which are now illustrated. In Chapter 3, we also analyze how these Cold War beliefs came under attack from abroad (through the weakening of the Eastern and Western blocs, the emergence of the Sino-Soviet split, the development of the nonaligned movement) and at home (principally over the Vietnam War) and how commitment to them within the American leadership and the public was lost.

With the breakdown of the Cold War consensus, finalized by the Vietnam War, succeeding administrations attempted to bring forth new foreign policy perspectives to replace this shattered world view. From the late 1960s to the present, the dominant foreign policy beliefs of U.S. policy makers have shown a considerable degree of fluctuation from one administration to the next. We have witnessed movement from the realist approach adopted by the Nixon-

Ford administrations to the idealist approach of the Carter administration, then back to elements of the Cold War in the Reagan administration, especially in its first term. In turn, the Bush administration adopted a more realist approach as it sought to deal with the apparent ending of the Cold War. Finally, the Clinton administration has sought to retard the isolationist impulse in the post–Cold War era and has proposed a return to some familiar democratic principles as a guide to America's future foreign policy.

The second half of Part I focuses on the differing value emphases within these administrations and how they have produced differing U.S. foreign policy behavior during the past several decades. In Chapter 4, we compare the "realist" approach that President Richard Nixon and National Security Advisor Henry Kissinger brought to American foreign policy in the late 1960s and early 1970s with the "idealist" approach that President Jimmy Carter adopted in the late 1970s. Each administration adopted foreign policy perspectives that were at odds with the key values of the Cold War years: Nixon and Kissinger's approach was characterized by a policy of détente with the Soviet Union and China; Carter's approach placed emphasis on "global politics." The two administrations also differed with one another in their compatibility with America's historical foreign policy values: Nixon and Kissinger's approach challenged this past, with its "power politics" emphasis in dealing with other states; Carter's approach was more in tune with that past in that it sought to reintroduce a stronger moral content to U.S. actions abroad, especially with regard to global human rights. Neither approach, however, succeeded in maintaining the support of the American people for very long, and both came under attack from critics at home and abroad.

In Chapter 5, we survey the values and beliefs of the Reagan-Bush years. While the Nixon and Carter administrations attempted to replace the values of the Cold War, the Reagan administration—in large measure—attempted to restore them. Upon assuming office, the Reagan administration turned away from the global approach that the Carter administration had initially chosen and adopted a bipolar view of the world—one closely reminiscent of the containment and Cold War policies of three decades earlier. While this approach enjoyed some initial success, it, too, encountered substantial resistance. By the end of the first term and the beginning of the second term of the Reagan presidency, a discernible change in course had taken place. Reagan's earlier approach was replaced by one that sought to be more accommodative in bilateral relations with the Soviet Union even as it continued to challenge that nation for influence in other areas of the world.

The Bush administration adopted many of the values and beliefs of the second term of the Reagan administration, but it also sought to put its own stamp on foreign policy. Most notably, the Bush administration tried to adopt foreign policy values that would allow it to address the significant transformations that had taken place in the international Communist movement. In reality, the approach largely resembled a combination of realist and idealist beliefs without setting a clear course for the post–Cold War era.

In Chapter 6, the foreign policy approach of the Clinton administration is analyzed in some detail. Like the Bush administration, the first term of the Clinton administration had difficulty developing a coherent set of policies to follow from the principles that it thought important to promote.

CHAPTER

I

AMERICA'S TRADITIONS IN FOREIGN POLICY

Wherever the standard of freedom and Independence has been or shall be unfurled, there will her heart, her benedictions and her prayers be. But she goes not abroad, in search of monsters to destroy. She is the well-wisher to the freedom and independence of all. She is the champion and vindicator only of her own.

Secretary of State John Quincy Adams
July 4, 1821

Do not think...that the questions of the day are mere questions of policy and diplomacy. They are shot through with the principles of life. We dare not turn from the principle that morality and not expediency is the thing that must guide us and that we will never condone iniquity because it is most convenient to do so.

President Woodrow Wilson
October 1913

Politics, at its roots, deals with values and value differences among individuals, groups, and nations. Various definitions of the term *politics* attest to the central place that values play in political life. Political scientist Harold Lasswell has written, for example, that politics "is the study of influence and the influential.... The influentials are those who get the most of what there is to get."[1] What there is to get, Lasswell continued, is values, such as "*deference, income, and safety.*"[2] Drawing upon Aristotle and Max Weber, Robert Dahl notes that what seems to be common across different definitions of politics is that they deal with values such as power, rule, and authority.[3] David Easton's famous definition of politics is even more explicit in its assessment of the relationship between politics and values: "Politics is the authoritative allocation of *values.*"[4] According to this definition, authority structures (e.g., governments) distribute something, and that something is values.

Values refer to "modes of conduct and end-states of existence" that guide people's lives. They are "abstract ideals" which serve as an "imperative" for action.[5] Further, values are viewed as "goods" (not in a material, but in an ethical sense) that ought to be obtained or maintained by a person or a society. In the Declaration of Independence, for instance, the values of life, liberty, and the pursuit of happiness were explicitly stated as reasons for creating the United States. These values, moreover, came to serve as guides to political action in the earliest days of the nation. Indeed, such values have remained important to this day. Liberty, or freedom, is emphasized again and again by American political leaders as one value that differentiates this nation from so many others.

VALUES, BELIEFS, AND FOREIGN POLICY

Because the essence of politics is so closely related to achieving and maintaining particular values, the analysis of values and beliefs is a deliberate choice as the organizing theme for studying the foreign policy of the United States.[6] Further, since values and beliefs are the motivating forces for individual action—and because we shall make the assumption that foreign policy is ultimately the result of individual decisions—their importance for foreign policy analysis becomes readily apparent. Thus, by identifying the values and beliefs that American society fosters, we ought to be in a good position to understand how they have shaped our actions toward the rest of the world.

Social psychologists have provided an important analysis of the relationships among values, beliefs, and the behavior of individuals. Milton Rokeach defines beliefs as propositions "inferred from what a person says or does" and whose content "may *describe* an object or situation as true or false; *evaluate* it as good or bad; or *advocate* a certain course of action as desirable or undesirable." Individuals thus may have numerous beliefs, but some are more central than others in accounting for their behavior. These core beliefs are values. As Rokeach notes, "A value is a type of belief, centrally located within one's total belief system, about how one ought, or ought not, to behave, or about some end state of existence worth, or not worth, attaining." Although these values are likely to be few in number, they are crucial in understanding the attitudes and behaviors that an individual expresses.[7] By extension, then, nation-states would operate in the same way, since ultimately individuals comprise them.

The use of values and beliefs (or "ideas," as Judith Goldstein and Robert Keohane recently called them[8]) as our organizing scheme and focusing on nations and individuals contrasts with other principal models of analysis offered in recent years: the rational actor model, the organizational process model, and the governmental or bureaucratic politics model.[9] While each of these models has something to offer in helping us analyze foreign policy, none of them focuses sufficiently on the role of values and beliefs.

The rational actor model, for example, begins with the assumption that nations (like individuals) are self-interested and seek to maximize their payoffs (or outcomes) when making foreign policy decisions. In this model, the key to understanding foreign policy is to identify the policy preferences and their rank-ordering for a state. From a values perspective, however, the source of individual preferences and the relative ordering of those preferences have not been well explored. The organizational process model focuses more on identifying the decision-making routines by policy makers. As a result, foreign policy behavior is less the result of clear choices and more a function of organizations following standing operating procedures. In large measure, the values and beliefs of the policy makers are assumed and not fully analyzed. The bureaucratic politics model gives some attention to the role of values and beliefs (since each bureaucracy has institutional beliefs that it is seeking to maximize), but the primary explanatory focus is on the competition among the bureaucracies, based upon relative power and influence. Once again, though, the roles of values and beliefs within the bureaucracies are not brought into sharp focus. In this sense, while these foreign policy models have much to offer (and careful readers will note that we will use them in various ways throughout the book), an initial focus upon values and beliefs will enable us to provide a more complete picture for understanding the decisions made by American foreign policy makers.

Some Cautions with This Approach

There are some potential difficulties in focusing on values and beliefs and in assuming a direct analogy between individuals and nation-state behavior in analyzing American foreign policy. First, other factors such as the idiosyncratic personality traits of some leaders, the dynamics of the bureaucratic environment, and the restraints of the governmental process will intrude on any complete identification of a nation's values and beliefs.[10] While recognizing these factors and the wealth of research that has gone into their analysis by others, we contend that the role of underlying values and beliefs remains critically important and should not be overlooked in foreign policy analysis.

Even accepting this position, a second reason raises doubts about using this kind of values perspective: The very definition of national values is likely to be problematic. Whose values are we to identify? Should they be the values of political leaders or the public at large? With both the public and the elite, the array of values in a pluralist society is considerable, ranging from religiously based to more secularly driven values. While our analysis will focus primarily on particular values held by the political elites, the values and beliefs of the public, by necessity, will also be considered and examined as well.

A third caution in using the values approach to the study of American foreign policy is potentially more troubling. By focusing on values and beliefs, and using them as the basis for explaining U.S. foreign policy, we are close to relying on the national character (or, more generally, the political culture) explanation of behavior.[11] As A. F. K. Organski has asserted, the national character approach makes several key assumptions:

> (1) that the individual citizens of a nation share a common psychological make-up or personality or value system that distinguishes them from the citizens of other nations, (2) that this national character persists without major changes over a relatively long period of time, and (3) that there is a traceable relationship between individual character and national goals.[12]

Such assumptions are very difficult to make. Thus, there are limitations to the national character approach as a meaningful explanation of foreign policy, and it cannot be relied on completely. Its use in a more limited sense to identify the "basic attitudes, beliefs, values, and value orientations" of a society as a beginning point for analysis is appropriate, however, since individuals (and hence, nations) make decisions within the context of a particular array of values and beliefs.[13]

Some Rationales for This Approach

Although we acknowledge and recognize these limitations, we believe that this values approach is a sufficiently useful first step to warrant more coverage than it has received. Moreover, our analysis will not contend that certain values and beliefs do not change, although surely some principles are less changeable (and hence permanent) than others. Rather, we shall assess the changes in value emphasis and their consistency, especially in the past five decades, when the United States has been an active and continuing participant in the global arena.

Beyond the utility of the values approach to analyzing the foreign policy of any nation, it is especially germane to the study of American foreign policy for at least three additional reasons. First, the nation was explicitly founded on particular sets of values, and these values made the United States view itself as "different" (or "exceptional") from the nations of the Old World from which it originated. In this view, politics was not to be conducted upon the principles of power politics, but it was to be conducted on the basis of democratic principles. In the view of many, then, America should act in the world only on the basis of moral principles or in defense of such principles. Domestic values, at all times, were to be the guide to political behavior. Whether the United States lived up to these standards is debatable, but the inevitable desire to justify actions within a value context emphasizes the role of such principles as guides to U.S. foreign policy.

Second, since some American values toward international affairs have changed in recent years, an understanding of these changes is especially important for U.S. foreign policy analysis. As we shall discuss, America has moved from its isolationist past to an active globalism in the post–World War II years. Indeed, a particular set of values, often labeled the Cold War consensus, came to dominate the motivations of American policy actions from the late 1940s to at least the middle 1960s. In the post-Vietnam period (roughly 1973 and beyond), the value orientation of the various American administrations toward the world has changed a number of times—from the realism of the Kissinger-Nixon-Ford years, to the idealism of the Carter term, and back to the Cold War values of the Reagan administration. With the beginning of the "end of the Cold War" and with the onset of the post–Cold War years of the Clinton administration, American foreign policy values have again been undergoing change—with a new focus on selective global engagement and the promotion of democracy. With such discernible shifts throughout the recent history of U.S. foreign policy and the current searching for a definitive set of foreign policy values today, a knowledge of both past value approaches and their policy implications is important as the United States looks toward the twenty-first century.

Third, the lack of a foreign policy consensus at either the elite or mass levels in American society today further invites the use of a values approach. According to several national surveys, none of the foreign policy approaches of the post-Vietnam era has been fully embraced by the American public or its leaders. Both the public at large and the American leadership are divided as to the appropriate set of values to guide American policy for the future. While we shall discuss these divisions fully in Chapters 12 and 13, suffice it to say that values and beliefs will remain a useful way of understanding American foreign policy.

Finally, as we have noted, there have been efforts lately by analysts to reincorporate the role of values into the study of foreign policy and foreign policy decision making. Two well-known political scientists, Joseph Nye and Stanley Hoffmann, have written works assessing how ethical values may be or should be incorporated into international politics, generally, and particularly into foreign policy calculations. Even more recently, another analyst, through a careful review of several cases in the twentieth century, has sought to demonstrate the moral and ethical considerations that have been evident in American foreign policy.[14]

In this first chapter, then, we begin our analysis by sketching the historical values and beliefs of American society and then suggest how they have influenced our foreign policy toward the rest of the world, especially in the first century and a half of the nation.

THE UNITED STATES: A NEW DEMOCRATIC STATE

Numerous scholars have noted that the United States was founded upon values that were different from those of the rest of the world.[15] It was to be a democratic nation in a world governed primarily by monarchies and autocracies. Indeed, according to one historian, America's founders "didn't just want to believe that they were involved in a sordid little revolt on the fringes of the British Empire or of European civilization. They wanted to believe they were coming up with a better model,...a better way for human beings to form a government that would be responsive to them."[16] Thomas Jefferson stated this view best when he described the new American state as "the solitary republic of the world, the only monument of human rights...the sole depositary of the sacred fire of freedom and self-government, from hence it is to be lighted up in other regions of the earth, if other regions shall ever become susceptible to its benign influence."[17] Because of its democratic value emphasis, moreover, America developed with the belief that its society was unique and possessed a set of values worthy of emulation by others. In this sense, the country emerged as a deeply ideological society (although Americans do not readily admit it), and as one not always tolerant of those who hold contrary views.[18]

A Free Society

In 1776 the United States was explicitly conceived in liberty and equality in contrast to other nations, where ascription and privilege were so important.[19] It emerged as an essentially free society in a world that stressed authority and order. This new American state, to a large measure, was dynamic, classless, and free, in contrast to Europe, which was largely classbound and restrictive.[20] (Revolutionary France does not fit this description, but "classbound and restrictive" certainly describes politics under the Concert of Europe, the European power arrangement dominated by the conservative regimes of Prussia, Russia, and Austria after the defeat of Napoleon.[21]) Thus, the American Revolution was fought in defiance of the very principles by which Europe was governed. In this sense, there developed a natural aversion to European values—and foreign policies—which further reinforced America's beliefs in its own uniqueness.

The fundamental American beliefs that were perceived to be so different from European values of the time can be summarized in the notion of classical liberalism, especially as espoused by John Locke.[22] In this liberal tradition the individual is paramount, and the role of government is limited. Government's task is to do only what is necessary to protect the life and liberty of its citizens and to provide for their happiness. Citizens are generally left alone, free to pursue their own goals and to seek rewards based solely on their abilities.

Equality Before the Law

From such a concern for the individual, personal freedom and personal achievement naturally emerged as cherished values in American society. Yet equality before the law was also necessary to ensure that all individuals could maximize their potential on the sole basis of their talents. In a society that placed so much emphasis on the freedom of the individual, however, equality was viewed in a particular way. What was guaranteed was *not* equality of outcomes (substantive equality) but equality of opportunity (procedural equality) for all.[23] Although all citizens were not guaranteed the same ultimate station in life, all should (theoretically) be able to advance as far as their individual capabilities would take them. While equality of opportunity is thus important to American society, the freedom to determine one's own level of achievement remained the dominant characteristic of this new society. Indeed, in his second inaugural address in January 1997, President Clinton reaffirmed this distinction between substantive and procedural equality when he declared: "The preeminent mission of our new government is to give all Americans an opportunity—not a guarantee, but a real opportunity—to build better lives."[24]

The distinctive values of America were quickly recognized by one prominent visitor to the United States in 1831 and 1832. The French nobleman Alexis de Tocqueville was struck by the extraordinary amount of social and political democracy existing within the United States. In *Democracy in America,* his book cataloguing this visit, de Tocqueville was amazed at the level of social democracy ("The social condition of the Americans is eminently democratic; this was its character at the foundation of the colonies, and it is still more strongly marked at the present day"); its extent of equality ("Men are there seen on a greater equality in point of fortune and intellect, or, in other words, more equal in their strength, then in any other country of the world, or in any age of which history has preserved the remembrance"); and the degree of popular sovereignty ("If there is a country in the world where the doctrine of the sovereignty of the people can be fairly appreciated, where it can be studied in its application to the affairs of society, and where its dangers and its advantages may be judged, that country is assuredly America").[25] To be sure, de Tocqueville raised some concern about this equality and its implication for governance on domestic and foreign policy matters, but his admiration for America as a different kind of nation was indeed profound.[26]

Importance of Domestic Values

The early leaders of the new American state differed from their European counterparts in a third important way: the relationship between domestic values and foreign policy. Unlike the European states of the time, most of the new American leaders did not view foreign policy as having primacy over domestic policy or as a philosophy whereby the power and standing of the state must be preserved and enhanced at the expense of domestic well-being. Nor did these new leaders view foreign policy values and domestic policy values as distinct from one another, where one moral value system guided domestic action and another, by necessity, guided action between states. Instead, most early American leaders saw foreign policy as subservient to the interests of domestic policy and domestic values. One recent analysis of Thomas Jefferson's beliefs on the relationship between the domestic and foreign policy arenas best captures the predominant view at the outset of the American republic: "The objectives of foreign policy were but a means to the ends of posterity and promoting the goals of domestic society, that is, the individual's freedom and society's well-being."[27]

Dual Emphases on Isolationism and Moral Principle

Such values and beliefs came to have important consequences for foreign policy action by this new nation. Because the United States adopted a democratic political system, developed strong libertarian and egalitarian values domestically, and believed in the primacy of domestic over foreign policy, two important foreign policy traditions quickly emerged: an emphasis on isolationism in affecting whether to be involved abroad and an emphasis on moral principle in shaping that involvement.[28] Both traditions, moreover, were surely viewed as complementary to one another and were intended to assist in perpetuating unique American values: the former by reducing U.S. involvement in world affairs, and particularly those of Europe; the latter by justifying U.S. involvement abroad only for sufficient ethical reasons. At times, these two traditions pulled in different directions (one based on the impulse to stay out of world affairs, the other based on the impulse to reform world affairs through unilateral action), but both came to dominate the foreign policy action of the new state.

THE ROLE OF ISOLATIONISM IN AMERICAN FOREIGN POLICY

Since democratic values were so much at variance with those of the rest of the world, many early Americans came to view foreign nations, and especially European states, with suspicion.[29] They feared that the nation's values would be compromised by other states and that international ties would only entangle the United States in alien conflicts. From the beginning, therefore, there was a natural inclination in American society to move away from global involvement and toward isolationism. Throughout the greatest part of the history of this nation, in fact, isolationism best describes America's foreign policy approach.[30]

Although philosophical concepts influenced the isolationist orientation, it was also guided by some important practical considerations. First, the United States was separated geographically from Europe—the main arena of international politics in the eighteenth and nineteenth centuries—and from the rest of the world. Staying out of the affairs of other nations, therefore, seemed a practical course. Second, the United States was a young, weak country with a small army and a relatively large land mass, so seeking adversaries and potential conflicts abroad would hardly be prudent. Third, domestic unity—a sense of nationalism—was still limited and merited more attention than foreign policy. Finally, the overriding task of settling and modernizing the American continent provided reason enough to adopt an isolationist posture.[31]

Two Statements on Isolationism

Early in the history of the country, two statements—Washington's Farewell Address and the Monroe Doctrine—effectively portrayed isolationism and set limits on its application. The first president's Farewell Address of September 1796 was originally meant to thank the American people for their confidence in his leadership, but it also contained a series of warnings about problems that could arise and threaten the continuance of the Republic. Washington admonished American citizens not to become involved in factional groups (i.e., political parties), sectional divisions (e.g., East vs. West or North vs. South), or international entanglements. His comments on international involvements are instructive in explaining what isolationism was to mean in determining American foreign policy for a century and a half.

America's attitude toward the world, Washington said, should be a simple one:

> Observe good faith and justice toward all nations. Cultivate peace and harmony with all. In the execution of such a plan nothing is more essential than that permanent, inveterate antipathies against particular nations and passionate attachments for others should be excluded, and that in place of them just and amicable feeling toward all should be cultivated.[32]

He warned against the danger of forming close ties with other states:

> ...a passionate attachment of one nation for another produces a variety of evils. Sympathy for the favorite nations, facilitating the illusion of an imaginary interest in cases where no real common interest exists, and infusing into one the enmities of the other, betrays the former into a participation in the quarrels and wars of the latter without adequate inducement or justifications.[33]

And Washington provided a "rule of conduct" for the United States and admonished that any involvement in the Byzantine politics of Europe would not be in this country's best interest:

> The great rule of conduct for us in regard to foreign nations is, in extending our commercial relations to have with them as little political connection as possible. So far as we have already formed engagements let them be fulfilled with perfect good faith. Here let us stop. Europe has a set of primary interests which to us have none or a very remote relation. Hence she must be engaged in frequent controversies, the causes of which are essentially foreign to our concerns. Hence, therefore, it must be unwise in us to implicate ourselves by artificial ties in the ordinary vicissitudes of her politics or the ordinary combinations and collisions of her friendship or enmities.[34]

In sum, Washington suggested that while the foreign policy of the United States should not be totally noninvolved (because economic ties with some states were good and useful, and amicable diplomatic ties with others were commendable), he strongly opposed the establishment of any permanent political bonds to other countries. Moreover, he directly warned against any involvement in the affairs of Europe.

While Washington's Farewell Address outlined a general isolationist orientation to the world, the Monroe Doctrine set forth specific guidelines for U.S. involvement or noninvolvement in international affairs. This doctrine—named after President James Monroe's seventh annual Message to the Congress, on December 2, 1823—was promulgated in part as a response to the possibility of increased activities by the European powers in the affairs of the American continents, especially when some South American states were moving toward independence or had just achieved it.[35] Monroe's message contained several distinct and identifiable themes: a call for future noncolonization in Latin America by the European powers and a "maintenance of the *status quo*" there, a declaration about the differences in the political systems of Europe and America, and a statement indicating that the United States would not interfere in the affairs of Europe.[36]

Monroe stated the first of these themes by declaring that the American continents "are henceforth not to be considered as subjects for future colonization by any European power." Such involvement in the affairs of the Americas would affect the "rights and interests" of the United States. Near the end of the message, he highlighted the differences in policies between the United States and Europe toward each other and toward Latin America:

> Of events in that quarter of the globe [Europe] with which we have so much intercourse and from which we derive our origin, we have always been anxious and interested *spectators*.... In the wars of the European powers in matters relating to themselves we have never taken any part, nor does it comport with our policy so to do.... With the movements in this hemisphere we are of necessity more immediately connected and by causes which must be obvious to all enlightened and impartial observers. The political system of the allied powers is essentially different in this respect from that of America. These differences proceed from that which exists in their respective Governments.... We owe it, therefore, to candor and to the amicable relations existing between the United States and those powers to declare that we should consider any attempt on their part to extend their system to any portion of this hemisphere as dangerous to our peace and safety. With the existing colonies or dependencies of any European power we have not interfered and shall not interfere. But with the Governments who have declared their independence and maintained it, and whose independence we have, on great consideration and on just principles, acknowledged, we could not view any interposition...by any European powers in any other light than as the manifestation of an unfriendly disposition toward the United States.[37]

The Monroe Doctrine thus gave rise to the "two spheres" concept in American foreign policy by emphasizing the differences between the Western and Eastern Hemispheres—the New World versus the Old World.[38] As Washington had done earlier, Monroe's statement called for political noninvolvement in the affairs of Europe. But Monroe's message did more than Washington's; it specified that the U.S. policy of political noninvolvement in European affairs did not apply equally to Latin American affairs. By asserting that the "rights and interests" of the United States would be affected by European involvements in the Western Hemisphere, it stipulated that the United States did, indeed, have political interests beyond its borders—particularly in Latin America. In this sense, U.S. political isolationism did not wholly apply to the Western Hemisphere. Instead, U.S. political interests in Latin America became widespread, and they had their origins in the Monroe Doctrine.

Viewed together, these two messages can be a valuable guide in understanding this country's isolationist orientation toward global affairs. The principles enunciated in them generally reflected the diplomatic practices of the United States throughout much of the nineteenth century and into the twentieth, and their words became the basis of the nation's continuing foreign policy.

The Isolationist Tradition in the Nineteenth Century

As a result of the isolationist nature of foreign policy during the nineteenth century, there was a severe restriction on treaty commitments that would bind the United States *politically* to other states. In fact, one prominent historian has pointed out that the United States made no treaties of alliance between the treaty with France in 1778 and the Declaration of the United Nations in 1942.[39] A survey of American treaties, however, would show that the United States did in fact enter into a number of agreements on political matters with other states.[40] For example, the United States enacted agreements on extradition, navigation of the seas, treatment of nationals, and amity and friendship. None of these "political" treaties could be construed as "entangling" alliances, however; instead they served primarily to facilitate amicable trade relations with other states.

A summary of the kind of agreements made by the United States from its founding to the twentieth century and, for comparison, from 1947 to 1960 is displayed in Table 1.1.[41] The first column of data for the 1778–1899 period confirms the large emphasis upon economic ties and the limited political ties in the early history of the nation. Amity and commerce and claims (largely economic) constitute about 70 percent of the agreements. Even the agreements with more direct political elements, such as those dealing with consular activities and extradition, are largely routine matters for fostering good relations with other states, rather than highly controversial political issues. Only those pacts that deal with boundary issues and with territorial concessions (e.g., the Louisiana Purchase, the purchase of Alaska, the Oregon Treaty, or the Gadsden Treaty) might be placed in the more controversial category. Even those, however, still comprise less than 10 percent of all commitments. The single alliance was the treaty with France, which was ultimately left to lapse in 1800.[42]

By contrast, the data for 1947–1960—the initial period of America's active entry into global affairs—show a strikingly different pattern of commitments. First, the sheer number of agreements is markedly different from one period to the next—from just over 600 in a 120-year period to over 4,900 in a fourteen-year period. While economic agreements (amity and commerce) still constituted the largest single type (about 63 percent), alliances and multilateral commitments now constituted over 30 percent of all agreements. To be sure, these alliances ties were broadly defined—such as setting up military bases, establishing defense pacts and mutual security agreements, and sending military missions to particular nations—but they nevertheless demonstrated a much different level and scope of involvement than what occurred in the country's early years. Similarly, the number and kind of multilateral pacts are also distinctive in the two periods. For the more recent period, the number of such pacts were now over 10 times greater, and their content reflected a new dimension to such ties. At least 15 percent of the multilateral pacts in the immediate postwar years were now defense commitments; no such level was registered in the earlier period.

In short, then, the comparative data bring into sharp relief the fact that America's global involvement in the late eighteenth century and the entire nineteenth century was very different than today. The first 120 years of the

TABLE 1.1

Content of International Agreements by the United States

Content	Years 1778–1899	Years 1947–1960
Alliance	1	1,024
Amity and Commerce	272	3,088
Boundary	32	4
Claims	167	105
Consular Activities	47	212
Extradition	47	12
Multilateral	37	469
Territorial Concessions	18	4
Total	621	4,918

Sources: Calculated from Igor I. Kavass and Mark A. Michael, *United States Treaties and Other International Agreements, Cumulative Index 1776–1949,* Vol. 2 (Buffalo, NY: Wm. S. Hein & Co., Inc., 1975); and from Igor I. Kavass and Adolf Sprudzs, *United States Treaties Cumulative Index 1950–1970,* Vol. 2 (Buffalo, NY: Wm. S. Hein & Co., Inc., 1973). For a discussion of how the table was constructed, see the text and note 41.

Republic produced relatively few international agreements, and even these were largely restricted to fostering amicable relations and sound commercial ties between the new American states and the rest of the world.

An illustration or two will more fully demonstrate the limited extent of any political commitments in these early pacts. Under the Treaty of Amity and Commerce between the United States and Sweden, both parties committed themselves to neutrality in case of war and agreed to help each other's ships at sea if they were subject to attack by third parties.[43] Similar kinds of commitments were made in treaties with Prussia, Tripoli, Tunis, and others in the early years of the Republic. Even a subsequent Treaty of Peace and Friendship between the United States and Tripoli (November 4, 1796, and January 3, 1797) emphasized the common effort to facilitate freedom of shipping for the two contracting parties more than the political bonds between the nations. Document 1.1 excerpts the main elements of the pact to illustrate this point more fully.

This type of treaty hardly bound the United States to other societies in any large degree. Instead, such treaties further typify the essential kind of international commitment that the young nation wanted: agreements to facilitate and enhance commerce. Further, commercial ties covered virtually all areas of the world, ranging from Europe to South America to the Far East—where agreements were made with Japan, China, and Siam, among numerous others. In essence, Washington's principle that political ties should be avoided while economic ties were facilitated was generally honored in the first century of the United States.

A brief survey of the diplomatic history of the United States during the nineteenth century gives further evidence of a commitment to the principles of Washington and Monroe. For example, President James K. Polk, in

DOCUMENT 1.1

Treaty of Peace and Friendship Between the United States and Tripoli

Article 1.
There is a firm and perpetual Peace and friendship between the United States of America and the Bey and subjects of Tripoli of Barbary, made by the free consent of both parties, and guaranteed by the most potent Dey & regency of Algiers.

Article 2.
If any goods belonging to any nation with which either of the parties is at war shall be loaded on board of vessels belonging to the other party they shall pass free, and no attempt shall be made to take or detain them.

Article 3.
If any citizens, subjects or effects belonging to either party shall be found on board a prize vessel from an enemy by the other party, such citizens or subjects shall be set at liberty, and the effects restored to the owners.

Article 6.
Vessels of either party putting into the ports of the other and having need of provissions *[sic]* or other supplies, they shall be furnished at the market price. And if any such vessel shall so put in from a disaster at sea and have occasion to repair, she shall be at liberty to land and reembark her cargo without paying any duties. But in no case shall she be compelled to land her cargo.

Article 7.
Should a vessel of either party be cast on the shore of the other, all proper assistance shall be given to her and her people; no pillage shall be allowed; the property shall remain at the disposition of the owners, and the crew protected and succoured till they can be sent to their country.

Article 8.
If a vessel of either party should be attacked by an enemy within gunshot of the forts of the other she shall be defended as much as possible. If she be in port she shall not be seized or attacked when it is in the power of the other party to protect her. And when she proceeds to sea no enemy shall be allowed to pursue her from the same port within twenty four hours after her departure.

Article 9.
The commerce between the United States and Tripoli,—the protection to be given to merchants, masters of vessels and seamen,—the reciprocal right of establishing consuls in each country, and the privileges, immunities and jurisdictions to be enjoyed by such consuls, are declared to be on the same footing with those of the most favoured nations respectively.

Article 11.
As the government of the United States of America is not in any sense founded on the Christian Religion—as it has in itself no character of enmity against the laws, religion or tranquility of Musselmen,—and as the said States never have entered into any war or act of hostility against any Mehomitan nation, it is declared by the parties that no pretext arising from religious opinions shall ever produce an interruption of the harmony existing between the two countries.

continued on next page

DOCUMENT 1.1

Treaty of Peace and Friendship Between the United States and Tripoli (continued)

Article 12.
In case of any dispute arising from a violation of any of the articles of this treaty no appeal shall be made to arms, nor shall war be declared on any pretext whatever. But if the Consul residing at the place where the dispute shall happen shall not be able to settle the same, an amicable referrence *[sic]* shall be made to the mutual friend of the parties, the Dey of Algiers, the parties hereby engaging to abide by his decision. And he by virtue of his signature to this treaty engages for himself and successors to declare the justice of the case according to the true interpretation of the treaty, and to use all the means in his power to enforce the observance of the same.

Source: Excerpted from Hunter Miller, ed., *Treaties and Other International Acts of the United States of America,* Vol. 2 (Washington, DC: U.S. Government Printing Office, 1931), pp. 364–366.

his first annual Address to the Congress on December 2, 1845, reemphasized the tenets Monroe had set down twenty-two years earlier: "It should be distinctly announced to the world as our settled policy, that no future European colony or dominion shall, with our consent, be planted or established on any part of the North American continent.[44] While Polk did not explicitly allude to the ongoing dispute with the British over the Oregon Territory in his reaffirmation of Monroe's policy, the implication (in the view of at least one noted diplomatic historian) was quite clear.[45] Similarly, Polk expressed concern over rumors that the British were about to obtain land in the Yucatan. In a message to Congress (April 29, 1848), Polk said that the "United States would not permit such a deal, even with the consent of the inhabitants.[46]

During this same period the United States concluded the Clayton-Bulwer Treaty, which stipulated that neither Britain nor the United States would ever "obtain or maintain for itself any exclusive control" over a canal across the isthmus at Panama and that "neither will ever exert or maintain fortification commanding the same, or in the vicinity thereof, or fortify, or colonize, or assume, or exercise any dominion over Nicaragua, Costa Rica, the Mosquito Coast, or any part of Central America."[47] While this pact was later viewed as a mistake by some because it gave some standing to the British in the hemisphere, it did allow continued involvement by the United States in the political affairs in Latin America. Consistent with the prescriptions of the Monroe Doctrine, it also tried to regulate European affairs in the area.[48]

Late in the nineteenth century, during the presidency of Grover Cleveland, American policy makers again invoked the principles of the Monroe Doctrine to support Venezuela's claim against the British over a boundary dispute between British Guiana and Venezuela. On July 29, 1895, Secretary of State Richard Olney sent a note to the British stating that they were violating the Monroe Doctrine and that the United States could not permit any weakening of this policy. The British, with good reason, rejected this interpretation. President Cleveland responded angrily, asked Congress for funds to establish a boundary commission to investigate the dispute; he got them quickly, thus fueling war fever over this relatively minor issue.[49] The incident, too, illustrates the continuing influence of the Monroe Doctrine on American foreign policy throughout much of the nineteenth century.[50]

The Isolationist Tradition in the Early Twentieth Century

Despite the appeal of imperial expansion for some American leaders, global isolationism and noninvolvement continued to be the guiding principle toward much of European interaction. Only when moral principle justified interventionist policy into European affairs, as the case of World War I surely illustrates and as we discuss shortly, was isolationism abandoned temporarily. Even then, though, interventionism was largely a last resort and was justified in strong moral tones by the Wilson administration. By contrast, several social, economic, and political actions, largely directed toward Europe, illustrate the preferred isolationist sentiment that continued to dominate American thinking and policy in the early decades of the twentieth century.

In social policy, perhaps the most notable development in the early twentieth century was the passage of the National Origins Act of 1924. This legislation restricted further immigration from Southern and Eastern Europe and forbid immigration from the Orient. It was largely a reaction to the fear of the development of communism within the country (or the so-called "red scare") and the fear of aliens that had also shaken the country. Importantly, it represented an attempt to control foreign influences within the United States through more stringent regulation of immigration. In economic policy, the Smoot-Hawley tariff of 1930 was passed, imposing high tariff barriers for selling foreign products in the United States. Such protectionist legislation was yet a further attempt to isolate the United States from the effects of global economic influences. Further, in the words of one analyst, "the belief...that the Depression stemmed from forces abroad against which the United States had to insulate itself...also gave a 'protective' tariff an irresistible symbolic appeal."[51] In the political arena, the isolationist impulse was equally pronounced. After American involvement in World War I, a "return to normalcy" was the dominant theme. This theme implied a more isolationist and pacifist approach toward world affairs and was manifested in American rejection of membership in the League of Nations, established after World War I, its refusal to recognize the Soviet Union (until 1933) and other regimes of which it disapproved, its attempt to outlaw international war with the signing of the Kellogg-Briand Pact in 1928, and its effort to limit global armament through a series of conferences in the 1920s and again in the early 1930s. In addition, a strong pacifist movement emerged with over fifty peace societies developing across the country in the 1920s. The efforts to eliminate international war were viewed as partial reparation for involvement in World War I and as an effort to prevent such involvement in the future. Thus, international reform was wholly consistent with domestic reform in the minds of many Americans.[52]

Involvement in Latin America in the Twentieth Century

Isolationism and noninvolvement were not the guiding principles toward Latin America in the new century, however. Instead, the 1904 Roosevelt Corollary to the Monroe Doctrine further refined the meaning of that doctrine and expanded U.S. involvement in the Western Hemisphere. As a means of blunting possible European intervention into the affairs of some Western Hemisphere states that had not paid their debts, President Theodore Roosevelt extended the meaning of the Monroe Doctrine to include American intervention, if necessary, to protect the region.

In a letter to the Congress on December 6, 1904, Roosevelt outlined his rationale for this addition to the Monroe Doctrine:

> Chronic wrongdoing, or an impotence which results in a general loosening of the ties of civilized society, may in America, as elsewhere, ultimately require intervention by some civilized nation, and in the Western Hemisphere the adherence of the United States to the Monroe Doctrine may force the United States, however, reluctantly, in flagrant cases of such wrongdoing or impotence, to the exercise of an international police power. Our interests and those of our southern neighbors are in reality identical. They have great natural riches, and if within their borders the reign of law and justice obtains, prosperity is sure to come to them. While they thus obey the primary laws of civilized society they may rest assured that they will be treated by us in a spirit of cordial and helpful sympathy. We would interfere with them only in the last resort and then only if it became evident that their inability or unwillingness to do justice at home and abroad had violated the rights of the United States or had invited foreign aggression to the detriment of the entire body of American nations.[53]

Ironically, the Monroe Doctrine, which had been initiated to prevent intervention from abroad, was now used to justify American intervention in the Western Hemisphere.

This policy was quickly implemented in 1905 by American intervention into the Dominican Republic to manage its economic affairs and to prevent any other outside interference. Similar financial and military interventions followed on the basis of this experience. The United States became involved in the affairs of the Dominican Republic, Haiti, Nicaragua, and Mexico, with intervention in each of these countries throughout the early years of the twentieth century. American forces occupied the Dominican Republic from 1916 to 1924, Haiti from 1915 to 1934, Nicaragua from 1912 to 1925 and 1926 to 1933, and Mexico for a time in 1914. In addition, the United States established a protectorate over Panama from 1903 to 1939 and over Cuba from 1898 to 1934.[54]

The Monroe Doctrine in the Present Era

In recent decades, the Monroe Doctrine has hardly lost its relevance for American policy. In 1954, the United States supported a coup that overthrew the government of the Jacobo Arbenz Guzman regime in Guatemala, after Arbenz had initiated domestic reform programs and had received arms shipments from the Soviet bloc. Both the fear of communism in the Western Hemisphere and the tradition of the Monroe Doctrine figured prominently in American support for the coup.[55] After Fidel Castro had seized power in

MAP 1.1

U.S. Involvements in Central America and the Caribbean, 1898–1996

Source: The involvement data for 1898–1939 are taken from the map in Walter LeFeber's *The American Age* (New York: W. W. Norton and Company, 1989), p. 233. The subsequent American involvements have been added by the author.

Cuba in 1959, a U.S.-backed force of Cuban exiles was organized and trained to topple the Castro regime. In April 1961, the abortive Bay of Pigs invasion ended in disaster, but it was defended as an attempt to stop the spread of communism in the Western Hemisphere. In 1962, the American blockade against Cuba after the discovery of Soviet missiles in that country was again justified by the Monroe Doctrine. In his address to the nation during the Cuban Missile Crisis, President Kennedy noted how these missiles violated "the traditions of this nation and the Hemisphere."[56] In April 1965, when Communists were allegedly seizing power in the Dominican Republic, President Lyndon Johnson sent in some 23,000 U.S. and Organization of American States (OAS) forces to protect American citizens and to restore a government more favorable to the United States.

From the late 1970s and into the mid-1990s, the tenets of the Monroe Doctrine continued to shape American foreign policy in the Western Hemisphere. In September 1979, when the presence of 2,000 to 3,000 Soviet combat troops was revealed in Cuba, Senator Richard Stone of Florida cited the Monroe Doctrine as one reason the troops had to be removed. Secretary of State Cyrus Vance echoed the sentiments of this doctrine when he said that the presence of these forces would not be tolerated. When successful political revolutions occurred in El Salvador and Nicaragua in 1979, the United States immediately became concerned that these revolutions would produce "Soviet beachheads" at America's backdoor in the Western Hemisphere. Quick efforts were made to bolster the new moderate government in El Salvador with large amounts of economic and military assistance to meet the challenge from a guerrilla force, the Farabundo Marti National Liberation Front (FMLN).

By contrast, the Reagan administration challenged the new Marxist-led Sandinista government in Nicaragua and, by late 1981, had initiated a covert operation to support the *Contras*, a counterrevolutionary force committed to the overthrow of that new Nicaraguan government. When the funding for the Contras was stopped by the U.S. Congress from late 1984 to late 1986, Reagan administration officials devised a scheme to continue supporting the rebel Contra forces by secretly selling arms to Iran and transferring part of the proceeds to the Nicaragua rebels. This operation became known as the Iran-Contra affair (see Chapter 5). Through continued American support for the Contras and diplomatic efforts by the United States, but especially by the Central American states, a free election was arranged for February 1990 in Nicaragua. The U.S.-backed candidate, Violetta Chamorro, in a stunning upset to many observers, defeated the incumbent Sandinista leader, Daniel Ortega, for the presidency of Nicaragua. A government that was more consistent with U.S. interests was once again in power and the Monroe Doctrine seemed intact.

The United States worried about the corrupt regime of Manuel Antonio Noriega in Panama and its implication for American influence in that country. General Noriega, who had ruled Panama since the violent death of General Omar Torrigos in 1981, reportedly made huge profits from the drug trade that traversed Panama, and in turn became increasingly repressive in the treatment of his citizens, going so far as nullifying an election in May 1989 when the result did not go in his favor. The Reagan administration sought and obtained his indictment on drug smuggling in Miami and undertook various efforts to oust Noriega from power through American economic and diplomatic actions. In October 1989, a military coup covertly supported and encouraged by the Bush administration failed when the United States suddenly limited its level of involvement. Then, in December 1989, the United States employed a military force totaling about 25,000 to overthrow the Noriega regime. The effort promised to be successful, and Noriega was finally captured, brought to the United States, and convicted on drug trafficking charges.

As the Clinton administration sought to remove General Raoul Cedras and restore democratically elected President Jean-Bertrand Aristide to power in Haiti in 1994, the Monroe Doctrine hovered in the background as an important policy justification. While the administration was much more reluctant to intervene or remain in other trouble spots around the world (e.g., Bosnia, Somalia, or Rwanda), the proximity of Haiti to the United States and its location in the Western Hemisphere (as well as the promotion of democracy) became part of the rationale for American occupation of that country in September 1994. In announcing his determination on this policy matter, President Clinton first tied his actions to previous ones in the Western Hemisphere by Presidents Reagan and Bush, then made an explicit reference to the importance of this region to the United States. "Restoring Haiti's democratic government will lead to more stability and propriety in our region, just as our actions in Panama and Grenada did. Beyond the human rights violations, the immigration problems, the importance of democracy, the United States also has strong interests in not letting dictators—*especially in our own region*—break their word to the United States and the United Nations."[57]

While the effort to stabilize El Salvador, Nicaragua, Panama, and Haiti proved costly, the imperative to keep the Western Hemisphere free of outside powers and to keep the Monroe Doctrine alive continues largely unabated. Similarly, the American view, since at least Theodore Roosevelt, that it could use its power to establish order in this region, also is alive and well as the most recent occupation of Haiti demonstrates.

THE ROLE OF MORAL PRINCIPLE IN AMERICAN FOREIGN POLICY

The founding of the United States with a unique set of values, as well as the nation's development in the context of political isolationism, yielded another important dimension of America's foreign policy: a reliance on moral principle as a guide to world affairs.[58] Americans never felt very comfortable with international politics (especially power politics as practiced in the Old World), and they had largely honored the imperative to stay away from foreign entanglements. This policy of political noninvolvement generated a distinct approach to the world when the country occasionally did become involved in international politics. As political scientist John Spanier and others have argued, discernible American attitudes developed toward such important political concepts as the balance of power, war and peace, and force and diplomacy.[59] More generally, the role of moral values (as opposed to political interests) became an important feature of American policy making. On occasion, this moral fervor produced policies that had the quality of crusades seeking to right a perceived wrong as the United States did become involved in global affairs.

Before we proceed, we ought to add a note here about moral principles and their relationship to policies followed by all nations. Our discussions are not intended to convey that moral principle is absent in the action of other nations and that only the actions of the United States are based upon such principles. To be sure, all nations are governed by particular value codes, although they are clearly different (or at least have different emphases) as we move from one state to another. What we do mean to communicate, however, is that the United States, as a nation, has been particularly sensitive to reconciling its actions with moral principle, perhaps more so than many other nations. As we shall subsequently discuss, the faithfulness to those principles in action has not always been sustained; yet, the very concern for moral principle is an important characteristic of U.S. foreign policy, especially when compared to other national traditions at the beginning of the American Republic.

Moral Principle and the Balance of Power

The balance of power concept, which has dominated policy making in Europe since the inception of the nation-state system there, is predicated on several key assumptions. First, it assumes that all states are interested in preventing large-scale war and in preserving the existence of at least the major states in the international system. Second, it is based on the view that all states are fundamentally motivated in their foreign policy behavior by power considerations and national interests. Third, it assumes that states are willing and able to join alliances (and to change alliances) to prevent the dominance of any one state. Fourth, it assumes that there will be few domestic political constraints preventing states from acting in the political arena.[60] The essence of the balance of power concept is the adroit use of diplomacy and bargaining, but it maintains that force and violence can—and should—be used to perpetuate the system.

Until recently, the United States has tended to reject philosophically virtually all the key assumptions of balance of power politics.[61] American society has maintained that foreign policy should be motivated not by interests and power considerations but by moral principles; domestic values have been seen as the sole basis for foreign policy behavior. As Henry Kissinger, a critic of American antipathy toward power politics, has observed: "It is part of American folklore that, while other nations have interests, we have responsibilities; while other nations are concerned with equilibrium, we are concerned with the legal requirements of peace."[62]

The views of war and peace and force and diplomacy in American society follow from its views of power politics. Because Americans have rejected the balance of power concept, most would find little comfort in Karl von Clausewitz's dictum that war is "the continuation of political activity by other means."[63] Instead, Americans have generally perceived war and peace as dichotomous: Either war or peace exists. Intermediate conditions in which limited force is used (e.g., uses of military force to settle border disputes or short-term interventions to achieve some limited objectives, such as the liberation of Kuwait from the Iraqis in February 1991 by the United States) are not wholly understandable or tolerable to many Americans. When war does break out, and the country does have to get involved, an all-out effort should be made to win the war. If the cause is sufficiently important in the first place, should not the effort be complete and total? Alternatively, if the cause is not important, why should U.S. forces be committed at all?

The continued impact of this view of war and peace to the present is illustrated by public reaction to three recent "limited wars" engaged in by the United States. For many Americans, the conduct of the Korean and Vietnam wars was perceived as extraordinarily frustrating because an all-out military effort was not undertaken. Instead, a mixture of military might and diplomacy was employed. As a result, the outcomes were not wholly satisfactory—prolonged stalemate in the first, defeat in the second.

Even the highly successful effort of the United States in the third, the Persian Gulf War of 1991, still did not end satisfactorily for some because political restraints entered the process once again. In particular, segments of the public (including the American general in charge of coalition forces against Iraq) were unhappy that the United States did not "finish the job" at the end of that war. Instead of stopping the war north of Basra in Iraq after a hundred hours of combat and significant Iraqi casualties, some Americans wanted the U.S. to go all the way to Baghdad and eliminate the government of Saddam Hussein.

Similarly, the U.S. view of force and diplomacy parallels the attitudes toward peace and war. Americans generally believe that when a nation resorts to force, its use should be sufficient to meet the task at hand. There should be no constraints of "politics" once the decision to use force has been made. As a consequence, combining force and diplomacy (as in the balance of power approach) is not understandable to large segments of the American people because it appears to compromise the country's moral position. Again, the Korean and Vietnam wars illustrate this point. In both instances, "talking and fighting" were not well understood or well received by many Americans. The efforts by Richard Nixon and Henry Kissinger to combine force and diplomacy (a policy of "coercive diplomacy") were criticized by both the political right and the political left because they suggested a certain amoralism in American foreign policy efforts.

American diplomacy, too, has historically been heavily infused with this moral tradition. Historian Dexter Perkins has noted that this kind of reliance on moral principle has produced a certain "rigidity" in dealing with other nations. Diplomacy, by its very nature, requires some compromise on competing points, he argues. However, when "every question is to be invested with the aura of principle, how is adjustment to take place?"[64] Similarly, Spanier has noted that, given that moral principle is so prevalent in American policy making, it has traditionally been difficult for Americans to understand how compromise is possible or necessary on some questions in global politics.[65] When to compromise, and over what principles, remains a source of debate for many Americans.

Moral Principle and International Involvement

Prior to 1947, when the United States finally committed itself to global involvement, American engagement in global affairs was generally tied to explicit violations of international ethical standards by other states. Four prominent instances—the War of 1812, the Spanish-American War, World War I, and World War II—illustrate the importance of moral principle as a justification for U.S. involvement and foreign policy actions.[66]

War of 1812. The first instance when isolationism was abandoned in the name of moral principle was the War of 1812. When the U.S. Congress finally voted a declaration of war against Great Britain in June 1812, it did so only after various efforts to avoid involvements with the dominant European powers of the time—France and England—and only after what it perceived as continuous violations of an important principle of international law: freedom of the seas for neutral states.[67] Under a series of policy directives to limit Napoleon's power and enhance its own, the British government barred American commerce from France or any continental ports that barred the British. Further, it barred any neutral American vessel that had not passed through a British port or paid British customs duties from carrying on commerce. U.S. ships violating such standards were subject to seizure. (France, under Napoleon, enacted similar restrictions on American shipping, but, for a variety of reasons, the United States responded with greater hostility to the British strictures.[68]) Such British actions infuriated the United States, and American leaders characterized them as blatant violations of freedom of the seas. In addition to the seizure of American vessels, the British went further in their effort to control the seas through the practice of impressment, which involved seizing sailors off American vessels and forcing them into the British navy (because they were alleged to be deserters from the Royal Navy). Impressment, too, further challenged America's freedom of commerce and the seas and was seen as besmirching U.S. national honor. While America's involvement in this war proved costly and ultimately unpopular and the final results largely confirmed the status quo, it does suggest the potency of moral principle in guiding early American action.[69]

Spanish-American War. In the Spanish-American War (1898), a variety of arguments based on moral principle was advanced to justify American actions: the harsh Spanish treatment of the Cubans, the sinking of the American battleship *Maine*, and the personal affront to President William McKinley by the Spanish ambassador in a private letter. (The ambassador portrayed McKinley as a "bidder for the admiration of the crowd" and as a "common politician."[70]) Fewer arguments for American participation were cast on the basis of how it might affect the national interest; instead, in one view, moral arguments provided the dominant rationale.[71]

World War I. American participation in World War I in 1917 and 1918 was also cast in terms of the same kind of moral imperative, rather than in response to the demands of the balance of power in Europe. Only for sufficient ethical cause did the United States feel compelled to enter this European conflict. In this case, the ethical justification was provided by Germany's violation of the principle of freedom of the seas and the rights of neutrals through its unrestricted warfare campaign on the open seas.[72]

The outrage that developed in 1915 with the sinking of the British passenger ship the *Lusitania* (and later, the *Sussex*), with the accompanying loss of American lives, provided sufficient reason to abandon isolationism temporarily. The proximate events that precipitated United States entry into the war, however, were the German announcement of its unrestricted submarine warfare in February 1917 and Germany's Zimmermann Telegram to Mexico that sought to prod that country into war with the United States.[73] Even as the United States embarked on this course, continued moral justification was reflected in the slogans devised to boost American participation; World War I was to be a "war to end all wars" and a campaign to "make the world safe for democracy."

World War II. Finally, U.S. participation in World War II from 1941 to 1945 also reflected the ethical roots of the country's foreign policy behavior. Although the United States was assisting the allies before its formal involvement, U.S. reentry into world conflict could be justified only in terms of some moral violation. The Neutrality Act of 1939, for example, had reduced the restrictions on arms sales and allowed the United States to supply its allies, France and Britain. The Destroyers for Bases deal with Great Britain—in which the United States gained naval and air bases in Newfoundland and some Caribbean islands in exchange for fifty destroyers—occurred in September 1940.[74] In March 1941, moreover, the Congress passed the Lend-Lease Act as another way to help the allies.[75] Nevertheless, it was not until the Japanese bombing of Pearl Harbor, Hawaii, on December 7, 1941, "a date which will live in infamy" as President Franklin Roosevelt described it, that the United States was accorded a wholly satisfactory reason for plunging the country into the conflict.[76] Then the United States, consistent with its attitude, felt compelled to seek "absolute victory," as Roosevelt said. A total war effort was mounted that ultimately led to the unconditional surrender of the Japanese in September 1945, only a few months after the victory in Europe had been secured.

Implications for U.S. Involvement

As these four instances demonstrate, the United States has been reluctant to give up its isolationism and did so only for identifiable moral reasons. That is, the United States traditionally agreed to international involvement only in response to perceived violations of clearly established principles of international law and not to respond to the requirements of power politics, as many other states have done. As a consequence, sustained American activities in the world of power politics have been decidedly few in the past and have been entered into only in special circumstances.

After each of the first three involvements discussed here, the United States generally moved back to its favored position of isolationism; moreover, none brought about a basic change in American foreign policy orientation. (The significance of World War II is considerably different, and Chapter 2 discusses its impact on U.S. foreign policy.) After the War of 1812, for example, the immediate reaction was the reaffirmation of the policy of noninvolvement in European affairs by the Americans and the call for no European involvement in Western Hemispheric affairs via the Monroe Doctrine of 1823.

The strong American impulse toward isolationism was perhaps most vividly demonstrated in the rejection of the idealistic foreign policy proposed by President Woodrow Wilson at the end of World War I. "Wilsonian idealism," as it came to be called, attempted to shake the United States from its isolationist moorings and encourage America to be a continuing participant in global affairs. This idealism, largely borne out of President Wilson's personal beliefs, consisted of several key tenets. First, moral principle should be the guide to U.S. actions abroad. Second, the Anglo-American values of liberty and liberal democratic institutions are worthy of emulation and promotion worldwide. Indeed, they are necessary if world peace is to be realized. Third, the old order, based upon balance of power and interest politics, must be replaced by an order based upon moral principles and cooperation by all states against international aggression. And fourth, the United States must continue to take an active role in bringing about these global reforms.[77] For Wilson, then, moral principle would serve as a continuing guide to global involvement, but the interests of humankind and global reform would take precedence over any narrowly defined national or state interest.

The most complete statement of the new world that Wilson envisioned was probably summarized in his Fourteen Points, which he offered to a joint session of the U.S. Congress in January 1918 and which became the basis for the Paris Peace Conference at the end of World War I.[78] This new order would ban secret diplomacy and foster international trade among nations. It also emphasized self-determination and democracy for nations and set forth several specific requirements for resolving nationality and territorial issues in Central Europe at the time. (A summary of Wilson's Fourteen Points is presented in Document 1.2). Point 14 of this plan, however, was particularly notable—and ultimately troubling to many Americans—because of its explicit rejection of isolationism. This point called for the establishment of a collective security organization—a League of Nations—which was to rid the world of balance of power politics and create a world order based on universal principles. The League was to be an organization that would exploit the cooperative potential among states and emphasize the role of collective (i.e., universal) action to stop warfare and regulate conflict. As such, it would require each participant to be involved in the affairs of the international system. If the United States were to join such an organization, it would be permanently involved in global politics and would be an active participant in this global reform effort.

Wilson's collective security proposal would have moved the United States away from isolationism, and it would have produced a strong moral cast to American involvement and to global politics generally. As one of Wilson's harshest critics put it, Wilson's idealism was not far from the isolationism that was ultimately embraced by the United States after World War I. Both

DOCUMENT 1.2

Wilson's Fourteen Points

I. Open covenants of peace, openly arrived at....
II. Absolute freedom of navigation upon the seas....
III. The removal, so far as possible, of all economic barriers and the establishment of an equality of trade conditions among all the nations....
IV. Adequate guarantees given and taken that national armaments will be reduced to the lowest point consistent with domestic safety.
V. A free open-minded, and absolutely impartial adjustment of all colonial claims....
VI. The evacuation of all Russian territory and such a settlement of all questions affecting Russia...[and] an unhampered and unembarassed opportunity for the independent determination of her own political development and national policy....
VII. Belgium...must be evacuated and restored without any attempt to limit the sovereignty which she enjoys in common with all other free nations.
VIII. All French territory should be freed and the invaded portions restored, and the wrong done to France by Prussia in 1871 in the matter of Alsace-Lorraine, which has unsettled the peace of the world for nearly fifty years, should be righted....
IX. A readjustment of the frontiers of Italy should be effected along clearly recognizable lines of nationality.
X. The peoples of Austria-Hungary...should be accorded the freest opportunity of autonomous development.
XI. Rumania, Serbia, and Montenegro should be evacuated; occupied territories restored; Serbia accorded free and secure access to the sea; and the relations of the several Balkan states to one another determined by friendly counsel along historically established lines of allegiance and nationality....
XII. The Turkish portions of the present Ottoman Empire should be assured a secure sovereignty, but the other nationalities...under Turkish rule should be assured...[an] opportunity of autonomous development, and the Dardanelles should be permanently opened as a free passage to the ships and commerce of all nations....
XIII. An independent Polish state should be erected...[with] political and economic independence and territorial integrity...guaranteed by international covenant.
XIV. A general association of nations must be formed under specific covenants for the purpose of affording mutual guarantees of political independence and territorial integrity to great and small states alike.

Source: Taken from a speech by President Woodrow Wilson to a joint session of the U.S. Congress as reported in *Congressional Record*, January 8, 1918, 691.

Wilsonianism (as this critic pejoratively called this idealism), and later the isolationism between World War I and World War II, were largely the same side of the coin—with one more extreme than the other—and were equally divorced from political interests and political reality. In this sense, "both [isolationism and Wilsonianism] have a negative relation to the national interest of the United States outside the Western Hemisphere.... Wilsonianism applies the illusory expectations of liberal reform to the whole world, isolationism empties of all concrete political content the realistic political principle of isolation and transforms it into the unattainable parochial ideal of automatic separation."[79] Put differently, Wilson's approach put too much emphasis on transforming global politics in line with American ethical beliefs, while the isolationism of the interwar years was not a shrewd political strategy as had been the isolationism of the early Republic. Instead, this new isolationism was simply an insular effort at stopping all international ties.

Yet Wilson's plan for a League of Nations did become a reality for a time, but without the participation of the United States; the U.S. Senate failed to pass the Versailles peace treaty by the necessary two-thirds vote. On two of three different roll calls, the treaty failed even to obtain majority support in the upper chamber of the U.S. Congress.[80] Despite America's long-standing rejection of balance of power politics, it remained unwilling to increase its global involvement in order to destroy this system. Instead, the United States reaffirmed its isolationist beliefs and reverted to "normalcy" in the 1920s and remained in that posture throughout the 1930s as well.

The return to isolationism was also manifested in another way in the interwar years. As the situation in Europe began to polarize, and conflict seemed once again imminent, the United States passed a series of neutrality acts in 1935, 1936, and 1937. These acts sought to prevent the export of arms and ammunition to belligerent countries and to restrict travel by American citizens on the vessels of nations involved in war.[81] The ultimate aim was to reaffirm U.S. noninvolvement and to reduce the prospects of the United States being drawn into war through these means. Although President Roosevelt had by 1939 asked for and received some alterations in the neutrality acts of the past,[82] it was not until the Japanese attack that the United States was again fully shaken from its isolationist stance.

Concluding Comments

The reliance on isolationism and moral principle largely forms the essence of America's past in foreign policy,[83] and these values and beliefs continue to affect the country's orientation to the world to this day. To be sure, the American approach to the world, however, would be altered in response to the shock of World War II, the substantial destruction of the major European powers of France, Britain, and Germany, the emergence of the Soviet challenge, and the onset of the Cold War. Noninvolvement in global affairs was rejected, even as a commitment to the pursuit of moral principles served as a guide to policy.

With the collapse of the Soviet Union and the end of the Cold War, the appeal of these traditional values has reemerged, as the United States looks to shape a new foreign policy for the twenty-first century. The Clinton administration, for example, has struggled to stem the appeal of isolationism to some, even as it has sought to promote and sustain American involvement abroad. The perfection of democracy at home and the promotion of democracy abroad—principles consonant with America's past—have now been invoked to serve as the *raison d'être* for America's global actions.

In the next five chapters, we will highlight the changes in America's values and beliefs in the foreign policy area during the post–World War II years and in the post–Cold War period as well. We seek not only to demonstrate how these historical traditions have changed in emphasis or application from administration to administration, but also to illustrate how these traditions have continued to influence the various administrations and their policies. In Chapter 2 we specifically examine the global political and economic factors that shook the United States from its isolationist moorings and propelled it into global politics. At the same time, we shall see how moral principle as a guide to policy remained largely intact.

Notes

1. Harold D. Lasswell, *Politics: Who Gets What, When, How* (New York: Whittlesey House, 1936), p. 3.
2. Ibid. Emphasis in original.
3. Robert A. Dahl, *Modern Political Analysis*, 2nd ed. (Englewood Cliffs, NJ: Prentice-Hall, Inc., 1970), pp. 4–6. Also see Christian Bay, *The Structure of Freedom* (New York: Atheneum Publishers, 1965), pp. 20–21, for another discussion of the definition of politics.
4. David Easton, *The Political System* (New York: Alfred A. Knopf, Inc., 1953), p. 90. Emphasis added.
5. Milton Rokeach, *Beliefs, Attitudes and Values* (San Francisco: Jossey-Bass, Inc., 1968), pp. 124, 159–160.
6. We shall use the terms "values" and "beliefs" interchangeably throughout this book. These concepts (along with attitudes), while distinct, are very closely related to one another, as discussed in Rokeach, *Beliefs*, pp. 113 and 159–160.
7. See Milton Rokeach's discussion under "Attitudes" in the *International Encyclopedia of the Social Sciences* (New York: The Macmillan Company and The Free Press, 1968), pp. 449–457. The quotations are from pp. 450 and 454, respectively. Emphasis in original.
8. Judith Goldstein and Robert O. Keohane, "Ideas and Foreign Policy: An Analytic Framework," in Judith Goldstein and Robert O. Keohane, eds., *Ideas and Foreign Policy: Beliefs, Institutions, and Political Change* (Ithaca and London: Cornell University Press, 1993), pp. 3–30. Some of the discussion of the models following in the next paragraph draws upon Goldstein and Keohane.
9. Graham Allison, *Essence of Decision* (Boston: Little, Brown and Co., 1971).
10. A book that surveys the research done within the context of these various factors to explain foreign policy is Lloyd Jensen, *Explaining Foreign Policy* (Englewood Cliffs, NJ: Prentice-Hall, Inc., 1982).
11. For a discussion of how the political culture concept can be used to explain a nation's behavior, see Gabriel Almond and Sidney Verba, *The Civic Culture* (Boston: Little, Brown & Co., 1963). A discussion of American political culture is in Donald J. Devine, *The Political Culture of the United States* (Boston: Little, Brown & Co., 1972). The approach that we adopt falls more generally within the societal and belief system determinants of foreign policy. For a good summary discussion of these approaches—and some recent research on them—see Jensen, *Explaining Foreign Policy*, pp. 45–105.
12. A. F. K. Organski, *World Politics* (New York: Alfred A. Knopf, Inc., 1968), p. 87.
13. Kenneth W. Terhune, "From National Character to National Behavior: A Reformulation," *Journal of Conflict Resolution* 14 (June 1970): 259. For more discussion of Terhune and others on national character, see Howard Bliss and M. Glen Johnson, *Beyond the Water's Edge: America's Foreign Policies* (Philadelphia: J. B. Lippincott Co., 1975), pp. 93–98.
14. See Joseph S. Nye, *Nuclear Ethics* (New York: The Free Press, 1986), Stanley Hoffmann, *Duties Beyond Borders: On the Limits and Possibilities of Ethical International Politics* (Syracuse: Syracuse University Press, 1981), and Robert W. McElroy, *Morality and American Foreign Policy: The Role of Ethics in International Affairs* (Princeton,

NJ: Princeton University Press, 1992). The McElroy volume brought the Nye and Hoffmann books to my attention at p. 3, for which I am grateful.

15. See, for example. Seymour Martin Lipset, *The First New Nation* (Garden City, NY: Anchor Books, 1967); Russel B. Nye, *This Almost Chosen People* (East Lansing: Michigan State University Press, 1966); John G. Stoessinger, *Crusaders and Pragmatists* (New York: W. W. Norton and Company, 1979), pp. 3–7; Edmund Stillman and William Pfaff, *Power and Impotence: The Failure of America's Foreign Policy* (New York: Vintage Books, 1966), pp. 15–59; Paul A. Varg, *Foreign Policies of the Founding Fathers* (East Lansing: Michigan State University, 1963), pp. 1–10; and John Spanier, *American Foreign Policy Since World War II*, 9th ed. (New York: Holt, Rinehart and Winston, 1982), pp. 1–14. Spanier's essay is perhaps the best brief treatment of this and related topics discussed here. Its utility here will be readily apparent.

16. This characterization was made by Professor Frank A. Cassell, chairman, Department of History, University of Wisconsin-Milwaukee, in a 1989 Independence Day interview. See Jerry Resler, "Living On: U.S. as Model Would Please Founder" *Milwaukee Sentinel*, July 4, 1989, part 4, p. 1.

17. Quoted in Robert W. Tucker and David C. Hendrickson, "Thomas Jefferson and Foreign Policy," *Foreign Affairs* 69 (Spring 1990): 136.

18. George F. Kennan made this point about the ideological roots of American society by noting the isolated development of the United States and the Soviet Union. This development in relative isolation from the rest of the world produced a strong sense of righteousness. See his "Is Detente Worth Saving?" *Saturday Review*, March 6, 1976, 12–17. For others who would judge America as an ideological society, see, for instance, Nye, *This Almost Chosen People*, and Stillman and Pfaff, *Power and Impotence*. Stanley Hoffmann would not entirely agree. See his *Gulliver's Troubles, or the Setting of American Foreign Policy* (New York: McGraw-Hill, 1968), pp. 114–117.

19. Lipset, in *The First New Nation*, uses the values of equality and achievement as the basis of his analysis.

20. This description, as noted in Spanier, *American Foreign Policy*, p. 7, was true for most Americans, but not all. Some were clearly excluded from the political process—notably blacks, women, Indians, and many who were propertyless.

21. Gordon A. Craig and Alexander L. George, *Force and Statecraft*, 3rd ed. (New York and Oxford: Oxford University Press, 1995), pp. 27–31.

22. On his view of the goals and limits of government, see John Locke, *Two Treatises of Government*, portions of which are reprinted in William Ebenstein, *Great Political Thinkers: Plato to the Present*, 3rd ed. (New York: Holt, Rinehart and Winston, 1965), pp. 404–408, in particular. Also see the discussion of classical liberalism in Everett C. Ladd, Jr., "Traditional Values Regnant," *Public Opinion* 1 (March/April 1978): 45–49, and Charles W. Kegley and Eugene R. Wittkopf, *American Foreign Policy: Pattern and Process*, 4th ed. (New York: St. Martin's Press, 1991), pp. 249–250.

23. These values are discussed in Ladd, "Traditional Values and Regnant," and some evidence is presented on the current American commitment to these values and beliefs.

24. "Transcript of President Clinton's Second Inaugural Address to the Nation," *New York Times*, January 21, 1997, A12.

25. Alexis de Tocqueville, *Democracy in America*, edited and abridged by Richard D. Heffner (New York: New American Library, 1956), pp. 49, 54, and 56 for the quoted passages.

26. See ibid. and David Clinton, "Tocqueville's Challenge," *The Washington Quarterly* 11 (Winter 1988): 173–189.

27. Tucker and Hendrickson, "Thomas Jefferson and Foreign Policy," p. 139. For a discussion of how Jefferson's views were shared by other early leaders, see pp. 143–146. On the difficulty of Jefferson's actually making this distinction work, see pp. 146–156.

28. See Spanier, *American Foreign Policy*, pp. 6 and 12. Many others, of course, agree with this assessment of the role of these two traditions. See, for instance, Varg, *Foreign Policies*, and Dexter Perkins, *The American Approach to Foreign Policy* (Cambridge, MA: Harvard University Press, 1962). Previously, "isolationism" and "moralism" were used as summary terms. The use of "moralism," however, may have a pejorative connotation

for some (and it has surely been used that way). That is not the intent here. Rather, it is to convey the important role that values have played in the way America has thought about its involvement in the global arena. Hence, moral principle as a guiding tradition will be used here.

29. Dexter Perkins, *Hands Off: A History of the Monroe Doctrine* (Boston: Little, Brown & Co., 1941), pp. 3–26. For a vivid picture of how one prominent American viewed Europe, see Daniel J. Boorstin, *America and the Image of Europe: Reflections on American Thought* (New York: Meridian Books, 1960), p. 21, in which he quotes Thomas Jefferson while traveling in France: "For this whole chapter in the history of man is new.... Before the establishment of the American States, nothing was known to history but the man of the old world, crowded within limits either too small or overcharged, and steeped in the vices which that situation generates." This passage is also cited in Stillman and Pfaff, *Power and Impotence*, p. 16.
30. See Cecil V. Crabb, Jr. *Policy-Makers and Critics: Conflicting Theories of American Foreign Policy* (New York: Frederick A. Praeger, Inc., 1976), pp. 1–33, for an extended discussion of this isolationist tradition.
31. See ibid., pp. 7–15, for a discussion of several different dimensions of isolationism in America's past.
32. "Washington's Farewell Address," *Annals of The Congress of the United States*, 4th Cong., 2nd sess., 1786–1797, 2877.
33. Ibid.
34. Ibid., p. 2878.
35. Albert Bushnell Hart, *The Monroe Doctrine: An Interpretation* (Boston: Little, Brown & Co., 1916), pp. 20–68.
36. These themes are succinctly discussed in Evarts Seelye Scudder, *The Monroe Doctrine and World Peace* (Port Washington, NY: Kennikat Press, 1972), pp. 15–20. The quote is at p. 19. Emphasis in original.
37. "President's Message," *Annual of the Congress of the United States*, 18th Cong., 1st sess., 1823–1824, 22–23. Emphasis added.
38. Several scholars have emphasized how the Monroe Doctrine, more than any other policy statement, formalized and solidified the U.S. isolationist tradition in world affairs—at least toward Europe. See, for instance, Perkins, *The Evolution of American Foreign Policy*, 2nd ed. (New York: Oxford University Press, 1966), pp. 33–38; Nye, *This Almost Chosen People*, p. 184; and Spanier, *American Foreign Policy*, p. 6.
39. Thomas A. Bailey, *The Man on the Street: The Impact of American Public Opinion on Foreign Policy* (New York: MacMillan, Inc., 1948), p. 251.
40. A survey of all international agreements during the early history was undertaken using the listing compiled by Igor I. Kavass and Mark A. Michael, *United States Treaties and Other International Agreements Cumulative Index 1776–1949* (Buffalo, NY: William S. Hein and Company, Inc., 1975), pp. 3–130. For the latter period, the data source was Igor I. Kavass and Adolf Sprudzs, *United States Treaties Cumulative Index 1950–1970*, vol. 2 (Buffalo, NY: William S. Hein and Company, Inc., 1973), pp. 11–444, and some additional agreements from the first source for the years 1947–1949 at pp. 526–615.
41. The table was constructed using the sources listed in note 40. The category labels were derived largely form the descriptions of the agreements given in the first source. For manageability and convenience, agreements in different years in the 1778–1899 period were segmentally categorized (e.g., 1778–1799, 1800–1850, etc.), and the overall results were collapsed and categorized. For the second part of the table (1947–1960), the same categories were used. While the content of the categories is relatively self-evident, the alliance, amity and commerce, and multilateral categories deserve some comment. The alliance category consisted primarily of formal military commitments, but it also included establishing military bases, signing mutual security agreements, and sending military missions to other countries. The amity and commerce category included a wide array of commercial, health and sanitation, technical cooperation, educational, aviation, and postal agreements, among others, and commitments for friendly relations with other states. The multilateral category included all agreements that were designated as such by the source. The actual content of those pacts covered a wide array of issues, but

the multilateral designation was retained to show the degree to which the United States committed itself to groups of other states during this period. Finally, some agreements overlapped the categories, and some judgments were made to place them into one category rather than another. Others categorizing the pacts might likely come up with a different classification and slightly different results. It is unlikely, however, that the general pattern of the results would be changed.

42. Perkins, *The Evolution of American Foreign Policy*, p. 30, reports that the French alliance was not renewed in that year.
43. The treaty text is given in Hunter Miller, ed., *Treaties and Other International Acts of the United States of America*, vol. 2 (Washington, DC: U.S. Government Printing Office, 1931), pp. 123–150.
44. Thomas A. Bailey, *A Diplomatic History of the American People* (New York: F. S. Crofts & Co., 1942), p. 238.
45. Ibid.
46. Hart, *Monroe Doctrine*, p. 115.
47. Robert H. Ferrell, *American Diplomacy: A History* (New York: W. W. Norton & Co., Inc., 1975), p. 231.
48. Ibid., pp. 231–232. For the controversy over whether the Clayton-Bulwer Treaty really regulated European involvement in the Western Hemisphere, see Hart, *Monroe Doctrine*, pp. 122–125; and Bailey, *Diplomatic History*, pp. 292–295. The Hay-Pauncefote Treaty of 1901 annulled the Clayton-Bulwer Treaty and enabled the United States to become the sole guarantor of the canal. See Ferrell, *American Diplomacy*, p. 400.
49. For a discussion of the various challenges to the Monroe Doctrine in the latter half of the nineteenth century, see Scudder, *Monroe Doctrine*; and Hart, *Monroe Doctrine*.
50. See Perkins, *The Evolution of American Foreign Policy*, pp. 35–36, on this point and on the general applicability of the Monroe Doctrine and its declining influence as well (pp. 32–36).
51. Robert Dallek, *The American Style of Foreign Policy* (New York: Alfred A. Knopf, 1983), p. 110. The discussion here is based upon pp. 92–122. Dallek also discusses the competing motivations that shaped policy during the interwar years and how these motivations often appear to be contradictory with one another.
52. Ibid., p. 96–97, in which Dallek discusses the various implications of the pacifist movements in this time period.
53. *Congressional Record*, December 6, 1904, 19.
54. Ferrell, *American Diplomacy*, pp. 395–415. The American occupations and protectorates in the Caribbean are outlined by Walter LaFeber, *The American Age: United States Foreign Policy at Home and Abroad Since 1750* (New York: W. W. Norton & Company, 1989), p. 233.
55. Walter Lefeber, *Inevitable Revolutions: The United States in Central America* (New York: W. W. Norton and Company, 1984), pp. 111–126, especially pp. 118–123. Clearly, however, Lefeber does not fully accept this interpretation of events in Guatemala in the early 1950s.
56. President Kennedy's address to the nation can be found in Robert F. Kennedy, *Thirteen Days* (New York: Signet, 1969), pp. 131–139. The quoted passage is at p. 132.
57. President William J. Clinton, "Remarks by the President in Television Address to the Nation," September 15, 1994. Emphasis added. Further, this speech makes references to "our region," as well as "our hemisphere," as part of this policy justification.
58. See Dexter Perkins, *American Approach*, pp. 72–97, for a cogent discussion of moral principles as a guide in American foreign policy.
59. See Spanier, *American Foreign Policy*, pp. 9–11; and Stoessinger, *Crusaders and Pragmatists*, pp. 5–7.
60. A discussion of the assumptions, aims, and means of the balance of power can be found in Edward V. Gulick, *Europe's Classical Balance of Power* (Ithaca, NY: Cornell University Press, 1955), pp. 3–91.

61. Changes in American policy makers' attitudes and beliefs toward a balance of power system occurred dramatically during the years in which Henry Kissinger was responsible for formulating American policy. This will be discussed in Chapter 4.
62. Henry A. Kissinger, *American Foreign Policy*, expanded ed. (New York: W. W. Norton & Co., Inc., 1974), pp. 91–92.
63. Carl von Clausewitz, *On War*, ed. and trans. Michael Howard and Peter Paret (Princeton: Princeton University Press, 1976), p. 87. Spanier, *American Foreign Policy*, p. 10, also raises this point and discusses the dichotomous view of war and peace upon which we draw.
64. Perkins, *American Approach*, p. 77.
65. Spanier, *American Foreign Policy*, p. 11.
66. These instances are discussed in both George F. Kennan, *American Diplomacy 1900–1950* (New York: Mentor Books, 1951); Robert Endicott Osgood, *Ideals and Self-Interest in America's Foreign Relations* (Chicago: The University of Chicago Press, 1953); and Farrell, *American Diplomacy*, pp. 123–153.
67. Harry L. Coles, *The War of 1812* (Chicago: The University of Chicago Press, 1965), pp. 1–37, and Farrell, *American Diplomacy*, pp. 136–141.
68. Coles, *The War of 1812*, pp. 1–37; and Farrell, *American Diplomacy*, pp. 136–141.
69. Ibid., p. 142.
70. Kennan, *American Diplomacy 1900–1950*, p. 14; and Farrell, *American Diplomacy*, p. 353.
71. For a critical assessment of the impact of popular sentiment on this conflict, see Kennan, *American Diplomacy 1900–1950*, pp. 15–16.
72. Ferrell, *American Diplomacy*, pp. 456–462; and Kennan, *American Diplomacy 1900–1950*, pp. 50–65.
73. Ferrell, *American Diplomacy*, pp. 468–469.
74. Ibid., pp. 556–558.
75. P.L. 77-11, March 11, 1941. 55 Stat 31.
76. Speech by President Franklin D. Roosevelt to a joint session of Congress. The quotation can be found in the *Congressional Record*, 77th Cong., 1st sess., Vol. 87, December 8, 1941, 9519.
77. On Wilson's beliefs, see John G. Stoessinger, *Crusaders and Pragmatists: Movers of Modern American Foreign Policy*, 2nd ed. (New York: W. W. Norton and Company, 1985), pp. 8–27; and Michael H. Hunt, *Ideology and U.S. Foreign Policy* (New Haven, CT: Yale University Press, 1987), pp. 125–136, especially at pp. 129–135.
78. For a listing of the Fourteen Points and a discussion of the Paris Conference, see Ferrell, *American Diplomacy*, pp. 482–92. The depiction of the new order draws upon Hunt, *Ideology and U.S. Foreign Policy*, p. 134.
79. Hans J. Morgenthau, "The Mainsprings of American Foreign Policy" in James M. McCormick, ed., *A Reader in American Foreign Policy* (Itasca, IL: F. E. Peacock Publishers, Inc., 1986), p. 46.
80. Robert Farrell, *American Diplomacy: The Twentieth Century* (New York: W. W. Norton & Company, 1988), p. 153.
81. See the text of the Neutrality Act of 1935 (August 31, 1935) or the Neutrality Act of 1936 (February 29, 1936) for a full treatment of the restrictions on arms exports and travel by Americans. Both are reprinted in Nicholas O. Berry, ed., *U.S. Foreign Policy Documents, 1933–1945: From Withdrawal to World Leadership* (Brunswick, OH: King's Court Communications, Inc., 1978), pp. 25–27, 32.
82. See the Neutrality Act of 1939 (November 4, 1939), reprinted in ibid., pp. 58–60.
83. See Howard Bliss and M. Glen Johnson, *Beyond The Water's Edge: America's Foreign Policies*, chap. 4, for a discussion of other values that have shaped the American style. Also see Hoffmann, *Gulliver's Troubles*, chaps. 5 and 6.

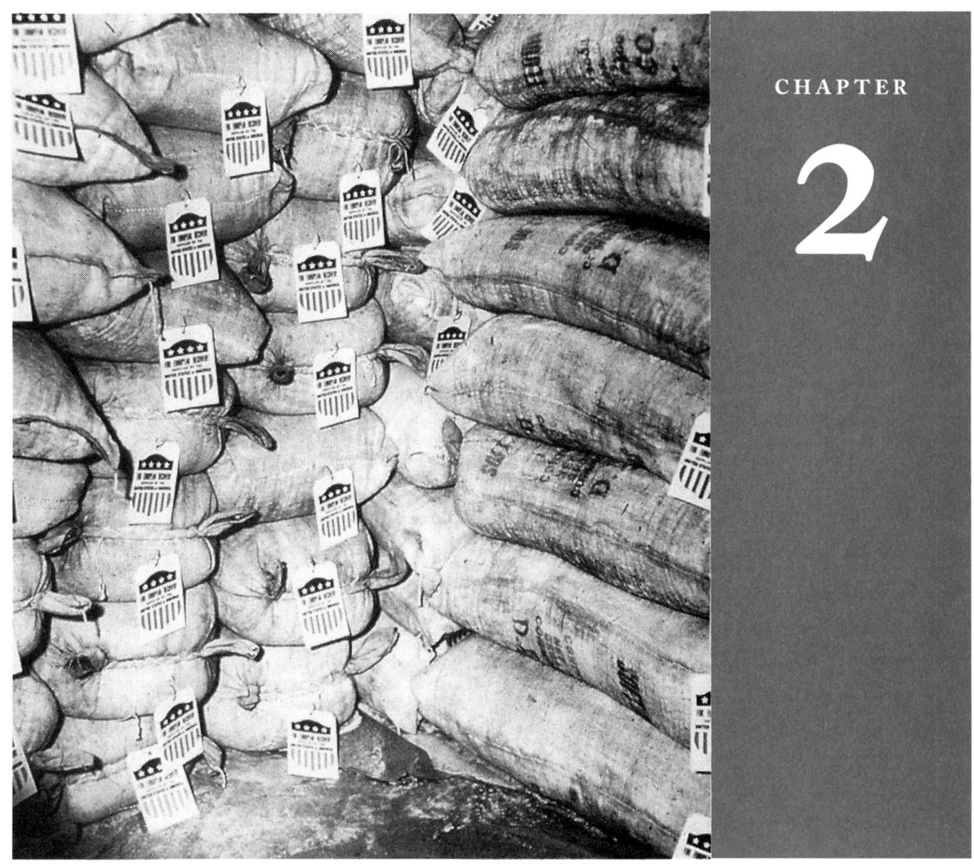

CHAPTER

2

AMERICA'S GLOBAL INVOLVEMENT AND THE EMERGENCE OF THE COLD WAR

It is logical that the United States should do whatever it is able to do to assist in the return of normal economic health in the world.... Our policy is directed not against any country or doctrine but against hunger, poverty, desperation and chaos. Its purpose should be the revival of a working economy in the world so as to permit the emergence of political and social conditions in which free institutions can exist.

Secretary of State George C. Marshall
Address at Harvard University
June 5, 1947

It is clear that the main element of any United States policy toward the Soviet Union must be that of a long-term, patient but firm and vigilant containment of Russian expansive tendencies.

Mr. X [George F. Kennan]
"The Sources of Soviet Conduct"
Foreign Affairs, July 1947

World War II plunged the United States fully into global affairs. By the end of 1941, the country had fully committed itself to total victory, and its involvement was to prove crucial to the war effort. Because of its central importance to allied success, and its substantive involvement in international affairs, the United States found it difficult to change course in 1945 and revert to the isolationism of the past. To be sure, the first impulse was in this direction. Calls were heard for massive demobilization of the armed forces, cutbacks in the New Deal legislation of President Franklin Delano Roosevelt, and other efforts toward political and economic isolationism.[1] However, at least three sets of factors militated against such a course and propelled the United States in the direction of global power: (1) the global political and economic conditions of 1945 to 1947; (2) the decision of leading political figures within the United States to abandon isolationism after World War II; and, most important, (3) the rise of an ideological challenge from the Soviet Union.

In this chapter, we first examine these factors and how they led to the abandonment of isolationism and the adoption of globalism by the United States. In turn, we set forth the military, economic, and political dimensions of this new globalist involvement—summarized under the rubric of the containment doctrine—and discuss how this involvement became both universal in scope and remained moral in content. As will be shown in Chapter 3, moreover, the containment doctrine produced a distinct set of foreign policy values, beliefs, and actions on the part of the United States.

THE POSTWAR WORLD AND AMERICAN INVOLVEMENT

The international system that the United States faced after the defeat of Germany and Japan was considerably different from any that it had faced in its history: The traditional powers of Europe were defeated or had been ruined by the ravages of war; the global economy had been significantly weakened by that war; and a relatively new power, the Soviet Union, equipped with a threatening ideology, had survived the war—arguably in better shape than any other European power. Yet, the United States was in a relatively strong political, economic, and military position. Such conditions seemed to imply the need for sustained U.S. involvement, despite its isolationist past. Yet, such a decision for involvement was made neither quickly or automatically; rather, it seemed to come about over the course of several years and largely through the confluence of several complementary factors. We begin our discussion, therefore, with a brief description of three of these factors and suggest how they interacted with one another to move the United States toward sustained global involvement.

The Global Vacuum: A Challenge to American Isolationism

The first important factor that contributed to America's decision to move away from isolationism was the political and economic conditions of the international system immediately after World War II. The land, the cities, and the homes, along with the economies, of most European nations had been devastated by the war. Sizeable portions of the land had been either flooded, scorched from battle, or confiscated for military operations. Even the land that remained for cultivation was in poor condition. Hunger was widespread, and a black market in food flourished. The industrial sectors of these nations, along with the major cities, were badly damaged or in total ruins. London, Vienna, Trieste, Warsaw, Berlin, Rotterdam, and Cologne, among others, bore the scars of war. Millions of people were homeless, too. By one estimate, 5 million homes had been destroyed, with many more millions badly damaged. In a word, Europe was a "wasteland."[2]

European economies were weak, in debt, and driven by inflation. Britain, for example, had to use up much of its wealth to win the war and, with a debt of about $6 billion at war's end, had to rely upon American assistance to remain solvent.[3] France, the Netherlands, Belgium, and other European states were in no better shape. Each had to rely, in varying degrees, upon American assistance to meet its financial needs. Foreign and domestic political problems also faced these states. Several British and French colonies were demanding freedom and independence. In Syria, Lebanon, Indochina, and later Tunisia, Morocco, and Algeria, for instance, indigenous movements were seeking independence from France. The British were confronted by independence efforts in India, Burma, Ceylon, and Palestine, among others. Britain faced domestic austerity, while the French struggled at home with governmental instability and worker discontent. With such problems at home and abroad, neither of these states was in a position to assert a very prominent role in postwar international politics.

The conditions in Germany and Italy further contributed to the political and economic vacuum in Europe. Both of these powers had been defeated, and Germany was divided and occupied. Italy had a huge budget deficit in 1945–46 (300 billion lire by one estimate) as well as an extraordinarily high rate of inflation. Germany, too, was in debt, owing nearly nine times more than at the beginning of World War II.[4] Overall, then, Europe, which for so long had been at the center of international politics and for so long had shaped global order, was ominously weak, both politically and economically. None of the traditional European powers seemed able to exert its traditional dominance in global politics.

In contrast to the postwar portrait of Europe, the United States was healthy and prosperous. Its industrial capacity was intact, and its economy was still booming. In the middle 1940s, the United States had growing balance of trade surpluses and huge economic reserves. For example, while

Europe had trade deficits of $5.8 billion and $7.6 billion in 1946 and 1947, the United States in those same years had trade surpluses of $6.7 billion and $10.1 billion. Furthermore, American reserve assets—about $26 billion—were substantial and growing.[5]

The military might of the United States, too, seemed preeminent at that time. American troops occupied Europe and Japan. The nation had the world's largest navy ("The Pacific and the Mediterranean had become American lakes," in the words of one historian[6]). And, of course, the United States alone had the atomic bomb. In this sense, the United States possessed the capacity to assume a global role. Moreover, the international environment seemed highly conducive to both the possibility, and the necessity, for America to play a dominant role in global affairs.

American Leadership and Global Involvement

A second factor that encouraged the United States to abandon its isolationist strategy was the change in world view among American leaders during and immediately after World War II. Most important, President Franklin Roosevelt had long concluded that America's response to global affairs after World War I had been ill-advised and that such a response should not guide American policy after World War II.[7] Instead, Roosevelt had decided that continued American involvement in global affairs was necessary and, early on in the war, had revealed his vision of world order in the postwar period.

Roosevelt's Plan. The first necessity in Roosevelt's plan was the total defeat and disarming of the adversaries, with no leniency shown toward aggressor states. Second, there must be a renewed commitment on the part of the United States and others to prevent future global economic depressions and to foster self-determination for all states. Third, there must be the establishment of a global collective security organization with active American involvement. Finally, above and beyond these efforts, the allies in war must remain allies in peace in order to maintain global order.[8]

This last element of the plan was the core of Roosevelt's global blueprint.[9] American involvement in world affairs and its cooperation with the other great powers were essential. Indeed, Roosevelt's design envisaged a world in which this postwar cooperation among the four principal powers (United States, Great Britain, USSR, and China) would yield a system in which they acted as the "Four Policemen" to enforce global order. In other words, unlike Wilson's League of Nations, where all states would act to stop warfare and regulate conflict, only the great powers would have this responsibility. Such a vision bore a striking and unmistakable resemblance to traditional balance of power politics, although Roosevelt was unwilling to describe it in such terms.

Strategy: Building Wartime Cooperation. To make this global design a reality, two major tasks confronted Roosevelt's diplomatic efforts during the war. One was directed toward building wartime cooperation, which would continue after the war. The other was directed toward jarring the United States from its isolationist moorings and positioning the country in such a way that it would retain a role in postwar international politics. To realize the first goal, the building of cooperation with the Soviet Union was deemed essential. Roosevelt, unlike some of his advisors and some State Department officials, believed that cooperation with the Soviet Union was possible after the end of World War II. He believed that the Soviet Union was motivated, in the shorthand of Daniel Yergin, more by the "Yalta Axioms" (the name is taken from the 1945 wartime conference in which political bargains were struck between East and West) than by the "Riga Axioms" (the name is taken from the Latvian capital city where a U.S. mission was located which "issued constant warning against the [Soviet] international menace" in the 1920s and 1930s.[10]

In the Yalta view, the Soviet Union was much like other nations in terms of defining its interests and fostering its goals based on power realities (the Yalta Axioms) rather than being driven primarily by ideological considerations (the Riga Axioms). As Yergin contends, "Roosevelt thought of the Soviet Union less as a revolutionary vanguard than as a conventional imperialist power, with ambitions rather like those of the Czarist regime."[11] Because of this perceived source of Soviet policy, Roosevelt judged that the Grand Alliance would be able to continue on a "businesslike" level as long as each recognized the interests of the other. Moreover, since the Soviet Union would be concerned about the reconstruction of its economy and society after the devastation of the war, it would have even further incentives to seek postwar stability and peace.

According to one well-known political analyst, there was another reason why Roosevelt thought that this cooperation could continue: the power of personal diplomacy.[12] Because Roosevelt had steered American policy toward the recognition of the Soviet Union, shared Stalin anxiety over British imperialism, and seemed to recognize Soviet interest in the Baltics and Poland, cooperation would be possible.

To facilitate postwar cooperation with the Soviets, Roosevelt made a concerted effort throughout the war to foster good relations with them. The United States extended Lend-Lease assistance to the Soviet Union (albeit not as rapidly as the Soviet Union wished) and agreed to open up a second front against the Germans to relieve the battlefield pressure placed on them (albeit not as soon as the Soviet Union wanted). Through the several wartime conferences—Teheran, Cairo, Moscow, and Yalta—Roosevelt gained an understanding of the degree of Soviet insecurity regarding its exposed western borders and the need to take this factor into account in dealing with them. At the same time, though, he became increasingly convinced that he could work with "Uncle Joe" Stalin and that political bargains and accommodations with the Soviets were possible.

Strategy: A Role in Postwar International Politics. Among the wartime conferences, the one that bears most directly upon postwar arrangements was the Yalta Conference, held in that Crimean resort during February 1945. Not only did this conference achieve agreement on a strategy for the completion of the war effort, but also it appeared to achieve commitments on the division and operation of postwar Europe. Such understandings were important since they signaled continued American interest and involvement in global affairs—specifically Europe's—but they also signaled that the competing interests of states were subject to negotiation and accommodation. Spheres of influence and balance of power politics were expressly incorporated in these agreements, and the major powers were to possess the greatest amount of importance in fulfilling them.[13]

Specifically, Roosevelt, Stalin, and British Prime Minister Winston Churchill agreed to zones of occupation of Germany by the Americans, British, French, and Russians. Second, they provided some territorial concessions to the Soviets at the expense of Poland. (In turn, Poland was to receive some territory from Germany.) Third, the wartime leaders allowed an expansion of the Lublin Committee, which was governing Poland, to include some Polish government officials who were in exile in London as a way of dealing with the postwar government question in Poland. Fourth, they proclaimed the Declaration of Liberated Europe, which specified free elections and constitutional safeguards of individual freedom in the liberated nations. And, finally, the conferees produced an agreement on the Soviet Union's joining the war against Japan and the veto mechanism within the Security Council of the United Nations.[14]

In light of subsequent events, Roosevelt has been highly criticized for the bargains that were made at Yalta. The Soviets got several territorial concessions and were able in the space of a few short years to gain control of the Polish government as well as other Eastern European governments. Roosevelt's rationale was that only by taking into account the interests of the various parties (including the Soviets) was a stable postwar world possible. Moreover, he also appeared to consider the Soviet sense of insecurity along its western border in making some of these arrangements. Finally, and perhaps most importantly, Soviet troops already occupied these Eastern European states.[15] Any prospects of a more favorable outcome for the Western states appeared to be more in the realm of hope than a real possibility. Despite these criticisms, the Yalta agreements do mark the beginning of an American commitment to global involvement beyond the wartime period. In addition, with the agreement on the operation of the Security Council and the subsequent conference on the United Nations Charter in San Francisco during April 1945, the United States was rather quickly moving itself toward global involvement.[16]

The Rise of the Soviet Challenge

This commitment to international involvement was no less true for President Roosevelt's successor, Harry S Truman, and his principal foreign policy advisors. But this commitment was expanded and solidified by the rise of the Soviet ideological challenge that developed by late 1946 and early 1947.

Although Truman's foreign policy approach was not nearly as well developed as that outlined by Roosevelt's postwar plan, there was no inclination on the part of President Truman to reject continued American involvement in the world. Three sets of factors seem to have shaped his commitment to involvement: (1) his Wilsonian idealism, (2) the wartime situation existing when he assumed office, and (3) the views of his principal foreign policy advisors.

MAP 2.1

Europe Divided Between East and West After World War II

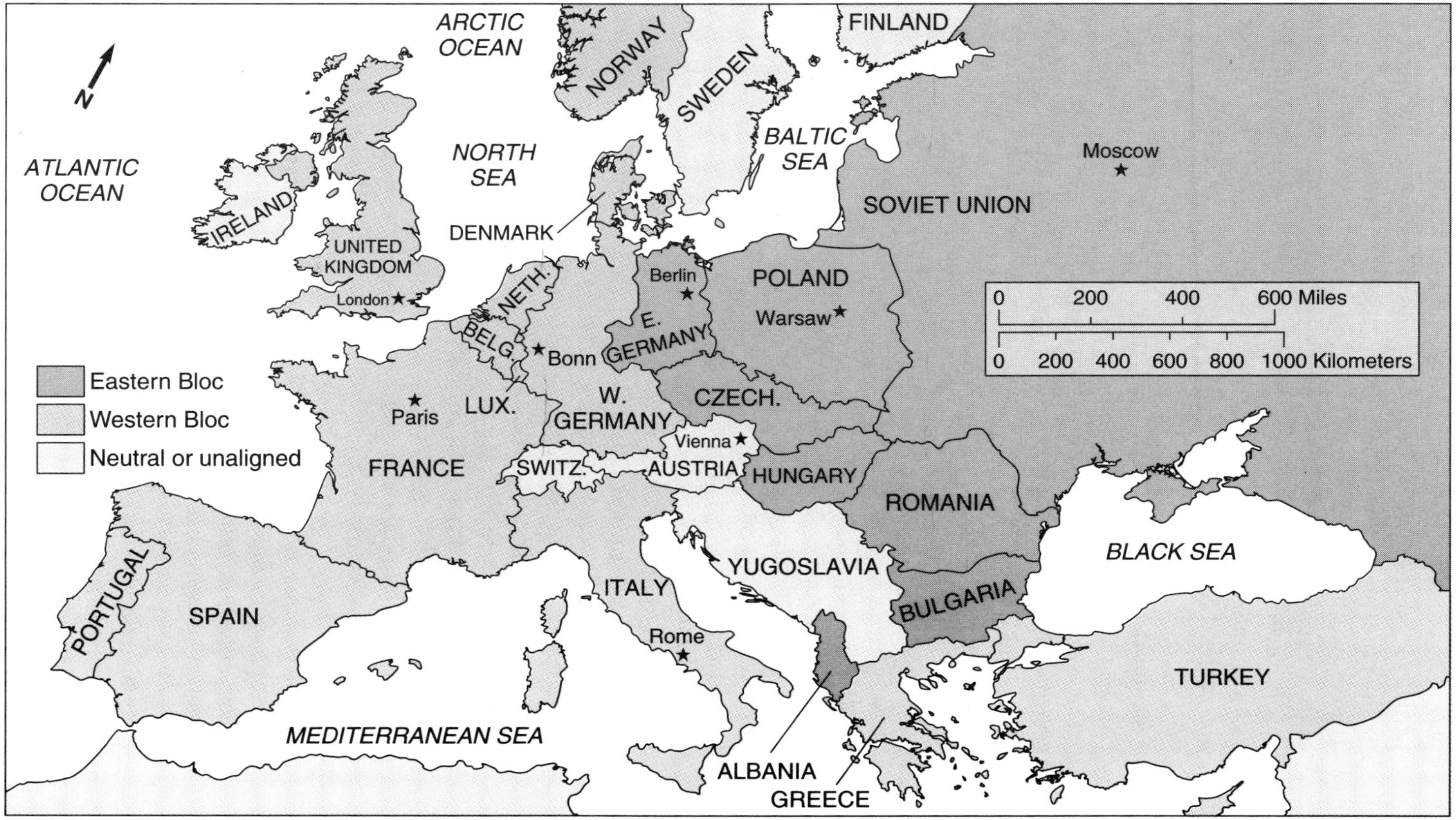

Wilsonian Idealism. Truman, prior to assuming the presidency, had displayed a commitment to an international role for the United States. In particular, he agreed with Woodrow Wilson that America should participate in world affairs, particularly through a global organization. As a consequence, Truman worked in the Senate to gain support for the emergent United Nations. At the same time, like Wilson, he tended to see the United States as a moral force in the world and was somewhat suspicious of the postwar design epitomized by the Four Policemen plan.[17] Nonetheless, he supported and worked to put Roosevelt's plan into practice.

Wartime Situation. Truman's commitment to global involvement was aided by the circumstances at the time he became president. President Roosevelt had died just after the Yalta agreements on postwar Europe had been concluded, just prior to the United Nations Conference in San Francisco, and just before the Allies had been ultimately successful in World War II. As a result, Truman felt the Yalta agreements had to be implemented, the United Nations needed to become a reality, and the war had to be won. In all of these areas, President Truman forged ahead along the lines of his predecessor.

Views of Truman's Advisors. Truman's closest advisors were also influential in reinforcing the commitment to a global role for the United States. In particular, such key advisors as Admiral William D. Leahy, Ambassador Averell Harriman, Secretary of State Edward R. Stettinius, and Secretary of War Henry Stimson all counseled for a continuance of a leading role for the United States.[18] Later, such men as Secretary of State James Byrnes, Under Secretary of State (and later Secretary of State) Dean Acheson, and Navy Secretary James V. Forrestal became Truman's key policy advisors. These new advisors also tended to favor an active global involvement, especially with their less favorable view of the Soviet Union, although, according to historian Ernest May, "their prejudices and predispositions can serve as only one small element" in the change of American policy toward the Soviet Union.[19]

Nevertheless, the issue soon became less one of whether there should be American global involvement and more a question of the degree of that involvement. Fueled by negative assessments of the Soviet Union by seasoned diplomatic observers, Truman's advisors increasingly focused upon the threat posed by international communism generally and by the Soviet Union specifically.[20] In time, the shape of America's postwar global role became largely a consequence of the perceived intentions of Soviet ideology.

Truman's Early Position. In the first months after assuming office, President Truman followed Roosevelt's strategy for peace and American involvement by trying to maintain great-power unity. As he said: "I want peace and I am willing to work hard for it:...to have a reasonably lasting peace, the three great powers must be able to trust each other." Likewise, he remained faithful to the requirements of the Yalta agreements and tried to cajole Stalin to do the same by telling Soviet Foreign Minister Molotov to "carry out your agreements."[21]

A Changing Environment. But by the time of the Potsdam Conference (July 1945), President Truman was increasingly urged to be tough with the Soviets, while still seeking postwar cooperation. Although the accommodation that came out of Potsdam over German reparations and German boundaries, as well as other agreements, were deemed tolerable, American officials ultimately came away uneasy over the future prospects of Soviet-American relations.[22] Subsequent meetings in London (September 1945), over peace treaties for Finland, Hungary, Romania, and Bulgaria, and in Moscow (December 1945), over adherence to the Yalta accords, reinforced this uneasiness and continued to highlight the growing suspicion between the United States and the Soviet Union.[23]

The end of the 1945 and early months of 1946 seemed to mark a watershed in Soviet-American relations.[24] By this time, the American public, Congress, and the president's chief advisors were increasingly lobbying for tougher action against Soviet noncompliance with the Yalta agreements and with its efforts to undermine governments in Eastern Europe. Coupled with these domestic pressures were ominous statements by Stalin and Churchill about American and Soviet intentions toward the world.

Stalin Attacks Capitalism. In a speech on February 9, 1946, Soviet leader Joseph Stalin alarmed American policy makers by attacking capitalism, suggesting the inevitability of war among capitalist states, and calling for significant economic strides to meet the capitalist challenge. At the outset of the speech, Stalin noted the dangers from capitalist states: "Marxists have repeatedly declared that the capitalist world economic system conceals in itself the elements of general crisis and military clashes...." Near the end, Stalin asserted that "the party intends to organize a new powerful advance in the national economy.... Only under these circumstances is it possible to consider that our country will be guaranteed against any eventuality."[25]

While the meaning and intent of Stalin's remarks inevitably fostered some debate (one analysis suggested that Stalin really did not want a "new war" and said so through 1947), and it should be noted that these comments "constituted about one–tenth of the address,"[26] the ultimate effect was quite profound on American policy makers. Indeed, in the assessment of two prominent diplomatic historians of this period, the meaning of these passages was clear. Stalin was suggesting that "war was inevitable as long as capitalism existed," and "that future wars were inevitable until the world economic system was reformed, that is, until communism supplanted capitalism...."[27]

Churchill's Response. On March 5, 1946, Winston Churchill reciprocated by articulating the West's fear of the East. In his famous "iron curtain" speech at Westminster College in Fulton, Missouri, Churchill called for "a fraternal association of the English-speaking peoples...a special relationship between the British Commonwealth and Empire and the United States" to provide global order since "from Stettin in the Baltic to Trieste in the Adriatic, an iron curtain has descended across the Continent. Behind that line lie all the capitals of the ancient states of Central and Eastern Europe." Moreover, these states and many ancient cities "lie in what I must call the Soviet sphere," Churchill continued, "and all are subject in one form or another, not only to Soviet influence but to a very high and, in many cases, increasing measure of control from Moscow."[28] This speech marked a frontal attack on the Soviet Union, and, like Stalin's February speech, suggested the impossibility of continued Soviet-American cooperation in the postwar world because of the differing world view held by each nation. Importantly, President Truman seemed to be giving some legitimacy to such a view, since he accompanied Churchill to Missouri.[29]

Kennan's Perception from Moscow. At about the same time as these two important speeches were delivered, George Kennan, an American diplomat serving in Moscow at the time, sent his famous "long telegram" to Washington. (The actual date of the message is February 22, 1946.) In this lengthy message, Kennan outlined his view of the basic premises of the Soviet world outlook, the "Kremlin's neurotic view of world affairs," the "instinctive Russian sense of insecurity," and its "official" and "subterranean" actions against free societies. Its policies, Kennan argued, will work vigorously to advance Soviet interests worldwide and to undermine Western powers. "In general," Kennan noted near the end of the message that "all Soviet efforts on [an] unofficial international plane will be negative and destructive in character, designed to tear down sources of strength beyond reach of Soviet control."

Kennan, however, put it even more succinctly in the concluding section of the telegram:

> ...we have here a political force committed fanatically to the belief that with US there can be no permanent modus vivendi, that it is desirable and necessary that the internal harmony of our society be disrupted, our traditional way of life be destroyed, the international authority of our state be broken, if Soviet power is to be secure. Finally, it is seemingly inaccessible to considerations of reality in its basic reactions. For it, the vast fund of objective facts about human society is not, as with us, the measure against which outlook is constantly tested and reformed, but a grab bag from which individual items are selected arbitrarily and tendentiously to bolster an outlook already preconceived.[30]

In essence, this view of the Soviet Union has come to be summarized as the Riga Axioms (in contrast to the Yalta Axioms, which President Roosevelt had adopted). Ideology, and not the realities of power politics, was the important determinant of Soviet conduct.

These statements by Stalin and Churchill and the circulation of Kennan's "long telegram" within the Washington bureaucracy increased the clamor for a changed policy toward the Soviet Union.[31] They produced a "get tough" policy on the part of the United States. And they permanently changed the role of the United States in global affairs.

AMERICA'S GLOBALISM: THE TRUMAN DOCTRINE AND BEYOND

The immediate response to these calls for a "get tough" policy was reflected in American policy over Soviet troops remaining in Iran in March 1946.

Under the Tripartite Treaty of Alliance signed by Iran, the Soviet Union, and Great Britain in January 1942, Allied forces were to be withdrawn from Iranian territory within six months after hostilities had ended between the Allies and the Axis powers. By March 2, 1946—six months after the surrender of Japan—all British and American forces had indeed withdrawn from Iran, but Soviet forces had not. Instead, the Soviets were sending additional troops into Iran, were continuing to meddle in Iranian politics, and apparently had designs on Turkey and Iraq from their Iranian base.[32]

With such circumstances, the American leadership decided to stand firm on the withdrawal of Soviet forces. Secretary of State James Byrnes and British Foreign Minister Ernest Bevin gave important speeches that made the West's position clear. In a late February 1946 speech, Secretary Byrnes had asserted:

> We have joined our allies in the United Nations to put an end to war. We have covenanted not to use force except in the defense of law as embodied in the purposes and principles of the [U.N.] Charter. We intend to live up to that covenant.
>
> But as a great power and as a permanent member of the Security Council *we have a responsibility to use our influence to see that other powers live up to their covenant....*
>
> We will not and we cannot stand aloof if force or threat of force is used contrary to the purposes and principles of the Charter. We have no right to hold our troops in the territories of other sovereign states without their approval and consent freely given...[33]

Later, on March 16, Secretary of State Byrnes reiterated American resolve in another speech by repeating some of the themes from the earlier address, although, in addition, he urged an extension of the expiring military draft and called for the adoption of universal military service in the future. The target of such proposed measures was unmistakable.

Faced with British and American resolve and with an imminent UN Security Council session on the Iranian issue, the Soviet Union began to seek a negotiated solution. In early April 1946, an agreement was reached that called for the withdrawal of all Soviet forces from Iran by the middle of May 1946.[34]

Thus, when America adopted a tougher policy line toward the Soviet Union, it was able to achieve results. Despite the initial success of this firmer course in early 1946, the real change in America's policy toward the Soviets (and ultimately toward the rest of the world) was not fully manifested until a year later.

The occasion for the formal pronouncement of this sharp turn in policy, from one of accommodation to one of confrontation, was over the question of aid to Greece and Turkey to enable them to combat threats to their security. The Greek government was under pressure from a Communist-supported national liberation movement, while Turkey was under political pressure from the Soviet Union and its allies over control of the Dardanelles (the straits that provide access to the Mediterranean from the Soviet Union's Black Sea ports) and over territorial concessions to the Soviets in Turkish-Soviet border areas.[35] Because the British, in February 1947, had indicated to the Americans that they could no longer aid these countries, the burden apparently now fell to the Americans if these states were to remain stable.

Accordingly, President Truman decided to seek $400 million in aid for these Mediterranean states.

The granting of aid itself was not a sharp break from the past, since the United States had provided assistance in 1946.[36] What was dramatic about the aid request was its *form, rationale, and purpose.* The form of the request was a formal speech by President Truman to a joint session of Congress on March 12, 1947. The rationale for the request was even more dramatic: a need to stop the expansion of global communism. And the purpose was startling: to commit the United States to a global strategy against this Communist threat.

In his speech, in which he announced what has come to be known as the Truman Doctrine, the president first set out the conditions within Greece and Turkey that necessitated this assistance. Then he more fully outlined the justification for his policy and identified the global struggle that the United States faced. The United States, he said, must *"help free peoples to maintain their free institutions and their national identity against aggressive movements that seek to impose upon them totalitarian regimes."* Moreover, such threats to freedom affect the security of the United States: "*...totalitarian regimes imposed upon free peoples, by direct or indirect aggression, undermine the foundations of international peace and hence the security of the United States.*" At this juncture in history, President Truman continued, the nations of the world face a decision between two ways of life: one free, the other unfree; one based "upon the will of the majority," the other based upon "the will of a minority," one based upon "free institutions," the other based upon "terror and oppression." The task for the United States, therefore, is a clear one, he concluded "*...we must assist free peoples to work out their own destinies in their own way.*" The challenge to the Soviet Union was now clearly drawn. And the Cold War had begun.[37]

The specific policy that the United States was to adopt in this struggle with the Soviet Union was the containment strategy. This term was first used in an anonymously authored article in *Foreign Affairs* magazine in July 1947. (Its author was quickly identified, though, as George Kennan, by then the head of the Policy Planning Staff at the Department of State in Washington, and the article actually grew out of his original "Long Telegram" sent to the State Department a year earlier.) According to Kennan, the appropriate policy to adopt against the Soviet challenge was "a long-term patient but firm and vigilant containment of Russian expansive tendencies." Specifically, he called for the application of "counter-force at a series of constantly shifting geographical and political points," against Soviet action. By following such a policy, the United States may, over time, force "a far greater degree of moderation and circumspection...and in this way...promote...tendencies which must eventually find their outlet in either the break-up or the gradual mellowing of Soviet power."[38]

Kennan identified a number of conditions within the Soviet system that would aid this containment policy in achieving the prescribed goal. The population "in Russia today," he noted, "is physically and spiritually tired." The impact of the Soviet system on the young remains unclear. The performance of the Soviet economy "has been precariously spotty and uneven."[39] And the issue of succession is surely incomplete:

> ...the future of Soviet power may not be by any means as secure as Russian capacity for self-delusion would make it appear to the men in the Kremlin. That they can keep power themselves, they have demonstrated. That they can quietly and easily turn it over to others remains to be proved.[40]

Although Kennan was confident that a steady course by the United States would be successful, he was not precise in stating what the actual substance of the counterforce or containment toward the Soviet Union should be. As a result, the response by American policy makers was to embark upon a series of sweeping military, economic, and political initiatives from 1947 through the middle 1950s to control international communism, a direction that Kennan was actually to criticize later.[41]

ELEMENTS OF CONTAINMENT: REGIONAL SECURITY PACTS

The first, and probably principal, containment initiative was the establishment of several regional politico-military alliances. In Latin America, the *Rio Pact* (formally known as the Inter-American Treaty of Reciprocal Assistance) was signed in September 1947 by the United States and twenty-one other American republics. In Western Europe, the *North Atlantic Treaty Organization* (NATO) was set up in April 1949 by the United States, Canada, and ten (later thirteen) Western European nations. In Asia, two important pacts were established: the *ANZUS Treaty* of September 1951,[42] and the Southeast Asia Collective Defense Treaty of September 1954. The former treaty involved the United States, Australia, and New Zealand, while the latter included the United States, the United Kingdom, France, Australia, New Zealand, Pakistan, the Philippines, and Thailand and formed what became known as the *Southeast Asia Treaty Organization* (SEATO). For the SEATO treaty, a protocol was added to provide security protection for South Vietnam, Cambodia, and Laos. (This protocol would become most important in light of America's subsequent involvement in the Vietnam War.)[43] Map 2.2 portrays these organizations and the areas covered by each and also summarizes the principal goals of each organization and the nations that comprise the membership.

One other collective security organization, the *Central Treaty Organization* (CENTO), was also established during this time period, although the United States was not a direct member. This organization evolved out of a bilateral pact of mutual cooperation between Iraq and Turkey (the so-called Baghdad Pact of February 1955) and was formally constituted in 1959 with the inclusion of the United Kingdom, Pakistan, and Iran. However, through an executive agreement with Turkey, the United States pledged to support the security needs of CENTO members and to provide various kinds of assistance. In addition, the United States actively participated in CENTO meetings and assisted with the pact's joint undertakings. Because of the active involvement in the operation of the organization by the United States and because of its indirect pledge of support, CENTO was actually another link in the global security arrangements the United States initiated

MAP 2.2

United States Collective Defense Arrangements

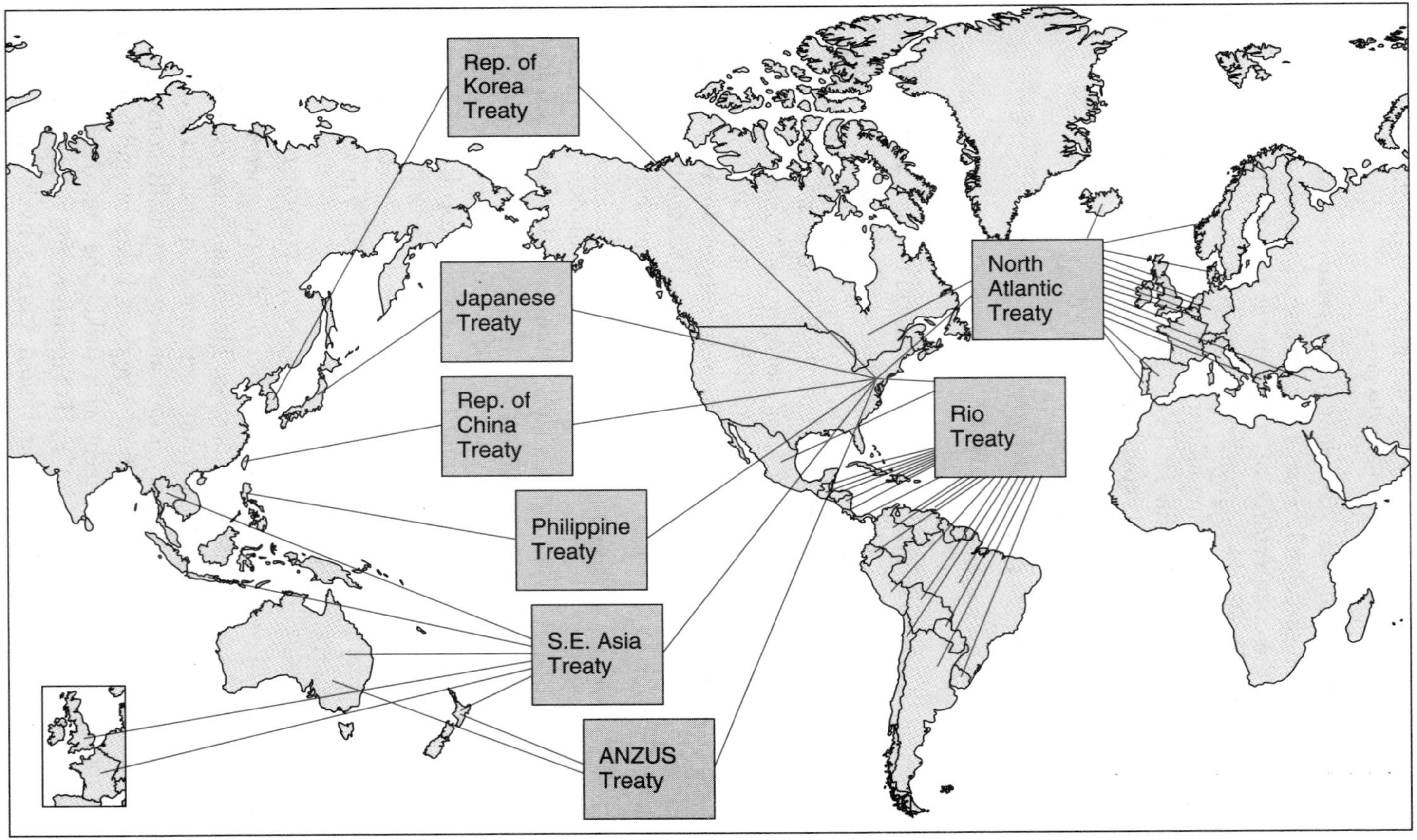

Rep. of Korea Treaty
Japanese Treaty
Rep. of China Treaty
Philippine Treaty
S.E. Asia Treaty
ANZUS Treaty
North Atlantic Treaty
Rio Treaty

Multilateral Pacts

Rio Treaty, or the Inter-American Treaty of Reciprocal Assistance (22 Nations)

A treaty signed September 2, 1947, which provides that an armed attack against any American state, "shall be considered as an attack against all the American States and...each one...undertakes to assist in meeting the attack...."

Membership: United States, Mexico, Cuba, Haiti, Dominican Republic, Honduras, Guatemala, El Salvador, Nicaragua, Costa Rica, Panama, Colombia, Venezuela, Ecuador, Peru, Brazil, Bolivia, Paraguay, Chile, Argentina, Uruguay, and Trinidad and Tobago

North Atlantic Treaty (16 Nations)

A treaty signed April 4, 1949, by which "the Parties agree that an armed attack against one or more of them in Europe or North America shall be considered an attack against them all; and...each of them...will assist the...attacked by taking forthwith, individually and in concert with the other Parties, such action as it deems necessary, including the use of armed force...."

Membership: United States, Canada, Iceland, Norway, United Kingdom, Netherlands, Denmark, Belgium, Luxembourg, Portugal, France, Italy, Greece (joined in 1952), Turkey (1952), Federal Republic of Germany (1955), and Spain (1982)

ANZUS Treaty (3 Nations)

A treaty signed September 1, 1951, whereby each of the parties "recognizes that an armed attack in the Pacific Area on any of the Parties would be dangerous to its own peace and safety and declares that it would act to meet the common danger in accordance with its constitutional processes."

Membership: United States, New Zealand, and Australia

Southeast Asia Treaty (7 Nations)

A treaty signed September 8, 1954, whereby each party "recognizes that aggression by means of armed attack in the treaty area against any of the Parties...would endanger its own peace and safety" and each will "in that event act to meet the common danger in accordance with its constitutional processes."

Membership: United States, United Kingdom, France, New Zealand, Australia, Philippines, and Thailand

Bilateral Pacts

Philippine Treaty

A treaty signed August 30, 1951, whereby each of the parties recognizes "that an armed attack in the Pacific Area on either of the Parties would be dangerous to its own peace and safety" and each party agrees that it will act "to meet the common danger in accordance with its constitutional processes."

Membership: United States and the Philippines

Japanese Treaty

A treaty signed January 19, 1960 (replacing the original security treaty of September 8, 1951), whereby each party "recognizes that an armed attack against either Party in the territories under the administration of Japan would be dangerous to its own peace and safety and declares that it would act to meet the common danger in accordance with its constitutional provisions and processes."

Membership: United States and Japan

Republic of Korea Treaty

A treaty signed October 1, 1953, whereby each party "recognizes that an armed attack in the Pacific area on either of the Parties...would be dangerous to its own peace and safety" and that each party "would act to meet the common danger in accordance with its constitutional processes."

Membership: United States and the Republic of Korea

Republic of China Treaty

A treaty signed December 2, 1954, whereby each of the parties "recognizes than an armed attack in the West Pacific Area directed against the territories of either of the Parties would be dangerous to its own peace and safety..." and that each "would act to meet the common danger in accordance with its constitutional processes." The territory of the Republic of China is defined as "Taiwan (Formosa) and the Pescadores."

Membership: United States and the Republic of China

Source: U.S. Department of State, Bureau of Public Affairs, September 1977 and April 1981.

in the immediate postwar years. All of these defense agreements had provisions for assistance when confronted by armed attacks, threats of aggression, or even internal subversion in the case of SEATO. For the ANZUS, SEATO, Rio, and CENTO pacts, however, the response was not automatic. Instead, in the main, each of the signatories agreed "to meet the common danger in accordance with its constitutional processes."[44] NATO is usually identified as an exception among these pacts for at least two reasons: (1) the commitment by the parties to respond to an attack appears to be more automatic than the other pact, and (2) the organizational structure within NATO developed much more fully than in the other pacts.

First, Article 5 of the NATO agreement seemed to call an automatic armed response on the part of the signatories to an attack:

> The Parties agree that an armed attack against one or more of them in Europe or North America shall be considered an attack against them all, and consequently they agree that, if such an armed attack occurs, each of them...will assist the Party or Parties so attacked forthwith, individually, and in concert with the other Parties, such action as it deems necessary, including the use of armed force, to restore and maintain the security of the North Atlantic area.[45]

Yet constitutional scholar Michael Glennon has cautioned against too facile an interpretation of this article. As he noted, a party to the pact could take actions it "deems necessary," but troops are not necessarily required automatically. Indeed, at the time, Secretary of State Dean Acheson, in commenting on this treaty provision—both in a public address and in a congressional hearing—downplayed the automaticity of troop commitments, since, he acknowledged, only Congress had that authority. However, both Acheson and congressional allies of the Truman administration vigorously opposed a reservation to the NATO treaty that would have spelled out the limited nature of the commitment more fully. The Truman administration apparently wanted to maintain some ambiguity over the meaning of this article, both to accommodate critics at home and to reassure allies abroad.[46] In this sense, the commitment in the NATO treaty does appear to be a bit different than in the other pacts during this time.

Second, the members of the NATO pact also established an integrated military command structure and called for the commitment of forces to NATO (although the forces remained under ultimate national command) by each of the member states. In both of these ways, then, NATO proved the most important of the regional security pacts, since it involved the area of greatest concern for American interests and because Europe was regarded as the primary area of potential Soviet aggression.

In addition to the regional military organizations that were set up, a series of bilateral defense pacts were established in Asia to combat Soviet and Chinese aggression. Bilateral pacts were completed with the Philippines (1951), Japan (1951), the Republic of Korea (1953), and the Republic of China (Taiwan–1954). These pacts resulted from two major political events in Asia in the late 1940s and early 1950s—the Communist triumph in China and the war that broke out in Korea.

By October 1949, Mao Zedong had won the civil war and had established the People's Republic of China. He quickly sought close ties with the leader of the Communist world—the Soviet Union—and the United States immediately viewed the Communist movement as increasingly powerful and challenging to U.S. and Western interests. As a result, the United States refused to recognize Mao's regime and discouraged other states from doing so. (Indeed, formal diplomatic relations would not develop until three decades later, in 1979.) Instead, the United States continued to support its ally in the Chinese civil war, Chiang Kai-shek, who had fled to the island of Taiwan, and recognized his government, the Republic of China, as the official government of all China. The United States also began to deploy its Seventh Fleet in the Taiwan Straits to discourage any attempts by the mainland to invade Taiwan or, conversely, for the island government to seek to invade the mainland.[47]

The second major upheaval in Asia was the Korean War, which lasted from 1950 to 1953. In June 1950, North Korea attacked South Korea. In response, American forces were dispatched to South Korea under United Nations auspices to fight what became a protracted war. During this war, Chinese Communist "volunteers" assisted the North Koreans. The involvement of both Communist powers raised concern over the aggressive intentions of these states and served as further motivation for the establishment of defense pacts in the area. The Korean War is discussed in more detail in a later section of this chapter, since it is often cited as the first real test of containment and the event that brought the Cold War to fruition.[48]

With these bilateral treaties in the early 1950s, the mosaic of global security was largely completed. Moreover, a quick look at Map 2.2 indicates that the United States was quite successful in forming alliances in most areas that were not directly under Soviet control.

Nevertheless, two prominent regions, Africa and the Middle East, were still not directly covered by these security arrangements. Here too, however, some elements of containment were evident. In Africa, for instance, the European colonial powers still held sway, and thus the region was largely under the containment shield through these allied states.[49] The security efforts in the Middle East region were more complex. Although the regimes in this area at this time were mainly traditional monarchies, stirrings of nationalism and pan-Arabism within Egypt under Gamal Abdel Nasser and the spread of these sentiments throughout the region made treaty commitments difficult. Added to these factors were America's close ties to Israel over the festering Arab-Israeli conflict. Despite these hindrances, the United States did initiate one important security proposal to the nations in this volatile area: the so-called Eisenhower Doctrine.

This doctrine arose from a speech given by President Eisenhower to a joint session of Congress over perceived trouble in the Middle East and the need for the United States to combat it. "If power-hungry Communists should either falsely or correctly estimate that the Middle East is inadequately defended, they might be tempted to use open measures of armed attack," President Eisenhower declared. To combat this eventuality, he asked Congress for authority to extend economic and military assistance as needed and "to use armed forces to assist any such nation or group of such nations requesting assistance against armed aggression from any country controlled by international communism."[50] U.S. security commitments were now truly global in scope.

ELEMENTS OF CONTAINMENT: ECONOMIC AND MILITARY ASSISTANCE

The second set of initiatives to implement the containment strategy focused upon economic and military assistance to friendly nations. From the late 1940s and through the middle and late 1950s, substantial aid (reaching over $10 billion in 1953) was provided to an ever-expanding set of nations throughout the world. While the initial goal of these assistance efforts was to foster the economic well-being of the recipient societies, the ultimate rationale, especially after 1950, became strategic and political in content: to ensure the stability of those states threatened by international communism and to build support for anticommunism on a global scale. Three important programs reflect the kinds of assistance initiated by the United States during this period as well as its change in orientation over time:

1. The Marshall Plan
2. The Point Four program
3. The mutual security concept[51]

The Marshall Plan

Proposed in a speech by Secretary of State George Marshall at the Harvard commencement exercises in June 1947, the Marshall Plan is the best-known U.S. assistance effort. Marshall called for the Europeans to draw up a plan for economic recovery and pledged American economic support to implement such an effort. As a consequence of this speech and subsequent European-American consultations, President Truman asked Congress for $17 billion over a four-year period from 1948 to 1952 to revitalize Western Europe. The enormity of such an aid commitment becomes apparent when compared to the approximately $1 billion of assistance offered to Eastern Europe after the collapse of the Iron Curtain in 1989 and 1990. Its size is also reflected in the fact that the Marshall Plan aid program constituted about 1.2 percent of the GNP of the United States at the time. Over recent years, the amount of U.S. development assistance has constituted well under 0.5 percent of the GNP. In 1989, it constituted only 0.15 percent of the GNP.[52]

The rationale for the Marshall Plan was to rebuild the economic system of Western Europe. As a key trading partner for the United States, a healthy Europe was important to the economic health of America. Beyond these economic concerns, though, there were political concerns. If Europe did not recover, the region might well be subject to political instability and perhaps Communist penetration and subversion. According to Gilbert Winham's imaginative analysis of the decision making over the Marshall Plan, this "threat" dimension became particularly important in the late stages of deliberations (February through April 1948, just prior to the enactment of the plan).[53] In this sense, by the time of its formal passage by Congress, the European Recovery Program, or Marshall Plan, had clear elements of the containment strategy even though its initial motivations were primarily economic.

Point Four

While the Marshall Plan proved remarkably successful in fostering European recovery, President Truman also envisioned a larger plan of assistance for the rest of the world. His Point Four program was announced in his inaugural address of January 20, 1949. (The name was derived from the fact that this was the fourth major point in his suggested courses of action for American policy.) The aim of this program was to develop on a global scale the essentials of the Marshall Plan, which was then underway in Western Europe. Unlike the Marshall Plan, though, Point Four was less a cooperative venture with participating states and more a unilateral effort on the part of the United States, although America's allies might also become involved. In essence, the program was to provide industrial, technological, and economic assistance to the underdeveloped nations of the world. As President Truman announced:

> We must embark on a bold new program for making the benefits of our scientific advances and industrial progress available for the improvement and growth of underdeveloped areas.... I believe that we should make available to peace-loving peoples the benefits of our store of technical knowledge in order to help them realize their aspirations for a better life. And, in cooperation with other nations, we should foster capital investment in areas needing development.[54]

In this sense, the Point Four program was an imaginative and substantial commitment to global economic development by the United States.

The Mutual Security Concept

While Point Four had some of the same ambitious economic—and undoubtedly political—motivations as the Marshall Plan, the program never really received sufficient funding authorization from the Congress.[55] Instead, this strategy of global assistance was rather quickly replaced by a new approach that was more explicitly political in content, the mutual security concept. The mutual security approach emphasized aiding nations to combat communism and to strengthen the security of the United States and the "free world." In addition to the change in rationale for aid, the kind of assistance also changed from primarily economic and humanitarian aid to military assistance by the early and middle 1950s. While economic aid was not halted during this period, its purpose changed. Now economic assistance was more likely given to bolster the overall security capability of friendly countries.

These changes in aid policy can be explained by the deepening global crisis that the Untied States perceived in the world. Tensions between the Soviet Union and the United States were rising over Soviet actions in Eastern Europe and its potential actions toward Western Europe. The Korean War had broken out, apparently with Soviet compliance. Subsequently, the Chinese Communists entered this conflict, again evoking concern over Communist intentions. Domestically, too, there was an increased sense of Communist threat, led by the verbal assaults of Senator Joseph McCarthy of Wisconsin on various individuals and groups for being "soft on communism" and by the vigorous debate concerning communism. All in all, America's national security was perceived to be under attack, and this required some response.

The first real manifestation of this new aid strategy was the Mutual Defense Assistance Act of 1949.[56] This act, signed after the completion of the NATO pact and after the Soviets had tested an atomic bomb, provided for military aid to Western Europe, Greece, Turkey, Iran, South Korea, the Philippines, and the "China area." The strategic location of these countries is quite apparent; most bordered the Soviet Union or mainland China. Although the amount of aid called for in this act was relatively small, its significance lay in the face that it was the initial effort in military aid by the United States.

A later act, the Mutual Security Act of 1951, marked the real beginning of growth in military assistance amounts. Equally important, the introductory language of the act dramatically illustrated the linkage between this new aid policy and American security. The aim of this act was

> to maintain the security and to promote the foreign policy of the United States by authorizing military, economic, and technical assistance to friendly countries to strengthen the mutual security and individual and collective defenses of the free world, [and] to develop their resources in the interest of their security and independence and the national interest of the United States....[57]

With successive mutual security acts like these, American global assistance, and particularly military assistance, increased sharply. Furthermore, the number of recipient countries also began to grow. As Figure 2.1 shows, military assistance came to dominate the total assistance effort. Even with the addition of food aid under Public Law 480 in 1954 and with the inclusion of some technical and developmental assistance to particular countries (e.g., Yugoslavia and Poland),[58] the proportion of military assistance was often greater than nonmilitary assistance until about 1960. By this time, a new approach to aid, one motivated more explicitly by development considerations, was already being contemplated and was finally implemented under the Kennedy administration in 1961, with the establishment of the Agency for International Development (AID).

In general, the political rationale dominated aid policy and the choice of aid recipients prior to the emergence of AID. Nations that were "neutral" or "nonaligned" in the Cold War struggle between the United States and the Soviet Union were viewed skeptically and were not likely to receive economic or military assistance from the United States.[59] Instead, aid was intended to save America's friends from Soviet (and Chinese) communism.

ELEMENTS OF CONTAINMENT: THE DOMESTIC COLD WAR

The third element in the containment strategy was primarily domestic. Its aim was to make the American people aware of the Soviet threat and to change American domestic priorities to meet it. In essence, this aspect of containment might be labeled the domestification of the Cold War. One

FIGURE 2.1

Patterns in Foreign Aid, 1945–1970 (Net Grants and Credits)

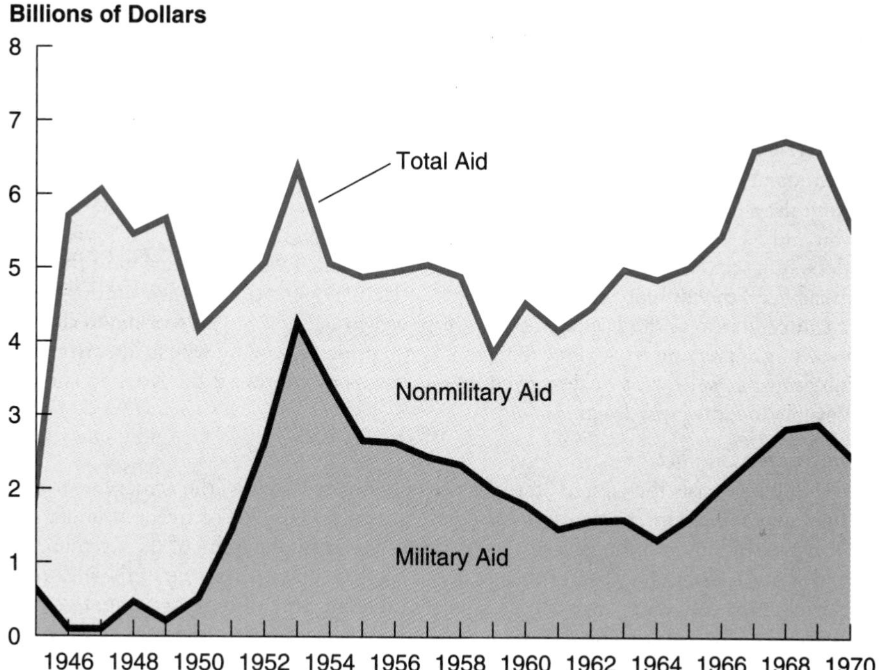

Source: *The Statistical History of the United States from Colonial Times to the Present* (New York: Basic Books, Inc., 1976), pp. 274 and 872.

important document, completed by the National Security Council in April 1950 and entitled NSC-68, summarized the goals of this effort and provided a good guide to the subsequent domestic and international changes that occurred to meet the perceived Communist threat. Along with the Korean War, which we discuss in the next section, NSC-68 solidified America's commitment to the containment policy course.

NSC-68: Defense

NSC-68 was the result of a review of American foreign and domestic defense policies by State and Defense Department officials under the leadership of Paul Nitze. (Since the report remained classified until 1975, it also gives us a unique picture of the thinking of American officials without the restraint that might characterize documents written for public disclosure.) The document itself is a rather lengthy statement that begins by outlining the nature of the current international crisis between the Soviet Union and the United States and then goes on to contrast the foreign policy goals of Washington and Moscow in much the same vein as the Truman Doctrine, albeit in much harsher language. (Document 2.1 excerpts portions of NSC-68 that depict these alternate views of the world.)

DOCUMENT 2.1

Excerpts from NSC-68, April 14, 1950

Fundamental Design of the United States

The fundamental purpose of the United States is laid down in the Preamble of the Constitution.... In essence, [it] is to assure the integrity and vitality of our free society, which is founded upon the dignity and worth of the individual.

Fundamental Design of the Kremlin

The fundamental design of those who control the Soviet Union and the international communist movement is to retain and solidify their absolute power, first in the Soviet Union and second in the areas now under their control. In the minds of the Soviet leaders, however, achievement of this design requires the dynamic extension of their authority and the ultimate elimination of any effective opposition to their authority.... The United States, as the principal center of power in the non-Soviet world and the bulwark of opposition to Soviet expansion, is the principal enemy whose integrity and vitality must be subverted or destroyed by one means or another if the Kremlin is to achieve its fundamental design.

Nature of the Conflict

The Kremlin regards the United States as the only major threat to the achievement of its fundamental design. There is a basic conflict between the idea of freedom under a government of law, and the idea of slavery under the grim oligarchy of the Kremlin.... The idea of freedom, moreover, is peculiarly and intolerably subversive of the idea of slavery. But the converse is not true. The implacable purpose of the slave state to eliminate the challenge of freedom has placed the two great powers at opposite poles. It is this fact which gives the present polarization of power the quality of crisis.

The assault on free institutions is world-wide now, and in the context of the present polarization of power a defeat of free institutions anywhere is a defeat everywhere....

In a shrinking world, which now faces the threat of atomic warfare, it is not an adequate objective merely to seek to check the Kremlin design, for the absence of order among nations is becoming less and less tolerable. This fact imposes on us, in our own interests, the responsibility of world leadership. It demands that we make the attempt, and accept the risks inherent in it, to bring about order and justice by means consistent with the principles of freedom and democracy.... Coupled with the probable fission bomb capability and possible thermonuclear bomb capability of the Soviet Union, the intensifying struggle requires us to face the fact that we can expect no lasting abatement of the crisis unless and until a change occurs in the nature of the Soviet system.

Source: *A Report to the National Security Council, April 14, 1950*, pp. 5–9. Declassified on February 27, 1975, by Henry A. Kissinger, Assistant to the President for National Security Affairs.

An example of how Soviet policy is characterized in the document makes this point as well:

> The Kremlin's policy toward areas not under its control is the elimination of resistance to its will and the extension of its influence and control.... The means employed by the Kremlin in pursuit of this policy are limited only by considerations of expediency. Doctrine is not a limiting factor; rather it dictates the employment of violence, subversion, and deceit and rejects moral considerations.[60]

purpose / a doctrine:

NSC-68 analyzed four different policy options for the United States in responding to the Soviet challenge: (1) continuing the current policies; (2) returning to isolationism; (3) resorting to war against the Soviet Union; or (4) "a rapid build-up of political, economic and military strength in the Free World." After careful analysis of each one along military, economic, political, and social aspects, the study recommends that a rapid buildup of American and allied strength "is the only course which is consistent with progress toward achieving our fundamental purpose. The frustration of the Kremlin design requires the free world to develop a successfully functioning political and economic system and a vigorous political offensive against the Soviet Union."[61]

What makes NSC-68 particularly distinct from the other elements of containment is its emphasis upon a domestic response to the Soviet Union. While the report calls for aiding allies and promoting anticommunism around the world, it offers substantial commentary on the need for building up America's military capacity and eliciting greater support against the Soviet challenges at home.

The U.S. military, NSC-68 contended, was inferior to that of the Soviets in number of "forces in being and in total manpower." The amount of U.S. defense spending was also relatively low, about 6 to 7 percent of the GNP as compared to more than 13 percent of GNP by the Soviet Union. In response, NSC-68 called for a rapid buildup of the American military establishment to counteract the Soviet challenge. Indeed, it went beyond this important general demand by proposing a new policy on military budgeting approach: In the future, it may be necessary to meet defense and foreign assistance needs by the reduction of federal expenditures in other areas. Further, taxes increases may also be necessary![62]

In effect, this policy was to place defense spending as the number-one priority in the budgeting process of the U.S. government. Instead of defense being a residual category of the budget, it was to become the focal point of future allocation decisions. The rest of the budgetary items would become residual categories.

NSC-68 had at least one other significant statement on military planning. In the body of the report (and not specifically in its conclusions), the document calls for the United Sates to "produce and stockpile thermonuclear weapons in the event they prove feasible and would add significantly to our net capability."[63] Although this reference is relatively oblique in the context of the entire report, it was significant in terms of timing. During this period, the Truman administration was embroiled in a policy debate on whether to go forward with the building of the H-bomb.

NSC-68: Internal Security

A second previously unaddressed area in the report was the moral capabilities of the United States. This area was also vulnerable to Soviet actions, and the Soviets might well seek to undermine America's social and cultural institutions by infiltration and intimidation:

> Those that touch most closely our material and moral strength are obviously the prime targets, labor unions, civic enterprises, schools, churches, and all media for influencing opinion. The effort is not so much to make them serve obvious Soviet

> ends as to prevent them from serving our ends, and thus to make them sources of confusion in our economy, our culture and our body politic.[64]

Thus the development of internal security and civilian defense programs was suggested. NSC-68 contended, moreover, that the government must "assure the internal security of the United States against dangers of sabotage, subversion, and espionage." It must also "keep the U.S. public fully informed and cognizant of the threats to our national security so that it will be prepared to support the measures which we must accordingly adopt."[65] In essence, there should be efforts to protect the American people against subversion and to gain their support for Cold War policies.

To a considerable degree, these recommendations became American policy in the early 1950s, sparked, as we shall see, by American involvement in the Korean War. Defense expenditures escalated to a level of more than 10 percent of the GNP in the early 1950s and generally stayed above 8 percent throughout the 1960s. Similarly, defense spending as a percentage of the federal budget rose sharply in the fifties to more than 50 percent and remained over 40 percent for all the years of the Johnson administration. A parallel growth pattern occurred in the size of the United States armed forces, with the number of people under arms reaching over 22 per 1,000 population in the early fifties and remaining about 14 per 1,000 population throughout the heart of the Vietnam War years. Figure 2.2 provides a summary view of these trends during the 1946–1968 period.[66] Additionally, the H-bomb program was given the go-ahead, and nuclear weapons became a part of defense strategy.

Efforts to ensure internal security were undertaken, too. As we have already noted, Senator Joseph McCarthy initiated his campaign against "Communists" within the government. In addition to his unswerving attacks, the public raised questions about Communist subversion within America. The various investigations by the House Un-American Activities Committee of the 1950s and 1960s reflect this growing concern with possible Soviet penetration. FBI and CIA activities in this area were also prevalent, as the Church Committee investigations of intelligence activities were to reveal in the mid-1970s. Furthermore, efforts to employ loyalty oaths also reflected this trend toward national security consciousness. In short, political attacks, from the schoolrooms to the boardrooms, produced a sense of widespread fear about veering too far from the mainstream on foreign policy issues. To a remarkable degree, a foreign policy consensus was the result of the political and psychological effects of the Cold War. Foreign policy debate became a casualty of the political environment. Moreover, when debate did occur, it was more often on foreign policy tactics than on fundamental strategy.[67]

THE KOREAN WAR: THE FIRST MAJOR TEST OF CONTAINMENT

Although the events in Greece and Turkey stimulated the emergence of containment policy in 1947, the first major test of this policy, and what brought

FIGURE 2.2

National Defense Expenditures and U.S. Armed Forces per 1,000 Population, 1946–1968

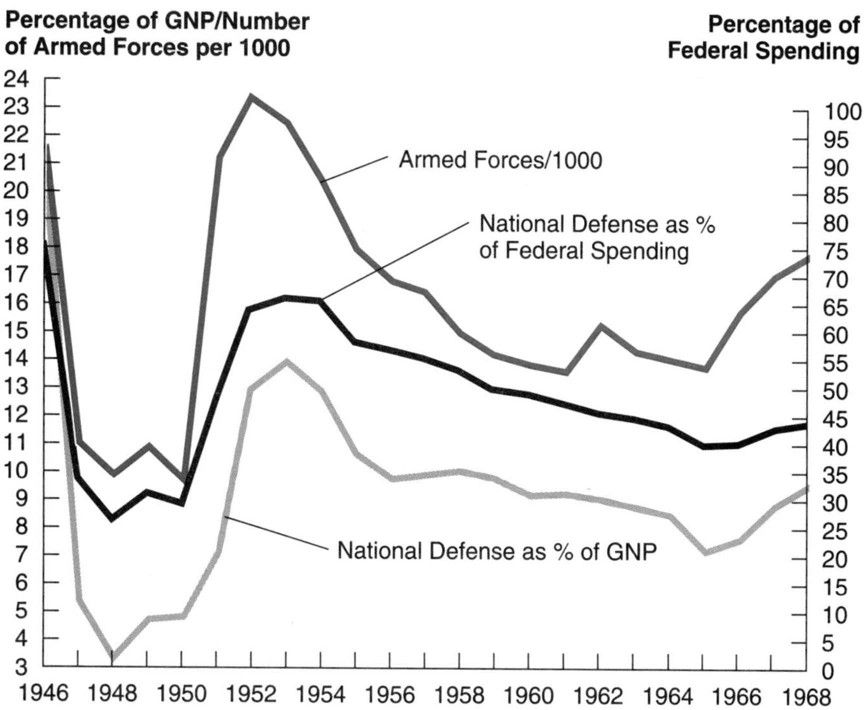

Sources: The data for national defense as a percentage of federal spending and GNP are taken from Alice C. Moroni, *The Fiscal Year 1984 Defense Budget Request: Data Summary* (Washington, DC: Congressional Research Service, 1983), p. 13. Total National Defense data, rather than only Department of Defense data, are used here. The two totals are usually very close (p. 14). The armed forces percentages were calculated from total population (Part 1, p. 8) and armed forces (Part 2, p. 1141) data in U.S. Bureau of the Census, *Historical Statistics of the United States, Colonial Times to 1970,* Bicentennial Edition, Parts 1 and 2 (Washington, DC: U.S. Government Printing Office, 1975).

the Cold War fully into existence, occurred in Korea in 1950. On June 25, 1950, North Korea attacked South Korea, which quickly engaged the Soviet Union, China, and the United States in a confrontation on the Korean peninsula. For the United States, too, it provided the *raison d'etre* for fully implementing the various elements of the containment strategy outlined above.

American Involvement in Korea

A brief description of the situation on the Korean peninsula, the origins of the conflict, and the extent of U.S. involvement illustrates that conflict's significance for American postwar policy. First of all, Korea had been annexed by the Japanese in 1910 and was finally freed by American and Soviet

MAP 2.3

The Korean War, 1950–1953

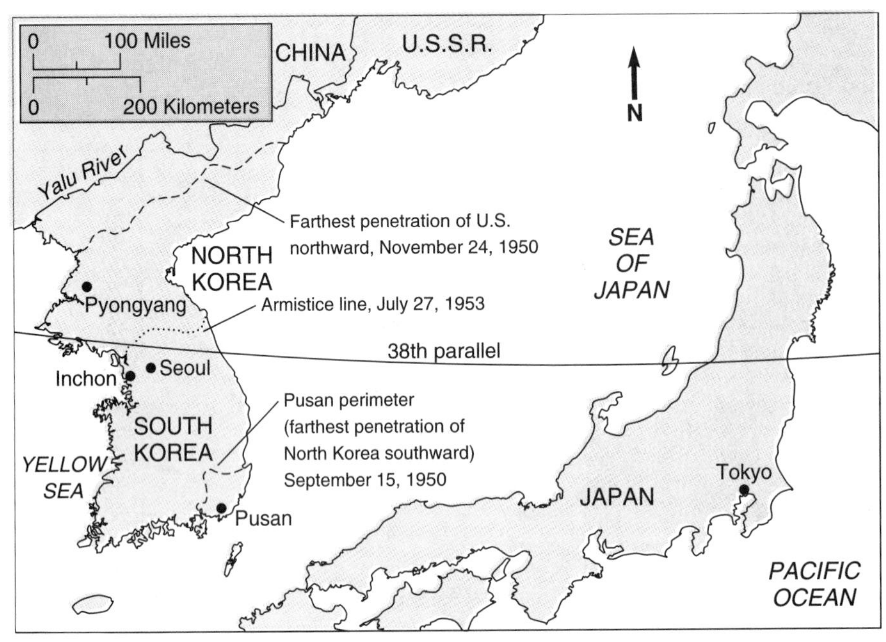

forces at the end of World War II. By agreement between the two countries, Korea was then temporarily divided along the 38th parallel, with Soviet forces occupying the North and U.S. forces occupying the South (see Map 2.3). Despite several maneuvers by both sides, this division assumed a more permanent cast when a UN-supervised election in the South resulted in the establishment of the Republic of Korea on August 15, 1948, and when the adoption of a constitution in the North resulted in the creation of the Democratic People's Republic of Korea on September 9, 1948.[68] Each regime claimed to be the government of Korea, and neither would recognize or accept the legitimacy of the other. While Soviet and American occupying forces left in 1948 and 1949, respectively, the struggle between the two regimes (with the support of their powerful allies) was not finished.

This struggle soon erupted into sustained violence in mid-1950. When the North Koreans attacked South Korea, their powerful allies were quickly brought back into this conflict. Indeed, the United States viewed this attack on the South as Soviet-inspired and Soviet-directed.[69] While a great deal of scholarship has been directed at whether this view was accurate,[70] a former under secretary of state at the time, U. Alexis Johnson, has made the essential point over this debate: "Whatever prompted Kim [Il-Sung, the North Korean leader] to order the attack, this is certain: At the time no responsible official in the United States or among our allies seriously questioned that the aggression was Soviet-inspired and aimed principally at testing our resolve."[71] With this overriding perception, the United States had little recourse but to respond and to make the containment doctrine a reality.

Within days, President Harry Truman ordered American air and naval support for the beleaguered South Korean troops and dispatched the Seventh Fleet to patrol the Formosa Strait to prevent Communist Chinese actions against the nationalist government on Taiwan. In addition, Truman sought and quickly obtained both United Nations Security Council condemnation of the attack and support for a collective security force to be sent to aid the South Korean forces under U.S. direction. (The UN action was made possible by the Soviet Union's boycott of UN Security Council sessions because the China seat had not been given to the Communist government led by Mao Zedong. As a result, the Soviet Union was unable to exercise its veto.) Although some fourteen other nations ultimately sent forces to aid the South Koreans, the bulk of the war effort was carried by the Americans.[72] Indeed, the commander of all UN and U.S. forces in Korea was General Douglas MacArthur.

Initially, the American-led effort in Korea fared badly. Allied troops were driven to a small enclave around Pusan in Southeast Korea, and the North Koreans were on the verge of overrunning the entire peninsula. In September 15, 1950, however, General MacArthur executed his Inchon landing near Seoul behind North Korean lines, and, within a matter of weeks, proceeded across the 38th parallel into North Korea. While this invasion was brilliant as a strategic move, the Chinese became alarmed as MacArthur's forces moved ever northward, coming within miles of the Chinese border.[73]

While the Chinese had warned the West indirectly, through India in September 1950, that they would not "sit back with folded hands and let the Americans come to the border,"[74] the warning was not believed by U.S. policy makers. Beginning as early as mid-October 1950, Chinese People's Volunteers began crossing into North Korea to aid that government's forces. By late November 1950, the total Chinese forces totaled more than 300,000 fighting alongside the North Koreans against the UN and U.S. forces. The massive Chinese intervention drove allied forces back across the 38th parallel, the "temporary" dividing line between North and South Korea. Stalemate ensued.

General MacArthur proposed that U.S. forces carry the war into China as a way to resolve the conflict. Because President Truman had ordered him not to make public statements without administration approval and because administration policy was to limit the conflict, Truman fired General MacArthur for insubordination. This action caused an outpouring of support for MacArthur and a vilification of President Truman.[75] By and large, the American people continued to support the proposition that, once a war was undertaken, it should be fought to be won; it should not be limited by political constraints. The Truman administration felt otherwise; as General Omar Bradley, chairman of the Joint Chiefs of Staff, put it: "So long as we regarded the Soviet Union as the main antagonist and Western Europe as the main prize" a massive invasion of China "would involve us in the wrong war at the wrong place at the wrong time and with the wrong enemy." In other words, involvement in the land war in Asia would lead "to a larger deadlock at greater expense" and would do little to contain Soviet designs on Western Europe.[76]

By July 1951, truce talks were arranged and fighting ceased for the most part by the end of the year. An armistice, however, did not come about for another year and a half, as a prolonged controversy developed over the repatriation of prisoners of war, and as an American election occurred with Korea as an important issue. An uneasy peace eventually did result with the establishment of a demilitarized zone between North and South Korea. The first test of containment, however, brought numerous lessons for American policy makers for the future course of the Cold War.[77]

Korea and Implications for the Cold War

Political scientist Robert Jervis argues that American involvement in Korea "shaped the course of the Cold War by resolving the incoherence which characterized U.S. foreign and defense efforts in the periods 1946–1950 and establishing important new lines of policy."[78] American involvement resolved that incoherence by moving the United States to match its perceived sense of threat from the Soviet Union and international communism with policies consistent with that threat. New actions were undertaken in at least three different areas, and the political rhetoric of the late 1940s became policy during the 1950s.

The first policy effect of the Korean war was a sharp increase in the American defense budget and the militarization of NATO. While NSC-68 had called for such military increases, they did not result until U.S. involvement in Korea and were largely sustained after it. Note from Figure 2.2 how high military spending (either as a percentage of the GNP or as a percentage of the budget) remained throughout much of the 1950s. Similarly, the establishment of an integrated military structure of NATO and the eventual effort to rearm West Germany followed directly on the heels of American involvement in Korea. The threat of Soviet expansionism had been made real with the actions in Asia.

A second effect of the Korean War was that it brought home to American policy makers the need to maintain large armies and to take action against aggression, wherever it appeared. Limited wars, too, may be necessary, however unpopular at home.[79] In this view, if the United States did not confront aggression in one dispute, American resolve in others would be questioned. Indeed, the Korean experience had already raised this doubt. After all, Secretary of State Dean Acheson had seemed to indicate, in a speech in January 1950, that the Korean peninsula was not within the American "defense perimeter" in Asia.[80]

A third effect of the Korean War was to solidify the American view that a Sino-Soviet bloc promoting communist expansion was a reality and that there was a need to combat it. The Chinese intervention on the side of the North Koreans illustrated the extent to which China was controlled by the Soviet Union. Indeed, the views that "China and Russia were inseparable were products of the war."[81] Moreover, the various bilateral pacts in

Asia were established after the Korean War was underway. In sum, then, the outbreak of the Korean War and American involvement were to bring about a most dramatic correspondence between U.S. policy beliefs and its actions.

Yet a fourth impact, beyond Jervis's discussion, seems reasonable, especially if we keep in mind the date on which NSC-68 was issued (April 1950) and when the Korean War began (June 1950). In many ways, the actions in Korea gave further credence to the global portrait outlined in NSC-68, as well as the need to make rapid changes in the security arrangements of America and the free world. Moreover, in relatively short order, that is exactly what happened.

Finally, a preeminent American diplomatic historian of this generation, John Lewis Gaddis, has summarized the principal importance of the Korean War in this way: "the real commitment to contain communism everywhere originated in the events surrounding the Korean War, not the crisis in Greece and Turkey [in 1947]."[82]

Concluding Comments

In Chapter 1, we noted that isolationism and moralism were America's twin pillars from the past. The Cold War period and the containment policy appear to represent a sharp break from this heritage, at least with respect to isolationism. On one level, of course, the United States did abandon isolationism for a policy of globalism.[83] On another level, globalism was largely a unilateralist approach on the part of the United States, a strategy of going it alone in the world, or at least attempting to lead other nations of the world in a particular direction. In other words, much as the original isolationism was unilateralist; so, too, was the containment policy. It was a strategy by the United States to reshape global order through its own design and largely through its own efforts.

The heritage of moral principle is more readily evident in the Cold War period and containment policy. The universal campaign that the United States initiated was highly consistent with its past. Moral accommodation with the values of Russian communism, and all communism, was simply not acceptable. In fact, some even sought to "roll back" communism rather than just contain it. Like the efforts in America's past (the War of 1812, the Spanish-American War, World War I, and World War II), then, the containment strategy represented an all-out attempt, in this case, to confront the moral challenge from the Soviet Union and all it represented. Moral values, moreover, served as a primary justification for American policy once again.

In the next chapter, we examine more fully the values and beliefs that shaped the U.S. approach to the world during the height of the Cold War. A Cold War consensus among American leaders and the public was developing in the late 1940s and the early 1950s, and the Korean War only served to solidify it. This consensus provided the rationale for the complete implementation of the containment policy during the rest of the 1950s and 1960s and guided U.S. policy during the several decades until it was challenged by the emergence of the Sino-Soviet split, the nonaligned movement, the Cuban Missile Crisis, and the Vietnam War.

Notes

1. Joseph M. Jones, *The Fifteen Weeks* (New York: The Viking Press, 1955), pp. 89–89.
2. The term is from Richard Mayne's Chapter 2 title in his *The Recovery of Europe 1945–1973* (Garden City, NY: Anchor, 1973), pp. 27–52. The discussion here draws upon this chapter as well as p. 14 on the extent of decolonization.
3. Ibid., pp. 39–40.
4. Ibid.
5. Stephen E. Ambrose, *Rise to Globalism: American Foreign Policy 1938*–1976 (New York: Penguin Books, 1976), p. 16. A good discussion of the economic strength of the United States in the immediate postwar period can be found in Joan Edelman Spero, *The Politics of International Economic Relations*, 2nd ed. (New York: St. Martin's Press, 1981), pp. 23–30, 33–41. The economic data cited are at p. 36.
6. Ambrose, *Rise to Globalism*, p. 16.
7. John Lewis Gaddis, *The United States and the Origins of the Cold War 1941–1947* (New York and London: Columbia University Press, 1972), p. 1. See also Daniel Yergin, *Shattered Peace: The Origins of the Cold War and the National Security State* (Boston: Houghton, Mifflin Company, 1977), pp. 42–68.
8. Gaddis, *Origins of the Cold War*, p. 2.
9. Yergin, *Shattered Peace*, pp. 43–46.
10. Ibid., pp. 17–68. The quote about Riga is at p. 19.
11. Ibid., p. 55.
12. Michael MccGwire, "National Security and Soviet Foreign Policy," in Melvyn P. Leffler and David S. Painter, eds., *Origins of the Cold War: An International History* (London and New York: Routledge, 1994), p. 61.
13. See the discussion of the Yalta agreements in Robert H. Ferrell, *American Diplomacy: A History* (New York: W. W. Norton & Co., Inc., 1975), pp. 594–603.
14. Ibid.
15. James Lee Ray, *Global Politics*, 2nd ed. (Boston: Houghton Mifflin Company, 1983), p. 30.
16. For some evidence that the United States was already planning a sustained global involvement during World War II, see Melvyn P. Leffler, "National Security and U.S. Foreign Policy," in Melvyn P. Leffler and David S. Painter, eds., *Origins of the Cold War: An International History* (London and New York: Routledge, 1994), pp. 18–19.
17. Yergin, *Shattered Peace*, pp. 71–73.
18. Ibid. Also see Gaddis, *Origins of the Cold War*, pp. 200–206.
19. Ernest R. May, *"Lessons" of the Past* (New York: Oxford University Press, 1973), pp. 20–22. The quotation is from p. 22.
20. See ibid., pp. 22–32, for a discussion of the views of these diplomatic assessments and their impact on Truman and his advisors.
21. Harry S Truman, *Year of Decision* (New York: Doubleday & Co., Inc., 1955), p. 99. The earlier passage is quoted in Gaddis, *Origins of the Cold War*, p. 232.
22. For a recent description and assessment of the Potsdam Conference, see Charles L. Mee, Jr., *Meeting at Potsdam* (New York: M. Evan & Co., Inc., 1975).
23. Gaddis, *Origins of the Cold War*, pp. 263–281.
24. Ibid., pp. 282–312.
25. Both passages were originally from *Pravda*, the Communist party newspaper, and were quoted in B. Thomas Trout, "Rhetoric Revisited: Political Legitimation and the Cold War," *International Studies Quarterly* 19 (September 1975): 264 and 266.
26. The "new war" remark is quoted from Pravda and is from ibid., p. 265, as is this assessment. The second quotation is from ibid at p. 269.
27. The first quote is from Walter Lafeber, *America, Russia, and the Cold War 1945–1975.* (New York: John Wiley & Sons, Inc., 1976), p. 39, and the second is from Gaddis, in *Origins of the Cold War*, p. 299.

28. The text of the speech can be found in Robert Rhodes James, ed., *Winston S. Churchill, His Complete Speeches 1897–1963*, vol. VII: 1943–1949 (New York: Chelsea House Publishers, 1974), pp. 7285–7293. The quoted passages are at pp. 7289 and 7290, respectively.
29. Yergin, *Shattered Peace*, p. 176.
30. The complete text of the "long telegram" can be found in Kenneth M. Jensen, ed., *Origins of the Cold War: The Novikov, Kennan, and Roberts' "Long Telegrams" of 1946* (Washington, DC: United States Institute of Peace, 1991), pp. 17–31. The quoted phrases are at pp. 20, 23, 28 and 29. The last passage can also be found in George F. Kennan, *Memoirs 1925–1950* (Boston: Little, Brown & Co. Inc., 1967), p. 557.
31. Interestingly, a few months after Kennan's "long telegram" was sent from Moscow to Washington, the Soviet Ambassador to the United States, Nikolai Novikov, sent a telegram to Moscow in September 1947. That telegram, dubbed the "Novikov Telegram," and only made public in the summer of 1990, "mirrored" the Kennan "long telegram" in that it depicts the inherent designs of the United States for world domination and for challenging the Soviet Union. In essence, the Soviets, too, seemed to be having increasing misgivings about continuing U.S.-Soviet cooperation in the postwar years. The complete text of the telegram can be found in Jensen, *Origins of the Cold War: The Novikov, Kennan, and Roberts' "Long Telegrams" of 1946*, pp. 3–16.
32. The discussion draws upon Jones, *The Fifteen Weeks*, pp. 48–58, especially at pp. 48–49 here.
33. Quoted in ibid., p. 54. Emphasis in original.
34. Ibid., p. 56. Jones does point out that the Soviets apparently got some concessions for their withdrawal.
35. Lafeber, *America, Russia, and the Cold War*, pp. 50–59, provides a useful description of the situation in Greece at this time, while Jones, *The Fifteen Weeks*, pp. 59–77, describes the situations in Greece and Turkey during 1946 and 1947.
36. These characteristics of the Truman Doctrine are from Lafeber, *America, Russia, and the Cold War*, p. 53.
37. The "Truman Doctrine" speech can be found in *House Documents, Miscellaneous*, 80th Cong., 1st sess., Vol. 1 (Washington, DC: Government Printing Office, 1947), Document 171. Emphasis added here. John Lewis Gaddis in his book, *Strategies of Containment* (New York: Oxford University Press, 1982), pp. 65–66, asserts that the Truman Doctrine was not so much meant as a call to attack "communism" as it was to attack "totalitarianism" in general. Truman's reference to two ways of life referred to totalitarianism vs. democracy. Only later did the commitment to contain communism really develop. See his "Was the Truman Doctrine a Real Turning Point?" *Foreign Affairs* 52 (January 1974): 386–402.

    The source of responsibility for the Cold War and its exact date of origin are topics of great debate among scholars. Some argue that the Cold War was initiated by the Soviet Union, with its expansionist policies in Eastern Europe; others contend that the United States was responsible, with its attempt to use its great power to restructure global order; still others see a more complex process of mutual causation.

    When the Cold War began is also controversial. Did it begin in 1947 (as we tend to argue) or was it put into place much later (e.g., with the outbreak of the Korean War)? Our intention is not to resolve this issue, but rather to make the reader aware of the controversy surrounding the Cold War concept. Besides Gaddis and Yergin, some other literature to consult on this topic includes the following: Gar Alperovitz, *Atomic Diplomacy: Hiroshima and Potsdam* (New York: Random House, 1965); D. F. Fleming, *The Cold War and Its Origin, 1917–1970* (New York: Doubleday & Co., Inc., 1961); and Howard Bliss and M. Glen Johnson, *Consensus at the Crossroads: Dialogues in American Foreign Policy* (New York: Dodd, Mead & Co., Inc., 1972). More recent discussion on the Cold War and containment can be found in John Lewis Gaddis, "Containment: A Reassessment," *Foreign Affairs* 55 (July 1977): 873–887; Eduard Mark, "The Question of Containment: A Reply to John Lewis Gaddis," *Foreign Affairs* 56 (January 1978): 430–441; Robert Jervis, "The Impact of the Korean War on the Cold War," *The Journal of Conflict Resolution* 24 (December 1980): 563–592; and Charles S. Maier, ed., *The Origins of the Cold War and Contemporary Europe* (New York: New Viewpoints, 1978).

38. George Kennan has reprinted his July 1947 article from *Foreign Affairs* entitled "The Sources of Soviet Conduct" in his *American Diplomacy 1900–1950* (New York: Mentor Books, 1951). The quoted passages are at pp. 99 and 105. It has also been reprinted in *Foreign Affairs* 65 (Spring 1987): 852–868.
39. Mr. X [George Kennan], "The Sources of Soviet Conduct," in James M. McCormick, *A Reader in American Foreign Policy* (Itasca, IL: F. E. Peacock Publishers, Inc., 1986), pp. 68–69.
40. Ibid., pp. 70–71.
41. George Kennan, in his *Memoirs 1925–1950*, pp. 354–367, contends that the implementation of containment by such sweeping actions was not what he had intended. He envisioned a more limited, more measured response than what resulted. Also see his views on the Truman Doctrine at pp. 313–324. A more recent summary of Kennan's views on containment are available in "Containment Then and Now," *Foreign Affairs 65* (Spring 1987): 885–890.
42. ANZUS was also seen as protection against Japanese expansion into the South Pacific in light of the experience of World War II, as well as an anti-Communist alliance in the face of the Korean War. For an extended discussion of ANZUS from the perspective of one of the partners, see Malcom McKinnon, *Independence and Foreign Policy: New Zealand in the World Since 1935* (Auckland: Auckland University Press, 1993).
43. A brief description of the development of these organizations, and the charter of each one, can be found in Ruth C. Lawson, *International Regional Organizations: Constitutional Foundations* (New York: Praeger, 1962). The subsequent discussion of CENTO is also based upon this source.
44. The Rio Pact did not have this language, but it did state that the "Contracting Parties may determine the immediate measures which it may individually take in fulfillment of the obligation." Quoted in Michael Glennon, *Constitutional Diplomacy* (Princeton: Princeton University Press, 1990), p. 207.
45. *NATO Handbook* (Brussels: NATO Information Service, 1980), p. 14.
46. This discussion draws upon the analysis and documentation by Glennon, *Constitutional Diplomacy*, pp. 209–214. The statements from Acheson are at pp. 210–211.
47. On the evolution of American strategy policy toward China and Asia in the late 1940s and early 1950s, see Thomas H. Etzold, "The Far East in American Strategy, 1948–1951," in Thomas H. Etzold, ed., *Aspects of Sino-American Relations Since 1784* (New York: New Viewpoints, 1978), pp. 102–126. On the sending of U.S. forces into the Taiwan Straits, see the discussion in the subsequent section on the Korean War.
48. On the Korean War, see Allen S. Whiting, *China Crosses the Yalu* (Stanford: Stanford University Press, 1960), and John W. Spanier, *The Truman-MacArthur Controversy and the Korean War* (New York: W. W. Norton & Company, Inc., 1965). On the importance of the Korean War in actually instigating the containment policy and producing the Cold War, see Gaddis, "Was the Truman Doctrine a Real Turning Point?" and Jervis, "The Impact of the Korean War on the Cold War."
49. In fact, the original NATO pact (subsequently altered in January 1963)) covered "the Algerian Departments of France" in its security network. In this limited sense, a small part of Africa was originally included in NATO. See Article 6 of the NATO charter in *NATO Handbook*, p. 14 on this point.
50. The speech by President Eisenhower can be found in *House Documents, Miscellaneous*, 85th Cong. 1st sess., Vol. 1 (Washington, DC: U.S. Government Printing Office, 1957–1958), Document 46. The first quote is from this document. The latter quote is from Public Law 85–7, which was passed on March 9, 1957, to put the Eisenhower Doctrine into effect.
51. This section draws largely upon the fine summary of American foreign aid policy between 1945 and 1964 presented in *Congress and the Nation 1945–1964* (Washington, DC: Congressional Quarterly Service, 1965), pp. 160–186.
52. The text of Secretary of State Marshall's address can be found in *New York Times*, June 6, 1947, 2. The Soviet Union and Eastern European states were invited to participate in the Marshall Plan under the original formulation. While Poland and Czechoslovakia had shown some initial interest, the Soviet Union quickly vetoed their efforts. See Ferrell,

American Diplomacy, pp. 634–635. The percentage of GNP for the Marshall Plan was calculated from data presented in U.S. Bureau of Census, *Historical Statistics of the United States, Colonial Times to 1970*, Bicentennial Edition. Parts 1 and 2 (Washington, DC: U.S. Government Printing Office, 1970). Aid effort over time by the United States can be found in the yearly reports by *Development Co-Operation* (Paris: Organization for Economic Cooperation and Development). The datum for 1989 is from Joseph C. Wheeler, *Development Co-Operation* (Paris: Organization for Economic Cooperation and Development, December 1990), p. 91.

53. Winham, Gilbert, "Developing Theories of Foreign Policy Making: A Case Study of Foreign Aid," *The Journal of Politics* 32 (February 1970): 41–70. For other case studies of the Marshall Plan, see Morton Berkowitz, P. G. Bock, and Vincent Fuccillo, *The Politics of American Foreign Policy* (Englewood Cliffs, NJ: Prentice-Hall, Inc., 1977), pp. 20–38; and Jones, *The Fifteen Weeks*, pp. 239–256.
54. President Truman's inaugural address can be found in *Senate Documents, Miscellaneous*, 81st Cong., 1st sess., Vol. 1 (Washington, DC: Government Printing Office, 1949), Document 5.
55. See Robert A. Pastor, *Congress and the Politics of U.S. Foreign Economic Policy 1929–1976* (Berkeley: University of California Press, 1980), p. 269.
56. *Congress and the Nation 1945–1964*, p. 166.
57. The Mutual Security Act of 1951 can be found as Public Law 82-165, passed on October 10, 1951.
58. Aid was given to some countries in order to bolster their economies and their political will to retain some independence from Moscow. See *Congress and the Nation 1945–1964*, pp. 161–162.
59. Secretary of State John Foster Dulles was particularly noted for the suspicion with which he viewed the actions of neutral or nonaligned states in international politics.
60. *A Report to the National Security Council, NSC-68*, Washington, DC, April 14, 1950, p. 13
61. Ibid., p. 54.
62. Ibid., p. 57. The quoted phrase on military strength is at p. 31, and the information on spending is at p. 25 in NSC-68. On these points and others on NSC-68, see John C. Donovan, *The Cold Warriors: A Policy-Making Elite* (Lexington, MA: D. C. Heath and Company, 1974), pp. 81–96.
63. *A Report to the National Security Council, NSC-68*, p. 39.
64. Ibid., p. 34.
65. Ibid., p. 63. These passages are actually from an earlier report, NSC 20/4 in NSC-68.
66. Similar data are reported in James L. Payne, *The American Threat* (College Station, TX: Lytton Publishing Company, 1981), p. 291. For an extended treatment of what the authors call the "militarization of American foreign policy" over the post–World War II decades, see Charles W. Kegley and Eugene R. Wittkopf, *American Foreign Policy: Pattern and Process*, 4th ed. (New York: St. Martin's Press, 1991), pp. 72–111.
67. See Howard Bliss and M. Glen Johnson, *Beyond the Water's Edge: America's Foreign Policies* (Philadelphia: J. B. Lippincott Co., 1975), pp. 3–10, for a discussion of the "costs of consensus" and for another set of assumptions comprising the postwar consensus.
68. For various accounts of the Korean War, and upon which we relied for this summary, see John G. Stoessinger, *Why Nations Go To War*, 5th ed. (New York: St. Martin's Press, 1990), pp. 55–83, especially at p. 61; Spanier, *The Truman-MacArthur Controversy and the Korean War*, especially pp. 23–26; Young W. Kihl, *Politics and Policies in Divided Korea: Regimes in Contest* (Boulder, CO: Westview Press, 1984), pp. 27–42; and Whiting, *China Crosses the Yalu*.
69. Stoessinger, *Why Nations Go to War*, p. 61; and Spanier, *The Truman-MacArthur Controversy*, pp. 23–26, for example.
70. John Merrill in his *Korea: The Peninsular Origins of the War* (Newark, DE: University of Delaware Press, 1989) has catalogued five different kinds of explanations for the outbreak of the war: (1) Moscow ordered the North Koreans to invade the South; (2) the

South Koreans provoked the North into an attack; (3) the South Koreans, in conjunction with the United States, initiated the war; (4) the deeply divided North Koreans "sprang the war on their unsuspecting Soviet allies"; and (5) the war was the result of regional politics initiated by the Soviet Union "to bring the independently minded Chinese leadership back into line and to frustrate American plans to establish a permanent military presence in Japan." The quoted passages are at pp. 19 and 48, respectively. Another recent study, quoting a North Korean official, argues that Stalin "reluctantly consented" to the surprise attack on the South. The author writes: "Stalin was giving a nod to the general idea of an invasion but had made consultations with Mao a condition for his unequivocal assent to any future detailed plan of action." See Sergei N. Goncharov, John W. Lewis, and Xue Litai, *Uncertain Partners: Stalin, Mao, and the Korean War* (Stanford: Stanford University Press, 1993), p. 144. The first quotation is Goncharov and others' quote of the North Korean official, while the second is their judgment. Historian Bruce Cumings has written a two-volume examination of the Korean War. In *The Origins of the Korean War, Volume II: The Roaring of the Cataract, 1947–1950* (Princeton: Princeton University Press, 1990), Cumings leaves open the question of who started the war by examining three "mosaics" of possible caution: North Korea launched an attack; South Korea launched an attack; or South Korea provoked a North Korea attack (see p. 568). By the end of the discussion (at pp. 618–619), he does not decide among these mosaics. Finally, in July 1994, South Korean officials announced that Soviet documents provided to them by Russian President Boris Yeltsin a month earlier "showed that Soviet dictator Josef Stalin and Chinese leader Mao Tse-tung approved Kim Il-Sung's attack on South Korea in June 1950." See Sam Jameson, "Kim Plotted Korean War, South Claims," *Des Moines Register*, July 21, 1994, 10A.

71. Quoted in Frederick H. Hartmann and Robert L. Wendzel, *America's Foreign Policy in a Changing World* (New York: HarperCollins College Publishers, 1994), p. 222. The original source is U. Alexis Johnson, *The Right Hand of Power* (Englewood Cliffs, NJ: Prentice-Hall, 1984), p. 99.

72. Stoessinger, *Why Nations Go to War*, p. 67.

73. See the chronology of events in Whiting, *China Crosses the Yalu*, and in John E. Mueller, *War, Presidents, and Public Opinion* (New York: John Wiley and Sons, Inc., 1973), among others, upon whom we rely.

74. As quoted in Whiting, *China Crossees the Yalu*, p. 93.

75. On the firing and its implications for American foreign policy, see Spanier, *The Truman-MacArthur Controversy and the Korean War*.

76. Bradley is quoted in Robert H. Ferrell, *American Diplomacy: The Twentieth Century* (New York: W. W. Norton & Company, 1988) at pp. 284–285.

77. Mueller, *War, Presidents, and Public Opinion*, pp. 25–27.

78. Jervis, "The Impact of the Korean War on the Cold War," p. 563.

79. These effects are derived from ibid.

80. In a speech to the Press Club on January 12, 1950, Secretary of State Dean Acheson had indicated that the U.S. "defensive perimeter runs along the Aleutians to Japan and then goes to the Ryukyus. We hold important defense positions in the Ryukyu Islands, and these we will continue to hold.... The defensive perimeter runs from the Ryukyu to the Philippine Islands." Korea thus was outside this defense line. See Dean Acheson, *Present at the Creation* (New York: W. W. Norton & Company, Inc., 1969), p. 357.

81. Jervis, "The Impact of the Korean War on the Cold War," p. 584.

82. Gaddis, "Was the Truman Doctrine a Real Turning Point?" p. 386.

83. For an extended discussion of the following argument in a similar vein, see Edmund Stillman and William Pfaff, *Power and Impotence* (New York: Vintage Books, 1966), but especially at pp. 15, 58–59.

CHAPTER

3

THE COLD WAR CONSENSUS AND CHALLENGES TO IT

Let every nation know, whether it wishes us well or ill, that we shall pay any price, bear any burden, meet any hardship, support any friend, oppose any foe to assure the survival and the success of liberty.

President John F. Kennedy
Inaugural Address, January 1961

In honor of the men and women of the armed forces of the United States who served in the Vietnam War. The names of those who gave their lives and of those who remain missing are inscribed in the order they were taken from us.

Inscription on the Vietnam Veterans Memorial
Washington, D.C.

From the Cold War environment, and the initial encounter of the Korean War, an identifiable foreign policy consensus developed among the American leadership and the public at large. This consensus was composed of a set of beliefs, values, and premises about America's role in the world and served as an important guide for U.S. behavior during the heart of the Cold War period (the late 1940s to the late 1960s). In the first part of this chapter, we shall undertake (1) to identify the principal components of the Cold War consensus, (2) to illustrate how strongly the key values of this consensus were held within American society, and (3) to provide a brief description of how the Cold War evolved in the first three decades after the end of World War II. In particular, we will show how the Cold War consensus largely prevailed in shaping American policy making during this period, but that the Cold War interactions between the United States and the Soviet Union also reflected both periods of hostility and periods of accommodation.

In the second half of the chapter, we will discuss how the Cold War consensus came under challenge during the 1960s from a variety of sources: (1) a changing international environment, particularly in the Third World, Eastern Europe, and Western Europe, which made implementing the containment policy more difficult; (2) the American domestic environment, particularly as a result of the Cuban Missile Crisis and the Vietnam War, which made policy making more difficult; and (3) the emergence of new political leadership in the late 1960s and 1970s with alternate views for achieving global order even in the face of Soviet and Communist challenge. In sum, both anticommunism and containment, as the cornerstones of American foreign policy, would be modified but not abandoned as the United States entered the 1970s. And some of the chill of the Cold War would be removed.

KEY COMPONENTS OF THE COLD WAR CONSENSUS

Lincoln P. Bloomfield has compiled an extensive list of U.S. foreign policy values in his book, *In Search of American Foreign Policy*.[1] Table 3.1 reproduces a portion of his list, and it shall serve as a starting point for our discussion of the Cold War consensus.

America's Dichotomous View of the World

First of all, Bloomfield reminds us of the dichotomous view most Americans held of the world—one group of nations led by the United States and standing for democracy and capitalism, another group led by the Soviet Union and standing for totalitarianism and socialism. Even this dichotomy was not wholly accurate because the United States came to define the "free world" not in a positive way—by adherence to democratic principles of individual liberty and equality—but in a negative way—by adherence to the principles of anticommunism. Thus the "free world" could equally include the nations of Western Europe (including the dictatorships of Spain and

TABLE 3.1

The American Postwar Consensus in Foreign Policy

1. Communism is bad; capitalism is good.
2. Stability is desirable; in general, instability threatens U.S. interests.
3. Democracy (our kind, that is) is desirable, but if a choice has to be made, stability serves U.S. interests better than democracy.
4. Any area of the world that "goes socialist" or neutralist is a net loss to us and probably a victory for the Soviets.
5. Every country, and particularly the poor ones, would benefit from American "know-how."
6. Nazi aggression in the 1930s and democracy's failure to respond provides the appropriate model for dealing with postwar security problems.
7. Allies and clients of the United States, regardless of their political structure, are members of the Free World.
8. The United States must provide leadership because it (reluctantly) has the responsibility.
9. "Modernization" and "development" are good for poor, primitive, or traditional societies, and they will probably develop into democracies by these means.
10. In international negotiations the United States has a virtual monopoly on "sincerity."
11. Violence is an unacceptable way to secure economic, social, and political justice—except when vital U.S. interests are at stake.
12. However egregious a mistake, the government must never admit having been wrong.

Source: *In Search of American Foreign Policy: The Humane Use of Power* by Lincoln P. Bloomfield. Copyright 1974 by Oxford University Press, Inc. Reprinted by permission of the author.

Portugal through the mid-1970s) and the military regimes of Central and South America because they embraced anticommunism. Such an "alliance" provided a ready bulwark against Soviet expansion.

U.S. Attitudes Toward Change

While a substantial part of such a "free world" structure was grounded in this abiding concern over Soviet expansion, a second concern also permeated this thinking: U.S. attitudes toward stability and change. During this period, change in the world was viewed suspiciously. It tended to be seen as Communist-inspired and, therefore, something to be opposed. Stability was generally the preferred global condition.

Change was feared because it might lead to enhanced influence (and control) for the Soviet Union. This gain in influence could occur directly (by a nation's formal incorporation into the Soviet bloc) or indirectly (by a state's adopting a "neutral" or "nonaligned" stance in global affairs). As a consequence, Americans also tended to be skeptical of new states following the "nonaligned" movement initiated by Prime Minister Nehru of India and President Tito of Yugoslavia, among others. At this time, such a movement represented a "loss " for America's effort to rally the world against revolutionary communism.

Change was even more troublesome for the United States when it appeared in a nationalist and revolutionary environment. While the United States tended to have philosophical sympathy for such nationalist and anticolonialist efforts, the global realities, as viewed by American policy makers, often led them to follow a different course. J. William Fulbright, senator from Arkansas and former chairman of the Senate Foreign Relations Committee, described this dilemma for America when dealing with forces of nationalism and communism in a revolutionary setting:

> ...we are simultaneously hostile to communism and sympathetic to nationalism, and when the two become closely associated, we become agitated, frustrated, angry, precipitate, and inconstant. Or, to make the point by simple metaphor: loving corn and hating lima beans, we simply cannot make up our minds about succotash.[2]

The resultant American policy, as Fulbright goes on to state, was often to oppose communism rather than to support nationalism.

American Intervention to Stall Communism

This fear of change was manifested in yet a more dramatic way: the several American military interventions (either directly or through surrogates) in the 1950s and 1960s to prevent Communist gains. A few instances will make this point. In 1950, of course, U.S. military forces were sent to South Korea to assist that government's defense from the attack by the North Koreans. In 1953, the United States was involved in the toppling of Prime Minister Mohammed Mossadegh of Iran and the restoration of the Shah. In 1954, the CIA assisted in the overthrow of the Jacobo Arbenz Guzman government in Guatemala because of the fear of growing Communist influence there. In 1958, President Eisenhower ordered 14,000 marines to land in Lebanon to support a pro-Western government from possible subversion by Iraq, Syria, and Egypt.

The early 1960s saw the occurrence of three more interventions for a similar reason. In April 1961, the Bay of Pigs invasion of Cuba by Cuban exiles was attempted without success. This effort was designed to topple the Communist regime of Fidel Castro, who had seized power in 1959, and was planned and organized by the CIA. In 1965, President Lyndon Johnson ordered the marines to land in Santo Domingo, Dominican Republic, to protect American lives and property from a possible change in regimes there. Communist involvement in this unrest was the rationale. Finally, of course, the prolonged involvement in Vietnam, beginning in a substantial way in the early 1960s (although having a history back to at least 1946), was justified by the desire to prevent the fall of South Vietnam, and subsequently all of Southeast Asia, to the Communists.[3]

Beyond these direct interventions, the military was used in another way as an important instrument of American policy during the heart of the Cold

TABLE 3.2

Use of American Military Force During Eight Administrations, 1946–1988 (Categorized by Regions)

Administration	Latin America	Europe	Middle East and North Africa	Rest of Africa	Asia	Total
Truman	5	16	7	1	6	35
Eisenhower	18	6	13	2	19	58
Kennedy	17	6	4	2	11	40
Johnson	13	11	6	5	13	48
Nixon	6	2	9	—	12	29
Ford	—	1	4	1	6	12
Carter	3	2	4	4	5	18
Reagan	25	1	35	4	9	74
Regional Totals	87	45	82	19	81	

Sources: Calculated by the author from Barry M. Blechman and Stephen S. Kaplan, *Force Without War: U.S. Armed Forces as a Political Instrument* (Washington, DC: The Brookings Institution, 1978), pp. 547–553, for the years 1946–1975; Philip D. Zelikow, "The United States and the Use of Force: A Historical Summary," in George K. Osborn, Asa A. Clark IV, Daniel J. Kaufman, and Douglas E. Lute, eds., *Democracy, Strategy, and Vietnam* (Lexington, MA: D. C. Heath and Company, 1987), pp. 34–36, for the years 1975–1984; and for 1985–1988 from data generously supplied by James Meernik of the University of North Texas. See the text and these sources for a definition of what constitutes an incident in which military force is used.

War period. Two foreign policy analysts, Barry M. Blechman and Stephen S. Kaplan, provide some useful data on this topic in their examination of the "armed forces as a political instrument." According to these analysts, "*[a] political use of the armed forces occurs when physical actions are taken by one or more components of the uniformed military services as part of a deliberate attempt by the national authorities to influence, or to be prepared to influence, specific behavior of individuals in another nation without engaging in a continuing contest of violence.*"[4] Thus, a naval task force that is moved to a particular region of the world, troops put on alert, a nonroutine military exercise begun, and the initiation of reconnaissance patrols can all be illustrations of this use of armed forces when they are characterized by specific political goals directed at another country.

Using these criteria, then, Bechman and Kaplan identified some 215 incidents from 1946 to 1975. For the period that marked the height of the Cold War (1946–1968), some 181 incidents occurred. The top half of Table 3.2 shows the breakdown of these incidents from the administrations of Truman through Johnson. President Eisenhower used these military instruments most frequently (although he was in office longer than the other presidents), but Presidents Kennedy and Johnson had the highest average use of these types of military instruments during their tenures. Further, Latin American and Asia were the most frequent areas of these incidents for all the presidents from Truman through Johnson. For President Truman, as one might suspect, Europe commanded the greatest attention in the use of this kind of military force.

Overall, then, even though the number of direct military interventions is relatively limited, the use of military armed forces as a political instrument was quite frequent during the period of the Cold War consensus. Moreover, Blechman and Kaplan conclude that "when the United States engaged in these political-military activities, the outcomes of the situations at which the activity was directed were often favorable from the perspective of U.S. decision makers—at least in the short term."[5] In the long term though, Blechman and Kaplan were less optimistic; nevertheless, this consequence of the Cold War consensus appeared to be popular among policy makers.

The bottom half of Table 3.2 shows the American use of force for the last two decades of the Cold War—from President Nixon through President Reagan.[6] During this period, the use of American force waned somewhat, with a decline from 181 incidents during the first two decades to 133 incidents during the last two decades of the Cold War. This decline in the use of force occurred across all areas of the world when compared with the two earlier decades, except for the Middle East and North Africa region. In this region, the incidents of the use of American force rose dramatically, from thirty incidents through 1968 to fifty-two incidents during the 1969 through 1988 period—a 60 percent increase from the first two decades of the Cold War. With the dramatic events in this region for all American administrations—from the Yom Kippur War of 1973 during the Nixon administration and the Egyptian-Israeli and Syrian-Israeli disengagement agreements during the Ford administration to the Camp David Accords for President Carter and the Lebanon involvement during the Reagan administration—this increase becomes more understandable, but the rise is still quite remarkable.

When the use of force in this latter part of the Cold War years is analyzed by administration, all presidents—except President Reagan—had relied less on the use of military force than did their predecessors during the first two decades of the Cold War. By contrast, President Reagan accounted for over 55 percent of all the use of American forces during these two decades. Further, his administration was the most frequent initiator of the use of American force among any postwar American president. This conclusion holds even when we take into account that Reagan served longer than any of the other presidents surveyed here, except for President Eisenhower. Yet, comparing the eight years of the Reagan administration with the eight years of the Eisenhower administration, the Reagan administration's usage of force was still slightly more than a quarter larger (seventy-four incidents versus fifty-eight incidents).

Thus, displays of force and occasional violence came to be justified to defend American interests. Challenges to national security (increasingly defined as global security) were not to go unmet. Instead, confronting potential aggressors was essential to world peace. The so-called "Munich syndrome," the fear of appeasing an aggressor as Chamberlain had done with Hitler, became another theme of American Cold War thinking. In short, drawing upon historical analogies as a guide to present policy was an important source of this kind of response to aggression.[7]

TABLE 3.3

Attitudes Toward Stopping the Spread of Communism, 1950–1951

In general, how important do you think it is for the United States to try to stop the spread of communism in the world—very important, only fairly important, or not important at all?

Survey Date	Very Important	Fairly Important	Not Important	Don't Know
January 1950	77%	10%	5%	8%
April 1950	83	6	4	7
June 1951	82	7	4	7

Source: Eugene R. Wittkopf, *Faces of Internationalism: Public Opinion and American Foreign Policy*, Table 6.1 (p. 169). Copyright 1990, Duke University Press. Reprinted with permission.

The United States as Model

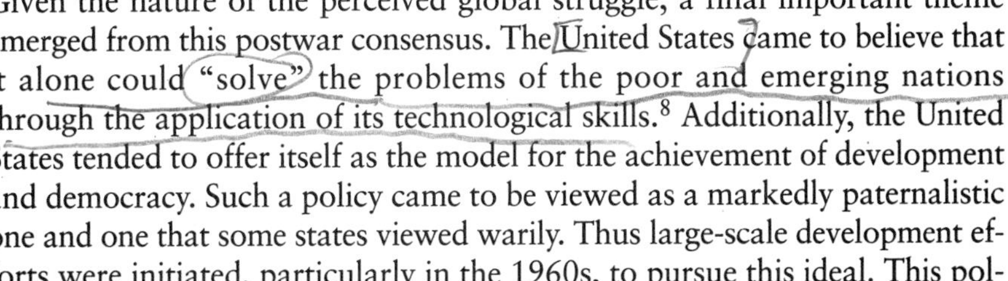

Given the nature of the perceived global struggle, a final important theme emerged from this postwar consensus. The United States came to believe that it alone could "solve" the problems of the poor and emerging nations through the application of its technological skills.[8] Additionally, the United States tended to offer itself as the model for the achievement of development and democracy. Such a policy came to be viewed as a markedly paternalistic one and one that some states viewed warily. Thus large-scale development efforts were initiated, particularly in the 1960s, to pursue this ideal. This policy, however, led to frustration for Americans when development did not occur as rapidly as envisioned or when democracy did not result. Nonetheless, this belief during the 1950s and 1960s, seems to summarize nicely the general value orientation that the United States employed to achieve its view of global order and to oppose the strategy of the Soviet Union.

THE PUBLIC AND THE COLD WAR CONSENSUS

Bloomfield's list provides an excellent summary of Cold War consensus, but it does not convey how deeply held these views were among the American public during the late 1940s and 1950s. Fortunately, some limited public opinion survey data are available and provide additional support for Bloomfield's generalizations.[9] In particular, these survey results depict prevailing American attitudes toward the perceived threat from international communism, the use of American troops to combat it abroad, and, more generally, how the public thought relations should be conducted with the Soviet Union.

Table 3.3 summarizes the results to a survey question asked on three different occasions in 1950 and 1951: "In general, how important do you think it is for the United States to try to stop the spread of communism in

TABLE 3.4

Attitudes Toward the Threat of Communism, 1948

Question Wording A: Do you think it makes much difference to the United States whether the countries in Western Europe go Communist or not?

Question Wording B: Do you think it makes much difference to the United States whether Germany goes Communist or not?

Question Wording C: How about China? [Do you think it makes much difference to the United States whether China goes Communist or not?]

Question Wording D: And how about the small countries in South America? [Do you think it makes much difference to the United States whether they go Communist or not?]

Question Wording E: Do you think it makes much difference to our country whether China goes Communist or not?

Question Wording F: How about Mexico—Do you think it would make much difference to our country whether or not Mexico were to go Communist?

Questions Wording G: And how about the countries in South America? [Do you think it makes much difference to our country whether they go Communist or not?]

Region/ Country	Survey Date	Question Wording	Yes	No	Don't Know
Western Europe	July 1948	A	80%	10%	10%
Germany	July 1948	B	80	9	11
China	July 1948	C	73	14	13
South America	July 1948	D	70	15	15
China	November 1948	E	71	17	12
Mexico	November 1948	F	82	8	10
South America	November 1948	G	80	8	12

Source: Eugene R. Wittkopf and James M. McCormick, "The Cold War Consensus: Did It Exist?" *Polity* 22 (Summer 1990): 633.

the world?" On average, 80 percent of the American public identified stopping communism as a "very important" goal of the United States and another 8 percent said that this goal was a "fairly important" goal. Only 5 percent of the American public saw stopping communism as "not important." When the public had been asked a similar question two years earlier about the threat of communism spreading to specific regions and countries, the results were virtually the same (Table 3.4). Between 70 and 80 percent of the public agreed with the statement that if Western Europe, South America, China, or Mexico were to go to Communist it would make a difference to the United States.

The public also was quite willing to use American force to stop the spread of communism, even if it meant going to war. In two surveys, one in 1951 and another in 1952, the public was asked the following: "If you had

TABLE 3.5

Attitudes Toward the Use of Troops to Respond to Communist Attacks, 1950

Do you think the United States should or should not go to war with Russia if any of these things happen?

	Survey Date	Should	Should Not	No Opinion
1. Communist troops attack Philippines	July 1950	82%	9%	9%
2. Communist troops attack the American Zone in Germany	July 1950	80	12	9
3. Communist troops attack Formosa	July 1950	58	25	16

Source: Source: Eugene R. Wittkopf, *Faces of Internationalism: Public Opinion and American Foreign Policy*, Table 6.6 (p. 178). Copyright 1990, Duke University Press. Reprinted with permission.

to choose, which would you say is more important—to keep communism from spreading, or to stay out of another war?" Less than 30 percent of the public chose to stay out of war, and about two-thirds of the public was quite willing to take action to stop the spread of communism. Further, when the public was asked about the use of American forces to stop Communist attacks against particular countries or regions, the response was usually overwhelmingly favorable. For Communist attacks against the Philippines, the American-occupied zone in Germany at the time (and what eventually became West Germany), or Formosa, the public favored going to war with the Soviet Union if these attacks happened (Table 3.5). Similarly, the public favored using force if Central or South America were attacked by another country (Table 3.6). Indeed, the public appeared willing to sustain a worldwide effort to stop communism, including the use of armed forces.

Short of force, the American public also expressed support for efforts to stop communism. It was generally quite willing to provide economic and military assistance to countries threatened by international communism. As political scientists Benjamin Page and Robert Shapiro report: "By March 1949, for example, NORC [National Opinion Research Center] found solid support for military aid to Europe (60% approving), for continuing the Marshall Plan (79%), and for maintaining or increasing the level of [European] recovery spending (60%)."[10] Further, in surveys by the NORC between January 1955 and January 1956, the average level of support for using economic aid to help countries opposing Communist aggression was about 81 percent. Similarly, support for use of military assistance in six surveys in 1950 and 1951 averaged 57 percent among the American public.[11]

Finally, by the end of World War II, the public was highly suspicious of dealing with the Soviet Union. As Page and Shapiro also report, a large majority of the American people felt as early as March 1946 that the United States was "too soft" in dealing with the Soviet Union. Moreover, by March 1948, that percentage increased even more, to 84 percent of the public.[12]

TABLE 3.6

Attitudes Toward the Use of Troops in Central and South America, 1947–1954

Question Wording A: Suppose some country attacked one of the countries in South America. Would you approve or disapprove of the United States sending armed forces along with other American countries to stop the attack?

Question Wording B: Suppose some big country attacks a South American nation. Would you approve or disapprove of the United States using its armed forces to help stop the attack?

Question Wording C: How about South America—Would you approve or disapprove of the United States using its armed forces to help stop any attack on a country in South America?

Question Wording D: Suppose some country in South or Central America does set up a Communist government. Would you favor trying to get them out, even if we have to use armed force?

Survey Date	Question Wording	Favorable Response	Not Favorable	Don't Know/Not Qualified/No Opinion
June 1947	A	72%	12%	16%
April 1949	B	62	19	19
September 1949	C	50	30	20
June 1954	D	65	26	9

Source: Taken from a portion of Table IV in Eugene R. Wittkopf and James M. McCormick, "The Cold War Consensus: Did It Exist?" *Polity* 22 (Summer 1990): 641.

Further, they report that the percentage of the American public expecting cooperation with the Soviet Union dropped precipitously from mid-1945 through mid-1949 to roughly 20 percent and that this drop occurred across all educational levels in American society.[13] This wariness of the Soviet Union, moreover, was to continue throughout the Cold War years.

In ten different surveys between April 1948 and November 1953, the American public was asked to respond to the following question: "How do you feel about our dealings with Russia—Do you think the United States should be more willing to compromise with Russia, or is our present policy about right, or should we be even firmer than we are today?" About 60 percent of the respondents chose a response that called for the United States to "be even firmer." A policy of "compromise" never enjoyed more than a 10 percent level of support in the surveys. When the American public was asked its views on trading with the Soviet Union or about working out "a business arrangement to buy or sell more goods to each other," a majority occasionally supported such a position even during the height of the Cold War.[14] In this sense, the public appeared to support some contact with the Soviet Union, but that contact was to be primarily one that the United States had historically fostered with other states—a commercial relationship.

In short, however, after summarizing a wealth of American survey data on the early Cold War period, Page and Shapiro conclude: "The U.S. public accepted the logic of the Cold War and favored appropriate policies to carry it out."[15]

CHRONOLOGY 3.1

Six Phases of the Cold War, 1945–1972

Phase I	1945–1947 Preliminary Skirmishing	
	1. International Standing	U.S. advantage
	2. Military Power	probably a Soviet advantage
	3. Economic Power	overwhelming U.S. advantage
	4. Domestic Policy Base	uncertainty in both
Phase II	1948–1952 Soviet Union Assertive	
	1. International Standing	U.S. advantage
	2. Military Power	marginal Soviet advantage?
	3. Economic Power	decisive U.S. advantage
	4. Domestic Policy Base	U.S. advantage
Phase III	1953–1957 United States Assertive	
	1. International Standing	U.S. advantage
	2. Military Power	U.S. advantage
	3. Economic Power	U.S. advantage
	4. Domestic Policy Base	U.S. advantage
Phase IV	1958–1963 Soviet Union Assertive	
	1. International Standing	declining U.S. advantage
	2. Military Power	uncertain U.S. advantage
	3. Economic Power	U.S. advantage
	4. Domestic Policy Base	probable U.S. advantage
Phase V	1963–1968 United States Assertive	
	1. International Standing	marginal U.S. advantage
	2. Military Power	clear U.S. advantage
	3. Economic Power	U.S. advantage
	4. Domestic Policy Base	declining U.S. advantage
Phase VI	1968–1972 Soviet Union Assertive	
	1. International Standing	roughly equal
	2. Military Power	marginal U.S. advantage?
	3. Economic Power	U.S. advantage
	4. Domestic Policy Base	Soviet advantage

Note: The year 1972 was added to the end of phase VI, since the article used as a source was written in that year.

Source: Zbigniew Brzezinski, "How the Cold War Was Played," *Foreign Affairs* 51 (October 1972): 203–204. Reprinted by permission of FOREIGN AFFAIRS, October 1972, Copyright 1972 by the Council on Foreign Relations, Inc.

PATTERNS OF INTERACTIONS DURING THE COLD WAR, 1946–1972

Even with these deeply held views that constituted the Cold War consensus and the evident hostility between the United States and the Soviet Union, the Cold War interactions between these two states were not played out in a straight-line fashion of either increasing or decreasing levels of hostility. Instead, the Cold War was largely a series of ebbs and flows, from periods of greater to those of lesser hostilities and from periods of greater to those of lesser advantage by one power over the other. Neither party obtained all the goals that had motivated this conflict, but neither party was able to vanquish the other. As these nations changed in their capabilities and as the international system changed, the nature of the Cold War changed and the first major attempt at accommodation occurred by the early 1970s.

Zbigniew Brzezinski has nicely captured these ebbs and flows in U.S.-Soviet relations over the height of the Cold War and has categorized them into six different phases through 1972.[16] Chronology 3.1 summarizes these phases along four dimensions: the relative international standing of these rivals in each phase, their relative military capabilities toward one another, their relative economic capabilities toward one another, and the relative stability of their domestic political environment.

As the table suggests, the early phases of the Cold War, as discussed in Chapter 2, were marked by uncertainty in the relationship between the two powers. By the 1948–1952 period, however, the Soviet Union was in a more assertive policy pattern, and the United States was largely relegated to respond to the Soviet challenge, whether that challenge occurred in Eastern Europe, with the fall of Czechoslovakia, Hungary, and Poland and the Berlin blockade of 1948–1949, or in Asia, with the establishment of communism in China and the outbreak of the Korean War. Hostility and conflict were sharp and intense.

By the 1953–1957 phase, though, the United States was in a better position to respond to this challenge. Indeed, in Brzezinski's estimation, the United States was preeminent on numerous fronts—politically, militarily, economically, and domestically—during these years. U.S. military capability was enhanced with a large increase in its long-range nuclear bomber fleet, its adoption of a nuclear strategy of massive retaliation, and the conventional arms buildup in Western Europe. The American economy was expanding, and the gap in the strengths of the two economies was widening. The United States was also in a strong position politically, and was largely able to work its political will in international affairs through the several alliance structures that it had created globally.

Even during this period of American ascendancy and intense rivalries between the two emerging superpowers, though, there were some nascent efforts at accommodation. After Stalin's death in 1953, President Dwight Eisenhower made a conciliatory speech to the Soviet Union, which responded with some informal contacts. In 1955, an Austrian State Treaty was agreed upon, in which Soviet and American troops would be withdrawn from that country. Austria became a neutral, demilitarized state in Central Europe, and tensions were reduced somewhat in that region of the world.[17] In July of that same year, the "spirit of Geneva" blossomed with a summit conference among the leaders of the United States, the Soviet Union, France, and Great Britain.[18] Similarly, Soviet Premier Nikita Khrushchev, at the Twentieth Party Congress, renounced the inevitability of war among the capitalist states—an important Stalinist tenet—and raised the prospect that some longer-term accommodation with the West might be possible.[19] "Peaceful coexistence" had entered the lexicon of American-Soviet diplomacy, but rivalries were still intense.

In the next phase of the Cold War, roughly about 1958 and beyond, hostilities heated up once again. The Soviets attempted to engage in a truly global policy and expanded their activities in Europe, the Middle East, Africa, Asia, and even in the Western Hemisphere. Soviet Premier and Communist Party Secretary Nikita Khrushchev proclaimed his nation's support for "national liberation struggles" around the world and attempted to place the United States on the defensive in numerous trouble spots. In Europe, for example, the United States and the Soviet Union faced off over the future of Berlin in 1958–1959 and 1961.[20]

In November 1958, the Soviet Union proposed to sign a separate peace treaty with the East German government, ending its control over the Soviet sector of Berlin and allowing the East Germans to control access to the British, French, and American sectors. (Since Berlin was located about 100 miles inside East Germany, it was particularly vulnerable to such action.) Its aim was to establish a "free city" of West Berlin, albeit under the ultimate control of the East German government, and to eliminate Western influence there. The Soviet Union did not act immediately, however. Instead, it served notice that the Soviet Union would give the West six months to solve this problem before it effected this change in status for Berlin. The United States viewed this declaration as an ultimatum and stood firm to resist it, although some accommodation by the West as to the number of military forces in Berlin was proposed. The Soviet deadline passed without incident, however, and no immediate change in the status of Berlin occurred. By mid-1959, the crisis over Berlin was further moderated when President Eisenhower invited Soviet Premier Nikita Khrushchev to visit the United States for an "informal conversation" on numerous matters, including Berlin. The first American visit by a Soviet leader served to provide a brief thaw in the Cold War.

In 1961, the Berlin issue was raised anew by Khrushchev with a newly elected American president, John F. Kennedy. The Soviet demands were essentially the same, a peace treaty that would include giving East Germany controls over access to Berlin, an end to all access rights by the Western allied powers, and the establishment of West Berlin as a "free city" within East German territory. President Kennedy responded by indicating U.S. determination to defend West Berlin, and he took several actions to demonstrate that resolve. He called for an increase in military spending by the United States, ordered reserve units to active duty, and stepped up efforts in procuring new conventional weapons. Premier Khrushchev answered with "one of the most belligerent speeches of his career" and spoke determinedly about the Soviet Union's intention to resist this "military hysteria" in the United States.[21] In a matter of days, on August 13, 1961, the Soviet Union and the East German government began to seal East Berlin from the West by building a wall of wire and eventually of mortar. The Berlin Wall was a response to the actions of the U.S. and its allies in Berlin and to the extraordinary flow of East German refugees to West Berlin. Moreover, the Berlin Wall—which stood until November 9, 1989—came to serve as a prominent symbol of the Cold War and the deep ideological and political gulf that existed between East and West.

In the developing world, three other confrontations occurred that reflected how the East versus West dimension dominated global politics during this period. In the central African republic of Congo (later called Zaire), the United States and the USSR found themselves supporting opposite sides in a civil war that erupted after that nation gained independence from Belgium in June 1960. Both powers sent considerable resources to bolster their allies as the Cold War was played out in an arena far from either power's territory. The United Nations eventually assumed a major role in this dispute and attempted to diffuse it by sending peacekeeping forces. In the Western Hemisphere, a similar phenomenon took place. With Fidel Castro's successful revolution in Cuba and his eventual declaration that he was a Marxist-Leninist, a second confrontation between East and West was played out with the Bay of Pigs in April 1961. In Asia, too, the United States and the Soviet Union were deeply involved in the civil war in Laos. The United States pressed for the status quo—a neutral government in Laos—while the Soviet Union backed forces attempting to overthrow that regime. In this instance, a Declaration and Protocol on the Neutrality of Laos was reached in July 1962.[22]

In the third confrontation, the Cold War reached its climax with the Cuban Missile Crisis of October 1962 and its aftermath and with the escalation of the Vietnam War. During this period, the United States once again asserted its globalist posture and challenged the Soviet Union and its allies. Changes in governments from Brazil to Algeria and from Ghana to Indonesia produced a global environment more favorable to U.S. interests. Yet, as Brzezinski contends, this "new phase did not involve a return to the mutual hostility of the fifties."[23] Instead, further efforts at accommodation persisted. The negotiation of the Limited Test Ban Treaty in 1963 and the Nuclear Non-Proliferation Treaty in 1968, the opening of a "hot line" between Washington and Moscow, the beginning of a more differentiated strategy toward Eastern Europe on the part of the United States, and the continuance of superpower summitry—all suggested that the tenor of the Cold War was changing. Many of these events, and several international shifts, had a profound impact on the stability of the Cold War consensus. We shall discuss them in more detail in the second part of this chapter.

The final phase in Brzezinski's description of how the Cold War evolved is dated from 1969, with Richard Nixon's assumption of the presidency, and ends roughly with the Moscow Summit of 1972. At that summit, the Strategic Arms Limitation Talks (SALT I) produced two important nuclear arms pacts—an agreement limiting offensive arms and an agreement limiting defensive arms (the Anti-Ballistic Missile Treaty). The significance of these agreements lay in the mutual recognition by each superpower of the destructive capacity of its nuclear arsenal and the need to address this common dilemma. Equally significant, this summit—and indeed this entire period—recognized the essential equivalence of the United States and the USSR in international affairs. (Note that in Chronology 3.1 neither power dominates across all four policy arenas, as had largely been the case previously.) As a result, agreements for greater political, economic, and social agreements were struck in addition to the military accords. The intense chill of the Cold War was replaced by the spirit of detente ("relaxation of tensions") between the superpowers.

This period of detente proved to be somewhat short-lived, lasting at most until December 1979, when the Soviet invasion of Afghanistan occurred. Detente, however, was frayed and unraveling earlier, from the mid-1970s onward, as disputes between the two superpowers arose over the lack of fidelity to political, military, and economic agreements struck in 1972 (see Chapter 4). Similarly, elements of the Cold War were resurrected during the Reagan years, and especially during his first term. Only toward the end of the Reagan administration and with the ascendancy of Mikhail Gorbachev in the Soviet Union was the Cold War thaw under way once again (see Chapter 5). Despite these ebbs and flows in the Soviet-American relationship and the resurgence of the Cold War in the early 1980s, the values and beliefs of the Cold War consensus were beginning to be challenged as early as the mid- to late 1960s. It is to those challenges that we now turn to complete the discussion of this consensus and its impact on U.S. foreign policy.

CHALLENGES TO THE COLD WAR CONSENSUS

While this East versus West approach as reflected in the Cold War consensus provides the basic prism for viewing international politics during the administrations from Truman through Johnson, it did begin to meet resistance. The predominant challenge came from the changing world environment—a world that was increasingly multipolar rather than bipolar. New power centers began to appear within the Communist world, among the Western allies, and between the developed world and the Third World.[24] Other serious challenges to the postwar consensus were over the limits of American power as exercised in the Cuban Missile Crisis in October 1962, but even more so over America's Vietnam policy, particularly from 1965 to the early 1970s. While these latter two challenges were initiated abroad, their impact was profoundly manifested at home. In particular, Vietnam policy produced a full-blown domestic debate over the conduct of American foreign policy and is often cited as having signaled the death knell of the Cold War consensus.

Sino-Soviet Split

The policy split between the People's Republic of China and the Soviet Union, the two largest Communist powers, challenged the Cold War assumption about the basic unity of international communism and the degree to which communism was directed from Moscow. Throughout the height of the Cold War, the United States had treated communism as a monolithic movement that everywhere took its orders from the Soviet Union. When China and the Soviet Union became increasingly antagonistic toward one another in the late 1950s and early 1960s, the West, and the United States in particular, were challenged to rethink their assumption about Communist unity.

In many ways, the Sino-Soviet split should not have been surprising to U.S. policy makers. Both historical rivalries and social-cultural differences had long characterized Soviet-Chinese relations. Historically, the Soviet Union had always wanted to gain access to and control over Asia, and, in turn, had always feared the growth of Chinese influence. Likewise, the Chinese had always perceived the Russians as an "imperialist" power and as a threat to their sovereignty and territorial integrity. Territorial disputes date back at least to the signing of the Treaty of Nerchinsk in 1659 and continued into the nineteenth and twentieth centuries as the disintegration of China took place at the hands of the outside powers—including the Russians.[25]

On a cultural level, too, deep suspicions have always permeated Soviet and Chinese views of one another. The Soviets viewed the "Mongols" from the East with grave concern, while the Chinese regarded the Soviet commissars with similar apprehension. To the Chinese, the Soviets were "foreigners" and "barbarians," intent upon destroying the glories of Chinese culture and society. Although the other "imperialist" powers were driven from China with Mao's successful revolution of 1949, the Soviets never left. Their continued presence reinforced the hostility on the part of the Chinese toward the Soviets.

Despite these profound suspicions of one another, a formal alliance was still forged between the Soviet Union and the People's Republic of China in 1950. This pact raised the belief in official Washington that past differences were resolved, rather than temporarily shelved. In fact, mutual self-interest apparently dictated this formal tie. The China of Mao Zedong, although successful in its domestic revolution, was still weak and hardly independent. The Soviets, badly in need of global partners in a world of capitalist powers, had much to gain by allying with their new ideological partner.[26] In a world that both China and the USSR viewed as hostile to Communist states, an alliance of these two socialist regimes seemed essential.

But new differences between the two Communist giants quickly began to arise and were superimposed on the disputes of the past. The new difficulties were mainly economic and ideological. Although the Soviet Union provided economic and technological assistance to China, neither was sufficient. Such low aid levels frustrated the Chinese aim of self-sufficiency, a goal that the Soviet Union did not share. Furthermore, the Soviet Union refused to help the Chinese build an independent nuclear force. This singular technological failure has been identified by some as the catalyst for the reemergence of the Sino-Soviet split.[27]

On an ideological level, Mao's brand of communism, unlike what Soviet Premier Nikita Khrushchev was enunciating, did not call for a policy of "peaceful coexistence" with the West.[28] Nor did it call for emulating the Soviet model of heavy industrialization as the road to modernization and socialism. Further, the Soviets and the Chinese disagreed over the de-Stalinization movement, engaged in a rather continuous debate over the degree of diversity allowable among Communist states and parties, and adopted differing views on the nature of the worldwide revolutionary movement.[29] In short, Mao's proclamations on the "correct" interpretation of Marxism-Leninism were increasingly perceived as direct challenges to Soviet leadership of the Communist world.

By the late 1950s and into the early 1960s, the traditional Sino-Soviet split emerged full blown once again. American officials slowly began to recognize this global reality and the need for a policy that did not homogenize the Communist powers.

Disunity in the East and West

A second fissure in America's view of the Communist world as wholly unified occurred in Eastern Europe. While the differences that emerged within Warsaw Pact—the military alliance between the Soviet Union and its Eastern European neighbors—were nowhere as severe as the Sino-Soviet split, they again suggested that some change was needed in the unidimensional way in which the U.S. viewed and approached the Communist world during the Cold War.

Uprisings in East Germany in 1953 and Poland in 1956, outright revolt in Hungary later in the same year, and the call for communism "with a human face" in Czechoslovakia by 1968—all signaled a changed Eastern Europe. Considering also Yugoslavia's long-standing independent Communist route, Albania's departure from the Warsaw Pact in 1968, and Romania's break with Eastern Europe over the recognition of West Germany in 1967, Eastern Europe was hardly the model of alliance unity. It soon became apparent to American observers that exploiting the internal differences within the Eastern bloc was yet another way of moving these nations away from Soviet control. Furthermore, Eastern European nations themselves sought to expand economic advantage through diplomatic contact and recognition.[30] Failure to seize available economic and political opportunities could prove highly dysfunctional for the long-term American policy of combating international communism. Yet such opportunities would be lost if the world were conceptualized and treated only through the strict East Bloc versus the West Bloc dichotomy.

But fissures in this unified East versus unified West definition of global politics were not confined to disharmony among the Communist states. If the Soviet Union faced challenges from the People's Republic of China and Eastern Europe, America faced several challenges within its own NATO alliance. By the early 1960s, the United States could no longer automatically expect the Western European states to follow its foreign policy lead. More accurately, the United States could no longer dictate Western policy. With the economic recovery of France and West Germany and the emergence of the European Common Market, a number of European states wanted to exercise a more independent role in world affairs—or at least not be so subservient to American policy prescriptions.

The best example of this fissure within the Western bloc was the foreign policy pursued by France under President Charles de Gaulle (1958–1969), the undisputed leader of this challenge to U.S. leadership. Under de Gaulle's guidance, France sought to restore some of its lost glory by reducing its strong linkage with the United States, weakening overall American influence over Western Europe affairs, and improving ties with the Soviet Union and Eastern Europe. De Gaulle's ultimate goal, in fact, was to break the "hegemonic" hold of both the Soviet Union and the United States on Europe and to establish a "community of European states" from the "Atlantic to the Urals."[31] In this global design, France would be able to reassert its central role in European politics.

To accomplish this, de Gaulle undertook a series of initiatives to reduce American influence on the continent and to weaken Soviet control as well. First, in 1958, shortly after gaining the French presidency, de Gaulle reportedly proposed a three-power directorate for the NATO alliance. Under this proposal, policy decisions within the Western alliance could result only with the unanimous consent of the United States, Great Britain, and France. In effect, such a proposal would give France a veto over NATO policy. Second, de Gaulle, despite American objections, announced his plan to develop an independent French nuclear force, the *force de frappe*, and refused to join American and British (and later, German) plans for an integrated nuclear force. Third, and perhaps most dramatically, de Gaulle announced in 1965 that France was withdrawing from the military structure of NATO the next year. This last act was probably the single most potent challenge to Western unity. The appearance of political divisions within the NATO structure became a reality with de Gaulle's military withdrawal.

Both the Kennedy and Johnson administrations favored a strong, unified Europe, closely allied to the United States. De Gaulle did not favor such prominent U.S. involvement in European affairs. Instead, President de Gaulle took a series of actions to reshape Western European politics more in accord with his views and as a further means of frustrating American dominance. Thus he sought to reshape the European Common Market, increase French-German ties (at the expense of American-German relations), and isolate Great Britain from European affairs. De Gaulle attempted to reduce the supranational components of the Common Market—the power of the European commission, for example—and to increase the emphasis on intergovernmental components within the organization. In effect, he wanted to allow the member states, especially France, more control over Common Market policy. To accomplish this, he proposed the Fouchet Plan, which was both a broadening of coverage of the Common Market concept to include political, cultural, and defense activities within a European union and a lessening of centralized control. Although this plan was ultimately rejected, it caused considerable controversy and division within the European Community.

President de Gaulle, on two different occasions (1963 and 1967), vetoed British entry into the Common Market. Both vetoes were blows to American prestige, since the United States had pushed hard for British membership. The first veto was a particular affront because de Gaulle gave as a reason for his veto the fact that Britain was too closely tied to the United States and might well be a surrogate for the Americans in European affairs. In essence, Britain was not sufficiently independent of the Americans to be admitted into European membership.

In yet a third step to combat American influence in Europe and to increase European independence, de Gaulle sought, largely unsuccessfully, to forge a strong alliance between France and West Germany. His strategy, once again, was to break the close ties between the United States and the Federal Republic. In the main, he was rebuffed by successive German chancellors, although he did manage to put into effect a German-French Treaty of Friendship in January 1963. Even the utility of the treaty as a lever against German-American ties was weakened because a preamble that was strongly pro-American was added to the pact by the German Bundestag.[32]

Bridges Across East and West

Although de Gaulle's actions were not the only source of dissension within the Western alliance, they did represent the most consistent pattern of moving away from the bipolar world of the Cold War. But de Gaulle's challenge to a bipolar world did not stop with these actions toward America and Western Europe. He also opened up a series of contacts with Eastern Europe and took policy steps clearly at odds with the bloc-to-bloc relations of the previous decade. Such actions alarmed the Americans because de Gaulle was operating unilaterally and outside the policy of the Western Alliance; they undoubtedly pleased the Eastern Europeans because they granted these nations some legitimacy in the eyes of the West; and they probably caused a mixed reaction among the Soviets because, while granting recognition to Eastern Europe, they had the potential effect of undermining Warsaw Pact unity.

De Gaulle's strategy toward Eastern Europe was first to increase social, cultural, and economic ties and then to proceed toward political accommodation. For instance, educational exchanges between France and Eastern Europe were increased dramatically in the early to middle 1960s. Tourism between France and the East was increased. Trade relations were expanded, too. (In actual totals, though, German, British, and Italian trade increased more than did French trade with Eastern Europe during the 1960s.) More importantly, however, France initiated political contacts at the highest levels of government with the Eastern Europeans.

In the first part of his campaign to "build bridges" to the East, de Gaulle sent his foreign affairs minister to several Eastern European countries. This action was dramatic in itself and was in response to the visits to France by numerous political officials from Eastern Europe. But even more dramatic was de Gaulle's decision to visit Eastern Europe himself. He subsequently made official visits to the Soviet Union in June 1966, Poland in September 1967, and Romania in May 1968. Additionally, he had accepted invitations to visit Czechoslovakia, Hungary, and Bulgaria, although these trips were not made before he left office.[33] The significance of these visits cannot be overstated. Since Western policy was not to yield any official diplomatic recognition to the Eastern European governments because of their failure to recognize West Germany, de Gaulle's behavior was a sharp break with the past.

Throughout these visits, differences between France and Eastern Europe were still evident over the question of Germany (with the Eastern Europeans continuing to call for the recognition of the East German regime and de Gaulle steadfast in his support of the Federal Republic). Nevertheless, mutual calls for reconciliation were made. Moreover, de Gaulle's characterization of Europe's division into blocs as "artificial" and "sterile" epitomizes his continuing effort to break the political divisions of the Cold War.[34] His effort gave impetus to greater contact between Eastern and Western Europe. For instance, West Germany's policy toward Eastern Europe

(*Ostpolitik*) was slowly nurtured during the 1966 to 1969 period and came to fruition after 1969. French initiatives were important harbingers of changes in the politics of the European continent. For Americans, these initiatives once again demonstrated the difficulties of conducting policy based on biopolarity in a world that was multipolar.

The Nonaligned Movement

In the post–World War II years, another major political force was unleashed: the desire for independence by colonial territories, especially throughout Asia and Africa. In fact, over ninety nations were granted or achieved political independence from the colonial powers from 1945 through 1980. Sixteen states became independent in the years from 1945–1949, nine states in the 1950–1959 period, forty-three states from 1960–1969, twenty-five states from 1970 through 1979, six states from 1980–1989, and twenty-three states from 1990–1995 (see Chronology 3.2).[35] This surge of independence began in Asia and northern Africa. Pakistan, India, and the Philippines, among others, gained independence in the late 1940s, while Tunisia, Cambodia (Kampuchea), Morocco, Libya, and Malaysia, among others, gained their sovereignty by the middle 1950s. The decolonization of Africa mainly occurred in the early 1960s, although Ghana and Guinea led the way by gaining independence in the late 1950s. By the end of the 1960s, in fact, some sixty-eight new nations were part of the international system, and this process continued into the 1970s, albeit at a slower pace.

This decolonization movement proved to be a third major challenge to the bipolar approach that was at the base of American foreign policy during the Cold War years. These new states generally refused to tie themselves into the formal bloc structures of the Cold War and, instead, preferred to follow an independent, nonaligned foreign policy course. Moreover, these new states actually started a nonaligned movement to demonstrate their independence.

The founder of this nonaligned movement was Jawaharlal Nehru of India, who as early as 1946 had stated that India "will follow an independent policy, keeping away from the power politics of groups aligned one against another."[36] He continued his efforts on behalf of this movement once he reached power in India, and he then proceeded to help organize the Conference of Afro-Asian States held at Bandung, Indonesia, in 1955. This conference is sometimes cited as the initial effort toward the development of a nonaligned movement, since it was the first time that former colonial territories met without the presence of European powers. However, the tone of the debate and the principles adopted later were criticized as not fully reflecting the principles of nonalignment.[37]

The more formal institutionalization of this movement was the Belgrade Conference in September 1961. Spurred on by the organizational efforts of leaders such as Tito of Yugoslavia, Nasser of Egypt, Nkrumah of Ghana, and Sukarno of Indonesia, as well as Nehru, this conference of twenty-five nations produced a statement of principles for those nations seeking a "third way" in world politics. Several critical passages in the

CHRONOLOGY 3.2

The Growth of New Nations, 1945–1995

Nations Gaining Independence 1945–1949

Bhutan
Burma
Germany, East
Germany, West
India
Indonesia
Israel
Jordan
Korea, North
Korea, South
Laos
Lebanon
Pakistan
Philippines
Sri Lanka
Taiwan

Nations Gaining Independence 1950–1959

Cambodia
Ghana
Guinea
Libya
Malaysia
Morocco
Sudan
Tunisia
Vietnam

Nations Gaining Independence 1960–1969

Algeria
Barbados
Benin
Botswana
Burkina Faso
Burundi
Cameroon
Central African Republic
Chad
Congo
Cyprus
Equatorial Guinea
Gabon
Gambia
Guyana
Ivory Coast
Jamaica
Kenya
Kuwait
Lesotho
Madagascar
Malawi
Maldives
Mali
Malta
Mauritania
Mauritius
Nauru
Niger
Nigeria
Rwanda
Senegal
Sierra Leone
Singapore
Somalia
Swaziland
Tanzania
Togo
Trinidad and Tobago
Uganda
Western Samoa
Zaire
Zambia

Nations Gaining Independence 1970–1979

Angola
Bahamas
Bahrain
Bangladesh
Cape Verde
Comoros
Djibouti
Dominica
Fiji
Grenada
Guinea-Bissau
Kiribati
Mozambique
Oman
Papua New Guinea
Qatar
St. Lucia
St. Vincent and the Grenadines
São Tomé and Principe
Seychelles
Solomon Islands
Suriname
Tonga
Tuvalu
United Arab Emirates

Nations Gaining Independence 1980–1989

Antiqua and Barbuda
Belize
Brunei
St. Kitts and Nevis
Vanuata
Zimbabwe

Nations Gaining Independence 1990–1995

Armenia
Azerbaijan
Belarus
Bosnia and Herzegovina
Croatia
Czech Republic
Eritrea
Estonia
Georgia
Kazakhstan
Kyrgyzstan
Latvia
Lithuania
Macedonia
Moldova
Namibia
Russia
Slovakia
Slovenia
Turkmenistan
Ukraine
Uzbekistan
Yemen

Sources: The dates of independence for the new nations from 1945–1990 were taken from Bruce Russett and Harvey Starr, *World Politics: The Menu for Choice*, 4th ed. (New York: W. H. Freeman and Company, 1992), pp. 593–599. The source for the other data was Central Intelligence Agency, *The World Factbook 1993* (Washington, DC: Office of Public and Agency Information, n.d.).

Declaration of the Belgrade Conference of Heads of State and Government of Nonaligned Countries are worth quoting because they demonstrate the rejection of the bloc politics of the Cold War and outline the policy course that these states wanted to pursue:

> The participating countries consider...that the principles of peaceful existence are the only alternative to the cold war and to a possible general nuclear catastrophe. The non-aligned countries represented at this Conference do not wish to form a new bloc and cannot be a bloc. They sincerely desire to cooperate with any Government which seeks to contribute to the strengthening of confidence and peace in the world...They consider that the further extension of the non-committed area of the world constitutes the only possible and indispensable alternative to the policy of total division of the world into blocs, and intensification of cold war policies. The non-aligned countries provide encouragement and support to all peoples fighting for their independence and equality.[38]

In effect, these states not only wanted to reject bloc politics, they also wanted to expand the areas of the world that were part of the nonaligned movement. They saw their contribution to world peace as directly opposite to the way world politics had been conducted up to that time—that is, taking an active part in world affairs through their own initiatives and in their own way without going through coordinated actions of a bloc of states. More specifically, these states rejected military alliances with, or military bases for, the superpowers so that the politics of the Cold War could be extended through such intermediary states. In this sense, nonalignment did not mean noninvolvement or total rejection of global politics, but it did mean the rejection of the way international politics had been played during the Cold War.[39]

This movement proved highly successful, and adherents to its beliefs rapidly increased in number. In the space of less than a decade, the membership had doubled, with fifty-three nations attending the Third Summit Meeting in Lusaka, Zambia, in September 1970.[40] These new members came primarily from colonial territories as they gained their independence in the early to middle 1960s. Essentially, then, the new participants in world politics were joining the ranks of the nonaligned. These states wanted neither to infringe upon their newly gained independence by the formal incorporation into the East-West bloc structures nor to return to the influence of their former colonial powers, the nations that largely composed these blocs. The United States thus found that the new states would not join in its efforts against international communism.

At the same time, the United States was always a bit skeptical of the nonaligned movement and its degree of independence in world politics. Indeed, a continuous debate existed from the movement's inception over how "nonaligned" the movement was. The organization's policy pronouncements have often been more critical of the actions West than of the East, and it was typically more critical of capitalism than socialism. Further, several prominent nations within the organizations had close ties with the Soviet Union. Cuba, Vietnam, and Afghanistan, among others, could hardly be viewed as "nonaligned" in global politics during the entire history of this movement.

Despite this anomaly within the nonaligned movement, the movement itself provided yet another reason for American policy makers to conclude

MAP 3.1

Cuba

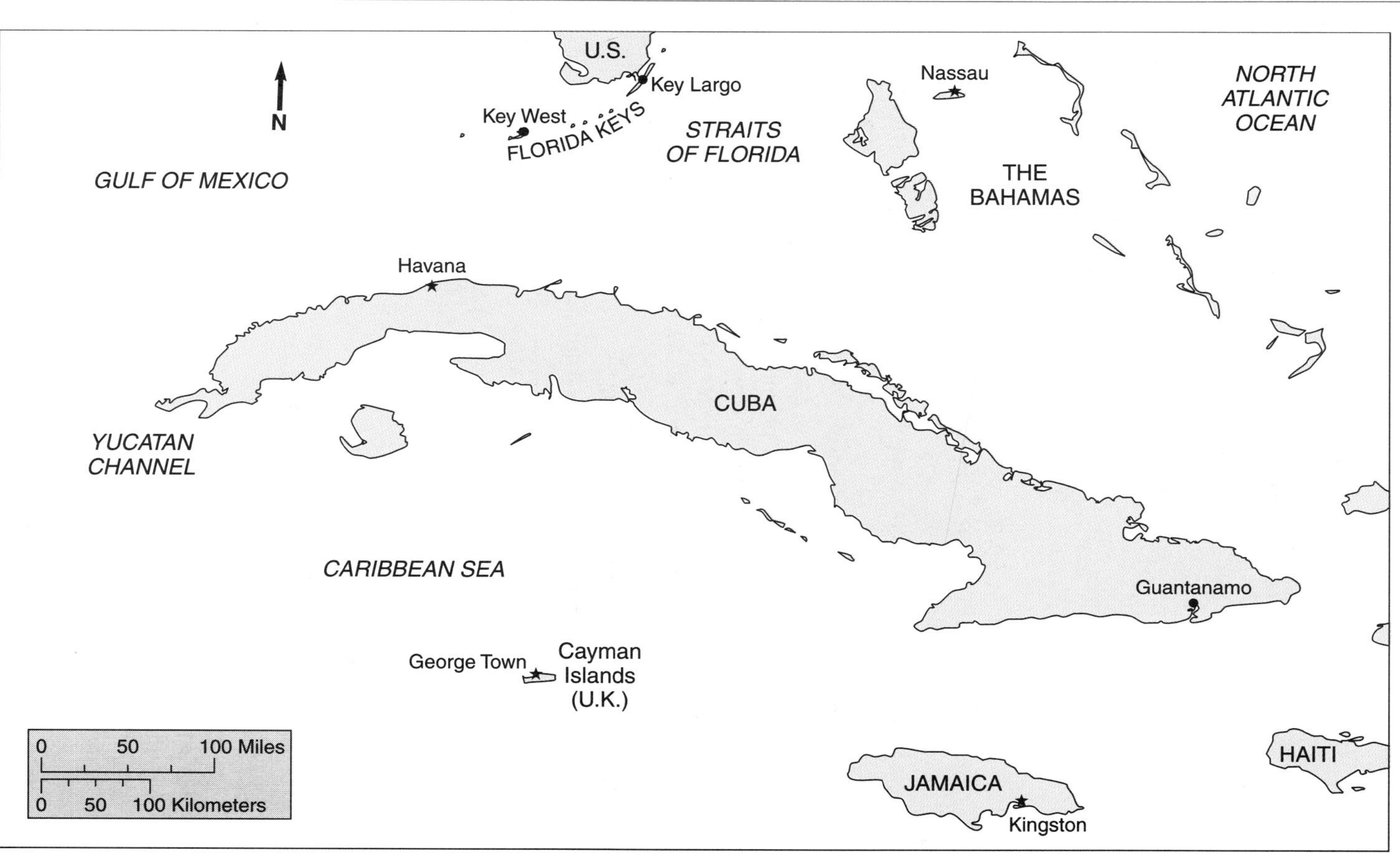
N
U.S.
Key Largo
Key West
FLORIDA KEYS
STRAITS
OF FLORIDA
Nassau
THE
BAHAMAS
NORTH
ATLANTIC
OCEAN
GULF OF MEXICO
Havana
CUBA
YUCATAN
CHANNEL
CARIBBEAN SEA
Guantanamo
George Town
Cayman
Islands
(U.K.)
0 50 100 Miles
0 50 100 Kilometers
JAMAICA
Kingston
HAITI

that global politics would not conform to their image of East versus West; they were further confronted with the need to consider their policy toward this new and powerful movement and, ultimately, toward international politics in general.

The Missiles of October: The First Crisis of Confidence

The last important challenge to America's Cold War consensus—prior to Vietnam—was the Cuban Missile Crisis. Although both of these episodes were foreign policy events, their impact was as much domestic as it was foreign, and they profoundly affected American thinking about the world. These episodes brought home to American leaders and to the American people—in most dramatic fashion—the limits of the United States in influencing the Soviet Union and Third World areas. Both events illustrate the limited extent to which American beliefs and values were able to create the global design envisioned by the Cold War consensus.

The Cuban Missile Crisis of October 16–28, 1962, was the closest that the United States and the Soviet Union had come to nuclear confrontation since the advent of atomic power. Cuba, under the leadership of Fidel Castro since 1959, had by this time declared itself a "Marxist-Leninist" state and had sought assistance from the Soviet Union against alleged American intrigues. The crisis centered on the introduction of "offensive" intermediate-range ballistic missiles into Cuba by the Soviet Union during the fall of 1962. Such Soviet actions were in violation of its stated commitment to introduce only "defensive" weapons into Cuba.

Upon the discovery of the missiles on October 16, 1962, President John Kennedy set out to devise an appropriate strategy to remove these missiles from territory only ninety miles from American shores. After a week of highly secret deliberations through his Executive Committee of the National Security Council, President Kennedy finally announced on October 22, 1962, that a naval quarantine would be set up 800 miles around Cuba to interdict the further shipment of missiles. Furthermore, President Kennedy threatened the Soviet Union with a nuclear response if the missiles in Cuba were used against the United States. In addition, a series of other measures, ranging from actions through the Organization of American States and the United Nations to bilateral contacts with the Soviet Union, were undertaken to remove the missiles already in place.

After another week of tense confrontation and exchanges of diplomatic notes, an agreement was worked out for the removal of the missiles by the Soviet Union under United Nations supervision. The United States also pledged that it would not attempt to overthrow the Castro regime in Cuba. Subsequent revelations about the crises through a series of review conferences in the late 1980s and early 1990s among American, Soviet, and Cuban participants now reveal that an informal exchange was struck between the United States and the Soviet Union. The Soviet Union would remove its threatening missiles from Cuba, and the United States would remove its threatening missiles from Turkey.[41]

The Missile Crisis has long been subject to analysis and reanalysis, and various lessons have been gleaned from it for Soviet-American relations during the Cold War and for nuclear relations generally.[42] First, the crisis fully brought home to both Soviet and American leaders (and their populaces) that nuclear annihilation was a real possibility. Mutual assured destruction or MAD, was no longer an abstract theory. While the United States may have been relatively safe from Soviet nuclear attacks in the 1950s, the development of intercontinental missiles—and even intermediate range missiles that had been placed in Cuba—demonstrated that this condition no longer existed. Americans were now vulnerable to Soviet nuclear power, just as the Soviets were to the U.S. nuclear arsenal.

More recently, political analysts Len Scott and Steve Smith conclude that, with the new data available on the crisis, this lesson is even clearer today. As they report, "recent sources seem to show absolutely clearly that U.S. decision-makers were extremely worried about the prospect of any Soviet nuclear response, so much so that the result was to nullify the enormous nuclear superiority that the United States enjoyed at the time."[43] Two other analysts, James Blight and David Welch, writing from new material and from the review conference discussions, identify the "perceptions of risks" as the first "meta-lesson" to be drawn from the Cuban Missile Crisis.[44]

Put differently, mutual survival proved more important than the unilateral interests of either country during this episode. Despite their avowed antipathy toward one another, then, neither the Soviet Union nor the United States would want to back the other into a corner where all-out war (and nuclear holocaust) or surrender were the only options. This caution was also reflected in the various personal accounts of the decision making during the crisis and in the importance that was attached to "placing ourselves in the other country's shoes."[45]

Such caution also yielded a second lesson: Both the United States and the Soviet Union were capable of evaluating in a rational way their national interests and global consequences—a lesson that was especially important for American policy makers. Because of the Cold War consensus, Americans had tended to view skeptically the decision making of the Soviet Union. Being so consumed by Marxist-Leninist ideology, would the Soviets be able to assess the costs and the consequences of their actions and respond prudently? The answer was clearly yes, as reflected in the outcome of the crisis, and in the subsequent scholarly research on this event.[46] Rational policy making with the Soviet Union might just be possible.

Yet, some very recent assessments also make clear the need to go beyond the rational policy-making assumption in drawing any lessons from this dramatic crisis episode. First, reliance on the "rational actor" assumption, only, fails to account "for the values and priorities of the president. For that, cognitive models are required."[47] That is, an understanding of the values, beliefs, and perceptions of the leaders and the roles these factors played is important for understanding the successful resolution of the crisis and is a useful lesson to take away from this confrontation. Second, organizational and bureaucratic factors in policy making (see Chapters 9 and 10) actually produced more nuclear risks during the crisis than previously thought. Policy managers were, in fact, less successful in controlling the details of their subordinates in the field than many might want to believe.[48] One recent book that focuses on the crisis, for example, makes this point dramatically by noting that, during this period, "the U.S. nuclear command system clearly did not provide the certainty in safety that senior American leaders wanted and believed existed at the time."[49]

Finally, and most important, the episode suggested that the Soviet Union and the United States were going to be major participants in international relations for a long time and that each state might just as well devise policies that would acknowledge the interests and rights of the other. Neither superpower would be able to dislodge the other from its place in world politics. For the Americans, any vision of "rolling back communism" was illusory at best; for the Soviets, any vision of capitalist collapse was similarly myopic. Thus the Americans and the Soviets each learned that accommodation with their major adversary was possible—and necessary—for mutual survival. In this sense, and somewhat ironically, the nuclear showdown over the missiles in Cuba has been cited as the beginnings of detente between the Soviet Union and the United States.

In sum, then, the Cuban Missile Crisis—even with the Soviet humiliation over the removal of its missiles from Cuba—challenged the Cold War view that the Soviet Union or communism could be quickly and easily dislodged from global politics. A foreign policy based solely upon this assumption was therefore likely to remain frustrating and self-defeating. (Although this point is difficult to demonstrate, the Soviet Union probably learned similar lessons about the United States.) At the same time, and equally important, the Cuban Missile Crisis illustrated the possibility of negotiating with an implacable foe—even over the most fundamental of questions—and accommodating a world of different political and social systems.

THE VIETNAM DEBACLE

American involvement in Vietnam began at the end of World War II and lasted for almost thirty years, until the evacuation of American embassy personnel from Saigon at the end of April 1975. That involvement spanned six administrations, from President Truman to President Ford, and it was guided largely by the values and beliefs of the Cold War consensus. This involvement, however, produced the most divisive foreign policy debate in the history of the Republic, and it ultimately produced a major foreign policy defeat for the United States as well. At home, the most important outcome of the Vietnam War was that it signaled a halt to the Cold War foreign policy approach—at least until the emergence of the Reagan administration in the 1980s. Before we assess the overall impact of Vietnam, let us present a brief sketch of American involvement there.

The Origins of Involvement, 1945–1963

Although President Roosevelt gave the first hints of American interest in Indochina when he indicated a preference for an international trusteeship arrangement over countries that today are Cambodia, Laos, and Vietnam near the end of World War II, the events of the immediate postwar years

MAP 3.2

Vietnam, 1954–1975

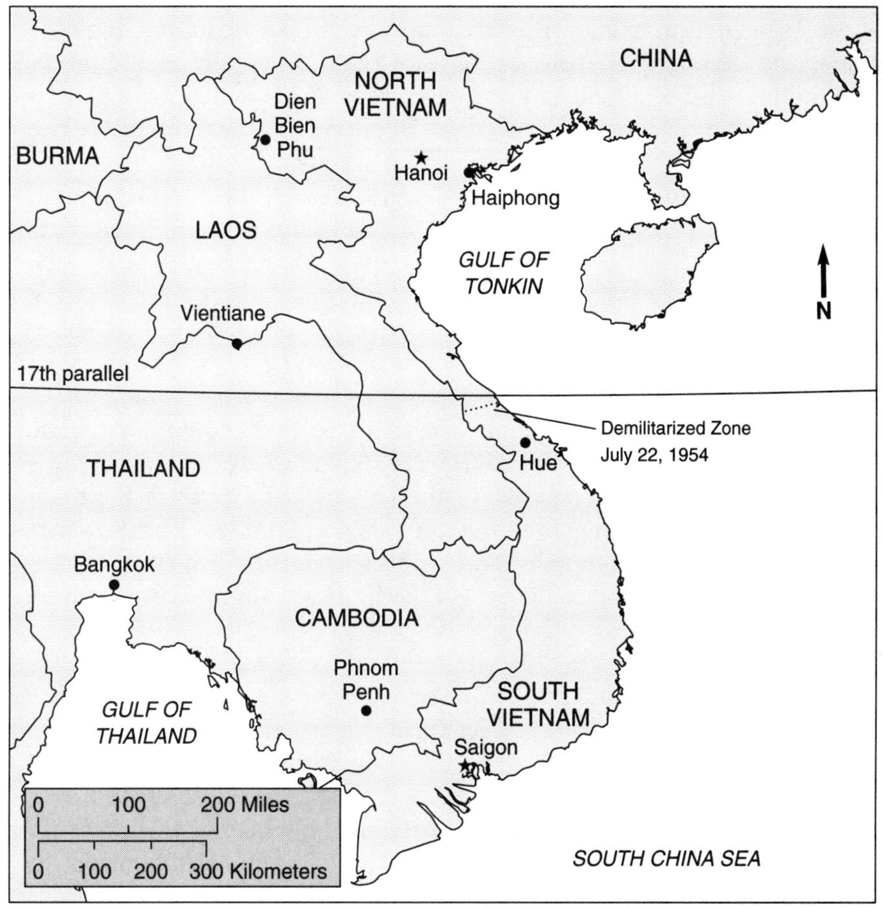

and the rise of the Cold War propelled the United States in a different direction. While the Truman administration had serious reservations about identifying itself with colonialism, Soviet actions toward Eastern Europe, Communist success in China, and uncertainty about the political leanings of Ho Chi Minh—the leader of the Vietnamese independence movement—ultimately moved the United States to assume "a distinctly pro-French 'neutrality.'" As a result, the United States began providing clandestine economic and military assistance to France in the late 1940s in its war against the Vietminh (the followers of Ho Chi Minh).[50] In addition, the Truman administration was not prepared to lose another country to communism or to forfeit the valuable raw materials of the region such as rubber, oil, tin, and tungsten. As a result, French domination was therefore preferred to "Commie domination of Indochina," as Secretary of State Dean Acheson later put it.[51]

After the outbreak of the Korean War, which seemed to confirm Washington's suspicions about Soviet global intentions, American involvement deepened as did the war in Indochina against the French. More than $133 million of military hardware was committed to the French for Indochina, and another $50 million was sent in economic and technical assistance to the governments that the French had established there. Throughout the rest of the Truman administration, the United States provided more and more military and economic assistance. In fiscal year 1951, military aid totaled $426 million and economic aid was an additional $22 million, while in fiscal year 1952, the amounts reached $520 million and $25 million, respectively. Such aid constituted 40 percent of the total costs of the ongoing war for the French against the insurgents in Indochina.[52] Most important, perhaps, by now the Truman administration had begun to commit American prestige into a war that was still being fought by the French.

The Eisenhower administration took the rationale for American involvement in Vietnam one step further by invoking much of the language of the Cold War over the conflict there and by continuing to increase assistance to the non-Communist and French-backed Vietnamese government. President Eisenhower and his assistants, for example, invoked diplomatic and strategic language tying American security to what happened in Southeast Asia and regularly used language of the Cold War to describe the threat posed by the Vietminh. In a 1954 news conference, President Eisenhower referred to the "falling dominoes" in Southeast Asia, and Secretary of State John Foster Dulles hinted at the role of the Chinese Communists in causing the unrest in Indochina.[53]

Yet, the Eisenhower administration did not go much beyond providing economic and military assistance throughout its years in office. In fact, it explicitly ruled out the use of American force to rescue the French from defeat at the decisive battle of Dien Bien Phu with the Vietminh in 1954, and instead sought to achieve a negotiated outcome between the French and the Vietminh at a 1954 Geneva conference on Indochina.[54] The results of that conference were incomplete at best. They called for an armistice between the parties, a temporary division of the country at the 17th parallel, and elections in 1956 to unify the country. The United States neither signed these accords nor endorsed them, and the all-Vietnam election scheduled for 1956 was never held. Nonetheless, these accords did purchase some breathing room for the non-Communist forces in Vietnam, and the United States promptly proceeded to help such forces.

Indeed, the United States quickly became the principal supporter of the non-Communist government of Premier (later President) Ngo Dinh Diem in South Vietnam. Diem, who had been invited back to Vietnam after spending time in the United States, Belgium, and France to serve as prime minister in mid-1954, came to be identified as "America's Mandarin," as he sought to replace French influence with close American ties.[55] Moreover, President Eisenhower and Secretary of State Dulles believed Diem represented the best prospect for developing a non-Communist Vietnam. Between 1955 and 1961 the United States provided $1 billion in aid to Diem, and by 1961, South Vietnam was the fifth largest recipient of U.S. foreign assistance.[56]

Even with this massive assistance, the stability of the Diem government was still precarious. On the one hand, the Diem government in South Vietnam still had not rallied much domestic support. Instead, the regime had become even more authoritarian as it sought to maintain its hold on power. On the other hand, North Vietnam had decided to change its tactics from a "political struggle" to an "armed struggle" in its effort to achieve a united Vietnam. And in another important development, the National Liberation Front of South Vietnam, the Vietcong, was officially founded in 1960, with its membership rising to 300,000 within one year.

Upon taking office, therefore, President Kennedy expanded military and economic assistance to South Vietnam and contemplated sending in American military forces to prevent the fall of South Vietnam to communism. Yet, he did not quite take that step. Instead, he incrementally enlarged the number of American military "advisors" in South Vietnam from 685 when he took office to about 16,000 by the time of his assassination.[57] Even so, President Kennedy appeared to commit the United States to the defense of South Vietnam, although, by one account, he did not give an "unqualified commitment to the goal of saving South Vietnam from Communism."[58] Nonetheless, President Kennedy's actions had taken the United States further down the path to military involvement and may well have continued in that direction had he remained in office.[59]

American Military Involvement in Vietnam, 1964–1975

It was, however, President Lyndon Johnson who fully changed the U.S. involvement in South Vietnam from a political to a military one. He both broadened and deepened America's commitment to preserve a non-Communist South Vietnam and was ultimately the one who decided to send in American combat forces.

As the stability of the South Vietnamese government worsened (some nine changes of government occurred from the time of the coup against President Diem in November 1963 until February 1965) and as North Vietnamese and Vietcong successes increased, the Johnson administration sought a new strategy to hold on to South Vietnam.[60] At least as early as February 1964, American clandestine operations were under way against North Vietnam. Ultimately, these actions led to attacks by the North Vietnamese upon two American destroyers, the *Maddox* and the *C. Turner Joy* in the Gulf of Tonkin, off the North Vietnamese coast, in August 1964. These attacks were quickly used by the Johnson administration to seek congressional approval of the presence of American military in Southeast Asia.[61] In a matter of hours, Congress approved the Gulf of Tonkin resolution, which authorized the president to take "all necessary measures" in Southeast Asia (see Chapter 7).

For the Johnson administration, this resolution became the equivalent of a declaration of war, and U.S. retaliatory airstrikes were quickly ordered. By December 1964, air attacks against North Vietnamese infiltration routes through Laos had begun. By February 1965, "Operation Rolling Thunder," a bombing strategy to weaken North Vietnam resistance and bring it to the negotiating table, was initiated. By March 1965, the first American ground troops landed, and a rapid buildup in these forces was ordered in July of that year.[62] Indeed, the number of forces continued to escalate until they ultimately reached over a half million American soldiers by late 1968.

Despite this vast commitment of personnel and materiel, the war continued to go badly for the South Vietnamese and the United States. The Tet offensive (named after the occurrence of the lunar new year) perhaps more than any other event brought this home to Americans. This offensive consisted of widespread attacks by the North Vietnamese and the Viet Cong over a six-month period beginning at the end of January 1968. While the offensive was ultimately a military failure for the North Vietnam, costing it tens of thousands of lives, it was a political success in that it demonstrated the vulnerability of South Vietnam, despite years of war. Moreover, the impact of this offensive within the United States was immediate—with a sharp drop in the American public's optimism about the war.[63] Additionally, the political pressure on President Johnson became so severe that, in March 1968, he voluntarily withdrew from considering a reelection campaign.

President Richard Nixon, elected as Johnson's successor in part on a commitment to change Vietnam policy, did adopt a different strategy. He began to decrease American military involvement through a policy of "Vietnamization" of the war—a policy whereby the South Vietnamese military would replace American soldiers—and also pursued the peace negotiations (begun originally in mid-1968 in Paris) through both open and secret channels. The Vietnamization program proceeded fairly quickly, but a negotiated settlement proved more difficult.

With Vietnamization, American forces in Vietnam were reduced from about 543,000 shortly after President Nixon took office to about 25,000 by the end of his first term.[64] As part of this Vietnamization strategy, the Nixon administration invaded Cambodia in April 1970, with the expressed purpose of wiping out the North Vietnamese sanctuaries or safe havens in that county in order to accommodate the departure of American forces and to bolster the South Vietnamese government against further attack. To many Americans, though, this action appeared to be a widening of the war. Protests erupted across the United States, and tragedy struck on two college campuses (Kent State University and Jackson State University) where student protesters were killed. Further opposition to the war resulted.

After one final North Vietnamese offensive in the spring of 1972 had been repulsed and after further American bombing of the North near the end of the negotiations, a settlement was finally arranged. After continuous involvement by the United States since 1965 and the loss of more than 58,000 American lives and countless Vietnamese, a cease-fire agreement, formally called "The Agreement on Ending the War and Restoring the Peace," was signed on January 27, 1973.[65] The agreement called for the withdrawal of all Americans and the return of prisoners of war. In addition, it allowed the North Vietnamese to keep their military forces in South Vietnam, and it left open the question of the future of South Vietnam. On balance, the agreement was less a "peace with honor," as it was portrayed at the time, and more a mechanism for enabling the United States to leave Vietnam.[66]

Although the cease-fire reduced the level of fighting and provided a way for the United States to extricate itself from Vietnam, it did not totally end the war or end American involvement. The end of American involvement really came two years later, during the Ford administration. With the fall of Saigon and the final evacuation of all American personnel, American involvement ceased on April 30, 1975. The fall of Saigon represented a humiliating defeat for a policy based on preventing Communist success in that Southeast Asian country. This defeat produced searching policy reflection at that point, but not before the basic premises of America's Vietnam involvement had come under scrutiny and intense debate.

Some Lessons from Vietnam

Several political and military explanations have been offered for the American defeat. Some have focused, for example, on the military tactics that the United States used in responding in Vietnam and the very nature of "limited war."[67] The use of a policy of "graduated response" did not allow the United States to take maximum advantage of its military capabilities. Others point to the failure to adjust the military strategy to the nature of the unconventional war in Vietnam and the futility of the "search-and-destroy" (i.e., forces sent to find the enemy and destroy them) approaches against the adversary.[68] Still others point to the political problems associated with the war. The "legitimacy" of the South Vietnamese government remained a problem, and its shaky domestic support weakened its efforts.[69] By contrast, the determination and will of the North Vietnamese were much greater than many had suggested. Even under the pressure of intensive bombing and high causalities, they continued to fight. Yet, other explanations focus on the loss of support for the war back home and the nature of American leadership.[70] Both the American public and the Congress ultimately were unwilling to sustain support for the war. Some no longer supported the war because they believed that it was not being prosecuted fully, while others did so because they no longer believed that it was moral or ethical to engage in this conflict. Hence this foreign policy defeat, and various explanations for it, produced a significant reexamination of the Cold War consensus and contributed substantially to undermining (or at least revising) it.

American policy toward Vietnam, of course, was guided by an elegant, albeit simple, theory about Southeast Asia. Dubbed the "domino theory" after President Eisenhower's reference as early as 1954, this theory was derived directly from the assumptions of the Cold War consensus. The theory contended that change is a function of "wars of liberation," inspired by Communist forces (in this case, the Chinese Communists). Success of one of these wars of liberation would eventually produce wars in neighboring countries. In time, the whole region would be lost to the Communist movement. As a consequence, preventing the fall of one of the "dominoes" (i.e., South Vietnam) was essential to preventing the collapse of the whole region to international communism. Table 3.7 summarizes the assumptions and the important deductions characterizing the domino theory as applied to Southeast Asia and South Vietnam.[71]

The domino theory made many assumptions consistent with the Cold War consensus: The world was divided between Communists and anti-Communists; change is inspired by communist forces; American security is directly threatened by political change in Third World areas, and the Unit-

TABLE 3.7

The Domino Theory in Southeast Asia

Basic Value Imperative: Contain the influence of Communist China

Axiom 1: If South Vietnam falls, then wars of liberation are encouraged in Southeast Asia.

Axiom 2: If wars of liberation occur, then other countries will go Communist.

Axiom 3: If Southeast Asia goes Communist, then Communist China will gain influence.

Policy Prescription: South Vietnam must be defended.

ed States has the responsibility for maintaining global order. Virtually all of these assumptions—and the overall utility of the domino theory—were challenged in the domestic debate that developed over Vietnam policy.

The U.S. Role. The first general consequence of such domestic turmoil was the questioning of the U.S. role in the world. Should the United States be responsible for political activity everywhere in the world—especially in a country half a world away with only the most tangential relationship to American national security? Was the American public willing to support and legitimize such actions? Was the public willing to support a policy that had only the most lofty goals in international affairs? The American public's response to these questions by the early 1970s was generally a resounding "No." There were limits to American power; there were limits to America's responsibility; and there were limits to how much globalism the American public would tolerate. The role of the United States would need to be much more limited in scope.

Questions of Strategy. A second general lesson learned from the Vietnam case was a greater hesitancy in fighting limited war, and a belief that a different strategy would need to be pursued in doing so. By the late 1970s and early 1980s, the U.S. military leadership became increasingly uneasy about suggestions to quickly deploy American forces abroad and came to demand from their political leaders clearer missions, adequate resources, and a reasonable "exit" strategy. This Vietnam "lesson" was most poignantly played out during the Persian Gulf War of 1991, when General Colin Powell, Chairman of the Joint Chiefs of Staff, and General Norman Schwartzkopf, commander of American forces in the Middle East region, sought and obtained an overwhelming force level to displace the Iraqis from Kuwait.

Open Public Debate. The Vietnam experience also had a third consequence for American foreign policy at home. Foreign policy goals now became a ready source of public debate. Public opinion challenged the leadership policy on Vietnam. By 1968 and early 1969, a majority of the

FIGURE 3.1

The "Mistake" Question on Vietnam

Percentages of responses to the question: "In view of the developments since we entered the fighting in Vietnam, do you think the U.S. made a mistake sending troops to fight in Vietnam?" (Gallup Organization data)

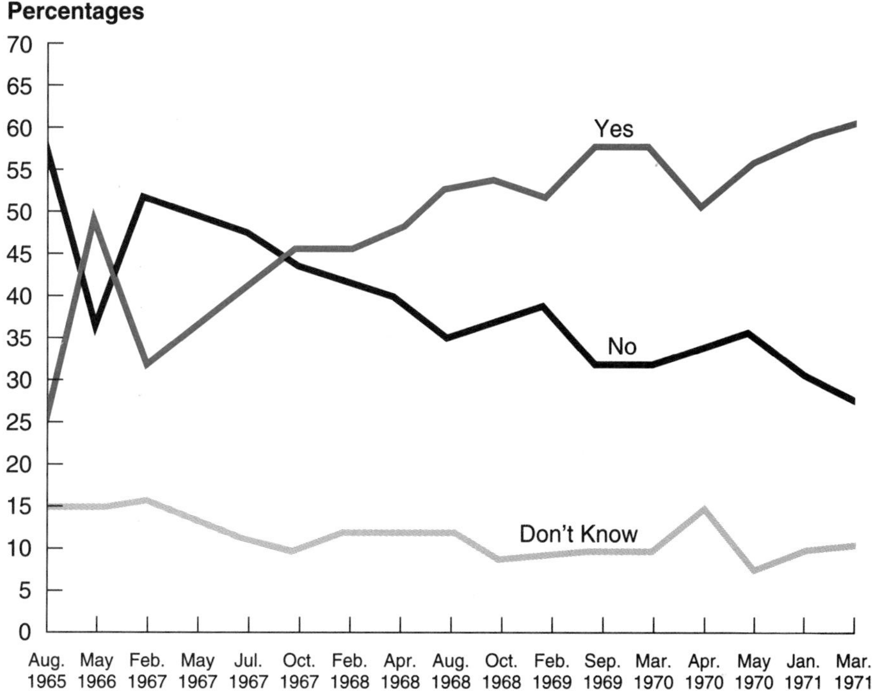

Source: Adapted from a portion of Table 3.3 in John E. Mueller, *War, Presidents and Public Opinion* (New York: John Wiley & Sons, Inc., 1973), pp. 54–55.

American public viewed Vietnam as a "mistake."[72] (See the public opinion data in Figure 3.1.) Moreover, after the Tet offensive of 1968, the number of "hawks" declined, although the public still did not favor immediate withdrawal. By late 1969, however, the support for withdrawal rose to almost the 70 percent level.[73] In the Congress, too, divisions were apparent between "liberals" and "conservatives" and between "hawks" and "doves" on foreign policy matters.[74] Such divisions stand in sharp contrast to the philosophies of just a few years earlier when "liberals" and "conservatives," despite their differences on domestic matters, often stood together on foreign policy issues. After the Vietnam experience, no such harmony was evident. Foreign policy matters had now become a subject for domestic debate.

Consensus Collapse. The fourth general consequence followed from these earlier ones and is directly germane to our discussion of the Cold War consensus. The value and belief consensus that had guided the conduct of foreign policy since the end of World War II was shattered. No longer could the American foreign policy elite depend on general support for their foreign policy goals and actions. And America's foreign policy elite were equally divided among themselves about the relative role of the United States in world affairs.

Concluding Comments

More than any other action, the Vietnam War appears responsible for ultimately shattering the Cold War consensus and producing a reassessment of America's approach to international affairs. Moreover, the public, as well, had seemingly changed views from what it had embraced in the 1950s. While in the post-Vietnam era, the threat of communism remained real to most Americans, they were no longer as enthusiastic about using economic and military aid or American soldiers to combat it. Furthermore, the public was much more favorable to greater accommodation with the Soviet Union and less inclined to confrontation with that nation.[75]

Thus, Vietnam, coupled with the other Cold War challenges that we have discussed, produced a foreign policy vacuum at home. The nation was ready for new ideas for dealing with the rest of the world. A unique opportunity existed for succeeding presidents to develop a new foreign policy approach. Each new administration for the next two decades attempted to initiate this new change of direction. In the following chapters, we survey the realist and idealist approaches of the Nixon and Carter administrations, a modified Cold War approach by the Reagan administration, and pragmatic approach by the Bush administration, and we evaluate their relative success in shaping a new direction in U.S. foreign policy for the remaining Cold War years.

Notes

1. Lincoln P. Bloomfield, *In Search of American Foreign Policy: The Humane Use of Power* (New York: Oxford University Press, Inc., 1974).
2. J. William Fulbright, *The Arrogance of Power* (New York: Vintage Books, 1966), p. 77. His conclusion on American policy choice in this dilemma is on p. 78.
3. See the Rusk-McNamara Report to President Kennedy in *The Pentagon Papers, New York Times* edition (New York: Bantam Books, Inc., 1971), p. 150, for a statement of American objectives in Southeast Asia.
4. Barry M. Blechman and Stephen S. Kaplan, *Force Without War* (Washington, DC: The Brookings Institution, 1978), p. 12. The examples are from p. 13. Emphasis in original.
5. Ibid., p. 517. Their skepticism over the long term is at p. 532.
6. The use of force data for mid-1975 through late 1984 were taken from Philip D. Zelkow, "The United States and the Use of Force: A Historical Summary," in George K. Osborn, Asa A. Clark IV, Daniel J. Kaufman, and Douglas E. Lute, eds., *Democracy, Strategy, and Vietnam* (Lexington, MA: D.C. Heath and Company, 1987), pp. 34–36, while the data for 1985–1988 were generously supplied by James Meernik of the University of North Texas from his current research on this topic.
7. As Ernest May points out, however, American policy makers have often used historical analogies badly by preparing for the *last* war. See his *"Lessons" of the Past*, especially his discussion of the Korean War and Truman's use of the 1930s as the analogue for U.S. policy, pp. 81–86.

8. On this "skills thinking" in the American approach to foreign policy, see Stanley Hoffmann, *Gulliver's Troubles, or the Setting of American Foreign Policy* (New York: McGraw-Hill, 1968), pp. 148–161.

9. See, for example, the discussion of polling results from the early Cold War period in Benjamin I. Page and Robert Y. Shapiro, *The Rational Public: Fifty Years of Trends in Americans' Policy Preferences* (Chicago: University of Chicago Press, 1992). I am also indebted to Eugene Wittkopf for sharing some public opinion poll results with me and allowing their inclusion here. A more complete analysis of some of the public opinion data from the Cold War years discussed here is presented in Eugene R. Wittkopf and James M. McCormick, "The Cold War Consensus: Did It Exist" *Polity* (Summer 1990): 627–653.

10. Page and Shapiro, *The Rational Public*, p. 201. They also note, however, in this same passage some shifting in levels of support in response to particular events, although the overall message is one of considerable support for the Cold War (see p. 202).

11. Wittkopf and McCormick, "The Cold War Consensus: Did It Exist?" p. 635.

12. Page and Shapiro, *The Rational Public*, p. 200.

13. Ibid., pp. 203–204.

14. Ibid., p. 648.

15. Page and Shapiro, *The Rational Public*, p. 202.

16. Zbigniew Brzezinski, "How the Cold War Was Played," *Foreign Affairs* 51 (October 1972): 181–204. Our subsequent discussion of these phases is drawn from his work and from the others cited below (see note 17).

17. See John Lewis Gaddis, *The Soviet Union and the United States: An Interpretative History* (New York: John Wiley and Sons, Inc., 1978), pp. 214–215; and Seyom Brown, *The Faces of Power* (New York: Columbia University Press, 1983), p. 92.

18. Gaddis, *The Soviet Union and the United States: An Interpretative History*, p. 215.

19. Paul Marantz, "Prelude to Detente: Doctrinal Change Under Khrushchev," *International Studies Quarterly* 19 (December 1975): 510.

20. Brown, *The Faces of Power*, pp. 138–145.

21. Ibid., p. 222–233. The quotes are at p. 229, with the second one from Khrushchev.

22. Ibid., p. 214.

23. Brezezinski, "How the Cold War Was Played," p. 194.

24. In his review and critique of Henry Kissinger's approach to international politics, Richard Falk identifies some of these characteristics as the basis for the growth of multipolarity and shows how they fit into Kissinger's foreign policy design. See Richard Falk, "What's Wrong with Henry Kissinger's Foreign Policy," *Alternatives* 1 (March 1975): 86. An earlier analysis of the "challenge to consensus" can be found in Howard Bliss and M. Glen Johnson, *Beyond the Water's Edge: America's Foreign Policies* (Philadelphia: J. B. Lippincott, 1975), pp. 1–26. Their analysis focuses primarily on the impact of Vietnam.

25. For an informative discussion of these historical antipathies, see Harrison E. Salisbury, *War Between China and Russia* (New York: W. W. Norton and Company, Inc., 1969), pp. 13–52. Also see John G. Stoessinger, *Nations in Darkness: China, Russia, and America*, 3rd ed. (New York: Random House, 1978), pp. 212–218; and Robert C. North, *The Foreign Relations of China*, 2nd ed. (Encino and Belmont, CA: Dickenson Publishing Company, Inc., 1974), pp. 112–122, for two other lucid discussions of this dispute.

26. Stoessinger, *Nations in Darkness*, pp. 214–215.

27. For an examination of the centrality of military issues in the Sino-Soviet split, see North, *The Foreign Relations of China*, pp. 41–46, 121.

28. Ibid., pp. 116–120.

29. These issues and others are discussed in Donald S. Zagoria, *The Sino-Soviet Conflict 1956–1961* (Princeton, NJ: Princeton University Press, 1962).

30. The extent of these East-West contacts is analyzed in Josef Korbel, *Detente in Europe: Real or Imaginary?* (Princeton, NJ: Princeton University Press, 1972).

31. For a summary of de Gaulle's vision of European and global politics, see ibid., pp. 40–60; Alfred Grosser, *French Foreign Policy Under de Gaulle* (Boston: Little, Brown,

1965), especially pp. 13–28; Edward A. Kolodziej, *French International Policy under de Gaulle and Pompidou* (Ithaca, NY: Cornell University Press, 1974); Edward A. Kolodziej, "Revolt and Revisionism in the Gaullist Global Vision: An Analysis of French Strategic Policy," *The Journal of Politics* 33 (May 1971): 448–477; Roy C. Macridis, "The French Force de Frappe," and William G. Andrews, "de Gaulle and NATO," in Roy C. Macridis, ed., *Modern European Governments: Cases in Comparative Policy Making* (Englewood Cliffs, NJ: Prentice-Hall, 1976), pp. 75–116. These sources were used for our discussion here.

32. On this point, see Josef Joffe, "The Foreign Policy of the German Federal Republic," in Roy C. Macridis, ed., *Foreign Policy in World Politics*, 5th ed. (Englewood Cliffs, NJ: Prentice-Hall, Inc., 1976), p. 141.
33. This discussion draws upon Korbel, *Detente in Europe*, pp. 40–60.
34. Ibid., p. 58.
35. The number of newly independent states from 1945–1980 was calculated from Appendix B, "Characteristics of States in the Contemporary International System," in Bruce Russett and Harvey Starr, *World Politics: The Menu for Choice* (San Francisco: W. H. Freeman and Company, 1981), pp. 575–583. For the period from 1981–1990, the same appendix in the fourth edition of this book was used, pp. 533–541. Table 3 also shows the independent states for 1990 and beyond. Virtually all of these states are associated with the end of the Cold War and thus do not fit within the general argument of the nonaligned movement. The numbers of these new states do illustrate the continuation of this global trend, however. The source of the data for this grouping is Central Intelligence Agency, *The World Factbook 1993* (Washington, DC: Office of Public and Agency Information, n.d.).
36. Richard L. Park, "India's Foreign Policy," in Roy C. Macridis, ed., *Foreign Policy in World Politics*, 5th ed. (Englewood Cliffs, NJ: Prentice-Hall, Inc., 1976), p. 326.
37. On this point, see the discussion in Peter Willetts, *The Non-Aligned Movement: The Origins of a Third World Alliance* (London: Frances Pinter Ltd., 1978), p. 3.
38. These passages are drawn from more extensive extracts from the Belgrade Declaration, which are presented in Roderick Ogley, ed., *The Theory and Practice of Neutrality in the Twentieth Century* (New York: Barnes and Noble, Inc., 1970), pp. 189–194. The quoted passages are at pp. 191 and 192.
39. For two important discussions of the notion of nonalignment, see Cecil V. Crabb, Jr., *The Elephants and the Grass: A Study of Nonalignment* (New York: Frederick A. Praeger, 1965); and Willets, *The Non-Aligned Movement*, especially pp. 17–31.
40. See Table 1.1 in Willetts, *The Non-Aligned Movement*, for a summary of the various nonaligned conferences and their membership.
41. Theodore Sorensen, one of President Kennedy's advisors and who edited Robert Kennedy's book on the missile crisis, now acknowledges "that the missile trade had been portrayed as an explicit deal in the diaries on which the book was based, and that he [Kennedy] had seen fit to revise that account in view of the fact that the trade was still a secret at the time, known to only six members of the ExComm." This quote is from James G. Blight and David A. Welch, *On the Brink: Americans and Soviets Reexamine the Cuban Missile Crisis*, 2nd. ed. (New York: The Noonday Press, 1990), p. 341. This admission was made by Sorensen at the 1989 Moscow Conference on the Cuban Missile Crisis.
42. See ibid., but also see Len Scott and Steve Smith, "Political Scientists, Policy-makers, and the Cuban Missile Crisis," *International Affairs* 70 (October 1994): 659–684, which seeks to summarize and analyze various old and new interpretations of events and lessons from the crisis by incorporating the findings from the various academic analyses and the review conferences held on this topic.
43. Ibid., p. 681.
44. Blight and Welch, *On the Brink*, p. 347.
45. Robert F. Kennedy, *Thirteen Days* (New York: Signet Books, 1969), p. 124.
46. See, for example, the study of Ole R. Holsti, Richard A. Brody, and Robert C. North, "The Management of International Crisis: Affect and Action in American-Soviet Relations," in Dean G. Pruitt and Richard C. Snyder, eds., *Theory and Research on the Causes of War* (Englewood Cliffs, NJ: Prentice-Hall, Inc., 1969, pp. 62–79.

47. Scott and Smith, "Political Scientists, Policy-makers, and the Cuban Missile Crisis," p. 680.
48. See ibid. throughout, but especially at pp. 682–683.
49. Scott Sagan, *The Limits of Safety: Organizations, Accidents, and Nuclear Weapons* (Princeton, NJ: Princeton University Press, 1993), p. 151, as quoted in Scott and Smith, "Political Scientists, Policy-makers, and the Cuban Missile Crisis," p. 682.
50. George C. Herring, *America's Longest War: The United States and Vietnam* (New York: Alfred A. Knopf, Inc., 1986), pp. 7–10. The quote is at p. 10.
51. Quoted in ibid., p. 15.
52. These data are primarily from Leslie H. Gelb with Richard K. Betts, *The Irony of Vietnam: The System Worked* (Washington, DC: The Brookings Institution, 1979), p. 46. But also see Herring, *America's Longest War: The United States and Vietnam*, pp. 18 and 19, for the first two pieces of data.
53. Gelb with Betts, *The Irony of Vietnam: The System Worked*, pp. 50 and 51.
54. See the chapter on "The Decision Not to Intervene in Indochina 1954," in Morton Berkowitz, P.G. Bock, and Vincent J. Fuccillo, *The Politics of American Foreign Policy* (Englewood Cliffs, NJ: Prentice Hall, Inc., 1977), pp. 54–74. Also see *The Pentagon Papers, New York Times*, edition, pp. 13–22; Herring, *America's Longest War: The United States and Vietnam*, pp. 41–42; and Timothy J. Lomperis, *The War Everyone Lost—and Won* (Washington, DC: CQ Press, 1984), p. 48, on the Geneva Accords.
55. On the role of the United States in backing Diem and the "America's Mandarin" label, see Stanley Karnow, *Vietnam: A History* (New York: The Viking Press, 1983), pp. 206–239.
56. On the level of support, see Herring, *America's Longest War: The United States and Vietnam*, p. 57.
57. The information in this paragraph and the previous one is from *The Pentagon Papers*, pp. 76, 78 and 83.
58. Ibid., p. 107.
59. See Richard K. Betts, "Misadventure Revisited." in James M. McCormick, ed., *A Reader in American Foreign Policy*, (Itasca, IL: F. E. Peacock Publishers, Inc., 1986), p. 100, for this assessment.
60. On the changes in Vietnamese governments, see Lomperis, *The War Everyone Lost—and Won*, p. 62.
61. See *The Pentagon Papers* at pp. 236–237 for the chronology of events in 1964. For the controversy of what really happened in the Gulf of Tonkin, see Herring, *America's Longest War: The United States and Vietnam*, pp. 119–123.
62. *The Pentagon Papers*, pp. 308–309 and pp. 459–461.
63. Lomperis, *The War Everyone Lost—and Won*, pp. 76–79. On the Tet offensive, also see Karnow, *Vietnam: A History*, pp. 515–566.
64. Ibid., p. 82. On the Cambodian invasion, see pp. 83–85.
65. According to the fact sheet issued by the Vietnam Veterans Leadership Program of Houston, Inc., 57,704 deaths occurred in the Vietnam War. The number of names inscribed on the Vietnam Veterans War Memorial in Washington, DC, however, is 58,132. On the last "Easter Invasion," see Lomperis, *The War Everyone Lost—and Won*, pp. 87–90.
66. Ibid., p. 94, for terms of the negotiated settlement and Herring, *America's Longest War: The United States and Vietnam*, pp. 255–256, for this assessment of it.
67. One recent assessment of this view is George C. Herring, *LBJ and Vietnam: A Different Kind of War* (Austin: University of Texas Press, 1994) at pp. 178–186, although he also focuses significantly on the role of President Johnson and his leadership style.
68. On these explanations, ibid., pp. 276–278.
69. See Lomperis, *The War Everyone Lost—and Won*, for the thorough examination of the national legitimacy question. For many lessons of Vietnam, see Gelb with Betts, *The Irony of Vietnam: The System Worked*, pp. 347–369.
70. See ibid. and Herring, *LBJ and Vietnam: A Different Kind of War.*

71. I am indebted to Professor Cleo Cherryholmes of Michigan State University for originally providing me with this formalization of the domino theory over 25 years ago.

72. See Table 3.3 on public opinion survey results regarding support and opposition to the Vietnam War in John E. Mueller, *War, Presidents and Public Opinion* (New York: John Wiley, 1973), pp. 54–55.

73. Page and Shapiro, *The Rational Public*, pp. 232–235.

74. For one summary of the literature on domestic policy/foreign policy divisions among liberals and conservatives, see Bruce Russett, "The Americans' Retreat from World Power," *Political Science Quarterly* 90 (Spring 1975): 1–21, especially pp. 14 and 15.

75. Wittkopf and McCormick, "The Cold War Consensus: Did It Exist?" discusses the public's view in the post-Vietnam period.

CHAPTER

4

NIXON´S REALISM AND CARTER´S IDEALISM IN AMERICAN FOREIGN POLICY

...the United States will participate in the defense and development of allies and friends, but...America cannot—and will not—conceive all *plans, design* all *programs, execute* all *the decisions and undertake* all *the defense of the free nations of the world.*

President Richard Nixon
"U.S. Foreign Policy for the 1970s"
February 18, 1970
Emphasis in original

...we are now free of that inordinate fear of communism which once led us to embrace any dictator who joined us in that fear.... It is a new world that calls for a new American foreign policy—a policy based on constant decency in its values and on optimism in our historical vision.

President Jimmy Carter
Commencement Address at the University of Notre Dame, May 1977

With the breakdown of the Cold War consensus seemingly finalized by America's agonizing defeat in the Vietnam War, succeeding administrations attempted to bring forth new foreign policy approaches to replace this shattered world view. In this chapter, we discuss the values and beliefs that the Nixon and Carter administrations brought to U.S. foreign policy. Each relied upon considerably different value perspectives to inform foreign policy making. The Nixon administration, primarily through its secretary of state and national security advisor, Henry A. Kissinger, sought to employ a "power politics" or "realist" approach to U.S. policy, while the Carter administration tried to employ a "global politics" or "idealist" approach.[1] Neither approach, however, succeeded in producing a new foreign policy consensus; instead, each met with substantial criticism and resistance. Each approach in its own way, however, brought a distinct and identifiable worldview to U.S. foreign policy after the height of the Cold War.

REALISM AND IDEALISM AS FOREIGN POLICY CONCEPTS

Realism and idealism are two concepts that require some discussion before we proceed.[2] Each has been widely used to describe the behavior of individuals and states in the study of foreign policy. Each is an *ideal type*, a phenomenon in which individuals and states are closer to one approach than the other, but do not match either perfectly. Earlier postwar presidents (e.g., Truman or Eisenhower) may have combined elements of realism and idealism, but none matched these characteristics as well as Nixon and Carter in their foreign policy behavior. In this sense, realism and idealism serve as important ways to think about foreign policy actions of these administrations even if these concepts do not fully describe them.

The realist approach is based upon several key assumptions about world politics: (1) the nation-state is the primary actor in world politics; (2) interest, defined as power, is the primary motivating force for the action of states; (3) the distribution or balance of power (predominantly military power) at any given time is the key concern that states must address; and (4) the quality of state-to-state relations (and not the character of domestic politics within another state) is the primary consideration that should shape how one nation responds to another. For the realist, since human nature is ultimately flawed, efforts at universal perfection in global politics are myopic, shortsighted, and ultimately dangerous. Instead, moral considerations in foreign policy are largely derived from what is good for the state and for its place in international politics.

In this view, foreign policy is a highly conflictual process between states, with each seeking to further its interests and with each warily monitoring the activities of others. Balance of power politics predominates because all states are concerned about the relative distribution of power at any one time, and all states are trying to maximize their own power and standing in international affairs.

The idealist approach starts with a different set of assumptions: (1) the nation-state is only one, among many, participants in foreign policy; (2) values, rather than interests, are predominant in shaping foreign policy responses; (3) the distribution of power is only one of many values of concern to the idealist, with social and economic issues equally as important as military ones; and (4) overall global conditions, not state-to-state relations, dominate foreign policy considerations. For the idealist, human nature can be changed, improving humankind is a laudable goal, and universal values should be the basis of action.

In this view, foreign policy should be a cooperative process between states and groups. Joint efforts ought to be undertaken to address the problems facing humankind, whether they be political, military, economic, or social. International institutions (e.g., international and regional organizations) are crucial to shaping global politics, and balance of power politics are largely to be eschewed.

REALISM AND THE NIXON ADMINISTRATION

The Nixon administration adopted a foreign policy approach more closely approaching the realist tradition than did earlier post–World War II presidents. Its approach was based upon the principles of the "balance of power" and was to be anchored in a global equilibrium among the United States, the Soviet Union, and the People's Republic of China (and later, Japan and Europe). This realist perspective was to enable the United States to play a more limited global role and to utilize substantial amounts of regional power (and power centers) to foster American interests worldwide. At the same time, it would allow the United States to remain an important, even dominant, participant in global affairs. One should keep in mind that this new realism in foreign policy was precipitated by the events surrounding the Vietnam War (see Chapter 3). Indeed, the Nixon administration was as much consumed by the events in Vietnam as it was in reordering superpower relations. Both factors pointed the United States in the direction of a different approach to foreign policy, however.

The Nixon Approach to Foreign Policy

Several dimensions of the Nixon policy design were foreshadowed in a *Foreign Affairs* article that the future president wrote for the April 1967 issue, almost two years before he took office.[3] First of all, he emphasized two main points: (1) the importance of bringing the People's Republic of China back into the world community; and (2) the more limited role for the United States in regional disputes in the future. The United States, Nixon wrote, "cannot afford to leave China forever outside the family of nations. There is no place on this small planet for a billion of its potentially most able people to live in angry isolation." At the same time, Nixon argued that a "policy of firm restraint" must be employed to persuade Peking to accept the "basic rules of international civility."

Nixon also foreshadowed a change in American policy toward regional conflict: "Other nations must recognize that the role of the United States as world policeman is likely to be limited in the future." If U.S. assistance is requested, it must come only after a regional collective effort has been attempted and failed and only when a collective request is made to the United States. Unlike the Vietnam experience, direct intervention by the United States must be reduced or limited.

Other essential elements of President Richard Nixon's approach to the world, however, were described more fully in his State of the World Address to the Congress in early 1970, although that statement was actually an expansion on some remarks that the president had made on Guam and in a speech to the nation on the Vietnam War in 1969.[4] In the 1970 statement, he outlined his conception of how to build a new "structure of peace" in the world. Three principles shaped the "Nixon Doctrine" and were driven in no small measure by his desire to shape a role for the United States after America's departure from Vietnam:

1. Peace would require a partnership with the rest of the world.
2. Peace would require strength to protect U.S. national interests.
3. Peace would require a willingness to negotiate with all states to resolve differences.

What these principles meant was that the role of the United States was to be diminished and its power was to be shared with others in terms of preserving world order. Such a design also meant that the United States would act to protect its interests and would do so primarily through the use of military might. Furthermore, the United States would welcome the opportunity to negotiate with other states to resolve outstanding differences.

Such a conception was some distance from the postwar consensus that had put so much stock in the ability of the United States to carry the burden of the responsibilities in the "free world." In addition, President Nixon made two other important observations in this speech. First of all, he recognized that the world was multipolar: "Today, the nature of that world has changed—the power of individual Communist nations has grown, but international Communist unity has been shattered." Second, he acknowledged the power of nationalism in the developing world. Moreover, he implied that this nationalism should not be equated with the increase in Communist penetration: "Once, many feared that they [the new nations] would become simply a battleground of cold-war rivalry and fertile ground for Communist penetration. But this fear misjudged their pride in their national identities and their determination to preserve their newly won sovereignty."

In all, then, this design pointed to a different foreign policy approach for the United States and represented a sharp break with the postwar consensus.[5]

Henry Kissinger and World Order

While President Nixon's statements outlined the key components of a new policy approach, the new national security advisor, and later secretary of state, Henry Kissinger, provided a more complete exposition of what the policy design would look like in practice. To appreciate Kissinger's approach, we must begin with his basic philosophy of international politics, which was developed from a number of years of academic writing and from practical foreign policy experience in previous administrations.

For Henry Kissinger, the essential problem in the postwar world was a structural one: the lack of a legitimate international order.[6] Both the United States and the Soviet Union had tended to think of the world in terms of absolutes and had tried to impose their own views of world order in international politics. Neither had succeeded. As a result, a "revolutionary" and multipolar international system appeared, characterized by (1) the emergence of many states and new centers of power, (2) the growth of vast new technologies that has created great disparities in power, and (3) the appearance of a diversity of political purposes by these states. All these forces made it difficult to establish or maintain any legitimate order. Thus, according to Kissinger, the most important challenge confronting the United States was "to develop some concept of order in a world which is bipolar militarily but multipolar politically."

To create such order, Kissinger argued, the United States must think more along the lines of balance of power politics. While America's idealism of the past should not be abandoned, the requirements of global equilibrium should give some "perspective" to such idealism. The United States should not be afraid to pursue its interests; it should not be afraid to pursue equilibrium; and it should not be afraid to think in terms of power.[7]

What Kissinger proposed was an international order in which stability was a fundamental goal—in contrast to absolute peace, a goal so essential in America's past. Only by achieving a stable international system would international peace really become possible. Kissinger himself points to the dangers of blindly seeking peace without the concern for international stability:

> Whenever peace—conceived as the avoidance of war—has been the primary objective of a power or a group of powers, the international system has been at the mercy of the most ruthless member of the international community. Whenever the international order has acknowledged that certain principles could not be compromised even for the sake of peace, stability based on an equilibrium of forces was at least conceivable.
>
> Stability, then, has commonly resulted not from a quest for peace but from a generally accepted legitimacy. "Legitimacy" ... should not be confused with justice. It means no more than an international agreement about the nature of workable arrangements and about the permissible aims and methods of foreign policy.[8]

In short, the achievement of stability—in which competing powers recognize the rights of one another—held the best prospect for achieving international peace because no state would attempt to impose its views on the international system.

To achieve stability and an equilibrium of forces, the legitimacy of states and of the international system had to be recognized. A prerequisite for such legitimacy was for states to accept the rights and interests of other nations and contain their revolutionary fervor. Henry Kissinger (and President Nixon) therefore proposed a "structure of peace" that would be

FIGURE 4.1

The Principal Participants in the Balance of Power System Conceptualized by Nixon and Kissinger

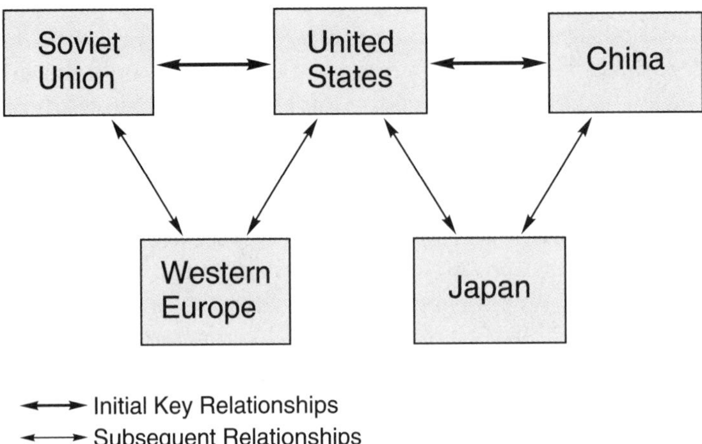

composed of a "pentagonal" balance of power among the United States, the Soviet Union, the People's Republic of China, Western Europe, and Japan.[9] The emphasis would be to gain some accommodation among the first three, with Western Europe and Japan added later to this global design.

An important requirement of this design was that deviations from respecting the rights and interests of other states would not go unpunished. If, for example, a state took actions outside its "traditional area of interest," other states should take action to demonstrate that violations of the required "norms of international conduct" would not be tolerated. For instance, if the Soviet Union provided economic or military support to revolutionary forces in Angola—an area where it had no historical tie—as it did in 1975, some response must be made. The response could take the form of reducing the quality of the bilateral relationship between the United States and the Soviet Union (e.g., reducing trade or the prospects of future arms negotiations) or in the multilateral relationship in the third area itself (e.g., giving direct assistance to the factions opposing the Soviet-backed group in Angola). Whichever strategy is employed, some action must be taken. The intent of such action is to bring home to the offending state the limitations of acceptable international behavior and demonstrate that attempts at expansion (and upsetting international stability) would not go unpunished. In this way, conflict itself would contribute to stabilizing the international order.

This approach to violations of acceptable norms of international behavior came to be known as "linkage" in the operation of the Kissinger system. Put differently, this concept meant that the character of behavior in one foreign policy arena (e.g., completing bilateral trade agreements) was inevitably linked to the character of behavior in another foreign policy arena (e.g., aiding insurgents in a Third World nation). It is significant to note that the Nixon-Kissinger approach did *not* link foreign and domestic arenas. For Nixon and Kissinger, linkage did not mean, for example, predicating the completion of arms agreements on changes in domestic conditions within the Soviet Union. Nonetheless, the importance of this concept to the Nixon-Kissinger approach should not be minimized; it was indeed at the heart of their foreign policy strategy.

By getting all states to accept the legitimacy of the rights and interests of one another and by employing the notion of linkage, Kissinger believed that the United States would go a long way to achieving the stability that he sought. In the short run, the success of this strategy meant the abandonment by the United States, the Soviet Union, and the People's Republic of China of their universal goals of transforming international politics to their own ends. Furthermore, it meant that a policy of cooperation would be mixed with a policy of competition in the relationship among these states. This approach, which became labeled "detente" or relaxation of tension between the superpowers, was an attempt to build some predictability into international politics. In the long run, if this approach could be institutionalized, a global order, based upon balance of power principles, would be a reality.

Domestic Values and Foreign Policy

Aside from bringing a policy of accommodation with adversaries to American foreign policy, Henry Kissinger also challenged four other precepts of past American approaches to the world. He believed that diplomacy (or the "statesman" as he labeled him in his essay on the subject[10]) was the key to the resolution of disputes and to the operation of international politics. As he said, "negotiation is the mechanism of stability because it presupposes that maintenance of the existing order is more important than any dispute within it." Moreover, he was willing to negotiate outstanding differences between states as the principal means of achieving stability. As we suggested in Chapter 1, such reliance on diplomacy was directly at variance with America's traditional approach to global politics.

But Kissinger's challenge to the past did not stop with his heavy reliance on diplomacy; he also took a different attitude toward the use of force and the combining of force with diplomacy. His attitude may best be summarized as, "Negotiate when possible, use force when necessary." Furthermore, Kissinger believed in the use of relative levels of force in efforts to achieve foreign policy goals. Such an attitude toward force and the use of degrees of force was again wholly at odds with America's past. Recall our discussion in Chapter 1 where we noted that Americans were not disposed to such distinctions. Force and diplomacy were rarely bedfellows in the minds of many, and when force was used, all-out force was the standard.

Kissinger challenged the postwar consensus and America's traditional approach in two other significant ways. His view was that domestic values should not dominate American foreign policy. Policy should not become excessively moralistic; when it does, he argued, policy becomes dangerous, especially in a pluralistic world.[11] America should be guided by its historical values, but it should seek to evoke them in the world rather than try to impose them on it.

In this same vein, Kissinger wanted a clear demarcation between the operation of domestic politics and foreign policy. He viewed these two arenas as separate and distinct. The imposition of standards of conduct across these two areas should be minimal. In particular, Kissinger did not want the U.S. Congress imposing conditions on the ability of a nation's "statesman" to operate in the international system. Thus, he vigorously opposed the imposition of restraints on trade with the Soviet Union because of its treatment of Jews who sought to emigrate. While human rights standards were perfectly acceptable in domestic politics, these standards were, he believed, unacceptable in the conduct of foreign policy. Put differently, the domestic policies of a nation mattered less to Kissinger than the way that nation treated the United States in foreign affairs. The principal guide to American foreign policy should be the condition of relations *between* the two nations, not the domestic conditions *within* another nation. In essence, Kissinger was acting in a way consistent with the traditional European and balance of power view of international politics. His view becomes more understandable if one recalls that he was born in Germany and his initial exposure to international politics was largely in the 1930s, before his emigration to the United States.[12]

THE NIXON-KISSINGER WORLDVIEW IN OPERATION

Many of the foreign policy beliefs of Richard Nixon and Henry Kissinger became policy for the United States. This section illustrates the correspondence between their views on world order, the use of force and diplomacy, and the role of domestic values and American foreign policy actions from 1969 through 1976.[13] The following section will also offer some important criticisms that arose concerning this realist approach to foreign policy.

Developing Sino-Soviet-American Detente

Almost immediately upon assuming office, National Security Advisor (and later, Secretary of State) Henry Kissinger and President Nixon set out to establish the model of world order that they proposed. By November 1969, the first discussions with the Soviet Union over nuclear accommodation were under way. The Strategic Arms Limitation Talks (SALT) were initiated in Geneva and proceeded through several sessions before agreement was reached in 1972. At the Moscow Summit in May 1972, President Nixon and Soviet President Leonid Brezhnev signed the SALT I accords, which consisted of two agreements. One, the Interim Agreement on Offensive Strategic Arms, called for limitations on the offensive nuclear weapons that the Soviet Union and the United States were allowed; the other, the Anti-Ballistic Missile Treaty, limited the development of defensive nuclear weapons systems by the two superpowers. These pacts signaled the first agreements to stabilize a structure of world order between the two superpowers and to institute a stable "balance of terror" between them. They became synonymous with the notion of detente. Document Summary 4.1 provides greater details on both of these agreements and the other agreements at the summit.

The Moscow Summit meetings produced more than military accommodation between the United States and the USSR; they also produced a series of political, economic, and social/cultural arrangements. A political agreement ("Basic Principles of Relations Between the United States and the Union of Soviet Socialist Republics") was reached, in which the principle of linkage was presumably institutionalized because each country pledged not to take advantage of the other, either "directly" or "indirectly." An economic commitment was made to improve trade relations between the two countries, and a Joint Commission was established for that purpose. Four social/cultural agreements were also signed in Moscow. These agreements called for U.S./Soviet cooperation on protecting the environment, enhancing medical science and public health cooperation, undertaking joint space activities (including the 1975 Apollo-Soyuz flight), and science and technology.[14] The essence of detente with the Soviet Union was in place with these 1972 agreements because broad avenues of cooperation were opened in the context of a relationship that was still competitive. An important part of the three-pronged global order seemed to be operating.

These agreements, moreover, were signed at the same time that the United States was bombing Hanoi, the North Vietnamese capital, and blockading Haiphong, Hanoi's harbor, in the American effort to bring "peace with honor" to the war in Vietnam. Thus, the effort to stabilize global relationships among the strong went forward even at a time of sharp U.S.-USSR disagreement over policy in Asia. Consistent with Kissinger's beliefs, negotiated efforts to achieve global stability proved more important than any existing conflict in the world. In short, the Soviet Union appeared willing to submerge ideological conflict in Asia for a larger attempt at world order.

Similar efforts at achieving global stability were initiated with the other major player in the Nixon-Kissinger design: the People's Republic of China. In late 1970, Premier Zhou Enlai gave the first hints of an interest in establishing contact with the United States.[15] The United States responded quickly and positively. By mid-year 1971, Henry Kissinger made a secret trip to Peking in order to pave the way for a visit by an American president to that long-isolated country. On July 15, 1971, President Nixon appeared on American radio and television with the shock announcement: He had been invited to the People's Republic of China, had accepted the invitation, and would go there as soon as arrangements could be worked out. Nixon visited China in February 1972 and, by any analysis, enjoyed a huge success.

The Shanghai communique resulted from this meeting and was issued from that Chinese city on February 28, 1972.[16] While the communique reflected the differing world views of the two nations, it did provide areas of global and bilateral commonalities. (See Document Summary 4.2 for the areas of agreement and disagreements in the communique.) For instance, it reflected some movement on the question of Taiwan through confirmation by both sides that there was only "one China"; it opposed "hegemony" in the world (a not-so-subtle strategy by the United States to use the "China card" to influence Soviet behavior); and it called for efforts at normalization of relations (although full diplomatic relations would not be achieved until

DOCUMENT SUMMARY 4.1

Major Agreements from the Moscow Summit, May 1972

POLITICAL AGREEMENT

Basic Principles of Relations Between the United States and the Union of Soviet Socialist Republics

This agreement committed both countries to conduct their relations on a basis of peaceful coexistence while recognizing their differences in ideology and in social systems. It also committed them to "do their utmost to avoid military confrontations and to prevent the outbreak of nuclear war" and "to recognize that efforts to obtain unilateral advantage at the expense of the other, *directly* or *indirectly*, are inconsistent with these objectives."

MILITARY AGREEMENTS

Strategic Arms Limitation Talks—SALT I Accords

- Anti-Ballistic Missile (ABM) Treaty

This treaty limited each country to two ABM sites within its territory. One in each country would be around its capital and another around a land-based missile site. It also limited the number of ABM launchers for each of those sites. In effect, the agreement severely restricted this defensive kind of nuclear weapons system. The agreement was of unlimited duration.

- Interim Agreement on Strategic Offensive Arms

This five-year interim agreement limited the number of land-based and sea-based intercontinental missile launchers to 1,054 and 710 for the United States and 1,618 and 950 for the Soviet Union. In addition, the United States could possess 44 ballistic missile submarines and the Soviet Union 62.

Agreement on Prevention of Incidents at Sea

This agreement provided for procedures to prevent incidents at sea between the Soviet and American navies and in the air space of their navies at sea.

ECONOMIC AGREEMENTS

Commitment to a U.S.-USSR Trade Agreement

No formal agreement was made, but a joint communique committed the two countries to achieve this goal "in the near future."

Creation of a U.S.-Soviet Joint Commercial Commission

The purpose of this commission was to explore ways to increase commerce between the two countries.

SOCIAL/CULTURAL AGREEMENTS

Agreement on Cooperation in the Area of Medical Science and Public Health
Agreement on Cooperation in the Exploration and Use of Outer Space
Agreement on Science and Technology
Agreement on Cooperation in Environmental Protection

Source: Abstracted from the agreements and the joint communique, from the *Department of State Bulletin*, June 26, 1972, pp. 898–899, 918–927.

DOCUMENT SUMMARY 4.2

Key Elements of the Shanghai Communique, February 27, 1972

AREAS OF DISAGREEMENT

Competing Worldviews

The U.S. side stated: Peace in Asia and peace in the world requires efforts both to reduce immediate tensions and to eliminate the basic causes of conflict. The United States will work for a just and lasting peace; just, because it fulfills the aspirations of peoples and nations for freedom and progress; secure, because it removes the danger of foreign aggression. The United States supports individual freedom and social progress for all the peoples of the world, free of outside pressure or intervention.

The Chinese side stated: Wherever there is oppression, there is resistance. Countries want independence, nations want liberation, and the people want revolution—this has become the irresistible trend of history. All nations, big or small, should be equal; big nations should not bully the small and strong nations should not bully the weak. China will never be a superpower and it opposes hegemony and power politics of any kind.

The Taiwan Question

The Chinese side reaffirmed its position:...the Government of the People's Republic of China is the sole legal government of China; Taiwan is a province of China which has long been returned to the motherland; the liberation of Taiwan is China's internal affair in which no other country has the right to interfere.

The U.S. side declared: The United States acknowledges that all Chinese on either side of the Taiwan Strait maintain there is but one China and that Taiwan is a part of China. The United States Government does not challenge that position. It reaffirms its interest in a peaceful settlement of the Taiwan question by the Chinese themselves.

AREAS OF AGREEMENT

Anti-hegemony Clause

Neither [country] should seek hegemony in the Asia-Pacific region and each is opposed to efforts by any other country or group of countries to establish such hegemony.

Both sides are of the view that it would be against the interests of the peoples of the world for any major country to collude with another against other countries, or for major countries to divide up the world into spheres of interest.

Normalization of Relations

The two sides agreed that it is desirable to broaden the understanding between the two peoples....

Both sides view bilateral trade as another area from which mutual benefit can be derived, and agreed that economic relations based on equality and mutual benefit are in the interest of the peoples of the two countries....

The two sides expressed the hope that the gains achieved during this visit would open up new prospects for the relations between the two countries. They believe that the normalization of relations between the two countries is not only in the interest of the Chinese and American peoples but also contributes to the relaxation of tension in Asia and the world.

Source: "Text of Joint Communique Issued at Shanghai, February 27," *Department of State Bulletin*, March 20, 1972, pp. 435–438. The substantive elements are quoted directly from the communique.

the Carter administration); and it opened up trade and other contacts between the American and Chinese peoples. Overall, the content of the communique did not provide the areas of cooperation that the Moscow meeting would, but it had the seeds of such cooperation. Nonetheless, it was remarkable in a more profound sense: After more than thirty years, formal contact between harsh adversaries was begun. The Asian component of the Kissinger-Nixon global design seemed to be falling into place as well.

The last component of this detente strategy was the Final Act of the Conference on Security and Cooperation in Europe signed in Helsinki, Finland, on August 1, 1975.[17] It was signed after President Nixon had left office, but while Henry Kissinger still dominated policy, and it signaled efforts at expanding detente from involving only the superpowers to including all European states.

The conference itself was composed of thirty-five countries from East and West Europe and the United States and Canada from North America. The Final Act (or the Helsinki Accords as they are sometimes called) was a "political statement," rather than a legally binding treaty of international law. It was composed of three "baskets" of issues, with each basket containing provisions for enhancing cooperation among the signatory nations. The first basket dealt with principles of conduct toward one another and ways to reduce military tension among them; the second dealt with efforts to enlarge cooperation in economic, technological, and environmental arenas; and the third dealt with a series of measures for fostering closer social/cultural interaction among participants. Document Summary 4.3 summarizes these "baskets" more fully. The Final Act, however, was not viewed as an end in itself; instead, it was seen as the beginning point of an evolving cooperative process in Central Europe, much as the Moscow and Shanghai agreements of 1972 were viewed. In this sense, with the Helsinki Accords, the "relaxation of tensions" and the stability of the international order that Nixon and Kissinger had envisioned expanded to all of Central Europe.

Force and Diplomacy in the Third World

Two major events demonstrate the importance of the combined use of force and diplomacy to Nixon and Kissinger's foreign policy approach. The first involved negotiations over ending the Vietnam War, the second entailed the use of "shuttle diplomacy" in the Middle East. From the outset of Kissinger's tenure as national security advisor, he saw negotiations as the key to the resolution of the Vietnam War.[18] A two-track system of secret and open negotiations was put into effect immediately. These negotiations, however, did not produce quick results. In addition, the process of the war itself continued to deteriorate, from the American perspective, and protests at home continued to increase. In an attempt to get the negotiations back on track, force—and in this case the escalation of force—needed to be added to the diplomatic track. For Nixon and Kissinger, force could be used to demonstrate resolve concerning their bargaining position and to prod their adversary to serious negotiations.

On at least three occasions, the use of escalating force was combined with the ongoing Vietnam negotiations in efforts to produce diplomatic re-

DOCUMENT SUMMARY 4.3

A Description of the Three "Baskets" of the Helsinki Accords, August 1, 1975

BASKET 1

The Declaration of Principles on Political Relations Among the States

This basket contains ten principles to guide the conduct of relations among the thirty-five signatory countries. These principles range from respect for "sovereign equality," the "inviolability of frontiers," and "respect for human rights and fundamental freedoms" to "cooperation among states," "the peaceful settlement of disputes," and "nonintervention in the affairs of states." This basket also contains a series of proposals (called "confidence-building measures" or "CBMs") that states should undertake to contribute to stability in Europe.

BASKET 2

A Call for Economic, Scientific, Technical, and Environmental Cooperation Among the States

This basket contains a series of recommendations for enhancing East-West cooperation in all of these areas. Efforts should be undertaken, for example, to encourage industrial cooperation, reduce trade barriers, promote joint scientific research, and support environmental cooperation.

BASKET 3

A Call for Humanitarian Cooperation Between East and West

This basket calls for the "freer movement of people, ideas, and information" between East and West. The reunification of families, binational marriages, and freer travel should be encouraged; greater exchange of information should be allowed; and cultural and educational cooperation should be promoted.

Source: Abstracted from "Conference on Security and Cooperation in Europe," *Department of State Bulletin,* September 26, 1977, pp. 404–410.

sults. First, in April 1970, Kissinger and Nixon agreed to an American "incursion" into Cambodia, a neutral country—essentially escalating the war (although secret bombing attacks had previously occurred). This action was undertaken to demonstrate U.S. resolve on the issue and as a way to move the North Vietnamese toward serious negotiations. Second, about two years later (May 1972), when negotiations were again stalled, the bombing and blockading of Hanoi and Haiphong were used for the same expressed goal. Kissinger apparently had some doubts about the decision to blockade Haiphong because it might wreck the upcoming Moscow summit and the signing of the SALT I accords. Although he believed that a more intensive bombing campaign might be sufficient to show resolve, he ultimately acquiesced in the policy decision by the president.[19] Third, force and diplomacy were combined in the so-called "Christmas bombing" of December 1972. After Kissinger had so solemnly announced that "peace is at hand" in late October 1972, and that only a few details were left to negotiate, the final negotiations abruptly hit a snag. As a consequence, President Nixon intensified the bombing of North Vietnam as a way to reopen negotiations and to bring about the successful completion of the Paris agreements. While there is some dispute over the extent to which Kissinger concurred with the bombing decision from the outset, he did not publicly challenge it. Instead, he went on record as supporting it.[20] Further, debate remains over the extent of impact the bombing had on altering the terms of the settlement. In the words of one historian, George C. Herring, "the bombing did not produce a settlement markedly different from the one that United States had earlier rejected.... The changes were largely cosmetic, enabling each side to claim that nothing had been given up."[21] In any event, and as we noted in Chapter 3, by late January 1973, a Vietnam disengagement was signed in Paris.

The other major illustration of the importance of diplomacy and force as the keystone of American policy for Nixon and Kissinger (and later, President Gerald Ford) occurred in the Middle East. After the Arab initiation of force in the Yom Kippur War of October 1973, and the imposition of the oil embargo by the Arab oil states, the United States first used American military assistance to reinforce Israel, but then Kissinger used his considerable diplomatic skills to negotiate a series of disengagement pacts among Egypt, Syria, and Israel. These agreements began to untangle the Middle East conflict, but they had, perhaps, more importance in turning the oil spigot back on for the United States. The negotiations were to demonstrate to the Arab states (and particularly the Arab oil states) that the United States was serious about resolving the Middle East conflict.

Intermittently, over a period of months from 1973 through 1975, Henry Kissinger "shuttled" between Cairo, Tel Aviv, and Damascus to hammer out two disengagement agreements over the Sinai Peninsula, between Egypt and Israel, and one over the Golan Heights, between Syria and Israel. Such diplomatic actions brought into sharp relief the central role that negotiations placed upon the "statesman." Although Kissinger's further efforts were ultimately stalled by intransigence on both sides, even his efforts to that point illustrated how diplomacy could be a powerful tool in moving toward international order.

Human Rights and Foreign Policy Action

Finally, there indeed appeared to be a separation between American domestic values and American foreign policy actions during the tenure of Nixon and Kissinger. This separation was perhaps best illustrated in policy toward authoritarian and totalitarian regimes. Nixon and Kissinger were reluctant to bring to the attention of the Chilean and Greek juntas their concerns about violations of human rights because of the overriding importance of such states to establishing global order. Similarly, U.S. policy toward South Africa continued tacit support for that regime, despite its apartheid policy of legally separating races in social and political life. Once again, strategic considerations became an important motivating force for the Nixon administration.

Toward totalitarian regimes, Nixon and Kissinger seemed to operate on a similar dichotomy. For instance, Kissinger opposed giving any official Washington recognition to Alexsandr Solzhenitsyn when he was expelled from the Soviet Union, just as he opposed the Jackson-Vanik Amendment to the Trade Act of 1974. This amendment essentially made free emigration policy a requirement for any U.S. trading partner seeking most-favored-nation status. Because the Soviet Union enforced a restrictive emigration policy, most-favored-nation trading status was denied them. Domestic politics in any state were to be subordinated to the requirements of international politics. To the extent that domestic situations within another state were to be addressed, these were to be done through "quiet diplomacy"—secret representations to the offending regime.

CRITICISMS OF THE NIXON-KISSINGER APPROACH

Despite the policy successes that Nixon and Kissinger brought to U.S. foreign policy in the 1970s, their foreign policy approach was subject to criticism both for the content of its policy and for its style of policy making. These criticisms came from analysts on both the left and the right sides of the political spectrum, and even from the foreign policy establishment.

From the Left

On the left, the most telling critique was offered by political scientist Richard Falk in an essay aptly entitled "What's Wrong with Henry Kissinger's Foreign Policy?"[22] His criticisms focused upon the lack of moral content in Kissinger's policy and its irrelevance to the last quarter of the twentieth century. Kissinger's concern with order and stability in international politics ignored the more important questions of peace and justice in global affairs. In Falk's view, the most pressing issues of international politics were not power and domination, as Kissinger emphasized, but hunger, poverty, and global inequity, which Kissinger did not. Yet, his policy approach had no direct way to deal with these important concerns.

Instead, Kissinger's global order was predicated upon preserving the nation-state system and attempting to manage that system by moderating conflict among a few, strong Northern Hemisphere states. Such a view represents the "underlying conceptual flaw in Kissinger's approach," according to Falk.[23] This "cooperative directorate among great powers" that Kissinger envisioned was shortsighted in more fundamental ways as well:

> It accepts as inevitable the persistence of large-scale misery and repression. It enables the disfavored many to be kept under control by the favored few. The global structure of control that Kissinger envisages and endorses tempts change-minded groups to adopt some variant of "desperate politics" to achieve their goals of liberation from social, political and economic oppression.[24]

The antirevolutionary nature of Kissinger's policies and his indifference to the character of domestic regimes with which those policies dealt further eroded the prospect for meaningful global reform through his foreign policy. Although Kissinger emphasized stopping of "revolutionaries" of the right or left, his policy was mainly directed at controlling those from the left. In this sense, his policy approach was little different than the staunch anti-communism of an earlier era. His "tendency to remove the moral question from the sphere of international diplomacy"[25] enhanced his ability to gain support within the United States from liberal and conservatives alike, but it did not add to the moral character of U.S. policy.

In a 1972 campaign address, Senator and presidential nominee George McGovern also criticized the Nixon-Kissinger approach for its outdated pentagonal design and for its lack of moral character. McGovern argued that the "five-corner, balance of power thesis attempts to force onto the contemporary world a naive prenuclear view dating back to the 19th century and before."[26] The United States ought to stand for more than that narrow vision and it ought to reflect "our attitudes towards ourselves, towards our country, and towards the rest of mankind." His proposed "New Internationalism" would use American power to achieve "elemental human dignity" and to support a new kind of interventionism in which the United States provides "agricultural and technical assistance...the building of roads and schools...the training of skilled personnel, in concert with other nations and through multilateral institutions."[27]

From the Right

On the right, the Kissinger approach was also criticized in terms of moral relativity. In particular, political conservatives viewed the policy of detente as morally bankrupt because it gave legitimacy and equality to regimes to which the United States had not done so in the past. Indeed, the opening to the People's Republic of China was particularly troubling, since the United States had never recognized or interacted with the regime of Mao Zedong. Suddenly, this situation changed almost overnight. While the change was not as abrupt with the Soviet Union, the effect was largely the same.

William Buckley, a leading conservative spokesperson, put this criticism in a slightly different way. He argued that the detente policy was based upon an "ideological egalitarianism" that implied that there were no fundamental differences between the American, Soviet, and Chinese societies. As he noted in a televised interview with Henry Kissinger, the Chinese had been most often described as "warlike," "ignorant," "sly," and "treacherous" in a 1966 American poll in the United States. One month after President Nixon's return from China in 1972, however, the description had changed dramatically. Now, the Chinese were most often described as "progressive," "hard-working," "intelligent," "artistic," and "practical."[28] Yet, the regime in Beijing (at that time) had hardly changed its policy at all; only American policy had changed. Detente, therefore, had the effect of reducing the ideological distinction between the United States and these Communist states almost overnight.

Yet a third criticism from the right, and hardly divorced from the other two, is that detente is a strategy that connotes a "no win" strategy against communism. By accepting the legitimacy of these other key states and by working with them, these states are perpetuated, not undermined, which presumably had been the U.S. aim for three decades.

General Criticisms of the Nixon-Kissinger Detente

From yet another quarter, another kind of criticism was leveled at the detente policy that Nixon and Kissinger pursued. Former under secretary of state in the Kennedy and Johnson administrations George Ball, writing near the end of Kissinger's time in office, did not see the policy as particularly new or as necessarily advantageous to the United States for several reasons.[29] First, ever since World War II, the United States and the West had tried to obtain better relations with the Soviet Union. Indeed, America's initiatives of the late 1960s and early 1970s were grounded largely in earlier Western European efforts. Second, the results of detente were not all that advantageous to the West. While the SALT accords were useful, the other agreements struck with Moscow produced few tangible results and may have been too high a price to pay for SALT. After all, SALT was in the bilateral interests of both countries. Third, the detente policy approach had not produced the kind of superpower cooperation envisaged in the "Basic Principles" agreement at the 1972 Moscow Summit. The Soviets, for example, had not been cooperative in resolving the Middle East conflict, or at least Kissinger had not been able to engage them in such cooperation.

Finally, Ball charged that the style of policy making by Nixon and Kissinger in the pursuance of their foreign policy agenda was inappropriate for a great power and for a democratic society. Kissinger's "lonely cowboy" approach to policy making limited the foreign policy agenda that could be pursued. The result was "a policy that ignore[d] relations with nations that happen...to be outside the spotlight, and...encourage[d] a practice of haphazard improvisation."[30] Further, this "policy of maneuver," by the "Master Player," as Ball characterized the approach, was built on secrecy and personalism that were hardly consistent with a democratic society. By tradition, policies, and their rationales, must be fully explained to the American public—something that Nixon and Kissinger were not wont to do.

In a more recent biography, Walter Isaacson seems even harsher in his judgment of Kissinger's foreign policy approach, especially his penchant for secrecy. In fact, Kissinger's efforts to open negotiations with China were kept so secret that an odd situation developed: "...the Foreign Ministries of China, Pakistan, Romania, and the Soviet Union all knew about the American initiative to China, but the U.S. State Department did not."[31] In addition, of course, the American public and the U.S. Congress were also kept in the dark. Indeed, Kissinger's foreign policy approach was such that Isaacson was led to characterize his work, variously, as "duplicitous," "secretive, even deceitful," "furtive," and "underhanded."[32] Nonetheless, Kissinger had the unique ability to charm and ingratiate himself with the press and Washington notables as he almost singularly operated the foreign policy machinery of the U.S. government.

A Break with Tradition

In short, opponents (and even admirers) appeared on both the political right and the political left to charge that the Nixon-Kissinger "power politics" strategy was fundamentally amoral and inconsistent with America's past, and that its style of decision making challenged democratic traditions at home. Despite these fundamental criticisms, America's approach to the world had come full circle during the eight years of Nixon-Ford and Kissinger. American policy had indeed moved away from an emphasis on both moral principle and isolationism; instead it had embraced the basic elements of realism. From an initial postwar moral crusade, driven largely by fervent anticommunism, the United States had now adopted an approach driven by the principles of pragmatism and "power politics." However, support for this approach was to wane rather quickly, and the 1976 presidential election was fought, at least in part, on the morality of American foreign policy. That election produced a new president—one committed to a foreign policy based on moral standards.

IDEALISM AND THE CARTER ADMINISTRATION

Jimmy Carter ran for president in 1976 on the theme of making American foreign policy compatible with the basic goodness of the American people; he came to office pledged to restore integrity and morality to American diplomacy. With those fundamental concerns, President Carter introduced a policy approach that was closer to the idealist approach than that of earlier presidents after World War II. His approach sought to reorient the focus of America's foreign policy away from a singular emphasis on adversaries, and especially the Soviet Union (as had characterized Nixon-Ford-Kissinger) toward a policy with a truly global emphasis. Four major policy areas would be highlighted: (1) emphasizing domestic values in foreign policy, (2) improving relations with allies and resolving regional conflict, (3) deemphasizing the Soviet Union as the focus of U.S. policy, and (4) promoting global human rights.[33] Despite his initial idealism, however, by the last year of his term, Carter had reverted to a policy much more consistent with the realist policies of previous postwar presidents.

The Carter Approach to Foreign Policy

From the outset, President Jimmy Carter highlighted the importance of domestic values as a guide to American foreign policy. In this sense, his approach was consistent with a reliance on moral principle so evident in America's historical past and in sharp contrast with the previous two administrations. For his presidency, domestic values were to be preeminent in the shaping of America's foreign policy; the United States must "stand for something" in the world. Even more, America should serve as a model for other nations.

In his inaugural address, President Carter stated these beliefs forcefully. He said: "Our Nation can be strong abroad only if it is strong at home. And we know that the best way to enhance freedom in other lands is to demonstrate here that our democratic system is worthy of emulation."[34] He went on to say that the United States would not act abroad in ways that would violate domestic standards. In a similar vein, during his 1977 Notre Dame commencement address, President Carter again emphasized the moral basis of American policy: "I believe we can have a foreign policy that is democratic, that is based on fundamental values, and that uses power and influence which we have for humane purposes."[35]

In addition to emphasizing this moral basis of policy, President Carter also called for a different style of foreign policy—one that would be "open and candid," and not one that was a "policy by manipulation" or based on "secret deals." Such references were apparently to what he saw as the style adopted during the years that Henry Kissinger was at the helm of American foreign policy.

Finally, while the president recognized that moral principle must guide foreign policy, he acknowledged that foreign policy cannot be "by moral maxims." The United States would have to try to produce change rather than impose it. In this sense, Carter believed that there were limits to what the United States could do in the world. Although these limits would need to be recognized, America could not stand idly by. The United States should try to play a constructive and positive role in shaping a new world order. This role should be through an American policy "based on constant decency in its values and on optimism in our historical vision."[36]

Carter and Global Order: New States and Old Friends

The focus of the Carter administration also reflected its view of the world. To begin with, its policy would not be simply one of anticommunism inherited from the past. (President Carter said, "We are now free of that inordinate fear of communism which once led us to embrace any dictator who joined us in that fear.") Instead, the Carter administration proposed a policy of global cooperation, especially with the newly influential countries in Latin America, Africa, and Asia, but also with the industrial democracies of the world. The aim of such an effort would be "to create a wider framework of international cooperation suited to the new and rapidly changing historical circumstances."[37] Moreover, this policy sought to move beyond one seeking global stability among the strong to a policy that recognized the reality of the new states and their place in the world order.

The philosophical basis for such a policy cannot be attributed only to Carter himself; it also reflects the influence of one of his principal foreign policy advisors, Zbigniew Brzezinski. Writing in *Foreign Policy* in the summer of 1976 and interviewed later by Elizabeth Drew for *The New Yorker* in 1978, Brzezinski echoed these themes.[38] In his view, the greatest danger in the world was international anarchy, not the potential domination of the Soviet Union. America, Brzezinski wrote, was "indispensable" in addressing these issues. "For all its shortcomings, America remains the globally creative and innovative society." The failure of the United States "to project a constructive sense of direction would hence contribute directly to major global economic and political disruption." America must not be afraid of change in the world; in fact, it must seek change in order to confront the new global agenda that faces humankind.

Within this same global context, crucial regional trouble spots of the world were to be important areas of American foreign policy concentration. Efforts at resolving the seemingly intractable problems of the Middle East were to have a high priority in the Carter administration. The festering problems of southern Africa—Rhodesia, Namibia, and South Africa, for example—would need solutions if a more just and peaceful global order were to evolve. Similarly, the problems with Panama and the Canal, and the potential of this issue for generating hostility toward the United States in the Western Hemisphere, also formed part of this strategy of addressing regional conflicts as a stepping-stone to a more stable international order.

A second major focal point within this global approach was the improvement of relations with Western Europe and Japan. This emphasis upon better trilateral relations was again in part a response to the previous administration's emphasis on improving relations with adversaries. For instance, Kissinger's much heralded "Year of Europe" for 1973 was essentially stillborn as pressing Middle East problems arose. As a result, fissures began to appear in ties with America's traditional friends. Economic, political, and military differences with its principal postwar allies therefore were to be difficult problems for the Carter administration.

Economic fissures were fueled by global inflation and skyrocketing oil prices. The Europeans and the Japanese were concerned about American inflation and its effect on their economies, while the Americans were disappointed with the failure of the Europeans (and especially the Germans) and the Japanese to expand their economies as a means of assisting the rest of the continent out of recession. Similarly, trade imbalances between the Japanese and the Americans were producing increased friction. To the Carter administration, however, better economic coordination among the developed democracies was a necessity for the late 1970s.

Accompanying these economic woes, political differences had emerged. A consistent complaint of the Europeans and the Japanese was that they had been inadequately consulted during the height of detente between the United States and the Soviet Union and during the initial period of rapprochement between the United States and the People's Republic of China. Too often, the allies contended, they were merely informed of decisions made by the superpowers. Thus, their status as important U.S. partners seemed to have been undermined. In essence, better political coordination would also be essential to refurbish and strengthen alliance ties.

Finally, the Americans wanted the Europeans and the Japanese to increase their military efforts to confront the increased Soviet defense buildup in both Eastern Europe and East Asia. The Europeans and the Japanese, however, were reluctant to do so, given their domestic economic woes. At the same time, these nations were worried about America's commitment to their defense. Would the Americans have the Europeans and Japanese increase their defenses as a means of lessening U.S. efforts? Better military coordination would be needed as well.

Carter and the Soviet Union

With such a global emphasis, the centrality of the Soviet-American relationship was downgraded. To be sure, detente policy with the Soviet Union would not be abandoned, but it would be placed in a larger context of global issues. In particular, President Carter was committed to joint efforts at strategic arms control; thus, this aspect of the Soviet-American tie would be the continuing and central part of the relationship. The broad comprehensive detente approach of the previous administrations, however, would not be the aim of the Carter administration. Economic, sociocultural, and political cooperation could continue, but only on the basis of mutual advantage. What was crucial here was that such cooperation would not be linked to the overall quality of the relationship. In this sense, the "linkage" notion of the past would be jettisoned.[39]

In essence, Carter's approach to the Soviet Union assumed that the world order of the late 1970s and early 1980s would not be achieved merely by harnessing the Soviet-American relationship. Detente had neither produced stability in U.S.-Soviet relations nor had it addressed the crucial global and regional issues. Instead, it had encouraged a variety of critics at home and abroad and had diverted attention from important global concerns. In short, the heart of international politics in this period had moved beyond this bilateral relationship, and any vision of an improved world along the Kissinger design was not politically feasible.

Carter's initial approach toward the Soviet Union deeply offended and confused it. This approach was offensive because the Soviet Union had long commanded the bulk of America's attention since 1945 and because it had gained superpower status only five years before in the series of Moscow agreements of May 1972. Now this status was apparently being denied. It confused the Soviets because they saw themselves as the critical nation that could affect conflict in the world, especially in the nuclear age. Despite their centrality to questions of war and peace, the Carter administration seemed to be shoving them aside. The Soviets did not quite know how to react to America's emphasis on moral principle and on globalism as espoused by Jimmy Carter, nor to the emphasis on human rights.

Carter and Human Rights

Indeed, the pivotal new focus of the Carter administration was the emphasis on human rights.[40] The role of this policy in the Carter administration can be gleaned from his inaugural address:

> Our commitment to human rights must be absolute.... Because we are free, we can never be indifferent to the fate of freedom everywhere. Our moral sense dictates a clear-cut preference for those societies which share with us an abiding respect for individual human rights. We do not seek to intimidate, but it is clear that a world which others can dominate with impunity would be inhospitable to decency and a threat to the well-being of all people.[41]

At his Notre Dame commencement address, too, President Carter reaffirmed this commitment to human rights. Outlining the premises of his foreign policy, he began his presentation by enunciating the central role of human rights once again:

> We have reaffirmed America's commitment to human rights as a fundamental tenet of our foreign policy.... We want the world to know that our nation stands for more than financial prosperity.[42]

Such a human rights philosophy was to provide the key moral principle for guiding American foreign policy. The United States would not conduct "business as usual" with nations that grossly and consistently violated the basic rights of its citizens. Instead, America would require states to change their domestic human rights behavior if they wished amicable relations with the United States. While President Carter made it clear that the human rights criterion would not be the only consideration, he also believed "that a significant element in our relationships with other governments would be their performance in providing basic freedoms to their people."[43]

The human rights issue appealed to Jimmy Carter because of his strong personal and religious beliefs about individual dignity, but also because of the issue's strong domestic appeal, especially after Vietnam, Watergate, and revelations about CIA abuses. The "something" that the United States would stand for in the world would now be something that it had historically embraced, the freedom of the individual. At the same time, the human rights issue appealed across the political spectrum and thus would be domestically attractive. Conservatives would like this policy because it would presumably condemn Communist nations for their totalitarian practices, while liberals would like it because the United States would now reexamine its policy toward authoritarian states.

Although the human rights campaign tapped American moral traditions, President Carter also believed that it would improve America's standing abroad: "Our country has been strongest and most effective when morality and a commitment to freedom and democracy have been the most clearly emphasized in our foreign policy." Furthermore, President Carter thought that human rights "might be the wave of the future," and he wanted the United States to be involved in it.[44]

THE CARTER WORLDVIEW IN OPERATION

In the main, Carter's initial foreign policy strategy was well received by the American public—especially in light of the traumatic events of the early 1970s. His approach represented a reemergence of American idealism with a clear emphasis on traditional American values and beliefs. As political scientist Stanley Hoffmann has noted, President Carter "was determined to redefine the national interest to make it coincide with the moral impulse" of the United States.[45] In this sense, Carter succeeded. Coupled with the idealism of the Carter approach, however, was the realization of the limits of American power. While the United States could assist in the shaping of global order, it did not have the power to direct the international system of the 1970s—a system that was so diverse and complex that no nation or set of nations could impose its views of international order. In this sense, the Carter approach was partly compatible with the previous Kissinger approach: The United States must evoke a global order through its actions. However, the focal point of this new order was considerably different from the past.

In this section, we shall evaluate the Carter worldview in three crucial areas—improving human rights, dealing with the Soviet Union, and resolving Third World conflicts. Such an analysis will enable us to understand more fully the abrupt change in policy by President Carter in the last year of his presidency.

Improving Human Rights

Definition and Policy. Almost immediately, the Carter administration faced the problem of clearly defining human rights and establishing a consistent application of this policy on a global basis. What President Carter apparently had in mind originally was the humane treatment of individuals: their freedom from torture and arbitrary punishment for expressing political beliefs. Yet such a policy was not sufficiently defined by his spokespersons.

Early on the Carter administration seemed to assert a much broader interpretation of human rights policy. In this official description, human rights policy fell into three main categories, and the United States would encourage change in each worldwide:

1. First, the right to be free from governmental violation of the integrity of the person. Such violations include torture; cruel, inhuman, or degrading treatment or punishment; arbitrary arrest or imprisonment....
2. Second, the right to fulfillment of such vital needs as food, shelter, health care, and education....
3. Third, the right to enjoy civil and political liberties such as freedom of thought, religion, assembly, speech, and the press; freedom of movement both within and outside one's country; freedom to take part in government.[46]

In this sense, the human rights notion was broadened to include political, economic, and social rights. Nonetheless, according to Lincoln Bloomfield, who dealt with human rights issues on the National Security Council during the last two years of the Carter administration, the priority was still on individual civil and political liberties more than on economic and social rights.

Further, after an initial review and refinement of the policy, there seemed to be a slight downplaying of the human rights criterion for foreign policy; human rights would be one consideration in determining U.S. foreign policy toward another nation, and President Carter and Secretary of State Cyrus Vance had indicated as much. Secretary Vance cautioned against "mechanistic formulas" for the human rights campaign, and President Carter recognized the limitation of "rigid moral maxims" in his Notre Dame speech.[47] From the initial rush of enthusiasm over human rights, then, a detectable pullback appeared underway.

Implementation. A second problem also arose. How was the human rights campaign going to be put into effect? How far was the United States willing to go to produce human rights change? Was it willing to cut off all contact with the nations allegedly pursuing human rights violations? Was the United States going to stop all diplomatic, economic, or military ties to offending states? Or, alternatively, was the United States going to continue these ties or modify them in line with more responsive behavior by the other nations? After all, was not this a better way to exercise influence over another nation than by stopping all contacts, and thus all means of influence? In short, what were the best tactics for encouraging human rights improvements in target nations?

Indeed, aid—and particularly military aid—was cut off to principal offender nations such as Chile, Argentina, Uruguay, Guatemala, Nicaragua, Vietnam, Cambodia, Uganda, and Mozambique.[48] Economic aid was used to encourage continued human rights improvements for another group of states. But the primary instrument used toward states with poor human rights records was diplomatic "jawboning"—publicly and privately bringing to the attention of the foreign governments American dissatisfaction with their human rights practices. Clearly, there were limits as to how much the United States could or wanted to do in the human rights area.

At the same time, efforts were made to make certain that the United States complied fully with existing human rights standards, especially as required by the Helsinki Accords (or more formally, the Statement of Principles of the Conference on Security and Cooperation in Europe) of August 1975. President Carter, for example, removed travel restrictions on American citizens to Cuba, North Korea, Vietnam, and Cambodia (Kampuchea).[49] Furthermore, President Carter sought and gained repeal of the Byrd Amendment, which had allowed trade with Rhodesia and which had violated international sanctions toward that country's illegal minority regime.[50] Despite these actions, though, the Carter administration was unable to persuade the Congress to ratify all the components of what came to be called the "International Human Rights Bill." This "bill" consists of three United Nations agreements—the Universal Declaration of Human Rights (1948), the International Covenant on Economic, Social, and Cultural Rights (1966), and the International Covenant on Civil and Political Rights (1966). The United States signed all three, but the U.S. Senate had failed to ratify the last two. Further, the Carter administration had failed to get congressional approval for the International Convention on the Elimination of All Forms of Racial Discrimination, as well as the Covenant on the Prevention and Punishment of the Crime of Genocide.[51]

Applicability. A third major problem was: To whom should the human rights policy apply? The paradox of the Carter policy was evident when nations saw, on the one hand, the United States calling for the free exercise of human rights, particularly in the Soviet Union and in Latin America, but, on the other hand, the United States providing economic and military assistance to nations often cited as having serious human rights violations—such as South Korea, the Philippines, and Iran, among others. Juxtaposing the human rights policy against the demands of realpolitik became a central dilemma for the Carter administration and a constant target of attack by its critics.

The apparent problem of selective application was criticized from two different directions. From one perspective, neoconservative critics, perhaps best represented by Jeane Kirkpatrick, argued that the human rights standards as practiced by the United States against "moderately repressive," but friendly, regimes was, in effect, undermining these states and American global influence. The unintended result of this action might well be the replacement of these imperfect regimes by ones opposed to U.S. interests—for example in Iran and Nicaragua. Whatever the merits of human rights (and Mrs. Kirkpatrick would argue that they are considerable), the requirements of global balance of power politics could not be wholly jettisoned.[52] In this sense, quiet efforts—as well as intergovernmental, semigovernmental, and nongovernmental efforts—were necessary to pursue human rights in the international system.[53]

Critics from a different perspective argued that the U.S. human rights policy was yet another way to impose American values on the international system. Moreover, it reflected both the lack of political realism and the importance of American moral principle in shaping foreign policy. In this respect, it was another of America's attempts to shape global politics. As well intentioned as was the human rights goal, it was inappropriate for the diverse international system and would ultimately be dysfunctional for global order. Such a refrain was heard from Third World leaders and even from some American allies, notably France and Germany.

Positive Effects. The overall effect of the Carter administration's human rights campaign is obviously difficult to measure.[54] While the number of countries with an improved human rights record did increase slightly during the Carter years, much greater gains were necessary if global human rights conditions were to be changed substantially. Such a limited result is as much as admitted in one of the State Department's annual human rights reports to the Congress. The report concludes that "the distance covered is still small in comparison to the distance that remains to be traveled before people throughout the world are secure from the excesses of government power, find opportunities to feed, clothe, and educate their children, and see before them a future of freedom and equality."[55]

To be sure, some tangible instances of improved global human rights were registered by the Carter administration. The Dominican Republic made a turn toward democracy; elections were announced for 1978 in Peru, Ecuador, and Bolivia; improved conditions were evidenced in Colombia, Malaysia, Honduras, Morocco, and Portugal, among others; political prisoners were released in Sudan, Nepal, Indonesia, Haiti, and Paraguay in the first year of the policy; and instances of torture apparently did show a decline.[56] More significantly, perhaps, American prestige in various areas of the world was enhanced. The United States began to stand for particular political values in world affairs. As a result, a more receptive attitude toward American initiatives was forthcoming throughout the world, and especially within the developing world.

Perhaps the greatest demonstration of this human rights impact was in Africa. The black nations of southern Africa, in particular, began to have confidence in the Carter administration and American policy toward that region. Through the vigorous efforts of Andrew Young, President Carter's ambassador to the United Nations, the "front-line" states around white-ruled Rhodesia (Angola, Botswana, Mozambique, Tanzania, Zambia) began to believe that the Carter administration was willing to seek a just solution to the problems of that nation (now Zimbabwe), Namibia, and South Africa itself. Moreover, the pivotal African state of Nigeria also began to express confidence in the American administration by receiving President Carter for an official visit.[57]

President Jimmy Carter, writing in his memoirs, *Keeping Faith*, seemed to place the greatest benefit of his human rights policy on the intangible change of atmosphere and attitude toward individual liberties on a worldwide scale during his years in office. As he notes, "The lifting of the human spirit, the revival of hope, the absence of fear, the release from prison, the end of torture, the reunion of a family, the newfound sense of dignity" were the ultimate measure of the worth of the human rights policy.[58] For him, that was satisfaction enough to have made it worthwhile.

Negative Effects. On the negative side, the human rights campaign caused friction with friendly—but human rights–deficient—nations. Relations with Nicaragua, Argentina, Brazil, Iran, and South Korea, among others, were strained by these calls for human rights efforts. Further, the human rights policy contributed to problems in Soviet-American relations. The policy was particularly challenging to detente because it implied an "intervention" into the internal affairs of other states. Nonintervention in internal affairs, by contrast, had been the benchmark of the detente approach that evolved under the Nixon-Ford-Kissinger administration.[59]

Beyond the apparent violation of national sovereignty, the human rights policy threatened the Soviet Union for a more fundamental reason: Fostering individual freedom of expression and tolerating diversity directly affronted totalitarian control at home and foreshadowed a weakening of Soviet control over Eastern Europe. Thus when President Carter wrote a letter to Andrei Sakharov, perhaps the leading Soviet scientist and dissident, or expressed support for Vladimir Bukovsky, the leader of the Helsinki Monitoring Group in the Soviet Union, the tension in East-West relations was exacerbated. While President Carter acknowledged that these kinds of actions "did create tension between us and prevented a more harmonious resolution of some of the other differences," he disputes the claim, however, that the human rights issue singularly affected overall Soviet-American relations: "I cannot recall any instance when the human rights issue was the *direct* cause of failure in working with the Soviets on matters of common interest."[60]

The Soviet Union challenged and attacked Carter's human rights policy. The Soviets contended that the United States itself was guilty of human rights violations because of the lack of economic rights for its citizens—insufficient employment, inadequate health care, and unsatisfactory social welfare benefits. Furthermore, the atmosphere for conducting relations between the United States and the Soviet Union was affected by the human rights campaign, as Foreign Minister Andrei Gromyko implied in April 1977, after initial arms control discussions had broken down."[61]

Dealing with the Soviet Union

The essential aim of the Carter administration was to downgrade the dominance of the Soviet-American relationship in the foreign policy of the United States and to concentrate efforts primarily on the other areas of the world. As one analyst has aptly put it, the goal was to contain the Soviet Union, not by directly confronting it as in the past, but "by drying out the pond of possible Soviet mischief" through resolving global issues.[62] If global problems were addressed, global intrusions by the Soviets would be much less likely, and the Soviet Union would be contained.

Despite the intentions of the Carter administration to de-emphasize the Soviet-American relationship, it never really was possible to do this. The distance between the Carter administration's perception of what policy should be and its ability to achieve it was greatest in this particular area. Moreover, Carter's failure to establish a clear and consistent policy toward the Soviet Union was probably the greatest shortcoming of his initial foreign policy plan. Ironically—especially in light of his basic approach—the failure to establish such a policy hindered the attempt to give greater priority to other global issues and to achieve more success in those areas.

At least three different reasons may be cited for the overall inconsistency of Carter's policy toward the Soviet Union.

Soviet Centrality. First of all, the Soviets would not allow the United States to downgrade their centrality to global politics. The Soviet Union's prestige was damaged by the Carter policy. Since the Soviet Union had placed a great effort on achieving superpower military and political parity and had finally achieved it with the 1972 agreements, it was unwilling to yield to playing "second fiddle" on global issues. Thus, the Soviets challenged Carter on human rights, but they also attacked him on arms control, despite their desire for it. More important, the Soviets challenged Carter's attempt to focus on Third World issues. The Soviets sought to make inroads into the Western Hemisphere, especially in Central America through Cuba (or so the United States believed). The Soviets, too, were not restraining the Vietnamese in Asia and were continuing their military deployments there. Finally, the Soviet Union continued its pressure on Western Europe through an increase in its own military capabilities.[63]

Competing Perspectives in the Administration. A second factor also contributed to the lack of a consistent policy toward the Soviet Union: a division within the Carter administration itself over how to deal with the Soviet Union. In other words, how convinced was the American leadership that it wanted to move away from a Soviet-focused foreign policy? Such a question particularly emphasized the competing perspectives of Carter's two top advisors, Secretary of State Cyrus Vance and National Security Advisor Zbigniew Brzezinski. More specifically, it focused on the conflicting views within the thinking of Brzezinski himself. While Secretary Vance appeared to be committed to Carter's globalist perspective and wanted to deal with the Soviets on a piecemeal basis without linkage, Brzezinski, by now, seemed to be of two minds in dealing with the Soviets.[64]

Although Brzezinski was in many ways the originator of the global perspective for the Carter administration, once in office as national security advisor, he seemed to interpret international events through the Soviet-American prism. Brzezinski had formally rejected the notion of "linkage" as the guide to American policy in dealing with the Soviets, yet he adopted a policy stance that seemed markedly close to it. In fact, the first time that the Soviets took significant actions in a "third area"—by supporting the sending of Cuban troops to Ethiopia—aspects of the original Kissinger formula for dealing with the Soviet-American relationship were resurrected by Brzezinski. He wanted to confront the Soviets directly and to downgrade any remaining elements of the detente relationship.

To Brzezinski, these activities in the Horn of Africa should affect the SALT negotiations, and he said so directly.[65] Moreover, he used language strongly reminiscent of linkage in discussing this issue:

> In the nuclear age, we can't have stability unless detente is general and reciprocal. What we have to establish is that the rules of the games have to be the same for both sides. I think that the Horn is a basic test of that. I think if we don't establish some reciprocity and some mutual restraint and don't make it binding, especially in its military favor, then we're going to get a reaction against detente that is going to make some things that are desirable impossible to achieve—such as SALT.[66]

Others within the Carter administration—Secretary of State Cyrus Vance and Secretary of Defense Harold Brown, as well as the president himself—were not willing to go as far as Brzezinski on this issue. While Brzezinski eventually lost out in this debate, it was this kind of dispute over how to deal with the Soviets, and especially how multilateral events were to affect bilateral relations between the two superpowers, that dominated the Carter administration agenda during its first three years.

Beginning with this rather dramatic example over the Horn of Africa, President Carter and his advisors were groping for a coherent policy toward the Soviet Union. Speeches by the president at Wake Forest University and the U.S. Naval Academy demonstrated efforts to pursue a more vigorous foreign policy toward that nation. Nonetheless, a conciliatory policy continued to hold sway throughout 1978.[67] In fact, the same general approach was followed until late 1979 and the Soviet invasion of Afghanistan. Despite the Carter intention of reducing the American fixation on its foreign policy relationship with the Soviet Union, the internal policy making debate among Carter and his advisors had just the opposite effect.

American Domestic Attitudes. A third factor that made it difficult for the United States to move away from a perception of the Soviets as dominant in foreign policy matters was the nature of American domestic beliefs. A real dualism existed in the minds of the American public. While most Americans supported detente efforts by a wide margin, they were also increasingly wary of growing Soviet power vis-à-vis the United States. Additionally, the American public continued to see the Soviet Union as central to U.S. foreign policy.[68]

Accompanying this dual attitude was a shift away from support for cuts in defense spending, which had been so strong in the immediate post-Vietnam years. By 1977, and especially by 1978, support for more defense spending was increasing, and the public's willingness to favor military force against Soviet incursions was also becoming more evident.[69] Thus, from the viewpoint of domestic politics, the Soviet-American relationship still seemed very crucial, and the Carter administration was no doubt aware of these changing beliefs and the need to accommodate them in the foreign policy arena.

For various reasons, then, the Soviet-American relationship could not be removed from its dominant role in American foreign policy matters despite the Carter administration's initial hopes. Moreover, the inability of the administration to integrate fully the primacy of this relationship into its foreign policy design and its "strategic incoherence" when it tried to do so plagued the administration throughout its four years.[70]

Resolving Third World Conflicts

The area of greatest success for the Carter administration in implementing its global design was in addressing particular Third World conflicts. During his administration, President Carter was able to alleviate, if not resolve, conflict in Central America over the Panama Canal, in the Middle East between Egypt and Israel, and in southern Africa over Rhodesia and Namibia. Finally, although Carter's establishment of formal diplomatic relations between the People's Republic of China and the United States can hardly be characterized as dealing with a Third World conflict, it was important for lessening regional conflict in Asia.

The Panama Canal. Perhaps the greatest arena of success was the resolution of the Panama Canal dispute. For more than two decades, the United States had negotiated over the transfer of the Canal and the Canal Zone to sole Panamanian sovereignty. The failure to resolve this dispute was one of those regional issues that was undermining American influence in Central and South America, and was one of the issues that President Carter was determined to address during his presidency.

Indicative of the importance of this issue was the fact that the first Presidential Review Memorandum emanating from the Carter administration dealt with the Panama Canal.[71] With such a central priority, the American and Panamanian negotiators set out to reach an agreement. In a few short months, they succeeded. By September 1977, moreover, the two treaties that constituted the agreement were ready for an elaborate signing ceremony in Washington. All Latin American countries were invited to witness the signing of these two pacts, and it was a triumphant occasion for the Carter administration.

One of the pacts, the Panama Canal Treaty, called for the total transfer of Canal control to Panama by the year 2000, with intermediate stages of transfer during the twenty-two years of the pact. The second agreement, the Neutrality Treaty, would become effective in the year 2000 and was of unlimited duration. This pact states that the Canal would be permanently neutral, secure, and open to the vessels of all nations in time of peace and war. Moreover, the United States and Panama agreed to maintain and defend this neutrality principle. Document Summary 4.4 summarizes these treaties.

While the signing of the treaties was a success for Carter, the task of getting them passed by the U.S. Senate proved to be an even greater triumph for his administration.[72] Through a long and arduous personal lobbying

DOCUMENT SUMMARY 4.4

The Panama Canal Treaties, September 1977

Panama Canal Treaty
This treaty abrogates any earlier treaty arrangements between the United States and Panama and allows the United States to operate the Panama Canal until December 31, 1999. At that time, the control of the Canal will revert to Panama. The Panama Canal Company will be dissolved, and the Panama Canal Commission, composed of Americans and Panamanians, will operate the Canal until its reversion. The canal administrator will be an American, with a Panamanian as a deputy until 1990; after 1990, the canal administrator will be a Panamanian, with an American as a deputy until the year 2000.

Treaty Concerning the Permanent Neutrality and Operation of the Panama Canal
This treaty enters into effect at the same time as the Panama Canal Treaty and guarantees that the Canal "shall remain secure and open to peaceful transit by vessels of all nations on the terms of entire equality," whether in times of war or peace. Panama and the United States each "shall have the discretion to take whatever action it deems necessary, in accordance with its constitutional processes, to defend the canal against any threat to the permanent regime of neutrality."

Sources: These summaries are drawn from "Text of Treaties" and "Letters of Submittal," *Department of State Bulletin,* October 17, 1977, pp. 438–485 and 496–498; and Department of State, "Panama Canal: The New Treaties," Department of State Publication 8924, November 1977, pp. 7–12.

effort—even in the face of opposition by the American public—President Carter saw the Neutrality and Panama Canal Treaties passed by identical votes, 68 to 32, on March 16, 1978, and April 18, 1978, respectively.[73] President Carter viewed these pacts, moreover, as clearly compatible with his goals of reducing regional conflicts and fostering global justice. Both of these goals, moreover, would minimize anti-American feelings and enhance American prestige and influence abroad.[74]

The Middle East. In the Middle East, a constant regional trouble spot, the initial strategy of the Carter administration was to seek a comprehensive settlement through a Geneva conference, cosponsored with the Soviet Union. This approach did not get very far because the Israelis were reluctant to participate and the Arabs demanded maximum Palestinian participation.[75] The Israeli fear was that it would be outvoted in such a conference by the larger number of Arab states and the Soviet Union. Hence the outcome of such a meeting would be far from their liking.

In November 1977, however, President Anwar Sadat of Egypt took a dramatic step to move the peace process along. He announced that he was willing to go to Jerusalem to seek peace. Prime Minister Menachem Begin of Israel quickly issued an invitation for President Sadat to speak to the Israeli Parliament. On November 19, 1977, President Sadat landed in Jerusalem for three days of discussions with the Israelis.[76] The importance of this visit cannot be overstated. It broke the impasse that had set into the

MAP 4.1

Israel and Its Neighbors, 1977

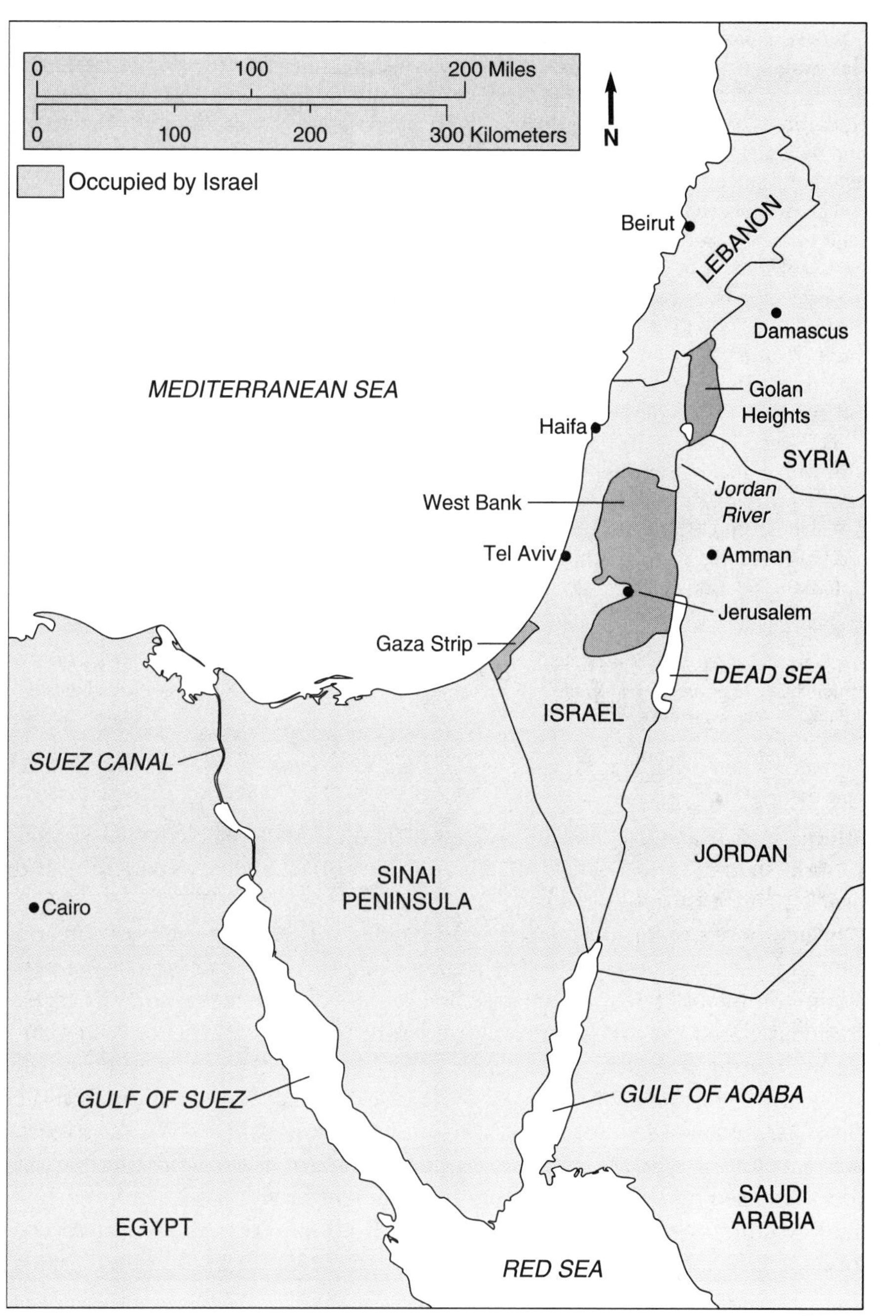

DOCUMENT SUMMARY 4.5

The Camp David Accords Between Egypt and Israel, September 1978

Framework for Peace in the Middle East
This framework called for a "just, comprehensive, and durable settlement of the Middle East conflict through the conclusion of peace treaties based upon Security Council Resolutions 242 and 338 in all their parts." (The resolutions called for an exchange of land by Israel—the territories seized in the June 1967 war—for peace with their Arab neighbors—an end to the state of war with Israel.) It consisted of two parts.

The first part of the framework dealt with resolving the conflict over the West Bank of the Jordan and the Gaza Strip, which Israel had seized. This portion called for the establishment of a self-governing authority within these territories "for a period not exceeding five years." By at least the third year of that self-governing authority, "negotiations will take place to determine the final status of the West Bank and Gaza and its relationship to its neighbors and to conclude a peace treaty between Israel and Jordan...." These negotiations will involve representatives from Egypt, Israel, Jordan, and "representatives of the inhabitants of the West Bank and Gaza...."

The second part of the framework called for Egypt and Israel "to negotiate in good faith with a goal of concluding within three months from the signing of this Framework a peace treaty between them." [This treaty was ultimately signed in March 1979 in Washington, D.C. Under this treaty, Israel returned the Sinai Peninsula to Egypt, and Israel and Egypt ended their state of war, recognized one another, and established diplomatic relations.]

Source: This description is drawn from the framework, which was printed in Department of State Publication 8954, *The Camp David Summit* (Washington, DC: Office of Public Communications, Bureau of Public Affairs, September 1978).

Middle East peace process since the shuttle diplomacy of Henry Kissinger; it established the precedent of face-to-face negotiations between Arabs and Israelis; and it raised hopes for real progress.

Such hopes were soon dashed. Both sides still held strong positions on the fundamental questions of the return of Arab lands and Israeli security. By the summer of 1978, an impasse had set in—despite mediation efforts by President Carter. At this juncture, President Carter himself took a bold gamble by inviting President Sadat and Prime Minister Begin to Camp David, Maryland—the presidential retreat—for in-depth discussions on the Middle East. As a result of thirteen days of intense negotiations, "A Framework for Peace in the Middle East" was agreed to by the two competing parties and witnessed by President Carter.[77] (Document Summary 4.5 summarizes the key components of this framework.) Both adversaries attributed the success of the Camp David meetings to the personal efforts of Jimmy Carter.

The signing of the Camp David Accords on September 17, 1978, was another highlight of the Carter foreign policy. Some real progress had been made in addressing the Middle East conflict. Furthermore, in March 1979, a peace treaty—based on the Camp David framework—was signed between Egypt and Israel. A comprehensive peace settlement, however, ultimately eluded the Carter administration, as all the Arab states except Egypt refused to accept and participate in the Camp David framework.

MAP 4.2

Southern Africa

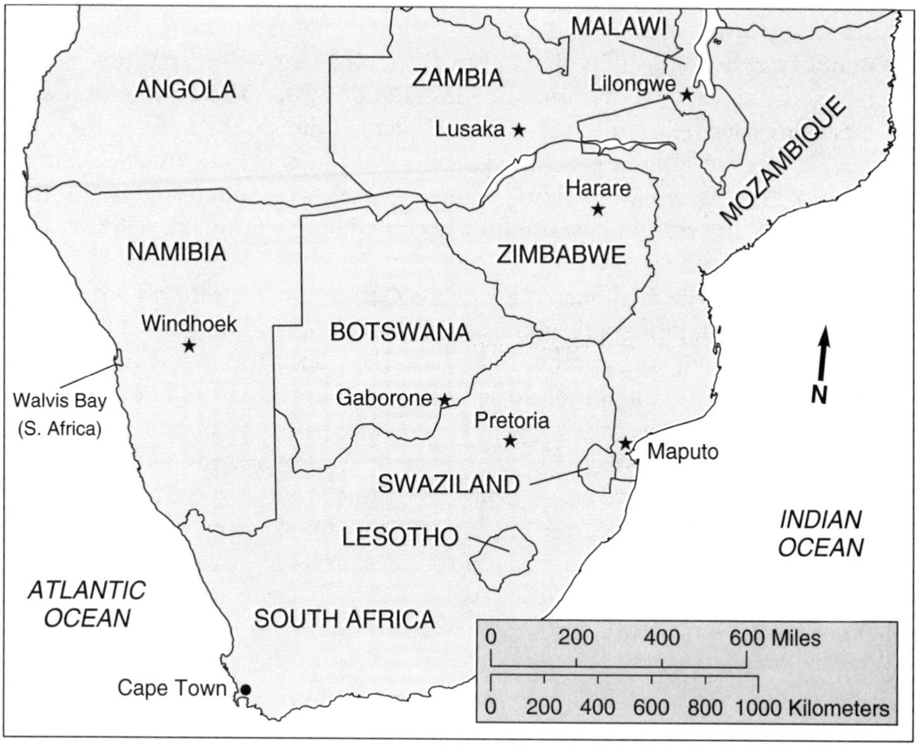

Rhodesia, Namibia, and South Africa. The third region of the world where the Carter administration achieved some success was in southern Africa over the questions of Rhodesia and Namibia. The role of the United States was not as direct as in the Panama Canal and the Middle East, but it was nonetheless important. Specifically, the Carter administration adopted a strong stand for black majority rule in these areas and assisted the British in achieving a successful outcome for Rhodesia, now Zimbabwe. The United States, with the assistance of other Western states, maneuvered the South African government to accept a UN resolution on the transfer of power in Namibia.[78]

In the case of Rhodesia, the Carter administration ceased trade with the white-dominated government and imposed economic sanctions on it in the first year of its term, bringing U.S. policy in line with long-standing UN sanctions. Even when the white minority government and some black leaders had reached an "internal settlement" in 1978, the administration refused to lift sanctions because dissident factions in exile outside the country had not participated in the settlement. By adopting such a stance, despite considerable opposition within Congress, the United States gave impetus to the British efforts toward a comprehensive settlement involving all parties. Such a settlement was ultimately worked out in the Lancaster House negotiations in London during the fall of 1979, and the agreement was put into effect in 1980.[79] Majority rule was obtained in former Rhodesia, and the Carter administration rightly claimed credit for its role.

The same policy posture was adopted toward South Africa—a firm stance against apartheid and a call for the transfer of control of Namibia to majority rule. Under U.S. policy pressure and that of other states, South Africa did agree to UN Resolution 435 on this transfer. The transfer of power met numerous snags and was not implemented during the Carter years. (In fact, it was not fully implemented until 1990.) Nonetheless, the decision to promote the American domestic values of respecting human rights and fostering majority rule won praise for the United States throughout Africa.

People's Republic of China. Finally, the Carter administration's decision to establish formal diplomatic relations with the People's Republic of China on January 1, 1979, was another major foreign policy success. Although this decision caused some initial difficulties with Taiwan (since relations were broken with this government), it was generally hailed as an important milestone in American foreign policy. Opening relations with Peking reduced hostilities between two important states and had the potential of easing conflicts in East Asia. At the same time, though, this step created another uncertainty in America's approach to its traditional adversary, the Soviet Union, and reinforced the Soviet view that the Carter administration was more interested in dealing with other states than with it.

REALISM IN THE LAST YEAR: A RESPONSE TO CRITICS

By 1979, the Carter foreign policy was already subject to considerable criticism on the grounds that it was inconsistent, incoherent, and a failure. According to one critic, it was leading to a decline in America's standing abroad.[80] While some successes in Carter's global approach might be identified, too many problems were evident, without a clear strategy for dealing with them. A revolution occurred in Iran, replacing the Shah (whom the Carter administration had supported) with a markedly anti-American regime; a revolution succeeded in Nicaragua, with the United States adopting a policy that pleased neither the Somozistas nor the Sandinistas; the Middle East peace effort was in a holding pattern with Arab rejection of the Camp David framework; and Soviet power continued to grow without an American response. On all these fronts, a certain malaise seemed to have set into the Carter foreign policy, marked by indecision and inability to act, and for such reasons, a change in policy direction might well have been anticipated. Yet two international events ultimately proved critical to the Carter foreign policy change.

The seizure of American hostages in Iran in November 1979, and the Soviet invasion of Afghanistan a month later were the watershed events in the global approach of the Carter administration.[81] Despite the administration's effort to move away from concentrating on the Soviet Union, these two events brought that nation back into focus for America—the former indirectly, because it raised the prospect of Soviet inroads into the Middle East and Southwest Asia; the latter directly, because it projected the Soviet Union into the center of global affairs once again. Map 5.2 visually portrays the geographical and strategic importance of Iran and Afghanistan in Southwest Asian and Middle Eastern affairs.

American Hostages in Iran

The November 1979 seizure and holding of more than fifty Americans in the U.S. Embassy in Tehran, Iran, produced perhaps the Carter administration's greatest foreign policy challenge. It also produced a clear change in policy orientation and direction by the Carter administration, with a new national self-interest now dominating its agenda. Rather than trying to accommodate Third World demands, as had been attempted in previous years, the United States now took a variety of steps, from breaking diplomatic relations, to seizing Iranian assets, to imposing sanctions, and ultimately attempting a military rescue of the hostages as a means of demonstrating resolve. Such actions also connoted a return to a realist perspective in foreign policy and away from the idealism that President Carter had initially tried to pursue. Unfortunately, this strategy failed to yield quick results, and the American hostages were not freed for 444 days—until immediately after President Carter left office on January 20, 1981.

Soviet Invasion of Afghanistan

The Soviet invasion of Afghanistan also had a pronounced effect on President Carter's view of the Soviet Union and on his foreign policy approach as well. Regarding Carter's new view of the Soviet Union after this invasion, it was poignantly summarized by the president himself in an ABC television interview at the time: "My opinion of the Russians has changed most drastically in the last week [more] than even in the previous 2½ years before that."[82] The invasion also had an immediate impact on his approach to foreign policy. President Carter promptly moved away from his global approach, with the Soviet Union only one among many countries. Instead he now adopted the bilateral approach of the past, with the Soviet-American relationship at the center of his policy making. New policy actions quickly followed from this new orientation. While not all the earlier initiatives were jettisoned, the issue areas that the Carter administration had emphasized early on in its term were given a secondary role.

The Carter administration adopted a series of responses to the Soviet Union over the invasion of Afghanistan. The ratification of the SALT II treaty was shelved in the U.S. Senate; high technology sales to the Soviet Union were halted; Soviet fishing privileges in American waters were restricted; and a grain embargo was imposed upon the Soviet Union.[83] A little later, an American boycott of the 1980 Summer Olympics in Moscow was announced.

Global Events and Soviet-American Relations

Global events now were increasingly interpreted through lenses that focused on their effect on Soviet-American relations. The principal U.S. efforts during this year were to rally its friends to contain the Soviet Union. Moreover, it was during this time period that such global goals as arms transfer controls were downplayed as a signal to the Soviets of American resolve. For instance, discussions were held with the Chinese about providing them with arms. Furthermore, the United States began an effort to shore up its ties in the Persian Gulf and in Southwest Asia. Military aid was quickly offered to Pakistan, and National Security Chief Zbigniew Brzezinski made a highly publicized trip to the Khyber Pass to illustrate American determination over Afghanistan. Contacts were also made with friendly regimes in the Middle East to gain base and access rights for the United States in case of an emergency. Finally, the development of the U.S. Rapid Deployment Force—an elite military force that could respond quickly to an emergency anywhere in the world—was given a top priority.

As a further signal to the Soviet Union, President Carter in his 1980 State of the Union Address warned the Soviets that "an attempt by any outside force to gain control of the Persian Gulf region will be regarded as an assault on the vital interests of the United States. It will be repelled by use of any means necessary, including military force."[84] Quickly labeled the Carter Doctrine, this statement was highly reminiscent of an earlier era, with its Cold War rhetoric and its reliance on the essential elements of containment. Nonetheless, it accurately set the tone for the final year of the Carter administration and the policy shift that had occurred in the administration.

Foreign Policy and the 1980 Campaign

Despite President Carter's attempt to change foreign policy direction, the perception of ineffectiveness continued to haunt his administration. As a consequence, foreign policy, with particular emphasis on the Iranian and Afghan experiences, became an important campaign issue in the 1980 presidential election.[85] Now, however, instead of focusing on a foreign policy that was "good and decent," as in 1976, the Republican challenger to President Carter, Ronald Reagan, called for a policy to "make America great again." Such a policy was surely a call to move away from the idealism of the early Carter years. Yet—and ironically—it was a call to pursue the kind of foreign policy that President Carter himself had tried to initiate in his last year in office.

Concluding Comments

The Nixon and Carter administrations offered different approaches to American foreign policy, as the Cold War was challenged. Each approach sought, albeit in different ways, to change the emphasis from the globalism of the Cold War and its basic tenets. The greatest value change that the Nixon years brought to U.S. policy was a movement away from the emphasis on moral principle and greater acceptance of traditional realism as the basis of actions toward the rest of the world. At least until the last year of its time in office, the Carter administration sought to continue the limited globalism of the Nixon years (defined more with an emphasis upon trilateral and Third World relations than upon superpower ties) but to change from the largely singular moral emphasis on anticommunism to a more comprehensive, morally based approach, best exemplified by its human rights campaign. As we have discussed, though, neither succeeded completely, and both faced challenges.

In the next chapter, we shall survey yet another approach to American foreign policy in the post-Vietnam era. The administration of Ronald Reagan sought less to impose a new value approach and more to restore an earlier one—best epitomized by the Cold War consensus. While the Reagan administration would continue the moral emphasis of the Carter administration (although now the target would once again be global communism, not global human rights violations), it would seek to restore an American globalism more reminiscent of an earlier era than had its immediate predecessors.

Notes

1. The approach of the Ford administration (1974–1976) is not treated separately here because Henry Kissinger continued to serve as national security advisor (through 1975) and as secretary of state (through 1976).
2. For a detailed listing of the assumptions of realism and idealism, see Charles W. Kegley, Jr., "The Neoliberal Challenge to Realist Theories of World Politics: An Introduction," in Charles W. Kegley, Jr., *Controversies in International Relations Theory* (New York: St. Martin's Press, 1995), pp. 4–5. For a classic statement on realism, see Hans J. Morgenthau, *Politics Among Nations: The Struggle for Power and Peace* (New York: Alfred A. Knopf, 1973), pp. 3–15, or Kenneth N. Waltz, *Theory of International Politics* (Reading, MA: Addison-Wesley Publishing Company, 1979). For a recent statement of the idealism/liberalism tradition in international politics, see Robert O. Keohane and Joseph S. Nye, Jr., *Power and Interdependence*, 2nd ed. (Glenview, IL: Scott, Foresman/Little Brown, 1989).
3. Richard M. Nixon, "Asia After Viet Nam," *Foreign Affairs* 46 (October 1967): 111–125. The quoted passages are at pp. 121, 123, and 114.
4. Richard M. Nixon, *U.S. Policy for the 1970s, A New Strategy for Peace.* A report to the Congress (Washington, DC: Government Printing Office, February 18, 1970). The quoted passages are at pp. 2 and 3. For the earlier statements on some of these principles, see Richard M. Nixon, "Informal Remarks in Guam with Newsmen, July 25, 1969," and "Address to the Nation on the War in Vietnam, November 3, 1969" in *Public Papers of the Presidents of the United States, Richard Nixon 1969* (Washington, DC: U.S. Government Printing Office, 1971), pp. 544–556 and pp. 901–909, respectively. Indeed, the "Nixon Doctrine" is sometimes referred to as the "Guam Doctrine."
5. For a more detailed and recent treatment of the Nixon approach to foreign policy, including some more comparisons with earlier post–World War II approaches and America's historical traditions, see Henry Kissinger, *Diplomacy* (New York: Simon & Schuster, 1994), pp. 703–718. The careful reader will note that Kissinger's description of Nixon's approach closely follows the key points made about Kissinger himself and his approach in the next section.
6. This section draws upon Kissinger's important essay "Contemporary Issues of American Foreign Policy." It is printed as Chapter 2 in Henry A. Kissinger, *American Foreign Policy*, 3rd ed. (New York: W. W. Norton and Company, Inc., 1977), pp. 51–97. The quoted passage is at p. 79.

7. Ibid., pp. 91–97.
8. Henry A. Kissinger, *A World Restored: Metternich, Castlereagh and the Problems of Peace 1812–1822* (Boston: Houghton Mifflin Company, 1957), p. 1.
9. President Nixon's commitment to the balance of power and to this pentagonal world can be found in *Time*, January 3, 1972, and quoted in Kissinger, *Diplomacy*, p. 705: "I think it will be a safer world and a better world if we have a strong, healthy United States, Europe, Soviet Union, China, Japan, each balancing the other, not playing one against the other, an even balance."
10. For a description of the characteristics of the "statesman," see Kissinger's essay "Domestic Structure and Foreign Policy," in James N. Rosenau, ed., *International Politics and Foreign Policy*, rev. ed. (New York: Free Press, 1969), pp. 261–275. The quoted passage on the importance of negotiations to stability is at p. 274.
11. Kissinger, *American Foreign Policy*, pp. 120–121.
12. For a further analysis of the dimensions of Kissinger's approach described here, and a strong critique of it, see Falk, "What's Wrong with Henry Kissinger's Foreign Policy," *Alternatives* I (1975): 79–100.
13. Once again, the analysis includes the years through 1976, even though President Ford came to office in August 1974, because Henry Kissinger continued to dominate the foreign policy apparatus as Secretary of State.
14. "U.S.-U.S.S.R. Exchanges Programs," *GIST* (Washington, DC: Department of State, April 1976).
15. See the excerpts from Henry Kissinger's *White House Years* (Boston: Little, Brown, 1979) on China in *Time*, October 1, 1979, 53–58.
16. The Shanghai Communique is reprinted in Gene T. Hsiao, ed., *Sino-American Detente and Its Policy Implications* (New York: Praeger Publishers, Inc., 1974), pp. 298–301.
17. This discussion draws upon "Conference on Security and Cooperation in Europe," *Department of State Bulletin* 77 (September 26, 1977): 404–410. The notion of "baskets" to summarize their work came from the conference itself (p. 405).
18. See his essay in *American Foreign Policy*, expanded ed. (New York: W. W. Norton and Company, 1974), pp. 99–135.
19. See John G. Stoessinger in his *Henry Kissinger: The Anguish of Power* (New York: W. W. Norton and Company, 1976), pp. 62–63. For another analysis of Kissinger's belief systems generally, see Harvey Starr, *Henry Kissinger: Perceptions of International Politics* (Lexington, KY: University Press of Kentucky, 1984); and, for an application of Kissinger's belief system toward the Vietnam War, see Stephen G. Walker, "The Interface Between Beliefs and Behavior: Henry Kissinger's Operational Code and the Vietnam War," *The Journal of Conflict Resolution* 21 (March 1977): 129–168.
20. Ibid., p. 73.
21. George C. Herring, *America's Longest War: The United States and Vietnam 1950–1975*, 2nd ed. (New York: Alfred A. Knopf, 1986), p. 255.
22. Falk, "What's Wrong with Henry Kissinger's Foreign Policy," pp. 79–100.
23. Ibid., p. 98.
24. Ibid., p. 99.
25. Ibid., p. 88.
26. George McGovern, "A New Internationalism," in William Taubman, *Globalism and Its Critics* (Lexington, MA: D. C. Heath and Company, 1973), p. 163.
27. Ibid., p. 167.
28. William F. Buckley, Jr. "Politics of Henry Kissinger," Transcript of *Firing Line* program, originally telecast on the Public Broadcasting System, September 13, 1975, p. 5. Mr. Buckley was quoting from Gallup Polls.
29. George W. Ball, *Diplomacy for a Crowded World* (Boston: Atlantic Monthly/Little Brown, 1976), pp. 108–129.
30. Ibid., p. 15. The other quotes are from pp. 13 and 14.

31. Quoted in "Little Heinz and Big Henry," *New York Times Book Review*, September 6, 1992, 21. The original passage is in Walter Isaacson, *Kissinger: A Biography* (New York: Simon & Schuster, 1992), p. 339.
32. Quoted in "Little Heinz and Big Henry," p. 21.
33. This global perspective (and changes in it) is discussed in part in Leonard Silk's brief analysis of an address by Zbigniew Brzezinski, "Economic Scene: New U.S. View of the World," *New York Times*, May 1, 1979, D2; and in an address by Cyrus Vance, "Meeting the Challenges of a Changing World" (Washington, DC: Bureau of Public Affairs, Department of State, May 1, 1979).
34. Jimmy Carter, "Inaugural Address of President Jimmy Carter: The Ever-Expanding American Dream," *Vital Speeches* 43 (February 15, 1977): 258.
35. Jimmy Carter, "Humane Purposes in Foreign Policy," Department of State News Release, May 22, 1977, p. 1 (Commencement Address at the University of Notre Dame).
36. Ibid., p. 2.
37. Ibid., pp. 1 and 5.
38. Zbigniew Brzezinski, "America in a Hostile World," *Foreign Policy* 23 (Summer 1976): 65–96; and Elizabeth Drew, "A Reporter at Large: Brzezinski," *The New Yorker* (May 1, 1978): 90–130. The quotations are from "America in a Hostile World," at p. 91 and p. 94, respectively.
39. See the discussion in Drew, "A Reporter at Large: Brzezinski," over the extent to which linkage was applied, especially pp. 117–121.
40. Although the Carter administration is usually identified with human rights, congressional action on this issue began at least in 1973 with hearings by the International Organizations and Movements Subcommittee, headed by Donald Fraser. On this point, see the discussion in Harold Molineu, "Human Rights: Administrative Impact of a Symbolic Policy," in John C. Grumm and Stephen L. Wasby, eds., *The Analysis of Policy Impact* (Lexington, MA: Lexington Books, D. C. Heath and Company, 1981), pp. 24–25.
41. "Inaugural Address of President Jimmy Carter: The Ever-Expanding American Dream," p. 259.
42. "Humane Purposes in Foreign Policy," p. 2.
43. Jimmy Carter, *Keeping Faith* (New York: Bantam Books, 1982), p. 145.
44. Ibid., pp. 142 and 144.
45. Stanley Hoffmann, "Requiem," *Foreign Policy* 42 (Spring 1981): 3.
46. These descriptions are from *Human Rights and U.S. Foreign Policy* (Department of State Publication 8959, Washington, DC: Bureau of Public Affairs, 1978), pp. 7–8. Secretary of State Cyrus Vance had outlined these same categories in a speech to the University of Georgia School of Law on April 30, 1977 (*Department of State Bulletin* 76 [May 23, 1977]: 505–508).
47. Lincoln P. Bloomfield, "From Ideology to Program to Policy," *Journal of Policy Analysis and Management* 2 (Fall 1982): 6.
48. In reality, some nations (Argentina, Brazil, Guatemala, for example) simply rejected American military assistance after attacks on their human rights records by the United States. See Charles W. Kegley, Jr., and Eugene R. Wittkopf, *American Foreign Policy: Pattern and Process*, 2nd ed. (New York: St. Martin's Press, 1982), p. 595.
49. "The President's News Conference of March 9, 1977," in *Weekly Compilation of Presidential Documents* 13 (March 14, 1977): 328–329.
50. Rhodesia was an "illegal" regime in this instance, since its minority leaders had unilaterally declared its independence from Great Britain, without British approval in 1965.
51. Louis Rene Beres, *People, States, and World Order* (Itasca, IL: F. E. Peacock Publishers, Inc., 1981), p. 51.
52. These arguments are developed in Jeane J. Kirkpatrick, "Dictatorships and Double Standards, " *Commentary* 68 (November 1979): 34–45; and "Human Rights and American Foreign Policy: A Symposium," *Commentary* 79 (November 1981): 42–45.

53. See, for example, the proposal by William F. Buckley, Jr., in his "Human Rights and Foreign Policy," *Foreign Affairs* 58 (Spring 1980): 775–796. Also, see Arthur Schlesinger, Jr., "Human Rights and the American Tradition," *Foreign Affairs* 57 (Winter 1978/1979): 503–526, for his view on intergovernmental and nongovernmental organizations.
54. For one effort to compare the Carter administration with its successor Reagan administration in the human rights area, see David Carleton and Michael Stohl, "The Foreign Policy of Human Rights: Rhetoric and Reality from Jimmy Carter to Ronald Reagan," *Human Rights Quarterly* 9 (May 1985): 205–229.
55. Department of State, *Report on Human Rights Practices in Countries Receiving U.S. Aid.* Submitted to the Committee on Foreign Relations, U.S. Senate and Committee on Foreign Affairs, U.S. House of Representatives (Washington, DC: Government Printing Office, 1979), p. 5.
56. Ibid., pp. 4–5; Bloomfield, "from Ideology to Program to Policy," p. 9; and Warren Christopher, "The Diplomacy of Human Rights: The First Year," Speech to the American Bar Association, February 13, 1978 (Washington, DC: Department of State, 1978).
57. See Colin Legum, "The African Crisis," in William P. Bundy, ed., *America and the World 1978* (New York: Pergamon Press, 1979), pp. 633–651.
58. Carter, *Keeping Faith*, p. 150.
59. See, for example, the Helsinki Accords discussed above and summarized in Document Summary 4.3 regarding this principle.
60. The quotations are from *Keeping Faith*, p. 149. Emphasis in original. The support for Bukovsky is cited in Bloomfield, "From Ideology to Program to Policy," p. 9.
61. Christopher S. Wren, "After a Rebuff in Moscow, Detente Is Put to the Test," *New York Times*, April 1, 1977, IA and 8A.
62. Stanley Hoffmann, "Carter's Soviet Problem," *The New Republic* 79 (July 29, 1978): 21. On this point and for a discussion of other Carter difficulties discussed here, see Stanley Hoffmann, "A View from at Home: The Perils of Incoherence," in William P. Bundy, ed., *America and the World 1978* (New York: Pergamon Press, 1979), pp. 463–491.
63. Most significantly, perhaps, the Soviet Union began the deployment of the SS-20s, its intermediate-range ballistic missiles, in the late 1970s.
64. Such a dualism in Brzezinski's thinking about the Soviets probably should not have been unexpected. His academic career had been largely made on the basis of a strong anti-Soviet view. Thus, his concern with global issues was a more recent phenomenon in his thinking.
65. Drew, "A Reporter at Large: Brzezinski," p. 117.
66. Ibid., p. 118.
67. Hedley Bull, "A View from Abroad: Consistency Under Pressure," in William P. Bundy, ed., *America and the World 1978* (New York: Pergamon Press, 1979), pp. 444–445.
68. John E. Rielly, ed., *American Public Opinion and U.S. Foreign Policy 1979* (Chicago: The Chicago Council on Foreign Relations, 1979), pp. 5 and 15.
69. Bruce Russett and Donald R. Deluca, "'Don't Tread on Me': Public Opinion and Foreign Policy in the Eighties," *Political Science Quarterly* 96 (Fall 1981): 381–399.
70. Hoffmann, "Requiem," p. 11.
71. Carter, *Keeping Faith*, p. 157.
72. See the fine case study of congressional decision making on the treaties by William L. Furlong, "Negotiations and Ratification of the Panama Canal," in John Spanier and Joseph Nogee, eds., *Congress, the Presidency, and American Foreign Policy* (New York: Pergamon Press, 1981), pp. 77–106.
73. A New York Times /CBS Poll in April 1978, indicated that Americans opposed the treaties 5 to 3 and that those figures had been stable over the previous six months. See this discussion in "Americans' Support for Israel Declines, a Poll Finds," *New York Times*, April 14, 1978, 1A and 10A. President Carter in his discussion of Panama Canal poll results reports a more optimistic picture. See *Keeping Faith*, pp. 159, 162, and 167.

74. Ibid., p. 184.
75. Ibid., p. 292.
76. Ibid., pp. 296–297.
77. Department of State Publication 8954, *The Camp David Summit* (Washington, DC: Office of Public Communications, Bureau of Public Affairs, September 1978).
78. See UN Security Council Resolution 435 in *Resolutions and Decisions of the Security Council, Security Council Official Records: Thirty-Third Year* (New York: United Nations, 1979), p. 13, for the resolution that South Africa eventually said that it would work to put into effect.
79. See Henry Wiseman and Alastair M. Taylor, *From Rhodesia to Zimbabwe: The Politics of Transition* (New York: Pergamon Press, 1981).
80. For an analysis of the Carter foreign policy from this perspective, see Robert W. Tucker, "America in Decline: The Foreign Policy of 'Maturity,'" in William P. Bundy, ed., *America and the World 1979* (New York: Pergamon Press, 1980), pp. 449–488.
81. The impact of these events on Carter foreign policy is discussed in Richard Burt, "Carter, Under Pressure of Crises, Tests New Foreign Policy Goals," *New York Times*, January 9, 1980, A1 and A8, upon which we rely.
82. "My Opinion of the Russians Has Changed Most Drastically," *Time*, January 14, 1980, 10.
83. These actions are outlined in a speech that President Jimmy Carter gave to the nation on January 4, 1980. The speech can be found in *Vital Speeches of the Day* 46 (January 15, 1980): 194–195.
84. Jimmy Carter, "State of the Union 1980," *Vital Speeches of the Day* 46 (February 1, 1980: 227.
85. Poll results suggested that the failure to secure the quick release of the American hostages contributed significantly to the electoral defeat of Jimmy Carter in 1980.

CHAPTER

5

A RENEWAL AND END OF THE COLD WAR: THE REAGAN-BUSH YEARS

What I am describing...is a plan and a hope for the long term—the march of freedom and democracy which will leave Marxism-Leninism on the ashheap of history as it has left other tyrannies which stifle the freedom and muzzle the self-expression of the people.

President Ronald Reagan
Address to Members of the British Parliament
June 8, 1982.

The world leaves one epoch of cold war and enters another epoch.... The characteristics of the cold war should be abandoned.

Former Soviet President Mikhail Gorbachev
at the Malta Summit
with President George Bush
December 1989

Just as Jimmy Carter shifted away from the foreign policies of the Nixon-Ford-Kissinger years, Ronald Reagan sought to chart a different course than Carter. Ronald Reagan campaigned for the presidency on the principle of restoring American power at home and abroad, and his foreign policy was aimed at reflecting such power. Whereas Jimmy Carter attempted to move away from the power politics of the Kissinger era and away from a foreign policy that focused directly on adversaries—and particularly the Soviet Union—Ronald Reagan embraced the need for power—especially military power—and the need to focus on the Soviet Union and its expansionist policy. During its second term, however, the Reagan administration sought and successfully obtained some accommodation with the Soviet Union, although without altering its anti-Soviet approach in Third World areas.

George Bush, Reagan's vice president, was elected president in November 1988, less on a commitment to change the course of U.S. foreign policy and more as a result of the American people's desire for continuity in the United States's approach to the world. Unlike Reagan, Bush came to office less as a foreign policy ideologue and more as a pragmatist without a strongly held worldview. In this sense, President Bush's initial foreign policy impulse leaned toward maintaining continuity with the recent past, rather than seeking change. However, his commitment to continuity was challenged by the dramatic events that began at the end of his first year in office: the demise of the Soviet empire, the emergence of new political, economic, and social openness in Eastern Europe, and the movement toward the reunification of Germany.[1]

By 1990, President Bush had modified the course of American foreign policy, away from one driven by the anti-Communist principles of the past and toward one driven by the changes in the Soviet Union and Eastern Europe. Iraq's invasion of Kuwait, and the American and allied response to it, gave further impetus for seeking a new direction for American foreign policy. Indeed, shortly after the beginning of the Persian Gulf War, President Bush acknowledged as much, when he announced that "we stand at a defining hour" in our foreign policy.[2] In that pursuit, the Bush administration sought to advance a new rationale for America's global involvement using the old rubric of a "new world order."

In this chapter, then, we review the foreign policy values, beliefs, and approaches of these two administrations toward the end of the Cold War. For the Reagan administration, we outline the effort to reassert the principles of the Cold War and the actions to seek Soviet-American accommodations. For the Bush administration, we outline the dramatic events that ultimately led to the demise of the Cold War and the Soviet Union, and we examine the initial efforts to build a "new world order" in American foreign policy for the 1990s. In addition, we assess the Persian Gulf War of 1991, which proved to be the major foreign policy challenge of the Bush presidency after the collapse of the Cold War, and evaluate how it affected American foreign policy in the early 1990s.

VALUES AND BELIEFS OF THE REAGAN ADMINISTRATION

Ronald Reagan did not bring to the presidency a fully developed foreign policy design, but he did bring to the office a strongly held worldview. For him, the prime obstacle to peace and stability in the world was the Soviet Union, and particularly Soviet expansionism. The principal foreign policy goal of the United States, therefore, was to be the revival of the national will to contain the Soviet Union and the restoration of confidence among friends that America was determined to stop communism. Furthermore, the United States must make other nations aware of the dangers of Soviet expansionism.

The ideological suspicion with which President Reagan viewed the Soviet Union was stated rather dramatically at his first news conference in January 1981:

> I know of no leader of the Soviet Union, since the revolution and including the present leadership, that has not more than once repeated, in the various Communist Congresses they hold, their determination that their goal must be the promotion of world revolution and a one-world socialist or Communist state—whichever word you want to use.
>
> Now as long as they do that and as long as they, at the same time, have openly and publicly declared that the only morality they recognize is what will further their cause: meaning they reserve unto themselves the right to commit any crime; to lie; to cheat, in order to obtain that, and that is moral, not immoral, and we operate on a different set of standards, I think when you do business with them—even at a detente—you keep that in mind.[3]

Indicative perhaps of the lack of fundamental change in the Reagan administration's approach to the Soviet Union throughout its first term was a speech by the president himself in early 1983. Echoing this first news conference, President Reagan assailed the morality of the Soviet Union once again and denounced it as an "evil empire." The United States, in his judgment, remained in a moral struggle with that nation. Referring specifically to the ongoing discussion of the nuclear freeze issue, President Reagan made his point in this way:

> So in your discussions of the nuclear freeze proposals, I urge you to beware the temptation of pride—the temptation blithely to declare yourselves above it all and label both sides equally at fault, to ignore the facts of history and aggressive impulses of an evil empire, to simply call the arms race a giant misunderstanding and thereby remove yourself from the struggle between right and wrong, good and evil.[4]

Such a consistently hostile view of the Soviet Union brought to mind comparisons with the U.S. foreign policy orientation of the 1950s, when the Cold War consensus was dominant. It surely stood in contrast to Jimmy Carter's view only four years earlier that "we are now free of that inordinate fear of communism."[5] Instead, President Reagan's view implied the centrality of the Soviet Union and its foreign policy objectives to American actions abroad. Indeed, to many observers, such a posture suggested the emergence of a new Cold War.[6]

THE POLICY APPROACH OF THE REAGAN ADMINISTRATION

Despite the ideological cohesion that seemed to permeate the Reagan administration, the translation of that perspective into a working foreign policy was not readily apparent to outside observers. In fact, charges were immediately hurled about that the Reagan administration really had no foreign policy because it appeared to have no coherent strategy for reaching its goals. Critics complained that rhetoric served as policy. Such a failing was particularly accented since the Reagan administration had come into office determined to bring coherence and consistency to foreign affairs, which they charged the Carter administration had failed to do.[7]

Yet this criticism is a bit overstated, since Secretary of State Alexander Haig did provide a statement of principles and the underlying rationale for dealing with the world early in his tenure. Describing his approach as a "strategic" one, Secretary Haig asserted that American foreign policy behavior was based upon four important pillars:

1. The restoration of our economic and military strength
2. The reinvigoration of alliances and friendships
3. The promotion of progress in the developing countries through peaceable changes
4. A relationship with the Soviet Union characterized by restraint and reciprocity.[8]

None of these pillars should be pursued independently, and policy initiatives in any one of these areas must support the others. The glue that would hold these "pillars" together was the Soviet-American relationship because, as Secretary Haig indicated, "Soviet-American relations must be at the center of our efforts to promote a more peaceful world."[9] A survey of Reagan administration behavior with respect to each of these pillars will reveal how the Soviet-American concern came to dominate each one.

Rebuilding American Strength

The Reagan administration quickly called for an increase in military spending. It proposed a $1.6 trillion defense buildup over a six-year period (1981–1986). While the buildup was across the entire military—from a larger navy to a modernized army and air force and from the development of a new rapid deployment force to better pay for military personnel—the strategic modernization plan attracted much of the attention in the early part of the Reagan presidency.[10]

Under this plan, each component of the America's nuclear triad—the array of land-based missiles, sea-based nuclear missiles, and intercontinental nuclear-armed bombers—would be modernized. First, a new and more powerful land-based missile, the MX or missile experimental, would be added to the American arsenal. Second, a new sea-based missile, the Trident II, and larger Trident submarines would be developed as well. Third, the B-1 bomber would replace the aging B-52s, which had constituted the third leg of the triad system. Moreover, the B-1 was intended to last until the Stealth aircraft or B-2, a new and technologically superior bomber, became available. Although the Carter administration had canceled the B-1 bomber, it had initiated the improvements in the other two legs of the triad; the difference that characterized the Reagan administration was that it would pursue all these modernizations more vigorously than before. Finally, the strategic command and control structures, the technical communication facilities that provide direction for U.S. nuclear forces,[11] would be upgraded to guard against any possible first strike from the Soviet Union.

In addition, the Reagan administration pursued two other actions to improve America's nuclear capability—one regional, the other global. On a regional level, the Reagan administration proposed to carry out the NATO alliance's Dual Track decision of 1979. According to that decision, new intermediate-range or theater nuclear weapons would be deployed in Western Europe if negotiations on theater nuclear arms control failed. In short, both cruise missiles and new intermediate range missiles would be developed and deployed as ways of improving regional European defense against the Soviet Union, and as a further means of improving the strategic forces in those two areas. On a global level, President Reagan added yet one other element to America's nuclear arsenal. He called for the United States to "embark on a program to counter the awesome Soviet missile threat with measures that are defensive." Such a defensive missile system against the Soviet threat "could pave the way for arms control measures to eliminate...[nuclear] weapons themselves."[12] Formally called the Strategic Defense Initiative (SDI) but more commonly known as "Star Wars"—after the popular motion picture—this proposal was viewed by critics as a further escalation of the arms race. Yet to the Reagan administration, the SDI proposal was a further component of its effort to rebuild America's military might and to confront Soviet power directly.

The success of the Reagan administration in achieving all of these military efforts was ultimately incomplete, but, as Table 5.1 shows, the administration did go some distance in rebuilding U.S. military strength.

Reinvigorating Allies

The reinvigoration of the allies meant basically to upgrade the military strength of the West and to have the allies support the political leadership of the United States globally. In the military area, the United States succeeded in having the Western Europeans go forward with the rearmament component of the Dual Track decision—the deployment of the 572 Pershing II and cruise missiles began by late 1983, after arms negotiations stalled.[13] In

TABLE 5.1

Major Weapons Systems Sought and Obtained by the Reagan Administration, 1981–1988

Weapons System	Policy Goal	Policy Outcome
MX Missile	200 deployed missiles	50 missiles deployed
B-1B Bomber	100 operational bombers	100 bombers approved by Congress
Trident (D5) Missile	Full development of these submarine-launched missiles	Complete Trident program approved by Congress
Intermediate-range missiles in Europe	Deployment of 464 cruise missiles and 108 Pershing II missiles	Deployment started in November 1983
	Treaty to remove all such American and Soviet missiles from Europe	INF Treaty of December 1987 eliminated all intermediate-and medium-range missiles
Strategic Defense Initiative ("Star Wars")	Funding over six years totaling $30 billion	Funding over six years totaled $16 billion

Source: Abstracted from "Reagan Administration National Security Scorecard" in *Nucleus* 10 (Fall 1988): 5.

addition, the United States wanted the Europeans to accept a greater defense burden as a means of counteracting growing Soviet power in their region and wanted the Japanese to assume greater military responsibility in East Asia. Appeals were made for the Europeans to follow the American lead in enacting sanctions against the Soviet Union and Poland after the imposition of martial law in the latter nations in late 1981, although the success was limited. The United States also tried to stop the Europeans from completing the natural gas pipeline arrangement with the Soviet Union at about the same time and, later, the Reagan administration sought (without success) to impose sanctions on the Europeans themselves over their failure to follow American wishes.[14]

Bolstering Friends in the Developing World

The meaning of the third pillar—a commitment to progress in the Third World—was to reflect a sharp shift in strategy toward American friends in the developing states. As compared to the Carter years, the Reagan administration changed policy in three distinct ways. First of all, unlike President Carter, who expressed a sympathy for Third World aspirations, the Reagan administration challenged those nations to pull themselves up by their own bootstraps and to seek improvement through the efforts of private enterprise. Prior to a meeting of twenty-two developed and developing states in

1981, President Reagan called for a strategy that allowed "men and women to realize freely their full potential, to go as far as their God-given talents will take them. Free people build free markets that ignite dynamic development for everyone."[15]

The administration soon developed the Caribbean Basin Initiative as a model for utilizing the private sector to stimulate development. While economic assistance to the Caribbean would be increased by $350 million under this plan, preferential trade access to the American market for the Caribbean states and increased American investments in the region were the key development components of this initiative. Most important, perhaps, the administration would encourage private U.S. investment in the Caribbean Basin by seeking tax breaks for American investors, by developing new international insurance facilities through private sources and multilateral banks (e.g., Inter-American Development Bank) to protect investors, and by working with each country to facilitate private-sector development.[16]

The second major shift policy was the increased reliance on military assistance as an "essential" element of U.S. policy. Although the Reagan administration committed itself to economic development, it contended that such modernization could take place only in the context of political stability. To implement this policy, the Reagan administration scrapped the arms transfer policy of the Carter administration and, following a plan more attuned to its philosophical orientation, announced that it would provide military assistance to "its major alliance partners and to those nations with whom it has friendly and cooperative security relationships." Furthermore, the directive noted, the United States would not endanger its own security by engaging in unilateral action to restrict the transfer of weapons abroad. Instead, "we will deal with the world as it is, rather than as we would like it to be."[17]

The third shift in policy toward the developing world focused on how regional conflicts would be analyzed and acted upon by the United States. Regional conflicts would not be analyzed on the basis of regional concerns only. Conflicts in the developing world had to be recast into the underlying global conflict that the Reagan administration saw in the world. In turn, U.S. actions in these regional disputes must recognize that global reality. Therefore the emphasis was on how regional conflicts affected U.S.-Soviet relations. The aim was to build a "strategic consensus" against the Soviet Union and its proxies.[18] Only after the danger posed by the Soviet Union in these conflicts was addressed could regional concerns be brought into the resolution of the conflicts.

Restraint and Reciprocity with the Soviet Union

The fourth pillar of the Reagan administration's approach to foreign policy focused directly on the Soviet Union. Only if the Soviet Union demonstrated restraint in its global actions would the United States carry on normal and reciprocal relations with it. In this sense, the familiar linkage notion of the Kissinger years was at the heart of any relationship with the Soviet Union. Specifically, Secretary Haig stated that the United States would "want greater Soviet restraint on the use of force. We want greater Soviet respect for the independence of others. And we want the Soviets to abide by their reciprocal obligations, such as those undertaken in the Helsinki Accords." No area of international relations could be left out of this restraint requirement. "We have learned that Soviet-American agreements, even in strategic arms control, will not survive Soviet threats to the overall military balance or Soviet encroachments...in critical regions of the world. *Linkage is not a theory; it is a fact of life that we overlook at our peril.*"[19]

THE REAGAN WORLDVIEW IN OPERATION

With these four pillars as the primary guide to U.S. foreign policy, a brief survey of American actions toward the Soviet Union, Central America, southern Africa, and the Middle East will illustrate how the Reagan administration put these principles into action.

Policy Actions Toward the Soviet Union

Because the Soviet Union had exercised neither policy restraint nor reciprocity in the past, the Reagan administration did not seek to improve relations immediately. Instead, the United States sought to rally other states against the Soviet Union and adopted several initial measures to prod it to exercise international restraint. First, administration officials publicly criticized the Soviet Union. President Reagan and Secretary Haig attacked the Soviet system as bankrupt and on the verge of collapse, charging the Soviets with fomenting international disorder.[20] Second, the administration took direct steps to demonstrate American resolve. In addition to its strategic modernization plan, the administration called for producing and stockpiling the neutron bomb, a new kind of weapon (originally proposed during the Carter years) that killed people but did not destroy property. Most significant, perhaps, the United States promptly imposed sanctions upon the Soviet Union and Poland in 1981 to show its dissatisfaction with the imposition of martial law by Poland's Communist government and Soviet support for that action.[21]

Third, some actions were *not* taken—to demonstrate that normal relations could not occur until the Soviet Union showed restraint. In this connection, the two most important omissions were the failure to move rapidly on arms control and the failure to engage in summit meetings. In fact, arms control discussions were initially put on the back burner until the arms buildup was completed by the United States. Additionally, questions of a summit meeting between the Soviet and American presidents were put off with the comment that the conditions were not appropriate and that little valuable discussion would result.

Despite a relationship that was marked primarily by harsh rhetoric and strong action, some initial cooperative elements were still evident. Moreover, they illustrate the anomalies that were present even in a relationship that was marked by such hostilities. In the economic area, the Reagan administration lifted the grain embargo in April 1981—an embargo President Carter had put into effect after the Afghanistan invasion—despite its commitment to isolating and punishing the Soviet Union. Within a year, the administration sought to expand grain sales to the Soviet Union and eventually agreed to a new five-year grain deal.[22] In the military area, the administration also stated that it would continue to adhere to the SALT I and SALT II limitations if the Soviets would.[23] This stance was adopted even though the former pact had expired in 1977, and the latter had not been ratified by the U.S. Senate and had been called "fatally flawed" by Reagan supporters during the 1980 election campaign. In the diplomatic area, Secretary of State Haig met with Soviet Foreign Minister Andrei Gromyko during his visit to the UN General Assembly in the fall of 1981, despite the chilly political atmosphere. Finally, the intermediate nuclear force (INF) talks—talks on nuclear missiles with ranges only within Europe—reluctantly were begun by the Reagan administration during November 1981 much earlier than expected given the overall political climate. Seven months later, President Reagan also initiated the Strategic Arms Reduction Talks (START)—talks on intercontinental nuclear weapons—despite the seeming confrontational environment.[24]

By November 1983, neither of these talks had reached any agreement, and the United States went ahead with its deployment of intermediate missiles in Europe.[25] That action had an immediate effect on the already deteriorating relationship between the two superpowers. The Soviet Union walked out of the INF negotiations and, within one month, declared that it would not proceed with the Strategic Arms Reduction Talks either. Further, the Soviets took a number of other provocative actions over the next few months to show its displeasure with Reagan administration policy: It resumed and expanded the deployment of its intermediate range nuclear missiles in Central Europe; it announced the deployment of more nuclear submarines off the American coasts in retaliation for the new American weapons in Western Europe; and it withdrew from the 1984 Olympic Games in Los Angeles, claiming that its athletes would not be safe there.[26]

The consequence of this barrage of various charges and actions by both superpowers was that Soviet-American relations by the middle of 1984 were "at the lowest level for the entire postwar period."[27] The "restraint and reciprocity" that the Reagan administration had initially set out to achieve had not been accomplished, but the plan of restoring the Soviet Union to the center of American foreign policy and building up U.S. defenses was well under way.

Policy Action Toward the Third World

Central America. In Central America, the response of the Reagan administration toward the unrest in El Salvador reflected its basic foreign policy approach (see Map 5.1). The administration quickly moved to interpret the ongoing civil war in El Salvador as Soviet and Cuban directed. Calling El Salvador a "textbook case" of Communist aggression, the Reagan administration issued a white paper outlining the danger there. The administration wanted

> the American people and the world community [to] be aware of the gravity of the actions of Cuba, the Soviet Union, and other Communist states who are carrying out what is clearly shown to be a well-coordinated, covert effort to bring about

MAP 5.1

Central America

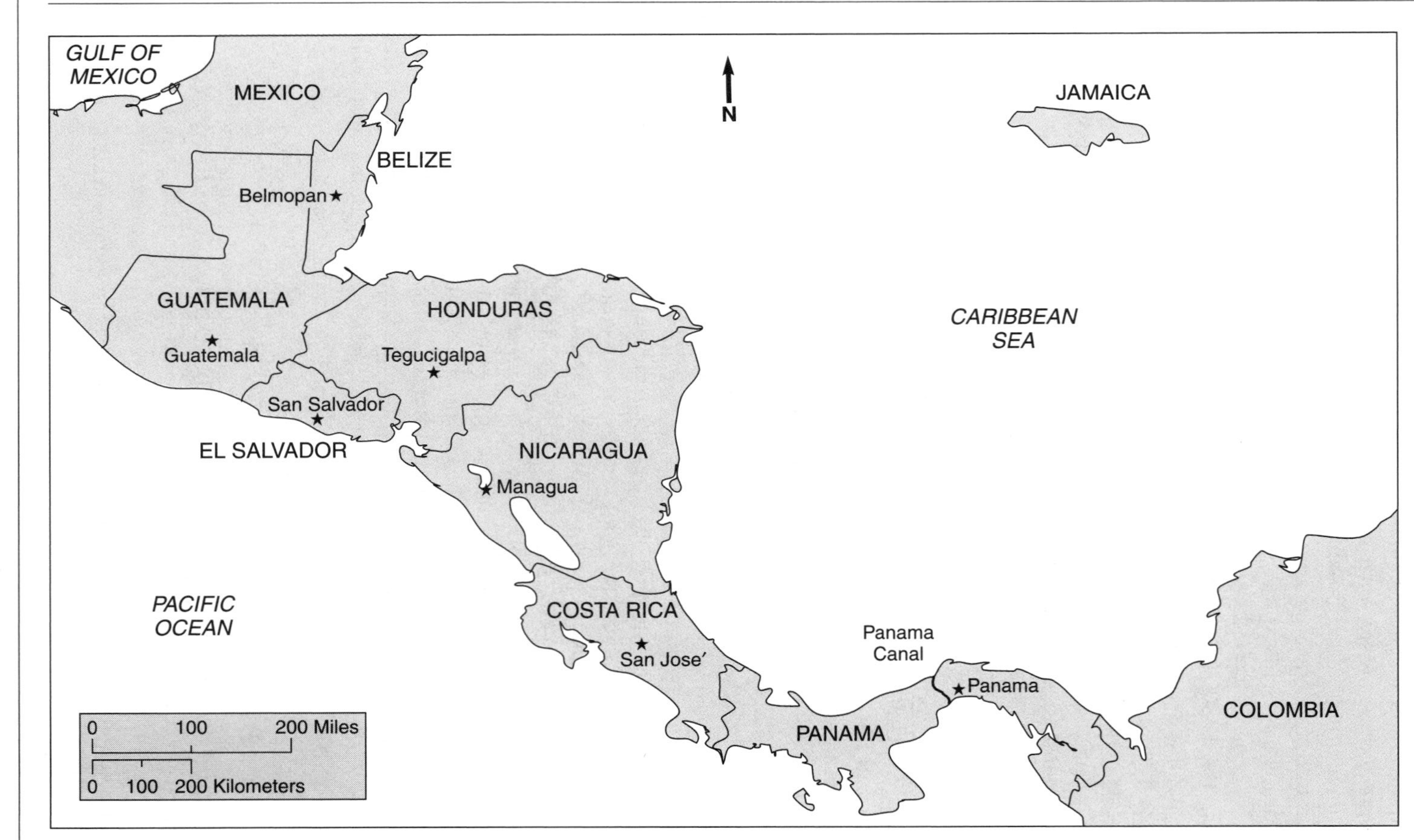

> the overthrow of El Salvador's established government and to impose in its place a Communist regime with no popular support.[28]

Furthermore, testifying at a House Foreign Affairs Committee hearing in March 1981, Secretary of State Haig charged that the Communist attack on El Salvador was part of a "four-phased operation" aimed at the ultimate Communist control of Central America.[29]

Military assistance and the threat of military action were the principal instruments used by the U.S. government to respond to the situation. Military aid totaling $25 million was immediately proposed for the government of El Salvador in its struggle with rebel forces, with more to come. The number of military advisors was increased from twenty to fifty-five by the spring of 1981.[30] Over the next several years, El Salvador and its neighbor, Honduras, became leading recipients of U.S. foreign assistance.

A similar policy approach, and some of the administration's harshest rhetoric, was directed toward El Salvador's neighbor, Nicaragua. President Reagan described the Sandinista-led government of Nicaragua as "a Communist reign of terror," and Nicaraguans themselves as "Cuba's Cubans" for its assumed involvement in aiding the Salvadoran guerrillas.[31] He also quoted directly from the Truman Doctrine of four decades earlier to justify the need for American action in the region ("I believe that it must be the policy of the United States to support free peoples...").[32]

Charging that the Nicaraguan government was arming the guerrillas in El Salvador, the Reagan administration, upon taking office, cut off $15 million of economic aid to that country.[33] Press leaks further indicated that the Reagan administration was exploring military actions against Cuba and Nicaragua. By early 1982, in fact, the Reagan administration apparently had a clandestine operation underway in Honduras—supporting Nicaraguan rebels, or *Contras*, opposed to the Sandinista government.[34]

The hardline policy of containing communism in Latin America was perhaps manifested most dramatically with the American invasion of the Caribbean island of Grenada in October 1983. After Marxist Prime Minister Maurice Bishop was killed on October 19, 1983, and after a more radical group seized control, the United States agreed to join forces with the five members of the Organization of Eastern Caribbean States "to restore order and democracy" in Grenada. This action was officially taken to ensure the safety of between 800 and 1,000 Americans—mostly medical students—and to "forestall further chaos."[35] Within a few days, the American control of the island was achieved, the Marxist regime had been replaced, and the return to a Western-style democracy was under way. The intervention, moreover, demonstrated that the Reagan administration would confront Marxist regimes and use military force, if necessary.

Southern Africa. In southern Africa, the Reagan administration's actions followed a similar pattern against potential Communist gains. The administration adopted a policy of "constructive engagement" toward South Africa and linked any settlement in Namibia (or Southwest Africa) to the removal of Soviet-backed Cuban forces from Angola. These policies were predicated upon several key beliefs. First, South Africa was staunchly anti-

Communist, and, as a result, the United States should not seek a confrontational approach toward it. Second, the conflict in the region really had East-West overtones that could not be overlooked. After all, South Africa was confronted by a Marxist regime in Angola, which was backed by Cuban soldiers and Soviet arms.[36] Third, only when the South Africans felt more confident of American support could the United States try to exert influence upon them to change their apartheid policy and to seek a solution to the question of Namibia. In this region, the strategic concern of controlling communism produced a markedly different approach than the Carter administration had adopted (see Chapter 4).

The Middle East. In the Middle East, the administration's primary strategy was aimed at stopping any potential Communist gains as well. No new initiatives were proposed, nor was there much effort to proceed with the Camp David framework, inherited from the Carter administration. Instead, as elsewhere, the Reagan administration attempted to rally the Arab states against the Soviet Union and to engage the Israelis in a strategic understanding. A new Persian Gulf command, with the Rapid Deployment Force as part of that structure, was announced. Negotiations were held with several Middle East states regarding American base and access rights in the regions. Egypt, Sudan, Somalia, and Oman, for example, agreed to joint military exercises with the United States during November 1981,[37] and the United States also obtained military cooperation from the Israelis.[38]

The most dramatic examples of using military assistance to bolster American influence against the Soviet Union also occurred in this region. The United States agreed to sell technologically advanced aircraft equipment and the Airborne Warning and Control System (AWACS) aircraft to Saudi Arabia in October 1981. The administration also agreed to supply forty F-16 fighter aircraft to Pakistan (an arms deal worth more than $3 billion) as part of its strategy for Southwest Asia.[39]

The Reagan administration's emphasis on global concerns over local concerns ultimately proved short-lived in this volatile region. By the summer of 1982—and wholly as a result of Israel's invasion of Lebanon and its advance all the way to Beirut—the Reagan administration was fully immersed in local issues in the Middle East. As a result, the Reagan administration had to respond to local issues, not global ones. The administration sought to negotiate a cease-fire between the Israelis and the surrounded Palestinian forces in West Beirut and a withdrawal of Syrian and Israeli forces from Lebanon itself. Moreover, even President Reagan moved into a mediator posture with a new policy initiative (labeled the Reagan Initiative) to serve as a follow-up to the Camp David framework. The initiative called for a Palestinian homeland federated with Jordan, an end to Israeli settlements in the West Bank, and security for Israel.[40]

The depth of American involvement in the area even reached the point of deploying American military personnel on two different occasions. The administration sent a contingent of American Marines into Lebanon in August 1982, as part of an effort to evacuate the Palestine Liberation Organization (PLO) members from Beirut, where they had been surrounded by the Israelis. This mission was successfully completed without any major incident. In September 1982, however, the Marines were again dispatched to Lebanon as part of a Multinational Force (MNF), composed of military personnel from several Western nations. While the MNF was to serve as a "peacekeeping" force between the various Lebanese factions and to facilitate a negotiated settlement among them, the task proved elusive and ultimately disastrous.[41] As factional feuding continued, the role of the MNF became increasingly unclear. In time, the American Marines, encamped at the Beirut airport, became identified with the central government and became the target for snipers from the other Lebanese factions. More than that, the Marines became the target of a terrorist bombing on October 23, 1983, which killed some 241 Americans in an attack on their barracks. Although the Reagan administration originally intended to deal with regional issues in a global context, it became deeply involved in "local issues" in the Middle East without a well-conceived policy.

CHALLENGES TO THE REAGAN APPROACH

Despite the efforts of the Reagan administration to redirect the focus and content of American policy to the Soviet danger, the rest of the world would not easily follow its lead. Concern—and at times rejection—over the ideological tone and substance of the Reagan foreign policy came from both international and domestic sources. Such challenges both made it difficult for the Reagan administration to continue the ideological consistency that it originally intended and contributed to some modification in it over time.

Foreign Policy Differences

The Western European states, for example, were reluctant to follow the Reagan administration's political lead in dealing with the Soviet Union. Whether it was over martial law in Poland or the building of a natural gas pipeline from the Soviet Union to Western Europe, the Europeans were more concerned with preserving contacts with Eastern Europe, not disrupting them. In short, the European's did not go as far as the Reagan administration wished in confronting the Soviet Union.[42] Similarly, while the Europeans were committed to the Dual Track decision of 1979, they were unsure (and uneasy) about President Reagan's commitment to pursuing negotiations seriously. With his harsh rhetoric, his strategic modernization plan, and his reluctance to proceed very quickly with arms control talks, President Reagan did not seem to be following a policy of arms restraint. Secretary of State Haig's and President Reagan's comments about the possibility of a demonstration nuclear explosion and a limited nuclear war—actions highly threatening to the Europeans—were not reassuring.[43] Further, the hundreds of thousands of demonstrators filling the streets of London, Rome, Berlin, and Bonn in protest of the Reagan arms policy created further political difficulties for European leaders.[44] Finally, some European and Latin American states failed to support either the American approach to the situation in El Salvador or its policy toward Nicaragua. Early on, France and Mexico proposed to initiate negotiations between the government in El Salvador and the political arm of the rebel movement.[45] Similarly, the international Socialist movement, led by Willy Brandt of West Germany, also sought to get negotiations started.

Domestic Differences

Domestic challenges arose as well. Although the public was willing to support some increase in defense spending at the time the Reagan administration took office, the situation had changed considerably by 1983. By then, 45 percent of the American public indicated that the United States was spending too much on the military, and only 14 percent indicated that the United States was spending too little. By contrast, in 1981, only 15 percent of the public had indicated that the United States was spending too much on defense, and 51 percent indicated that the United States was spending too little.[46]

Like its European counterpart, the nuclear freeze movement within the United States also gained quick public support, with opinion polls consistently showing more than 60 percent of the American public supporting a "mutual and verifiable freeze" of nuclear weapons between the Soviet Union and the United States.[47] This movement was able to turn out more than 700,000 people to demonstrate in New York City in June 1982—one of the largest single demonstrations in American political history. The composition of the demonstration—individuals from a wide variety of political and social backgrounds—reflected the diversity of support for this movement.[48]

Similarly, domestic challenges arose over Central American policy. In particular, concern was expressed over potential American involvement in the region, especially now that more American advisors were being sent there. Would American combat forces be sent to the region? Was this involvement the beginning of another Vietnam-like quagmire in which American involvement would slowly escalate? This kind of fear caused Secretary of State Haig to rule out the use of American troops in Central America.[49] Further, some argued, local conditions, such as poverty and inequality, ought to be given greater credibility in explaining the political unrest in the region than the Reagan administration was allowing.

POLICY CHANGE: ACCOMMODATION WITH THE SOVIET UNION

In the aftermath of his resounding election to a second term in November 1984, with the largest electoral vote total in American history (525 out of a possible 538) and with one of the largest percentages of the popular vote (59 percent), President Reagan immediately announced that his administration would continue to do "what we've been doing."[50] In reality, some change did occur. While generally he did not abandon his hard-line position on Soviet expansionism in Third World areas, President Reagan actually came to embrace a much more accommodationist approach to the Soviet Union in his second term.

Sources of Change

At least three factors contributed to this movement away from the previous hard-line approach of the Reagan administration toward the Soviet Union: (1) a change in the policy stance of the American leadership; (2) the emergence of new leadership and "new thinking" in the Soviet Union; and (3) the domestic realities of the arms race between the superpowers. Although it is difficult to specify which of these factors (and presumably others as well) weighed most heavily in this policy change—or to show fully how they interacted with one another—a discussion of each will portray the change in approach from only four years earlier.

Policy Shifts. Secretary of State George Shultz, who had replaced Alexander Haig in June 1982, seemingly signaled a change in emphasis by the Reagan administration. In October 1984, Shultz indicated that the Soviet behavior in all areas of the world would not automatically be linked to the quality of relations between the Soviet Union and the United States. Unlike former Secretary of State Alexander Haig's characterization of linkage as a fact of life, Shultz declared that

> clearly linkage is not merely a "fact of life" but a complex question of policy. There will be times when we must make progress in one dimension of the relationship contingent on progress in others.... At the same time, linkage as an instrument of policy has limitations; if applied rigidly, it could yield the initiative to the Soviets, letting them set the pace and the character of the relationship.... In the final analysis, linkage is a tactical question; the strategic reality of leverage comes from creating facts in support of our overall design.[51]

A little later, Shultz summarized the principal U.S. foreign policy goal: "We must learn to pursue a strategy geared to long-term thinking and based on both negotiation and strength simultaneously, if we are to build a stable U.S.-Soviet relationship for the next century."[52]

In his second inaugural address, President Reagan reiterated his post-election commitment to better relations with the Soviet Union, especially in the area of nuclear arms control. He indicated that the United States would seek to reduce the cost of national security "in negotiations with the Soviet Union." These negotiations, however, would not focus just on limiting an increase in nuclear weapons, but they would "reduce their numbers."[53] To appreciate how dramatic a change had occurred, recall how the Reagan administration initially rejected arms control negotiations.

"New Thinking." A second factor that contributed to the possibility of accommodation between the two superpowers was the 1985 selection of Mikhail Gorbachev as the general secretary of the Communist party of the Soviet Union, and eventually as president of the Soviet Union. Gorbachev's rise to power was critical, because he brought with him several important conceptual changes to Soviet foreign policy thinking and a commitment to improving relations with the United States. In fact, he added two major concepts to the political lexicon of the 1980s and 1990s, *perestroika* and *glasnost*. Perestroika referred to the "restructuring" of Soviet society in an effort to improve the economy, while glasnost referred to a new "openness" and movement toward greater democratization within the Soviet system.

Such "new thinking" by the Soviet leadership, as Gorbachev himself called it, came to have important implications for Soviet-American relations. In contrast to earlier desires for "nuclear superiority," the Soviet leadership began to embrace the concepts of "reasonable sufficiency" as a nuclear weapons strategy in dealing with the West and to recognize the need for greater "strategic stability" in the nuclear balance as well. In such an environment, nuclear arms accommodation between the two superpowers became a viable option. Furthermore, the Soviet leadership indicated that the struggle between capitalism and socialism had changed, and political solutions, rather than military ones, ought to be pursued.[54]

The Sustained Arms Race. Yet a third factor may well have been the most pivotal for both nations: the increasing domestic burden of sustained military spending. In both societies, the military burden of continued confrontation was distorting and undermining the domestic health of their economies. In the Soviet Union, the basic needs of its people could not be met, as more and more resources were spent on the military. Gorbachev's hope of restructuring the Soviet system could not be realistically undertaken as long as military spending consumed so much of the wealth of the society. In the United States, with military budgets approaching $300 billion per year and federal budget deficits increasing, the health of the economy remained in question. Further, no longer could the Reagan administration count on public support for increased military spending. Public opinion polls in 1982 and 1986 indicated that the public favored keeping military expenditures about the same (although no great sentiment appeared for defense cuts).[55]

The Return of Soviet-American Summitry

The first significant manifestation of a changed policy was the reemergence of summitry between American and Soviet leaders. Ironically, considering his initial reluctance to talk with the Soviet, President Reagan ultimately held more summits with Soviet leaders than any other American president. In the space of about three and half years, he held five summits with President Gorbachev.[56] Each of these summits proved to be important building blocks for improving Soviet-American ties. Because Table 5.2 provides a detailed summary of each of these summits, we shall only highlight some key points from the most important ones.

The first summit between President Reagan and General Secretary Mikhail Gorbachev was held in Geneva, Switzerland, on November 19–21, 1985, and it was called the "Fireside Summit" for the backdrop in which the talks were held. No important agreements emerged; rather, it was an opportunity for both leaders to get to know each other better and to exchange views on numerous issues, including arms control, human rights, and regional conflicts. In effect, this summit was really a prelude to the next one.[57]

The second and third summits were arguably the most important ones of the Reagan presidency. The October 1986 summit, held in Reykjavik, Iceland, focused largely on seeking progress in the nuclear arms talks underway

TABLE 5.2

The Five Soviet-American Summits During the Second Term of the Reagan Administration

Location and Date	Objectives; Accomplishments
1. Geneva Switzerland November 19–21, 1985	The "Fireside Summit"; a "get-acquainted" summit that reached some minor agreements and focused upon an agenda for the future.
2. Reykjavik, Iceland October 11–12, 1986	Arms Control Talks; progress on intermediate nuclear forces agreement; proposal for 50% reduction in strategic nuclear weapons.
3. Washington, D.C. December 8–10, 1987	Signing of the Intermediate Nuclear Forces (INF) Treaty; sought progress on strategic arms reduction agreement.
4. Moscow, USSR May 29–June 2, 1988	Exchange of ratification documents on INF Treaty; further discussions on other nuclear arms control efforts and other bilateral and multilateral issues.
5. New York, N.Y. December 7, 1988	Farewell meeting between Reagan and Gorbachev; initial meeting between President-elect Bush and Gorbachev.

between the Soviet Union and the United States. The most significant products of this summit were agreements in principle to reduce all strategic nuclear weapons 50 percent over a five-year period and to limit intermediate-range nuclear forces to 100 warheads for each side.[58] These commitments were significant for advancing work on a strategic arms reduction (START) agreement and on an intermediate nuclear forces (INF) agreement. Disagreement remained, however, over negotiations on space-based missiles (the "Star Wars" defense systems), threatening to undermine the work in the other two areas. Still, the INF discussions were eventually separated from the other talks and that action quickly led to the completion of the Intermediate Nuclear Forces (INF) Treaty (discussed below), which was signed at the third summit.

The fourth summit, held in Moscow in late May and early June 1988, was primarily to exchange instruments of ratification of the new INF Treaty, seek further progress in strategic arms negotiations, and discuss other key global issues.[59] The fifth and final Soviet-American summit of the Reagan administration was a brief one-day meeting in New York City in December 1988 in conjunction with President Gorbachev's visit and speech to the United Nations.[60] It was an opportunity for a final exchange of views before Reagan left office and for the new President-elect, George Bush, to meet the Soviet leader.

The INF Treaty

The most important manifestation of progress in Soviet-American relationship in Reagan's second term was the completion of the Intermediate

TABLE 5.3

Key Components of the Intermediate Nuclear Forces (INF) Treaty

Treaty Articles
requires the Soviet Union and the United States to eliminate all intermediate-range missiles within three years of the effective date of the treaty and all medium-range missiles within 18 months

Memorandum of Understanding on Data Exchange
requires the Soviet Union and the United States to provide each other with data on the number, location, and character of their intermediate-range and medium-range nuclear missiles

Elimination Protocol
provides specific guidelines and procedures for the destruction of all missiles, launchers, support structures, and support equipment for these intermediate-range and medium-range nuclear missiles

The Inspection Protocol
provides for a wide variety of on-site inspections by each side upon the other for up to 13 years after the treaty enters into force

Special Verification Commission
establishes this commission for the purpose of resolving immediately any problem that is identified by either party.

Source: Abstracted and adapted from "The INF Treaty: What's in It?" in *Arms Control Update* (Washington, DC: Arms Control and Disarmament Agency, January 1988): pp. 4–5.

Nuclear Forces (INF) Treaty. This treaty culminated a long series of negotiations that had originally begun in November 1981, broke off in November 1983, and resumed again after a joint Soviet-American agreement to link all nuclear arms negotiations—one track on intermediate nuclear forces, a second on strategic nuclear forces, and a third on defense and space arms—in a set of "New Negotiations" in January 1985.[61] After the 1986 Reykjavik summit, however, the INF talks were selected for accelerated action, while, after the 1987 Washington summit, the defense and space talks were downgraded and the main outlines of a strategic agreement were adopted but not formally signed during the Reagan years. Only the INF Treaty was wholly completed.

The treaty, summarized in Table 5.3, called for the elimination of all medium-range nuclear weapons within three years and all intermediate-range nuclear weapons within eighteen months.[62] It also prohibited the United States and Soviet Union from ever again possessing such weapons. Further, it provided a series of on-site inspections for each party and set out exacting procedures on how these nuclear weapons should be destroyed. Finally it established a Special Verification Commission, which would be continuously in session to deal with any issues that may arise. Such a commission stood in sharp contrast to earlier arms control agreements in which such commissions had to be called into session or only met periodically.

Under this new arrangement, problems or concerns would be immediately addressed by the two parties.

The military significance of the INF Treaty has been questioned. It required relatively few nuclear missiles to be destroyed, and each superpower retained a formidable arsenal with which to destroy one another and the world at large. The political significance of the pact, however, is less debatable. The INF Treaty represented the first nuclear arms reduction pact in human history, and it gave real momentum to arms control and arms reduction for the future. With the incorporation of on-site inspection into the pact, it initiated a new departure in the verification of arms control agreements between the superpowers.

POLICY CONTINUITY: REAGAN DOCTRINE AND THE THIRD WORLD

Although actions toward the Soviet Union represented an important source of change, policy toward the Third World—and the perceived role of the Soviet Union in causing unrest there—remained an important constant during the second term of the Reagan administration. This continuity was reflected in the formal emergence of the "Reagan Doctrine," a policy of supporting anti-Communist movement in various locations around the world, and it was demonstrated most dramatically by the sustained support of the Nicaraguan Contras, even as Congress cut off military support for that operation from 1984 to 1986. This latter episode, known as the "Iran-Contra affair" (to be discussed in detail later in this section), reflected the administration's determination to "stand tall" against perceived Communist penetration in Central America. At the same time, the episode produced a major inconsistency in policy: The Reagan administration secretly abandoned its official policy of an arms embargo toward Iran in an attempt to free American hostages in the region.

The Reagan Doctrine

By 1985, the administration's support for anti-Communist forces in the Third World had gained such prominence and permanency that it took on a name of its own—the "Reagan Doctrine." Unlike U.S. policy that focused on containing the expansion of communism, the Reagan Doctrine espoused "providing assistance to groups fighting governments that have aligned themselves with the Soviet Union."[63] Despite the thaw in relations with the Soviet Union during Reagan's second term, the strategy was still pursued vigorously and proved to be the main thread of continuity with the hardline policy of anticommunism that was so prominent in 1981.

What this policy meant in reality was that several anti-Communist movements across three continents received both covert and overt American economic and military assistance and political encouragement in their fights against the Communist governments in power. In Asia, for example, the United States continued to support the Afghan rebels in their battle with the

Soviet troops and the Soviet-backed Kabul government. In Kampuchea (present-day Cambodia), the United States also clandestinely funneled aid to groups opposing the government supported by the occupying Vietnamese troops. In Africa, the Reagan administration persuaded Congress to repeal its prohibition on aid to forces opposing the Angolan government, and it continued to support rebel leader Jonas Savimbi and his National Union for the Total Independence of Angola (UNITA) in its fight against the Marxist-supported government there. In Central America, of course, the Reagan administration continued to support the Nicaraguan Contras against the Sandinista government, even as Congress diligently attempted to end such aid.

A useful indicator of how institutionalized the Reagan Doctrine became was the 1985 foreign aid authorization bill. While that bill not only included some nonmilitary humanitarian aid for the Nicaraguan rebels, support for other anti-Communist rebel groups was publicly acknowledged with a $5 million allocation to the Cambodian rebels and a $15 million "humanitarian" allocation to the Afghan people.[64] As alluded to above, the congressional prohibition on aid to rebel forces in Angola was formally rescinded in this legislation.

Policy Actions Under the Reagan Doctrine

At least two policy successes resulted from the Reagan Doctrine. In Asia, through continued American support of the Afghan rebels and through the decision by President Gorbachev to reduce the Soviet Union's worldwide activity, an agreement on Afghanistan was reached in August 1988. Under UN mediation, Afghanistan, Pakistan, the United States, and the Soviet Union signed an agreement to provide for the total withdrawal of Soviet troops by February 1989. Pakistan and Afghanistan also agreed not to interfere in the domestic affairs of each other, and the United States and the Soviet Union agreed to serve as guarantors of those commitments.[65] In southern Africa, a similar outcome occurred that was favorable to the Reagan Doctrine. Although the Reagan administration had supported independence for Namibia from South Africa through UN-supervised elections, that commitment was conditioned upon the removal of Soviet-backed Cuban troops from neighboring Angola. As an incentive for a political settlement, the Reagan administration had provided support to UNITA, an opposition group in Angola. In late December 1988, an agreement was signed among Angola, Cuba, and South Africa that called for a phased withdrawal of all Cuban troops from Angola by July 1991, the withdrawal of South African troops from Namibia by the end of 1990, and the completion of elections in Namibia by the end of 1990.[66]

At least two other policy actions were taken that were consistent with the principles of the Reagan Doctrine. Substantial economic and military assistance continued to flow to the government of El Salvador as that government sought to defeat Marxist-backed forces within its country. In the Middle East, the Reagan administration responded swiftly and decisively to a terrorist attack in Germany in which Americans were the target. Based upon its intelligence, the American government claimed that Libya was the source of the attack, and President Reagan quickly ordered a retaliatory air strike against Libya in April 1986, with the headquarters of President Muammar al-Gadhafi among its targets.

The Iran-Contra Affair, 1984–1986

The episode that best illustrates the extent to which the administration embraced the Reagan Doctrine was the Iran-Contra affair during 1984 through 1986. This affair brought together two vexing foreign policy problems for the Reagan administration.[67] The first was the question of dealing with the Sandinista government in Nicaragua. The Reagan administration viewed the Sandinistas, who had overthrown the Nicaraguan dictator Anastasio Somoza in 1979, as avowed Marxists, intent upon spreading revolution throughout Central America. The second was the question of dealing with Iran and its government led by Ayatollah Khomeini. That government had seized American hostages in November 1979, held them hostage for 444 days, released them only on the day of President Reagan's inauguration. To deal with these two policy questions, the Reagan administration supported the Nicaraguan Contras fighting against the Sandinistas in various ways, including the use of U.S. clandestine assistance, and continued observance of President Carter's trade sanctions against Iran, including a prohibition on U.S. arms sales to that country.

Beginning in 1984, however, policies toward Nicaragua and Iran faltered, and eventually unravelled by the middle of 1985. Iran's actions in support of terrorism caused the first challenge to the Reagan administration's policy. As a result of the U.S. presence in a multinational peacekeeping force in Lebanon in 1982 and 1983, anti-American sentiment and terrorism against the United States rose significantly. In October 1983, terrorists bombed American Marine barracks in Lebanon. In early 1984, three Americans were seized in Beirut. The next year, four more Americans were taken as hostages. Both the American public and President Reagan became increasingly impatient over the hostage situation. Indeed, by the middle of 1985, President Reagan decided to reverse the long-standing policy of an arms embargo against Iran in an attempt to free U.S. hostages.

Yet the Reagan administration's policy reversal toward Iran was not done in isolation; it quickly became tied to an attempt to save its policy of aiding the Nicaraguan Contras. In October 1984, Congress had cut off all American military assistance to the Nicaraguan Contras with the passage of the most restrictive version of the Boland Amendment (see Chapter 8). In light of this congressional action, high administration officials almost immediately undertook efforts to keep the Contras together in "body and soul," as President Reagan had instructed. What ultimately emerged from these efforts was a covert operation by private operatives to raise money and provide support for the Nicaraguan rebels. These were at least two means of raising money to support the Contras: One was through contributions by private individuals and other governments, the other was through the clandestine sale of arms to the Iranian government and the transfer of profits to the Nicaraguan rebels. Importantly, throughout the entire episode and during the investigations afterwards, President Reagan consistently denied both that he knew that the arms sales profits were being transferred to the Contras and that the arms sales to Iran were tied solely to the freeing of American hostages held in Lebanon.

Through a complex covert arms operation and Contra resupply effort, directed by Lt. Col. Oliver North of the National Security Council staff, several shipments of arms were sold to Iran and some profits from those sales were transferred to the Contras in 1985 and 1986. While three hostages were released from Lebanon during the arms sales period, three more hostages were seized before the affair was disclosed publicly. On the narrow goal of gaining the release of hostages through arms sales, the policy hardly proved a net success. Throughout the period of these operations, these activities were never reported to Congress as required by the Intelligence Oversight Act and other governing legislation. Indeed, Congress only learned of this covert operation when CIA Director William Casey briefed the intelligence committees on November 21, 1986, but after the episode had been revealed in the press.

The Iran-Contra affair affected both procedural and policy aspects of American foreign policy during the latter years of the Reagan administration. It damaged both the clarity and credibility of the administration's policy and challenged the way the Reagan Doctrine was being carried out. It had a profound effect upon congressional-executive relations and upon public support for foreign policy. The affair also resulted in two separate investigations—one by the executive branch (the Tower Commission, named after its chair, former Senator John Tower of Texas), the other by Congress (the Iran-Contra committees in the House and Senate)—which sought to identify exactly what went on and what changes were needed to ensure that similar episodes would not occur in the future. In general, the congressional investigation found that standard procedures were not followed in making policy decisions, that Congress was misled, that dishonesty and excessive secrecy pervaded the process, and that the president should have known, if he did not, about the diversion of funds from the arms sales to the Nicaraguan rebels. The executive branch investigation reached many of the same conclusions.[68]

Policy Change and Reagan: Philippines, PLO, and South Africa

Although policy adherence to the Reagan Doctrine marked the administration's approach to the Third World, three important policy changes did occur in different regions of the world. One was in Southeast Asia, a second in the Middle East, and the third in Africa.

The Aquino Victory. The first change was over the Philippines and the movement toward democracy under Corazon Aquino in 1985 and 1986. The United States had long supported the government of Ferdinand Marcos, principally because of his anti-Communist credentials and because of the need to maintain two strategic U.S. bases on Philippine soil (a naval base at Subic Bay and an air base at Clark Field). Yet Marcos's dismal human rights record and authoritarian rule had long been a source of embarrassment and concern to U.S. policy makers. With the assassination of Senator

Benigno Aquino, Jr., the leading opposition politician to Marcos, and the rise in strength of the New People's Army—a Marxist opposition group—and other nationalist opposition groups, the Reagan administration came under increasing pressure to reevaluate its policy. By 1984, the reevaluation had begun, and a National Security Council directive anticipated a post-Marcos period.[69]

When President Marcos suddenly agreed to hold a "snap election" in early 1986 to demonstrate his popularity, Corazon Aquino, wife of the assassinated senator and a political novice, agreed to run against him. Although Marcos was declared the election winner, accusations of voter fraud were rampant. Opposition groups surrounded the presidential palace and called for Marcos to give up power. At that juncture, the Reagan administration threw its full support behind the opposition candidate, Corazon Aquino, and informed Marcos that he should resign. Within a matter of days, he left the country and took up exile in Hawaii.

The significance of this action for the Reagan administration was that it represented a clear departure from previous policy, away from maintaining stability through support for authoritarian rule and toward the promotion of human rights and democracy. This action seemed to be particularly at odds with an administration that had previously supported Third World stability as the less dangerous way to thwart potential communist expansion.

U.S.-PLO Dialogue. A second illustration concerned the question of talking with the Palestine Liberation Organization (PLO) in any Middle East peace negotiations. Since 1975, as part of the commitments associated with second disengagement agreement between Israel and Egypt, the United States had pledged to Israel that it would have no contact with the PLO until at least two conditions were met: (1) the PLO recognized the right of the state of Israel to exist; and (2) the PLO accepted UN resolutions 242 and 338 as the basis for negotiations in the Middle East.[70] Over the years, a third condition for any contact between the PLO and the United States was added: (3) the PLO would have to renounce the use of terrorism.[71] Although a variety of efforts was undertaken by Secretary of State George Shultz in the mid-1980s, no real accommodation occurred among the parties to the ongoing dispute.

In November 1988, however, the Palestine National Council, the political assembly of the PLO, took a dramatic step to change the situation. First, it declared an independent Palestinian state in the area occupied by Israel and sought recognition from abroad. Second, and most importantly for U.S. policy, it moved to accept the first American condition for discussion between the parties and accepted in part the second condition. On the third condition, however, it only "condemned" terrorism and did not renounce it. By the middle of December 1988, however, Yasir Arafat, head of the PLO, sensing the political value of discussions with the United States, announced his full acceptance of the three explicit conditions for U.S.-PLO dialogue and his renunciation of terrorism. Within a matter of hours, President Reagan determined that Arafat's statement met American conditions and announced a shift in American policy.[72]

Opposition to Apartheid. The third arena of change was South Africa. Although all American administrations, including Reagan's, had long opposed South Africa's policy of apartheid—segregation of the races—the Reagan administration had followed a policy of "constructive engagement" in which "quiet diplomacy" was seen as the best way to elicit change in that strategically important country. By August 1985, however, Congress had become impatient with such a strategy and was on the verge of passing a compromise bill that would have imposed economic sanctions on South Africa as a more tangible way to effect change. In a clear reversal of policy, and undoubtedly as an attempt to rescue the initiative from Congress, President Reagan issued an executive order imposing virtually the same set of sanctions that Congress had proposed.[73]

In 1986, however, the Reagan administration failed to take any further action against South Africa. At the same time, Congress pressed ahead and passed a new, tough sanctions bill, the Anti-Apartheid Act of 1986, over President Reagan's veto. The policy change that President Reagan had originally put into place after congressional prodding in 1985 was now made permanent by an act of Congress in 1986. In this sense, the policy change on the part of the Reagan administration was less its own and more the result of congressional action.

VALUES AND BELIEFS OF THE BUSH ADMINISTRATION

In contrast to the Reagan administration's initial ideological approach, the Bush administration assumed office mainly seeking continuity but also willing to pursue modest change in foreign policy direction. Although the commitment to continuity was quickly challenged by the dramatic events in central Europe and the Middle East, the foreign policy values and beliefs of the Bush administration remained markedly unchanged throughout its four years in office.

"Pragmatic" and "prudent" were favorite terms used to describe the Bush administration's basic values in directing American foreign policy.[74] President Bush did not come to office with a grand design or with a "vision thing" (as he himself might have said) for reshaping international politics. Instead, his administration's approach really reflected the values, beliefs, and temperament of Bush himself, a moderate, middle-of-the-road professional politician who was well trained in foreign affairs. After all, President Bush had a wealth of foreign policy experience—as director of the CIA, American representative to the People's Republic of China, ambassador to the United Nations, and vice president of the United States. Although at various times he claimed to be from Texas, Connecticut, or Maine, Bush had spent most of the twenty years prior to taking office deep within the establishment of Washington and was fully steeped in the foreign policy emanating from the nation's capital. Thus, he was prepared for the "give and take" of Washington and global politics.

The Commitment to Continuity: A Problem-Solver, Not a Visionary

Although President Bush might have described himself as a policy conservative, he was more than that. He was a problem-solver who worked well with those with whom he disagreed.[75] His underlying political philosophy might best be summarized in this way: Getting results are more important than claiming ideological victory; getting results are the best way to achieve political success.

Because of his cautious nature and his willingness to pursue pragmatic policies, President Bush's initial impulse was less an effort to initiate his own foreign policy approach and more an effort to assure continuity with the last half of the Reagan administration. To be sure, his initial foreign policy action was to call for a complete review in an attempt to separate himself from previous policy. When the review was completed, however, the shape of policy looked only modestly different from that of the Reagan administration during its second term.

The tenets of realism (Chapter 4) come the closest to describing the general principles of Bush's foreign policy making. Bush essentially wanted to deal with the world as it existed and sought only those changes that would not be too unsettling for the international system as a whole. Further, the Bush administration was much more interested in relations with the strong (e.g., the Soviet Union and China) than with the weak (e.g., the Third World nations). In this sense, his policy orientation came closer to the balance of power approach that Nixon, Kissinger, and Ford brought to U.S. policy than to the staunchly anti-Communist, ideological approach of the Reagan years or the idealism of the Carter years. While these earlier principles continued to hold sway, the rapid unravelling of the Cold War from 1989 to 1991 compelled the Bush administration to adopt broader values and beliefs—largely from America's past—to guide U.S. policy for the future.

The personal style of decision making by President Bush gave further reason for asserting that personal values entered into the foreign policy process. Unlike the disengaged style of Reagan, Bush was actively involved in policy making—usually with a relatively small group of advisers. According to observers, he continuously "worked the phone" to accomplish his foreign policy objectives. Since he has served around the world and was vice president for eight years, he did indeed have a close working relationship with leaders from many nations. This personal dimension was most evident during the last half of 1990 and the early part of 1991, as Bush put together, and kept together, the anti-Iraq coalition prior to and during the Persian Gulf War.

Critics of the Bush administration viewed the president's initial pragmatic and cautious approach as indecisive, deliberate, and "ad hoc." Most agreed that the designs of policy were nonexistent or, more charitably, still emerging. As Theodore Sorensen, a former Kennedy administration official, put it, the early part of the Bush administration was "all tactics, no strategy." Moreover, Sorensen argued that "there is a difference between caution and timidity, and Mr. Bush has been excessively timid in his proposals on arms reductions, ethics, and education." Additionally, "he reacts but rarely initiates."[76] Another analyst, William Hyland, a former official in the Ford administration, was more supportive of the Bush administration's deliberate foreign policy approach. "It is the nature of the problems, however, not the style, that has dictated this approach," he contended at the time. When some initial decisions were required, the administration "avoided confrontation with wise compromises" in its early days.[77]

Other questions could be raised about Bush's "hand-on" approach to policy making and the dangers that may result from it. During his administration's decision to support the failed coup attempt in Panama in October 1989, for example, the president was apparently deeply involved in tactical decision making, perhaps much to his regret. By contrast, and perhaps indicative of his later style, he took a more detached approach to conducting the Persian Gulf War and left most tactical decisions to his military advisors. Even in this case, however, he did not stay too far away from the details, with constant briefings and updates.[78]

Bush's Foreign Policy Team: "Sensibly Conservative"[79]

The foreign policy team that occupied Washington in the Bush years, conducted the initial policy review, and made policy decisions generally lent credence to this pragmatic, cautious—yet realist—description of the Bush administration's approach to foreign policy. Like Bush, the people chosen for the key cabinet and national security positions in the administration were individuals without strong ideological posture but given to practical solutions to problems. His choices for secretary of state, James Baker, and national security advisor, Brent Scowcroft, for instance, shared his commitment to incremental change in global affairs. They also were two individuals who could work well with each other and who enjoyed enormous credibility on Capitol Hill. According to one long-time foreign policy analyst, "The Baker-Scowcroft combination is the most competent-looking pair of people any new president has put in those jobs.[80]

The other key foreign policy participants in the Bush cabinet largely shared similar characteristics. At the State Department, Baker's top assistant as deputy secretary of state (and later acting secretary of state when Baker left to run the 1992 presidential campaign) was Lawrence Eagleburger. Eagleburger had been in the Foreign Service for twenty-seven years and had worked with Kissinger Associates, a private international consulting firm headed by Henry Kissinger, between government appointments.[81] At the National Security Council, Scowcroft's top aide, Robert Gates, was perhaps more conservative than his boss, but he appeared to be a team player. Indeed, President Bush nominated him as CIA director in 1991.

At the Department of Defense, the appointment of Richard Cheney reflected a choice of a policy maker of the same calibre as the others. While Cheney, a former member of Congress, had a conservative voting record, he was also viewed as pragmatic and reasonable in his approach to policy questions. His experience as chief of staff during the Ford administration demonstrated his pragmatic approach particularly well, and his handling of policy making during the Persian Gulf troop buildup and during the war itself won him high marks from several quarters.

The same holds true for still other top policy makers. At the CIA, William Webster, Bush's first director and a holdover from the Reagan administration, was generally recognized as a top-flight professional without the ideological fervor of his predecessor, William Casey. At Treasury, Nicholas Brady, a personal friend of the president and a former U.S. senator, came from this moderate policy tradition, as did Carla Hills, the U.S. Trade Representative.

Despite the admiring characterization of the administration's foreign policy advisors as "closely integrated and coherent" and "a parallel-minded team," a danger existed that few dissenters resided within the inner circle of advisors.[82] While the absence of such advisors may have appeared a problem, the personal Bush strategy of consulting widely diminished the potency of this criticism.

POLICY APPROACH OF THE BUSH ADMINISTRATION

As a mechanism for looking to the future, President Bush called for a "policy review" at the very outset of his administration, as we have said. The review process, centered in the National Security Council system, inevitably involved the entire foreign policy machinery. Moreover, it took almost four full months to complete and its results were mainly announced not through a single document, but through a series of speeches that Bush gave in April and May 1989.[83] While the speeches failed to reveal much in the way of new foreign policy departures from the Reagan administration, they conveyed a positive approach toward working with the Soviet Union and Europe.

The Policy Review: Initial Ideas and Proposals

The Soviet Union. The commencement address at Texas A&M University in 1989 is probably the most important statement about the Bush administration's approach because of the considerable amount of ground it covered in dealing with the Soviet Union and the approaching end of the Cold War. As President Bush said, "We are approaching the conclusion of an historic postwar struggle between two visions: one of tyranny and conflict, and one of democracy and freedom.... And now, it is time to move beyond containment to a new policy for the 1990s—one that recognized the full scope of changes taking place around the world and in the Soviet Union itself." His administration, he continued, would "seek the integration of the Soviet Union into the community of nations."

To achieve that aim, however, President Bush outlined a number of changes in Soviet foreign policy that the United States would seek. First, the Soviet Union must change some of its global commitments (e.g., its support for the Sandinista regime in Nicaragua at the time and its ties with Libya). Second, the Soviet Union must undertake several changes in Eastern Europe, including reducing Soviet troops there, abandoning the Brezhnev

Doctrine, and the tearing down of the iron curtain.[84] Third, the Soviet Union must work closely with the West in addressing conflicts in Central America, southern Africa, and the Middle East. Finally, it must also demonstrate a substantial commitment to political pluralism and human rights and must join with the United States in "addressing pressing global problems, including the international drug menace and dangers to the environment."

If these actions were undertaken, the response of the United States to the Soviet Union would be positive. President Bush indicated that he would seek completion of the START negotiations, move toward approving verification procedures to permit the implementation of two signed—but unratified—treaties between the United States and the Soviet Union limiting the size of nuclear tests, and support a renewal of the "open skies" policy between the two nations. Further, as soon as the Soviet Union would reform its emigration laws, the United States would seek a waiver of the requirements of the Jackson-Vanik amendment for the Soviet Union, freeing up trade between the two countries.[85]

National Security. Juxtaposed against this proposed strategy of Soviet-American cooperation, President Bush reaffirmed the commitment to a strong national security strategy for the 1990s, largely consistent with the tradition of the Reagan administration, in his Coast Guard Academy graduation address. The United States would continue "to defend American interests in light of the enduring reality of Soviet military power." It would also seek to "curb the proliferation of advanced weaponry;...check the aggressive ambitions of renegade regimes; and...enhance the ability of our friends to defend themselves." The Bush administration's security strategy was formulated on two key principles: One was to maintain an effective nuclear deterrent through the deployment of the MX missile, the continuance of the SDI initiative, and the development and deployment of a new single-warheaded and mobile missile, the Midgetman; the other was a renewed commitment to arms control and arms reductions in both conventional and nuclear weapons.

Europe. In his other early speeches, President Bush's comments were primarily directed to the future of Eastern Europe. He first applauded the emergence of democracy in Poland, offered various forms of assistance by the United States and the international community, and expressed a hope for future changes in Eastern Europe as well. He later expressed American support for the uniting of Europe into a single market in 1992, for the development of new mechanisms of consultation and cooperation with Europe, and for the maintenance of U.S. military forces in Europe "as long as they are wanted and needed to preserve the peace in Europe."

In his Mainz, West Germany, address, on the occasion of the fortieth anniversary of the NATO alliance, President Bush set forth his view of a new Europe: "Let Europe be whole and free.... The Cold War began with the division of Europe. It can only end when Europe is whole." Four proposals were advanced to reach this goal: (1) "free elections and political pluralism in Eastern Europe;" (2) "glasnost [openness] to East Berlin," with the Berlin

Wall coming down; (3) East and West Europe cooperating on environmental issues; and (4) East and West working to reduce the degree of militarization in Central Europe.

Third World Trouble Spots. Apparently missing from these speeches was a strategy for dealing with the rest of the world. Yet, as revealed during the height of the Persian Gulf War, Bush's Pentagon and CIA advisors had previously given the general direction for dealing with Third World trouble spots in the earlier review:

> In cases where the U.S. confronts much weaker enemies, our challenge will be not simply to defeat them, but to defeat them decisively and rapidly.... For small countries hostile to us, bleeding our forces in protracted or indecisive conflict or embarrassing us by inflicting damage on some conspicuous element of our forces may be victory enough, and could undercut political support for U.S. efforts against them.[86]

Early Actions: A Mix of Moderation, Caution, and Realism

Unlike the bold speeches on the future of Eastern Europe and on ties with the Soviet Union or even the apparent advice on Third World trouble spots, the early policy actions of the Bush administration mainly reflected its impulses of pragmatism and moderation, albeit occasionally mixed with political realism. U.S. policy behavior in four major trouble spots reflected this policy mixture and set the tone for the reaction of the Bush administration to the major political changes that occurred in Central Europe in late 1989 and throughout 1990.

Support for the Nicaraguan Contras. The first instance of the administration's pragmatism and moderation involved policy accommodation with Congress over future support for the Nicaraguan Contras. Realizing that Congress was in no mood to provide further military support, the Bush administration quickly fashioned a bipartisan proposal that provided some support for the Contras, as the president wanted, and which committed the United States to the ongoing Central American peace, as Congress wanted.[87] The package called in $50 million of nonmilitary aid to the Contras and pledged the Bush administration to employ diplomatic and economic measures to pressure the Sandinistas to open up their political system. Further, in yet another effort to cement congressional-executive cooperation, the Bush administration agreed to allow four congressional committees the right to suspend any aid after November 30, 1989.[88] Fortuitously, this policy moderation paid off for both Congress and the administration. The Sandinistas government held to its earlier promise to hold nationwide elections in February 1990. And in a stunning result, the opposition won a convincing victory over the Sandinistas.

Cambodia. This same kind of policy moderation and pragmatism occurred in dealing with the ongoing civil war among the four parties competing to control the government of Cambodia. During the summer of 1990, in a sharp break with previous policy, the Bush administration withdrew its support from the three parties opposed to the Vietnamese-supported government in Cambodia and agreed to have direct talks with the Vietnamese government over the future of Cambodia.[89] This strategy, formulated in cooperation with the Soviet Union, was intended to motivate all parties to accept a UN peace plan for resolving the dispute, first through an internationally supervised cease-fire and then through an internationally supervised election. Within two months of this change in American policy, the four competing parties in Cambodia committed themselves to using the UN framework for settling the conflict.[90] The pragmatic approach of the Bush administration had produced some success.

Panama and Noriega. Policy accommodation, however, was not practiced everywhere by the Bush administration. Its actions toward Panama indicated the willingness to use force to defend American interests and, in effect, to take actions consistent with tenets of political realism. The Panamanian government of General Manuel Antonio Noriega had long been a source of annoyance and trouble for the Reagan administration, and had become so for the Bush administration as well. In February 1988, Noriega, a longtime CIA operative, was indicted on drug trafficking charges by a federal grand jury in Florida and was widely reported to be involved in numerous other unsavory international activities. Although the Reagan administration decided to impose economic sanctions on Panama and to use those and other economic measures as a way to force Noriega's resignation as the head of government,[91] none of these efforts proved successful.

The Bush administration also had to take several measures before it was finally successful against Noriega. First, when Noriega nullified Panama's national election results in May 1989—an election in which the opposition apparently won—the Bush administration asked the Organization of American States (OAS) to investigate. The OAS condemned the actions of the Noriega government and asked that he step down, but Noriega refused. Second, President Bush declared that Noriega's handpicked regime was illegitimate, called for the installation of the democratically elected government, and stated that the American ambassador to Panama, who had been called to Washington for consultations, would not return. In addition, Bush had earlier ordered more American forces into Panama, and, for political effect, the military had conducted exercises in Panama. All of these measures failed to budge Noriega's hold on power. Next, the Bush administration threw lukewarm support behind a coup attempt in October 1989, but it, too, failed within hours, much to the embarrassment of President Bush.[92] Finally, and as a last resort, President Bush ordered 13,000 American troops into Panama (in addition to the 11,000 already stationed at U.S. bases there) in December 1989. The invasion succeeded in a matter of days, and Noriega was captured and returned to the United States to stand trial on the drug trafficking charges. In essence, the Bush administration opted for and sustained a realistic approach in choosing the intervention course.

People's Republic of China. President Bush displayed the same reliance on political realism in his policy toward the People's Republic of China. During

May and early June 1989, massive pro-democracy demonstrations, calling for political reforms within the country, occurred in Beijing and other Chinese cities. The Chinese government tolerated these demonstrations for a time, but it finally decided to put them down militarily. In a violent and bloody assault on the demonstrators in Beijing's Tiananmen Square, the Chinese military killed hundreds, and perhaps thousands, of demonstrators.[93]

The Bush administration reacted initially by condemning the Chinese actions as violations of human rights and throwing its support behind the democracy movement within China. It immediately imposed a series of economic sanctions through an executive order; stopped arms sales; suspended visits between U.S. and Chinese military officials; offered humanitarian and medical assistance to those injured in the military crackdown; and instructed the U.S. immigration service to be sympathetic to Chinese students in the United States wishing to extend their stay. Yet, President Bush still wanted to maintain some ties with China, even in the context of continuing repression: "I understand the importance of the relationship with the Chinese people and the Government, it is in the interest of the United States to have good relations."[94] Indeed, the Bush administration vetoed legislation that would have allowed Chinese students to stay in the United States after their visas had expired, and it authorized high U.S. government officials to meet with Chinese officials, even though a ban on such visits was in effect.

These latter actions set off congressional protests at home over the administration's commitment to promoting global human rights and democracy. The response by the administration was framed largely in terms of realist politics. Despite the unacceptability of Chinese government actions, the administration reasoned, global realities compelled the United States to pursue a foreign policy based upon continued contact with the Beijing government in an effort to affect its actions. Political realism, not domestic moral principles, guided the actions of the Bush administration.

POLITICAL CHANGE AND EASTERN EUROPE

While Nicaragua, Cambodia, Panama, and China demonstrate the mixture of moderation and realism practiced by the Bush administration toward regional trouble spots, the imminent changes in Eastern Europe and within the Soviet Union were to pose the greatest challenge to its policy approach. Yet, in large measure, the Bush administration pursued the same policy mix, even as the Soviet Empire and the Soviet Union itself unraveled. Moderate and pragmatic responses, albeit occasionally infused with doses of political realism, were still the governing principles.

The events of 1989 and 1990 can only be described as monumental in that they shook the foundations of U.S. foreign policy. In the space of less than two years, the Soviet Empire collapsed, with most of the states of Eastern Europe moving from socialist states to capitalist ones and from nondemocratic (Communist) states to democratic ones; the future of a divided Germany was resolved through reunification by the end of 1990; and, by the end of 1991, the Soviet Union itself was dissolved. In effect, the central

CHRONOLOGY 5.1

The Democratization of Four Eastern European Nations, 1989–1990

POLAND

April 1989—The Communist party of Poland and Solidarity, the Polish trade union movement, agree on the legalization of Solidarity and the holding of a national election in June.

June 1989—The first democratic elections are held, with Solidarity candidates winning virtually all available seats in the upper and lower houses of parliament.

August 1989—Tadeusz Mazowiecki of the Solidarity movement is named the prime minister of Poland, although the presidency is still controlled by the Communist party leader, General Jaruzelski.

October 1989—The Polish government announces the "full introduction of market mechanisms and institutions" during 1990 and 1991.

November 1990—Presidential elections are held, and the founder of Solidarity, Lech Walesa, is elected president. Communist party power has thus been replaced in both parliament and the presidency.

HUNGARY

January 1989—Hungarian parliament initiates legislation to guarantee individual liberties.

June 1989—Communist officials allow opposition groups to negotiate for the establishment of a multiparty system in Hungary.

October 1989—The Communist party is officially disbanded and a new party, the Socialist party, replaces it. The parliament establishes the Republic of Hungary to replace the Hungarian People's Republic. A popular referendum is held on the form of government for the nation.

March–April 1990—Free parliamentary elections are held, with the Communist party candidates badly defeated.

CZECHOSLOVAKIA

November 1989—Massive demonstrations call for the resignation of the Communist party and for democratic reforms.

November–December 1989—A series of changing Communist party governments seek to maintain control, but they are rejected by the populace.

December 1989—Popular playwright Vaclav Havel, the leader of Civic Forum, the leading opposition organization, is elected president by the parliament.

June 1990—Free and democratic parliamentary elections are held, with the Communist party candidates faring badly.

issues of the Cold War—a divided Europe and Soviet-American antagonism—were seemingly resolved by these series of events.

Because the political changes were so substantial, a brief sketch of them is necessary to put American foreign policy in the early 1990s into perspective and to appreciate the subsequent policy responses of the Bush and Clinton administrations.

The Collapse of the Soviet Empire

The initial changes within Eastern Europe began in Poland in early 1989.[95] Although *Solidarity*, the banned Polish trade union movement, had operated for many years in Poland, its success in gaining legal status by April

CHRONOLOGY 5.1

The Democratization of Four Eastern European Nations, 1989–1990 (continued)

EAST GERMANY

September 1989—East Germans begin fleeing the country through Austria, Hungary, and Czechoslovakia and through seeking asylum in West German embassies.

October–November 1989—Massive demonstrations calling for democratic reform occur in Leipzig and other East German cities.

October 1989—Long-time Communist party leader Erich Honecker is forced to resign. The communist government resigns in early November.

November 1989—East Germany opens the Berlin Wall and allows free travel in that divided city.

December 1989—The Communist party gives up its monopoly on political power.

March 1990—Free and democratic elections are held in East Germany with conservative and anti-communist parties gaining power.

October 1990—East and West Germany are reunited into the Federal Republic of Germany.

Sources: Peter Hayes, ed., "Chronology 1989" *Foreign Affairs: America and the World 1989/90,* 69 (1990): 218–230; Peter Hayes, ed., "Chronology 1990" *Foreign Affairs: America and the World 1990/91,* 70 (1991): 212–222; Elizabeth A. Palmer, "East Bloc Political Turmoil...Chronology of Big Changes," *Congressional Quarterly Weekly Report,* December 9, 1989, 3376–3377; *The 1990 World Book Yearbook* (Chicago: World Book, Inc., 1990); and *Encyclopedia Britannica 1990 Book of the Year* (Chicago: Encyclopedia Britannica, Inc., 1990).

1989 rapidly set in motion the democratic reform process. By June 1989, Solidarity or Solidarity-backed candidates won all of the available seats in the lower house and 99 out of 100 seats in the upper house in free elections. By August 1989, a Solidarity member was chosen as the first non-Communist prime minister in an Eastern European state since the end of World War II, and a little more than a year later (November 1990), the founder of the Solidarity movement, Lech Walesa, was elected president.

Hungary and Czechoslovakia followed a similar pattern. In Hungary, the parliament took the first steps to guarantee individual liberties to its citizens in January 1989, and, by October 1989, it adopted a number of sweeping democratic reforms. Parliamentary elections were held in March and April 1990, with the democratic parties and their coalition partners capturing most of the seats. In Czechoslovakia, the change to democracy was even more rapid and equally nonviolent. While the first popular demonstrations for democracy occurred there later (November 1989) than elsewhere, once started, democratic change occurred quickly. By early December, Vaclav Havel, the playwright and leader of the reform movement, was named as president. By June 1990, free and democratic parliamentary elections were held in Czechoslovakia with democratic reform candidates faring very well.

In East Germany, pressures for democratic reform began as early as August 1989, when East Germans fled to West Germany, using Hungary, Czechoslovakia, and Austria as access routes, or sought asylum in the West German embassies in East Berlin. By October 1989, the number of East Germans seeking asylum numbered almost 11,000. Popular demonstrations

CHRONOLOGY 5.2

The Division and Reunification of Germany, 1945–1990

February 1945—The Yalta Conference decides upon zones of occupation in Germany by the four major allied powers. Eventually, Britain, France, the United States, and the Soviet Union have zones of occupation. Berlin, the German capital, is also divided into these four occupation zones.

September 1949—The Federal Republic of Germany is formed from the Western zones of Germany (occupied by Britain, France and the U.S.).

October 1949—The German Democratic Republic is established in the Soviet zone of occupied Germany. Berlin remains divided among the four allied powers.

August 1961—The Berlin Wall is built by the Soviet Union and East Germany to keep East and West divided.

December 1972—The Basic Treaty is signed between East and West Germany, calling for two German states in one German nation. The division between the two states remains, even as they begin some social, economic, and political contacts.

August–October 1989—Thousands of east Germans seek to escape to the West through third countries, and thousands of others call for democratic reforms in East Germany.

November 1989—The Berlin Wall is opened by East Germany, and calls for German reunification begin. West German Chancellor Helmut Kohl offers a plan for the confederation of East and West Germany.

February 1990—East German Prime Minister Hans Modrow announces plans for the reunification of the two Germanys. The foreign ministers from the four allied countries and from East and West Germany agree upon the mechanism for discussing the reunification of Germany.

May–August 1990—Social, economic, and legal agreements are reached on reunification between East and West Germany with the economic union initiated on July 1.

September 1990—The four allied powers formally relinquish their rights over Germany and grant full sovereignty to the German state.

October 3, 1990—The formal unification of East and West Germany takes place under the name of the Federal Republic of Germany.

December 2, 1990—Democratic elections are held in the new German state.

Sources: Peter Hayes, ed., "Chronology 1989" *Foreign Affairs: America and the World 1989/90,* 69 (1990): 218–235; Peter Hayes, ed., "Chronology 1990" *Foreign affairs: America and the World 1990/91,* 70 (1991): 212–226; Elizabeth A. Palmer, "East Bloc Political Turmoil...Chronology of Big Changes," *Congressional Quarterly Weekly Report,* December 9, 1989, 3376–3377; Thomas L. Friedman, "Four Allies Give Up Rights in Germany," *New York Times,* September 13, 1990, A1 and A6; and "One Germany: Next Steps," *New York Times,* July 18, 1990, A4.

followed, and by March 1990, free and democratic elections were held in East Germany, with the conservative Alliance for Germany obtaining the greatest percentage of votes.

Nascent democratic movements characterized other Eastern European states, but their turn to democracy was slower and generally much less complete. Bulgaria, Romania, Yugoslavia, and Albania experienced calls for reform, but democratic reform was less certain in each case. Elections in Bulgaria, Romania, and Albania produced regimes that grew out of the former Communist parties or that were closely allied with them. Within the former Yugoslavia, a series of successor states emerged, but the degree of democratic reform was less certain immediately. Instead, intercommunal violence developed among the religious and ethnic groups within some of these new states (e.g., Bosnia) and between others (e.g., Serbia and Croatia).

The Unification of Germany

The unification of Germany was the second major Eastern European event of 1989–1990 and the one most directly related to the ending of the Cold War. Germany, which had been consciously divided by the victorious allies at the Yalta Conference in February 1945, and which had existed as two separate states from 1949 to 1990 was formally reunited on October 3, 1990.[96] Despite the pace of events elsewhere in Eastern Europe during the previous two years, both the ease and speed of this reunification—from mid-1989 through the end of 1990—were spectacular by any assessment. While the pressures for reunification began with the massive East German emigration to the West in August 1989, the opening of the Berlin Wall—the most tangible symbol of a divided city in a divided nation—on November 9, 1989, ignited even more calls for political reunification.

Despite Soviet President Mikhail Gorbachev's contention on November 15, 1989, that German unification "is not a matter of topical politics,"[97] West German Chancellor Helmut Kohl first proposed a "confederation" of the two Germanies in late November 1989. While the major wartime allies—the United States, France, Britain, and the USSR—still retained rights over the future of Germany and, in particular, Berlin, this obstacle was quickly overcome. At a February 1990 meeting of the foreign ministers from these allied countries and from East and West Germany, a formula was agreed upon for the eventual reunification of Germany. These so-called "four plus two" talks called for the two Germanys to discuss their plans for reunification and then to meet with the four allied powers to resolve remaining security matters.

By May 1990, East and West Germany had worked out the terms for completing reunification. Existing borders were agreed upon; an economic union was initiated on July 1, 1990; a treaty setting out the legal and social bases of the new union was signed on August 31, 1990; a formal treaty among the allied powers, renouncing their rights and powers over German affairs, was completed on September 12, 1990;[98] and formal reunification, under the name of the Federal Republic of Germany, took place on October 3, 1990.[99] Finally, democratic parliamentary elections across the unified German state were held in December 1990.

POLITICAL CHANGE AND THE SOVIET UNION

The Soviet Union itself was not immune to the changes that were sweeping Eastern Europe. While the changes in the Soviet state were not as rapid in 1989 and 1990 as they were elsewhere in Eastern Europe, change quickened by 1991, eventually producing the demise of the state itself. Initially, reform efforts were undertaken largely within the limits of maintaining a modified Socialist system. After a coup attempt by Soviet hard-liners against these reforms failed in August 1991, change accelerated once again. Calls

CHRONOLOGY 5.3

Political Change Within the Soviet Union, 1985–1991

March 1985—Mikhail Gorbachev is named general secretary of the Communist party after the death of Konstantin Chernenko.
June 1985—Gorbachev calls for new economic policies and initiates the process of *perestroika* (restructuring) with an initial economic reform plan proposed in October 1985.
July–September 1985—Long-time foreign minister Andrei Gromyko is replaced by Eduard Shevardnadze, a close ally of Gorbachev. Prime Minister Nikolai Tikhonov retires and is succeeded by Nikolai Ryzhkov.
June 1986—Gorbachev announces his intention to open up the Soviet system by establishing a program of *glasnost* (openness), in which government censorship would be reduced.
November 1986—The Supreme Soviet, the national parliament, approves legislation that would allow some private enterprise by Soviet citizens.
July 1988—Gorbachev proposes a restructuring of the Soviet government: the president would be given more power but would be chosen by a more representative national parliament; key officials would have limited terms; multiple candidates would be allowed in elections; and more authority would be granted to local governing bodies. The plan is quickly approved by the Communist party and later by the Supreme Soviet.
March 1989—The first national elections to the new parliament, the Congress of People's Deputies, are held. Multiple candidates are on the ballot, and numerous Communist party members are defeated. Two months later, Gorbachev is elected president of the Soviet Union by this body.
February 1990—The Central Committee of the Communist Party of the Soviet Union recommends that Article 6 of the Soviet constitution—granting the Party a monopoly on power—be changed.
March 1990—Lithuania, a Baltic republic forcefully incorporated into the Soviet Union in 1940, declares its independence from Moscow and forms a new non-Communist government. This action sparks calls for independence in many of the other Republics within the Soviet Union.
October 1990—The "Gorbachev Plan" for economic *perestroika* is approved by the Supreme Soviet, but it calls for a slower transition to a market economy than the 500-day Shatalin Plan that was originally proposed.
December 1990—Eduard Shevardnadze, foreign minister of the USSR, resigns his post and warns that reform efforts are being threatened by reactionary forces and that dictatorship may reemerge in the Soviet Union.

were now made for greater regional autonomy and greater democratization, and the future of the Soviet Union as a unified state appeared in doubt. By late 1991, moreover, the Baltic republics had achieved independence, and a looser confederation emerged among the Soviet republics. By December 1991, the Soviet Union itself collapsed. New nations replaced the former union and challenged long-held American thinking on foreign policy.

Changes Within the Soviet Union Before the August 1991 Coup

Two kinds of changes occurred within the Soviet Union before the August 1991 coup: (1) efforts at institutionalizing democratic political reforms and

CHRONOLOGY 5.3

Political Change Within the Soviet Union, 1985–1991 (continued)

January 1991—Reform efforts are stalled as Soviet troops are ordered into several republics to halt independence movements. Several citizens are attacked and killed in Lithuania.
April 1991—Nine republics of the Soviet Union agree in principle to sign a new Union Treaty in which more power would be granted to the republics, although central authority would be retained.
June 1991—Boris Yeltsin, an advocate of more rapid change within the Soviet Union and an opponent of Gorbachev, is popularly elected as president of the Russian Republic, the largest republic within the Soviet Union.
August 18, 1991—The "State Committee for the State of Emergency," a group of close associates to Gorbachev, seizes power in the Soviet Union and ousts him from office. Popular opposition, led by Russian President Boris Yeltsin, quickly develops, and within three days the coup collapses.
August–September 1991—Gorbachev returns to power, albeit in a politically weakened condition, while Boris Yeltsin's relative influence increases. Gorbachev quickly announces the end of the Communist party's role within the Soviet Union and appoints officials committed to hastening reform. Virtually all of the Soviet republics demand autonomy, however, and the future unity of the Soviet Union appears threatened.
September 2, 1991—A proposal is submitted to the Congress of People's Deputies to create a more confederative Soviet Union in which political power would be devolved to the constituent Republics, although the central government would maintain military and security powers.
September 5,1991—The Congress of People's Deputies approves a new interim confederative arrangement for the Soviet Union.
December 25, 1991—The Soviet Union is formally dissolved.

Sources: Kay King, ed., "Chronology 1985" *Foreign Affairs: America and the World 1985* 64 (1986): 654; Sara Robertson, ed., "Chronology 1986" *Foreign Affairs: America and the World 1986* 65 (1987): 667–668; Peter Hayes, ed., "Chronology 1988" *Foreign Affairs: America and the World 1989/90* 68 (1989): 226–230; Peter Hayes, ed., "Chronology 1989" *Foreign Affairs: America and the World 1989/90* 69 (1990): 218–230; Peter Hayes, ed., "Chronology 1990" *Foreign Affairs: America and the World 1990/91* 70 (1991): 212–222; "Gorbachev's Six Years," *The Wall Street Journal,* August 20, 1991, A10; Serge Schmemann, "Gorbachev, Yeltsin, and Republic Leaders Move to Take Power from Soviet Congress," *New York Times,* September 3, 1991, A1 and A6; and Serge Schmemann, "Soviet Congress Yields Rule to Republics to Avoid Political and Economic Collapse," *New York Times,* September 6, 1991, A1 and A6.

Western-style market reforms; and (2) pressures for greater autonomy and even independence by some of the constituent republics.

The efforts at democratic political reform within the Soviet Union were essential parts of Mikhail Gorbachev's implementation of *glasnost* and *perestroika,* the mechanism for making the country more efficient and competitive globally. In March 1989, for example, in the freest election since the 1917 Revolution, voting was held for seats in the new legislative body, the Congress of People's Deputies.[100] Later in the year, an effort was even undertaken to eliminate the "leading role" of the Communist party in the Soviet Union. By February 1990, the party adopted a platform that opened up the Soviet system to more than one party.[101] In 1990, more reforms were tried, albeit with mixed success. Local and constituent republic elections were held, and the Supreme Soviet, the national legislature of the USSR, approved new press freedom.

Market reform progressed more slowly. By the second half of 1990, a plan for a 500-day transition to a market economy was developed, but that one as well as less dramatic versions of it were shelved by the end of the year. During the last months of 1990 and early 1991, however, Gorbachev moved toward slowing down and even halting the political and economic liberalizations that he had initiated. Many of the internal reforms within the Soviet Union appeared stalled by the middle of 1991, and economic conditions worsened.

The other dramatic internal changes within the Soviet Union were the pressures for independence by several of the constituent Republics. The three Baltic states of Latvia, Lithuania, and Estonia took the boldest steps in this regard by passing various measures declaring their independence or eventual independence from the central government in Moscow. In addition, other republics, such as Georgia and Armenia and even the largest Soviet Republic, Russia, sought to achieve greater independence. Hence, Gorbachev and the rest of the Soviet leadership were required to devote a considerable amount of time and resources, including the use of economic sanctions and military force, to hold the USSR together.

After the Coup: The Collapse of the Soviet Union

While President Gorbachev had sought to produce change inside the Soviet Union within the context of maintaining strong central authority, impetus for even greater change occurred after a coup in late August 1991. On the day prior to the signing of the proposed union treaty, in which greater power would have in fact been dispersed to the constituent Republics, a group of hard-line Communist party members and government officials (the "State Committee for the State of Emergency") deposed Mikhail Gorbachev and seized power briefly. The "three-day coup" (August 18–21, 1991) collapsed due to (1) massive protests in Moscow led by the popularly elected president of the Russian Republic, Boris Yeltsin, (2) the apparent failure of the KGB to attack the protestors surrounding the Russian parliament, and (3) the virtually unified international condemnation. Upon his return to power, Gorbachev called the failed coup "a majority victory for perestroika" and pledged "to move ahead democratically in all areas."[102]

Ironically, the coup attempt had the effect of pressuring for even greater reform within the Soviet Union and further weakening the central government. With Gorbachev's power effectively curtailed in this new environment, he felt compelled to abandon his role as general secretary of the Communist party. Indeed, he called for a disbanding of the party itself because of its role in the coup. Furthermore, he consulted with the president of the Russian Republic, Boris Yeltsin, over the appointment of a number of key political offices and named several key officials from that republic to leadership posts within the central government.

Increased demands for independence by the constituent republics raised doubts about the future of the Soviet Union as a unified state. Within weeks of the coup, in fact, Lithuania, Latvia, and Estonia finally obtained their independence, and a new transitional confederative arrangement was devised between the central government and most of the Republics. Eventually, a new constitution would be formulated for a new Soviet state structure, with more policy control to the constituent Republics.[103] As with political change in Eastern Europe, the process of reform within the Soviet Union took on a life of its own, aided ironically by a coup that sought to topple the effort. By December 1991, the pressure's for formal dissolution of the Soviet Union were rapidly building and, on December 25, 1991, the Soviet Union was formally dissolved, some seventy-four years after the Bolshevik Revolution of 1917.

AFTER THE COLD WAR: POLICY TOWARD CENTRAL EUROPE

Throughout the period of these changes in Central Europe and the Soviet Union, the Bush administration was largely an interested spectator, not an active participant. Its policy approach was to encourage change in Central Europe and in the Soviet Union without trying to shape it directly. The administration also was careful to avoid any actions that would embarrass the Soviet Union or the Eastern European governments as they sought to undertake change. Similarly, the United States sought to refrain from any actions that might appear as "gloating" over the extraordinary movement to democracy and capitalism in these countries. In short, its pragmatic and cautionary approach toward U.S. foreign policy remained intact, even in a context of dynamic global change, and its policy goal as well: a "Europe whole and free."

Perhaps indicative of the policy caution on the part of the United States was President Bush's restrained reaction on the day that the Berlin Wall was opened between East and West—undoubtedly one of the most dramatic moments in recent political history. Although President Bush claimed that he was "elated" by the development, he went on to justify his reserve by indicating that "I'm just not an emotional kind of guy," and that "We're handling this properly with the allies..." Another administration official acknowledged the largely rhetorical nature of U.S. policy and argued for the measured American reaction to changing events: "I admit that when all is said and done it is a policy largely of stated desires and rhetoric. But what would you have us do? What we are dealing with in Eastern Europe, and to a lesser extent in the Soviet Union, is a revolutionary situation."[104]

Policy Toward Central Europe and Germany

Once these revolutionary changes were well underway, however, the Bush administration did outline tangible policy positions toward Central Europe, the reunification of Germany, and future relations with the Soviet Union. Toward Central Europe, the principal policy response was to provide some economic assistance to these new democracies and to encourage other European states (and particularly the European Community) to do so as well.

In visits to Poland and Hungary in 1989, for example, President Bush offered aid to both countries, and by the end of that year, Congress had approved an aid package that totaled over $900 million. The funds would aid efforts to stabilize the economy; foster private enterprise; provide food aid, trade credits, and environmental funds; and support agricultural programs, technical training, and scholarship and exchanges with the United States.[105] In November 1990, President Bush visited Czechoslovakia and promised economic assistance to that country as well, and Congress in turn earmarked $370 million to assist the newly developing democracies in Central Europe.[106]

Toward the future of Germany, the Bush administration added elements of realism to its accommodative stance, especially after the collapse of the Berlin Wall in November 1989. Beginning as early as December 1989, the Bush administration policy adopted the view that German reunification should proceed, that Germany's full sovereignty should be restored, and that other states (including the United States) would necessarily lose some of their rights over German territory. Somewhat later, it also made clear that it would accept only a reunified Germany that allowed the state to remain a full member of NATO.[107] This clear policy position proved significant in bringing about a unified Germany. In this respect, the Bush administration had clearly decided on its view of Germany's future and the kind of Central Europe that it sought.

Policy Toward the Soviet Union Through 1991

Prior to the breakup of the Soviet Union, the Bush administration's policy toward that nation was cautiously optimistic, albeit not fully developed. The administration sought first to end the Cold War formally and then to establish the foundation for a long-term cooperative relationship with the Soviet Union. In 1989 and 1990, two major summits were held, and important agreements were signed to reach the first goal; and several agreements and understanding's on political, military, and economic cooperation were initiated to move toward the second goal.

The Malta and Washington Summits. The Malta Summit was held in November 1989, and proved to be a watershed conference in ending the Cold War between the United States and the Soviet Union. As President Gorbachev indicated at that summit: "The world leaves one epoch of cold war and enters another epoch" and "the characteristics of the cold war should be abandoned."[108] At Malta, too, the Bush administration and the Soviet leadership committed themselves to make rapid progress on nuclear and conventional arms control. The Bush administration also threw its support behind the internal reforms initiated within the Soviet Union and pledged to assist the Soviet Union in joining the world economy. The administration did so after the Soviet Union had indicated its willingness to accept the ongoing changes in Central Europe, and after it had decided that internal reforms within the Soviet Union were consistent with U.S. interests.[109] In a matter of months, the Soviet Union gained observer status in the General Agreement on Tariffs and Trade (GATT) with U.S. assistance.[110]

If the Malta Summit set the tone for the end of the Cold War and for future relations, the leaders took several concrete steps to solidify the new relationship at the June 1990 Washington Summit. Agreements were signed (1) calling for the destruction of a substantial portion of each nation's chemical arsenal by the year 2002, (2) pledging both parties to accelerate negotiation on the Strategic Arms Reduction Treaty (START) and the Conventional (i.e., non-nuclear) Arms Forces in Europe (CFE) Treaty, and (3) initiating several cultural exchange pacts between the countries.[111] In an unexpected move at this summit, the United States agreed to a treaty that would normalize trade and economic ties with the Soviet Union and grant it most-favored nation (MFN) status. The Bush administration, however, placed an important condition on its signing of the treaty; it would not send the treaty for the Senate's advice and consent until the Soviet law on emigration was changed.[112] In December 1990, the Bush administration, however, temporarily lifted a portion of the Jackson-Vanik amendment and approved up to $1 billion in loans to assist the Soviet Union in meeting 1990–91 winter food shortages. Seven months later, the administration granted another waiver and offered new agricultural credits totaling $1.5 billion.[113]

CSCE and CFE. Toward the end of 1990, the Bush administration made three other important commitments that served as the capstone for the ending of the Cold War in Central Europe and setting the stage for European politics for the 1990s and beyond.[114] First, at the Conference on Security and Cooperation in Europe (CSCE) in November 1990, the United States and its NATO allies and the Soviet Union and its Warsaw Pact allies signed the Conventional Armed Forces in Europe (CFE) Treaty, which provided for a substantial reduction in conventional forces on both sides. Second, these states also signed a declaration of nonaggression between the two sides to end, officially, the Cold War. Third, the parties to the CSCE (which includes the United States, Canada, and virtually all European states) signed an agreement to give the CSCE a greater role in future European affairs. Under this "Paris Charter for a New Europe," the CSCE was to become the central mechanism for dealing with peace and security in Central Europe. Finally, and in another important symbol of the end of the Cold War in Central Europe, the Warsaw Pact—the military alliance among the Soviet Union and its former satellites in Eastern Europe—was formally disbanded at the end of March 1991.

New Political, Military, and Economic Cooperation. Yet another sign of the importance that the Bush administration attached to the new relationship with the Soviet Union was signaled in its attitude and policy toward the Soviet Union's effort to dissuade the Baltic Republics (Lithuania, Latvia, and Estonia) from pursuing independence in the spring of 1990 and the winter of 1991. In both instances, the Gorbachev government used economic sanctions and Soviet troops to stop these efforts. Although the Bush administration decried these actions, it did not do much more. (In January 1991, though, the Bush administration postponed a planned summit meeting, ostensibly because of the Persian Gulf War, but undoubtedly due to

DOCUMENT SUMMARY 5.1

Key Components of the Strategic Arms Reduction Treaty, July 1991

Limitations on Numbers of Nuclear Warheads and Delivery Vehicles

	U.S.	USSR
Total nuclear delivery vehicles (land-based and sea-based ballistic missiles and intercontinental bombers) allowed	1,600	1,600
Total accountable warheads on all nuclear delivery vehicles allowed	6,000	6,000
Total warheads on land-based or sea-based ballistic missiles allowed	4,900	4,900
Total warheads allowed on mobile land-based missiles	1,100	1,100
Nuclear warheads not covered by the treaty	c. 4,400	c. 2,000

Inspection and Verification Provisions

- Exchange of information between the U.S. and the USSR on all strategic offensive weapons would take place prior to treaty signing.
- Twelve types of on-site inspections would be allowed under the agreement.
- Several types of cooperative procedures will be implemented to ensure verification.

Duration and Implementation of the Treaty

The treaty will be implemented over a seven-year period and will last for fifteen years. It may be continued in intervals of five years thereafter.

Sources: Eric Schmitt, "Senate Approval and Sharp Debate Seen," *New York Times,* July 19, 1991, A5 (including the accompanying table entitled "New Limits on Strategic Weapons"); and Office of Public Affairs, U.S. Arms Control and Disarmament Agency, "Strategic Arms Reduction Talks," *Issues Brief,* April 25, 1991.

Soviet action in Lithuania.) In effect, the Bush administration's commitment to political realism surfaced once again.

In July 1991, the Bush administration took two additional steps—one military, another economic—as part of its new policy approach toward the Soviet Union. In the military area, President Bush and President Gorbachev met after the London economic summit among leaders of the industrial democracies (United States, France, Britain, Canada, Germany, Italy, Japan, and the European Community) and completed work in principle on a Strategic Arms Reduction Treaty (START).[115] (The agreement was formally signed about two weeks later at a hastily arranged summit in Moscow.) Under this agreement, the first in which the long-range nuclear arsenals of the two superpowers would actually be reduced, each side would trim the number of nuclear warheads and the number of nuclear delivery vehicles (land-based missiles, sea-based missiles, and intercontinental bombers) in their arsenals. (Document Summary 5.1 provides details on these numbers.) Furthermore, the agreement would allow twelve types of on-site inspections by each side and would require each side not to interfere in efforts by the other to monitor compliance. Moreover, it would be put into place over seven years and last for fifteen years (unless replaced by another agreement). This agreement concluded negotiations begun in June 1982 and represented a remarkable change in Soviet-American relations.

In the economic area, an agreement, also completed after the London economic summit, called for economic assistance for the Soviet Union by the industrial democracies. While these countries would not provide immediate financial aid to the Soviet Union, they did agree upon several different measures to aid the economic reform under way there. These included "special association" status for the Soviet Union with the International Monetary Fund and the World Bank (much as President Bush had done earlier), cooperation between the Soviet Union and all international economic institutions, the restoration of trade between the Soviet Union and its Central European neighbors, and closer contacts among the leaders of the industrial democracies and the Soviet Union.[116] While these actions may not have gone as far as the Soviet Union had initially hoped, they represented an extraordinary change in the economic relationship among the United States, the West, and the Soviet Union.

In the aftermath of the August coup within the Soviet Union and with the movement to a more confederative state in late 1991, the Bush administration faced calls to initiate new and wider economic and political ties with the constituent republics and the newly independent Baltic states. The Bush administration proceeded with diplomatic recognition for Lithuania, Latvia, and Estonia, albeit after several European states and the European Community had done so,[117] and promised to supply humanitarian aid to the Soviet Union as needed, albeit to the constituent Republics, not the central government.[118] Yet, there were limits as to how far it would go in providing massive economic assistance. In general, the Bush administration did not deviate from its policy announced after the London summit which, in effect, withheld economic aid until significant and sustained policy reforms were carried out.

THE SEARCH FOR A NEW WORLD ORDER?

With the international politics of the post–World War II period forever altered by the collapse of the Soviet Empire and the Soviet Union, the Bush administration sought to devise a new rationale and direction for U.S. foreign policy. The change was first hinted at in an address that President Bush gave to the UN General Assembly in September 1989, but it was more fully outlined in speeches to a joint session of Congress in September 1990, and the State of the Union address in January 1991, after Iraq's invasion of Kuwait.[119] The future direction, President Bush said, was to build "a new world order."[120]

President Bush described the new world order in this way: "a new era—freer from the threat of terror, stronger in the pursuit of justice, and more secure in the quest for peace, an era in which the nations of the world, East and West, North and South, can prosper and live in harmony." Such a world would be different from the one that had existed over the past forty-five years. It would be "a world where the rule of law supplants the rule of the jungle, a world in which nations recognize the shared responsibility for freedom and justice, a world where the strong respect the rights of the weak."[121] In his State of the Union address, President Bush summarized this new world order as a condition "where diverse nations are drawn together in common cause to achieve the universal aspirations of mankind: peace and security, freedom, and the rule of law."[122]

Yet, President Bush was quick to add that the United States had a special role to play in creating this new world:

> For two centuries, America has served the world as an inspiring example of freedom and democracy. For generations, America has led the struggle to preserve and extend the blessings of liberty.... American leadership is indispensable....we have a unique responsibility to the hard work of freedom.[123]

The new world order that the Bush administration envisioned, in effect, represented a reaffirmation of the traditional values that had shaped the birth of the nation and its foreign policy actions in its earliest years (see Chapter 1). Unlike the foreign policy at the beginning of the Republic, however, the emphasis on traditional values was coupled with a commitment to sustained American involvement. In both tone and emphasis, moreover, the new world order of the Bush administration had the ring of Wilsonian idealism, which emphasized the League of Nations and collective security at the end of World War I. With the demise of the old order, the Cold War system, the new world order of the Bush administration envisioned an order grounded in the cooperation of all states and based upon greater involvement of the collective security actions of the United Nations. To be sure, Bush did not convey the same fervor in calling for this new system as had Wilson, and he continued to embrace the principles of political realism from time to time. Nonetheless, Bush did see his approach as an important departure from America's recent past (Cold War) behavior. His search to create a new world order quickly faced at least three major tests: the Iraqi invasion of Kuwait, the formation of policy toward a post-Communist Russia, and the new challenges from global disorder in Bosnia, Somalia, and Haiti.

The Persian Gulf War

The event that sparked the effort to think about a new world order was Iraqi President Saddam Hussein's invasion of Kuwait on August 2, 1990. Iraq's action raises the question of whether the initial cooperation between the United States and the (then) Soviet Union could be sustained in another arena and whether the global community could rally around a common task. As events were to unfold, the first test of the new world order appeared to succeed: Soviet-American cooperation was sustained; the global community was largely supportive of this effort as well; and aggression was reversed.

U.S.-Iraqi Relations, 1984–1990. In some respects, the vigorous response of the Bush administration to Iraq's action may have been unexpected. On the one hand, the United States had sought to better relations with Iraq during the 1980s: Diplomatic relations had been restored in 1984, after

MAP 5.2

The Persian Gulf and Southwest Asia

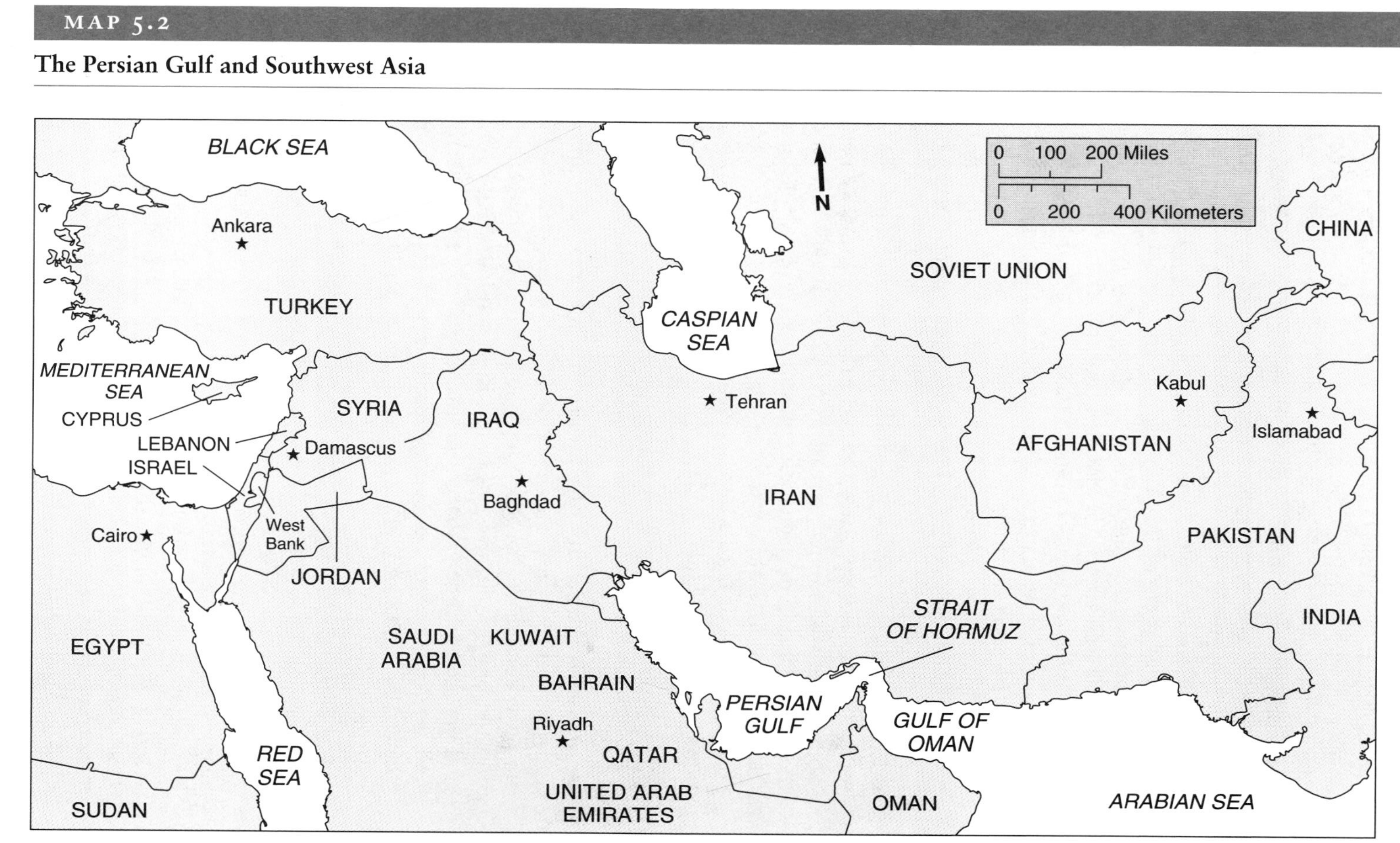

being ruptured since 1967, and the United States had "tilted" toward Iraq during the Iran-Iraq War. On the other hand, the Reagan administration had its quarrels with Iraq: It had been displeased over Iraq's apparent mistaken attack upon the USS *Stark* in the Persian Gulf in May 1987, resulting in the death of thirty-seven American sailors, and it had protested to Iraq in 1988 over its use of chemical weapons against its Kurdish ethnic minority.[124]

In keeping with its realist principles, however, the Bush administration decided early on to try to foster better relations with Iraq for both strategic and economic reasons. Iraq's location in the Persian Gulf area was important in efforts at achieving stability in the region, and its considerable oil reserves made Iraq crucial for global energy concerns. When Congress sought in early 1990 to enact economic sanctions against the Iraqi government over its abysmal human rights policy and the apparent effort to develop weapons of mass destruction, the administration argued against such an option.[125] Later, in the summer of 1990, when Iraq complained that Kuwait was responsible for keeping oil prices low (and hence hurting the Iraqi economy) by overproducing its oil quota, called for an OPEC meeting to raise oil prices, and threatened an invasion of Kuwait, the Bush administration's policy position did not really change. Indeed, the American ambassador in Baghdad actually seemed to reassure Saddam Hussein of U.S. disinterest in these questions: "I have direct instructions from President Bush to seek better relations with Iraq," and that "we have no opinion on the Arab-Arab conflicts, like your border disagreement with Kuwait." Furthermore, in testimony on Capitol Hill only days before the intervention, the administration did not issue any warning when asked about a possible Iraqi invasion into Kuwait.[126]

Response to the Seizure of Kuwait. Despite the Bush administration's equivocal attitude in the summer of 1990, its response to the Iraqi invasion was immediate: It condemned the Iraqi action and called for its withdrawal from Kuwait, froze all Iraqi and Kuwaiti assets in the United States, and imposed a trade embargo on Iraq as well. The European Community and the Arab League condemned the invasion, too. Most important, the Soviet Union joined the United States in opposing the action in a joint statement issued by Secretary of State James Baker and Soviet Foreign Minister Eduard Shevardnadze.[127] A few weeks later, President Bush and President Gorbachev arranged a meeting in Helsinki, Finland, to deal with this crisis and concluded by jointly stating that "Iraq's aggression must not be tolerated."[128] Within a matter of a few weeks, about 100 nations had condemned Iraq's invasion of Kuwait.

On August 8, 1990, the Bush administration announced that it was sending about 150,000 American forces into Saudi Arabia and the surrounding region for the purpose of helping that country defend its homeland against possible Iraqi aggression. President Bush outlined four policy goals that the United States sought to achieve in taking this action against Iraq: (1) "the immediate, unconditional, and complete withdrawal of all Iraqi forces from Kuwait"; (2) "the restoration of Kuwait's legitimate government"; (3) the protection of American citizens in Iraq and Kuwait; and (4) the achievement of "security and stability" in the Persian Gulf.[129] Two days later, the

CHRONOLOGY 5.4

The Persian Gulf War, 1990–1991

August 2, 1990—Iraqi forces invade Kuwait and seize control of that nation. The United Nations Security Council condemns the Iraqi action and calls for the unconditional withdrawal of Iraq from Kuwait.
August 2–4, 1990—The United States, France, Britain, and the European Community condemn the invasion and impose economic sanctions against Iraq. The Arab League condemns the Iraqi action as well.
August 8, 1990—President Bush announces that the United States will send American forces to Saudi Arabia to protect that country from Iraqi aggression and to seek to restore independence for Kuwait. Operation Desert Shield begins.
August 10, 1990—The Arab League votes to send forces to defend Saudi Arabia. Over the next few weeks, other countries make similar commitments, and, in all, some twenty-eight nations form the anti-Iraq coalition of military forces in and around Saudi Arabia.
September 9, 1990—Soviet President Mikhail Gorbachev and President George Bush meet in Helsinki, Finland, and issue a joint statement calling for Iraq "to withdraw unconditionally from Kuwait."
August–November 1990—The United Nations Security Council passes ten resolutions calling for economic sanctions against Iraq, authorizing various measures to enforce those sanctions, and condemning its annexation of Kuwait and its holding of foreign nationals and diplomats.
November 8, 1990—President Bush announces that American forces in the Persian Gulf will be increased to enable them to possess an offensive capability.
November 29, 1990—The United Nations Security Council votes to authorize member states to "use all necessary means" to enforce the previously passed UN resolutions, but allows Iraq until January 15, 1991, to comply with the resolutions.
January 12, 1991—The U.S. Senate, by a vote of 52–47, approves a resolution authorizing the president to implement the UN resolutions; the House of Representatives does likewise by a vote of 250–183.
January 16, 1991—The allied coalition forces begin a massive bombing attack against Iraq and occupied Kuwait. Operation Desert Storm begins.
February 23, 1991—A massive ground assault is undertaken by allied forces to expel Iraq from Kuwait.
February 27, 1991—President Bush declares that "Kuwait has been liberated," and calls for a suspension of hostilities by the allied coalition at midnight, February 28.
March 3, 1991—The United Nations Security Council passes a resolution suspending the Persian Gulf War, placing the liabilities for the war upon Iraq. Allied and Iraqi commanders meet in southern Iraq to formalize the cease-fire and set the terms of peace and the procedures for the exchange of prisoners of war.
April 3, 1991—The United Nations Security Council passes a resolution formally ending the Persian Gulf War and requiring Iraq to destroy chemical and biological weapons, renounce terrorism, use a portion of its oil income to repair damage in Kuwait, and accept the "inviolability" of the frontier between Iraq and Kuwait.

Sources: Peter Hayes, ed., "Chronology 1990" *Foreign Affairs: America and the World 1990/91* 70 (1991): 226–232; Andrew Rosenthal, "Bush Calls Halt to Allied Offensive; Declares Kuwait Free, Iraq Beaten; Sets Stiff Terms for Full Cease-fire," *New York Times,* February 28, 1991, A1; R. W. Apple, Jr., "U.S. Says Iraqi Generals Agree to Demands 'On All Matters'; Early P.O.W. Release Expected," *New York Times,* March 4, 1991, A1 and A6; "New U.S. Hint about Hussein," *New York Times,* March 4, 1991, A6; Paul Lewis, "UN Security Council Drafts Plan to Scrap Most Deadly Iraqi Arms," *New York Times,* March 27, 1991, A1 and A6; Paul Lewis, "UN Votes Stern Conditions for Formally Ending War; Iraqi Response Is Uncertain," *New York Times,* April 4, 1991, A1 and A7; and "UN Conditions," *Des Moines Register,* April 4, 1991, 14A.

Arab League also voted to send forces to Saudi Arabia to stop further Iraqi aggression.[130] Within a matters of weeks, at least twenty-eight nations from virtually every continent had sent forces to Saudi Arabia on behalf of this effort to defer further Iraqi aggression and to seek to get Iraq out of Kuwait as well. Other nations (e.g., Germany and Japan) pledged financial assistance.[131]

The UN Security Council also quickly took concerted actions against the Iraqi government over its invasion of Kuwait. Within hours of the invasion, the Security Council condemned the invasion and further demanded the immediate withdrawal of Iraq. In all, the UN Security Council passed ten resolutions against Iraq's invasion of Kuwait over the next several months. The resolutions sought to tighten the economic and political noose around Iraq to force it to leave Kuwait. They imposed mandatory economic sanctions against Iraq, invalidated Iraq's annexation of Kuwait, and condemned Iraq's holding of foreign nationals and diplomats. They also expanded the embargo to include sea and air embargoes as well. What was remarkable about these actions was not only their rapidity but also the unanimity among the permanent members on the Security Council (the United States, the Soviet Union, Britain, China, and France). Because of the Cold War and the existence of the veto power available to the permanent Security Council members, UN collective action for peace had always proved difficult.

The Hundred Hours War. On November 29, 1990, the Security Council passed its most significant resolution. It authorized member states "to use all necessary means to uphold and implement" the previous UN resolutions unless Iraq left Kuwait by January 15, 1991.[132] In effect, this resolution authorized the nations of the world to use force to expel Iraq from Kuwait. This call for collective security was only the second time in which the UN Security Council has authorized such action (the other was over the North Korean invasion of South Korea in 1950).

When Iraq failed to leave Kuwait by the January 15 deadline and after the U.S. Congress had given the president the authority to use American forces to implement this last UN resolution, the anti-Iraq coalition, now totaling over a half million troops, initiated a massive bombing attack against Iraq. While it initially failed to budge the Iraqis, by mid-February, Iraq agreed to withdraw from Kuwait, albeit with conditions attached. The anti-Iraq coalition, led by the Bush administration, rejected that plan and imposed a twenty-four-hour ultimatum on February 22, 1991, for the Iraqis to begin to leave Kuwait. When the deadline passed unanswered, the allied coalition mounted a massive ground, air, and sea assault to drive Iraq out. On February 27, 1991, President Bush declared that "Kuwait is liberated" and announced the suspension of hostilities beginning at midnight on February 28. On March 3, 1991, the United Nations Security Council passed a resolution ending the hostilities and placing responsibilities upon the Iraqis for their invasion of Kuwait; on the same day, military commanders met in southern Iraq to formalize the terms of the military cease-fire and to work out arrangements for the exchange of prisoners of war.[133] Finally, on April 3, 1991, the United Nations Security Council passed a resolution formally ending the war and requiring Iraq to (1) destroy all of its chemical and biological weapons and ballistic missile systems with a range of more than 150 kilometers, (2) pay reparations to Kuwait, (3) reject support for international terrorism, and (4) respect the sovereignty of Kuwait.[134]

Ensuring a lasting peace within Iraq, and the region generally, ultimately proved more difficult than winning the short war. Almost immediately after the coalition victory, rebellions broke out in the North and South of Iraq.[135] In the North, the Kurdish people, an ethnic minority, rebelled against the Iraqi government but failed. In the South, the Shiite population, a religious Muslim minority, attempted to rebel against the authorities in Baghdad, but they too failed. Saddam Hussein thus remained in control, even as the country continued to suffer from the devastation of the war. Yet, the victors, and particularly the United States and NATO forces, imposed "no-fly zones" in the North and the South of Iraq to ensure the safety of these minority populations. Even so, UN inspectors confronted resistance as they tried to investigate Iraqi facilities suspected of producing nuclear materials—a problem that continued from the Bush to the Clinton administration.

By late July and early August 1991, a tangible result emerged from the Persian Gulf War: the real prospect for Middle East peace. A U.S.-Soviet–sponsored peace conference gained support from several Arab states and Israel. In late October 1991, the conference opened in Madrid, and the prospects for sustained Arab-Israeli-Palestinian negotiations looked promising. Significant results, however, were not to be obtained until the first year of the Clinton administration, as we shall discuss in Chapter 6. In a limited sense, though, the first test of the new world order appeared to have been met with coalitional unity achieved in the Persian Gulf War and with the emergence of Middle East peace talks.

Relations with a Post-Communist Russia

A second test of the new order arose over devising an appropriate set of policies toward Russia and the other successor states of the old Soviet Union. In keeping with the instincts of the Bush administration, the policies were cautionary and pragmatic in both the economic and political-military areas, but significant commitments were made. By April, 1992, the Bush administration decided to make a greater commitment to providing economic assistance to Russia and Ukraine, prodded on by its Group of Seven (G-7) partners; and, by the end of the Bush administration, another dramatic nuclear arms reduction agreement, the START II treaty, was completed with Russia.

Diplomatic. On the diplomatic front, the Bush administration moved quickly to establish diplomatic ties with the new republics and to foster closer ties with President Boris Yeltsin of Russia. In February 1992, President Bush and Yeltsin held discussions at Camp David, Maryland, on nuclear arms and on aid to Russia. In the same month, Secretary of State James Baker visited Moldova, Armenia, Azerbaijan, Tajikistan, and Uzbekistan to begin the normalization of relations with these new republics.[136] In

DOCUMENT SUMMARY 5.2

Key Components of the START II Treaty

	START II Phase One	START II Phase Two
Total Strategic Warheads	3,800–4,250	3,000–3,500
MIRVed land-based missile warheads	1,200	0
Submarine-launched ballistic missile warheads	2,160	1,700–1,750
Heavy land-based missile warheads	650	0
Total strategic nuclear delivery vehicles	1,600	1,600

Source: Abstracted from *U.S. Department of State Dispatch*, Vol. 4, no. 1, January 4, 1993, p. 6.

addition, Baker began the process of negotiating with Moscow and Yeltsin over future economic assistance and the implementation of the START agreements. The highlight of these diplomatic efforts between Moscow and Washington was the June 16–17, 1992, summit conference between President Bush and President Yeltsin in Washington. This summit marked a crucial juncture in the emerging relationship since it propelled Russia and America to make further progress in their economic and military relationship after the Cold War. Specifically, it produced the outlines for a further reduction in nuclear weapons held by the two countries (what was to become the START II treaty), enabled President Yeltsin to speak to the U.S. Congress and request American assistance to Russia, and allowed for the development of various bilateral agreements dealing with cooperation in outer space, curbs on weapons of mass destruction, and American business activities in Russia. The summit was an occasion for President Bush to announce that Russia would be granted most-favored-nation (MFN) trading status with the United States.[137]

Military. In the military area, two important actions were completed. In May, 1992, a protocol to the START treaty was signed in Lisbon, Portugal, to recognize that the Soviet Union, as the original signatory of the treaty, had broken up, and the new states had to be incorporated into the pact. As such, the protocol required that "Byelarus, Kazakhstan, Russia and Ukraine together shall assume the obligations" of the former Soviet Union as set out in the START treaty.[138] After the June summit, final negotiations on the START II treaty were also completed (although they took longer than perhaps anticipated), and the final document was officially signed on January 3, 1993, about two weeks before President Bush left office. The new treaty called for further significant reductions in the number of strategic nuclear warheads that the United States and Russia could possess. (Document Summary 5.2 provides some details of the treaty.) Under the pact, the United States and Russia would be required to reduce the number of strategic nuclear warheads to at least 3,500, in two phases, by 2003.[139] In addition, it called for the elimination of all multiple (or MIRVed) warheads on land-based missiles, prohibited warheads on either country's "heavy" (or the largest) land-based missiles, and maintained the total number of "strategic nuclear delivery vehicles" (or launchers) at 1,600. In an important stipulation, however, START had to be fully implemented before START II would come into effect.

Economic. In the economic area, progress occurred as well. In 1991 and early 1992, President Bush had been criticized for his failure to be more responsive to Soviet (and then Russian) requests for assistance. Criticism came from diverse sources: former President Nixon, Bush's ambassador to Moscow, Robert S. Strauss, and the eventual Democratic presidential candidate, Governor Bill Clinton.[140] Undoubtedly prodded in part by that criticism, President Bush announced on April 1, 1992, that the United States would participate in a $24 billion assistance program developed by the Group of Seven (G-7) to aid Russia. The plan was characterized "as a way for the United States and its allies to prevent economic collapse in Russia and stop a new authoritarianism from rising from the rubble of the Soviet empire."[141]

This American aid plan—with the Bush administration's urging—was eventually written into law with the passage of the Freedom Support Act in October 1992. Under this legislation, the United States committed itself to provide $410 million in aid, authorized a $12.3 billion increase in its support of the International Monetary Fund as a mechanism to aid Russia and the other former Soviet Republics, supported a $3 billion multilateral effort to stabilize the Russian currency, and offered various ways of increasing American cooperation and support for the former Soviet Republics. In a unique feature, the Freedom Support Act authorized $800 million from the U.S. defense budget to help the former Soviet Republics dismantle nuclear weapons and other weapons of mass destruction.[142]

These various components of the Freedom Support Act of 1992 reflected how far economic and political cooperation between the former Soviet Union and the United States had progressed in less than a year. At the same time, the implementation of this aid package and the expansion of democratic reforms within Russia and elsewhere in the former Soviet Union would continue to be a difficulty for the Bush administration and, in turn, for the Clinton administration as well.

New Global Disorders: Bosnia, Haiti, and Somalia

The third major test in creating a new global order was over the direction of American policy toward new global *disorders*. Three particular problems captured the attention of the Bush administration and epitomized the difficulty confronting American foreign policy after the Cold War: the outbreak of ethnic fighting in Bosnia, the overthrow of democracy in Haiti, and the scourge of starvation in Somalia. In each case, different American responses occurred. As a result, no clear direction appeared in U.S. foreign policy, which raised questions about the role of the United States in this new world order.

Bosnia. The eruption of ethnic fighting in the former Yugoslavia occurred quickly after the end of the Cold War. With the declaration of independence by several constituent Republics of that former country (e.g., Slovenia, Croatia, and Bosnia-Herzogovina in 1991 and 1992) and the determination of Serbia to maintain control of the former Yugoslav government and much of its territory, fighting among the differing ethnic and religious factions within Croatia and Bosnia quickly broke out. By early 1992, an uneasy truce was in place in Croatia, but by April 1992, an ethnic war erupted in Bosnia. The Bosnia conflict, moreover, would become the focal point of attention for the American administrations for the next several years. The fighting was among three major groups: Bosnian Serbs, Bosnian Muslims, and Bosnian Croats, and there was also a war between the Serbian government and the newly created Bosnian government—with the former seeking to extend greater Serbia and the latter seeking to maintain its independence.

The initial impulse of the Bush administration was to try to hold Yugoslavia together. It was reluctant to grant diplomatic recognition to the newly independent states carved out of the former Yugoslavia and instead sought a negotiated outcome. As Acting Secretary of State Lawrence Eagleburger said, "the [Yugoslav] republics' unilateral and uncoordinated declarations of independence, which we unsuccessfully opposed, led inexorably to civil war."[143] The preferred policy was to have the parties negotiate a settlement and to have the Europeans (through the European Union, for example) and the United Nations take the lead in assisting the conflicting parties. While the United States eventually supported UN sanctions on Yugoslavia and the imposition of a NATO-run "no fly zone" over Bosnia as mechanisms to stop the fighting and achieve a peaceful outcome, the Bush administration was unwilling to do much more. Indeed, Secretary of State James Baker declared that "we don't have a dog in that fight." By that assessment, the United States would limit its actions in aiding the restoration of peace and stability in the new era.[144]

Haiti. In Haiti, however, the Bush administration faced another kind of post–Cold War problem, the promotion and maintenance of democracy. Here, it adopted a different response. In September 1991, the democratically elected government of President Jean-Bertrand Aristide was overthrown in a military-led coup.[145] While the United States was committed to Aristide's restoration, the Bush administration primarily limited its action to diplomatic and economic measures. The administration, for example, cut off economic assistance to Haiti, and froze Haitian government assets in the United States. In turn, after the Organization of American States (OAS) enacted a trade embargo against Haiti, the Bush administration followed suit by participating in the embargo. Despite these and other efforts, no progress was made in restoring democracy, and the Bush administration was disinclined to do more.

By early 1992, another, and more complicating, problem arose over Haiti. Haitian refugees, seeking to flee the failing economy and the brutal regime there, took to a variety of boats and vessels in an attempt to reach American shores for asylum. Despite the efforts to help the Haitians, the

Bush administration ultimately ordered the U.S. Coast Guard to stop the vessels and return them with their occupants to Haiti. By the end of the Bush administration, democracy had not been restored to Haiti, and the Haitian refugees had become a presidential campaign issue. By these actions, the United States and the Bush administration were clearly limiting their actions in promoting and maintaining democracy after the Cold War.

Somalia. The unrest in Somalia raised yet a third type of post–Cold War issue for the United States and a third type of response.[146] With the breakdown of the government within Somalia—and despite the efforts of international aid providers—starvation was rampant in that country by 1992. Estimates of death by starvation ranged up to 350,000. Relief convoys were systematically hijacked by rival "clans" within Somalia, and several cities and outlying villages simply were not receiving intended food aid shipped to that country. In July 1992, the United Nations acted and authorized the sending of UN peacekeepers to Somalia to aid the humanitarian efforts. At the time, too, the Bush administration authorized American military transport aircraft to help with the relief process. Despite these efforts, the situation continued to deteriorate in Somalia.

By early December 1992, the UN Security Council passed a resolution authorizing the United States to lead an effort to provide humanitarian assistance to Somalia. In an action dubbed "Operation Restore Hope," the Bush administration decided to intervene militarily. The administration directed that 28,000 American troops be sent to Somalia to make certain that humanitarian assistance reached the neediest people. While this action was carefully limited to providing food assistance and was successful initially, the Clinton administration would later expand the mission, and problems would develop (see Chapter 6).

CHALLENGES AND RESPONSE TO THE NEW WORLD ORDER

Somalia evoked a markedly different response by the Bush administration to global disorders than had occurred in the earlier two cases. Was Somalia, then, the emerging model for establishing a new global order, or was the Bush administration's basic pragmatism operating in all of these instances after the Cold War? To many of the Bush administration's critics, of course, the answer was the latter. A coherent post–Cold War foreign policy had not been developed, and an "ad hoc" foreign policy approach remained. Despite these criticisms, former Acting Secretary of State Lawrence Eagleburger, as he was leaving office, defended the efforts of the Bush administration to create a new world order.[147] Indeed, he argued that the administration did much more than it is credited in pointing the way to a future foreign policy course for the United States. Moreover, he argued that the administration's alleged "ad hocism" in foreign policy was "a virtue, not a vice."

In particular, Eagleburger contended that the Bush administration successfully met three challenges. First, the Bush administration ended the Cold

War peacefully by dealing with several major crises successfully—ranging from the democratic revolution in Eastern Europe, to the reunification of Germany, and to the collapse of the Soviet Union. Second, the administration dealt with the "instabilities generated by the Cold War's demise" (e.g., the Persian Gulf War and Yugoslavia). Third, and what some may overlook, the Bush administration started the process of reform of the global institutions in terms of paving the way for the future. In particular, Eagleburger had in mind the development of NAFTA (the North American Free Trade Agreement), the trade organization among the United States, Canada, and Mexico; the creation of the Group of 24 [G-24] developed countries aiding Central and Eastern Europe; and the emergence of APEC (Asia-Pacific Economic Cooperation), an organization of eighteen nations stretching across the Pacific from China and Japan in Northeast Asia to Australia and New Zealand, and to the United States and Canada. These largely economic organizations will be pivotal for the future. In short, Eagleburger argued, "there was a strategy behind the President's conduct of foreign policy..." and "a certain degree of 'ad hocery' is a virtue, not a vice, when you are dealing with a world in crisis and chaos...."

Concluding Comments

Much ground has been covered in this chapter—from the renewal of the Cold War by the Reagan administration to the efforts of the Bush administration to develop a new approach to foreign policy after the end of the Cold War. Both administrations achieved some success in their policies, but both met failures as well. Neither set the United States on a clear course for the post–Cold War era.

The Reagan administration came to office in 1981 largely committed to restoring the values of the Cold War era, and it largely succeeded. It placed the Soviet Union at the center of American foreign policy, took actions to challenge the Soviets worldwide, and attempted to rally the rest of the nations of the non-Communist world against the Soviet challenge. During its second term, the Reagan administration moved from confrontation to accommodation with the Soviet Union, notably completing the first nuclear arms reduction treaty (the INF Treaty) in history. Toward the rest of the world, however, the Reagan administration continued to pursue a staunch anti-Communist policy with a more mixed result.

Although the Bush administration came to office focused primarily on some continuity, the end of the Cold War and the collapse of the Soviet Union compelled it to attempt a different course in foreign affairs. Instead of Soviet-American relations serving as the centerpiece for American foreign policy as they had for the past forty years, a new international order would be sought. That order would be based upon a shared set of global values, involve cooperation among nations, and be grounded in the leadership of the United States. While the Bush administration surely achieved some success in uniting a coalition in the Persian Gulf War around this vision, its efforts in other areas of the world—whether toward Russia, Somalia, Haiti, or Bosnia—met with a more mixed reception from the American people. Any new world order remained elusive.

In the next chapter, we complete our survey of the different value approaches of recent administrations by turning to the Clinton approach to foreign policy. Although that administration was determined to pursue a foreign policy grounded in a set of principles and guided by a clear strategy, it, too, found that enunciating principles was easier than implementing a strategy.

Notes

1. Throughout this chapter, before the breakup of the Soviet empire in 1989–1990, the use of the term "Eastern Europe" shall refer to those countries that were Communist allies of the Soviet Union (East Germany, Poland, Czechoslovakia, Hungary, Romania, Bulgaria) and formed part of the "Soviet bloc." After its breakup, the term "Central Europe" shall refer to these countries, since it is more descriptive of their proper geographical location.
2. "Text of President Bush's State of the Union Message to Nation," *New York Times*, January 30, 1991, A8.
3. "Transcript of President's First News Conference on Foreign and Domestic Topics," *New York Times*, January 30, 1981, A10.
4. "Excerpts from President's Speech to National Association of Evangelicals," *New York Times*, March 9, 1983, A18.
5. Jimmy Carter, "Humane Purposes in Foreign Policy," Department of State News Release, May 22, 1977, p. 1 (Commencement Address at the University of Notre Dame).
6. See, for example, Robert E. Osgood, "The Revitalization of Containment," William P. Bundy, ed., *America and the World 1981* (New York: Pergamon Press, 1982), pp. 465–502.
7. One American diplomat was quoted as saying "Aside from opposing the Soviets, we don't really have a foreign policy." See Hedrick Smith in "Discordant Voices," *New York Times*, March 20, 1981, A2.
8. See, for example, the following statements by Alexander Haig and issued by the Department of State, "A New Direction in U.S. Foreign Policy" (April 14, 1981); "Relationship of Foreign and Defense Policies" (July 30, 1981); and "A Strategic Approach to American Foreign Policy" (August 11, 1981). The four items here are quoted from the last one at p. 2. We shall rely upon this last one for our subsequent analysis.
9. Ibid. Later section subtitles are from these points.
10. On these plans, see, for example, *Congressional Quarterly Almanac 1981* (Washington, DC: Congressional Quarterly, Inc., 1982), pp. 240–241; and Stephen Webbe, "Defense: Reagan Plans Largest U.S. Military Buildup Since Vietnam...." *Christian Science Monitor*, May 1, 1981, 8–9. The latter article puts the buildup at $1.5 trillion.
11. Alexander Haig, "Arms Control and Strategic Nuclear Forces" (Washington, DC: Bureau of Public Affairs, Department of State, November 4, 1981). The elements of strategic modernization are drawn from that statement. On the importance of the "command and control" system, see John D. Steinbruner, "Nuclear Decapitation," *Foreign Policy* 45 (Winter 1981–82): 16–28. Also see Osgood, "The Revitalization of Containment," pp. 474–478; and Raymond Aron, "Ideology in Search of a Policy," in William P. Bundy, ed., *America and the World 1981*, pp. 504–508. These articles were also useful for our survey of policies in the various regions.
12. "Peace and Security," President Reagan Televised Address to the Nation, March 23, 1983, reprinted in *Realism, Strength, Negotiation: Key Foreign Policy Statements of the Reagan Administration* (Washington, DC: Department of State, May 1984), p. 43.
13. See William P. Bundy, " A Portentous Year," in William P. Bundy, ed., *Foreign Affairs: America and the World 1983*, 62 (1984): 499, on the centrality of the deployment issue in Soviet-American relations.
14. On June 18, 1982, President Reagan imposed sanctions on American subsidiaries or their licensees from continuing to supply the Soviets over the gas pipeline. See Josef

Joffe, "Europe and America: The Politics of Resentment (Cont'd)," in William P. Bundy, ed., *America and the World 1981* (New York: Pergamon Press, 1982), pp. 573–574.

15. The quotations are drawn from President Reagan's speech to the World Affairs Council of Philadelphia. Portions of it can be found in "Excerpts from Reagan Speech on U.S. Policy Toward Developing Nations," *New York Times*, October 16, 1981, A12. The same theme was struck a week later by President Reagan at Cancun, Mexico. See Howell Raines, "President Asserts Meeting in Cancun Was Constructive," *New York Times*, October 25, 1981, 1. Also see the detailed discussion of the Reagan approach to the Third World and its difference from the Carter approach in Osgood, "The Revitalization of Containment," pp. 486–495, upon which we also draw.
16. "Caribbean Basin Initiative, *GIST* (Washington, DC: Department of State, February, 1982).
17. The White House Office of the Press Secretary, press release on arms transfer policy, July 9, 1981.
18. See the survey of Reagan's foreign policy in the November 9, 1981, issue of *Newsweek*, in which there is "A Tour of Reagan's Horizon," pp. 34–43. The mention of "strategic consensus" for the Middle East is at p. 41, but the concept can be applied to all areas of the world during the Reagan administration.
19. Haig, "A Strategic Approach to American Foreign Policy," p. 3. Emphasis added.
20. See, for example, the "Text of Haig's Speech on American Foreign Policy," *New York Times*, April 25, 1981, 4, and his characterization of the Soviet Union. Also see the chronology in Bundy, ed., *America and the World 1981*, p. 728, for President Reagan's comment at his June 16, 1981, press conference in which he says that the Soviet Union "shows signs of collapse." (The quote is from Bundy.) The text of President Reagan's remarks can be found in "The President's News Conference of June 16, 1981," *Weekly Compilation of Presidential Documents* 17 (June 22, 1981): 633.
21. On the neutron bomb, see Leslie H. Gelb, "Reagan Orders Production of 2 Types of Neutron Arms for Stockpiling in the U.S.," *New York Times*, August 9, 1981, 1. On sanctioning the Soviet Union over Poland, see the President's statement in *Weekly Compilation of Presidential Documents* 17 (January 4, 1982): 1429–1430.
22. Steven Weisman's "Reagan Ends Curbs on Export of Grain to the Soviet Union," *New York Times*, April 25, 1981, 1, 6, discusses the lifting of the embargo. The expansion of grain sales is reported in John F. Burns, "U.S. Will Permit Russians to Triple Imports of Grain," *New York Times*, October 2, 1981, A1, D14. A five-year grain deal was eventually agreed to in July 1983: Steven R. Weisman, "A New Pact Raises Soviet Purchases of American Grain," *New York Times*, July 29, 1983, A1 and D9. Also see William G. Hyland, "U.S. Relations: The Long Way Back," in William P. Bundy, ed., *America and the World 1981*, pp. 542–543.
23. Bernard Gwertzman, "U.S. Says It Is Not Bound by 2 Arms Pacts With Soviet," *New York Times*, May 20, 1981, All.
24. On the Haig-Gromyko meeting and for prospects on arms control talks, see Bernard Gwertzman, "U.S. and Soviet Agree to Renew Weapons Talk," *New York Times.*, September 24, 1981, A1, A10.
25. A discussion of the INF negotiations can be found in Strobe Talbott, "Buildup and Breakdown," in William P. Bundy, ed., *America and the World 1983*, pp. 587–615. On the first deployment, see James M. Markham, "First U.S. Pershing Missiles Delivered in West Germany," *New York Times*, November 24, 1983, A14.
26. The cataloguing of these events and other Soviet actions can be found in the "Cooling Trend in Soviet Policy," *Christian Science Monitor*, May 25, 1984, 1. On the explanation for the withdrawal from the Olympics, see "U.S.-Soviet Ties Termed 'Worst Ever,'" *Des Moines Sunday Register*, May 27, 1984, 1.
27. The comment was by a Soviet official and is quoted in ibid.
28. "Communist Interference in El Salvador" (Washington, DC: Bureau of Public Affairs, Department of State, February 1981), p. 1. Special Report No. 80.
29. See the testimony of Secretary of State Alexander Haig in Foreign Assistance Legislation for Fiscal Year 1982, Hearing before the Committee on Foreign Affairs, the House of

Representatives, 97th Cong., 1st sess. (Washington, DC: U.S. Government Printing Office, 1981), p. 194.

30. See the chronology in Bundy, ed., *America and the World 1981*, p. 749.
31. Ibid.
32. Reagan Says Security of U.S. Is at Stake in Central America," *Des Moines Register,* April 28, 1983, 6A.
33. "No More Aid for Nicaragua," *Today*, April 24, 1981, 13.
34. In its November 8, 1982, issue, *Newsweek* devoted its cover story to the covert war against Nicaragua. See "A Secret War for Nicaragua," pp. 42–55.
35. The justification for the Grenada invasion is taken from President Reagan's remarks on October 25, 1983. They are reprinted in "Grenada: Collective Action by the Caribbean Peace Force," *Department of State Bulletin* 83 (December 1983): 67.
36. The Reagan administration sought congressional repeal of the Clark Amendment, an amendment passed in 1976 which prohibited aid to forces in Angola. The apparent aim of such an action was to allow the United States to support Jonas Savimbi and his UNITA forces, who were still fighting the Marxist government in Angola.
37. A chronology of these various actions is presented in William P. Bundy, ed., *America and the World 1981*, pp. 734–735. This chronology, and the subsequent ones in the other volumes of this series, were useful beginning points for unraveling the sequence of events in the Reagan administration.
38. This agreement was quickly suspended by the United States after the Israelis annexed the Golan Heights in December 1981. See Aron, "Ideology in Search of a Policy," p. 517.
39. Juan de Onis, "U.S. and Pakistanis Reach an Agreement on $3 Billion in Aid," *New York Times*, June 16, 1981, A1, A15. On the importance of both the AWACS and Pakistani sales, see Carol Housa, "Arms Sale Test, U.S.-Pakistan Ties," *Christian Science Monitor*, November 12, 1981, 3.
40. On the Reagan Initiative, see "Transcript of President's Address to Nation on West Bank and Palestinians," *New York Times*, September 2, 1982, A11.
41. The explanations for sending these forces into Lebanon are contained in the reports to Congress on August 24, 1982, and September 29, 1982, and in the Multinational Force Agreement between the United States and Lebanon of September 25, 1982. All of these are reprinted in *The War Powers Resolution: Relevant Documents, Correspondence, Reports*, Subcommittee on International Security and Scientific Affairs, House Committee on Foreign Affairs, December, 1983, pp. 60–63, 74–76.
42. See "Communique by the Common Market," *New York Times*, January 5, 1982, A7; and "Text of Declaration on Poland by The Foreign Ministers of NATO, *New York Times*, January 12, 1982, A8. Also see John Vincour, "Bonn Says Sanctions Are Not the Solution," *New York Times*, December 30, 1981, A1, A7. Also see Andrew Knight, "Ronald Reagan's Watershed Year?" in William P. Bundy, ed., *America and the World 1982* (New York: Pergamon Press, 1983), pp. 511–541.
43. The President's comment is in Bernard Gwertzman, "President Says Should Not Waiver in Backing Saudis," *New York Times*, October 18, 1981, 1; and the statement by Haig is reported in Gwertzman's "Allied Contingency Plan Envisions a Warning Atom Blast, Haig Says," *New York Times*, November 5, 1981, A1, A9.
44. In West Germany, the proposed location for most of the theater nuclear forces, the opposition to the deployment of such weapons during 1983 assisted the Greens (a new anti-nuclear and environmental party) in gaining some seats in the legislatures of the Laender (or state) governments and eventually in the Bundestag (the national parliament). See "Focus on The National Elections in West Germany on March 6, 1983," p. 6, and "Focus on the Results of the National Elections in the Federal Republic of Germany on March 6, 1983," p. 2. Both are published by the German Information Center.
45. Paul E. Sigmund, "Latin America: Change or Continuity?" in William P. Bundy, ed., *America and the World 1981*, p. 636.
46. George Gallup, "Military Budget Boost Loses Support, Poll Hints," *Des Moines Sunday Register*, February 27, 1983, 5A.

47. A *Newsweek* poll as reported in the April 26, 1982, issue, p. 24, found that 68 percent of those who had heard of the nuclear freeze movement favored or strongly favored it. A later *Newsweek* poll in the January 31, 1983, issue, p. 17 found that 64 percent of the public supported the nuclear freeze proposal.
48. The crowd estimates ranged from 500,000 to 700,000 or more as reported in Paul L. Montgomery, "Throngs Fill Manhattan to Protest Nuclear Weapons," *New York Times*, June 13, 1982, 1, 43. For a survey of how the freeze movement reflects a diverse American public, see "A Matter of Life and Death," *Newsweek*, April 26, 1982, 20–33.
49. In a March 1981 interview with Walter Cronkite, President Reagan rejected the use of U.S. armed forces. See Francis X. Clines, "President Doubtful on U.S. Intervention." *New York Times*, March 4, 1981, A1, A22. In a December 1981 interview, Secretary Haig ruled out American troops. On the interview, see Sigmund, "Latin America: Change or Continuity?" p. 641.
50. The quoted passages are from "Transcript of President's News Conference on Foreign and Domestic Issues," *New York Times*, November 8, 1984, 13. The discussion also draws upon Howell Raines, "Reagan Takes 49 States and 59% of Vote, Vows to Stress Arms Talk and Economy," and Hedrick Smith, "Reagan Faces Difficult Task in Leading Divided Congress," *New York Times*, November 8, 1984, 1, 10; Brad Knickerbrocker, "Defense & Diplomacy," *Christian Science Monitor*, Nov. 8, 1984, 1, 4; and James McCartney, "Reagan Faces Decisions on Arms Curbs, Nicaragua," *Des Moines Register*, November 8, 1984, 7A.
51. George Shultz, "Managing the U.S.-Soviet Relationship Over the Long Term," address before the Rand/UCLA Center for the Study of Soviet International Behavior, October 18, 1984, reprinted in *Department of State Bulletin* 84 (December 1984): 2.
52. George Shultz, "The Future of American Foreign Policy: New Realities and New Ways of Thinking," in James M. McCormick, ed., *A Reader in American Foreign Policy* (Itasca, IL: F. E. Peacock Publishers, Inc., 1986), pp. 379–392. The quotation is from p. 382.
53. "Text of Inaugural Address," *Des Moines Register*, January 22, 1985, 4A.
54. On the changes in Soviet foreign policy, see David Holloway, "Gorbachev's New Thinking," and Robert Levgold, "The Revolution in Soviet Foreign Policy," in William P. Bundy, ed., *Foreign Affairs: America and the World 1988/89* 68 (1989): 66–98.
55. John E. Rielly, ed., *American Public Opinion and U.S. Foreign Policy 1987* (Chicago: The Chicago Council on Foreign Relations, 1987), p. 6.
56. For summits by other presidents, see Harold W. Stanley and Richard G. Niemi, *Vital Statistics on American Politics* (Washington, DC: CQ Press, 1988), pp. 293–294.
57. See the "Concluding Remarks: President Reagan, November 21, 1985," reprinted in *Department of State Bulletin* 86 (January 1986): 11.
58. The Reykjavik Meeting," *GIST* (Washington, DC: Department of State, December, 1986).
59. Steven B. Roberts, "Reagan Says He Was Moved by Contacts with Russians," *New York Times*, June 2, 1988, A16. On the third summit, see R. W. Apple, Jr., "Reagan and Gorbachev Report Progress on Long-Range Arms and Mute 'Star Wars' Quarrel," *New York Times*, December 11, 1987, 1 and 10.
60. The occasion was purposely described by President Reagan as not "a working summit" because there was no set agenda. See President Reagan's statement of December 3, 1988, in the *Department of State Bulletin* 89 (February 1989): 3.
61. "Joint Statement, Geneva, January 8, 1985," *Department of State Bulletin* 85 (March 1985): 30.
62. The complete text of the INF Treaty and its protocols are available in *Arms Control and Disarmament Agreements: Texts and Histories of the Negotiations* (Washington, DC: United States Arms Control and Disarmament Agency, 1990), p. 345–444.
63. Michael Mandelbaum, "The Luck of the President," in William G. Hyland, ed., *America and the World 1985* (New York: Pergamon Press, 1986), p. 408.
64. *Congressional Quarterly Almanac 1985* (Washington, DC: Congressional Quarterly, Inc., 1986), pp. 40, 56 and 58.
65. Peter Hayes, ed., "Chronology 1988," *Foreign Affairs: America and the World 1988/89*, 68 (1989): 239.

66. For a summary of the accord on Angola and Namibia, see "Angola/Namibia Accords," *Department of State Bulletin* 89 (February 1989): 10–16.

67. Several sources were used to construct the description of events associated with the Iran-Contra affair. Among them were *Report of the Congressional Committees Investigating the Iran-Contra Affair* (Washington, DC: U.S. Government Printing Office, November, 1987); *Report of the President's Special Review Board* (Washington, DC: U.S. Government Printing Office, February 26, 1987); Peter Hayes, ed., "Chronology 1987" *Foreign Affairs: America and the World 1987/88*, 66 (1988): 638–676; Peter Hayes, ed., "Chronology 1988" *Foreign Affairs: America and the World 1988/89*, 68 (1989): 220–256; Clyde R. Mark, "Iran-Contra Affair: A Chronology," Report No. 86-190F (Washington, DC: The Congressional Research Service, April 2, 1987); and James M. McCormick and Steven S. Smith, "The Iran Arms Sale and the Intelligence Oversight Act of 1980," *PS* 20 (Winter 1987): 29–37. The Reagan quote on keeping the Contras' "body and soul together" can be found in *Report of the Congressional Committees Investigating the Iran-Contra Affair*, p. 4, and the quote about Poindexter can be found at p. 7 of this report.

68. David Hoffmann and Dan Morgan, "Tower Panel Details Administration Breakdown, Blames Reagan, Top Aides for Policy Failures," *Washington Post*, February 27, 1987, A1.

69. The change in support is from Sandra Burton, "Aquino's Philippines: The Center Holds," *Foreign Affairs: America and the World 1986* 65 (1987): 524–526.

70. Nadav Safran, *Israel: The Embattled Ally* (Cambridge, MA: The Belknap Press, 1978), p. 594.

71. Alan Cowell, "Arafat Urges U.S. to Press Israelis to Negotiate Now," *New York Times*, November 16, 1988, A1 and A10.

72. "U.S. Makes Stunning Move Toward PLO." *Des Moines Register*, December 15, 1988, 3A. On the Palestine National Council deliberations, see "The P.L.O.: Less than Meets the Eye," *New York Times*, November 16, 1988, A30, and Youssef M. Ibrahim, "Palestinian View: A Big Stride Forward," *New York Times*, November 16, 1988, A10.

73. This discussion is based upon *Congressional Quarterly Almanac 1985* (Washington, DC: Congressional Quarterly, Inc., 1986), pp. 39, 40, and 85, and *Congressional Quarterly Almanac 1986* (Washington, DC: Congressional Quarterly, Inc., 1987), pp. 359–362.

74. These concepts are discussed in and drawn from Charles W. Kegley, Jr., "The Bush Administration and the Future of American Foreign Policy: Pragmatism, or Procrastination?" *Presidential Studies Quarterly*, 19 (Fall 1989): 717–731, especially p. 717. On the Bush presidency, also see Barbara Kellerman and Ryan J. Barilleaux, *The President as World Leader* (New York: St. Martin's Press, 1991), pp. 210–216.

75. See Elaine Sciolino, "Bush Selections Signal Focus on Foreign Policy," *New York Times*, January 17, 1989, 1, for this depiction of Bush as a problem-solver and not as a visionary.

76. Theodore C. Sorensen, "Bush's Timid 100 Days," *New York Times*, April 27, 1989, 27.

77. William G. Hyland, "Bush's Foreign Policy: Pragmatism or Indecision?" *New York Times*, April 26, 1989, 25. The second quote is taken from capsule summaries of the main themes of the article.

78. Evan Thomas with Thomas M. DeFrank and Ann McDaniel, "Bush and the Generals," *Newsweek*, February 4, 1991, 27.

79. The description was written by Charles William Maynes and is quoted in Sciolino, "Bush Selections Signal Focus on Foreign Policy," p. 1.

80. Noted analyst I.M. Destler is quoted in John Felton, "Will Bush-Hill Honeymoon Bring Bipartisanship?" *Congressional Quarterly Weekly Report*, February 18, 1989, 334.

81. Sciolino, "Bush Selections Signal Focus on Foreign Policy," pp. 1 and 11; Elaine Sciolino, "Lawyer Is Picked for High State Department Post," *New York Times*, January 23, 1989, 3; and Clifford Krauss, "In Hot Spots Like Gulf, He's Baker's Cool Hand," *New York Times*, January 3, 1991, A4.

82. Sciolino, "Bush Selections Signal Focus on Foreign Policy," p. 1; and Thomas, "Bush and the Generals," p. 27.
83. The National Security Council staff confirmed that there was not a publically available summary of the "policy review" and that these speeches summarized the essence of the policy positions of the Bush administration at that time. The speeches which are quoted below were supplied by the NSC staff and consisted of the following: "Remarks by the President to the Citizens of Hamtramck," April 17, 1989; "Remarks by the President at Texas A&M University," May 12, 1989; "Remarks by the President at Boston University Commencement Ceremony," May 21, 1989; "Remarks by the President at the Coast Guard Academy Graduation Ceremony, " May 24, 1989; and "Remarks by the President at Rheingoldhalle," Mainz, Germany, May 31, 1989.
84. The Brezhnev Doctrine, named after Soviet President Leonid Brezhnev, reserved to the Soviet Union the right to ensure the maintenance of socialism in any country of Eastern Europe by taking all necessary actions, including military intervention.
85. See Chapter 8 for a complete discussion of the Jackson-Vanik Amendment.
86. Quoted in Maureen Dowd, "Bush Moves to Control War's Endgame," *New York Times*, February 23, 1991, 5.
87. John Felton, "Bush, Hill Agree to Provide Contras with New Aid," *Congressional Quarterly Weekly Report*, March 25, 1989, 655–657.
88. See *Congressional Quarterly Weekly Report*, April 15, 1989, 853–854.
89. Steven Erlanger, "Hanoi's Partial Victory,' *New York Times*, July 20, 1990, A1, A2.
90. Steven Erlanger, "Ending Talks, All Cambodia Parties Commit Themselves to U.N. Peace Plan," *New York Times*, September 11, 1990, A3.
91. The following discussion draws upon "U.S. Invasion Ousts Panama's Noriega," and "From U.S. Canal to Invasion...A Chronology of Events," *Congressional Quarterly Almanac 1989* (Washington, DC: Congressional Quarterly, Inc., 1990), pp. 595–609 and 606–607, respectively; and Stephen Engelberg, "Bush Aides Admit a U.S. Role in Coup and Bad Handling," *New York Times*, October 6, 1989, 1 and 8.
92. Ibid.
93. Nicholas D. Kristof, "Beijing Death Toll at Least 200; Army Tightens Control of City But Angry Resistance Goes On," *New York Times*, June 5, 1989, 1. A summary of the Bush administration's actions over this episode can be found in "Repression in China Leads to Sanctions," *Congressional Quarterly Almanac 1989* (Washington, DC: Congressional Quarterly, Inc., 1990), pp. 518–526, and it was used here.
94. "President's News Conference on Foreign and Domestic Issues," *New York Times*, June 9, 1989, 12.
95. The chronology of events in the next three sections is based upon several sources: Peter Hayes, ed., "Chronology 1989" *Foreign Affairs: America and the World 1989/90*, 69 (1990); 213–257; Peter Hayes, ed., "Chronology 1990" *Foreign Affairs: America and the World 1990/91*, 70 (1991): 206–248; "East Bloc Political Turmoil...Chronology of Big Changes" *Congressional Quarterly Weekly Report*, December 9, 1989, 3376–3377; and the chronologies in *The 1990 World Book, Yearbook* (Chicago: World Book, Inc., 1990), and the *1990 Britannica, 1990 Book of the Year* (Chicago: Encyclopedia Britannica, Inc., 1990). For changes in Yugoslavia and Albania in 1991, see "2 Republics Split From Yugoslavia," *Des Moines Register*, June 26, 1991, 1A and 12A, and Thomas L. Friedman, "300,000 Albanians Pour into Streets to Welcome Baker," *New York Times*, June 23, 1991, 1, 4.
96. Serge Schmemann, "Two Germanys Unite After 45 Years with Jubilation and a Vow of Peace," *New York Times*, October 3, 1990, A1 and A9.
97. Quoted in "German-NATO Drama: 9 Fateful Months," *New York Times*, July 17, 1990, A6. It provides a useful chronology of the reunification process, which we also used here.
98. "'Two Plus Four' Treaty Signed; Germany Regains Full Sovereignty," *The Week in Germany*, September 14, 1990, 1–2. The formal name of the treaty is "Treaty on the Final Provisions Regarding Germany."
99. The details of the unification treaty can be found in "Bonn, GDR Sign Unification Treaty," *The Week in Germany*, September 7, 1990, 1–2.

100. On these elections, see Bill Keller, "Soviet Savor Vote in Freest Election Since '17 Revolution," *New York Times*, March 27, 1989, A1 and A6.

101. "Reforms in the Soviet Union," *Des Moines Sunday Register*, February 11, 1990, 1C.

102. The quotations are taken, respectively, from "Gorbachev's First Remarks: 'They Failed,'" *New York Times*, August 23, 1991, A9, and his first post-coup press conference ("The Gorbachev Account: A Coup 'Against the People, Against Democracy,'" *New York Times*, August 23, 1991, A10).

103. See Serge Schmemann, "Gorbachev, Yeltsin and Republic Leaders Move to Take Power From Soviet Congress," *New York Times*, September 3, 1991, A1 and A6; "Excerpts From Soviet Congress: Time for Drastic Changes," *New York Times*, September 3, 1991, A7; and Serge Schmemann, "Soviet Congress Yields Rule to Republics to Avoid Political and Economic Collapse," *New York Times*, September 6, 1991, A1 and A6.

104. The president and the "senior Bush Administration policy maker" are quoted in Thomas L. Friedman, "U.S. Worry Rises Over Europe's Stability," *New York Times*, November 10, 1989, 10.

105. "Poland, Hungary Aid Launched in 1989," *Congressional Quarterly Almanac 1989* (Washington, DC: Congressional Quarterly, Inc., 1990), pp. 503–504.

106. Janet Hook, "101st Congress Leaves Behind Plenty of Laws, Criticism," *Congressional Quarterly Weekly Report*, November 3, 1990, 3709.

107. Karl Kaiser, "Germany's Unification," in William P. Bundy, ed., *Foreign Affairs: America and the World 1990/91* 70 (1991): 179–205.

108. The quotations are from "Transcript of the Bush-Gorbachev New Conference in Malta," *New York Times*, December 4, 1989, A12. Also see Andrew Rosenthal, "Bush and Gorbachev Proclaim a New Era for U.S.-Soviet Ties; Agree on Arms and Trade Aims," *New York Times*, December 4, 1989, A1 and A10, and Frances X. Cline, "Economic Pledges Cheer Soviet Aides," *New York Times*, December 4, 1989, A11.

109. "As Iron Curtain Falls, Superpowers Thaw," *Congressional Quarterly Almanac 1989* (Washington, DC: Congressional Quarterly, Inc., 1990), pp. 477–484.

110. Peter Hayes, ed., "Chronology 1990," *Foreign Affairs: America and the World 1990/91*, 70 (1991): 208.

111. "Text of the Statement on Long-Range Arms," "Summary of U.S.-Soviet Agreement on Chemical Arms," "The Other Agreements in Brief," *New York Times*, June 2, 1990, 8.

112. Not until the Moscow Summit of July 1991 did President Bush announce that he would ask Congress to grant MFN status to the Soviet Union, since free emigration legislation passed the Supreme Soviet in May 1991. See ibid. and R. W. Apple, Jr., "Bush Vows to Put Soviets in Group Favored in Trade," *New York Times*, July 31, 1991, A1, A4. Only in 1994 did Russia receive MFN status from the Clinton administration.

113. Andrew Rosenthal, "Bush, Lifting 15-Year-Old Ban, Approves Loans for Kremlin to Help Ease Food Shortages," *New York Times*, December 13, 1990, A1, A6, and "Bush Extends Credits to Soviet Union," *Congressional Quarterly Weekly Report*, June 15, 1991, 1605.

114. James Baker, "The Gulf Crisis and CSCE Summit," *Dispatch*, 1 (November 19, 1990): 273–274; Pat Towell, "Historic CFE Treaty Arms, Marks the End of Cold War," *Congressional Quarterly Weekly Report*, November 24, 1990, 3930–3932; and "CSCE Summit in Paris Shapes 'New Europe'" *The Week in Germany*, November 23, 1990, 1. The Warsaw Pact was officially disbanded as of March 31, 1991. See Christine Bohlen, "Warsaw Pact Agrees to Dissolve Its Military Alliance by March 31," *New York Times*, February 26, 1991, A1, A10.

115. R.W. Apple, Jr., "Superpower Weapons Treaty First to Cut Strategic Bombs," *New York Times*, July 18, 1991, A1 and A6; Thomas L. Friedman, "Bush and Gorbachev Close Era in U.S.-Soviet Relations," *New York Times*, July 18, 1991, A8; Eric Schmitt, "Senate Approval and Sharp Debate Seen," *New York Times*, July 19, 1991, A5 (including accompanying table entitled "New Limits on Strategic Weapons"); and Office of Public Affairs, U.S. Arms Control and Disarmament Agency, "Strategic Arms Reduction Talks," *Issues Brief*, April 25, 1991.

116. Steven Greenhouse, "7 Offer Moscow Technical Help," *New York Times*, July 18, 1991, A1 and A8, and "Excerpts From Talks by Gorbachev and Major: Investing and Accepting," *New York Times*, July 18, 1991, A6.

117. Andrew Rosenthal, "Baltics Recognized," *New York Times*, September 3, 1991, A1, A8.

118. Clifford Krauss, "U.S. and Britain Will Send Some Food Aid to Republics," *New York Times*, August 30, 1991, A10.

119. See George Bush, "Outlines of a New World of Freedom," an address before the 44th session of the UN General Assembly, New York City, September 25, 1989 and "Toward a New World Order," an address before a joint session of Congress, September 11, 1990. Both are published by the Department of State, Bureau of Public Affairs, Washington, DC. Also see "Text of President Bush's State of the Union Message to Nation," *New York Times*, January 30, 1991, A8.

120. President Bush's national security advisor, Brent Scowcroft, is given credit for developing this phrase and the strategy behind it. See Andrew Rosenthal, "Scowcroft and Gates: A Team Rivals Baker," *New York Times*, February 21, 1991, A6.

121. "Toward a New World Order," p. 2.

122. "Text of President Bush's State of the Union Message to Nation," p. A8.

123. Ibid.

124. Daniel C. Diller, ed., *The Middle East*, 7th ed. (Washington, DC: Congressional Quarterly, Inc., 1990), pp. 164–165.

125. Ibid., p. 3.

126. The first quoted passage is cited in Tom Matthews, "The Road to War," *Newsweek*, January 28, 1991, 56, while the second quoted passage is from Elaine Sciolino with Michael R. Gordon, "U.S. Gave Iraq Little Reason Not to Mount Assault," *New York Times*, September 23, 1990, 1. This entire *Newsweek* report (pp. 54–65) provides a useful background for the evolution of the crisis, and it was used for this section on the administration testimony on Capitol Hill just prior to the invasion.

In testimony to congressional committees after the Persian Gulf War had ended, Ambassador April Glaspie, provided a different account of her meeting with Saddam Hussein than the one released by Iraq in September 1990. While acknowledging the veracity of the often-quoted statements, she testified that she also told Hussein that "we would defend our vital interests, we would support our friends in the Gulf, we would defend their sovereignty and integrity," and that Arab-Arab conflicts ought to be settled "in a nonviolent manner, not by threats, not by intimidation, and certainly not by aggression." (See Thomas L. Friedman, "Envoy to Iraq, Faulted in Crisis, Says She Warned Hussein Sternly," *New York Times*, March 21, 1991, A1, A7.) Glaspie acknowledged that she did not tell Saddam Hussein that the United States would use force to defend Kuwait, and the diplomatic cable that she sent to the Department of State in late July 1990, reportedly, did not indicate a staunch stand by U.S. over potential Iraqi action against Kuwait. (The question on fighting over Iraq was asked by Congressman Lee Hamilton [D-Indiana] during congressional testimony. The testimony and the cable controversy are described in Russell Watson with Margaret Garrand Warner and Thomas M. DeFrank, "Was Ambassador Glaspie Too Gentle with Saddam?" *Newsweek*, April 1, 1991, 17).

127. Peter Hayes, ed., "Chronology 1990" *Foreign Affairs: America and the World 1990/91*, 70 (1991): 228.

128. The joint statement is reprinted in "US-USSR Statement" *Dispatch* 1 (September 17, 1990): 92.

129. George Bush, "The Arabian Peninsula: U.S. Principles," an address to the nation from the Oval Office of the White House, August 8, 1990, provided by the Department of State, Bureau of Public Affairs, Washington, DC.

130. See "How the Arab League Voted in Cairo," *New York Times*, August 11, 1990, 4.

131. The most commonly cited number of countries in the anti-Iraq coalition in public descriptions was twenty-eight nations, but see Steven R. Bowman, "Iraq-Kuwait Crisis: Summary of U.S. and Non-U.S. Forces," Washington, DC: Congressional Research Service, The Library of Congress, December 27, 1990, in which slightly more nations are identified as having contributed some contingent of forces.

132. UN Security Council Resolution 678 (1990), reprinted in Marjorie Ann Browne, "Iraq-Kuwait: U.N. Security Council Resolutions—Texts and Votes" (Washington, DC: Congressional Research Service, The Library of Congress, December 4, 1990). This source

provides complete texts and a summary of the previous 11 UN resolutions, while "U.N. Resolutions on Iraq," *New York Times*, February 16, 1991, 6, provides a summary of them. The latter source was used for the discussion here.

133. Andrew Rosenthal, "Bush Calls Halt to Allied Offensive; Declares Kuwait Free, Iraq Beaten; Sets Stiff Terms for Full Cease-fire," *New York Times*, February 28, 1991, A1; R.W. Apple, Jr., "U.S. Says Iraqi Generals Agree to Demands 'On All Matters'; Early P.O.W. Release Expected," *New York Times*, March 4, 1991, A1 and A6; and "New U.S. Hint About Hussein," *New York Times*, March 4, 1991, A6. On Iraqi and American battlefield deaths, see Patrick E. Tyler, "Iraq's War Toll Estimated by U.S.," *New York Times*, June 5, 1991, A5; and "The Reluctant Warrior," *Newsweek*, May 13, 1991, 22.

134. Paul Lewis, "UN Votes Stern Conditions for Formally Ending War; Iraqi Response Is Uncertain,"*New York Times*, April 4, 1991, A1, A7; and "UN Conditions," *Des Moines Register*, April 4, 1991, 14A.

135. On the outbreak of these rebellions, see, among others, "Apocalypse Near," *Newsweek*, April 1, 1991, 14–16.

136. This discussion draws upon Patricia Lee Dorff, ed., "Chronology 1992," *Foreign Affairs: America and the World 1992/93*: 215–218, 230–233.

137. Ibid. Also see Michael Wines, "Bush and Yeltsin Agree to Cut Long-Range Atomic Warheads: Scrap Key Land-Based Missiles," *New York Times*, June 17, 1992, A1, A6.

138. U.S. Senate, *The START Treaty*, Report of the Committee on Foreign Relations, United States Senate (Washington, DC: U.S. Government Printing Office, 1992), p. 3.

139. The treaty details are summarized more fully in "START II Treaty," *U.S. Department of State Dispatch* 4, January 4, 1993 (Washington, DC: Bureau of Public Affairs, 1993), pp. 5–7 from which our discussion draws.

140. See "Bush Signs Freedom Support Act," *Congressional Quarterly Almanac 1992* (Washington, DC: Congressional Quarterly, Inc., 1993), pp. 523–524.

141. Andrew Rosenthal, "Bush and Kohl Unveil Plan for 7 Nations to Contribute $24 Billion in Aid to Russia," *New York Times*, April 2, 1992, A1.

142. "Freedom Support Act Highlights," *Congressional Quarterly Almanac 1992* (Washington, DC: Congressional Quarterly, Inc., 1993), p. 526. Also see U.S. Department of Defense, "Semi-Annual Report on Program Activities to Facilitate Weapons Destruction and Nonproliferation in the Former Soviet Union," April 30, 1994.

143. Lawrence Eagleburger, "Charting the Course: U.S. Foreign Policy in a Time of Transition," *Dispatch* 4 (Washington, DC: Bureau of Public Affairs, 1993), p. 3.

144. Former Secretary of State James Baker is quoted in Elizabeth Drew, *On the Edge: The Clinton Presidency* (New York: Simon & Schuster, 1994), p. 139. The chronology of events here was drawn from that source and from Dorff, "Chronology 1992," pp. 221–230.

145. The sequence of events here draws upon Patricia Lee Dorff, ed., "Chronology 1991," *Foreign Affairs: America and the World 1991/92* 71 (1991/92): 217–220; and Dorff, "Chronology 1992," pp. 243–245.

146. The sequence of events draws upon ibid., pp. 248–251. Also see John R. Bolton, "Wrong Turn in Somalia," *Foreign Affairs* 73 (January/February 1994): 56–66.

147. Eagleburger, "Charting the Course: U.S. Foreign Policy in a Time of Transition."

CHAPTER 6

THE CLINTON ADMINISTRATION: FOREIGN POLICY AFTER THE COLD WAR

There are times when only America can make the difference between war and peace, between freedom and repression.... We cannot and should not try to be the world's policeman. But where interests and values are clearly at stake, and where we can make a difference, we must act and lead.

President William Clinton
October 22, 1996

The successor to a doctrine of containment must be a strategy of enlargement, the enlargement of the world's free community of market democracies.

Anthony Lake
National Security Advisor to President Clinton
September 1993

Bill Clinton ran for president on the theme of change—change in domestic policy and change in foreign policy.[1] With the end of the Cold War, candidate Clinton argued, American foreign policy must change to meet the challenges of the end of the twentieth century and to prepare for the twenty-first. What was needed as we enter this new era, Clinton claimed, was "a new vision and the strength to meet a new set of opportunities and threats." "We face," Clinton continued, "the same challenge today that we faced in 1946—to build a world of security, freedom, democracy, free markets and growth at a time of great change."[2] In candidate Clinton's view, the Bush administration had failed on both counts: to articulate such a vision and to put into place a foreign policy strategy for the post–Cold War era. Indeed, he argued, Bush's leadership was "rudderless, reactive, and erratic," while the country needed leadership that was "strategic, vigorous, and grounded in America's democratic values."[3]

In this chapter, we identify the approach and strategy of the Clinton administration and assess the extent to which it succeeded in putting them into operation. We begin by identifying and discussing the foreign policy principles or values and beliefs of the Clinton administration's foreign policy and the personnel selected to implement them. Then, we turn to survey numerous foreign policy actions to see how well they correspond to those expressed aims. Finally, with the changes in the political landscape at home, including Republican majorities in both Houses of Congress and with Clinton's reelection for a new term, we evaluate the problems and prospects for American foreign policy as we head toward the next century.

THE VALUES AND BELIEFS OF THE CLINTON ADMINISTRATION

Unlike the Bush administration—which critics claimed was guided by pragmatism and "ad hocism" in its foreign policy—the Clinton administration was determined to have a foreign policy rooted in a clear set of principles, derived from America's past and guided by a coherent and workable strategy, appropriate to the end of the Cold War. Moreover, domestic policy and foreign policy would be tied together in this approach. Indeed, only by shoring up America's economic and social strength at home would the United States be in a position to have an effective economic and security policy abroad. Candidate Clinton summarized his unified policy approach in this way: "We must tear down the wall in our thinking between domestic and foreign policy."[4]

Key Foreign Policy Principles

Over the years, Clinton or his representatives have sought to outline the administration's foreign policy on several different occasions. Although specifics have changed, some priorities have remained.

The first occasion was in the election campaign of 1991 and 1992, in which selected foreign policy campaign speeches outlined key goals.[5] Despite his effort to downplay foreign policy in the campaign, candidate Clinton remained committed to global engagement by the United States and sought to restore more idealism to American foreign policy—especially via a commitment to democratization and human rights across the world. Candidate Clinton, for example, chastised the Bush administration for its go-slow policy on aiding the democratization of Russia, its lack of moral content in policy toward Bosnia and Haiti, and its embracing of the Chinese government. In short, idealism would be fused back into American foreign policy.

The second occasion was in early 1993, when the new Clinton administration attempted to be more specific about the key values that he wanted to pursue. In particular, Secretary of State designate Warren Christopher summarized the Clinton administration's foreign policy principles under three simple, albeit not simplistic, headings—economic security of the United States, a strong, but flexible, defense, and the promotion of democracy.[6] At Christopher's Senate confirmation hearings prior to the inauguration, he summarized the meaning of these principles and announced that they would serve as the basis for the Clinton administration's foreign policy after the Cold War.[7]

The Economic Security of the United States. The Clinton administration claimed that its highest foreign policy priority was the economic security of the United States. The rationale for this principle was stated early on in the campaign by the future president: "Our first foreign priority and our first domestic priority are one and the same: reviving our economy. America must regain its economic strength to play our proper role as leader of the world."[8] Warren Christopher made this point forcefully as well. Foreign policy and global economic policy would no longer be divorced from one another as they so often had been in the past, Christopher declared, and he committed the Clinton administration to "advance America's economic security with the same energy and resourcefulness we devoted to waging the Cold War."[9]

To achieve this end of economic security, the Clinton administration would initially undertake several key *domestic* measures to improve foreign economic competitiveness and complete two major *foreign* initiatives as well. The administration would develop a domestic economic program making American companies and American workers more productive and more competitive abroad; it would seek to put in place a strategy to reduce U.S. foreign borrowing to support its budget deficits; and it would take the necessary action to make America a more reliable and capable trading partner. Structurally, too, the Clinton administration would add an "Economic Security Council" to the policy-making apparatus to complement the National Security Council and to ensure "that economics is no longer a poor cousin to old-school diplomacy."[10]

Abroad, this strategy would require rapid completion and implementation of two important international economic agreements then under discussion. The first was the completion of the North American Free Trade Agreement (or NAFTA) to create a more open trading order in the Western Hemisphere among the United States, Canada, and Mexico. The second was the completion of the Uruguay Round of the GATT negotiations among

117 nations. This pact would systematically lower tariff and nontariff barriers on global trade. Because the United States remained the leading trading nation in the world, these agreements would, the administration claimed, directly aid and enhance the American economy.[11]

While this economic goal would be a central foreign policy objective, it would not be accomplished in a vacuum. Some important caveats were quickly place upon its achievement by the new administration. Commercial goals, as Secretary Christopher noted, still would not surpass all other concerns in dealing with states abroad. Nonproliferation, human rights, and sustainable development in the Third World would remain as a part of the policy mix.[12] In other words, some hedging on the centrality of the economic goal was offered immediately.

A Strong, Flexible Defense. The second principle that the Clinton administration advanced was the need to maintain a strong, but more flexible, defense to meet both new and continuing security challenges. In this way, deterrence would remain an important function of the armed services, but America's defenses would also need to be prepared to meet new threats and undertake new missions. These threats would indeed be distinct from those of the Cold War years and would thus require sustained readiness.

The possible new threats—including the proliferation of nuclear, chemical, and biological weapons to several countries (e.g., Iraq and North Korea), enhanced conventional weapons, with new and more dangerous delivery systems (e.g., the Middle East), the dangers of ethnic rivalries in various regions of the world (e.g., the former Yugoslavia), and the possibility of disorder within the former Soviet Union—would require new missions for the American military as well. Peacekeeping, peacemaking, humanitarian assistance, surveillance of drug trafficking, and antiterrorism would likely become more regular staples of U.S. defense policy.

To provide this new defense posture for the United States, the Clinton administration initially proposed that the American military be streamlined in a way compatible with its new mission (e.g., greater reliance on rapid response capability and more integrated force structure across the Army, Navy, and Air Force). Still, the military must, as the Persian Gulf War demonstrated, be equipped with the latest technology to meet the variety of new circumstances. At the same time, the Clinton administration proposed that a less costly and more efficient military establishment could be developed. The defense budget would thus be cut more deeply than what the Bush administration had proposed, and these cuts would come both in the level of defense spending and in the number of personnel in uniform.

A caveat on the use of military force by the new administration was also outlined: The Clinton administration indicated that force would be used in a more calculated way in the future. Each American decision now would be more than one of intervening or not intervening in a given global situation. Instead, decision options must include more than "a choice between inaction or American intervention."[13] In addition, the Clinton administration supported meeting American security needs by encouraging other nations to act through the use of collective security mechanisms (e.g., the United Nations).

The Promotion of Democracy. The third foreign policy principle for the Clinton administration was the promotion of democracy. During the campaign, Bill Clinton promised to place a greater emphasis on promoting democracy abroad and attacked the Bush administration's support of the "status quo": "From the Baltics to Beijing, from Sarajevo to South Africa, time after time, George Bush has sided with the status quo rather than democratic change—with familiar tyrants than those would overthrow them—and with the old geography of repression rather than a new map of freedom." By contrast, he argued, "my administration will stand up for democracy."[14]

The promotion of democracy was postulated on the degree to which it comported with America's moral principles, and on how building democracy around the world would yield a safer and more peaceful international order. As both candidate and President Clinton was fond of noting in several early addresses: "Democracies don't go to war with each other"; "democracies don't sponsor terrorist acts against each other"; and democracies provide "nonviolent means for resolving disputes."[15]

Once again, however, Warren Christopher added some cautionary elements to the implementation of this principle. "Promoting democracy," he noted, "does not imply a crusade to remake the world in our image. Rather, support for democracy and human rights abroad can and should be a central strategic tenet in improving our security." Still the Clinton administration was prepared to "coordinate" all of the possible leverage available, including "trade, economic, and security assistance and debt relief" to achieve its goal. "Public diplomacy—or public prodding—can be useful in this effort as well."[16]

These three basic "pillars" of policy (as Christopher labeled them) were viewed by the Clinton administration as "mutually reenforcing." A strong economy would allow for a strong military, albeit one not burdening the domestic economy. A sound economy and a sound military would enable the United States to play a more vital role in promoting democracy by being able to leverage all its foreign policy activity. By this promotion of democracy, too, old threats would be pacified, new ones would be prevented, and new markets for American products and investments would be opened.

In reality, these initial principles were not very distant from the ones the Bush administration promoted during its last year in office. In a speech in Chicago in April 1992, Secretary of State James Baker had argued for a new American foreign policy. "Our idea," Baker said, "is to replace the dangerous period of the Cold War with a democratic peace—a peace built on the twin pillars of political and economic freedom." The policy to build this peace was "a straightforward policy of American leadership called 'collective engagement'...Collective engagement allows the United States to rally like-minded nations on behalf of peace and to draw on international institutions where they can play a constructive part."[17] Put differently, the United States would seek to create free markets and free peoples in carrying out its foreign policy and would cooperate with international institutions when it could. In this sense, the principles of the Clinton administration did not reflect very dramatic change, but the new administration would probably say that the differences lay in the implementation and consistency of their principles and policies.

The Strategy of Enlargement

The third occasion for outlining the Clinton approach occurred in September 1993, in the midst of policy problems that the Clinton administration faced over Bosnia, Somalia, Iraq, and North Korea. President Clinton and three of his key advisors—Christopher, National Security Advisor Anthony Lake, and UN Ambassador Madeleine Albright—tried once again to define America's post–Cold War course.[18] Lake, in particular, tried to move beyond a statement of principles to encapsulate the various policy actions into what he called a "strategy of enlargement." That policy would replace the policy of containment that had guided U.S. actions over the past forty-five years, with a strategy of the enlargement of the community of global democracies. Yet each of these policy makers also tried to emphasize some similar themes to give a greater focus to Clinton policy and to dispel doubts that had arisen over the various policy directions pursued by the administration. In all, we can identify four themes.

Commitment to Global Engagement. A first theme was that the United States would remain committed to global engagement. Despite some fears raised in various quarters that the United States was pursuing a "neo-isolationist" policy, the United States would stay engaged. This fear perhaps gained its greatest currency when the Undersecretary of State for Political Affairs (the third-highest position at the Department of State), Peter Tarnoff, had called a few months earlier for a lessening of American involvement around the world.[19] At the time, Secretary of State Christopher quickly rejected the idea, but Lake, Albright, Christopher, and President Clinton felt compelled to once again emphasize the global engagement of the United States. Secretary Christopher directly stated this commitment: "I want to assure you that the United States chooses engagement," while Ambassador Albright put it more colorfully: "Our nation will not retreat into a post–Cold War foxhole."

Unilateral or Collective Security. A second theme was an effort to clarify whether the United States would act alone to protect its national interest or rely upon collective security mechanisms (e.g., the United Nations). Once again, these statements were attempts to blunt criticism of "assertive multilateralism" which the administration had pointed to earlier (and which U.S. Ambassador to the United Nations Albright had endorsed) in American policy toward Somalia. A strict reliance on either unilateralism or multilateralism was rejected; instead, the United States would select the kind of action to achieve its goals on a case-by-case basis. As Secretary Christopher said: "That issue...creates a false polarity. It is not an 'either-or' proposition." Or as National Security Advisor Lake put it: "Only one overriding factor can determine whether the U.S. should act multilaterally or unilaterally, and that is America's interests."

The Use of Force. A third theme, and related to the second one, was over the use of American forces—an effort to clarify when they would be used, under what conditions, and under whose command. This theme emphasized that the use of American forces within a UN peacekeeping operation would be more closely scrutinized, with greater attention to defining the mission and identifying the endpoint of UN involvement, as Ambassador Albright noted. President Clinton, too, made similar references to these mission-related questions, although he continued to voice support for the creation of a "genuine UN peacekeeping headquarters with a planning staff...with a logistics unit that can be deployed on a moment's notice, and a modern operations center..."

A few months later, the Clinton administration began to codify these tougher positions on the use of American forces in peacekeeping operations. By May 1994, Presidential Decision Directive 25 (PDD-25) was in place. According to that directive, numerous conditions must exist before U.S. involvement: "a threat to international security," defined as the need for immediate relief efforts, a democratic challenge, or severe violations of human rights; "clear objectives" for the UN mission; "consent of the parties" for the intervention to take place; "the availability of enough money and troops; a mandate appropriate to the mission; and a realistic exit strategy."[20] In addition, the Clinton administration downgraded its commitment to the creation of a UN Army—a pledge that had been made in the campaign—and now called for fewer UN missions around the world.

Some Policy Priorities. A fourth major theme from these speeches was to identify the policy priorities and the basic strategy to guide American foreign policy. President Clinton in his address at the United Nations focused on three substantive policy areas: conflict resolution around the world, nuclear nonproliferation activities, and the promotion of sustainable development. Anthony Lake's statement, however, focused on the two value themes that the Clinton administration chose to emphasize: the promotion of democracy and the promotion of open markets. As Lake put it, "*the successor to a doctrine of containment must be a strategy of enlargement—enlargement of the world's free community of market democracies.*"[21]

Lake emphasized four key components of this strategy of enlargement:

> First, we should strengthen the community of major market democracies—including our own—which constitutes the core from which enlargement is proceeding.
>
> Second, we should help foster and consolidate new democracies and market economies where possible, especially in states of special significance and opportunity.
>
> Third, we must counter the aggression—and support the liberalization of states hostile to democracy and markets.
>
> Fourth, we need to pursue our humanitarian agenda not only by providing aid but also by working to help democracy and market economics take roots in regions of greatest humanitarian concern.[22]

What the Clinton administration was undoubtedly intending at this stage was to convey a more focused policy approach with the promotion of democracies and markets at the core. Those policy emphases, moreover, would occur first among allies like Europe and Japan (the first component), next among new states like Central Europe and Russia (the second component), and last among developing states (the fourth component). In addition, of course, the so-called "backlash" states like Iraq or North Korea (the third component) had to be contained and countered. This primacy on a promotion of democracy in policy was stated yet again by Lake about a year later, when he emphasized that policy progress would only be "through persistence and pragmatism." The United States would now be engaged in "the long struggle for democracy and the freedom and tolerance it brings."[23]

Despite the administration's effort to refocus American policy and to encapsulate it into some larger picture of global democratization, the policy approach appeared not to gain widespread support. Not only was the American public uneasy about this commitment to global democratization, but the scope of this policy was perhaps beyond what the United States really was willing to do. Further, as Henry Kissinger noted shortly after Lake's statement, while "the growth of democracy will continue as America's dominant aspiration,...it is much more difficult to translate into operational terms."[24] Indeed, the real strategy for implementation of this "enlargement" was not very effectively set out by the Clinton administration.

Finally, in January and February of 1995, Secretary Christopher once again tried to articulate the guiding principles of the Clinton administration's foreign policy approach with some important differences from earlier statements.[25] Most importantly, the guiding principles now numbered four: a commitment to be engaged and lead; a commitment to cooperative relations with powerful nations; a commitment to adapt and build economic and security institutions; and a commitment to support democracy and human rights. In turn, these principles would lead to focusing on five key areas of policy emphasis: "advancing the most open global trading system in history; developing a new European security order; helping achieve a comprehensive peace in the Middle East; combating the spread of weapons of mass destruction; and fighting international crime, narcotics and terrorism."[26]

While Secretary Christopher did set out some actions in each of these areas, suggesting more of a strategy than perhaps before, the cataloguing still has more of a piecemeal approach to foreign policy and less the shaping of a clear vision for the future. Indeed, one sharp critic summarized the Clinton approach as conducting foreign policy "as if it were on a supermarket shopping spree, grabbing whatever it takes a fancy to, without worrying about the costs or whether the product is the right brand, or is genuinely needed."[27] Similarly, what was fundamentally lacking, one congressional critic said was "a conception of what they want the world to look like in ten to 20 years."[28] Still, this listing does illustrate a bit of a moving away from the idealism portrayed on the earlier occasions and some greater nod toward realism. Note the emphasis on building new security orders and on stabilizing relations with major powers. Last, the Clinton administration also issued a national security strategy statement on two different occasions—one in July 1994 and the other in February 1995. Both largely reiterate the points made so far.[29]

Clinton's Foreign Policy Team: Carter Veterans and Close Friends

Unlike President Bush, who came to foreign policy with a broad background and interest, President Clinton, by virtually all accounts, was largely uninterested in foreign policy making. Indeed, his foreign policy background prior to assuming office was largely confined to his two years at Oxford University, some travels in Western and Eastern Europe, and his personal anguish over American involvement in the Vietnam War. By contrast, his interest and involvement in a variety of domestic issues (e.g., educational reform, economic development) as governor of Arkansas were considerable. Thus, while Clinton may have justifiably been described as a policy "wonk" on domestic issues, that label was surely less accurate on foreign policy issues. Indeed, his attitude toward foreign policy was perhaps best summarized by what the political writer Elizabeth Drew identified as the task given to Anthony Lake, Clinton's campaign foreign policy advisor and later his first national security advisor: "Keep foreign policy from becoming a problem—keep it off the screen and spare Clinton from getting embroiled as he went about his domestic business." One senior administration official acknowledged the accuracy of this assessment later in 1993: "We had hoped to keep foreign policy submerged."[30]

With President Clinton's limited interest in foreign policy and his apparent desire to keep foreign policy "submerged," the composition of his first foreign policy team thus became crucial for the refinement and implementation of his foreign policy agenda. Although Clinton had committed himself to appoint a cabinet that would "look like America" and did give some consideration to this idea, the top foreign policy posts of his first cabinet seemed more narrowly drawn: a very large number of previous foreign policy participants who had served in the Carter administration (e.g., Warren Christopher as secretary of state, Anthony Lake as national security advisor, and William Perry, his second secretary of defense), a few with Capitol Hill experience (most notably, the initial appointment of Les Aspin as secretary of defense and Madeleine Albright as U.S. ambassador to the United Nations), and some personal and campaign friends (e.g., Mickey Kantor as United States Trade Representative, Ron Brown as secretary of commerce, Samuel [Sandy] Berger as deputy national security advisor to Lake, and Strobe Talbott, first as ambassador at large for Russia, and later as deputy secretary of state).

By virtually all assessments, this foreign policy team, at least through two years of Clinton's first term, had considerable difficulty developing policy and explaining it to the American people and dealing with pressing global issues. After the appointment of William Perry to replace Les Aspin, a biting commentary in the British weekly, *The Economist*, noted that this appointment had now produced a "stealth" foreign policy team for the Clinton administration. It was comprised of "the little-known Mr. Perry, the camera-shy Anthony Lake, and the low-profile Warren Christopher as secretary of state." Each one seemingly competed, the analysts claimed, "for invisibility." Yet, "all too visible...are the global troubles they will have to cope with."[31]

While this summary is a bit overdrawn, it does convey the nagging personnel problem that the Clinton administration confronted in the foreign policy arena, especially early in its first term. "The whole national security apparatus of the President was in terrible disarray," in 1993 and 1994, by one later assessment. "There was poor central direction from the White House and a weak N.S.C. [National Security Council] staff—the worst since the first Reagan administration. They didn't know what they didn't know."[32] American foreign policy was being developed by a cacophony of voices without a strong leader or a strong spokesperson, resulting in a seemingly incoherent foreign policy to address the post–Cold War world. This difficulty was compounded somewhat by a president who appeared too detached to make foreign policy work effectively and by global events like Bosnia, Haiti, Somalia, and Russia that would not let the Clinton administration isolate foreign from domestic policy.[33]

While the performance of Christopher, Lake, and Perry improved from 1995 onward, and they enjoyed some foreign policy successes over Bosnia, Haiti, and the Middle East, the direction of American foreign policy remained unsteady, and a target of criticism. A frequent critic, Senator John McCain (R-Arizona), continued to fault the Clinton administration for its lack of "strategic coherence" in dealing with foreign policy, its "self-doubt" over the direction of American policy direction abroad and its failure to identify key American interests in carrying out policy.[34]

For the second term, some changes have been made. President Clinton's foreign policy team continues to draw from veterans of the Carter administration and close friends, but is also contains several with foreign policy experience from Clinton's first term. To replace Warren Christopher as secretary of state, President Clinton chose Madeleine Albright, who served as American ambassador to the United Nations during his first term. Anthony Lake was initially nominated to head the Central Intelligence Agency, from his post as national security advisor, but he eventually withdrew as the nominee in March 1997 after questions were raised about his management of the NSC staff and his failure to keep Congress informed on Bosnian policy during the Clinton administration's first term. George J. Tenet, the Deputy Director of the CIA at the time, and a former National Security Council staffer and Senate Intelligence Committee staff director, was nominated by President Clinton to replace Lake. Lake's deputy and Clinton's longtime personal friend, Sandy Berger, assumed the national security advisor post. To replace Secretary of Defense William Perry, President Clinton chose retiring Republican senator, William Cohen, a longtime student of defense and intelligence policy in the Senate. The appointment also reflected an attempt to reach across party lines to shape a bipartisan foreign and defense policy with Congress, especially since Cohen had been a frequent defender of congressional prerogatives in foreign affairs.[35]

While this new foreign policy team would best be characterized as solid (rather than distinguished) in their foreign policy credentials, it arguably has an opportunity to shape a clearer direction to foreign policy for the post–Cold War era. Madeleine Albright, the first woman secretary of state in

American history, is likely to be a more articulate and more outspoken secretary than Christopher had been. In this way, she may well be able to explain more fully the direction of foreign policy to the American public and the American Congress. Furthermore, with her different style, Albright may be able to rally more support internationally for the direction to be pursued by the United States. The new national security advisor, Sandy Berger, is likely to work in an accommodative way with Albright to forge a new direction and to use his expertise on policy toward Asia to fill a possible policy void under Albright.[36] Nonetheless, the role of national security advisor in controlling the interagency process within the foreign policy bureaucracy (see Chapter 10) will inevitably create some tension in the relationship. In some ways, the success of this team in forging a coherent and consistent policy may well hinge on the emerging relationship between Berger and Albright. Finally, because William Cohen has thought about the direction of defense policy and because he will have allies in the Republican-controlled Congress, where he served for twenty-four years, he may well be able to implement a new post–Cold War defense policy, something that was started, but not completed, by Les Aspin and William Perry in the first Clinton term.

POLICY ACTIONS OF THE CLINTON ADMINISTRATION

Although the Clinton administration had identified a set of principles to guide its foreign policy and made some efforts to improve its foreign policy decision-making team early on, the initial policy actions, as we noted, seemed less to flow consistently from those principles and more to assume the "ad hoc" approach of which the Bush administration had been accused. "Indecisive," "incoherent," and "inconsistent" too often became the catchwords for describing the foreign policy of the Clinton administration, whether it was toward Bosnia or Somalia or even toward China and Russia. Coupled with these regional policy problems, the Clinton team began by announcing a change in policy on gays in the U.S. military and on the use of foreign aid funds for abortion-related activities abroad. These two policy decisions, and the abrupt changes in regional policy that we shall discuss, produced sharp domestic reactions and immediately made national security and foreign policy a center of debate. Only during the last two years of its first term did the administration begin to obtain some stability in its foreign policy actions, albeit still with mixed results.

In the following sections we analyze several key foreign policy actions of the Clinton administration, assess its successes and failures, and evaluate the correlation between its stated principles and its actual foreign policy behavior.

Promoting American Economic Security

One principal area of policy consistency and policy success for the Clinton administration related to the commitment to promote "economic security" and to wed foreign policy and foreign economic policy. The North American Free Trade Agreement (NAFTA) and the pact altering the General Agreements on Tariffs and Trade (GATT) went a long way to accomplishing those tasks. Two other initiatives were begun by the administration to free up global trade in other areas of the world: the initiation of greater economic cooperation and coordination among the members of the Asia-Pacific Economic Cooperation (APEC) organization, an organization composed primarily of Pacific Rim countries and the United States, and the initiation of an organization for expanded trade among the nations of the Western Hemisphere. In addition to these initiatives, the Clinton administration made a concerted effort to free up trade between the United States and Japan and between the United States and the European Union. Overall, these actions reflected significant strides by the Clinton administration to ensure greater economic security. While some of the benefits would be long-term, others (e.g., in the case of NAFTA and Japan) would be more immediate.

NAFTA. The North American Free Trade Agreement, an agreement among the United States, Canada, and Mexico that was originally signed by the three countries in December 1992, was the Clinton administration's first step toward achieving its goal of greater economic security.[37] Although candidate Clinton had initially raised some doubts about supporting the ratification of the pact and wanted "side agreements" completed to deal with some perceived weak elements (e.g., environmental enforcement issues), President Clinton worked vigorously to persuade a reluctant Congress, and especially the House of Representatives, to approve the negotiated agreement in November 1993.

The pact itself contained several key provisions for improving U.S. trade and investment (see Document 6.1). First, all tariffs among the three member countries would eventually be eliminated. Some tariffs would be removed immediately under the pact, most would be removed over a ten-year period, and some sensitive areas (e.g., some agricultural commodities, glassware, footwear, and ceramics) would be eliminated over a fifteen-year period. To ensure that none of the three countries would be used as an "export platform" for non-NAFTA countries (i.e., initially exporting products to either Mexico, the United States, or Canada for eventual reexport within the NAFTA free trade area under tariff-free arrangements), strict "rules of origin" for products were incorporated into the pact as well. Items such as cars, footwear, chemicals, textiles, and apparel were particularly subject to stricter rules of origin, since these items were especially likely to be imported into one of the NAFTA countries and reexported to the others. Second, in the area of investment, NAFTA "guaranteed foreign investors national treatment."[38] That is, an American investor in Mexico or in Canada would be treated the same way as a Mexican investor in his country or a Canadian investor in her country. Previously, restrictions had been placed upon the other nations' investors; however, now these would be phased out. Third, services would be increasingly opened across borders. Financial services, telecommunications, and transportation, for example, would be given more equal treatment across the member countries, albeit with some re-

DOCUMENT SUMMARY 6.1

Key Components of the North American Free Trade Agreement Among Canada, Mexico, and the United States, Effective January 1, 1994

Tariffs—All tariffs on goods produced by the three countries and sold among them would be eliminated. These tariff reductions would occur over a five- to fifteen-year period. Strict "rules of origin" of goods would be observed.
Investments—All investments by the other agreement partners would be provided with "national treatment." Some restrictions were included, however, on national security grounds and, for example, in the areas of oil and the petrochemical industries for Mexico.
Services—Several areas, including banking, telecommunications, transportation, and government procurement, were to be opened to the agreement partners. Some restrictions still remained, however, in shipping, films, publishing, and oil and gas for the signatories.
Intellectual Property—Copyrights, industrial designs, trademarks, and other areas were provided protection under the pact.
Safeguards and Side Agreements—Under defined circumstances, temporary tariffs could be reimposed to protect some local industries. Side agreements were also completed to address environmental concerns and working condition issues among the participants.

Source: Abstracted from "NAFTA Provisions," *Congressional Quarterly Almanac 1993* (Washington, DC: Congressional Quarterly, Inc., 1994), pp. 180–181.

strictions and a phase-in period built in. Still, it would allow American countries greater access to these other economies and the prospect of expanded economic activities in each one. Fourth, the pact called for greater protection of intellectual property rights by fuller adherence by all parties (although it was mainly directed at Mexico) to international copyright conventions. Fifth, the pact also incorporated "safeguards" for a member country that was experiencing flooding of its market ("dumping") by another. Under certain conditions, temporary tariffs of up to four years could be imposed. For some agricultural commodities (e.g., orange juice and sugar), these "tariff snapbacks," as they were called, could be imposed when an agreed level of imports was reached. Finally, the pact incorporated a rapid dispute settlement mechanism when disputes arose among two of the NAFTA participants over questions of dumping or unfair trading practices.

A unique feature of this pact was the completion of three side agreements among the three nations. These agreements dealt with enforcing environmental standards and protecting worker rights. The pacts were not ironclad, however, in that they only established a Commission on Environmental Cooperation and a Commission on Labor Cooperation to seek compliance and recommend fines or sanctions for noncompliance. The commissions, however, would not be able to actually force a government to pay a fine for nonadherence to the environmental or labor violations.

Despite the attractive features of the pact, NAFTA was a highly controversial agreement—as the Clinton administration quickly found by the fall of 1993.[39] On the positive side, the aim of NAFTA was to expand the export market of the United States by quickly gaining access to the growing market in Mexico, whose population exceeded 85 million people. With an expanded trade area for American companies, U.S. exports would increase, American competitiveness would improve, and better and higher-paying jobs at home would result. In this sense, NAFTA would produce greater job security—and greater economic security. Further, the pact had some less-tangible political benefits: It encouraged the liberal economic policy reforms under way in Mexico; it demonstrated greater equality in dealing with a neighbor country somewhat suspicious of the United States; and it had the potential to stop the flow of Mexican immigrants to the United States—both legal and illegal—since NAFTA would also spark economic development at home and reduce the incentive to emigrate.

On the negative side, there were powerful arguments against NAFTA. While the long-term effect of creating high-skilled, high-paying jobs might be true, the short-term effect could be devastating for unskilled and semiskilled American workers. As American businesses saw the opportunity to expand into an economy with a cheaper labor market, they would do so. The result would be the dramatic loss of U.S. jobs in the short term and a further eroding of the economic well-being of the American working class. Ross Perot, the independent presidential candidate in 1992, referred to the resulting process as the "giant sucking sound" of jobs lost to Mexico. Moreover, he undertook an extensive lobby effort nationwide and coauthored a book entitled *Save Your Job, Save Our Country* to make this argument.[40]

The passage of NAFTA by the Congress was not an easy task for the Clinton administration. With public opinion polls showing substantial opposition to the pact over the summer and fall of 1993, the Clinton administration waged a vigorous campaign to win congressional approval. The President's efforts included making a number of deals, primarily with different agricultural groups, to win their support and the approval of their congressional representatives. The White House "found rural Democratic lawmakers more amenable to making deals than legislators from the northern and Rust Belt states, who tend to be linked to Big Labor and generally oppose[d] the pact."[41] Ultimately, presidential persuasion was successful—first in the House, where President Clinton had to rely more on Republicans than Democrats to ensure passage, and then in the Senate, where support was more widespread. The passage of NAFTA in late November 1993 was appropriately hailed as a key foreign policy success for the Clinton administration and wedded foreign policy and economic policy.

GATT. The GATT agreement, passed almost exactly a year later, at the end of November 1994, complemented the NAFTA accord and gave further credence to the Clinton administration's goal of economic security.[42] Discussions to complete this "Uruguay Round" of GATT (named for the fact that this "round," or set of negotiations, first started in Punta del Este, Uruguay, in 1986) had spanned two earlier administrations and sought to lower tariffs and broaden GATT coverage into areas such as agriculture, services, investment, and intellectual property rights.

The completed GATT accord had several key components (see Document 6.2). First, tariffs were to be reduced worldwide, covering roughly 85

DOCUMENT SUMMARY 6.2

Key Components of the General Agreement on Tariffs and Trade (GATT) Changes, Fully in Force by July 1, 1995

Tariffs—Tariffs worldwide will be cut on approximately 85 percent of all world trade. These tariffs will be reduced from an average of 5 percent on industrial products currently to 3 percent at the end of this process. Cuts will be made over a five- to ten-year period.
Agriculture—For the first time, agriculture will be covered under this pact. On average, agricultural subsidies will be cut by 36 percent worldwide, and agricultural products exported with the help of governmental subsidies will drop by 21 percent. Quotas in agriculture will be converted to tariffs.
Textiles—Quotas placed on textiles imported from developing countries to the developed countries will be eliminated over a ten-year period.
Services—These kinds of transactions will now be covered by the GATT accord.
Subsidies, Intellectual Property—Government subsidies for particular industries will now be lowered and international protection will be accorded intellectual property such as semiconductor chip designs, books, films, and music.
World Trade Organization—As this round of GATT enters into effect, a new and expanded trading organization will be established to regulate global trade for the future.

Sources: Abstracted from "Highlights of GATT Accord," *Congressional Quarterly Almanac 1993* (Washington, DC: Congressional Quarterly, Inc., 1994), p. 183; and "The Shape of the Accord," *New York Times*, December 15, 1993, C18.

percent of all trade. On average, tariffs on industrial products would be reduced from an average of about 5 percent to about 3 percent worldwide. These cuts would be put into effect gradually over a five- to ten-year period. Second, and one of the most important components of the pact, agricultural trade was to be included in the GATT system. Moreover, subsidies for agricultural products were to be reduced worldwide by 36 percent, and exports that were produced through the help of subsidies were to be reduced by 21 percent. Further, nontariff barriers (e.g., quotas) were to be converted to tariffs with the expectation that, over time, tariff barriers would be reduced as well. In all, these efforts were directed toward a more open and free market in agriculture worldwide. Third, textile quotas imposed by industrial countries on developing countries would be phased out during a ten-year period under the agreement. Fourth, GATT standards were now applied to the service sectors with the aim of creating more open markets, as well as intellectual property rights (e.g., on copyrighted materials). Fifth, some agreement was also reached on restricting subsidies to particular industries (e.g., the aircraft industry), since subsidized exports provided unfair advantage to particular countries in global trade. Finally, a new organization, the World Trade Organization, was incorporated into the GATT accord and, with the ratification of the Uruguay Round changes, formally replaced GATT.

While passage of the GATT accord proved less difficult than NAFTA, considerable executive branch lobbying was still necessary since some opposition arose, especially to the creation of the World Trade Organization.

(The concern was that American sovereignty on key economic policy matters would be yielded to this organization.) Still, GATT won passage easily in the House with almost two-thirds support and exactly three-quarters support in the Senate. The argument that freer trade would instill greater competitiveness in the American economy, expand economic growth, and create more jobs seemed to be supported as good foreign policy. Hence, the economic security goal of the Clinton administration appeared to be on track.

Additional Economic Initiatives. The Clinton administration initiated two additional efforts in pursuit of its economic security goal. One was directed toward a "market-opening agreement" among the Pacific Rim nations at the November 1994 APEC meeting in Indonesia.[43] APEC (or Asia-Pacific Economic Cooperation), an organization of seventeen nations across four continents, agreed "to develop a blueprint of what exactly free trade means—whether it applies to goods or services or both" and set the target of 2020 to reach the goal.[44] Such a goal was hailed by one prominent international economist who had been involved in drafting the APEC plan as "the biggest single trade initiative in history."[45] If successfully implemented, the plan would establish a free-trade area among countries that constitute more than half the global economy at present and account for more than 40 percent of global trade as well.[46]

The other effort was the "Summit of the Americas" conference held in Miami by thirty-four Western Hemisphere countries in December 1994. The summit's aim was to set in motion the creation of a free-trade zone throughout the Americas. The target date agreed upon for completing these talks was set at 2005, although the actual date for the elimination of all trade barriers was not set. Many Latin American nations wanted the process to be speeded up, with earlier completion of the free-trade pact. Since many of those states have reduced their tariffs over the last decade (thus allowing American products easier access to their countries), they wanted access to the U.S. market earlier than the 2005 target.[47] Still, clear progress was made at the summit with a strong commitment to the free-trade idea. Further, a more immediate result of the meetings was an invitation to Chile to begin the process of negotiating membership into NAFTA arrangements.

In short, these multilateral economic policy actions were fully compatible with the policy principles that the Clinton administration had set out initially. In many ways, the administration surely wanted its foreign policy identified with such economic actions, but, in general, it was not to be the case. Instead, the failures and shortcomings in the Clinton administration's policy in dealing with more traditional political and military issues—and, in some instances, its departure from professed foreign policy principles—actually came to define perceptions of its foreign policy behavior.

Promoting Stability and Democracy Abroad: The Problems of China, Bosnia, Somalia, and Haiti

Foreign policy difficulties were most evident when the Clinton administration sought to deal with political/military issues, such as those with

China, Bosnia, Somalia, and Haiti that it inherited from previous administrations, but it also sought to deal anew with issues involving Russia and Europe generally. Caught between promoting democracy and human rights and fostering global stability—and committed to changing courses from the Bush administration—the Clinton administration often vacillated in its decision making. Because the administration's expressed foreign policy principles sometimes clashed with one another, devising and implementing a consistent foreign policy strategy also remained a serious challenge. Of concern, too, were the halting policies that the Clinton administration adopted toward these trouble spots and the serious questions they raised about the future role of the United States in the post–Cold War era.

China. The nature of the relationship with the People's Republic of China offers a useful starting point to illustrate the clash of principles—the search for economic security versus the promotion of democracy—and the kind of difficulties that the Clinton administration faced from the outset of its administration. In 1992, candidate Clinton had argued that his administration's policy toward the dictators in Beijing would not follow the Bush administration's course (see Chapter 5). In particular, candidate Clinton had criticized Chinese violations of human rights, its selling of missile technology abroad, its restrictive trade policies, and the failure of the Bush administration to do much about those issues. The Bush administration basically continued diplomatic and economic relations without much interruption in the face of these problems, including the annual renewal of most favored nation (MFN) status for China. This pattern, it was promised, would not occur in a Clinton administration.

Yet virtually within days of winning the 1992 election, President-elect Clinton appeared to embrace the China policy of the Bush administration. After a meeting with President Bush in mid-November, Clinton now allowed that some progress had been made in U.S.-Chinese relations over the past several months by the outgoing administration and that there had been "more modernization" in Chinese actions in a number of areas. Further, "we create a lot of jobs with trade with China."[48] These post-election comments, in fact, foreshadowed the maintenance of past policy.

To be sure, the Clinton administration did complete a policy review, but it promptly renewed MFN status for China by late May 1993. In an important stipulation, the administration made subsequent renewal of MFN "conditional" on a July 1994 report by the secretary of state. Further renewal of MFN would occur only if the extension of this provision "will substantially promote the freedom of emigration" of Chinese citizens and if the secretary determines that China "is complying with" a 1992 agreement on the use of prison labor in products for export. In addition, the secretary of state, in making his recommendation on continuance, would need to determine whether China had made "significant progress" in several other areas: "taking steps to begin adhering" to international human rights standards, "releasing and providing an acceptable accounting" of political prisoners, especially those held as a result of the Democracy Wall and Tiananmen Square movements, "ensuring humane treatment of prisoners," "protecting Tibet's distinctive religious and cultural heritage," and "permitting international radio and television broadcasts into China."[49]

By the spring of 1994, President Clinton acknowledged that China had indeed failed to make significant progress in several of these areas, but his administration went ahead with MFN renewal anyway:

> I have decided that the United States should renew most-favored-nation trading status toward China. This decision, I believe, offers us the best opportunity to lay the basis for long-term sustainable progress in human rights and the advancement of our other interests with China.[50]

Moreover, President Clinton went even further than had the Bush administration by also announcing that it was "moving...to delink human rights from the annual extension of most-favored-nation trading status for China."[51] While the decision on renewing MFN for China might have been anticipated—given the Clinton administration's commitment to economic security questions—relations with China continued to deteriorate over several other issues in subsequent years.

The Clinton administration, for instance continued to be concerned over China's transferring of nuclear and missile technology to Iran and Pakistan, respectively, its increasing defense spending, and its sustained military activity in the South China Sea.[52] Human rights conditions did not improve, and one particular incident further clouded relations between the two countries. Harry Wu, a Chinese-born human rights activist who became an American citizen, secretly tried to enter China to document human rights abuse in mid-1995. He was seized by Chinese authorities and imprisoned for more than two months. He was subsequently convicted of espionage, sentenced to a long prison term, and then expelled from China. While American government efforts undoubtedly facilitated Wu's release, the incident revealed the considerable fissure between the two countries.[53]

Perhaps the episode that particularly revealed the low state of Sino-American relations, however, was the granting of a visa to President Lee Teng-hui of Taiwan to visit the United States. President Lee, an alumnus of Cornell University, had been invited to give the commencement address at his alma mater in the spring of 1995. Since the United States does not have formal diplomatic relations with Taiwan, and given the sensitive nature of relations among China, Taiwan, and the United States, this request became an important policy question for the United States. Initially, the Clinton administration indicated that the visa would not be granted but changed its mind after congressional resolutions supported President Lee's travel to the United States.[54] The decision was reversed in such a way that the Chinese learned "of the president's change of heart on television."[55] This change of mind infuriated the Chinese and further eroded Chinese-American relations.

Relations were drawn even tighter during Taiwan's presidential elections in March 1996. In an apparent effort to intimidate Taiwan, and to pressure the Taiwanese to elect a president more favorable than Lee Teng-hui, China undertook military exercises off Taiwan, including firing military rounds close to Taiwanese territory. In order to support Taiwan, the United

States ordered two aircraft carrier groups to head for the Taiwan Straits, the waterway between Taiwan and mainland China. When China declared that it would not allow these vessels in the Straits, the United States backed down, and a further crisis was avoided.[56] Relations between the two countries eroded further. In many ways, though, this issue paled in significance when compared to issues of ethnic unrest that the administration faced in other parts of the world, but the considerable indecisiveness throughout this decision-making situation magnified the difficulties that the administration confronted on other, more complex issues.

Bosnia. One such issue was the situation that developed in Bosnia-Herzegovina (hereafter Bosnia) in 1992 and reached tragic dimensions by the time that the Clinton administration assumed office. In the immediate post–Cold War era, Bosnia, like several other Republics (e.g., Croatia, Slovenia) in the former Yugoslavia (a country originally created by combining several different ethnic Republics and held together by the Communist lead-

MAP 6.1

The Former Yugoslavia

CHRONOLOGY 6.1

Important Policy Actions Relating to Bosnia-Herzegovina, 1992–1996

February 1992—In a referendum in Bosnia-Herzegovina, voters approve independence move.
April 1992—The United States and the European Community [now Union] recognize the independence of Bosnia; ethnic strife has already begun in the country.
May 1992—Bosnia, Croatia, and Slovenia admitted to the United Nations; UN Security Council imposes economic sanctions on Yugoslavia in an attempt to get the Serbian government of Yugoslavia to stop its attacks on Bosnia-Herzegovina.
June 1992—UN expands the size of the peacekeeping forces in Sarajevo; Bosnia-Herzegovina to assist in the humanitarian efforts there.
July 1992—Candidate Clinton attacks Bush administration policy over Bosnia and calls for U.S. bombing of Serbians in Bosnia to aid delivery of U.S. supplies.
September 1992—UN Security Council enlarges the peacekeeping force in Bosnia-Herzegovina, with up to 6,000 additional forces drawn from NATO countries.
October 1992—UN Security Council establishes a "no-fly zone" for military aircraft over Bosnia-Herzegovina and sets up a war-crimes commission to investigate reports of atrocities there; special UN envoys Cyrus Vance and Lord Owen of the European Community [now Union] propose a peace plan based upon power-sharing among ten ethnic subdivisions.
November 1992—UN expands trade sanctions against Yugoslavia by imposing a naval blockade to enforce them; NATO quickly agrees to use its force to implement the blockade.
December 1992—The United States says that Serbia is violating the "no-fly zone" over Bosnia and, within the month, NATO agrees to enforce the ban.
February 1993—The new Clinton administration calls for a diplomatic solution of the situation in Bosnia and supports the UN effort led by Vance and Owen for a partitioning of Bosnia among the major ethnic and religious groups; by the end of the month, the U.S. Air Force has begun to drop supplies to besieged Muslim towns in Bosnia-Herzegovina.
May 1993—The United States, Russia, Britain, France, and Spain agree on joint effort to seek a negotiated settlement going beyond Vance-Owen initiative.
June–July 1993—Bosnian Serbs reject Vance-Owen plan in referendum; an agreement is reached in principle to divide Bosnia into three ethnic Republics; siege of Sarajevo, the Bosnian capital, continues with only some temporary letups.
September 1993—President Clinton reiterates his earlier commitment to send American forces to enforce any Bosnian settlement, but he now qualifies that commitment, based upon congressional approval.
November–December 1993—Talks among Muslims, Croats, and Serbs are held, but break up quickly, with no progress.
February 1994—NATO approves American proposal for airstrikes against the Serbian forces in Bosnia.
April 1994—NATO forces undertake two air strikes against Bosnian Serbs positions around the UN "safe haven" of Gorazde to deter them from shelling the town.
November 1994—The Clinton administration announces the end to U.S. enforcement of the United Nations arms embargo that had been imposed against the Bosnian Muslims.
December 1994—The Clinton administration indicates that UN forces would be used to assist in the evacuation of UN peacekeepers from Bosnia if a request were made to do so.

CHRONOLOGY 6.1

Important Policy Actions Relating to Bosnia-Herzegovina, 1992–1996 (continued)

May 1995—The Bosnian Serbs resume attacks around Sarajevo, and NATO forces initiate air strikes around the Serb headquarters at Pale. In turn, the Serbs seize UN peacekeepers as hostages.

July 1995—Bosnian Serb forces overrun Muslim safe havens of Srebenica and Zepa. Thousands of Muslims are taken away and massacred in some of the worst instances of "ethnic cleansing." The House and the Senate pass a resolution to lift the arms embargo against Bosnia-Herzegovina in order to allow the Muslims to defend themselves. The Clinton administration threatens a veto of that resolution.

August 1995–October 1995—After an attack on Sarajevo once again, NATO initiates a bombing campaign to stop the attacks and to pressure for negotiations. Croatian forces, with the tacit approval of the United States, retake territories in the Krajina region from Bosnian Serbs, and the Bosnian Muslims seek territories around Sarajevo.

October 1995—U.S. efforts at a negotiated settlement produce a cease-fire among the competing factions and leads to an agreement to hold preliminary talks in Dayton, Ohio.

November 1995—Extended talks occurs among the presidents of Serbia, Bosnia, and Croatia in Dayton. An agreement is finally reached on implementing a political settlement based upon ethnic divisions within a multiethnic society. The Serb Republic and the Croat-Muslim Federation will comprise the two constituent parts of a coalition national government for Bosnia. Separate governments will operate in the constituent parts. NATO agrees to enforce the agreement to separate the parties, stabilize armistice lines, and assist with demobilization and disarmament efforts among the parties. It will also assist with elections by September 1996, although other international agencies will conduct the elections and provide reconstruction assistance.

December 1995—The Dayton Accords are formally signed in Paris. NATO authorizes the use of an Implementation Force (IFOR) sent to Bosnia to assist in carrying out the accords. The United States, along with more than twenty other nations (both NATO and non-NATO countries), sends forces to Bosnia as part of the IFOR arrangement.

January–July 1996—The implementation of the Dayton Accords progresses reasonably well and without major incident. The return of Bosnian refugees to their original homes proceed less well, and the increasing evidence of massive slaughters of Bosnians sustains the ethnic hostility. Indicted war criminals, particularly the Bosnian Serb leader, Radovan Karadzic, and the Serb military leader, Ratko Mladic, escape capture.

August 1996—Municipal elections, scheduled for September 1996, are cancelled because the return of refugees to their hometowns is largely unsuccessful.

September 1996—The presidential and parliamentary elections are held, largely without incident and with a 70 percent turnout. Ethnic-based parties succeed in each area of Bosnia, with the Muslim candidate in Bosnia garnering the largest number of votes and elected as the chair of the tripresidency, composed of a Serb, Croat, and Muslim.

December 1996—NATO replaces IFOR with a new Stabilization Force (SFOR), composed of about 8,500 Americans. This new force would remain in Bosnia for another eighteen months to facilitate the peace process.

Sources: Patricia Lee Dorff, ed., "Chronology 1992," *Foreign Affairs: American and the World 1992/1993* 72 (1993): 221–230; Patricia Lee Dorff, ed., "Chronology 1993." *Foreign Affairs: Agenda 1994* (New York: Council on Foreign relations, 1994), pp. 219–225; "Serbs in Their Sights," *The Economist*, April 16, 1994, 15–16; "U.S. Policy in Bosnia," *Congressional Quarterly Weekly Report*, December 10, 1994, 3515; and "Four Tortuous of (sic) Years of Talk, Broken Promises and War," *New York Times*, November 1, 1995, A9.

ership of Marshall Tito throughout the Cold War) sought independence. Indeed, in April 1992, a public referendum was held, and independence was supported and promptly declared.

Conflicts immediately arose, however, because Bosnia is a multiethnic and multireligious state composed of ethnic Serbs, ethnic Croats, and Muslims. Serbia (with Montenegro), the official successor to the Yugoslav government, opposed an independent Bosnia, especially one that did not allow for Serbian domination. Moreover, the Bosnian Serbs immediately took up their cause not only to protect their interests within Bosnia, but also to lead the charge for the completion of a greater Serbia. (Links between Serbia and the Bosnian Serbs existed, of course, but the question was how integrated they would be.) Bosnian Serbs, as the largest ethnic group in the Republic, with an estimated 44 percent of the population, sought to dominate the Bosnian Croats with about 17 percent and the Bosnian Muslims with about 31 percent of the population.[57] Fierce ethnic fighting broke out, beginning about April 1992, and "ethnic cleansing" (the euphemistic expression for genocide by one ethnic group against another, albeit especially by the Bosnian Serbs against the Muslims) quickly occurred and was well documented. The killings, and the continued killings, alarmed even the most disengaged observers.[58]

The UN Security Council passed a resolution in 1992 to send in a UN Protection Force (UNPROFOR) to Bosnia in an attempt to maintain a cease fire among the parties. The European Community (now European Union) also initially sought to play a negotiating role to try to get the parties together. The U.S. position, meanwhile, was largely to view the situation in Bosnia as a European problem and to follow the lead of the Europeans and the United Nations in resolving it. In effect, this policy meant the backing of sanctions imposed upon Serbia and in supporting a "no fly zone" over the Bosnian republic to prevent Serbian and Bosnian Serb military attacks. Beyond those actions, Bush's Secretary of State James Baker summarized the extent of American interest in that conflict by noting "we don't have a dog in that fight."[59] Such a policy, however, did not stop the fighting, and more and more fighting and bloodshed resulted, including massive destruction of historic cities such as Dubrovnik and Sarajevo within Bosnia. Moreover, the assaults on Sarajevo quickly brought to mind the actions in that city prior to the outbreak of World War I and at least raised the question of whether the Balkans was again to serve as a powder keg in global politics.

As with Chinese policy, candidate Clinton had been quite explicit about his disagreement with Bush administration policy and promised that the position on Bosnia would change once he took office. Once elected, President Clinton did, in fact, spend an extraordinary amount of foreign policy time on the Bosnian issue—perhaps more than any other foreign policy issue in the early days of his administration. The effort, however, turned into one of frustration, since his advisors could not agree—and he could not decide—on which policy course to follow.[60] Indeed, policy swings occurred toward Bosnia without much permanent change over the initial years of the Clinton administration.

In late February 1993, for example, the Clinton administration announced that it would largely endorse ongoing diplomatic efforts, led by UN and European Community envoys Cyrus Vance and David Owen, and seek to reinvigorate those discussions. As that option was being implemented—and being criticized—the administration did agree to have American aircraft help drop food to besieged Bosnian Muslims. At the same time, the administration sought to pursue a tougher policy against the Bosnian Serbs. In particular, the policy of lifting the arms embargo against the Bosnian Muslims and engaging in air strikes against the Bosnian Serbs became the principal policy option and the main source of debate among the key policy advisors. In particular, Clinton's key advisors were deeply divided over the utility of air strikes. Could they be carried out given the terrain and the weather in Bosnia? Would they be effective, or would they endanger innocent populations? How would they affect the Serbs?

The so-called lift and strike option (i.e., lifting the arms embargo against Bosnia and attacking the Bosnian Serbs with air strikes) was eventually chosen as a new step by the Americans, but a serious stumbling block quickly arose—the reaction of the Western allies. (The Clinton administration did not want to carry out the policy alone.) Secretary of State Warren Christopher was given the job of selling the policy option to the allies—particularly the British and French, who had large contingents in Bosnia as part of the peacekeeping forces and whose forces would be endangered by the strike option. The allies balked at the lift and strike option, and the Clinton administration backed down. Moreover, this interalliance dispute became public, and Clinton's policy vacillations became evident. Critics saw the situation as Clinton caving in to the allies, as America's global leadership faltering, and as the United States being indecisive.

One seemingly positive development did result from this attempted policy initiative. In their opposition to lift and strike, the Europeans proposed the creation of "safe areas" for the Bosnian Muslims. These were to be areas where Bosnian Muslims presumably would be safe and have access to adequate food and medicine. Still, by the spring of 1993, Bosnian policy in the West was being sarcastically described as "rift and drift," and was hardly distinguishable from the Bush policy.[61]

Three policy options—seeking a diplomatic solution, lifting the arms embargo on the Bosnian Muslims, and engaging in air strikes against the Bosnian Serbs—framed the discussion for the next two years for the Clinton administration. Moreover, the back and forth arguments over these options aptly serve as a metaphor for uncertain Bosnian policy and American policy generally. It should be noted that one option was always ruled out in these discussions—the use of American ground troops in Bosnia—a fact not lost on the British and French, who formed the bulk of the UN mission there. Yet, even the rejection of the use of American forces had two exceptions built in: (1) If a negotiated agreement were reached for Bosnia, the Clinton administration would pledge up to 25,000 troops to enforce the pact (later, this position was amended to include the proviso that congressional approval for this action would be necessary); and (2) the United States sent a force of 300 (later, a total of 500) Americans to Macedonia, another republic in the former Yugoslavia, as part of the UN peacekeeping effort to prevent the expansion of the Balkan war there.

Although the Clinton administration continued to argue for stronger military action against the Serbs, it also explored a negotiated settlement, since the NATO allies were so reluctant to use force.[62] In the summer of 1993, the Clinton administration supported a negotiated settlement, built upon an expansion and revision of the Vance-Owen plan of about a year earlier. New proposals centered on the creation of ten ethnic enclaves and a confederation among them. Another proposal called for establishing three separate republics. By July 1994 the so-called contact group, composed of the United States, Britain, France, Germany, and Russia, offered a complex proposal as the basis for negotiating a Bosnian peace. It called for Serb- and Muslim-controlled areas, some areas divided between the two, and UN-controlled and European Union–controlled areas as well. None of these discussions yielded any positive outcomes in the short term, and the fighting and shelling continued. Throughout the conflict, however, Bosnian Serbs forces held the upper hand and gained more and more territory, controlling up to 70 percent of Bosnia by the end of 1994.[63]

By November and December 1994, as the "safe haven" town of Bihac was surrounded by Serb forces (and unable to receive food supplies from the outside world), and as Sarajevo continued under siege, the Clinton administration shifted its policy again. It formally abandoned the effort to gain widespread support for air strikes and a lifting of the arms embargo (although it did announce that the United States would no longer enforce the embargo). Instead, a new effort (largely the European allies' position) was embraced: seeking a negotiated settlement by suggesting further changes in the contact group's plan for a settlement.[64] As those efforts appeared to be failing, former President Jimmy Carter stepped in and aided the process by serving as an independent mediator. A four-month truce was eventually negotiated and was endorsed by the Western powers. The prospect of some movement on the Bosnia question was raised once again, although without great expectation.

During the first two years, the administration's Bosnian policy could only be labeled a failure: The Clinton administration had not succeeded in promoting democracy and human rights or even obtaining much stability in that troubled land. To be sure, the Clinton administration had taken several different kinds of actions: it had unilaterally abandoned enforcing the arms embargo, although the ban was continued by others; it had undertaken some limited air strikes against the Serbs, and it had continued the UN "no-fly zones" over that country.[65] Yet, the situation had actually deteriorated. More land was now held by Serbs, a new negotiating position was advanced by the United States that was more favorable to the Bosnian Serbs (and thus appeared to reward aggression), and the plights of the Muslims and the largely Muslim-controlled Bosnian Government were worse. More significantly, the fighting and the bloodshed among the ethnic groups continued.

During 1995 and 1996, American policy prospects improved. The Carter-negotiated truce largely held until about March 1995, when periodic fighting erupted. By May, with the truce officially ended, more widespread fighting began. By the end of the month, in fact, Serb forces seized UN peacekeepers in retaliation for NATO bombing. By July 1995, the situations worsened yet again, when Serb forces overran two important Muslim safe havens, Srbrenica and Zepa, and subsequently massacred scores (or more) of Muslims.[66] A month later, a shocking, apparently Serbian, attack on a Sarajevo market further fueled the deteriorating situation in Bosnia.

These actions jolted the international community, and especially the United States, into action. The Congress passed a resolution in July 1995 calling for a unilateral American lifting of the arms embargo against the Bosnian Muslims to allow them to defend themselves. NATO decided to use air power to defend Bosnian Muslim areas and began an air campaign across different parts of Bosnia. The United States, too, apparently gave "a green light to the Croatian attack on Serb-occupied Krajina [in northwest Bosnia] in late July."[67] Most importantly, the United States began a new diplomatic initiative to bring peace to the area.

Through tortuous negotiations, led by Assistant Secretary of State Richard Holbrooke, and with the help of NATO airpower and Bosnian Muslim and Croat successes against the Serbs, a cease-fire accord was finally agreed to and signed by the parties on October 5, 1995.[68] Furthermore, the parties agreed to meet at Dayton, Ohio, in November to discuss a peace agreement. After several weeks of negotiations, the "Dayton Accords" were accepted by the parties and were formally signed on December 14, 1995, in Paris. The Accords provided for the continuance of a Croat-Muslim Federation and a Serb Republic within a single Bosnian state, with Sarajevo remaining as the capital and as a multiethnic city.

Under the Dayton agreement, NATO and other countries agreed to provide up to a 60,000 implementation force (IFOR) to put the agreement into effect by keeping the parties separate and aiding reconstruction efforts. The United States agreed to contribute about 20,000 personnel, the largest contingent of any single nation, to the implementation force. Despite considerable American domestic opposition and rancorous congressional debate (but ultimate congressional resolutions to support the deployment of American troops there), IFOR proved more successful than many initially suggested. National Bosnian elections were scheduled—and conducted—on September 14, 1996, to elect a federal government with a tripresidency—a Bosnian Muslim, Croat, and Serb—and a national legislature. While all did not go well—freedom of speech and movement were restricted prior to the elections, and local elections were repeatedly postponed because some Bosnians were denied the right to return to their home areas—on balance, the Dayton accords worked better than expected.

Nonetheless, by November 1996, NATO appeared prepared to keep forces in Bosnia beyond the December 1996 departure date that the Clinton administration had initially stated for American forces. Indeed, a new force, named the Stabilization Force (SFOR), was authorized by NATO to replace IFOR. This force, a scaled-down version of IFOR and composed of about 8,500 Americans and other NATO-country forces, would remain for another eighteen months. Even so, sustained peace in Bosnia, after the ultimate departure of NATO forces, seemed problematic, and the future of Bosnia as a united multiethnic nation remained unclear.

In short, while the Clinton administration had avoided an American quagmire in Bosnia, and it achieved some stability there, the long-term prospect for its policy remained clouded. Early on, the administration had sent mixed signals over what the American role would be in such emerging conflicts and trouble spots. Only later, roughly about mid-1995, did the administration begin to address Bosnia with a clear and consistent policy. Still, the extent of engagement and involvement by the United States in such conflicts was not easily determined by the Bosnian case.

Somalia. By late 1996, in another area of the world, Somalia, Clinton administration policy fared much worse than the outcome in Bosnia. As noted in Chapter 5, the Bush administration had originally sent some 28,000 Americans to initiate Operation Restore Hope. That operation sought to provide humanitarian aid to a country torn apart by a civil war and devastated by a massive famine. The initial effort proved highly successful, and it was largely a U.S.-led and U.S.-directed mission, although formally authorized under a United Nations Security Council Resolution (see Chronology 6.2).

During February and March 1993, however, the Clinton administration changed the nature of the mission by backing a UN Security Council Resolution that placed the operation more fully under UN direction and moved it beyond a humanitarian mission to what came to be called a "nation-building" one. UN Security Council Resolution 814 called for the special representative of the UN Secretary-General in Somalia to "assume responsibility for the consolidation, expansion, and maintenance of a secure environment throughout Somalia." This resolution went further by calling for the Secretary-General to solicit funding for "the rehabilitation of the political institutions and economy of Somalia."[69] At the time, U.S. Ambassador to the United Nations Madeleine Albright hailed this resolution and noted, with enthusiasm, that "we will embark on an unprecedented enterprise aimed at nothing less than the restoration of an entire country as a proud, functioning and viable member of the community of nations."[70]

In practical terms, this resolution put U.S. forces under UN command and put them in the business of trying to institute a stable government among the competing clans in that African nation. In June 1993, however, the situation began to deteriorate as nation-building proved to be an elusive goal. General Mohammed Farah Aidid, the leader of the largest clan in Somalia, and his followers were unsympathetic to this new UN mission, presumably because they would lose power and influence in the country. As such, they apparently attacked and killed twenty-three Pakistani UN peacekeepers and wounded many more.

As a result of this incident, the UN mission changed once again. The UN and U.S. forces were now directed by yet another UN Security Council resolution to attempt to capture those responsible for the initial attack. Fighting between the U.S./UN forces and the local clans escalated over the next several months, with loss of lives and with an expansion of American presence in Somalia once again. (Some drawdown in forces had occurred previously.)

CHRONOLOGY 6.2

American Policy Toward Somalia, 1991–1995

January 1991—After Somali leader Siad Barre is driven from power, fighting erupts among the different clans within the country, and a civil war ensues. In addition, a widespread drought adds to the unrest, and starvation threatens almost one-third of the population.
February–April 1992—Cease-fire among competing factions is arranged through the UN, but the fighting continues among the independent armies, factions, and bandits. The United Nations authorizes the sending of fifty monitors to observe the operation of the cease-fire.
July–August 1992—The UN Security Council authorizes an airlift of food and medical supplies to aid the Somalis and the sending of 500 armed peacekeepers. The Bush administration agrees to provide transportation for the peacekeeping forces. In August, the authorized number of peacekeepers is expanded to 3,000, and U.S. military aircraft delivers food assistance to Somalia.
December 1992—The United National Security Council passes a resolution authorizing that its members "use all necessary means to establish as soon as possible a secure environment for humanitarian relief operations in Somalia." The Bush administration initiates "Operation Restore Hope" and authorizes the sending of 28,000 American troops to Somalia. President-elect Clinton endorses the Bush administration's actions.
February–March 1993—American and UN officials agree that the United Nations forces will replace American forces in Somalia "in the relatively near future." The United Nations passes a resolution in March 1993, expanding the mission in Somalia. The resolution calls upon the Secretary-General's special representative there "to assume responsibility for the consolidation, expansion, and maintenance of a secure environment throughout Somalia" and states that financial help should be sought for "the rehabilitation of the political institutions and economy of Somalia."
May 1993—The United Nations assumes control of relief activities in Somalia.
June 1993—Fighting in Somalia continues and twenty-three Pakistani and UN peacekeepers are killed; UN passes a resolution condemning attack and authorizing the arrest of the attackers; and U.S. and UN forces initiate attacks upon clan leader, General Mohammed Farah Aidid, and his forces. More Somalis and some American UN peacekeepers are killed.
September 1993—More violence continues within Somalia, and calls are made for American reinforcements there.
October 1993—Eighteen Americans are killed in Somalia, and many are wounded. The U.S. Congress reacts to this violence by calling for the withdrawal of American forces promptly since the mission in that country remains unclear and has been expanded over the past several months.
March 1994—The deadline for withdrawal of all American forces has passed, and virtually all, except for a small contingent, have left Somalia.
September 1994—The last American soldier leaves Somalia on the day of the American invasion of Haiti.
March 1995—The United Nations withdraws the last of its peacekeepers from Somalia.

Sources: John R. Bolton, "Wrong Turn in Somalia," *Foreign Affairs* 73 (January/February 1994), 56–66; "A Somalia Chronology," *Congressional Quarterly Almanac 1993* (Washington, DC: Congressional Quarterly, Inc, 1994), p. 489; Patricia Lee Dorff, ed., "Chronology 1992," *Foreign Affairs: American and the World 1992/1993* 72 (1993): 248–251; Patricia Lee Dorff, ed., "Chronology 1993," *Foreign Affairs: Agenda 1994* (New York: Council on Foreign Relations, 1994), 241–245; and "Chronology—March 1995," *The World Almanac and Book of Facts 1996* (Mahwah, NJ: World Almanac Books, 1996), p. 52.

On October 3, 1993, American involvement reached its peak. On that day, as American forces tried to capture some of Aidid's assistants (and perhaps Aidid himself), they were met by a strong response. In all, eighteen Americans were killed, and many more were wounded. One dead American was dragged through the streets of Mogadishu, and a captured American was put on display.[71] These sights brought a quick response at home. Almost immediately, calls were heard in Congress for the withdrawal of all American forces. Ultimately, a compromise resolution was approved requiring all forces to be home by March 31, 1994.

By March 1995, in fact, the United Nations withdrew completely from Somalia. Immediately afterwards, looting and fighting among the rival clans reemerged. By the end of August 1996, by one assessment, Somalia was in as desperate situation as it had been when the United Nations had first directed its attention to that country.[72]

For American foreign policy, the actions in Somalia raised a number of important policy questions: What was the United States trying to accomplish? Why were American forces under UN command? Why were there not adequate forces and sufficient equipment to respond to the Americans under siege? (One account outlined how the fire fight went on for some sixteen hours before it was broken.[73]) What American interests were really at stake in Somalia? The Somalia case, much like the early action in Bosnia, raised questions about the Clinton administration's foreign policy goals of promoting democracy and stability, about its ability to conduct effective foreign policy, and about its role in UN peacekeeping missions.

Haiti. Policy toward restoring democracy to Haiti raised these kinds of questions yet a third time in the first year of the Clinton administration. Should the United States get involved in promoting or restoring democracy again? Is our national interest affected over what is happening in Haiti? Ultimately, the outcome of this episode proved more positive for the Clinton administration than the earlier two cases, but relevant policy making was still fraught with indecisiveness until the summer of 1994.

As noted in Chapter 5, the Bush administration had provided political exile to Haiti's democratically elected president, Jean-Bertrand Aristide, after his ouster in September 1991, and had taken numerous economic actions—including the freezing of assets of the new Haitian government and imposing trade restrictions—to effect the return of democracy to Haiti.[74] The Clinton administration, however, was committed to do more than the Bush administration had done to support democracy in the Western Hemisphere and to return Aristide to power in Haiti (see Chronology 6.3).

As a start, the Clinton campaign had promised that it would reverse the Bush administration policy of forcefully returning Haitians seeking asylum in the United States to Haiti. As in the case of China, however, this campaign pledge was quickly jettisoned, even before President-elect Clinton was inaugurated. As a result, the Bush administration's policy on returning Haitian refugees remained in effect. The Clinton administration did undertake a vigorous diplomatic effort to urge the restoration of democracy in Haiti. In addition, the United States agreed to expand sanctions against

CHRONOLOGY 6.3

American Policy Toward Haiti, 1991–1995

December 1990—Democratic elections are held in Haiti and Jean-Bertrand Aristide is elected president by an overwhelming majority of the people.
September 1991—Aristide ousted from power in a military coup and seeks exile in the United States.
February–June 1992—Ousted Haitian President Jean-Bertrand Aristide and leaders of Haitian parliament reach agreement on his return to power in Haiti. Haitian leaders of the military government install their own new premier, and Aristide remains in exile.
May–August 1992—President Bush issues an executive order instructing the U.S. Coast Guard to return all boats carrying Haitian refugees to their country. In August, the U.S. Supreme Court holds that the Coast Guard can continue to carry out this policy, but declares that it would hear additional arguments over whether this action violates U.S. law.
January 1993—President-elect Clinton said that he would continue the policy adopted by the Bush administration of returning Haitians seeking asylum in the United States, despite campaign pledges not to follow this policy. United Nations observers are allowed to enter Haiti to assess human rights conditions.
March 1993—The Clinton administration tells Aristide that it will increase its efforts to put him back in power in Haiti.
June 1993—The United Nations Security Council places trade sanctions on oil, arms, and financial activity on Haiti. U.S. Supreme Court backs America's Haitian refugee return policy being followed by the Bush and Clinton administrations. Governor Island's agreement is reached between Aristide and Haiti's de facto ruler, General Raoul Cedras, presumably paving the way for Aristide's return by October.
August 1993—UN sanctions lifted against Haiti as incentive for return of Aristide and restoration of democracy.
October 1993—Haitian supporters of military government prevent the landing of the American ship, USS *Harlan County*, carrying U.S. trainers for a new Haitian police force as part of the Governor's Island accord. Haitian leaders indicate that they are unwilling to carry out the accord, and the United Nations promptly reimposes sanctions on that country.
January 1994— Clinton administration had called for the Haitian military rulers to resign by January 15 or face new tougher sanctions.
March 1994—American sanctions were to be tightened against Haiti, and the Clinton administration offers a new proposal for the return of Aristide to power.
July 1994—Haitian leaders expel UN human rights observers. UN Security Council passes a resolution authorizing the use of all necessary means to remove the illegal rulers in Haiti and to restore democracy. The United States agrees to lead a multinational force in this effort. An increased number of Haitians are fleeing their country.
September 1994—President Clinton announces an impending intervention into Haiti to restore democracy. Former President Jimmy Carter, former chairman of the U.S. Joint Chiefs of Staff, General Colin Powell, and Senator Sam Nunn make a last-ditch effort to negotiate a peaceful settlement for the return of Aristide and the removal of the military government. An agreement is reached, and an American occupation force of about 15,000 peacefully intervenes to restore order and complete the transition of power.

continued on next page

CHRONOLOGY 6.3

American Policy Toward Haiti, 1991–1995 (continued)

October 1994—Democratically elected President Jean-Bertrand Aristide is restored to power in Haiti.
January 1995—The first American soldier is killed in Haiti from hostile fire.
March 1995—American forces are replaced by a UN Mission in Haiti (UNMH), although the United States would contribute 2,400 military personnel to this operation.

Sources: Patricia Lee Dorff, ed., "Chronology 1992," *Foreign Affairs: American and the World 1992/1993* 72 (1993): 243–245; Patricia Lee Dorff, ed., "Chronology 1993," *Foreign Affairs: Agenda 1994* (New York: Council on Foreign Relations, 1994), pp. 237–240; Elizabeth Drew, *On the Edge: The Clinton Presidency* (New York: Simon & Schuster, 1994); George Szamuely, "Clinton's Clumsy Encounter with the World," *Orbis* 38 (Summer 1994): 389–390; "Remarks by the President in Television Address to the Nation," September 15, 1994; and "Chronology—March 1995," *The World Almanac and Book of Facts 1996* (Mahwah, NJ: World Almanac Books, 1996), p. 52.

Haiti and the military government in power. In June 1993, moreover, the UN Security Council voted to impose an oil and arms embargo against Haiti and to freeze its assets.[75]

The United Nations, the Organization of American States, and the United States seemingly achieved some initial success when an agreement was signed between Aristide and Haiti's de facto ruler, Lieutenant General Raoul Cedras, on Governors Island in New York in July 1993. Under the terms of this pact, General Cedras would step down by October 30, 1993, and Aristide would return to power. In addition, a new cabinet would be in place earlier to assist the transfer of power, the international community (including the United States) would provide training to professionalize the police and military for a return to democracy, and significant foreign assistance would be provided to aid the redevelopment of the society and economy in Haiti.[76]

Despite this agreement, indications quickly appeared suggesting that the Haitian military had little intention of adhering to the pact. In September 1993, for example, armed Haitians attacked Aristide supporters within the country, and a month later, the reform-minded Minister of Justice was assassinated. A few days before this killing, another ominous event had occurred. The American troopship, USS *Harlan County*, which was carrying U.S. and Canadian engineers who were to help retrain the Haitian police and military, was turned away from Port-au-Prince harbor by a small group of Haitians. The action was significant because it was, in effect, an attack upon the Governors Island accord. The ship remained offshore for about two days, as the Clinton administration decided what to do. Eventually, the ship simply sailed away, and, with it, much of the prospect for the immediate return of Haitian democracy.

Within days, the Cedras government in Haiti issued additional demands for implementing the Governors Island accord, and it accused the Aristide side of not living up to the pact. The agreed return date of October 30 passed with Aristide still in the United States. As a result, the United Nations reimposed sanctions on Haiti and authorized those sanctions to be enforced through the use of warships around Haiti. The United States went further by freezing American assets of Haitian military personnel and blocking numerous kinds of financial transactions between the island nation and the United States.[77]

By early 1994, the Clinton administration demanded, to no avail, that the Cedras government resign by January 15 or face tougher sanctions.[78] In April, Randall Robinson, head of TransAfrica, an African-American lobbying group, began a hunger strike to protest U.S. inaction over Haiti, a protest that eventually got President Clinton's attention and, in part, stimulated action. By the next month, the UN Security Council imposed virtually total economic sanctions upon Haiti; a little later, the Clinton administration appointed a new special envoy to pursue the restoration of democracy in Haiti, and it imposed harsher U.S. sanctions.[79]

By July, as violence continued in Haiti and as the economic sanctions took effect, more and more people began to flee the nation for the United States. Haitian policy once again occupied the front burner in the Clinton administration as American military forces had to repatriate the fleeing Haitians or find "safe havens" for them. The number of boat people was staggering, and the fear of loss of life at sea further affected policy making.

At the end of July 1994, the UN Security Council took the ultimate action allowable under the organization's Chapter VII on collective security: It passed, with U.S. backing, a resolution authorizing the use of force to restore democracy. The Council also set down particulars for the UN's role over the next two years to facilitate the democratic process in that country once Aristide was restored to power. Accordingly, the UN mission in Haiti would last until February 1996.[80] With this resolution in hand, the Clinton administration moved to implement it over the next two months.

In a September 15, 1994, nationwide address, President Clinton virtually announced his intention to invade if the military ruling Haiti did not give up power promptly ("Your time is up—leave now or we'll force you from power").[81] In an attempt to avert a bloody and costly forced intervention, and with opposition by the public and Congress widespread at the time, President Clinton decided, at the last moment, to send three prominent Americans—former President Jimmy Carter, retired General Colin Powell, and Senator Sam Nunn— to Haiti to attempt to negotiate the military leaders' departure from power. At the eleventh hour, the group succeeded. An agreement was reached whereby Aristide would return in about a month's time and political authority would be restored to Aristide. To facilitate this agreement, the U.S. military would occupy Haiti as a prelude to further United Nations actions.

On September 19, 1994, American forces began landing in Haiti without opposition, and eventually a force totaling about 20,000 soldiers from roughly twenty-five nations occupied the country (although the largest contingent was American forces).[82] The operation went without a hitch, and no American life was lost from hostile fire until January 1995. The restoration of President Aristide took place on schedule, although about a year after the original date set in the Governors Island agreement. Still, the promotion of democracy in Haiti had appeared to yield success for the Clinton administration. Moreover, by early 1995, the operation had gone so well that the transfer of authority to the 6,000 member UN force (with one-half American soldiers) was scheduled to take place sooner than originally envisioned. These UN forces remained until March 1996.

Elections were held in Haiti, power was transferred to the new government, and democracy seemingly was operating. By the fall of 1996, however, the Haitian government had to call upon American security assistance because the new president, Rene Preval, suspected that some members of his personal security force were involved in assassination activities. Consequently, the president did not feel secure in the presidential palace and actually avoided that residence during a visit of high American officials in late August.[83] In short, there was fear, as evidenced by this action and others, that Haiti was still showing "every sign of remaining Haiti," as noted in the felicitous phrase of one critic a few months earlier and by the continuing political turmoil into mid-1997.[84]

While the promotion in Haiti of democracy and stability was seemingly successful, the same lingering questions remained for the Clinton administration: What was the role of the United States in the post–Cold War era? What was the role of the national interest as a guide to U.S. policy? And would the United States control its own forces in foreign operations? Although the success in Haiti aided the Clinton administration's standing with the public on foreign policy temporarily, Americans remained wary about the pursuit of these kinds of nation-building initiatives.[85]

Promoting Stability and Democracy Abroad: Central Europe, Russia, and the Middle East

The Clinton administration also sought to promote democracy in Central Europe (particularly in Russia) and to achieve stability in the Middle East. While policies in neither region produced the same level of controversy as the other areas just discussed, more muted debate continued to occur. Policy toward those regions, moreover, reflected more a continuity with the Bush administration and less an emphasis on change initiated by the Clinton administration. In neither region, however, did policy success come easily or was it very complete.

Central Europe and Russia. Although Russia did not command the center of attention in American foreign policy that it had during the Cold War, the Clinton administration gave considerable time to that country and to Central Europe generally. The policy aims were to make certain that Russia's economic and political reforms were encouraged and supported, that other countries in the region stayed on a democratic track, and that a new and more stable European security arrangement was initiated. Moreover, the Clinton administration had decided early on to stake its policy in the region on the survival of the democratically elected government of Boris Yeltsin. American policy decisions toward Russia and the region were, therefore, continuously sensitive to that concern.

In the economic area, for example, the Clinton administration made a concerted effort to provide more American assistance to aid the transformation of the Russian society than the Bush administration had done. Indeed, during the 1992 campaign, candidate Clinton had actually announced his commitment to aiding Russian efforts immediately after President Bush's own policy statement in April 1992, and he quickly criticized the Bush administration for being too slow and cautious.[86] Once in office, President Clinton moved quickly to provide assistance to Russia. At the Vancouver summit meeting in April 1993 between Yeltsin and Clinton, President Clinton promised $1.6 billion in aid to Russia covering such areas as agriculture, food and medicine, housing, dismantling nuclear weapons, industrial conversion, and private investment assistance. Beyond this aid commitment, President Clinton was effusive in his support of President Yeltsin and Russia:

> We stand with Russian democracy. We are with Russian reforms. We are with Russian markets. We support freedom of conscience, of speech and religion. We support respect for ethnic minorities. We actively support reform and reformers and you in Russia.[87]

Furthermore, the summit concluded with a commitment by Clinton and Yeltsin to develop a "new democratic partnership" between the two nations.[88]

Less than two weeks later, the industrial democracies, known as the Group of Seven (G-7) and composed of the United States, Canada, Germany, Britain, France, Japan, and Italy, announced a massive $28.4 billion aid package for Russia. A few months later in July 1993, another meeting of the G-7 promised $3 billion for a "Special Privatization and Restructuring Program," an effort to break up state-run industries in Russia.[89] In the first year of the Clinton administration, then, the Western nations, led by the United States, had committed a significant amount of aid to support Russian reform.

Yet, by early 1994, a report indicated that less than one-third of the 1993 pledges had actually been released to Russia.[90] One important reason was that the Russian government had not met some international conditions for receiving this aid (e.g., reducing its inflation levels, undertaking and completing several economic reforms). Given the considerable political turmoil in that country, which we describe in part in this section, the economic reforms were stalled and did not (or could not) proceed very rapidly. Still, the Clinton administration was not prepared to change course. Instead, it called for speedier release of these funds, even as the administration endorsed the "conditions" that had been placed on their release by the G-7 nations and the International Monetary Fund.[91] On balance, though, as the Russian efforts at economic and market reform faltered, the Clinton administration still sought to encourage the Yeltsin government.

In the political area, too, the Clinton administration steadfastly supported Yeltsin and Russian democracy, despite (or perhaps because of) political challenges within Russia. In March 1993, for example, the Russian parliament tried to restrict Yeltsin's presidential power and even sought to impeach him. While he successfully fended off these challenges and won a public referendum endorsing his reforms in April, threats to his leadership deepened by the autumn. After Yeltsin tried to dissolve the Russian parliament and that body voted to unseat him for his actions, a standoff occurred between the two. After several days, the Russian army finally sided with

Yeltsin and attacked the parliament building, known as the White House. Several parliamentarians were arrested and jailed, considerable damage occurred to the White House, and 187 people were killed.[92] The closest thing to a coup against the incipient Russian democracy, however, had been averted. Throughout these various political crises during 1993, the Clinton administration's policy was to support Yeltsin—since he had been democratically elected, since he was committed to reform, and since there was uncertainty of who might follow him.

By late 1994 and early 1995, Yeltsin was faced yet again with a major crisis. This time the dispute was over the use of massive military force, as well as the indiscriminate killing, to suppress an independence movement in the Chechen region of Russia. Considerable domestic and international pressures were applied to halt this Russian policy, but American government support for the Yeltsin government did not waiver. To be sure, President Clinton and Secretary of State Christopher raised questions about the brutality of the operation and sought its rapid end. Both, however, backed Russia's right to maintain the country's sovereignty and signaled U.S. opposition to any effort to undermine Yeltsin's continuance in office.

Through 1995 and into 1996, the Clinton administration continued to support Yeltsin, especially with the upcoming June 1996 presidential elections in Russia. With tacit Clinton administration backing, and with help from Americans experienced in U.S.-style election campaigns, Yeltsin succeeded in winning the initial election and then the run-off vote between the two highest finishers. In that second round, he defeated the Communist party candidate, Gennadi Zyuganov, by a substantial margin. Throughout the campaign and through the end of 1996, however, Yeltsin was faced with significant health problems, weakening his effectiveness in office and raising the question of the status of democracy and economic reform in Russia.

In the military and security areas, friction developed between the Clinton administration and Russia, but such disagreements were relatively minor when considering the broad areas of agreements. The first and most notable area of policy convergence was over nuclear arms reduction. While the Bush administration had signed the START treaty in 1991 and the START II treaty in January 1993, neither pact had been implemented by the parties. Although the U.S. Senate had consented in October 1992 to the ratification of START, the Russian government held up formal ratification until the other former Soviet Republics with nuclear weapons (i.e., Belarus, Kazakhstan, and Ukraine) agreed to turn over their weapons to Russia and to adhere to the Nuclear Non-Proliferation Treaty (NPT). While Belarus and Kazakhstan made these commitments in 1993, Ukraine was more reluctant and became an important policy problem for the United States and Russia.

In January 1994, these three states did reach an accord whereby Ukraine would ship its nuclear weapons to Russia for dismantling. Ukraine in turn would receive payments for this action.[93] Ukraine's commitment to the NPT proved more elusive, but finally, in December 1994, it made such a pledge. With that action, the START treaty was formally put into effect with an exchange of the instruments of ratification.[94] Moreover, the START

II treaty could then begin the process of ratification, and this agreement was ratified by the United States Senate in January 1996.

A second important area of nuclear cooperation between the United States and Russia was over managing the surplus nuclear weapons materials produced by the major arms reduction agreements in force or about to come into force (i.e., the Intermediate Nuclear Forces Treaty, the START treaty and the START II treaty). Without proper controls on dismantling the warheads and managing the fissile nuclear materials, public safety could be endangered, and nuclear proliferation could occur.[95] The magnitude of such materials was considerable. By some estimates, about 100 tons of plutonium and 500 tons of highly enriched uranium may be freed by these pacts.

In an effort to deal with these matters and to reduce the proliferation threat, the U.S. Congress passed legislation (the so-called Nunn-Lugar legislation) to provide assistance to Russia totalling $1.2 billion for fiscal years 1992–94. While this action was started in the Bush administration, the Clinton administration was largely responsible for implementing the legislation. The progress in this area was slower than originally envisioned, although by 1996 some headway was being made.[96]

The other major political/military initiative concerning Central Europe and Russia was the effort to change the structure of the North Atlantic Treaty Organization (NATO). In January 1994, the United States proposed to its NATO partners that the organization extend greater cooperation to the countries of the former Soviet Union and the Warsaw pact. This "Partnership for Peace" was an extension of the Bush administration's efforts to introduce political consultation through the North Atlantic Cooperation Council (NACC) to these countries.

Under the Partnership proposal—which would seemingly be equivalent to an associate membership in NATO—these signatory countries would "develop with NATO an individual Partnership Programme." Under such an individually designed program, the Partnership state would be invited to cooperate with NATO in maintaining openness in defense planning and budgeting, participate in various NATO training exercises, gain access to particular NATO technical data, and attend and participate in all NACC/Partnership meetings. In addition, Partnership states could send permanent liaison officers to NATO headquarters in Belgium. The members of NATO in turn would work with the Partnership states to evaluate their forces and capabilities and assist them in activities such as "planning, training, exercises and the development of doctrine." Finally, and perhaps most important, "NATO will consult with any active participant in the Partnership if that Partner perceives a direct threat to its territorial integrity, political independence, or security."[97] While such a pledge is considerably weaker than the NATO alliance (see Chapter 2), this consultation commitment did provide some degree of added security for these new states.

This Partnership proposal was advanced only after suggestions of creating full memberships in NATO were rejected. Russia, in particular, was concerned about an expanded NATO membership, since it might again be surrounded by an alliance that was meant to contain it. The Partnership for Peace proposal was perceived as less threatening, and ultimately the Yeltsin government acquiesced to the idea.

Indeed, the Partnership idea proved exceedingly popular. By October 1994, only ten months after its initiation, twenty-three countries had signed on to the arrangement, and by November 1995, another four countries had signed the Partnership for Peace. These countries included (listed in order of their signing, beginning in 1994): Romania, Lithuania, Poland, Estonia, Hungary, Ukraine, Slovakia, Latvia, Bulgaria, Albania, the Czech Republic, Moldova, Georgia, Slovenia, Azerbaijan, Finland, Sweden, Turkmenistan, Kazakhstan, Kyrgyzstan, Russia, Uzbekistan, Armenia, Belarus, Austria, Malta, and the former Yugoslav Republic of Macedonia.[98]

By the end of 1994, the United States had again advanced its proposal for full membership within NATO. In a speech to the NATO Council in December, Secretary of State Christopher proposed that the organization begin "a steady, deliberate and transparent" process for the expansion of NATO. The expansion of full membership will be done in a way "that increases stability for all of Europe—for members and non-members alike."[99] The proposal was immediately met with some harsh criticism from Russian President Boris Yeltsin, who saw it as an attempt to divide Europe and to isolate Russia: "We hear explanations to the effect that this is allegedly the expansion of stability just in case there are undesirable developments in Russia."[100] While the United States indicated that no nation would be excluded from this expansion, this proposal will likely produce more friction between the U.S. and Russia.

The issue of NATO expansion continued as a source of contention between the two countries. In late October 1996, President Clinton declared, in his only major foreign policy speech on the campaign trail, that he favored the full incorporation of some former Warsaw Pact countries of Eastern Europe for full NATO membership by 1999. That date would mark the fiftieth anniversary of the signing of the Atlantic Alliance after World War II. By May 1997, NATO and Russia had negotiated and signed an agreement, the Founding Act Between NATO and the Russian Federation, to ease Russia's opposition. This act called for closer cooperation and consultation between the parties and provided assurances to Russia on several security questions. In turn, the Clinton administration then announced its intention to support the admission of Hungary, Poland, and the Czech Republic to NATO at the organization's meeting in July 1997. At the Madrid meeting, NATO formally extended an invitation to those three countries to join the alliance. Hence, the alliance will consist of nineteen members by 1999.[101]

The Middle East. In the Middle East, the Clinton administration continued the peace process (initiated after the Persian Gulf War) between Israel and its Arab neighbors and here, too, some policy movement was achieved. In addition, the Clinton administration initiated an important policy change: It replaced the balance of power policy followed by the Bush administration against Iran and Iraq with a policy that it called "dual containment."

The agreements between Israel and the Palestine Liberation Organization in September 1993 and between Israel and Jordan in October 1994 were important foreign policy accomplishments for the Clinton administration in furthering the peace process in the Middle East. For both pacts, the American administration served in a mediator role and facilitated the agreements. The Clinton administration has also sought to extend this role to include obtaining a peace settlement between Syria and Israel. Indeed, President Clinton went to Syria as part of a Middle East trip in late 1994, and Secretary of State Warren Christopher held talks with both the Israelis and the Syrians as part of the effort to make this process work. No agreement, however, has yet been achieved, and the prospect for success appears to be at some distance in the future.

The first achievement in the Middle East was the Israeli-PLO Accord signed between PLO leader Yasir Arafat and Israeli Prime Minister Yitzhak Rabin in Washington on September 13, 1993. The agreement was the culmination of the talks that had begun in Madrid, Spain, in October 1991, but the agreement did not follow an easy course from those initial talks. As late as June 1993, the tenth round of discussions between the parties had ended in an impasse and, by August, the process was nearly dead.[102] Fortunately, the Norwegian foreign minister, Johan Jorgen Holst, had secretly been holding talks between the two adversaries since April 1992. Those Norwegian-brokered talks proved crucial to reaching the September 1993 accord.

In summary form, the Israeli-PLO Accord set out a timetable over how the two sides will "share the same living space" in Palestine.[103] In particular, the agreement developed a framework for the gradual withdrawal of the Israelis from the Gaza Strip and the West Bank, the election of a Palestinian Council, and future elections in the area. Moreover, the negotiations on a permanent arrangement, and the final status of the territories, would begin approximately two years after the accord went into effect, "and within five years the final status of who will control what is to be resolved."[104]

The immediate goals of the pact focused on putting into effect a Declaration of Principles between the parties and beginning the process of self-rule by Palestinians in the two areas of the seized territories, the Gaza Strip and Jericho. The Declaration of Principles, in effect, called for the parties to cooperate in a variety of policy areas—water, electricity, and trade promotion—and in the transfer of authority from the Israelis to the Palestinians in some others—education, culture, health, social welfare, taxation, and tourism.[105] These areas of cooperation, of course, meant mutual recognition and significant movement to reduce the long-standing levels of hostility between the two sides.

The original target date for the transfer of authority in Gaza and Jericho was April 13, 1994. However, this process was delayed because of the February 1994 massacre of Palestinians in Hebron by an Israeli extremist and by attacks by Hamas—an Iranian-backed Palestinian group opposed to the accord—on Israelis. Gaza and Jericho were ultimately returned to Palestinian self-rule. The process was hardly smooth, however, and various deadlines remained unmet. Violence in Israel and in the Palestinian-held territories disrupted the process. By January 1995, 195 Palestinians and 91 Israelis had been killed since the signing of the Israeli-PLO Accord.[106] The main tasks for the Clinton administration was to prod the parties to complete the implementation of the accord and to seek sufficient financial assistance for the Palestinian area under self-rule to make it viable.

On the day after the Israeli-PLO Accord was signed in September 1993, Jordan and Israel signed an agreement that was to be the "basis for resolving 45 years of hostility" between the two countries.[107] In July 1994, the two sides ended their state of belligerency against one another, and on October 26, 1994, they signed a full peace treaty.[108] President Clinton and Secretary of State Warren Christopher attended the treaty signing, which was held on the Israeli-Jordanian border, to signal American support for this initiative.

The treaty itself was wide-ranging. It included some general principles of good relations—including mutual recognition of the "sovereignty, territorial integrity and political independence" of one another and the development of "good neighborly relations of cooperation." Further, the agreement included commitments to enhance security arrangements between the two states, to facilitate economic cooperation (by removing the economic boycott against Israel and encouraging free trade), and to alleviate problems associated with refugees and displaced persons in the two countries. Finally, the treaty called for cooperative actions for dealing with historical and religious sites in the two countries and in fostering cultural and scientific exchanges between them.[109] In this sense, the treaty matched, and perhaps exceeded, the one signed during the Carter administration, almost two decades earlier, between Israel and Egypt.

In September 1995, the Israeli-PLO Accord of two years earlier was given greater definition and specification with another agreement between the parties, once again witnessed and officially signed in Washington, D.C. Under this agreement, Israeli forces would be withdrawn from much of the West Bank by April 1996 and control over the West Bank would pass to a Palestinian Council.[110] The implementation of this agreement became much more difficult to complete than to sign and became highly controversial in Israel. Indeed, Israel's Prime Minister, Yitzhak Rabin, was assassinated in November 1995 by a right-wing Israeli extremist opposed to the perceived concessions to the Arabs and the Palestinians.

This action slowed the implementation process, and the peace agreements between the Israelis and the Palestinians became a key issue in the Israeli election, scheduled for late May 1996. Despite the virtual open endorsement of Rabin's successor, Shimon Peres, by the Clinton administration, the opposition candidate, Benjamin Netanyahu, won a narrow victory promising peace with security—a way of calling for a delaying of the peace process. By late September 1996, the peace process deteriorated to the point that the Israeli government decision to open a tunnel exit close to Arab religious sites in Jerusalem sparked widespread violence throughout the West Bank and Gaza Strip. Scores of Israelis and Palestinians were killed,[111] and the peace process fostered by the United States seemed shattered.

The Clinton administration called a quick summit between Palestinian and Israeli leaders, but the results were limited. While the two sides agreed to resume talks, the Israelis refused to commit to a quick withdrawal of military forces from the West Bank town of Hebron, as called for in the earlier accords. Palestinian leader Yasir Arafat was reportedly deeply disappointed, and the renewed negotiations were slow to achieve many results. In short, the peace efforts fostered by the Clinton administration had stalled and were on the verge of collapse by the end of 1996.

A second major policy initiative in the Middle East for the Clinton administration was the adoption of a "dual containment" strategy toward Iran and Iraq. Under this strategy, first announced by a National Security Council aide in a May 1993 speech and more fully set forth by the national security advisor in early 1994,[112] the Clinton administration would not "depend on either Iraq or Iran to maintain a favorable balance and protect U.S. friends and interests in the gulf."[113] There were several reasons for this change from tilting toward one or the other of these two states (a policy followed as far back as the Nixon administration): The Cold War had ended, and Soviet influence was no longer a concern; both Iran and Iraq were now much weaker, there was no incentive to build up either one, and the overall regional balance was more favorable to the United States. More fundamentally, too, both states were following policies largely inimical to the interests of the United States, and, given the changed global and regional circumstances, a balance of power was no longer needed.

One critic, however, cogently pointed out several problems that dual containment may produce.[114] It would be largely a static policy and would be costly to maintain. Moreover, as either Iran and Iraq continued to rebuild after their recent wars, one may have designs upon the other state and beyond. The result would be a more dangerous situation for America's friends within the region and for the United States. Further, how would the United States respond if these two states were to reach an accommodation with one another?

Nonetheless, the Clinton administration implemented its dual containment policy in several ways. It periodically continued the sanctions imposed against Iran in the 1980s, refused any efforts at restoring diplomatic ties, and was "deeply concerned that some nations are prepared to cooperate with Iran in the nuclear field."[115] The administration has been even more determined in its behavior against Iraq. It has recommitted the United States to the full implementation of the UN restrictions against Iraq that were passed by the end of the Persian Gulf War (including the continued enforcement of the "no-fly zones" within Iraq). In addition, the administration took two significant military actions against Saddam Hussein's regime in 1993 and 1994. In June 1993, the United States undertook a missile attack upon the headquarters of Iraqi intelligence in retaliation over the Iraqi plot to assassinate former President Bush during his visit to Kuwait in April 1993. In October 1994, when Saddam Hussein moved forces into the southern part of Iraq and appeared to once again be threatening Kuwait, President Clinton initially ordered 36,000 American troops to Kuwait to serve as a deterrent.[116] Within a very short time, Saddam Hussein backed down and moved his troops out of this area, and the crisis abated.

In September 1996, yet another confrontation developed between the United States and Iraq. When the Iraqi military moved its forces into northern Iraq and supported one of the two competing Kurdish factions in the civil war there, the United States attacked some missile sites in southern Iraq and expanded the southern "no fly zone" as a further effort to bottle up Saddam Hussein's regime within Iraq and to deter his government from contemplating any actions toward the southern part of Iraq or toward Kuwait or Saudi Arabia, where U.S. interests were greatest.

The results of this Clinton administration action proved to be mixed. The administration's CIA director, John Deutch, admitted in congressional testimony that Saddam Hussein was initially stronger, rather than weaker, as a result of this episode. That is, Hussein gained greater control over northern Iraq by weakening the Kurdish population, and the attack in southern Iraq reflected only minor and temporary damage. Furthermore, the defeated Kurdish faction in northern Iraq looked toward Iran for support, since immediate American support was not forthcoming. In short, the Clinton administration's dual containment strategy was still functioning, but it was being challenged by the actions inside Iraq.

Reshaping the American Military: The Bottom-Up Review, the Nuclear Forces Review, and the Quadrennial Defense Review

A third principle that the Clinton administration advanced for guiding American foreign policy was reshaping the American military in a way to meet the challenges of the post–Cold War era. Two major reviews were initially undertaken to accomplish this goal: one dealing primarily with conventional forces of the United States, the other with its nuclear forces. Both reviews produced recommendations that would considerably change the military force structure and mission of the United States. In May 1997, yet a third review, the Quadrennial Defense Review, was issued by Secretary of Defense William Cohen and sought to map a defense strategy and policy into the next century.

Conventional Force Review. The first report, the Bottom-Up Review, was issued relatively quickly by the administration in October 1993, and it sought to be "a comprehensive review of the nation's defense strategy, force structure, modernization, infrastructure, and foundations."[117]

The core of the report was a call for a change in America's defense strategy—from one based on meeting a global Soviet challenge to one focusing on the new dangers and opportunities of the post–Cold War era. Unlike the Cold War years, when the principal danger emanated from the Soviet Union with its significant nuclear and conventional forces, new dangers arise from the spread of nuclear, biological, and chemical weapons to new states, the outbreak of regional aggression initiated by major regional powers or, alternately, by regional ethnic or religious hostilities, the failure of democracy and economic reforms in Central Europe, and the inability of a weak American economy to meet its national security needs.[118]

At the same time, there now existed several new opportunities for the United States to enhance its security worldwide. These come from the prospect of expanding U.S. security partnerships in various regions of the world and the building of a larger number of democratic nations in the international system. Further, opportunities now exist to improve regional deterrence with the end of the Cold War, to implement dramatic nuclear arms reductions armaments as the START and START II treaties suggest, and to maintain U.S. security generally at a lower cost.[119]

In order to face these new dangers and meet these new opportunities, the report recommended that America's military forces be designed to fight and win two major regional conflicts (MRCs) simultaneously, or virtually simultaneously. In particular, the review illustrated its approach by focusing upon potential major regional conflicts with North Korea and Iraq. In addition, the force structure of the United States would also have to be prepared to undertake other kinds of operations as well: (1) engaging in peace enforcement or intervention operations abroad; (2) pursuing normal peacetime operations overseas; and (3) maintaining the deterrence capabilities of the United States.

With these new kinds of missions, the American military would be changed in a number of ways. First of all, the size and configuration of the armed forces would be altered—more dramatically than what the Bush administration had proposed. The Army and Air Force would have the greatest cuts in their size, while the Navy and the Marine Corps would have the smallest cuts. The reasoning here was straightforward in that the latter would be needed to respond rapidly to various crisis situations. Second, while the United States would maintain a worldwide presence, greater reliance would be placed on allied and friendly nations, and more "periodic deployments" of American forces abroad would be used. Increased reliance would be placed on upgrading airlift and sealift capacities of the United States and the use of the propositioning of equipment and supplies. In turn, the National Guard and reserve forces would play a larger role in America's defenses. These decisions would allow for rapid response capabilities abroad, albeit with less stationing of troops overseas. At the same time, some important forward-based deployments would remain, with 100,000 American military forces in Europe and about an equal number spread throughout Asia.[120]

In particular, the readiness capability of the American military would be given a high priority, so that American forces could meet these new challenges. Still, the military budget under the Clinton administration would actually be reduced beyond the 25 percent reduction set forth by the Bush administration. It was estimated in the Bottom-Up Review that defense spending could be cut by $104 billion more, over fiscal years 1995–1999, than the baseline budget that the Bush administration had projected.

A related proposal was the announcement of the Counterproliferation Initiative by outgoing Secretary of Defense Les Aspin in December 1993. The first new threat identified in the Bottom-Up Review was the possible proliferation of the weapons of mass destruction (WMD). Under this new initiative, the United States would seek new ways to deal with this problem. In particular, the Clinton administration decided to transform the Strategic Defense Initiative of the Reagan and Bush administrations into the Ballistic Missile Defense Organization, as a means of possibly responding to theater nuclear weapons of these new threatening states. Further, greater efforts will be made to develop a strategy for fighting wars against these potential threats, and counterproliferation intelligence capability of the United States would need to be improved. Finally, cooperative efforts to deal with this proliferation threat would be undertaken with America's allies.

Nuclear Force Review. The second major defense review was the Nuclear Posture Review (NPR), completed a year later and announced by Aspin's successor at Defense, William Perry. The NPR called for a dramatic reduction in the nuclear forces of the United States, but the guiding principle was to bring U.S. forces in line with the requirements of the START II treaty when it was fully implemented.

All three components of the U.S. strategic nuclear triad would be affected by the proposed changes. First, the number of ballistic missile submarines would be reduced from eighteen to fourteen. Second, all B-1 bombers would be changed to a conventional role, and no more B-2 bombers would be added. In other words, the present number of twenty B-2 bombers would be the size of that air component. Third, the number of land-based missiles would be reduced to a contingent of 500 Minuteman missiles.

The Nuclear Posture Review also recommended change for the nonstrategic or theater component of U.S. nuclear forces. While dual-capable (i.e., both conventional and nuclear) aircraft would remain in Europe as would a small deployment of nuclear weapons, the report recommended that the options of dual-capable aircraft on carriers and cruise missiles on surface ships be eliminated. Finally, the report made a number of recommendations for maintaining and improving the safety and security of America's nuclear arsenal.[121]

These military restructuring efforts—both conventional and nuclear—were met with skepticism in several different quarters. On the one hand, some argued that these cutbacks would seriously damage the capability of the United States. While the Cold War was over, the dangers in international politics actually were more broadly based than before, and the United States military would be required to do more. While some changes could be made in the configuration of the forces, this view generally held that the Clinton proposal had cut too deeply. On the other hand, others saw the proposal as simply tinkering with the Bush administration changes and called for even greater cuts than the Bottom-Up Review suggested. The opportunity remained for creating a "peace dividend."

One comprehensive analysis suggested a series of searching questions about the Bottom-Up Review.[122] The Clinton administration had not really advanced a military strategy to guide its creation of the force structure, and it had not made a wholly convincing case for the two-MRC approaches. Indeed, why should America's force structure be based upon two MRCs? Why not base it upon one or three MRCs, for example? How do allies fit into this two-MRC design? Was this an approach for fighting the last war (i.e., the Persian Gulf War) and not appropriate for the kind of future conflicts that the U.S. might face (e.g., Somalia, Haiti)? Further, how capable will the American military be in dealing with peacekeeping and interventionary actions? How much training and capability will or do they have for these kinds of missions?

In an ironic way, the Bottom-Up Review may have been prologue for the Clinton administration: By the end of its second year in office, the Clinton administration was confronted by military situations resembling two MRCs—and perhaps more than two MRCs. Recall that we mentioned that the United States, in late 1994, not only intervened in Haiti, but also had sent forces into Kuwait as a deterrent against Saddam Hussein's action in southern Iraq. Yet a third situation also faced the Clinton administration at the time: the real threat of the North Koreans' proceeding to develop a nuclear capability. While the concurrent Haitian and Kuwaiti episodes had not strained the military's capabilities or its logistic support, according to one report, a simultaneous action on the Korean peninsula could pose just such a problem.[123]

Part of this difficulty was eased with the Clinton administration's conclusion of an agreement to reduce the prospect of North Korea's producing nuclear weapons. While this agreement was the culmination of long-standing negotiations, the final push was the result of some interventionary actions by former President Jimmy Carter in June 1994, when the impasse between the United States and North Korea appeared the greatest over the failure of the latter to adhere to international inspection requirements for its nuclear facilities.

In October 1994, however, the United States and North Korea came to an agreement. Under the pact, the North Koreans would halt efforts to become a nuclear power and open up two sites to international inspections, so the extent of their nuclear capability could be determined. More immediately, North Korea would "freeze" its graphite-moderated nuclear reactors. In turn, the United States pledged to seek support from an "international consortium" (most likely Japan and South Korea) to replace North Korea's present nuclear reactors with two light-water nuclear reactors to meet the North Korean energy needs. The United States would provide aid "to offset the energy foregone" because of this agreement. Further, relations between the United States and North Korea would begin a process of normalization, eventually reaching the ambassadorial level.[124]

Yet, within the same time period as this agreement was announced, the Department of Defense acknowledged that the readiness of part of the U.S. military was in doubt, with three of twelve divisions not at "peak readiness levels." Combined with this admission and with the results of the 1994 congressional elections, in which the victorious Republicans had promised more spending on defense, President Clinton promptly announced that he would seek $25 billion more in defense spending for the next six years. These moneys, moreover, were to be directed at this readiness concern. While one of Clinton's defense policy critics acknowledged that this action was "the first sign of recognition on the part of this Administration that this nation's military readiness and ability to defend its vital national interests in the world is in question," the action was still not enough to address the deep problems in the defense position of the United States.[125]

By one assessment, the military readiness of American forces was underfinanced by as much as $60 billion instead of $25 billion.[126] The problem was not only the amount of moneys committed to these activities, but also the decision by the Clinton administration to use some readiness funding to finance various operations around the world. One way to address this issue was by more careful use of American military forces abroad or by financing such peacekeeping activities from other sources. With the election of a new Congress in the November 1994 election, however, the Republican majority proposed within its "Contract with America" that defense spending increase and that peacekeeping activities be reduced as a way to increase American preparedness.[127]

In particular, the Republican majority proposed more spending on military readiness and the creation of a "firewall" between defense and other policy areas so the former will not be raided to pay for the latter. In addition, the Republicans called for instituting new procedures for the use of American forces in UN operations as a way of reducing the number of American peacekeeping missions under UN auspices, seeking greater control in the placement of American troops under UN commanders, and reducing American spending on UN operations.

In the area of defense budgeting, this new congressional majority achieved some success, albeit not as much as it had hoped. For both fiscal 1996 and fiscal 1997, the Congress passed, and President Clinton signed or let become law, defense appropriations bills that were above his funding requests (at $243 billion and $244 billion) by 3 percent and 4 percent, respectively. The fiscal 1997 funding levels, the administration acknowledged, were still insufficient for fighting two major regional conflicts simultaneously.[128] Thus, the goals of the Bottom-Up Review were not being maintained, even by a Republican Congress more intent on increasing defense spending. At the same time, however, these appropriations succeeded in reducing the cuts in personnel and in adding on more spending for maintenance and overhauls of military equipment. Significantly, too, these appropriations increased both spending on ballistic missile defense by 20 and 30 percent over the requests of the Clinton administration, and continuing spending on several new weapons programs as well.[129] On the effort to reduce the American UN peacekeeping efforts around the world, no legislation was successful, but the Republican Congress did put the Clinton administration on notice over these activities through extensive legislative debate, the passage of a bill in the House, and the efforts to include these agenda items in other legislation.[130]

Quadrennial Defense Review. The results of a third major review by the Clinton administration, the Quadrennial Defense Review, were announced in May 1997. While the review largely contained the same portrait of the global threat environment set out in the Bottom-Up Review (including the need for the United States to fight two MRCs "nearly simultaneously"), it also sought to begin to implement *Joint Vision 2010*, a plan developed by the military on future operational needs, and to set out an approach to meet American defense needs through 2015. In general, the review called for further streamlining of the size of the military force and its infrastructure, continued to emphasize the need for America's military communication and technological superiority, sought military procurement funding for weapons modernization, and committed the military to use available resources more efficiently. In particular, this review proposed reducing the total size of the American military from 1.42 million to 1.36 million personnel on active duty and undertaking two more rounds of base closing as a means of obtaining a better match between the size of the force and the defense infrastructure. Each branch of the military would undergo some downsizing under the proposed plan. At the same time, the review called for continued investment in "command, control, communications, computers, intelligence, surveillance, and reconnaissance (C4ISR) systems" and continued work on a missile defense system and on nuclear arms reductions. Importantly, and undoubtedly in response to its critics during the first term, the administration sought to end the "procurement holiday" by calling for an increase in funding on technological modernization "to roughly $60 billion by FY 2001." Overall, the goal of the review is to create a more efficient and better equipped military, as the United States enters the new century. As with the other reviews discussed here, however, congressional scrutiny and action will be required before these recommendations become reality.[131]

CLINTON FOREIGN POLICY TOWARD THE TWENTY-FIRST CENTURY

With a comfortable victory behind him in the 1996 election and with the start of a new term in 1997, the inevitable question is, What will be the shape and direction of President Clinton's foreign policy as America moves toward the twenty-first century? While a host of intangibles cloud any precise assessments, we can suggest some general trends in the style that the Clinton administration is likely to adopt in its second term, the key issues that are likely to shape its agenda, and the principal political challenges at home that will condition the Clinton administration's foreign policy responses.

Style and Strategy

At one level, the Clinton administration in its second term is likely to exude a more self-confident approach toward foreign policy than during its first term, for several reasons. First, President Clinton, unlike his approach during much of his first term, is more likely to be involved in addressing foreign policy issues. Emboldened by some successes toward the end of his first term (e.g., deploying American troops to Haiti and Bosnia successfully without major casualties, implementing the Dayton accords in Bosnia, facilitating the completion of agreements in the Middle East, and beginning to stabilize the relationship with Russia and China), President Clinton undoubtedly sees the possibilities of future foreign policy successes as a way to leave a lasting legacy from his presidency. In this sense, he is more likely to adopt a more hands-on and engaged foreign policy than in the first term.

Second, President Clinton and his foreign policy team have now largely abandoned the "assertive multilateralism" approach through the United Nations that Madeleine Albright, as U.S. Ambassador to the United Nations, called for in 1993. At her Senate confirmation hearings as secretary of state in early January 1997, Albright announced, with some irony, that now "we will defend firmly our own vital interests."[132] In late 1996, too, administration officials said that the president "has become more comfortable wielding force and working alone if necessary." Thus although working with the United Nations or allies will not be abandoned, unilateral action will be pursued.

Third, in its second term the Clinton administration is likely to be even more careful about deploying American force abroad. Since the experience of Somalia in 1993, the administration had already begun to reconsider the deployment of American troops, including the development of PDD-25, which we discussed earlier. Furthermore, the new secretary of defense, William Cohen, is likely to add even greater constraint on deploying the American military abroad. In the United States Senate, Cohen was quick to criticize presidential use of force without congressional involvement. That kind of stance will add further caution to the actions of the Clinton administration as it contemplates foreign intervention.

Fourth, the recent experience of the foreign policy team will also promote a more self-confident mode. In addition to a more assertive personality than Secretary of State Christopher, Secretary of State Albright has benefitted from her four years as U.S. Ambassador to the United Nations. Similarly, Samuel Berger's experience as deputy national security advisor will assist him as he moves up to the top position on the National Security Council. The appointment of George Tenet to head the intelligence community, after previous work on the National Security Council staff, will also aid policy coordination. The familiarity of the players with one another, and their experience in working together previously, should aid policy coordination and assist in avoiding the foreign policy pitfalls so evident during the first two years of Clinton's initial term.

Finally, despite a fresh vigor and style that the new foreign policy team brings to Clinton's second term, one problem has still not been adequately addressed: the need to develop a more coherent and comprehensive foreign policy strategy.[133] So far, the administration continues to rely on familiar themes. At her Senate confirmation hearings, for instance, Madeleine Albright outlined some of the same general principles that the administration had followed in its first term. Indeed, in one estimate, she outlined an approach that suggests that she would be "more a custodian than an innovator" in foreign policy. In particular, she did not seem to give much impetus to the promotion of human rights.[134] Without a better rationale and a more careful road map for foreign policy, the danger remains that policy will slip back into "ad hocism." In short, a fuller conceptual map for American foreign policy continues to be the central challenge for the Clinton administration in its second term.

Policy Challenges

The need for a coherent strategy is no more evident than when considering the myriad set of issues the Clinton administration faces in the second term, arguably issues that are more numerous and more intractable than in the first four years. At the top of the list of such challenges is future political/military policy toward Central Europe and China.[135] Will Russia continue on the path of democratic and economic reform, and will the United

States continue to provide assistance to that nation? Will Bosnia move toward an integrated society, or will it move toward partition? Will the December 1996 American commitment to maintain U.S. soldiers in Bosnia for another eighteen months as part of the new Stabilization Force, or SFOR, prove as useful and trouble-free as the Implementation Force, or IFOR, that it is replacing? Will NATO expansion become a reality? More importantly, how will this expansion affect American-Russian relations in particular and American relations with Central Europe in general?

In Asia, the key political/military issue, of course, will be future relations with China. The Clinton administration has opted for "constructive engagement" as its basic policy toward China for the time being. As disputes over a more open trading relationship with China, the selling of missiles to Pakistan and elsewhere, Chinese actions toward Taiwan and Hong Kong, and China's myriad human rights violations are resurrected or expanded, pressures for the Clinton administration to adopt a new policy of containment will inevitably develop. Indeed, as we approach the twenty-first century and as China continues on the path to becoming a superpower, policy choices and policy direction toward China may well prove to be the most critical component of maintaining a peaceful global order in the next century.

Regional conflicts may need to take a backseat to the major political/military issues in Europe and Asia, but they remain serious challenges for the Clinton administration as well. Two in particular stand out: those in the Middle East and those in Northeast Asia. In the Middle East, despite the recent successes, the talks between the Israelis and Palestinians remain fraught with problems. Arguably, progress between these two adversaries will be more difficult in the years ahead, owing to changed leadership in Israel and renewed efforts by various groups to disrupt the progress made so far. The Hebron agreement signed in early January 1997, calling for Israeli withdrawal from that West Bank city and the withdrawal from all the West Bank by August 1998, may aid progress, but suspicions remain high on both sides.[136] Complicating this lingering issue in the Middle East are continuing difficulties that Iran and Iraq pose for American interests. In Northeast Asia, the Korean question remains high on the agenda. The full implementation of the framework agreement between North Korea and the United States will remain the focal point of policy, as the Clinton administration seeks to prevent nonproliferation on the Korean peninsula. In addition, though, action on the reunification of North and South Korea, so long put off, will likely capture attention before the turn of the century.

Foreign economic policy, arguably the area of greatest first-term success for the Clinton administration, will continue to compete for attention (and often complicate dealing) with these political/military issues. Yet, the first-term economic initiatives will require expansion and development if they are to foster American prosperity on a continuing basis. First, pressures for expansion of NAFTA to the rest of the Western Hemisphere will likely increase, especially since administration attention faltered a bit in 1995 and 1996.[137] Second, while the Clinton administration gave a real impetus to APEC during its first term, reducing trade barriers and achieving tangible movement toward a free-trade area will be a demanding task. Third, the Clinton administration will need to move beyond rhetoric in establishing a new trans-Atlantic relationship between the United States (and NAFTA) and the European Union. Fourth, trade relations with Japan are a continuing bilateral challenge for the United States and the Clinton administration. Despite some halting progress during the first term, the open market between the two countries sought by the United States remains elusive, and the Clinton administration will once again need to devote considerable attention to achieve real progress. Still, and reflecting a change from the first term, political/military issues are currently likely to garner more attention than the economic ones.

With such a large plate of political/military and economic issues, principally with developed states, a fourth set of issues—policy toward some failed or failing states (e.g., Rwanda, Liberia, Somalia)—is likely to get lost in the shuffle. Indeed, the Clinton administration has already deemphasized the policies as foreign policy priorities (witness, for example, its halting approach to aiding Rwanda and Zaire in late 1996), and that trend will likely remain so during a second term—for several reasons. Both indifference and opposition among the American people and the Congress offer little incentive to the Clinton administration to address these issues. The Clinton administration itself has self-imposed restraints on American intervention through PDD-25 after the Somalia fiasco. Further, American unhappiness with the functioning of the United Nations further reduces the likelihood of dealing with these issues.

Finally, the size and shape of the defense posture of the United States overshadows all of these policy initiatives. While the restructuring of the American military has begun, critical decisions remain on defense spending, the size of the force, and the development of the next generation of weapons. As these decisions occur, they will go a long way in shaping the Clinton administration's response to the issues that we have identified, be it in China, Russia, or Africa. In this sense, the defense question will remain as an overarching national security issue in the second term of the Clinton administration.

Political Challenges

The Republican majorities in the U.S. Congress, first elected in 1994 and reelected in 1996, will give considerable definition to the Clinton administration's foreign policy.[138] Indeed, in some areas, those majorities have already left their imprint on policy and will continue to do so in the future.

In the area of foreign affairs spending, the Congress has imposed, and will continue to impose, budget cuts. Total spending on international affairs activities has declined dramatically, resulting in closed U.S. embassies and consulates around the world, and the United States remains in arrears in its payments to the United Nations. Furthermore, the Congress has sought to restructure and eliminate part of the Washington foreign affairs bureaucracy as a further way to curb spending (see Chapter 9). While Senator Jesse Helms, the chair of the Senate Foreign Relations Committee, recently hinted at some accommodation in resolving this impasse over restructuring of the bureaucracy (and the administration did announce in April 1997 its own restructuring initiative),[139] the area of foreign affairs spending will remain contentious, since the call for congressional spending restraint also conveys policy differences (e.g., America's reliance on the United Nations to carry out policy).

The Clinton administration's foreign aid spending has also been a target of the Congress. Not only have some in Congress called for the elimination of the Agency for International Development, the principal foreign aid agency of the United States government (see Chapter 9), but others have called for a more narrowly drawn list of foreign aid recipients. In addition, foreign aid to multilateral institutions (e.g., the World Bank) and toward some controversial programs (e.g., population control programs promoted by the Clinton administration) have also been targeted and have already received congressional cuts. Absent a growing external threat to the United States, these efforts to streamline the foreign assistance budget will continue in the years ahead.

In the area of defense spending, the Congress has taken a different tack. In general, Congress proposes more spending on military readiness, creating a "firewall" between defense and other policy areas, and it wants to ensure that American forces are used abroad only after careful consideration. The goal of the former action is to slow down the military restructuring proposed by Clinton and actually to reverse it in some areas. One important flashpoint between the Congress and the White House is over the building of a theater nuclear defense system—a system to safeguard America from a surprise nuclear missile attack. The Congress favors the research, development, and deployment of such a system, while the Clinton administration favors only spending on research. The resolution of this issue will likely outlast a second Clinton term. The goal of the latter action, regarding deployment of military forces, as noted earlier, was to reduce the number of American peacekeeping missions under UN auspices, to seek to control the placement of American troops under UN commanders, and to reduce American spending on the UN operations. In large measure, the Clinton administration has already moved in this direction and will continue to endorse this congressional position.

Concluding Comments

The Clinton administration came to office committed to creating a new foreign policy vision that was "strategic, vigorous," and based on "America's democratic values." To date, that vision and that kind of policy have not emerged. While policy has surely changed in selected social and economic areas, the Clinton administration's political and military policies have largely failed to achieve a clear focus and direction for the post–Cold War era. To be sure, the emphasis on free markets and on the promotion of democracy has been repeatedly proclaimed, but efforts in these two areas glean considerably different assessments. NAFTA and GATT will likely be seen as successes of the Clinton years, but the administration's political-military policy from Russia and Bosnia to Somalia, Haiti, and North Korea gets more mixed reviews.

As it embarks on a second term, the Clinton administration has still not yet created a clear vision and strategy for the post–Cold War years.

While the administration has committed the United States to continued global involvement, the shape and extent of that involvement has not been carefully spelled out. Further, the approach has not been fully embraced by the American people. Although the administration had initially proposed a rather expansive unilateral and multilateral involvement on several different fronts, more recent policy directions suggest a tilt toward a more selective involvement, especially on military issues (e.g., peacekeeping missions). On economic matters, global involvement will remain, with an emphasis on creating more open markets. On the question of democratic promotion and human rights, however, the administration appears headed toward a position more consonant with America's past actions: encouraging movement in that direction, but being less involved in nation-building itself.

Notes

1. Part of this chapter and its arguments appeared in James M. McCormick, "Assessing Clinton's Foreign Policy at Midterm," *Current History* 94 (November 1995): 370–374.
2. Governor Bill Clinton, "A New Covenant for American Security," Address at Georgetown University, December 12, 1991.
3. "Remarks of Governor Bill Clinton," Los Angeles World Affairs Council, August 13, 1992.
4. Ibid.
5. The speeches were in Washington, DC, Los Angeles, Milwaukee, and New York, from late 1991 through the election of 1992.
6. Warren Christopher, "Statement of Warren Christopher before the Committee on Foreign Relations of the United States Senate," January 13, 1993.
7. Ibid.
8. "Remarks of Governor Bill Clinton." Also see Thomas L. Friedman, "Clinton's Foreign-Policy Agenda Reaches Across Broad Spectrum," *New York Times*, October 4, 1992, 1 and 28.
9. "Statement of Warren Christopher before the Committee on Foreign Relations of the United States Senate."
10. "Remarks of Governor Bill Clinton."
11. Ibid.
12. "Statement of Warren Christopher before the Committee on Foreign Relations of the United States Senate."
13. Ibid.
14. "Remarks of Governor Bill Clinton."
15. "A New Covenant for American Society."
16. "Statement of Warren Christopher before the Committee on Foreign Relations of the United States Senate."
17. "James A. Baker III Delivers Foreign Policy Address," *The Council Chronicle*, a publication of the Chicago Council on Foreign Relations, June 1992, pp. 1 and 5.
18. The four speeches were: President Clinton, "Confronting the Challenges of a Broader World," address to the UN General Assembly, September 27, 1993; Secretary Christopher, "Building Peace in the Middle East," address at Columbia University, September 20, 1993; Anthony Lake, Assistant to the President for National Security Affairs, "From Containment to Enlargement," address at John Hopkins University School of Advanced International Studies, September 21, 1993; and Madeleine K. Albright, "Use of Force in a Post–Cold War World," remarks at the National War College, September 23, 1993. All quoted passages by the various individuals in the next several paragraphs are from these addresses.

19. J.F.O. McAllister, "Secretary of Shhhhh!," *Time International*, June 7, 1993, 26. A recent public opinion poll has not shown any tendency toward isolationism—65 percent of the American public "favor an active role for the United States in world affairs." See John E. Rielly, ed., *American Public Opinion and U.S. Foreign Policy 1995*, (Chicago: The Chicago Council on Foreign Relations, 1995) p. 13.
20. Elaine Sciolino, "New U.S. Peacekeeping Policy De-emphasizes Role of the UN," *New York Times*, May 6, 1994, A1 and A4. The quoted passages are taken from A4.
21. Lake, "From Containment to Enlargement." Emphasis in original.
22. Ibid.
23. Anthony Lake, "The Reach of Democracy," *New York Times*, September 23, 1994, A15.
24. The source is Henry A. Kissinger, *Diplomacy* (New York: Simon & Schuster, Inc., 1994). A portion was excerpted in *Time*, March 14, 1994. The quoted passage is from *Time* at p. 74.
25. "Principles and Opportunities for American Foreign Policy," address at the John F. Kennedy School of Government, Harvard University, Cambridge, Massachusetts, January 20, 1995. Also see "Secretary Christopher's Testimony Before the Senate Foreign Relations Committee," February 14, 1995.
26. "Principles and Opportunities for American Foreign Policy."
27. George Szamuely, "Clinton's Clumsy Encounter with the World," *Orbis* 38 (Summer 1994): 393.
28. The critic is Senator John McCain, and he is quoted in "Calling Dr. Kissinger," *The Economist*, January 14, 1995, 23.
29. See "A National Security Strategy of Engagement and Enlargement," The White House, July 1994 and February 1995.
30. Both quotes are from Elizabeth Drew, *On the Edge: The Clinton Presidency* (New York: Simon & Schuster, 1994), p. 138. The first is Drew's assessment (for a similar characterization, see p. 28), the other is her quoting of a senior official.
31. Ibid.
32. A former national security council staffer during the Bush administration is quoted in Tim Weiner, "Clinton as a Military Leader: Tough On-The-Job Training," *New York Times*, October 28, 1996, A1.
33. For a discussion of these two reasons that help explain the Clinton administration's difficulty in foreign policy, see Anthony Lewis, "Foreign Policy Morass," *New York Times*, October 11, 1993, A11.
34. John McCain, "Imagery or Purpose? The Choice in November," *Foreign Policy* 103 (Summer 1996): 20–34.
35. See, for example, Gordon Silverstein, *Imbalance of Powers* (New York: Oxford University Press, 1997), pp. 5–6 and Adam Clymer, "A Career Bipartisan: William Sebastian Cohen," *New York Times*, December 6, 1996, A1, A16. On the Lake controversy and the Tenet nomination, see Tim Weiner, "Lake Pulls Out as Nominee for C.I.A., Assailing Hearing as Endless Political Circus," *New York Times*, March 18, 1997, A1, A12; R.W. Apple, Jr., "New Times, High Cost," *New York Times*, March 18, 1997, A1, A12; and Tim Weiner, "Clinton Proposes Acting C.I.A. Chief as Agency Leader," *New York Times*, March 20, 1997, A1, A14; and Tim Weiner, "For 'the Ultimate Staff Guy,' a Time to Reap the Rewards of Being Loyal," *New York Times*, March 20, 1997, A14.
36. Steven Erlanger, "Albright May Be Facing Unfamiliar Tests," *New York Times*, December 7, 1996, 5.
37. The summary of the NAFTA pact, and some criticisms of it, is based upon the following: Ramesh Thakur, "The North American Free Trade Agreement," *Australian Journal of International Affairs* (May 1993): 77–98; "NAFTA Provisions," *Congressional Quarterly Almanac 1993* (Washington, DC: Congressional Quarterly, Inc., 1994), pp. 180–181; "Testimony of Ambassador Michael Kantor, United States Trade Representative," House Ways and Means Committee, September 14, 1993; and Peter Hakim, "NAFTA...and After: A New Era for the US and Latin America?" *Current History* 93 (March 1994): 97–102.

38. "NAFTA Provisions," *Congressional Quarterly Almanac 1993* (Washington, DC: Congressional Quarterly, Inc., 1994), p. 180.
39. For some of the issues raised by the agreement, see "Testimony of Ambassador Michael Kantor, United States Trade Representative," William A. Orme, Jr., "NAFTA: Myths Versus Facts," *Foreign Affairs* 72 (November/December 1993): 2–12; and Paul Krugman, "The Uncomfortable Truth About NAFTA," *Foreign Affairs* 72 (November/December 1993): 13–19.
40. B. Drummond Ayres, Jr., "On Trade, Perot Must Do What He Reviles: Lobby," *New York Times*, November 17, 1993, A11.
41. Keith Bradsher, "Clinton's Shopping List for Votes Has Ring of Grocery Buyer's List," *New York Times*, November 17, 1993, A11. Also see the chart of deals on the same page entitled "What the President Has Promised So Far."
42. The background and elements of GATT discussed in the subsequent paragraphs draw upon the following sources: "GATT Deal Reached; Fast Track Ok'd" and "Highlights of GATT Accord," in *Congressional Quarterly Almanac 1993* (Washington, DC: Congressional Quarterly, Inc., 1994), pp. 182–183; Keith Bradsher, "U.S. and Europe Clear the Way for a World Accord on Trade, Setting Aside Major Disputes," *New York Times*, December 15, 1993, A1 and C18; "Uruguay Round: Jobs for the United States, Growth for the World," publication from the Office of the United States Trade Representative, n.d.
43. Bob Benenson, "Free Trade Carries the Day as GATT Easily Passes," *Congressional Quarterly Weekly Report*, December 3, 1994, 3446.
44. Elaine Sciolino, "Leaders Agree on Free Trade for the Pacific," *New York Times*, November 16, 1994, A6.
45. The economist quoted was C. Fred Bergsten in Andrew Pollack, "Opening Asia's Door," *New York Times*, November 16, 1994, A6.
46. Ibid.
47. James Brooke, "On Eve of Miami Summit Talks, U.S. Comes Under Fire," *New York Times*, December 9, 1994, A4.
48. Quoted in Thomas L. Friedman, "Clinton Says Bush Made China Gains," *New York Times*, November 20, 1992, A11.
49. William J. Clinton, "Executive Order 12850—Conditions for Renewal of Most-Favored Nation Status for the People's Republic of China in 1994," in *Weekly Compilation of Presidential Documents* (Washington, DC: Government Printing Office, May 31, 1993), p. 983.
50. "The President's News Conference," May 26, 1994, which is printed in *Weekly Compilation of Presidential Documents* (Washington, DC: Government Printing Office, May 30, 1994), pp. 1166–1167.
51. Ibid., p. 1167. In the same statement, the Clinton administration announced that it was banning certain guns and ammunitions from import from China and would provide more support to those working for "the cause of human rights and democracy" in China.
52. Kenneth Lieberthal, "A New China Strategy," *Foreign Affairs* 74 (November/December 1995): 35, and "Asia's Arms Racing," *The Economist*, February 3, 1996, 29.
53. "Lawmakers Vow to Sustain Pressure on China," *Congressional Quarterly Weekly Report*, September 2, 1995, 2669.
54. Ibid.
55. McCain, "Imagery or Purpose? The Choice in November," p. 31.
56. Ibid.
57. The figures are from John J. Mearsheimer, "How to Stop the War in the Balkans," a lecture at Iowa State University, October 18, 1993.
58. For an extended discussion of the ethnic cleansing within Bosnia and the former Yugoslavia, see the cover story of *Newsweek*, January 4, 1993.
59. Quoted in Drew, *On the Edge: The Clinton Presidency*, p. 139.
60. A detailed discussion of the policy debate among advisers and the extended discussions on Bosnia in the first several months of the administration are carefully outlined in ibid., pp. 138–163.

61. Ibid., p. 159.
62. One exception in the use of force, in addition to the enforcement of the "no-fly zone," was over protection of one of the "safe areas" in April 1994. Earlier, an agreement was brokered, with U.S. assistance, for a pullback of forces from the safe haven of Gorazde as a means of stopping the shelling of that town. When the Serbs were caught violating the agreement, two air strikes were undertaken by the NATO forces to seek to enforce the ban.
63. See Craig R. Whitney, "NATO Turns from Force to Diplomacy in Bosnia," *New York Times*, December 3, 1994, 5 and Roger Cohen, "Maps, Guns, and Bosnia," *New York Times*, December 6, 1994, A1 and A3.
64. See Michael R. Gordon, "U.S., in Shift, Gives Up Its Talk of Tough Action Against Serbs," *New York Times*, November 29, 1994, A1 and A4, and Cohen, "Maps, Guns, and Bosnia."
65. In December 1994, the flights were temporarily halted. See Chuck Sudetic, "U.N. and NATO Agree to Halt Warplane Flights Over Bosnia," *New York Times*, December 3, 1994, 1 and 5.
66. This summary description is based upon *The World Almanac and Book of Facts 1996* (Mahwah, NJ: World Almanac Books, 1996), pp. 46, 52, 57, and 59.
67. Roger Cohen, "Taming the Bullies of Bosnia," *New York Times Magazine*, December 17, 1995, 78.
68. Ibid. The following paragraphs also draw upon "A Chilly Peace in Bosnia," in Helen E. Purkitt, ed., *World Politics 96/97*, 17th ed. (Sluice Dock, Guilford, CT: Dushkin Publishing Group/Brown and Benchmark Publishers, 1996).
69. Quoted from UN Security Council Resolution 814 in John R. Bolton, "Wrong Turn in Somalia," *Foreign Affairs* 73 (January/February 1994): 62.
70. Quoted in ibid.
71. See "Bloodbath: What Went Wrong?" *Newsweek*, October 18, 1993, 32; and Michael Elliott, "The Making of a Fiasco," *Newsweek*, October 18, 1993, 34–38.
72. See "Chronology—March 1995," *The World Almanac and Book of Facts 1996* (Mahwah, NJ: World Almanac Books, 1996), p. 52; and "Somalia—Still Breathing, in Its Way," *The Economist*, August 31, 1996, 37–38.
73. See, "Fire Fight from Hell," *Newsweek*, October 18, 1993, 39–43.
74. Patricia Lee Dorff, ed., "Chronology 1991," *Foreign Affairs: American and the World 1991/1992* 71 (1992): 219–220.
75. "A Haitian Chronology," *Congressional Quarterly Weekly Report*, September 17, 1994, 2579.
76. These agreement details are taken from Pamela Constable, "Haiti: A Nation in Despair, a Policy Adrift," *Current History* 93 (March 1994): 108–109.
77. Ibid., p. 109.
78. Szamuely, "Clinton's Clumsy Encounter with the World," p. 389.
79. "A Haitian Chronology," p. 2579.
80. UN Security Council Resolution 940 is reprinted in *New York Times*, August 1, 1994, A6.
81. William Jefferson Clinton, "Remarks by the President in Television Address to the Nation," September 15, 1994.
82. Larry Rohter, "2,000 U.S. Troops Land Without Opposition and Take Over Haiti's Ports and Airfields," *New York Times*, September 20, 1994, A1 and A6.
83. "Haitian President, Fearing Threat, to Be Guarded by U.S. Agents," *Des Moines Register*, September 14, 1996, 7A.
84. McCain, "Imagery or Purpose? The Choice in November," p. 32. On the political turmoil in 1997, see, for example, Larry Rohter, "Haiti Premier Quits, Saying Aristide Camp Undercut Him," *New York Times,* June 10, 1997, A9.
85. There was one other important U.S. mission under UN auspices in 1994. Some American forces were part of a humanitarian relief effort in Rwanda and Zaire to assist those

Rwandans fleeing the civil war in their homeland and then to facilitate return home for some as well. This mission did not seem to create the same amount of controversy as these others.

86. See candidate Clinton's comments quoted in *1992 Congressional Quarterly Almanac* (Washington, DC: Congressional Quarterly, Inc., 1993), p. 525.

87. Serge Schmemann, "Yeltsin Leaves Talks with Firm Support and More Aid," *New York Times*, April 5, 1993, A1 and A4.

88. Quoted in ibid., p. A1, from closing statements by the two leaders.

89. Thomas L. Friedman, "Clinton Asks Allies for Help to Speed I.M.F. Aid to Russia," *New York Times*, February 1, 1994, A4.

90. Ibid.

91. Ibid.

92. Patricia Lee Dorff, ed., "Chronology 1993," *Foreign Affairs: Agenda 1994* (New York: Council on Foreign Relations, 1994), pp. 226–229.

93. See R.W. Apple, Jr., "Ukraine Gives in on Surrendering Its Nuclear Arms, *New York Times*, January 11, 1994, A1, A5, and Jane Perlez, "Ukraine Hesitates on Nuclear Deal," *New York Times,* January 12, 1994, A1, A5.

94. See Jane Perlez, "Treaty to Cut A-Weapons Now in Effect," *New York Times*, December 6, 1994, A4.

95. For a more complete discussion of this surplus nuclear weapons issue, see James M. McCormick and Daniel B. Bullen, "Dealing with Nuclear Weapons Waste," *Midwest Newsletter, International Studies Association* 1 (September 1994): 1, 2, and 8; and Daniel B. Bullen and James M. McCormick, "The Management of Surplus Nuclear Weapons Materials," mimeo.

96. Lawrence German and Ira Reed, "Implementation of the Nunn-Lugar Threat Reduction Programs: An Exercise in Post-Cold War Cooperative Security," paper presented at the 1996 Annual Meeting of the American Political Science Association, August 29–September 1, 1996.

97. The descriptions here and the quoted passages are taken from "Partnership for Peace: Framework Document," printed in *NATO Review* 42 (February 1994): 29–30.

98. The listing is taken from the North Atlantic Organization (NATO) public data service provided on the internet, October 12, 1994 and the internet listing of February 5, 1996.

99. Opening Statement of U.S. Secretary of State Warren Christopher at the meeting of the North Atlantic Council, NATO Headquarters, Brussels, Belgium, December 1, 1994, provided on the internet by North Atlantic Treaty Organization (NATO) public data service.

100. Yeltsin is quoted in Elaine Sciolino, "Yeltsin Says NATO Is Trying to Split Continent Again," *New York Times*, December 6, 1994, A4. These comments were made at the Conference on Security and Cooperation in Europe, where the Russians also withheld completing their "Partnership for Peace" program even though they had signed the framework earlier.

101. Alison Mitchell, "Clinton Urges NATO Expansion in 1999," *New York Times*, October 23, 1995, A12; "Founding Act Between NATO and the Russian Federation," May 27, 1997, via the North Atlantic Treaty Organization (NATO) public data service on the Internet; Philip Shenon, "U.S., Defying Allies, Insists NATO Limit Expansion to 3," *New York Times,* June 13, 1997, A1 and A6; and Craig R. Whitney, "3 Former Members of Eastern Bloc Invited into NATO," *New York Times,* July 9, 1997, A1 and A7.

102. Michael C. Hudson, "The Clinton Administration and the Middle East: Squandering the Inheritance?" *Current History* 93 (February 1994): 51–52.

103. Thomas L. Friedman, "Dividing a Homeland," *New York Times*, September 15, 1993, A1.

104. Ibid., p. A7.

105. Edward P. Djerejian, Assistant Secretary for Near Eastern Affairs, "Recent Developments and Next Steps in the Middle East Peace Process," Statement before the Senate

Foreign Relations Committee, October 15, 1993, reprinted in *Dispatch* 4 (October 25, 1993): 745.

106. "This Week with David Brinkley," January 22, 1995.

107. Elaine Sciolino, "Jordon and Israel Agree on a Basis for Finding Peace," *New York Times*, September 15, 1993, A1.

108. See "Decades of Dealing at Arm's Length," *New York Times*, October 27, 1994, A6, and Clyde Haberman, "Israel and Jordon Sign a Peace Accord," *New York Times*, October 27, 1994, A1 and A6.

109. Excerpts from the treaty upon which we draw here can be found in "The Agreement: Establishing Principles for a Lasting Peace," *New York Times*, October 27, 1994, A7.

110. Alison Mitchell, "Arafat and Rabin Sign Pact to Expand Arab Self-Rule," *New York Times*, September 29, 1995, A1.

111. Serge Schmemann, "50 Are Killed as Clashes Widen From West Bank to Gaza Strip," *New York Times*, September 27, 1996, A1 and A6.

112. See Hudson, "The Clinton Administration and the Middle East: Squandering the Inheritance?" pp. 50–51, and Anthony Lake, "Confronting Backlash States, " *Foreign Affairs* 73 (March/April 1994): 45–55.

113. Ibid., p. 49.

114. F. Gregory Gause III, "The Illogic of Dual Containment," *Foreign Affairs* 73 (March/April 1994): 56–66.

115. Christopher, "Principles and Opportunities for American Foreign Policy."

116. Michael R. Gordon, "U.S. Sending 36,000 Troops to Counter Iraqi Buildup," *New York Times*, October 10, 1994, A1 and A4.

117. Les Aspin, Secretary of Defense, *Report on the Bottom-Up Review*, October 1993, p. iii.

118. Ibid., pp. 1–2.

119. Ibid., p. 2.

120. These forces were confirmed in Christopher, "Principles and Opportunities for American Foreign Policy."

121. The discussion of the Nuclear Posture Review is taken from "DOD Review Recommends Reduction in Nuclear Force," Office of the Secretary of Defense (Public Affairs), Washington, DC, September 22, 1994, and "Radio-TV Defense Dialog," The Federal News Reuter Transcript Service, September 22, 1994.

122. See Andrew F. Krepinevich, *The Bottom-Up Review: An Assessment* (Washington, DC: Defense Budget Project, February 1994).

123. Eric Schmitt, "Some Doubt U.S. Could Fight Two Wars," *New York Times*, October 17, 1994, A5.

124. The components of the pact are taken from Alan Riding, "U.S. and North Korea Sign Atom Pact, *New York Times*, October 22, 1994, 7, and the pact itself, "The Agreed Framework Between the United States and the Democratic People's Republic of Korea," Geneva, October 21, 1994. The quoted passages are from the latter.

125. The quoted phrases and passages are taken from Douglas Jehl, "Clinton to Ask Billions More in Spending for the Military," *New York Times*, December 2, 1994, A1 and A9. The critic quoted is Senator John McCain, Republican of Arizona.

126. Part of the following draws upon Dov S. Zakheim, "Our Unready Military," *New York Times*, December 30, 1994, A15.

127. For a discussion of the "Contract with America," upon which we draw here, see "New Majority's Agenda: Substantial Changes May Be Ahead," *New York Times*, November 11, 1994, A10; Pat Towell and Carroll J. Doherty, "GOP Strikes at Cutbacks, Peacekeeping Missions," and "National Security," in *Congressional Quarterly Weekly Report*, November 19, 1994, 3339–3340 and pp. 3373–3376, respectively. Pat Towell and Carroll J. Doherty, "Republicans Lay Seige to Clinton's Policy," *Congressional Quarterly Weekly Report*, December 3, 1994, 3452–3453; and Carroll J. Doherty, "GOP Sharpens Budgetary Knife Over International Programs," *Congressional Quarterly Weekly Report*, December 17, 1994, 3452–3453.

128. See "Defense Bill Enacted Despite Objections," *Congressional Quarterly Almanac 1995* (Washington, DC: Congressional Quarterly, Inc., 1996), p. 11–21; and Pat Towell, "Clinton Signs Republicans' Fortified Defense Bill," *Congressional Quarterly Weekly Report*, October 12, 1996, 2928.

129. Ibid., pp. 2929–2932 and "Defense Bill Highlights," *Congressional Quarterly Almanac 1995*, (Washington, DC: Congressional Quarterly, Inc., 1996), pp. 11-28–11-29.

130. "House Seeks to Trim 'Peacekeeping,'" *Congressional Quarterly Almanac 1995* (Washington, DC: Congressional Quarterly, Inc., 1996), pp. 9–16.

131. The quotes and information in this paragraph are from "Secretary of Defense Issues Quadrennial Defense Review," News Release, Office of the Assistant Secretary of Defense, May 19, 1997; and William S. Cohen, *Report of the Quadrennial Defense Review*, May 1997. Both were available via the Internet.

132. Quoted in Steven Erlanger, "Courtly Ritual Greets Albright on Capitol Hill," *New York Times*, January 9, 1997, A1.

133. For a recent statement of this criticism, see "America's World: Good Intentions," *The Economist*, November 23, 1996, 23.

134. "A Muted Madeleine Albright," *New York Times*, January 9, 1997, A14.

135. On the centrality of the Russian and NATO issues and on China, see "America's World: Good Intentions," pp. 24–25.

136. See "Israel's Leaders Vote to Withdraw Troops," *Des Moines Register*, January 16, 1997, p. 6A; and Serge Schmemann, "Accord on Hebron Gets Endorsement of Israeli Cabinet," *New York Times*, January 16, 1997, A1.

137. On this point, see "America's World: Good Intentions," pp. 23–24.

138. See the various discussions on the "Contract with America," after the 1994 election, and its implications. In particular, see "New Majority's Agenda: Substantial Changes May Be Ahead, " p. A10; Towell and Doherty, "GOP Strikes at Cutbacks, Peacekeeping Missions," and "National Security," pp. 3339–3340 and pp. 3373–3376, respectively; Towell and Doherty, "Republicans Lay Siege to Clinton's Policy," pp. 3452–3453; and Doherty, "GOP Sharpens Budgetary Knife Over International Programs," pp. 3452–3453.

139. Erlanger, "Courtly Ritual Greets Albright on Capitol Hill," p. A4; and "Fact Sheet: Reinventing State, ACDA, USIA and AID," White House Press Release, April 18, 1997, via the Internet.

2

THE PROCESS OF POLICY MAKING

Now that the reader is generally familiar with the basic values and beliefs that have shaped American policy over time, we shift our focus to policy making itself. In Part II, we examine in some detail the policy making process and how various institutions and groups—the executive, the Congress, several bureaucracies, political parties, interest groups, and the public at large—compete to promote their own values in American policy abroad. In this section, our goal is to provide essential information on who the principal foreign policy makers are, what their relative influence within the decision-making process is, and how their power has changed in the postwar period. In this way, the student may be better able to understand how and why particular values, beliefs, and policies are adopted by the United States toward the rest of the world.

Chapters 7 and 8 examine the institutional competition between the two most important participants in the foreign policy process, the president and the Congress. While each branch of government has constitutionally prescribed power over particular aspects of the formulation and conduct of foreign policy, each shares responsibilities in shaping America's foreign policy. Because these institutions share responsibilities, conflict inevitably occurs regarding who should hold sway over the process. Chapter 7 explains why the values and beliefs of the executive branch often dominate the foreign affairs machinery of the American government. Chapter 8 discusses the post-Vietnam through the post–Cold War efforts of the Congress to reassert some of its constitutional prerogatives and to engage more fully in a foreign policy partnership with the executive branch.

Chapters 9 and 10 focus upon the bureaucratic structures within the executive branch that compete for policy influence. At least three reasons justify this emphasis upon bureaucracies in analyzing American foreign policy: first, the growth of executive institutions associated with foreign affairs (e.g., the National Security Council, the Department of State, and the Department of Defense) and the expansion of policy activities by other bureaucracies not normally viewed as participants in foreign policy making (e.g., the Office of the United States Trade Representative, Department of the Treasury, the Department of Agriculture, and the Department of Commerce); second, the emergence of competition among bureaucracies over policy options (e.g., the National Security Council vs. the Department of State) and the importance of this competition in understanding policy; and third, the ability of some bureaucracies to dominate policy, not always with adequate control by the executive branch, the Congress, or the public at large (e.g., the Central Intelligence Agency). Chapter 9 examines the role of the Department of State, the National Security Council, and several key economic departments in the policy process, while Chapter 10 examines the impact of the Department of Defense and the intelligence community. In the latter chapter, too, we explain how policy making has been coordinated among these various bureaucracies by the president through a system of interagency groups.

The final participants in the foreign policy process are political parties, interest groups, the media, and public opinion. Political parties seek to influence foreign policy making by gaining control of the machinery of government—the presidency, the Congress, and the bureaucracy. Interest groups and public opinion attempt to influence foreign policy making, indirectly rather than directly, by influencing these institutions. The media are important transmission vehicles through which the public and the policy makers learn about important issues. The media also may provide a discreet influence on what issues are on the agenda, how they are analyzed, and how they are decided. Chapter 11 discusses the role of political parties and interest groups and their impact on foreign policy. In the first part of this chapter, we outline the bipartisan tradition that the Democrats and Republicans have often claimed to follow in policy making and demonstrate how this tradition has eroded significantly in the last two decades. Further, we show how the two parties are moving farther apart on foreign policy as ideological differences become stronger. In the second half of Chapter 11, we identify the myriad types of interest groups that attempt to influence foreign policy. To illustrate how influence has been exercised by interest groups, we focus in particular on two types that, arguably, have enjoyed the greatest success in the postwar period: economic interest groups and ethnic interest groups. Finally, Chapter 12 is devoted to a discussion of the role of the media and public opinion in the foreign policy making process. In the first part of this chapter, we analyze the growth in media coverage of foreign affairs and the differing roles, as analysts argue, that the media play in the foreign policy. In the second half of this chapter, we highlight several factors that limit the influence of public opinion on foreign policy making, but we also demonstrate that the public can and does affect the actions of foreign policy makers.

CHAPTER

7

THE PRESIDENT AND THE MAKING OF FOREIGN POLICY

It is the president who is responsible for guiding and directing the nation's foreign policy. The Executive Branch alone may conduct international negotiations, appoint ambassadors, and conduct foreign policy.... The president also serves as commander-in-chief of our armed forces....

President George Bush
Address at Princeton University, May 10, 1991

I think that, clearly, the Constitution leaves to the President, for good and sufficient reasons, the ultimate decision-making authority [in foreign policy].

President Bill Clinton
October 1993

In October 1993, when President Clinton was faced with possible congressional restrictions on his ability to use force in Haiti, he resisted strongly.

While the president acknowledged that he had a "big responsibility" to "appropriately consult with members of Congress," he, like virtually every president—at least since Franklin Roosevelt—sought to retain his control over foreign policy: "I think that, clearly, the Constitution leaves to the president, for good and sufficient reasons, the ultimate decision-making authority."[1] Presidential dominance, in short, is the usual way to characterize U.S. foreign policy making.

More than a decade earlier, two former presidents, Jimmy Carter and Gerald Ford, enunciated this long-standing view in a joint appearance. In foreign policy, there is "only one clear voice," Carter said, and that is the president's; Ford endorsed this view by adding that Congress is too large and too diverse to handle foreign policy crises.[2] Two recent secretaries of state have made the same point about the foreign policy responsibilities of the president: one colorfully through a metaphor from the Old West, the other through invoking the formal and implied powers from the Constitution. During his 1989 Senate confirmation hearings, President Bush's secretary of state, James Baker, asserted that "in the saloons of the old West...you never shoot the piano player. And Dean Acheson wrote that in foreign policy, the President was the piano player."[3] In addition, he appealed for a "kinder and gentler Congress" in foreign policy, allowing the president to play the tune. Eight years earlier in the same Senate setting, President Reagan's secretary of state, Alexander Haig, echoed this theme more formally: "...the Constitutional and traditional responsibility of the President for the conduct of foreign affairs must be reaffirmed...the authoritative voice must be the President's."[4]

Over the past three decades, however, the U.S. Congress has increasingly challenged the presidency by seeking a larger role in the making of American foreign policy. This congressional resurgence began in the early 1970s, fueled by the Vietnam and Watergate experiences, and resulted in several initiatives that sought to curb executive prerogatives in foreign affairs. That assertiveness continued in the 1980s with major roles for Congress in shaping Central American, Middle Eastern, and Soviet-American policy. As the Cold War ended and as Republican majorities were elected to Congress in the 1990s, congressional initiatives did not diminish. In 1995, in debates over foreign aid legislation, Congress sought to include restrictions on presidential power. Indeed, the debate between these two branches over the control of U.S. foreign policy persists to this day.

In this chapter and the following one, we examine the struggle between the president and Congress to make American foreign policy. In these two chapters the analysis explores the following themes: (1) why and how the executive has dominated the foreign policy process: (2) why and how Congress has tried to curb presidential power recently; and (3) what is likely to be the relationship between the president and Congress as we approach the twenty-first century.

CONSTITUTIONAL POWERS IN FOREIGN POLICY

Under the Constitution, both the legislative and executive branches of government have been delegated specific foreign affairs powers. Both branches, too, were directed to *share* some foreign policy responsibility with the other. This arrangement ensured that Congress and the president could each check the actions of the other in foreign policy, much as the two branches do in domestic policy. Throughout the history of the Republic, however, the division of these foreign policy powers between the legislature and the executive has not always been clear. Indeed, political disputes have often arisen over it. In order to appreciate American foreign policy making more fully, we begin our analysis by identifying the foreign policy powers of each branch and the areas of dispute between them.

Presidential Powers

Under Article II of the Constitution, the president is granted several foreign policy powers. First, the president is granted the plenary power to be chief executive, which extends to the foreign policy arena ("The Executive Power shall be vested in a President..." and "he shall take Care that the Laws be faithfully executed").[5] He is also granted the power to command the armed forces ("The President shall be Commander in Chief of the Army and Navy of the United States..."). And, the president is granted the power to be the chief negotiator and the chief diplomat ("He shall have power, by and with the advice and consent of the Senate, to make Treaties...shall appoint Ambassadors...and he shall receive Ambassadors and other public Ministers..."). The president, in short, is to wear at least three different hats in foreign policy: chief executive, chief diplomat, and commander in chief of the armed forces. With such power at his disposal, the president seemingly possesses the constitutional mandate to dominate foreign affairs.

This delegation in our Constitution of foreign policy powers to the executive branch represented a marked change from the arrangements under the earlier Articles of Confederation, which had no executive branch. During that period prior to 1787, it was Congress that controlled foreign policy through its Committee on Foreign Affairs. Such a process, however, did not work very well. Congress's inability to manage trade policy, maintain and protect America's national boundaries, and deal effectively with Britain and Spain contributed to the need for a new constitutional structure for the young Republic. Indeed, according to one assessment, "*the mismanagement of foreign affairs by Congress*" contributed to the holding of the Constitutional Convention.[6]

While the Founders at the Constitutional Convention agreed on the need to strengthen the national government over the states, they were divided over how strong the foreign policy powers of the executive should be. Although they were familiar with Locke's *The Second Treatise on Government*, in which various foreign policy prerogatives rested with the executive, and with Sir William Blackstone's *Commentaries on the Laws of England*, in which the king enjoyed significant prerogatives in foreign affairs as well, the Founders largely rejected these models. Instead, they were concerned about too much executive power and were careful to share presidential powers in making treaties, appointments, and war and peace with the legislative branch.[7] Even as strong a proponent of executive power as Alexander Hamilton was led to conclude that the president under the Constitution would have fewer substantive foreign affairs powers than the King of England.[8]

Congressional Powers

Under Article I of the Constitution, Congress does in fact enjoy several significant foreign policy powers. Congress has the right to make and modify any laws and to appropriate funds for the implementations of any laws ("No money shall be drawn from the Treasury, but in Consequence of Appropriations made by Law"). Congress has the right to provide for the national defense and to declare war (Congress is authorized to "provide for the common Defence...; To declare War...; To raise and support Armies...; To provide and maintain a Navy"). Congress is also delegated the responsibility to regulate international commerce ("To regulate commerce with foreign nations...") and to use the implied powers (the right to "make all Laws which shall be necessary and proper..." for carrying out its other responsibilities).

Constitutional scholar Louis Henkin has argued that Congress has even more powers, what he calls the "Foreign Affairs Powers." These are powers that are not explicitly derived from the Constitution, but derive from the fact that the United States has sovereignty and nationhood. Thus, Congress enjoys additional authority to support legislation to regulate and protect "the conduct of foreign relations and foreign diplomatic activities in the United States." These undefined powers, too, allow congressional legislation in such areas as immigration, the regulation of aliens, the authorization of international commitments, and the extradition of citizens to other states. Moreover, Henkin rather boldly concludes that today there is no matter in foreign affairs "that is not subject to legislation by Congress."[9] In this sense, Congress has a constitutional mandate to be involved in foreign policy, just as the executive branch does.

"The Twilight Zone" and Foreign Policy

While the nation's Founders delegated separate foreign policy responsibilities to each branch, they went further by stipulating the sharing of some foreign policy power between them as well. While the president is the chief executive of the United States, Congress decides what laws are to be enforced; while the president may command the armed forces, Congress decides whether wars should be initiated; and while the president may negotiate treaties, Congress (or more accurately, the Senate) must give its advice and consent. (Table 7.1 shows three areas of shared foreign policy powers as outlined in Articles I and II of the Constitution.)

The constitutional ideal of shared foreign policy powers is more easily described than it is put into effective operation. Often, the actions of one branch seemingly cross over into the responsibilities of another branch. The president will rely upon his commander-in-chief power to initiate conflict with another nation, even though only Congress has the power to declare war. Congress will seek to restrict the deployment of troops into a particular region, even though the president has the power to direct the deployment of armed forces. What has emerged, in the words of Supreme

TABLE 7.1

Some Foreign Policy Powers Shared Between the President and the Congress

President	Congress
A. *War making*	
"Commander in Chief of the Army and Navy of the United States"	the power "to declare war"; "to raise and support armies"; to "provide for the Common Defence"
B. *Commitment making*	
"He shall have Power...to make Treaties"	"provided two thirds of the Senators present concur"
C. *Appointments*	
"He shall nominate...and shall appoint Ambassadors"	"by and with the advice and Consent of the Senate"

Court Justice Robert Jackson, has been "a zone of twilight in which [the president] and Congress may have concurrent authority, or in which its distribution is uncertain."[10]

The result of this shared responsibility has been an historical tension over who ultimately controls foreign policy, owing to this constitutional ambiguity. Perhaps one of the earliest debates reflecting the ambiguity of these divided powers was provided by two Founders, Alexander Hamilton and James Madison, writing under pseudonyms in the early 1790s. Hamilton (or "Pacificus," as he wrote), in defense of President Washington's declaration of neutrality in 1793 (over France's war against Great Britain, Spain, and the Netherlands), made the classic case for a strong executive who would dominate foreign policy: The powers and responsibilities over foreign policy rested with the executive, Pacificus argued, except for those powers specifically delegated to Congress. Madison (or "Helvidius," as he wrote) viewed presidential powers in foreign affairs in a more limited way: Only those powers expressly delegated to the executive were allowed under the Constitution, and there was not such an unrestrained delegation of power to that branch.[11] Moreover, other foreign policy powers were necessarily left to Congress to serve as a counterweight to the presidency. In short, no exact division was spelled out between the two branches.

In the modern era, several scholars attest to the problem of delineating the foreign policy powers between the two branches. Historian Arthur Schlesinger, in his book, *The Imperial Presidency*, describes the division of power between the two governmental branches in the Constitution as "cryptic, ambiguous, and incomplete," thus contributing to policy making disputes between the two institutions.[12] Constitutional scholar Henkin notes that "the constitutional blueprint for the governance of our foreign affairs has proved to be starkly incomplete, indeed skimpy."[13] Edward S. Corwin, the noted scholar on constitutional and presidential power, has probably provided the most often cited summary of this dilemma: The Constitution has really provided "an invitation to struggle for the privilege of directing American foreign policy."[14]

A CYCLICAL INTERPRETATION OF FOREIGN POLICY DOMINANCE

To some analysts, a cyclical pattern of control has resulted from this "invitation to struggle": one branch dominating during a particular epoch, the other dominating during another. The exact period of executive or legislative dominance may not be the same for all analysts, however.[15] Others would see the presidency as having emerged as more successful than Congress over the history of the Republic, and especially in the post–World War II years. In this view, only in recent decades (i.e., in the post-Vietnam era) has the legislative branch attempted to wrest some foreign policy making from the executive branch. Both views merit our attention, although the latter view, especially as we focus upon the post–World War II era, will receive more detailed analysis here.

The Early Years of the Republic

According to the cyclical interpretation, during the early decades of the country, presidential dominance was on the rise, and congressional involvement in foreign policy was often limited. When President Washington took several unilateral actions—appointing diplomats abroad, refusing to share information on the Jay Treaty, and issuing a neutrality declaration over fighting between Britain and France —with only limited congressional involvement, presidential ascendancy was assured. Other early presidents—Adams, Jefferson, and Madison—largely followed this pattern, epitomized, for example, by the executive initiatives in securing the Louisiana Purchase and in issuing the Monroe Doctrine. (These particular actions are described in more detail in the next section.) To be sure, congressional involvement was not entirely abandoned in these early years, as illustrated by the role of Congress in precipitating the War of 1812. In particular, Congress sought to enact various embargo bills—especially against the British. As a result, political scientist Holbert Carroll has subsequently judged that a "congressional war" was actually initiated.[16]

With the presidency of Andrew Jackson and generally continuing until the presidency of Abraham Lincoln (with the exception of James Polk), the congressional role became more assertive in the foreign policy realm. Jackson, for example, deferred to Congress when actions seemed called for over attacks upon American ships off South America, and when France was reluctant to pay claims owed to the United States. When Texas revolted against Mexico and then sought American recognition as an independent state, President Jackson turned to the U.S. Congress to seek its guidance on American policy.

During the presidency of James Polk, presidential dominance arose once again. Without asking Congress for authorization, President Polk ordered the U.S. military into the territory that was in dispute between Texas and Mexico. What resulted was an attack upon American forces by Mexico, and a rather quick declaration of war by Congress.[17] With the presidency of Lincoln, however, this executive dominance in foreign policy extended even further as the Civil War president sought to hold the Union together. A wide range of executive actions were initiated without congressional involvement, as we catalog below, and the height of the powerful presidency was upon us.

Congressional Dominance After the Civil War

After the Civil War, however, the "golden age of congressional ascendancy" emerged.[18] Congress once again asserted its role, passing a resolution to stop the acquisition of future territories, after Seward's purchase of Alaska in 1867. In 1869, the Senate refused to take action on a treaty "permitting de facto annexation of Santo Domingo." Indeed, over the next thirty years or so, congressional–executive relations were so strained that the "Senate refused to ratify any important treaty outside of the immigration context."[19]

By roughly the turn of the century, however, the pendulum began to swing back toward the executive. From Presidents McKinley and Roosevelt to Wilson (and with Taft as the exception), the presidency reigned over foreign policy. Consider Teddy Roosevelt's robust action in the Western Hemisphere and McKinley's in Asia. President Wilson, too, sought to enlarge the role of the presidency in foreign affairs with his proposal of a global collective security system and his endorsement of the League of Nations. As the U.S. Senate rejected the Versailles Treaty and membership in the nascent League of Nations, presidential dominance waned once again. By the time of the "return to normalcy" of the interwar years, Congress largely shaped foreign policy through the passage of neutrality acts to keep America out of foreign involvement and through restrictive trade and immigration laws (e.g., the Smoot-Hawley Tariff and the National Origins Act).

Despite the congressional role in the nineteenth century and into the early twentieth century, political scientist Holbert Carroll aptly describes Congress's overall involvement in foreign policy as "episodic and fitful."[20] Moreover, the congressional involvement was to change dramatically with the emergence of World War II, when executive dominance emerged once again. President Roosevelt, for example, acted to aid the British with the "destroyers for bases" deal, an arrangement in which the United States sold fifty destroyers to Britain in exchange for access rights to British bases "in the Atlantic and Caribbean,"[21] and he got congressional approval for the Lend-Lease Act, an American aid effort to support the allies already in World War II. With the emergence of the Cold War, presidential power was to change even more dramatically. Indeed, by the late 1940s and early 1950s, executive dominance in foreign affairs was fully in place.

EXECUTIVE DOMINANCE AFTER WORLD WAR II: THE IMPERIAL PRESIDENCY

Some of the reasons for the growth of presidential power after World War II are the result of long-term historical trends, but other reasons are particularly associated with the rise of American globalism in the post–World War II years. In the main, though, the president has been the one to dominate foreign affairs matters owing to several key factors:

1. Important historical executive precedents
2. Supreme Court decisions
3. Congressional deference and delegation
4. Growth of executive institutions
5. International situational factors

We now turn to examine each of these factors in detail. We begin by revisiting the brief historical sketch of congressional/executive relations from the last section. Now, however, we focus on some specific executive precedents that emerged over the nineteenth and early twentieth centuries of the Republic and strengthened the president's hand in foreign policy. Then we turn to examine more contemporary factors (e.g., the Supreme Court decisions, a supportive Congress, and the growth of institutions) that have fostered executive power in foreign policy, even to this day.

1. Important Historical Executive Precedents

An important first factor that contributed to executive dominance of foreign affairs consists of those actions taken by the various presidents throughout history. By assuming that they possessed control of foreign policy over particular issues and by taking action, the early presidents set a pattern for how future executives would act. These precedents ranged across several key foreign policy areas: the right of the president to negotiate with other nations, the right to recognize other governments, the right to withhold information from the Congress on certain foreign policy matters, the right to initiate the conduct of foreign policy, the right to begin conflict and even war with other nations, and the right to make commitments with other governments. In this regard, the actions of the first president, George Washington, were particularly pivotal in establishing these precedents, since he put into effect the meaning of the Constitution "in response to events."[22] Other early presidents followed Washington's lead and were to give the presidency preeminence in these foreign policy areas.

Negotiating with Other Nations. In the area of representing the United States abroad, President Washington made it clear that the executive would be that representative. He sent personal emissaries to represent him in negotiations abroad and simply informed Congress of his actions. In 1791, for instance, President Washington informed the Senate that Gouverneur Morris, who was in Great Britain at that time, would confer with the British over their adherence to the treaty of peace. A short time later, Washington sent his friend Colonel David Humphrey to Spain and Portugal as his personal representative.[23] By such actions, Washington established the principle that the president would conduct relations with other states.

Recognizing Other Nations. President Washington established another important precedent: The chief executive would be the one to recognize other states. When Washington received Edmond Genet ("Citizen Genet"), the first minister to the United States from the French Republic, he went a long way toward legitimizing that nation's revolutionary government. Similarly, when Genet seemingly violated his power, it was up to Washington to send him home.[24]

Withholding Foreign Policy Information. In a similar vein, President Washington provided another precedent by declining to share important diplomatic information with the House of Representatives when negotiating the Jay Treaty. Although his rationale was that the House had no standing in the treaty process, the implications of his actions went further. In Corwin's view, the allowance of this precedent broadened presidential power so that "a President feels free by the same formula to decline information even to his constitutional partner in treaty-making...."[25]

Initiating Policy. President Washington also established the precedent of executive initiation of foreign policy. In unilaterally declaring neutrality between France and Britain in 1793, he began the process of presidential direction for foreign policy matters. After this declaration, Congress largely followed the president and passed a neutrality act in conformity with Washington's wishes.[26] President Monroe followed a similar approach with his unilateral declaration of the Monroe Doctrine in 1823, although the Congress still held the right to deny funding for any Western Hemisphere activity.

In sum, by these actions of sending emissaries abroad and receiving representatives from other states, President Washington gave meaning to the constitutional power of appointing and receiving ambassadors. In effect, the executive power in this area came to eclipse any congressional prerogative. When President Washington followed the Hamiltonian notion of inherent executive power by initiating foreign policy actions, he seemed to imply that the powers of the executive derived from the fact that the United States was a sovereign state and that the president was the representative of that sovereignty. In short, President Washington gave meaning to the characterization of the presidency by a future chief justice of the United Sates, John Marshall: "The President is the sole organ of the nation in its external relations, and its sole representative with foreign nations."[27]

Other early presidents followed Washington's lead of a strong executive carrying on relations with other states. For instance, President Adams used his executive power to extradite an individual under the Jay Treaty without congressional authorization. Likewise, Adams vigorously defended his right to recognize other states. President Jefferson, too, although a proponent of legislative dominance in the affairs of state, still exercised considerable individual control over the Louisiana Purchase. Still later, President James Monroe refused to relinquish the president's right to recognize other governments, especially with regard to several Latin American states. The result, as Corwin concludes, was to "reaffirm the President's monopoly of international intercourse and his constitutional independence in the performance of that function."[28] This presidential preeminence in the recognition of, and negotiation of relations with, other states continued through the rest of the nineteenth century and into the twentieth century. As a result, the president's right to recognize and to negotiate with states is little challenged to this day.

Initiating Conflicts and War. Another area in which actions by early executives set a precedent was in war making. Although Congress was granted the right to declare war under the Constitution, to what extent could the executive use military force without the explicit authorization of the legislative branch? Put differently, how far could the president go under the commander-in-chief clause of the Constitution before it intruded on the congressional prerogative to declare war?

Early presidents generally were quite careful about extending the meaning of the commander-in-chief clause, but not always. Only in the case of attacks upon Americans or American forces did the president occasionally provide immediate military responses. As Arthur Schlesinger points out, however, even in those instances, the early presidents were quite meticulous in involving Congress in any actions.[29] When President Thomas Jefferson was faced with the question of using force against Tripoli because of its attack upon American shipping, he did send U.S. frigates to the Mediterranean, but he supposedly limited them to defensive action only. Some recent evidence by Schlesinger, however, suggests otherwise. Jefferson apparently "sent a naval squadron to the Mediterranean under secret orders to fight the Barbary pirates, applied for congressional sanctions six months later and then misled Congress as to the nature of the orders."[30] Moreover, at about the same time, Jefferson sent a message to Congress declaring that "his actions...[were] in compliance with constitutional limitations on his authority in the absence of a declaration of war."[31] In this sense, executive assertiveness in war making may have begun quite early in the Republic.

To be sure, by the 1840s, however, some transformation in the commander-in-chief clause was already evident. President James K. Polk was instrumental in using his power as head of the armed forces to precipitate a declaration of war against Mexico. By moving American troops into land disputed with Mexico—resulting in a Mexican attack upon these forces—President Polk was able to obtain a war resolution from Congress.[32] By using his constitutional power as commander in chief, President Polk was able to force Congress's hand on the war powers.

The boldest precedents with the commander-in-chief clause came during the presidency of Abraham Lincoln. Combining the powers granted under this clause with the executive power to take care that the laws were carried out, President Lincoln effectively made the "war power" his own, as analyst Edward Corwin said. Because of the Civil War, President Lincoln, without consulting Congress, "proclaimed a blockade of the Southern ports, suspended the writ of habeas corpus in various places, and caused the arrest and military detention of persons 'who were represented to him' as being engaged or contemplating 'treasonable practices...'"[33] In addition, Lincoln enlarged the Army and Navy, pressed into service the state militias, and called into service 40,000 volunteers. Despite outcries that the president was going beyond his limits, neither Congress nor the courts challenged him. In fact, Congress gave approval to his actions after the fact, and the Supreme Court upheld his actions in the *Prize Cases* by a narrow margin of 5–4.[34] While these presidential actions were taken in the context of a civil war (and their relevance to foreign wars is debatable), the expansion of the presidential power in war making was not lost on future presidents.

While congressional acquiescence to Lincoln's actions did not produce any expansion of war making by his immediate successors, it did establish important precedents for later commanders in chief.[35] The dispatch of troops to China by President McKinley in 1900, the interventions by Presidents Theodore Roosevelt and William Howard Taft in the Caribbean in the early 1900s, and even the sending of American forces to Korea (albeit with a UN resolution) were done without congressional authorization.

Furthermore, the several interventions by the United States during the height of the Cold War (Lebanon, Bay of Pigs, Dominican Republic, and Vietnam) occurred without the benefit of congressional actions before the fact. Moreover, even Lyndon Johnson was able to boast that there was a large body of precedent for his Vietnam policy by citing the actions of previous commanders in chief. On one occasion, for instance, President Johnson was able to cite some 125 cases in which previous presidents took military action to protect American citizens. On another occasion, he was to cite some 137 cases in which earlier chief executives had unilaterally employed force to protect U.S. citizens.[36] Later on, during the Vietnam War, President Nixon justified the Cambodian invasion in 1970 by stating: "I shall meet my responsibility as Commander in Chief of our Armed Forces to take the action necessary to defend the security of our American men."[37]

The pattern has continued throughout the 1980s and into the 1990s as well. In 1982, President Reagan initially sent American troops into Lebanon as a "peacekeeping force" without congressional approval and justified that action through the commander-in-chief clause of the Constitution. (Only after some American lives were lost in this deployment did Congress insist on applying the requirements of the War Powers Resolution, a congressional resolution requiring congressional notification and involvement when the president uses force. See Chapter 8.) In April 1986, too, President Reagan unilaterally initiated a retaliatory attack against Libya over that country's involvement with a terrorist attack upon Americans in West Berlin. In December 1989, President Bush approved the U.S. intervention into Panama and justified it on the basis of his "constitutional authority with respect to the conduct of foreign relations," his responsibility "to protect American lives in imminent danger," and "as Commander in Chief" of American military forces.[38] In August 1990 and beyond, President Bush once again used a similar kind of constitutional rationale for sending some American military personnel into Saudi Arabia to protect that country from Iraq's Saddam Hussein, who had seized Kuwait. When the president actually decided to use force against Iraq over its seizure of Kuwait, he did seek congressional authorization, as we discuss below.

President Clinton expressed the same presidential prerogative with regard to the use of force in Haiti. When Congress raised the possibility of restricting Clinton's use of force to intervene in Haiti in September 1993, the president said he was determined to "strongly oppose" congressional restrictions on the right to use force there and elsewhere. In a sharply worded letter to the leaders in the Senate, President Clinton stated that he opposed several amendments at the time because they would "unduly restrict the ability of the President to make foreign policy" and because they would weaken the commander-in-chief power as well.[39] Even Clinton's assistant attorney general was put in the somewhat awkward position of justifying the president's determination to intervene in Haiti (despite his earlier academic writing arguing otherwise) by pointing to the "circumstances peculiar to the situation there."[40]

In 1995, President Clinton again objected strongly to proposed congressional actions reshaping the foreign affairs bureaucracies and reducing foreign aid and threatened to veto the legislation. "These [proposed] constraints," the president said, "represent nothing less than a frontal assault on the authority of the president to conduct the foreign policy of the United States and on our nation's ability to respond rapidly and effectively to threats to our security."[41] These kinds of actions, the administration argued, would undermine the foreign policy powers of the president and the commander-in-chief clause of the Constitution as well.

According to critics, then, the commander-in-chief clause had been expanded to include the power not only to conduct a war already begun, but to *initiate* a conflict if necessary. The growth of this executive precedent has caused Congress to react strongly to this apparent incursion into its area of responsibility. As we shall discuss in the next chapter, the War Powers Resolution was passed in an attempt to curb executive war making, but it has been far from successful.

Making Foreign Commitments. A final area of executive precedent was in the making of foreign policy commitments. Instead of relying on the treaty as the basic instrument of making commitments to other states, presidents have come to rely on the so-called executive agreement as a principal means of establishing bonds with other nations. By such precedent, the treaty power of Congress has been eroded, and congressional involvement in this aspect of foreign policy making has been weakened. In this way, once again, the president has enhanced his ability to make and carry out foreign policy by executive action only.

The executive agreement is an agreement made by the president or the president's representative, usually without congressional involvement, with another country. Its most important distinction from a treaty is that it does not require the advice and consent of the Senate, yet it has the same force of law as a treaty. An executive agreement actually may take two forms. One type is based solely on the constitutional power of the president; the other type is based on congressional legislation authorizing or approving the president's making a commitment with another nation. The former relies upon powers granted in Article II, and especially the commander-in-chief clause. An example would be an agreement made by the United Sates for use of naval facilities in Bahrain in 1971. A State Department official testified before Congress that the "President, as Commander in Chief, has constitutional authority to make arrangements for facilities for our military personnel." The latter type, the so-called statutory executive agreement, relies on some precise piece of earlier congressional authorization or a treaty. An example would be an agreement with Portugal for military rights on the Azores in 1971, which was based upon a 1951 Defense Agreement between the two countries in accordance with the NATO Treaty.[42]

Overall the statutory executive agreement is the more prevalent form of the executive agreement and the more controversial.[43] While the statutory agreement allows Congress to be involved procedurally in the agreement process, the extent of substantive congressional involvement remains an important question. It is not always clear that Congress is fully aware of the considerable discretion that it is affording the president in making commitments abroad or how far statutory authority is expanded to cover a contemplated executive agreement. In some instances, Congress may be providing legislation that might later be viewed as a "blank check" for presidential action.

Table 7.2 provides some data on the use of executive agreements (including both the statutory agreement and the "pure" constitutionally based agreements in one category) and treaties over the history of the Republic. As these data show, the executive agreement—instead of the treaty—was used moderately at first, but its use has grown dramatically in the last century or so.[44] By the 1889–1929 period, the number of executive agreements was almost twice that of the treaty form. By comparison, the executive agreement in the postwar period has virtually exploded in usage, dwarfing the treaty mechanism as the principal instrument of commitment abroad. Over the history of the nation, about 90 percent of all agreements have been executive in nature. Since 1950, though, 95 percent of all commitments have been made through executive agreements.

Despite the limited use of the executive agreement in the first century of the Republic, important commitments were still made via this route. For instance, the agreement between the British and the Americans to limit naval vessels on the Great Lakes (the Rush-Bagot Agreement of 1817) was made through an exchange of notes by executive representatives of both governments. Later, President McKinley agreed to the terms for ending the Spanish-American War by executive agreement. President Theodore Roosevelt entered into a secret agreement with Japan over Korea and into a "Gentlemen's Agreement" in 1907 to restrict Japanese immigration into the United States.[45]

In the modern era, the executive agreement was used frequently and for important commitments. The actions of President Franklin Roosevelt set the pattern for recent presidents. Roosevelt, for instance, completed the Destroyer-for-Bases deal of 1940 with an executive agreement. Similarly, the Yalta Agreement of 1945 was completed through this mechanism. President Truman followed this pattern with the Potsdam Agreement, also by executive agreement. Later, President Truman made an oral commitment to defend the newly independent state of Israel in 1948 and started a pattern of support for this nation through executive declaration.[46]

TABLE 7.2

Treaties and Executive Agreements, 1789–1992

Years	Treaties	Executive Agreements	% of Total as Executive Agreements
1789–1839	60	27	31%
1839–1889	215	238	57
1889–1929	382	763	67
1930–1939	142	144	50
1940–1949	116	919	89
1950–1959	138	2,229	94
1960–1969	114	2,324	95
1970–1979	173	3,040	95
1980–1989	151	3,457	96
1990–1992	52	981	95
Totals/Average %	1,543	14,122	90%

Sources: The agreement data for 1789–1988 are from Michael Nelson, ed., *Congressional Quarterly's Guide to the Presidency* (Washington, DC: Congressional Quarterly, Inc., 1989), p. 1104; while the agreement data for 1989–1992 are from *Treaties and Other International Agreements: The Role of the United States Senate,* A Study Prepared for the Committee on Foreign Relations, United States Senate (Washington, DC: U.S. Government Printing Office, 1993), p. 14. Column 3 was calculated by the author.

Following these initiatives, the other postwar chief executives proceeded to make numerous important political and military commitments through the executive agreement. As a Senate Foreign Relations subcommittee investigation reported in the late 1960s and early 1970s, numerous political, military, and intelligence commitments (some verbal and some secret) were extended to a diverse group of nations, ranging from Thailand and Laos, to Spain, Ethiopia, and the Philippines, among others, through executive action only. Congress was kept almost entirely in the dark about these commitments.[47]

A later analysis has also documented the extent to which important foreign military commitments have taken the form of executive agreements in the postwar years.[48] The commitment of military missions in Honduras and El Salvador in the 1950s, pledges to Turkey, Iran, and Pakistan over security in 1959, the permission to use the island of Diego Garcia for military purposes from the British in the 1960s, and the establishment of a military mission in Iran in 1974 were all done by executive agreement. Further, the analysis revealed that some "understandings" and arrangements with nations are handled by executive agreements. For instance, a message by President Nixon to aid the reconstruction of North Vietnam as part of a peace effort was handled in this way, and an "understanding" regarding the role of American military personnel in the Israeli-Egyptian disengagement agreement of 1975 was as well. Similarly, the Offensive Arms Pact of the Strategic Arms Limitation Talks (SALT I) took the form of an executive agreement.

More recently, presidents have carried out important commitments via executive agreements as well. Presidents Carter and Reagan completed the release of American hostages in Iran through an executive agreement. Moreover, the controversy over this unilateral executive action led to a court challenge *(Dames & Moore v. Regan)* during the Reagan administration, but the Supreme Court held that President Carter had the authority to carry out this pact by executive agreement even though the agreement nullified various judicial directives, returned Iranian assets, and altered private economic claims against Iran.[49] In October 1994, too, President Clinton completed a significant commitment with this instrument: An executive agreement between the United States and North Korea was signed over that country's future nuclear program. If this pact were fully implemented, North Korea would forgo any nuclear weapons development program, open up its nuclear power sites to international inspection, and receive two light-water nuclear power reactors from an international consortium (probably Japan and South Korea) in return.[50] Needless to say, with the rising fear of nuclear proliferation, this pact is highly significant for foreign policy.

Finally, various pledges at the superpower summits or presidential meetings have also taken this form. President Bush made unilateral commitments to former Soviet President Mikhail Gorbachev at summits in 1990 and 1991 regarding future relations, and President Clinton has taken similar actions with Russian President Boris Yeltsin, such as seeking to establish a "strategic relationship" between the two countries and greater economic cooperation. While Congress may still become involved in some of these commitments, especially if commitments are made to changes in the status of a nation under a treaty or convention (e.g., to grant most favored nation trading status to the former Soviet Union—now Russia— or China, for example) or when additional funding of some program is made (increased foreign aid for El Salvador, Haiti, Somalia, or Russia, for instance), the executive agreement remains a potent foreign policy tool for the president.

In sum, executive precedents in several different areas—negotiating with and recognizing other states, withholding information from Congress, initiating foreign policy actions, starting conflicts or interventions with other nations, and making unilateral commitments abroad—have given operational meaning to the delegation of executive foreign policy powers as outlined in Article II of the Constitution. In some instances, too, these precedents have expanded presidential authority in foreign policy well beyond what the Founders envisioned. As a result, precedents alone have contributed significantly to making the president the chief executive, the chief diplomat, and if necessary, the chief war maker in the conduct of foreign policy. However, this factor is only one of several that have allowed American presidents to dominate foreign policy making.

2. Supreme Court Decisions

The Supreme Court has also aided the president in gaining ascendancy in the foreign policy arena. With few exceptions, the Court's decisions have supported presidential claims to dominance over foreign policy matters. It has done so in two different, but important ways. First the Court, particularly in the twentieth century, has largely ruled on the merits in favor of the executive over the Congress on foreign policy matters. Second, and increasingly prevalent in recent decades, the Supreme Court and lower courts have refused to rule on cases challenging executive authority in foreign policy. The courts have done so either because the case under consideration raises political, not legal, questions (the "political question doctrine") or because the case is not ready for adjudication since all avenues have not been exhausted by the Congress or the plaintiff (the "ripeness" issue). Let us discuss these two different ways in greater detail.

Some Rulings Supporting the Executive. During the past century, when the Court has decided foreign policy cases, it has largely ruled in favor of the position supported by the executive branch. In turn, these decisions for the executive have become important precedents for the Court as other cases are brought before it. We highlight five important court decisions from the early twentieth century that illustrate the extent to which the Supreme Court has deferred to the president in matters dealing with international politics—even prior to America's extensive global involvement after World War II. We also discuss a ruling on the "legislative veto" from the 1980s that had significant implications for presidential foreign policy powers. By finding in support of the president in this instance, the Court once again provided the president considerable latitude in policy making and weakened the role of Congress.

CURTISS-WRIGHT. The most important and most sweeping grant of presidential dominance over foreign policy was set forth in the Supreme Court's decision in *U.S. v. Curtiss-Wright Export Corporation et al.* (1936).[51] In effect, this case gave special standing to the executive in foreign policy matters. A brief summary of the issues in dispute will make this clear.

The case dealt with a joint congressional resolution that authorized the president to prohibit "the sale of arms and munitions of war…to those countries engaged…in armed conflict" in the Chaco region of South America, if he determined that such an embargo would contribute to peace in the area. On May 28, 1934, President Franklin Roosevelt issued such a proclamation and put the resolution into effect. Later, in November 1935, he revoked this resolution with a similar proclamation. As a result of the original proclamation, however, the Curtiss-Wright Corporation was indicted on the charge that it conspired to sell fifteen machine guns to Bolivia, beginning in May 1934.

Several issues were raised before the Supreme Court by the corporation to deny any wrongdoing in this matter. Curtiss-Wright contended that the joint resolution was an invalid delegation of legislative power, that the joint resolution never became effective because of the failure of the president to find essential jurisdictional facts, and that the second proclamation (lifting the ban) ended the liability of the company under the joint resolution.[52] While the Court rejected all of the arguments, its reasoning on the first was the most important for enlarging presidential power in foreign affairs.

The Court held that the delegation of power to the executive—to apply the ban or not—was not unconstitutional because the issue dealt with a question of external, not internal, affairs. In these two areas, the Court said, the powers of delegation are different. In internal affairs, the federal government can exercise only those powers specifically enumerated in the Constitution (and such implied powers as are necessary and proper), but in the external area, such limitation do not apply. Because of America's separation from Great Britain, and as a result of being a member of the family of nations, the United States possesses external sovereignty and the powers associated with it. "The powers to declare and wage war, to conclude peace, to make treaties, to maintain diplomatic relations with other sovereignties, if they had never been mentioned in the Constitution, would have vested in the federal government as necessary concomitants of nationality."[53]

Most important, the Court held that the president was the representative of that sovereignty ("...the President alone has the power to speak or listen as a representative of the nation"). Therefore, the executive's powers in foreign affairs go beyond the actual constitutional delegation of power. Furthermore, the president is to be granted considerable discretion in his exercise of these powers as compared to the domestic arena. As the Court said, "it is quite apparent that if, in the maintenance of our international relations, embarrassment—perhaps serious embarrassment—is to be avoided and success for our aims achieved, congressional legislation which is to be made effective through negotiation and inquiry within the international field must often accord to the President a degree of discretion and freedom from statutory restriction which would not be admissible were domestic affairs alone involved."[54]

In light of such a view and numerous precedents that the decision cites, the Court held that the joint resolution was not an unlawful delegation of legislative power. Most important, the decision established that foreign policy and domestic policy were different arenas, with a special position for the president in the former. In sum, the *Curtiss-Wright* case made clear that the president's power in foreign policy could not be gleaned only from constitutional directives; there were "extra-constitutional" powers—tied to the sovereignty of the United States and the executive's role as the representative of that sovereignty. Subsequent cases and legal analyses have challenged this interpretation, but they have not fully undermined the notion of the executive's primacy in foreign affairs.[55]

MISSOURI V. HOLLAND. A second important Supreme Court decision, *Missouri v. Holland* (1920), clarified, and actually enlarged, the treaty powers given to the executive. In this case, the Court held that the treaty powers could not be limited by any "invisible radiation" of the Tenth Amendment to the Constitution.[56] Put differently, the power of the president in making treaties with other nations was ensured against any intrusion by states' right advocates.

The particulars of the case will once again point to the significance of the Court's decision. The dispute involved the constitutionality of the Migratory Bird Act, which was passed by Congress pursuant to a treaty between the United States and Great Britain. Missouri contended, however, that this act was void because Article I of the Constitution did not delegate the regulation of such birds to Congress; therefore, the states were reserved this power by the Tenth Amendment. In two earlier cases, moreover—before the treaty was signed—two U.S. district courts had voided such a congressional act. But now the Court decided differently, mainly because of the intervening treaty. Justice Holmes in his opinion for the majority wrote:

> Acts of Congress are the supreme law of the land only when made in pursuance of the Constitution, while treaties are declared to be so when made under the authority of the United States. We do not mean to imply that there are no qualifications to the treaty-making power; they must be ascertained in a different way. It is obvious that there may be matters of the sharpest exigency for the national well being that an act of Congress could not deal with but that a treaty followed by such an act could, and it is not lightly to be assumed that, in matters requiring national action, "a power which must belong to and somewhere reside in every civilized government" is not to be found.[57]

Justice Holmes argued further that the regulation of migratory birds was best left to the federal government. Although he acknowledged that the Constitution was silent on this issue, such silence was not sufficient to support the claim made by the State of Missouri. In addition, Justice Holmes held that "a treaty may override" the powers of the state.[58]

In sum, *Missouri v. Holland* was highly significant for the powers of national government versus the states, but it also aided the president. It legitimized his role of using the treaty process to add to the constitutional framework of the nation, in conjunction with the Senate; it arguably reduced the implied powers of the states and Congress, since those powers could be overridden through the treaty power; and it began a series of twentieth-century Court decisions giving special deference to the president in foreign affairs.

BELMONT AND PINK. The third and fourth important Supreme Court decisions, one prior to World War II and the other during the war [*U.S. v. Belmont* (1937) and *U.S. v. Pink* (1942)] deal with the legal status of executive agreements.[59] The decisions in these cases gave the president another means of enhancing his foreign policy powers.

The *Belmont* case involved whether the federal government could recover the bank account of an American national, August Belmont, who owned obligations belonging to a Russian company before the establishment of the Soviet Union. The bank accounts were held in the State of New York. The federal government tried to reclaim such accounts because, under the Litvinov Agreement—which established diplomatic relations between the United States and the Soviet Union—these accounts had been assigned to the U.S. government. While the state courts held that the federal government could not claim such accounts, the Supreme Court held otherwise. Justice Sutherland argued that the external powers of the United States must be exercised without regard to the constraint of state law or policies.

The *Pink* case also dealt with the legitimacy of the Litvinov Agreement and involved some of the same issues as the *Belmont* case. It was an action brought by the U.S. government against the New York State Superintendent of Insurance to acquire the remaining assets of the First Russian Insurance Company. When the Soviet Union was established, all properties—wherever located—were nationalized. Under the Litvinov Agreement, as we noted, all such assets were assigned to the American government. Superintendent Pink claimed, however, that the nationalization action had "no territorial effect" and that the U.S. government action was improper.[60] The Supreme Court held otherwise, and Justice Douglas stated the Court's view in this forceful passage:

> We hold that the right to the funds or property in question became vested in the Soviet Government as the successor to the First Russian Insurance Co.; that this right has passed to the United States under the Litvinov Assignment; and that the United States is entitled to the property as against the corporation and the foreign creditors.[61]

The *Belmont* and *Pink* cases are important because the Litvinov Agreement between the United States and the Soviet Union was an executive agreement. Thus, these decisions have been interpreted as giving legitimacy to executive agreements as the law of the land—without any congressional action—and the supremacy of those agreements over rights of an individual state (the State of New York in both cases) within the American union. Once again, too, these cases strengthened the president's hand in the conduct of foreign affairs. Moreover, Louis Henkin argues that the language and reasoning in the *Belmont* and *Pink* cases were sufficiently general to apply to any executive agreement and to ensure its supremacy over any state law.[62]

INS V. CHADHA. Perhaps the most important recent case was *Immigration and Naturalization Service v. Chadha* (1983). In this case, the Supreme Court found the "one-house legislative veto" unconstitutional. At the time of the *Chadha* decision, at least fifty-six statutes, including several important foreign policy statutes, contained one or more legislative vetoes.[63] The decision thus had far-ranging implications for congressional–executive relations generally and foreign policy in particular. It also illustrated the Court's continuing deference to the executive branch, often at the expense of the legislative branch. Some background on the legislative veto and the case itself will convey the significance of this ruling.

Originally devised in the 1930s, the legislative veto was a procedural device that allowed Congress "to relegate policy making authority to the executive branch in areas constitutionally delegated to the legislature," but which also "allowed Congress to retain ultimate oversight in the form of a veto power."[64] While this policy mechanism grew gradually until about 1960, its incorporation into new legislation expanded rapidly after that date. Foreign policy and defense legislation was hardly immune from this instrument. While the veto mechanism did not appear in foreign policy legislation until the 1950s and 1960s, immigration and defense legislation had such vetoes included as early as the 1940s.[65]

Specifically, the legislative veto works in the following way. Congress would explicitly incorporate a provision in a piece of legislation that allowed Congress to stop or modify the executive's subsequent implementation of the statute by simply declaring its objection. The legislative branch could register its "veto" of executive action in several different ways, depending upon how the statute was written: (1) by a single chamber passing by a simple majority a veto resolution (either the Senate or House); (2) by both chambers passing by a simple majority a veto resolution (called a concurrent resolution); or, in some instances, (3) by a committee in Congress passing by a majority a veto resolution.[66] The most important point is that none of these forms of veto resolutions allowed the executive to approve or disapprove the action. In other words, when the legislative veto was incorporated within an act of Congress, the legislative branch could pass legislation and then could, unilaterally, monitor and modify the implementation of that legislation by the executive branch. In this sense, congressional power was gained at the expense of executive power.

The particulars of the *Chadha* case will make clear how the legislative veto operated in this instance. The case involved an East Indian student who was born in Kenya and held a British passport. He overstayed his student nonimmigrant visa and was order deported by the INS. He appealed the deportation, and his deportation was suspended by immigration authorities. By a provision that was incorporated into previous immigration legislation, however, Congress (either the House or the Senate) could pass a simple majority resolution objecting to this suspension of the deportation order. In this case, the House of Representatives did so; in effect, the House called for Chadha's deportation promptly.

Once the case reached the Supreme Court, a majority of the justices held that this "legislative veto" in the earlier legislation was invalid for two important constitutional reasons. It violated the presentment clause of the Constitution.[67] That is, "every Bill which shall have passed the House of Representatives and the Senate, shall, before it becomes a Law, be presented to the President of the United States" for his consideration. Such a presentment did not occur in this case, since the House acted unilaterally to rescind the action of the executive branch. Second, the legislative veto also violated the principle of bicameralism (i.e., all legislation must be passed by majorities in both the House of Representatives and the United States Senate).[68] As such, the legislative veto could not stand.

Although the *Chadha* decision dealt only with the "one-House" legislative veto, the Supreme Court expanded its decision about two weeks later by declaring the "two-house" legislative veto as unconstitutional as well.[69] Since the legislative veto was a prominent device used by Congress in the 1970s and early 1980s to reign in executive power in foreign affairs (as we shall discuss in Chapter 8), the *Chadha* decision has had considerable impact on the extent of congressional resurgence.

Some Rulings Challenging the Executive. Although the president has usually gotten his way with the Court on foreign policy questions, we also need to highlight important instances in which he did not. One important case in the 1950s and two in the 1970s fit into this category. Still, even these successful challenges to executive power in foreign policy have been overshadowed by the precedents from the earlier cases and the nonrulings in favor of the president in numerous others (as we discuss shortly). Furthermore, the basis for deciding against the president in the 1970s cases was less an effort to reduce his foreign policy powers and more an effort to maintain some fundamental American freedoms.

YOUNGSTOWN SHEET & TUBE CO. ET AL. V. SAWYER. Unlike the earlier cases, the Supreme Court's decision in the *Youngstown* case restricted the foreign policy powers of the president, especially as those powers seem to delve into domestic policy. In so deciding, the Court thus preserved a role for Congress over some areas of foreign policy. In particular, the *Youngstown* case, decided in 1952, addressed the question of whether the chief executive and commander-in-chief clauses of the Constitution enabled the president to seize control of the nation's steel mills to avert a national strike and to protect national security. President Truman had made just such a claim and had issued an executive order to his secretary of commerce (Sawyer) to take over the operation of the steel mills.

The Court held that such action was unconstitutional. Justice Black wrote in the majority opinion for the Court that there was no statutory authorization for such action:

> The President's power, if any, to issue the order must stem either from an act of Congress or from the Constitution. There is no statute that expressly authorizes the President to take possession of property as he did here. Nor is there any act of Congress to which our attention has been directed from which such a power can fairly be implied.[70]

Likewise, Justice Black contended that there was no constitutional basis for such an action either:

> The order cannot properly be sustained as an exercise of the President's military power as Commander in Chief of the Armed Forces.... Even though "theater of war" be an expanding concept, we cannot with faithfulness to our constitutional system hold that the Commander in Chief of the Armed Forces has the ultimate power as such to take possession of private property in order to keep labor disputes from stopping production.... Nor can the seizure order be sustained because of the several constitutional provisions that grant executive power to the President.[71]

In sum, the *Youngstown* case made clear that there are indeed limits on the foreign policy powers of the president. This decision stands in contrast to the earlier cases that largely deferred to president's authority in foreign affairs and, indeed, afforded the president wide discretion as well.

In another intriguing aspect to this decision, Mr. Justice Jackson wrote a concurring opinion in which he, while agreeing with the decision, sought to set forth more fully the division of foreign policy powers between the president and Congress. In particular, Justice Jackson said that there were clear strictures on the foreign policy powers of the president:

1. When the President acts pursuant to an express or implied authorization of Congress, his authority is at its maximum, for it includes all that he possess in his own right plus all that Congress can delegate....
2. When the President acts in absence of either a congressional grant or denial of authority, he can only rely upon his own independent powers,

> but there is a zone of twilight in which he and Congress may have concurrent authority, or in which its distribution is uncertain....
>
> 3. When the President takes measures incompatible with the expressed or implied will of Congress, his power is at its lowest ebb, for then he can rely only upon his own constitutional powers minus any constitutional powers of Congress over the matter.[72]

Justice Jackson concluded that this particular case fell into the third category and was least sustainable for the executive branch. By one recent analysis, moreover, Justice Jackson's arguments sought to challenge the court's earlier decision in the *Curtiss-Wright* case.[73]

NEW YORK TIMES V. UNITED STATES AND U.S. V. NIXON. The two presidential defeats from the 1970s are arguably less sweeping in their implications for foreign policy than *Youngstown*, but they, too, convey important limitations on executive power. In *New York Times v. United States* (1971), popularly known as the *Pentagon Papers* case, the Court held that the executive's claims of national security could not stop the publication of these volumes chronicling American involvement in Southeast Asia. First-amendment freedoms proved to be more persuasive than any immediate national security needs. In *U.S. v. Nixon* (1974), the Court decided whether President Nixon must turn over tape recordings and records dealing with the Watergate investigation. The Supreme Court held that "neither the separation of powers nor the confidentiality of executive communications barred the federal courts from access to presidential tapes needed as evidence in a criminal case." At the same time, the Court was less than precise over whether specific claims of "national security" would have led to another result. As Chief Justice Burger put it, the president did not "claim...[a] need to protect military, diplomatic, or sensitive national secrets," as such.[74]

Nonrulings Supporting the President. A second important way in which the Court has supported the executive on foreign policy has been through nonruling—deciding not to decide cases brought before it. In doing so, the Court has allowed the executive actions that have already been taken to stand.

One justification for adopting this nondecision posture by the Court is the "political question" doctrine. In effect, the Court has held that the issue before it is a political, not a legal or constitutional, dispute between the branches of government, normally Congress and the presidency, and hence is not subject to judicial remedy. While the basis for the doctrine is not well developed or wholly understood in constitutional law, the doctrine seemingly has been invoked under several differing circumstances by the Court: when the Court believed it lacked the authority to decide the case because the constitutionally prescribed activities of another branch of government were involved, when the effective solution involved a political remedy that would favor one branch of government over another, and when the Court wanted to avoid a question brought before it.[75]

Another justification for the Court's nondecisions on foreign policy cases is the "ripeness" criterion, mentioned at the beginning of this section.

By this criterion, the Court has claimed that when members of Congress, for example, file suit against the president over the use of force abroad or the abrogation of a treaty, they must first use all available avenues within the political system (e.g., completing the legislative process and legislative routes) before pursuing a legal challenge. Only, then, the Court has held, may the issue be appropriate for judicial judgment.

Several recent cases have relied upon these two justifications as reasons for not ruling in particular cases, and a brief discussion of them will reveal the Court's rationale in each instance. In particular, the discussion will reveal how these nondecisions have strengthened the president's hand in policy making over the use of force as commander in chief and as well in the use of the treaty powers. The first two deal with treaty matters, while the next four deal with the president's powers as commander in chief.

The first treaty case deals with the breaking of the 1954 Mutual Defense Treaty with Taiwan (Chapter 2) as part of the process of establishing diplomatic relations with the People's Republic of China. In *Goldwater et al. v. Carter* (1979), several U.S. senators charged that President Carter could not terminate the 1954 Mutual Defense Treaty with Taiwan in establishing diplomatic relations with the People's Republic of China without either a two-thirds majority of the Senate or a majority of both houses of Congress. The Supreme Court, however, divided along several lines in rendering its judgment. Four justices held that the case was "nonjusticiable" because it involved a political issue, another said that is was not ripe for court action since Congress, as a body, had taken no formal action to challenge the president, and only one decided the case on the merits and argued that the president acted within his constitutional power to recognize states.[76] The upshot of this ruling was to dismiss the challenge to the president and his treaty powers.

The second treaty case deals with the constitutionality of President Carter's decision to transfer the Panama Canal back to Panama. In *Edwards v. Carter* (1978), sixty members of Congress charged that both Houses of Congress must approve any transference of property by Article IV of the Constitution. Such action cannot be done, they claimed, by self-executing treaties, such as the Panama Canal Treaty. (Self-executing treaties are those that can establish international obligations without implementing actions by Congress.[77]) While the District of Columbia Court of Appeals acknowledged that the disposal of American property was mentioned as a congressional power in the Constitution, the text was ambiguous. Furthermore, this power was not solely congressional, and the transference of the Canal was tied to a larger foreign policy action under the Panama Canal Treaties.[78] The Supreme Court ultimately let this decision stand by simply refusing to hear the case.

Several attempts were made to challenge the constitutionality of the Vietnam War in the 1970s, but, in virtually all instances, the Court refused to hear these cases since it judged them to deal with a political question between the two branches.[79] Much the same reasoning, albeit with an exception of two, prevailed in the cases dealing with presidential actions in El Salvador, Grenada, and the Persian Gulf during the 1980s. In *Crockett v. Reagan* (1983) twenty-nine members of Congress contended that the sending of U.S. military advisors and military aid to El Salvador was a violation of the War Powers Resolution and the Foreign Assistance Act. The former required presidential reporting to Congress of American forces sent abroad, the latter restricted aid to countries engaged in human rights violations (see Chapter 8). The lower court held that the issue was nonjusticiable because the issue was a "political question" between the branches and because it could not determine all the facts in the case. The Supreme Court refused to hear the case when it was appealed to it.

In *Conyers v. Reagan* (1985), eleven members of Congress, led by John Conyers of Michigan, charged that the executive branch had gone beyond its powers and had usurped Congress's war making powers in sending U.S. forces to invade Grenada. The district court dismissed the case by asserting that it lacked jurisdiction, and the appeals court held the issue as moot, since the invasion had ended. In *Lowry v. Reagan* (1987), 110 members of Congress wanted the president to report to Congress under the War Powers Resolution because American forces were being used to keep the Persian Gulf open during the Iran-Iraq War. Once again, the district court dismissed the case as a political matter between the two branches, and no further action was taken.[80]

Finally, in *Dellums v. Bush* (1990), fifty-four members of Congress sought a federal injunction to stop President Bush's right to go to war against Iraq without a congressional declaration of war or some congressional authorization. The federal district court in Washington, D.C., heard that case, but ruled against the members. The judge held that the issue was not "ripe" for decision because Congress as a body had not taken a formal stand on whether it wanted President Bush to seek a congressional authorization. While both leaving the door open for such a decision if Congress acted and rejecting the executive claim that the courts could not intrude into "political question" disputes, the judge's ruling did not formally restrict executive power in this area.[81] (As we shall discuss in the next chapter, however, President Bush did ultimately seek a congressional resolution to initiate the Persian Gulf War in January 1991.)

While the *Youngstown Steel* case (and particularly Justice Jackson's argument) seemed to argue strongly for a more balanced interpretation of constitutional powers over foreign policy, many of the recent cases reflect the extent to which the Supreme Court and other federal jurisdictions continue to defer to the executive in the conduct of foreign policy, often at the expense of Congress. (Document Summary 7.1 summarizes several cases and shows how these decisions and nondecisions have strengthened the president's power in foreign policy.) Indeed, constitutional analyst Gordon Silverstein sums up the Court's actions during the current period as a difficult one for the Congress when seeking to challenge the president on foreign policy. When "Congress is formally or clearly opposed" to the president, he argues, "the Court will support Congress."[82] Increasingly, however, the Court is demanding clearer and clearer direction when the Congress seeks to do so. If the Congress does not exhaust all avenues to assert its power (e.g., satisfying the ripeness criterion) or is at all unclear in its legislative intent or ambiguous in the language that delegates authority to the president, the Court is likely to support the executive. In recent decades, the executive has largely held sway.

DOCUMENT SUMMARY 7.1

Foreign Policy Powers and the Courts: Some Recent Rulings and Nonrulings Favorable to the President

I. Regarding the Treaty Powers

Edwards v. Carter [580 F. 2d 1055 (D.C. Cir. 1978)]
This case involved the constitutionality of the transfer of the Panama Canal from the United States to Panama. The members of Congress who brought the suit claimed that property could not be transferred through treaty, but instead needed the approval of both Houses of Congress, according to Article IV, section 3, clause 2 of the Constitution.

The Court of Appeals decided that property can be transferred internationally through the treaty power because the Constitution was ambiguous and the disposal of property was not solely the Congress's prerogative.

Goldwater et al. v. Carter [444 U.S. 996 (1979)]
This case concerned the constitutionality of President Carter's termination of the Mutual Defense Treaty with Taiwan. Several members of Congress, led by Senator Barry Goldwater, contended that the termination of the treaty should be subject to approval by a two-thirds majority in the Senate.

The Court held for the Carter administration because the issue was "political" in nature between the branches, because it was not ripe for judicial action since no confrontation had occurred between the two parties, and because the president possessed the "well-established authority to recognize, and withdraw recognition from, foreign governments."

II. Regarding the Commander-in-Chief Powers

Crockett v. Reagan [720 F. 2d 1355 (D.C. Cir. 1983), certiorari denied 467 U.S. 1251 (1984)]
The case involved a suit by twenty-nine members of Congress challenging the presence of U.S. military advisors and military assistance to El Salvador and the failure of the Reagan administration to comply with the War Powers Resolution and the war-making powers of the Congress.

The Court ruled that the case was a nonjusticiable political question and one in which it could not resolve the factual issues in dispute.

Conyers v. Reagan [765 F. 2d. 1124 (D.C. Cir. 1985)]
Eleven members of Congress claimed that the U.S. invasion of Grenada by the executive branch was unconstitutional because it violated the war powers of the Congress.

The district court held that it lacked jurisdiction. The District of Columbia Appeals Court held that the matter was moot, since the invasion had ended. It dismissed the suit.

Lowry v. Reagan [676 F. Supp. 333 (D.D.C. 1987)]
This case was brought by 110 members of Congress who wanted the president to report to the Congress under the provisions of the War Powers Resolution concerning the role of American forces in the Persian Gulf.

The district court dismissed the case because it involved a political question between the Congress and the executive and because it involved a dispute within the Congress as well.

continued on next page

DOCUMENT SUMMARY 7.1

Foreign Policy Powers and the Courts: Some Recent Rulings and Nonrulings Favorable to the President (continued)

Dellums v. Bush [752 F. Supp. 1141 (D.D.C. 1990)]
This case was brought by fifty-four members of Congress who sought an injunction to stop President Bush from going to war against Iraq in the Persian Gulf without a formal declaration or a congressional authorization, in light of the Congress's constitutional powers in this area.

The federal district court denied the injunction because the issue was not "ripe" for adjudication since Congress had not acted to stop this action. The court did hold that the petitioning members had standing and that the court could enter into a resolution that some might deem a political question.

III. Regarding Executive Power
INS v. Chadha [462 U.S. 919 (1983)]
After the House of Representatives vetoed the Immigration and Naturalization Service's suspension of a foreign student's deportation under a "legislative veto" provision contained in the legislation, the student challenged the power of the House to overrule the INS and the constitutionality of the "legislative veto."

The Court held that the one-house legislative veto as unconstitutional because it violated the presentment clause of Article I of the Constitution and the principle of bicameralism. That is, every bill must be passed by both Houses of Congress and must "be presented to the president" for his action.

Sources: The cases were drawn from the discussions in Warren Christopher, "Ceasefire Between the Branches: A Compact in Foreign Affairs," in James M. McCormick, *A Reader in American Foreign Policy* (Itasca, IL: F. E. Peacock Publishers, Inc., 1986); Jean E. Smith, *The Constitution and American Foreign Policy* (St. Paul: West Publishing Company, 1989); Gordon Silverstein, "Judicial Enhancement of Executive Power," in Paul E. Peterson, ed., *The President, the Congress, and the Making of Foreign Policy* (Norman and London: University of Oklahoma Press, 1994), p. 38; and the cases themselves.

3. Congressional Deference and Delegation

A third factor that has added to the presidential preeminence in foreign policy has been the degree of congressional support for presidential initiatives, particularly in the post–World War II period. In addition, Congress has sometimes gone further than giving its support to the executive; it has, on occasion, delegated some of its foreign policy prerogatives to the president. A brief survey of this factor will illustrate how the president's foreign policy control has been strengthened by congressional support and how it has met some challenge recently.

Congressional Leadership. Legislative support for the president in foreign policy can be seen in the statements and policy actions of members of both houses of Congress. This support was often couched in a commitment to bipartisanship in the conduct of foreign policy; "politics must stop at the water's edge" was a frequent postwar refrain. This tradition of bipartisanship probably dates from the pledge of Senator Arthur Vandenberg, Chairman of the Senate Foreign Relations Committee, to support President Harry Truman in his foreign policy efforts in the immediate post–World War II years. The Vandenberg Resolution, for example, worked out in close consultation with the Department of State and passed in June 1948, called upon the executive branch to proceed with the development of the North Atlantic Treaty and with reforms of the United Nations. What it also did, however, was to usher in an era of congressional–executive cooperation in the making of foreign policy. Throughout this era, and running to this day, the president has generally taken the initiative, and Congress has (as it did in the case of the Vandenberg Resolution) often legitimized an executive program.[83]

Leaders of Congress, and particularly leaders of the foreign affairs committees in both the House and the Senate, have often—until very recently—viewed their role primarily as carrying out the president's wishes in the foreign policy area. Thomas (Doc) Morgan, long-time chairman of the House Foreign Affairs Committee, stated this view directly: "Under the Constitution, the President is made responsible for the conduct of our foreign relations..." He saw himself as "only the quarterback not the coach of the team." Moreover, congressional scholar Richard Fenno reports that Chairman Morgan saw his committee, "in *all* matters, as the subordinate partners in a permanent alliance with the executive branch. And as far as he is concerned, the group's blanket, all purpose decision rule should be: support all executive branch proposals."[84]

Morgan's successor as chairman of the House Foreign Affairs Committee, the late Clement J. Zablocki, despite his activism for congressional reform, still adopted this bipartisan approach. According to the committee staff and State Department officials, Congressman Zablocki did attempt to work with the executive, generally trying to get the president's program through the committee.[85] At the same time, Zablocki allowed liberal critics ample opportunity to express their views. Further, despite his own moderate-to-conservative beliefs, Zablocki continued to express support—albeit not always enthusiastically—for such congressional initiatives as the nuclear freeze and the ending of covert aid to the Nicaraguan rebels.[86]

The late Senator J. William Fulbright, chairman of the Senate Foreign Relations Committee for fifteen years, also enunciated this commitment to bipartisanship in foreign affairs at least until 1965. As Chairman Morgan had done, Senator Fulbright relied upon a football analogy to express this support and deference for the president: "No football team can expect to win with every man his own quarterback.... The Foreign Relations Committee is available to advise the President, but his is the primary responsibility."[87] While this bipartisanship by Fulbright and the Senate Foreign Relations Committee waned with the deepening American involvement in Vietnam during the 1960s, the tradition of support for the president by the Committee was not entirely abandoned by subsequent leaders. Nonetheless, by the early 1980s, Senator Charles Percy, former chairman of the Senate Foreign Relations Committee, lamented the "partisan gap" that had developed over foreign policy and renewed the call for bipartisanship "if the United States is to maintain a leadership role in the world."[88]

By the early 1980s, and continuing to the present, any real semblance of policy cooperation between Congress and the executive "broke down;" the congressional leadership was not as willing to follow the lead of the president. Speakers of the House of Representatives Thomas P. ("Tip") O'Neill and Jim Wright clashed bitterly with the Reagan administration over Central American policy. The sending of American forces into Lebanon and the exchange of arms for hostages with Iran and the transfer of profits to the Nicaraguan contras (the so-called Iran-Contra affair) further weakened the notion of congressional support for executive action (see Chapter 5). The establishment of two committees in 1987 to hold hearings on executive decision making during the Iran-Contra affairs reflects the suspicion with which Congress held the president's explanation of this whole episode. Throughout these years of confrontation, calls for bipartisanship and for greater executive prerogatives in foreign affairs were never quite quelled by congressional debate over alleged executive abuses.

Sensing the need to renew the foreign policy process between Congress and the executive, President Bush called for the establishment of the "old bipartisanship" in his inaugural address. Some congressional leaders were responsive to this initiative. Proposals were made for increasing consultation between the White House and Congress by holding monthly meetings to review foreign policy issues, for congressional changes in the foreign aid bill to allow greater presidential flexibility in implementing it, and even for changing the restrictiveness of the War Powers Resolution.[89] While none of these could immediately reshape the suspicions of the immediate past, they do suggest the inclination by congressional leaders to defer to presidential leadership on foreign policy.

The chair of the House Foreign Affairs Committee at the time, Dante Fascell, generally applauded this call for bipartisan renewal, but he also wanted the democratic process to work. A moderate Democrat who often found himself in agreement with the Reagan and Bush policies on Central America, Fascell had been described as an effective builder and manager of political coalitions—a fact that allowed him to promote bipartisanship if he so chose. In his view, "a bipartisan foreign policy does not mean a unilateral decision by the president, rubber-stamped by the Congress." Yet, "if it gets to the point where consensus is asked for and consensus is reached on a specific policy decision, which the president will undertake, then obviously there is a responsibility for the congressional leadership to do what it can to drive that policy." If such a consensus were not reached, though, Fascell favored letting the "democratic process take over."[90]

Fascell's successor from 1993–1995, Lee Hamilton of Indiana, largely adopted this view on relations between Congress and the White House. While he was committed to making the constitutional system work, he also conveyed some deference to the foreign policy powers of the executive: "I do not fool myself about the role of Congress on foreign policy. It is an important actor, but presidential leadership is by far the most important ingredient in a successful foreign policy. Only the president can lead.... We in the Congress...can help and support him."[91]

Since the 1994 elections, the new Republican congressional foreign policy leadership, however, has been less ready to defer to a Democratic president who is perceived as weak on foreign policy. As such, they have generally been more assertive of a congressional role, and more confrontational than recent Democratic foreign affairs leaders toward President Clinton's initiatives in the foreign affairs realm. For example, both Senator Jesse Helms, chair of the Senate Foreign Relations Committee, and Congressman Benjamin A. Gilman, chair of the International Relations Committee, have offered legislation to restructure the foreign affairs bureaucracy within the executive branch and have proposed significant cuts in American foreign assistance. In this sense, any automatic deference toward presidential leadership seems to be waning.

Taking a position supportive of the president, House Speaker Republican Newt Gingrich, in addressing the House of Representatives in 1995, backed a measure to repeal the War Powers Resolution (see Chapter 8), strongly endorsing a bipartisan approach to foreign policy and expressing a willingness to defer to the president in this area: "As chief spokesman in the House Republican Party, I want to strengthen the current Democratic President because he's the President of the United States, and the President of the United States on a bipartisan basis deserves to be strengthened in foreign affairs and strengthened in national security. He does not deserve to be undermined and cluttered and weakened."[92] A few days later, in a joint appearance with President Clinton in New Hampshire, Speaker Gingrich invoked Senator Vandenburg and reiterated his earlier view by assuring the president of his intention to have Congress work with him on foreign policy matters in a spirit of bipartisanship.[93]

Supportive Legislative Behavior. Although the bipartisanship call by congressional leaders over the years is one indicator of legislative deference to presidential wishes on foreign policy matters, congressional action on executive branch proposals is an even better one. Aaron Wildavsky, in a 1966 article on the presidency, documented the level of congressional support for presidential initiatives, and then contended that

> In the realm of foreign policy there has not been a single major issue on which Presidents, when they were serious and determined, have failed. The list of their victories is impressive: entry into the United Nations, the Marshall Plan, NATO, the Truman Doctrine, the decisions to stay out of Indochina in 1954 and to intervene in Vietnam in the 1960s, aid to Poland and Yugoslavia, the test-ban treaty, and many more.[94]

Moreover, Wildavsky went on to demonstrate that on presidential proposals to Congress during the 1948 to 1964 period of his study, the president prevailed about 70 percent of the time in defense and foreign policy matters, but only 40 percent of the time on domestic maters.[95] Thus, the president is not only successful on foreign policy matters with Congress, but he is 75 percent more effective on foreign policy matters than on domestic policy matters. In this sense, Congress has been highly supportive of the president's wishes on issues beyond the water's edge.

Other studies have shown that this extraordinary support for the president's priorities in foreign policy has remained even into the 1970s and beyond, a period sometimes described as producing a congressional "revolution" in foreign affairs. LeLoup and Shull, for instance, demonstrate the congressional approval of presidential foreign policy initiatives remained high for the period of 1965 to 1975, although the average level of support has decreased to about 55 percent, compared to 70 percent for the 1948 to 1964 period.[96] Similarly, a considerable difference remained between congressional approval of foreign policy versus domestic policy issues advanced by the president (55 percent compared to 46 percent on average). Further, when LeLoup and Shull categorized the domestic policy questions into social welfare, agriculture, government management, natural resources, and civil liberties, presidential proposals in the foreign and defense area still received greater congressional support than any of the other individual issues.[97] Fleisher and Bond, in a study through the first term of the Reagan administration, found that presidential foreign policy success remained substantial in both the House and the Senate through the Reagan administration, although Nixon and Ford did not obtain as much support as did some of the other administrations. Similarly, Carter and Reagan did not do as well in the House as they did in the Senate, compared to earlier presidents.[98]

In our calculation of the degree of presidential success from Truman to Clinton on foreign policy voting in Congress, we also found that the recent presidents have been enormously successful in getting votes for issues on which they took a position. Table 7.3 shows the results of these calculations. Overall, presidential success has been greater, on average, in the Senate than in the House, but both chambers have been supportive of presidential votes. In the Senate, presidents averaged an 81 percent success rate and, in the House presidents won about 70 percent of the time.[99]

Still in another study, analyzing the impact of the president on the voting behavior of individual members of Congress, political scientist Aage Clausen found a high degree of congressional deference to the executive's positions on foreign policy issues. In his *How Congressmen Decide*, Clausen reported that legislative voting on "international involvement" issues showed a considerably different pattern than did legislative voting on issues involving agricultural assistance, social welfare, government management, and civil liberties during the years 1953–1964 and 1969–1970. Only on foreign policy questions did "presidential influence" significantly help to explain congressional action in both the House and the Senate. Moreover, this factor did better than region, constituency influence, and party.[100] Here again, then, we find that the role of the president is pivotal in the actions of Congress, especially as they relate to foreign policy matters.

Changing Legislative Behavior? Foreshadowing our discussion of congressional resurgence in the next chapter, some evidence exists that congressional support for the president on foreign policy matters has waned in recent years. Political scientist Lee Sigelman has shown that, when one examines "key votes," the degree of support for the president has declined in recent years, especially since 1973 and especially among the opposition party to the president in power.[101] Moreover, he suggests that despite what Wildavsky and others had contended earlier, the difference in congressional support for presidential initiatives on foreign policy versus domestic policy on key votes was never very great from 1957 to 1972 (74 percent vs. 73 percent) and has only slightly widened from 1973 to 1978 (60 percent vs. 57 percent).[102] In this sense, the argument about greater congressional sup-

TABLE 7.3

Presidential Victories on Foreign Policy Votes in the Congress: From Truman to Clinton

Administration	House		Senate	
Truman	68%	(N=78)	77%	(N=110)
Eisenhower	85	(N=94)	88	(N=217)
Kennedy	89	(N=47)	88	(N=109)
Johnson	86	(N=111)	81	(N=231)
Nixon	75	(N=85)	80	(N=181)
Ford	59	(N=46)	76	(N=106)
Carter	75	(N=180)	85	(N=215)
Reagan	64	(N=275)	84	(N=325)
Bush	48	(N=132)	77	(N=127)
Clinton (through 1996)	51	(N=122)	75	(N=80)

Note: Entries are the percentage of presidential victories on congressional foreign policy votes upon which the president took a position.

Sources: Calculated by the author and Eugene R. Wittkopf from congressional roll calls made available by the Inter-University Consortium for Political and Social Research and from reported votes in *Congressional Quarterly Weekly Reports* (various issues). The president's position was based upon *Congressional Quarterly Almanac* (various years) and *Congressional Quarterly Weekly Reports* (various issues) assessments for Eisenhower through Clinton and was determined for Truman by a survey of *Congressional Quarterly Almanac* and presidential papers in collaboration with Eugene R. Wittkopf of Louisiana State University.

port on foreign policy matters than on domestic matters is not demonstrable when key votes are examined. Nonetheless, the support by Congress for the president's foreign policy agenda even on key votes was still very high, at least until 1973.

LeLoup and Shull and our own analyses provide additional evidence that executive success with Congress has weakened somewhat in recent years. LeLoup and Shull demonstrate that the congressional approval of foreign policy initiatives for Nixon and Ford was considerably lower than for the other three presidents in their analysis (Eisenhower, Kennedy, and Johnson).[103] In this sense, the degree of congressional deference to executive proposals began to wane in the decade of the 1970s.

The data in Table 7.3 show a similar pattern for recent administrations, including the Clinton administration during its first term. This weakening of presidential success, however, is confined more to the House than to the Senate. Note that President Ford's success rate was only 59 percent in the House, Carter's was higher at 75 percent, but Reagan's at only 64 percent, Bush's lower still at 48 percent, and Clinton's only slightly higher at 51 percent. In the Senate, by contrast, Carter and Reagan are actually at about the same rate as the earlier administrations, although Ford's and Bush's success rates were a bit lower. President Clinton's support was quite high—

with an 88 percent success rate with a Democratic Senate during his first two years—but his average support fell to 75 percent for his first term, with Republican control of the Senate in the 104th Congress (1995–1996).

In contrast to Clausen's study noted above, more recent assessments of specific foreign policy issues show that partisanship and ideology are good predictors of congressional behavior. Analyses of congressional voting patterns on the antiballistic missile issue in the late 1960s and early 1970s, the Panama Canal Treaties in the late 1970s, the call for a nuclear freeze, the B-1 bomber debate, and the fight over aid to the Nicaraguan Contras in the 1980s demonstrate that ideology in particular was a potent factor in explaining individual member's votes, seemingly more important than presidential influence.[104]

Finally, Aaron Wildavsky acknowledged the substantial change in relations between Congress and the White House over the years. In a 1989 study, coauthored with Duane Oldfield, Wildavsky contended that his earlier argument was "time and culture bound." As the public and the political parties have become more ideological, the building of bipartisan support for the president has become much more difficult in the current era. Yet, Oldfield and Wildavsky argue that the president still has other means of exercising his power, much as our survey here suggests.[105] Overall, though, the foreign policy debate has become more politicized than in the past.

In the aggregate, then, while we can surely conclude that there has been some change in congressional deference to the executive, presidential success remains pronounced. Nonetheless, as we shall demonstrate in Chapter 8, specific areas of foreign policy did elicit changes in congressional procedures in dealing with the executive.

Legislative Delegation. Not only has Congress shown this deference by its approval of presidential actions, but it has occasionally gone even further in granting some of its powers to the executive. Most notably, this delegation of its foreign policy powers has occurred in authorizing the president to use armed forces as he sees fit, in affording the president discretion in the distribution of foreign aid, and in implementing trade policy abroad. In effect, these delegations transferred some congressional responsibility to the executive.

This transference of power in the post–World War II period has been most dramatic in the use of armed forces at the president's discretion. In the Formosa Resolution in January 1955, Congress granted to President Eisenhower the power to use armed forces to defend Quemoy and Matsu from attack by the Chinese Communists as well as to protect Formosa and the Pescadores Islands. The language was quite sweeping in its tone: "...the President of the United States is authorized to employ the Armed Forces of the United States *as he deems necessary....*"[106]

As we noted in Chapter 2, Congress also granted to President Eisenhower a broad mandate to deal with the threat of international communism in the Middle East. Popularly called the Eisenhower Doctrine, this congressional resolution appeared to grant to the president the right "to use armed forces to assist any such nation or group of nations requesting assistance against armed aggression from any country controlled by international communism" in the Middle East.[107] Once again, what was so remarkable about this resolution was the apparently broad grant of power given to the executive in the war-making area, although the Congress weakened the grant slightly by requiring the affected country to request assistance and by declaring that the United States (not the president per se) "is prepared to use armed forces to assist" such a country. Furthermore, President Eisenhower pledged to keep Congress informed about these activities.[108]

Perhaps the most famous grant of war-making power by Congress to the executive was the Gulf of Tonkin Resolution, approved by the House on a vote of 416–0 and in the Senate by 89–2 in August 1964 at the beginning of substantial American involvement in Vietnam. This resolution granted to the president the right "to take all necessary steps, including the use of armed forces, to assist any member or protocol state of the Southeast Asia Collective Defense Treaty requesting assistance...."[109] Moreover, the determination as to when to use these forces was left to the president, but he did have this prior congressional approval as a basis for action. This resolution was eventually viewed as the "functional equivalent" of war by the Johnson administration and was used to expand American involvement in Vietnam and Southeast Asia in the 1960s.[110]

Beyond these rather dramatic examples in the war-making area, Congress has had a tendency to grant to the executive considerable discretion in implementing trade and foreign assistance statutes. In recent foreign assistance legislation, for example, the president is still afforded latitude in authorizing development assistance "on such terms and conditions as he may determine," in providing economic support funds "on such terms and conditions as he may determine...to promote economic or political stability," and to provide military assistance in a similar fashion that "will strengthen the security of the United States." While this legislation also imposed considerable restrictions on the executive, considerable residual presidential authority still remains.[111]

The congressional delegation of trade responsibility to the president predates the Cold War years and goes back at least to the Reciprocal Trade Agreements Act of 1934. Under that act, the president was authorized to negotiate tariff reductions and implement such agreements. Moreover, these reductions could involve as much as 50 percent reduction without any congressional involvement. This process continued in subsequent reciprocal trade acts.[112] This procedure largely continued in more recent trade acts such as the Trade Act of 1974 and the Trade Act of 1979, in which the president was authorized to negotiate the elimination of nontariff barriers as well. In the words of one well-known trade analyst, I. M. Destler, the "Congress legislated itself out of the business of making product-specific trade law," despite the constitutional mandate that it shall "regulate commerce with foreign nations."[113]

In the Omnibus Trade and Competitiveness Act of 1988, too, the president's prerogatives were reaffirmed in negotiating and implementing trade legislation. The president was authorized to enter into tariff agreements, both bilaterally and multilaterally. He could also change the U.S. tariff schedules "if the President determines such action to be in the interest of the United States." While the legislation gave more power to the U.S. Trade

Representative in implementing many of the provisions, this representative would still be responsible to the president.[114] In this sense, too, the power of the executive office in this increasingly crucial area remains substantial.

In an even broader piece of congressional legislation enacted at the end of 1977, the International Emergency Economic Powers Act, the president was authorized to declare a national emergency to deal with any "extraordinary threat, which has its source in whole or substantial part outside the United States, to the national security, foreign policy, or economy of the United States." Under this authority, the president may "investigate, regulate, or prohibit" a wide array of actions, albeit largely economic ones.[115] In addition, however, this grant of authority was conditioned upon several requirements dealing with consulting and reporting to Congress. In this sense, the seemingly broad sweep of the legislation was actually to be more restrictive than what earlier legislation dating back to the Roosevelt era had allowed. Yet subsequent Supreme Court divisions in the early 1980s weakened the congressional role and, in the estimation of one analyst, "freed the president...to conduct widespread economic warfare merely by declaring a national emergency with respect to a particular country...."[116]

Part of this discretion is understandable in that individual cases might arise that Congress would not be able to foresee, or, alternatively, that Congress might not have the time or inclination to handle expeditiously. In this sense, presidential discretion was reasonable, since the presidential responsibility was to execute the law. At the same time, such discretion inevitably has led to a greater concentration of foreign policy power in the hands of the president—usually at the expense of the legislative branch.

4. Growth of Executive Institutions

A fourth reason for presidential dominance in foreign policy has been the expansion of executive institutions. Since the end of World War II, the foreign policy machinery of the president has grown quite substantially, while the capacity of Congress has grown only modestly. As a result, presidential control of the foreign policy apparatus and foreign policy information has increased sharply, leaving Congress at a distinct disadvantage in both areas.

With congressional passage of the National Security Act of 1947, the foreign policy machinery of the executive branch was both consolidated and enlarged.[117] This act provided for the establishment of the National Security Council, the Central Intelligence Agency, and the organization of the separate military forces under the National Military Establishment (later the Department of Defense). In addition, the civilian position of the secretary of defense was mandated to head this National Military Establishment, and the Joint Chiefs of Staff was organized to advise the secretary of defense.

All of these new agencies and individuals ultimately were to assist the president with the conduct of foreign policy. The National Security Council, for instance, composed of the president, vice president, the secretary of state, secretary of defense, and others that the president may designate, was "to advise the president with respect to the integration of domestic, foreign, and military policies relating to the national security...."[118] This council to the executive enabled him to make foreign policy with little involvement on the part of the other branches of government, and even without much involvement on the part of the rest of the executive branch. Moreover, as the National Security Council system has evolved—especially with the enhanced role of the national security advisor in more recent administrations—the executive control of the foreign policy machinery became firmly entrenched in the office of the president. One indicator of the growth of the National Security Council system is the size of the staffs under each succeeding president in the postwar years.

Under President Truman, for instance, National Security Council personnel numbered 20 in 1951. This total increased to 28 in 1955 under President Eisenhower; grew to 50 in 1962 under President Kennedy; remained at 50 in 1966 under President Johnson; rose to 75 under President Nixon; decreased to 64 under President Carter in 1979; and again declined to 62 in 1982 under President Reagan and to 61 in 1990 under President Bush. For the Clinton administration, the estimated number of National Security Council personnel for 1995 was 60, about the same size as under the three previous administrations. Thus, while the size of the National Security Council staff has fluctuated over time, it has surely grown from its initial years.[119] More importantly, it has grown in power and influence in the actual formulation of foreign policy within the executive branch (see Chapter 9).

The Central Intelligence Agency was established by the National Security Act for the purpose of developing intelligence estimates and for advising and making recommendations to the National Security Council. The agency also was to assist in coordinating the activities of other intelligence agencies within the U.S. government. Further, the CIA was "to perform such other functions and duties related to intelligence affecting the national security as the National Security Council may from time to time direct."[120] This last function was used as the rationale for "covert actions" by the American government as the CIA developed.

The National Security Act also begat the National Military Establishment in 1947. Under this provision of the act, the Departments of the Army, Navy, and Air Force came into existence, with the secretary of defense heading this overall organizational arrangement. By 1949, amendments to the act created the present Department of Defense to replace the National Military Establishment. Moreover, the secretary of defense, who was the head of this new cabinet department, was required to be a civilian and to be "the principal assistant to the President in all matters relating to the national security."[121]

Finally, the 1947 act provided for the creation of the Joint Chiefs of Staff. This group would consist of the Army and Air Force chiefs of staff, the chief of naval operations, and the chairman of the Joint Chiefs. Their duties would consist of preparing strategic plans and forces, formulating military policies, and advising the president and the secretary of defense on military matters.

By one congressional act, then, the president was provided an intelligence advisor (the director of the CIA), a military advisor (chairman of the Joint Chiefs of Staff), and a national security advisor (the secretary of defense). In addition, the president was provided with a bureaucratic mechanism for gathering intelligence (the Central Intelligence Agency), for making policy (the National Security Council), and for carrying out the military options (the National Military Establishment). All of these forums were in addition to the Department of State and the secretary of state, traditionally the principal foreign affairs bureaucracy and its spokesperson.

Later in the postwar period, some agencies were established to assist the president, and other agencies assumed a larger role in foreign policy matters. Three new agencies illustrate how the executive branch continued to gain greater control over various aspects of foreign policy. In 1961, the Agency for International Development (AID) was established by Congress to coordinate the distribution of foreign assistance abroad.[122] In the same year, the Arms Control and Disarmament Agency (ACDA) was mandated by Congress to coordinate arms control activities.[123] The director of ACDA was to be the principal advisor to the president on these foreign policy questions. In 1963, the Office of the Special Trade Representative was created by an executive order, and the duties of the individual who would be U.S. Trade Representative has been institutionalized and expanded in subsequent trade acts passed by Congress.[124] The U.S. Trade Representative, for instance, now has the responsibility for directing all trade negotiations and for formulating trade policy as well. Finally, the other bureaucracies within the executive branch that have become increasingly involved in international affairs include the Departments of Commerce, Treasury, Agriculture, and Justice, among others.[125] In short, with all of these agencies in place, the president, and the executive branch more generally, are in a better institutional position to shape foreign policy than the executives traditional rival, Congress.

Such structural and hierarchical arrangements have markedly aided the president and his advisors in gathering information and in making rapid foreign policy decisions. Indeed, it is estimated that, at any one time, over 35,000 people within the executive branch are working on matters related to foreign policy.[126] With all of these people ultimately answerable to the president and with all of these sources of information, centralized and quick decision making can *usually* result. Thus, the executive can *usually* respond quickly to an international situation, ranging from the use of military force, to negotiating arms control, to the distribution of foreign assistance. As we note in Chapters 9 and 10, however, bureaucratic politics can and does impede the assumed efficiency of the executive branch. The discerning student needs to keep this important exception in mind as we discuss the bureaucracies of the executive.

By contrast, Congress *usually* does not enjoy such advantages, and a number of its bureaucratic, procedural, and informational arrangements have been criticized. Congress is a large and often unwieldy body, with 535 members—who are sometimes described as parochial, not national or international, in their outlook. As constituency service has become an increasingly important mechanism for political survival, national and foreign policy interests may well suffer. Congress has a cumbersome bureaucratic system, with numerous committees and subcommittees claiming foreign policy responsibilities, and thus hindering quick foreign policy decision making. Congress does not enjoy many large independent information sources on foreign policy matters, and it has been often highly dependent upon the executive branch. Further, many complain that the size of congressional staffs has been inadequate to do the necessary background work on foreign policy questions.

Several of these criticisms about Capitol Hill are accurate, and some issues are being addressed by reforms within Congress, beginning in the 1970s and now continuing in the 1990s. Members are becoming more expert on foreign policy, and foreign policy issues can actually work to a member's advantage within a constituency, especially as the boundaries between domestic and foreign policy questions erode (e.g., agricultural trade policy for a midwestern member of Congress). Information sources have expanded, too. The General Accounting Office (GAO), an arm of the U.S. Congress, now has a National Security and International Affairs Division with eleven distinct subdivisions whose responsibilities are to investigate and to provide evaluations to members of the House and the Senate. The Congressional Research Service, a department within the Library of Congress, was expanded under the Legislative Reform Act of 1970 and now has a separate division, the Foreign Affairs and National Defense Division, to work on foreign policy analyses for members of Congress. The Office of Technology Assessment, also a creation of the 1970s, was another source of information on highly specialized topics for Congress (until it was eliminated during budget-cutting efforts in 1995).[127]

Beginning with the establishment of the Joint Committee on the Organization of Congress in 1992, members of the House and Senate held discussions into 1994 on how to streamline the congressional system and to make it more effective. While these reforms dealt largely with internal housekeeping matters within the two chambers (e.g., committee assignments for members, the budgeting process, and applicability of workplace rules), they would have an impact on the efficiency of Congress. In all, though, because of partisan bickering, these reforms were not enacted into laws.[128] In 1995, as the new Republican majority took control of the House and Senate, some changes did occur—with a reduction in the number of committees and subcommittees, new internal congressional rules on handling and expediting legislation, and the enactment of a bill applying national workplace rules to the House and the Senate. While, arguably, these reforms will have limited impact in the overall operation of Congress, they are meant to increase efficiency and accountability in carrying out the legislative process.

5. International Situational Factors

The final factor affects all of the previous ones. Throughout the greater portion of the years since World War II, the United States has made foreign policy within a Cold War environment. Such a perceived dangerous environment had the effect of muting foreign policy debate over long-term goals and instead focused on short-term tactics (see Chapter 2). Another consequence, given the dangerous global situation, was a tendency by both Congress and the American public to defer to the executive on foreign policy matters. If an emergency arose, the president, not Congress, could react immediately. If decisions had to be made about the use of force or diplomacy, the president, not Congress, had to be prepared to act quickly. Furthermore, with the advent of nuclear weapons and instantaneous global communication, centralized control of the foreign policy machinery seemed more necessary than ever. More generally, too, the president was often the most admired person among the American people, and this admiration was transferred to trust in his conduct of foreign affairs.[129] As a result, there was a tendency to defer to the executive, with the assumption that the "president knows best."[130]

In recent decades, such deference to the president has eroded somewhat, for a variety of domestic and international reasons, although this factor cannot be wholly dismissed as a source of presidential power. Now Congress and the public are more willing to question presidents on foreign policy matters. This new posture probably had its beginnings with the Watergate events of the early 1970s, when the credibility of President Nixon suffered greatly over that episode. President Ford's reputation, in turn, was hurt by his pardoning of the former president over the Watergate matter. Later on, President Carter's foreign policy credibility was diminished by his inability to deal effectively with the Iran hostage crisis.

In the 1980s, President Reagan had a similar difficulty, at least with regard to his Central American policy. Despite Reagan's overall popularity among the public and several addresses to the American people appealing for their support and that of their representatives in Congress, he was never able to obtain their approval for his Contra aid policy in Central America. Public opinion polls consistently opposed this aspect of his foreign policy throughout his term. Similarly, although President Bush enjoyed substantial popular support, he had to fight vigorously with Congress over his policy toward China after the Tiananmen Square massacre of June 1989, had to employ his veto power to stop restrictive trade policy toward Japan, and had to spar with that body over his right to conduct American policy unilaterally with Iraq over its seizure of Kuwait. Further, with the rapidly changing events in Central Europe and the Middle East, and with no evident consensus on what American policy should be in the world, President Bush had perhaps less than automatic support for his foreign policy agenda from the American people or its representatives.

With the end of the Cold War, President Bill Clinton, in particular, has failed to obtain this seemingly "automatic" deference that earlier presidents received on foreign policy matters. Several reasons appear to account for this situation. With a direct nuclear threat to the United States having diminished as a result of the demise of the Soviet Union, the public (and Congress) seem unwilling to defer to the president. With the public unsure of the future role of the United States in global affairs, and with the Clinton administration seemingly unable to define such a role, the public has been reluctant to embrace the policies of the president. With a president more interested in and more certain of his domestic policy agenda than his foreign policy agenda, the public has once again been unwilling to defer to the chief executive very readily. The result has been that President Clinton's handling of foreign policy has virtually always trailed his overall public support.

More significantly, President Clinton's public support on foreign policy has usually been below the 50 percent level (averaging in the mid-forties generally) and it actually fell to 34 percent support in August 1994 and 36 percent in April 1995.[131] More significant, perhaps, has been the limited impact of the so-called "rally around the flag" effect when the president does act. When the president's popularity and support increase, their levels remain modest. In this sense, this international situational factor, like some of the other factors discussed in this chapter, are under some scrutiny by the public and Congress.

Concluding Comments

Historical precedents as well as Supreme Court decisions and nondecisions continue to serve as important reservoirs of presidential domination of foreign policy making. Similarly, the capacity of the executive branch to control the foreign policy bureaucracy and the demands for rapid decision making in global events are usually supportive of the preeminence of the president in making American foreign policy (although the end of the Cold War may be altering the latter factor). While some legislative deference and delegation of power to the executive continues, these sources of executive strength began to change over the last two decades. Increasingly, these are now sources of challenge to presidential power in foreign policy, although the executive preeminence largely remains.

In Chapter 8, we shall examine the role of Congress more fully in foreign policy making. In particular, we shall focus upon the major areas in which Congress has tried to reassert its prerogatives and, at the same time, has sought to reduce the degree of executive dominance. After that analysis, we then turn to discuss how to address the inevitable policy making conflict between these two branches.

Notes

1. Thomas L. Friedman, "Clinton Vows to Fight Congress on His Power to Use the Military," *New York Times*, October 19, 1993, A18.
2. "The McNeil-Lehrer Report," Public Broadcasting Service, February 10, 1983.
3. "Excerpts from Baker's Testimony Before Senate Committee," *New York Times*, January 18, 1989, A16.
4. Alexander M. Haig, Jr., "Opening Statement at Confirmation Hearings" (Washington, DC: Bureau of Public Affairs, Department of State, January 9, 1981), p. 3. Current Policy No. 257.
5. Michael J. Glennon in his *Constitutional Diplomacy* (Princeton, NJ: Princeton University Press, 1990), p. 20, says that a "'plenary presidential power' is one that is not susceptible of congressional limitation." Thanks to James M. Lindsay for this point about plenary powers.
6. See Cecil V. Crabb, Jr., and Pat M. Holt, *Invitation to Struggle: Congress, the President, and Foreign Policy* (Washington, DC: Congressional Quarterly Press, 1980), p. 34. Emphasis in original. They cite two earlier studies on this point: "Foreign Affairs and the Articles of Confederation," in Paul A. Varg, *Foreign Policies of the Founding Fathers* (East Lansing, MI: Michigan State University Press, 1963), pp. 46–66; and Albert C. V. Westphal, *The House Committee on Foreign Affairs* (New York: Columbia University Press, 1942), pp. 14–15.

7. See Louis Fisher, *Presidential War Power* (Lawrence, KS: University Press of Kansas, 1995), pp. 1–6, for this argument. For an alternate view on the role of prerogative from Locke and executive power, see Arthur M. Schlesinger, Jr., *The Imperial Presidency* (Boston: Houghton Mifflin Company, 1973), p. 8, who claims that Founders were well acquainted with Locke's "Of Prerogative" and its implications. For a contrary view, see David Gray Adler, "The Constitution and Presidential Warmaking: The Enduring Debate," *Political Science Quarterly* 103 (Spring 1988): 1–36. At p. 32, he argues as follows: "There is not a scintilla of evidence whatever that the Framers intended to incorporate the Lockean Prerogative in the Constitution." Note, however, that Adler's argument is directed more narrowly to the war-making power than to the foreign policy prerogatives of the executive in general, as we discuss here.
8. *Federalist* No. 69 can be found in Clinton Rossiter, ed., *The Federalist Papers* (New York: A Mentor Book, 1961), pp. 415–423.
9. Louis Henkin, *Foreign Affairs and the Constitution* (Mineola, NY: The Foundation Press, Inc., 1972). The quotations are at pp. 74 and 76. An early court case, *Little v. Barreme* 6 U.S. 170 (1804) reveals the degree to which the Congress held sway over foreign policy and how the president must yield to its authority. See Glennon, *Constitutional Diplomacy*, pp. 3–8, for a discussion of this case.
10. Quoted in Louis Henkin, "Foreign Affairs and the Constitution," *Foreign Affairs* 66 (Winter 1987/1988): 285, from *Youngstown Sheet & Tube Co. v. Sawyer* (1952).
11. Cited in Henkin, "Foreign Affairs and the Constitution," p. 292.
12. Schlesinger, *The Imperial Presidency*, p. 2.
13. Henkin, "Foreign Affairs and the Constitution," p. 287.
14. Edward S. Corwin, *The President: Office and Powers 1787–1957* (New York: New York University Press, 1957), p. 171.
15. See Arthur Schlesinger, Jr., "Congress and the Making of American Foreign Policy," *Foreign Affairs* 51 (October 1972): 78–113; James L. Sundquist, *The Decline and Resurgence of Congress* (Washington, DC: The Brookings Institution, 1981), pp. 21–29; and Harold Hongju Koh, *The National Security Constitution* (New Haven, CT: Yale University Press, 1992). For a brief description of the "pendulum theory" of foreign policy powers between the president and Congress, see Thomas M. Franck and Edward Weisband, *Foreign Policy by Congress* (New York: Oxford University Press, 1979), pp. 5–6. Also, these are the sources for the discussion of the different phases in executive and legal dominance.
16. Holbert N. Carroll, *The House of Representatives and Foreign Affairs* (Pittsburgh: University of Pittsburgh Press, 1958), p. 10. Sundquist, *The Decline and Resurgence of Congress*, pp. 22–23, views this early period slightly differently, with seemingly more power for Congress.
17. In reality, Congress passed a resolution that acknowledged that "a state of war exists." This passage is quoted in Fisher, *Presidential War Power*, p. 33.
18. The quoted phrase is from ibid., p. 25.
19. The last two quoted passages are from Koh, *The National Security Constitution*, p. 86.
20. Carroll, *The House of Representatives and Foreign Affairs*, p. 14. Much of this section on the cyclical interpretation of foreign policy control also draws upon James M. McCormick, "Congress and Foreign Policy," *The Encyclopedia of U.S. Foreign Relations* (New York: Oxford University Press, 1997), pp. 312–328.
21. Fisher, *Presidential War Power*, p. 65.
22. Henkin, "Foreign Affairs and the Constitution," p. 290.
23. Corwin, *The President*, p. 206.
24. Henkin, "Foreign Affairs and the Constitution," p. 291.
25. Corwin, *The President*, p. 182.
26. Schlesinger, "Congress and the Making of American Foreign Policy," p. 82. Also see Fisher, *Presidential War Power*, pp. 21–22.
27. Quoted in Corwin, *The President*, p. 177.
28. Ibid., p. 188.

29. Schlesinger, "Congress and the Making of American Foreign Policy," pp. 83–87. Also, however, see the 1989 edition (and its epilogue) of *The Imperial Presidency* (Boston: Houghton Mifflin Company, 1989), p. 442 in particular.
30. Ibid.
31. Johnny H. Killian, ed., *The Constitution of the United States: Analysis and Interpretation* (Washington, DC: Congressional Research Service, 1987), p. 338.
32. Schlesinger, "Congress and the Making of American Foreign Policy," p. 86.
33. Corwin, *The President*, p. 229.
34. For a discussion of the *Prize Cases*, see *Guide to the U.S. Supreme Court* (Washington, DC: Congressional Quarterly, Inc., 1979), pp. 187–189.
35. Schlesinger, "Congress and the Making of American Foreign Policy," pp. 89–91. Also see pp. 91–95 for the interventions mentioned and others done by presidents without congressional authorization.
36. Francis D. Wormuth, "Presidential Wars: The Convenience of 'Precedent,'" in Martin B. Hickman, ed., *Problems of American Foreign policy*, 2nd ed. (Beverly Hills: Glencoe Press, 1975), p. 96.
37. Richard M. Nixon, "Cambodia: A Difficult Decision," *Vital Speeches of the Day* 36 (May 15, 1970): 451. This speech was originally delivered to the American public on April 30, 1970.
38. Taken from the "Letter to the Speaker of the House and the President Pro Tempore of the Senate on United States Military Action in Panama," *Weekly Compilation of Presidential Documents* 25 (December 25, 1989): 1985.
39. The quoted passages by the president are reported in Friedman, "Clinton Vows to Fight Congress On His Power to Use the Military," p. A1.
40. Neil A. Lewis, "At the Bar: For the Clinton Administration, a Constitutional Scholar Forges Opinions from Theory and Real Life," *New York Times*, June 9, 1995, B13. Moreover, this analysis points out, too, that the Assistant Attorney General (Walter E. Dellinger) was "at odds with almost all of the nation's leading constitutional scholars" in devising such a defense of presidential power.
41. Remarks by President Clinton in the White House Rose Garden on May 23, 1995, as reported in "This Legislation Is The Wrong Way," *Congressional Quarterly Weekly Report*, May 27, 1995, 1514.
42. These two examples are drawn from the testimony of U. Alexis Johnson, under secretary of state for political affairs, and reported in "Department Discusses Agreements on Azores and Bahrain Facilities," *Department of State Bulletin* (February 28, 1972): 279–284. The quoted passage is at p. 282. Johnson did add that Congress would have to approve the rental payment for the use of the Bahrain facilities.
43. For some evidence illustrating that the bulk of the executive agreements in the postwar period have been pursuant to statute, see Loch Johnson and James M. McCormick, "The Making of International Agreements: A Reappraisal of Congressional Involvement," *The Journal of Politics* 40 (May 1978): 468–478.
44. The agreement data are from Michael Nelson, ed., *Congressional Quarterly's Guide to the Presidency* (Washington, DC: Congressional Quarterly, Inc., 1989), p. 1104. Louis Fisher in his *The President and Congress: Power and Policy* (New York: Free Press, 1972), p. 45, reports similar data through 1970.
45. Schlesinger, *The Imperial Presidency*, pp. 86–88.
46. On this point, see "National Commitments," Senate Report 91–129, 91st Cong., 1st sess., April 16, 1969, 26.
47. The hearings on American commitments with other countries were held in 1969 and 1970 by a subcommittee of the Committee on Foreign Relations (Subcommittee on United States Security Agreements and Commitments Abroad), chaired by Senator Stuart Symington of Missouri. A summary of these hearings, popularly known as the Symington Subcommittee, is reported in "Security Agreements and Commitments Abroad," Report to the Committee on Foreign Relations of the United States Senate by the Subcommittee on Security Agreements and Commitments Abroad, December 21, 1970.

48. Loch Johnson and James M. McCormick, "Foreign Policy by Executive Fiat," *Foreign Policy* 28 (Fall 1977): 117–138.
49. Koh, *The National Security Constitution*, p. 138.
50. The pact was entitled "The Agreed Framework Between the United States and the Democratic People's Republic of Korea," and was signed in Geneva, Switzerland, on October 21, 1994.
51. 299 U.S. 304 (1936).
52. Ibid., p. 314.
53. Ibid., p. 318.
54. Ibid., pp. 319, 320. The "extra-constitutional" description below is from Henkins, *Foreign Affairs and the Constitution*, p. 22.
55. See Adler, "The Constitution and Presidential Warmaking: The Enduring Debate," pp. 30–36. See especially his discussion of the *Steel Seizure Case* and *Reid v. Covert* at p. 32 as particular challenges to this broad "extra-constitutional" interpretation of presidential power. For a detailed analysis of *Curtiss-Wright*, see Glennon, *Constitutional Diplomacy*, pp. 18–34.
56. 252 U.S. 433.
57. Ibid.
58. Ibid.
59. 301 U.S. 324 (1937) and 315 U.S. 203 (1942).
60. Jean Edward Smith, *The Constitution and American Foreign Policy* (St. Paul: West Publishing Company, 1989), p. 127.
61. 315 U.S. 234 (1942).
62. Henkin, *Foreign Affairs and the Constitution*, p. 185.
63. These statutes are listed in Appendix I of *INS v. Chadha* 462 U.S. 919 (1983).
64. Martha Liebler Gibson, "Managing Conflict: The Role of the Legislative Veto in American Foreign Policy," *Polity* 26 (Spring 1994): 442–443.
65. Joseph Cooper and Patricia A. Hurley, "The Legislative Veto: A Policy Analysis," *Congress & Presidency* 10 (Spring 1983): 1–24, especially at pp. 1 and 4.
66. For a fuller discussion of the origin and development of the legislative veto, see Gibson, "Managing Conflict: The Role of the Legislative Veto in American Foreign Policy," 441–472; Martha Liebler Gibson, *Weapons of Influence: The Legislative Veto, American Foreign Policy, and the Irony of Reform* (Boulder: Westview Press, 1992); and Cooper and Hurley, "The Legislative Veto: A Policy Analysis," pp. 1–24.
67. These details are taken from the *Chadha* decision and from David M. O'Brien, *Constitutional Law and Politics*, vol. 1 (W. W. Norton & Company, 1991), p. 355.
68. 462 U.S. 947–959 (1983).
69. Frederick M. Kaiser, "Congressional Control of Executive Actions in the Aftermath of the *Chadha* Decision," *Administrative Law Review* 36 (Summer 1984): 242.
70. 343 U.S. 585 (1952).
71. 343 U.S. 587 (1952).
72. 343 U.S. 635, 647 (1952).
73. Koh, *The National Security Constitution*, p. 108.
74. Quoted in Smith, *The Constitution and American Foreign Policy*, from the decision itself at p. 169. The earlier quotation is from Smith's analysis at the same page.
75. This discussion is gleaned and simplified somewhat from Henkin, *Foreign Affairs and the Constitution*, pp. 210–215. The "political doctrine" question is more complicated than this brief summary conveys and remains a complex issue of constitutional law.
76. Warren Christopher, "Ceasefire Between the Branches: A Compact in Foreign Affairs," in James M. McCormick, *A Reader in American Foreign Policy* (Itasca, IL: F. E. Peacock Publishers, Inc., 1986), pp. 253–254.

77. See Henkin, *Foreign Affairs and the Constitution*, p. 157.
78. Gordon Silverstein, "Judicial Enhancement of Executive Power," in Paul E. Peterson, ed., *The President, The Congress, and The Making of Foreign Policy* (Norman and London: University of Oklahoma Press, 1994), p. 38.
79. See, for example, *Altee v. Richardson* 411 U.S. 911 (1973).
80. The discussion is drawn from *Crockett v. Reagan* 720 F. 2d 1355 (1983); *Conyers v. Reagan* 765 F. 2d 1124 (1985); and *Lowry v. Reagan* 676 F. Supp. 333 (D.D.C. 1987).
81. Neil A. Lewis, "Lawmakers Lose War Powers Suit," *New York Times*, December 14, 1990, A9. Also see 752 F. Supp 1141 (D.D.C. 1990).
82. Silverstein, "Judicial Enhancement of Executive Power," pp. 23–45, especially pp. 34–45. The quoted passage is at p. 26.
83. On the Vandenberg Resolution, see James A. Robinson, *Congress and Foreign Policy-Making*, rev. ed. (Homewood, IL: The Dorsey Press, 1967), pp. 44–46. Also see Table 2-1 at p. 65, which shows the small degree of congressional initiation in foreign policy and the considerable degree of executive influence within Congress.
84. Richard F. Fenno, Jr. *Congressmen in Committees* (Boston: Little, Brown and Company, 1973), p. 71. Emphasis in original.
85. Interview, House Foreign Affairs Committee, Washington, DC, June 1982 and Department of State, Washington, DC, October 1981.
86. John Felton, "Foreign Affairs Committee Changes Seen Under Fascell," *Congressional Quarterly Weekly Report* 41 (December 10, 1983): 2622–2623. In fact, Zablocki was the principal sponsor of nuclear freeze resolutions in the House in 1982 and 1983.
87. Fenno, *Congressmen in Committees*, p. 163.
88. Charles H. Percy, "The Partisan Gap," *Foreign Policy* 45 (Winter 1981–82): 15.
89. On the "perpetual crisis in executive–legislative relations" during the Reagan years and on these proposals to improve this situation in the Bush years, see John Felton, "Will Bush-Hill Honeymoon Bring Bipartisanship?" *Congressional Quarterly Weekly Report* (February 18, 1989): 332–337. The quotations are from p. 335.
90. The description of Fascell is taken from Felton, "Foreign Affairs Committee Changes Seen Under Fascell," pp. 2622–2623. Despite Fascell's bipartisan inclination, one should not infer that he would be unwilling to challenge the executive. Fascell led the fight to suspend the testing of new anti-satellite weapons, favored by the Reagan administration, back in 1984 (see "Congressional Leader Urges Suspension of Space-Weapons Tests," *Des Moines Register*, May 21, 1984, 4A.).
91. Lee H. Hamilton, "American foreign Policy: A Congressional Perspective," speech at the Department of State, Washington, DC, December 14, 1993.
92. Quoted in Katharine Q. Seelye, "House Defeats Bid to Repeal 'War Powers,'" *New York Times*, June 8, 1995, A5.
93. The joint appearance was in Claremont, New Hampshire on Sunday, June 11, 1995, as shown on the Cable News Network (CNN).
94. Aaron Wildavsky, "Two Presidencies," *Trans-action* 3 (December 1966): 8.
95. Ibid. For several cogent arguments questioning the utility of roll-call analysis in evaluating presidential success, see James M. Lindsay and Wayne P. Steger, "The 'Two Presidencies' in Future Research: Moving Beyond Roll-Call Analysis," *Congress & The Presidency* 20 (Autumn 1993): 103–117. For some arguments supporting the use of roll-call analysis, see Jon R. Bond and Richard Fleisher, *The President in the Legislative Arena* (Chicago and London: The University of Chicago Press, 1990), pp. 66–71.
96. Lance T. LeLoup and Steven A. Shull, "Congress Versus the Executive: The 'Two Presidencies' Reconsidered," *Social Science Quarterly* 59 (March 1979): 707.
97. Ibid., pp. 712–713.
98. Richard Fleisher and Jon R. Bond, "Are There Two Presidencies? Yes, But Only for Republicans," *The Journal of Politics* 50 (August 1988): 747–767. Table 1 at p. 754 is the source of these conclusions. Also see their book which in part addresses this issue: Bond and Fleisher, *The President in the Legislative Arena*.

99. These results were calculated from roll-call data made available through the Inter-University Consortium of Political and Social Research (the Consortium bears no responsibility for the analyses and interpretations reported here) and from recorded votes reported in *Congressional Quarterly Almanac* (various years) and *Congressional Quarterly Weekly Report* (various issues). Foreign policy votes were identified for the Eisenhower through Clinton years on which the president took a position, based upon *Congressional Quarterly Almanac* and *Congressional Quarterly Weekly Report* assessments, and then the president's success or failure was calculated across each administration. The foreign policy votes for the Truman years were identified from the roll-call data, and Truman's position was determined by an assessment of available *CQ Almanacs* and presidential papers. The assistance of Eugene R. Wittkopf of Louisiana State University in identifying all the foreign policy votes, in collecting the Clinton votes, and in determining Truman's position on those particular votes is appreciated. A more detailed discussion of the data collection process is reported in James M. McCormick and Eugene R. Wittkopf, "Bipartisanship, Partisanship, and Ideology in Congressional-Executive Foreign Policy Relations, 1947–1988," *The Journal of Politics* (November 1990): 1077–1100.

100. Aage R. Clausen, *How Congressman Decide: A Policy Focus* (New York: St. Martin's Press, 1973), pp. 192–212, 222–230. Clausen qualifies this conclusion by stating that presidential influence "appears to be effective only on congressmen of the same party as the president" (p. 209).

101. See Lee Sigelman, "A Reassessment of the Two Presidencies Thesis," *The Journal of Politics* (November 1979): 1195–1205, especially 1200–1201. Drawing upon *Congressional Quarterly*, Sigelman defined a key vote as one involving "'a matter of major controversy,' 'a test of presidential or political power,' or 'a decision of potentially great impact on the nation and lives of Americans.'" The number of such votes ranged between 10 and 36 for the years of his study (p. 1199).

102. Ibid., pp. 1200–1201.

103. LeLoup and Shull, "Congress Versus the Executive: The Two Presidencies' Reconsidered," p. 710.

104. See Robert A. Bernstein and William Anthony, "The ABM Issue in the Senate, 1968–1970: The Importance of Ideology," *American Political Science Review* 68 (September 1974): 1198–1206; James M. McCormick and Michael Black, "Ideology and Voting on the Panama Canal Treaties," *Legislative Studies Quarterly* 8 (February 1983): 45–63; James M. McCormick, "Congressional Voting on the Nuclear Freeze Resolutions," *American Politics Quarterly* 13 (January 1985): 122–136; Richard Fleisher, "Economic Benefit, Ideology, and Senate Voting on the B-1 Bomber," *American Politics Quarterly* 13 (April 1985): 200–211; James M. Lindsay, "Parochialism, Policy, and Constituency Constraints: Congressional Voting on Strategic Weapons Systems," *American Journal of Political Science* 34 (November 1990): 936–960; and Eugene R. Wittkopf and James M. McCormick, "The Domestic Politics of Contra Aid: Public Opinion, Congress, and the President," in Richard Sobel, ed., *Public Opinion in U.S. Foreign Policy: The Controversy over Contra Aid* (Lanham, MD: Rowman & Littlefield Publishers, Inc., 1993), pp. 73–103.

105. Duane M. Oldfield and Aaron Wildavsky, "Reconsidering the Two Presidencies," *Society* 26 (July/August 1989): 54–59. The quotation is at p. 55. For a good summary of the recent debates over the "two presidencies" argument, see Steven A. Shull, ed., *The Two Presidencies: A Quarter Century Assessment* (Chicago: Nelson/Hall Publishers, 1991).

106. See P.L. 85-7, in *United States Statutes at Large*, Vol. 69 (Washington, DC: Government Printing Office, 1955), p. 7. Emphasis added.

107. P.L. 85-7, in *United States Statutes at Large*, Vol. 71 (Washington, DC: Government Printing Office, 1958), p. 5.

108. See Fisher, *Presidential War Powers*, pp. 107–110 for the controversies surrounding this resolution. Also see "'Eisenhower Doctrine' for the Middle East," *Congressional Quarterly Almanac 1957* (Washington, DC: Congressional Quarterly Inc., 1957), pp. 573–579. The quote indicating that America "is prepared to use armed forces" is at p. 573. Also see Gordon Silverstein, *Imbalance of Powers* (New York: Oxford University Press, 1997), pp. 78–79.

109. P.L. 88-408.

110. See the testimony by Undersecretary of State Nicholas Katzenbach in "U.S. Commitments to Foreign Powers," *Hearings* before the Committee on Foreign Relations, 90th Cong., 1st sess., August 16, 17, 21, 23, and September 19, 1967, p. 82. Two other resolutions were passed by Congress in 1962 "expressing the determination of the United States" to use armed forces if necessary to stop Cuban aggression and to defend Berlin. Neither resolution, however, expressly granted the presidential discretion that the Formosa and Gulf of Tonkin resolutions did. See P.L. 87-733 (October 3, 1962) and H. Con. Res. (October 10, 1962).

111. These passages are taken from the Foreign Assistance Act of 1961, as amended, and reported in *Legislation on Foreign Relations Through 1985* (Washington, DC: U.S. Government Printing Office, April 1986). The quoted passages are at pp. 32, 141, and 129, respectively.

112. See I. M. Destler, *American Trade Politics* (Washington, DC: Institute for International Economics and New York: The Twentieth Century Fund, June 1992), p. 12. Also see Sharyn O'Halloran, "Congress and Foreign Trade Policy," in Randall B. Ripley and James M. Lindsay, *Congress Resurgent: Foreign and Defense Policy on Capitol Hill* (Ann Arbor: The University of Michigan Press, 1993), pp. 283–303.

113. Destler, *American Trade Politics*, p. 13.

114. The quoted passage is from P.L. 100-418 at 102 Stat. 1143. A summary of the bill is in *Congressional Quarterly Almanac 1988* (Washington, DC: Congressional Quarterly, Inc., 1989), pp. 209–215.

115. 91 Stat. 1626.

116. Koh, *The National Security Constitution*, pp. 46–47. The quoted passage is at p. 47.

117. P.L. 253, in *United States Statutes At Large*, Vol. 61, part 1, 80th Cong., 1st sess., pp. 495–510.

118. Ibid., p. 496. The membership of the National Security Council has changed slightly over time. This membership represents the current required composition, although the president may invite other members to participate.

119. These data are taken from the Budget of the United States Government for the appropriate years.

120. P.L. 253, p. 498.

121. Ibid., p. 500.

122. See P.L. 87-194.

123. See P.L. 87-297.

124. *U.S. Government Manual 1989/1990,* July 1, 1989. p. 95.

125. For a discussion of the role of some of these bureaucracies in the foreign policy process, see Chapter 9.

126. Charles W. Kegley, Jr., and Eugene R. Wittkopf, *American Foreign Policy: Pattern and Process*, 3rd ed. (New York: St. Martin's Press, 1987), p. 340.

127. For a discussion of these services for Congress, see *Executive Legislative Consultation on Foreign Policy: Strengthening Foreign Policy Information Sources for Congress* (Washington, DC: Government Printing Office, February, 1982), pp. 27–37; Evelyn Howard, *The Congressional Research Service* (Washington, DC: Congressional Research Service, August 14, 1989); and General Accounting Office, *National Security and International Affairs Division: Organization and Responsibility* (Washington, DC: Government Printing Office, 1989).

128. See "No Action Taken on Congressional Reform," *Congressional Quarterly Almanac 1993* (Washington, DC: Congressional Quarterly, Inc., 1994), pp. 21–29.

129. For some evidence on how admired presidents have been in the postwar period, see John E. Mueller, *War, Presidents and Public Opinion* (New York: John Wiley & Sons, Inc., 1973), pp. 179–195.

130. The phrase is taken from Daniel Yankelovich, "Farewell to 'President Knows Best,'" in William P. Bundy, ed., *America and the World 1978* (New York: Pergamon Press, 1979),

pp. 670–693, who discusses this deferential tradition in the American public and its decline in the middle 1970s.

131. For some summary poll numbers on foreign policy support for the Clinton administration among the American public, see "Opinion Outlook" in various issues of *National Journal.* See, for examples, the following issues: January 14, 1995, p. 130; February 11, 1995, p. 385; March 11, 1995, p. 642; April 8, 1995, p. 889; and May 6, 1995, p. 1129.

CHAPTER 8

CONGRESSIONAL PREROGATIVES AND THE MAKING OF FOREIGN POLICY

The Framers...gave to Congress the responsibility for deciding matters of war and peace. The President, as Commander in Chief, was left with the power to "repel sudden attacks"...Whenever the President acts unilaterally in using military force against another nation, the constitutional rights of Congress and the people are undermined.

Constitutional scholar Louis Fisher
December 1995

It's very important for the President to seek approval of the Congress [before sending troops to Bosnia]. The title of Commander in Chief is one thing. But the power of the purse is the greatest power in our Constitutional system.

Senator Robert Byrd (D-West Virginia)
October 1995

The unrest at home over America's involvement in Vietnam, the perceived growth in the foreign policy powers of the president, and the weakening of executive authority as a result of the Watergate incident—all contributed to efforts by the legislative branch to reassert its foreign policy prerogatives beginning in the early 1970s. Congress achieved some success in placing limitations on the foreign policy powers of the president in four principal ways:

1. Requiring the executive to report all commitments abroad
2. Limiting the war powers of the president
3. Placing restrictions on foreign policy funding
4. Increasing congressional oversight of the executive branch in foreign policy making

By the mid 1990s, several of these limitations had become institutionalized practices between Congress and the president, others had been altered or largely abandoned, and, in some instances, new ones added. In this sense, the struggle over foreign policy continues between the two branches.

In this chapter, we review several of the foreign policy restrictions enacted by Congress over the past three decades, assess how well they have worked, and discuss how they have affected congressional-executive relations in American foreign policy making.

COMMITMENT MAKING

The first area of congressional resurgence in the 1970s involved commitment making by the executive. This effort to rein in executive power was not particularly new, since a similar attempt was undertaken in the 1950s, but it did prove to be more successful than the earlier one. The two efforts differed in several ways: The earlier effort took the form of a proposed constitutional amendment restricting the kind of treaties and executive agreements the president might initiate; the later focused upon requiring the president to report to Congress on commitments already made. The earlier effort was led by congressional conservatives, the latter by congressional liberals.

The Bricker Amendment

The 1950s effort at curbing the president was motivated by America's increasing global involvement and was led by Senator John Bricker of Ohio. In a series of constitutional amendments, Bricker proposed that any treaty or executive agreement that infringed upon the constitutional rights of American citizens shall be unconstitutional and that Congress shall have the right to enact appropriate legislation that will be required to put into effect any treaty or executive agreement made by the president. Bricker was concerned that the United Nations Treaty, and human rights treaties and agreements under consideration by the UN at the time, might commit the United States to particular domestic actions and, thus, reduce congressional or state prerogatives under the Constitution.[1] Bricker did not want actions to obtain constitutional legitimacy simply because a treaty or agreement had been agreed to by the president.[2] In effect, his amendment was designed (1) to alter the constitutional principle established for treaties in *Missouri v. Holland* and for executive agreements in *U.S. v. Belmont* and *U.S. v. Pink* (see Chapter 7), (2) to stop self-executing treaties (i.e., treaties not requiring implementing legislation on the part of Congress) from occurring, and (3) to ensure a larger congressional role in implementing all treaties and executive agreements domestically.

Several votes were taken in the Senate on these various amendment proposals. All failed. One ballot in 1954, however, came close to passage, failing by only one vote to obtain the necessary two-thirds majority needed to pass such a constitutional amendment in the Senate. Similar proposals were made throughout the mid-1950s, but support waned, and President Eisenhower's opposition to such legislation remained.

The Case-Zablocki Act

With the escalating involvement in Vietnam, primarily through presidential initiative, and with the revelations of secret commitments to a variety of other nations during the 1950s and 1960s, the congressional liberals of the 1970s sought to enact some limitations on executive commitments abroad.[3] In June 1969, the Senate passed a "sense of the Senate" resolution stating that the making of national commitments should involve the legislative as well as the executive branch (The National Commitments Resolution).[4] When the executive branch went ahead with executive agreements with Portugal and Bahrain, another "sense of the Senate" resolution was passed stating that agreements with these states for military bases or for foreign assistance should take the form of treaties.[5]

Although these resolutions provided an avenue for venting congressional frustration over executive actions abroad, they were largely symbolic, since they did not legally bind the executive branch to alter its previous policies. Nevertheless, these actions in the late 1960s and early 1970s foreshadowed stronger legislative measures in several different areas over the next few years.

By the middle of 1972, Congress did pass the first significant piece of legislation in the commitment-making area, the Case-Zablocki Act, named after Senator Clifford Case (R-New Jersey) and Congressman Clement Zablocki (D-Wisconsin). This law required the executive branch to report all international agreements to Congress within sixty days of their entering into force. (Classified agreements would be transmitted to the House Foreign Affairs [now, the International Relations] Committee and the Senate Foreign Relations Committee under an injunction of secrecy.[6]) Later, in 1977, this act was amended and strengthened to require that all agreements made by all agencies within the executive branch must be reported to the Department of State within twenty days for ultimate transmittal to Congress under the provision of the original act.[7]

Even with this reporting arrangement (further strengthened under the Foreign Relations Authorization Act of 1979), Congress has enjoyed only

TABLE 8.1

Late Reporting of International Agreements by the Executive Branch to the Congress, Selected Years

	Number				Percentage			
	1981	1988	1992	1978–1992	1981	1988	1992	1978–1992
Agreements transmitted to Congress	368	412	296	5457	100%	100%	100%	100%
Agreements reported after 60 days	99	79	56	1025	26.9	19.1	18.9	18.8
Reported late from the Department of State	69	39	38	547	18.8	9.5	12.8	10.0
Reported late from other agencies to the Department of State	30	40	18	265	8.2	9.7	6.1	4.9

Sources: Constructed from the information provided in *International Agreements*, Communication from the President of the United States, House Document 97-148, 97th Cong., 2nd sess., February 24, 1982; *Report on International Agreements Transmitted to the Congress after Expiration of the Sixty-Day Period Specified in the Case-Zablocki Act*, from the House Foreign Affairs Committee for 1988; and Committee on Foreign Relations, United States Senate. *Treaties and Other International Agreements: The Role of the United States Senate.* A Study Prepared for the Committee on Foreign Relations, United States Senate, by the Congressional Research Service. Washington, DC: U.S. Government Printing Office, November 1993, p. 188.

mixed success in obtaining all agreements in a timely fashion. While a large number of agreements (both public and classified) have been reported to Congress, the number of late transmittals to Congress remains quite substantial. In 1976, for example, 39 percent of all agreements were reported late; by the first half of 1978, the percentage had dropped to 32 percent.[8] By 1981, over 26 percent of all agreements were still transmitted to Congress beyond the sixty-day period. By 1988, reporting had improved, but almost one-fifth of all agreements were still reported late.[9] By 1992, the situation had changed very little with 19 percent of all agreements still being reported late.[10]

Moreover, while some agencies other than the Department of State had contributed to the tardiness of agreements in 1977, the bulk of the late agreements in 1981 had emanated from the Department itself. By 1988, both the Department of State and other agencies had about equally contributed to the tardiness in reporting. By 1992, however, the Department of State was again the most frequent agency that was late in reporting, with 38 of the late agreements coming from that department and 18 deriving from other agencies. Table 8.1 provides a summary of the agreements that were reported late in 1981, 1988, and 1992.

Late reporting or nonreporting prompted concern by Congress for at least two reasons. Not only are late reports inconsistent with the procedural requirements of the Case-Zablocki and Case legislation, but they could also affect the substance of policy. Although one can readily acknowledge that the late reporting of some executive agreements dealing with administrative details (e.g., water and electricity agreements for American bases in the Philippines) may not be terribly problematic, other executive agreements (e.g., intelligence agreements with other countries) may be. The failure of Congress to know about the latter type of agreements in a timely fashion may well preclude that body from taking any action or even staying informed on current policy. Both procedurally and substantively, then, prompt reporting of commitments abroad is important to the continuation of the role of Congress in foreign policy making.

Beyond the timeliness of reporting to Congress, the reports transmitted by the executive branch have not always been complete. In a recent assessment, congressional staff report that the agreements transmitted to them often lack sufficient detail to be informative and are "vague about the responsibility of the other party." State Department officials have responded to this criticism by noting that these kinds of reports are necessary because of "the inability of U.S. negotiators to make precise commitments pending implementing legislation, particularly authorized funding." Another factor complicating this reporting picture, and which further accounts for the lack of frequency and quality of the reporting, is the "nonbinding agreement." In a technical sense, these kinds of agreements—agreements of a political or moral character but not of a legal one with another party (e.g., the Helsinki Accords of 1975)—are not required to be transmitted under Case-Zablocki to Congress. As a practical matter, however, succeeding administrations have done so, although not as fully or as completely as Congress may have desired. Hence, dissatisfaction on information sharing regarding international commitment making continues to cloud the relationship between Congress and the president into the 1990s.[11]

Beyond Case-Zablocki

While the Case-Zablocki Act required only the reporting of commitments, it did signal congressional determination to participate in the agreement-making process. In fact, some members of Congress were sufficiently dissatisfied with the limitation of just the reporting requirement that they sought to go further in strengthening the legislative role in this entire process. Various attempts were made by members of the House and the Senate to allow Congress to have the right to reject a commitment made by the executive branch within a prescribed period of time (usually sixty days). In the Senate, for example, Senator Sam Ervin (D-North Carolina) introduced several measures that would have allowed both houses to veto any executive agreement within sixty days, while Senator John Glenn (D-Ohio) introduced a similar bill that would have allowed only the Senate the right of disapproval of these executive agreements.[12]

In the House, similar measures were introduced. Perhaps the most intriguing one on this topic was that advanced by Congressman Thomas (Doc) Morgan (D-Pennsylvania), then chairman of the House Foreign Affairs Committee. He proposed in the Executive Agreements Review Act of 1975 that both houses of Congress have the right of disapproval of executive agreements, but only for those involving "national commitments"—mainly those agreements regarding the introduction of American military personnel or providing military training or equipment to another country.[13]

In other words, this legislation attempted to involve Congress in the review of only "significant" executive agreements and did not burden itself with routine or trivial ties between states. Despite such congressional initiatives through the middle 1970s, none of these proposals became law.

The reform effort that came closest to going beyond the simple reporting of executive agreements was that undertaken by Senator Dick Clark (D-Iowa) on behalf of his Treaty Powers Resolution in 1976 and after. Under this resolution:

> ...the Senate may...refuse to authorize and appropriate funds to implement those international agreements which, in its opinion, constitute treaties and to which the Senate has not given its advice and consent to ratification.[14]

In other words, the Senate would be able to reject any measure that it thought should have been a treaty and, instead, had been done by executive action. While the Clark resolution was eventually reported out of the Senate Foreign Relations Committee on a tie vote in 1978 after narrowly surviving a vote to delete it, the resolution was replaced on the Senate floor by a weakened substitute measure offered by Senator John Glenn.[15]

The existence of this resolution did set the stage for the passage of some reform procedures between Congress and the executive that were incorporated into the Foreign Relations Authorization Act for Fiscal Year 1979, passed in October 1978.[16] Under the provisions of this act, the president must now report yearly to Congress on each agreement that was late (i.e., beyond the sixty-day reporting period) in being transmitted to Congress; the Secretary of State must now determine what arrangements constitute an international agreement; and oral agreements must now be "reduced to writing."[17] In effect, this act further strengthened the original idea behind Case-Zablocki, without going much beyond it.

At the same time, the Department of State worked out an informal arrangement with the Senate Foreign Relations Committee for periodic consultation regarding which international agreements should take the form of treaties. An exchange of letters between the Senate Committee and the Department of State in July 1978, in conjunction with the Senate's consideration of a (nonbinding) resolution, formally called the International Agreements Consultation Resolution, produced this arrangement.[18] This resolution was eventually passed by the Senate in September 1978, and explicitly pointed to "agreed procedures with the Secretary of State."[19]

In practice, these procedures involve the periodic transmittal of a list of agreements under negotiations by the Department of State (or other agencies) to the House and Senate foreign policy committees. These lists include "a citation of the legal authority for the agreement, and the expected form the agreement would take (treaty or executive agreement)." In turn, they "are circulated and filed in a manner similar to the procedures used for classified agreements under the Case [-Zablocki] Act." These lists are "selective," and are based on the administration's judgment "of the interests of the Congress." Furthermore, the use of these lists does not preclude more informal consultation between committee staff and the Department of State, although "a formal record" of such consultation "may not exist," in the assessment of one recent study.[20]

In sum, although Congress nurtured the beginning of a resurgence in the commitment-making area, it was unwilling to go very far. Except for the formal list procedure and more informal congressional staff–Department of State consultations, Congress has not ventured much beyond the reporting mechanism for trying to control agreement making by the executive. More extensive legislative action in the foreign policy realm would be taken by seeking to control Congress's war powers and by using the appropriations power.

WAR POWERS

Frustrated over the use of the commander-in-chief and executive clauses of the Constitution to intervene abroad, Congress adopted several measures to limit the war-making ability of the president in the 1970s. The first important action was the 1970 congressional repeal of the Gulf of Tonkin resolution, which had allowed the president a virtual free hand in conducting the Vietnam War.[21] Although the repeal was more symbolic than substantive, Congress, by this action, was beginning to assert its role in war making. The executive branch, however, still claimed it had the power to continue the war even without the resolution in place.

Spurred on by the Nixon administration's indifference to its repeal of the Gulf of Tonkin resolution, Congress proceeded to work on a proposal that would limit the war-making powers of the president more generally. The resulting War Powers Resolution, passed over President Nixon's veto in November 1973, remains by far the most significant congressional attempt to reassert its control over committing American forces abroad.[22]

Key Provisions of the War Powers Resolution

This resolution has several important provisions that require presidential consultation and reporting to Congress on the use of United States forces abroad, limit the time of deployment of such forces, and provide Congress a mechanism for withdrawing these forces prior to this time limit as well. These provisions are worth summarizing in detail.[23]

First, the president may introduce United States Armed Forces "into hostilities or into situations where imminent involvement in hostilities is clearly indicated by the circumstances" under only three conditions: "(1) a declaration of war, (2) specific statutory authorization, or (3) a national emergency created by attack upon the United States, its territories, or its armed forces." The significance of this provision is that, for the first time, Congress specified the conditions under which the president could use armed forces. Previously, and excepting a declaration of war, presidential power to use force abroad was more discretionary and ambiguous.

Second, the president "in every possible instance shall consult with Congress" before sending American forces into hostilities or anticipated hostilities and "shall consult regularly with Congress" until those forces have been removed. Put differently, the resolution expected Congress to be involved in the process from beginning to end.

Third, for those circumstances in which forces were introduced without a declaration of war, the president must submit a written report to the Speaker of the House and the President pro Tempore of the Senate within forty-eight hours of deploying American forces, explaining the reasons for the introduction of troops, the constitutional and legislative authority for taking such actions, and the "estimated scope and duration of the hostilities or involvement." Further, the president was directed to "report to the Congress periodically on the status of such hostilities or situation as well as on the scope and duration of such hostilities or situation" at least every six months, if troops remain that long.

Fourth, and perhaps its core feature, the resolution placed a time limit on how long these forces may be deployed. The resolution specifically authorized the president to use American forces for no longer than sixty days, unless there had been a declaration of war or a specific congressional authorization to continue the use of such forces beyond this period. An extension of thirty days was possible, according to the resolution, if the president certified that military requirements precluded troop withdrawal within the sixty-day period. In an important ambiguity in the resolution, however, unless the president reports under the appropriate section [Section 4 (a) (1)], the sixty-day time limit does not automatically begin. Alternately, however, Congress may begin the sixty-day clock by invoking the resolution itself.[24] In any event, the beginning of the sixty-day time limitation is a bit more ambiguous than an initial review of the resolution might suggest.

Finally, the congressional resolution included a provision that allowed Congress to withdraw the troops prior to the expiration of the sixty-day limitation. By passing a concurrent resolution (a resolution in both houses but without presidential approval) by a simple majority, Congress could specify that the troops be withdrawn from the hostilities immediately. Moreover, the resolution provided time limits on the hearings in committee on such a resolution and required that a vote must be taken expeditiously. In other words, safeguards were provided so that the concurrent resolution would not become tied up within Congress without ever reaching a vote.

The clear intent of this war powers legislation was to stop the president from introducing American troops abroad and getting them mired into a conflict without a clear objective. Put more simply, it was to reduce the possibility of future Vietnams. At the same time, the intent of the resolution was also to reassert the expressed war powers of Congress under Article I of the Constitution. Despite these combined aims, the resolution would not prevent the president from taking military action if and when necessary; instead, the War Powers Resolution would promote the sharing of responsibility between the executive and legislative branches for dispatching American military personnel abroad.

Despite its obvious legal requirements, the War Powers Resolution also had another important purpose: It served as a political and psychological restraint on presidential war making. By this legislation, the president would now have to calculate whether Congress and the American public would support the sending of American forces to foreign lands. In addition, he would need to provide a formal justification for his taking military action and might well have to submit to formal congressional scrutiny.

Presidential Compliance

The record of presidential compliance with the requirements of this resolution is, at best, mixed. Some of the reporting requirements and the time limitation on troop deployments, as specified in the War Powers Resolution, have been nominally adhered to since 1973, but controversy continues to surround the precise situations requiring its applicability, the extent and manner of presidential compliance with all aspects of the resolution, and its overall effectiveness in curbing the expansion of executive power in this area. In addition, the *Chadha* decision on the congressional veto, as noted in Chapter 7, has seemingly made the concurrent resolution provision of this law unconstitutional.

Over the last six administrations (through mid-1996), fifty-one reports had been forwarded to Congress in accordance with the procedures of the War Powers Resolution. President Richard Nixon did not submit any reports in his brief time in office after the enactment of the resolution. President Gerald Ford submitted four reports to Congress under the resolution: one for the evacuation of Vietnam refugees from Da Nang in early April 1975; another for the evacuation from Cambodia in mid-April 1975; a third for the evacuation from Saigon at the end of April 1975; and a fourth over the use of force to free the crew of the *Mayaguez* in May 1975. President Jimmy Carter sent up one report in April 1980, after the abortive attempt to rescue the American hostages in Iran.

Until the Clinton administration, the most frequent reporting had been done by President Ronald Reagan. Fourteen different reports were sent by President Reagan, including American participation in the Multinational Force and Observers (MFO) in the Sinai Peninsula in accordance with the Egyptian-Israeli Peace Treaty, the deployment of American forces to Lebanon on three different occasions, the dispatch of two Airborne Warning and Control Systems (AWACS) planes and other aircraft to Sudan, and the deployment of 1,900 members of the United States Army and Marines, supplemented with Navy and Air Force personnel to the Caribbean island of Grenada in October 1983.[25] Among other reports sent to Congress were ones outlining the use of American military forces in the attack upon Libya in retaliation for a Libyan-sponsored terrorist attack against Americans, the United States attack on Iranian vessels in the Persian Gulf, and the United States attack upon an Iranian airliner, also in the Persian Gulf.[26]

President Bush filed seven reports to Congress during his term in office. The first was on the occasion of providing United States air patrol support in December 1989 to the Corazon Aquino government in the Philippines to assist her in restoring order and in protecting the lives of American citizens. The second occurred after his sending of 25,000 American forces to invade Panama and to capture General Manuel Noriega in December 1989. The third took place in August 1990, when the United States sent a reinforced rifle company to Liberia to provide increased security at the United States Embassy in that country.[27] The fourth was his report to Congress in

August 1990 after his ordering of American forces into Saudi Arabia after the seizure of Kuwait by Iraq.[28] The fifth and sixth reports by the Bush administration also dealt with Iraq, one without mention of the War Powers Resolution and another with explicit mention of it. The final report by the Bush administration was a report on the deployment of United States armed forces into Somalia on a humanitarian mission to aid with the distribution of food supplies to needy Somalians.

The Clinton administration submitted twenty-five reports through early 1996, the most by any president since passage of the resolution.[29] These reports dealt with military deployments or use of force in Bosnia-Herzegovina—first to enforce the UN embargo and then the Dayton Accords through the Implementation Force (IFOR) ordered by NATO—but they also dealt with the sending of forces to Macedonia to deter Serb expansion there, the bombing attack on Iraq in retaliation for the reported unsuccessful assassination attempt against former President Bush in Kuwait, military actions in Somalia and Haiti (including the intervention of some 20,000 American soldiers in that country), and the use of United States military forces in Burundi to evacuate American forces from Rwanda. Chronology 8.1 summarizes presidential reporting to Congress consistent with the War Powers Resolution since the Ford administration.

CHRONOLOGY 8.1

The War Powers Resolution and Presidential Reports to Congress

Ford Administration (1974–1977)

April 4, 1975—Evacuation of Americans and other nationals from Da Nang to "safer areas" of Vietnam.

April 12, 1975—Evacuation of American personnel and other nationals from Cambodia.

April 30, 1975—Evacuation of Americans and other nationals from Vietnam.

May 15, 1975—American military action over the seizure of the American merchant vessel, *Mayaquez*, by Cambodian forces.

Carter Administration (1977–1981)

April 26, 1980—American military action over the abortive rescue attempt of American hostages in Iran.

Reagan Administration (1981–1989)

March 19, 1982—American military participation in the Multinational Force and Observers in the Sinai Peninsula to implement the Peace Treaty between Egypt and Israel.

August 24, 1982—American military forces to Lebanon to assist in the evacuation of the Palestine Liberation Organization.

September 29, 1982—American military forces to Lebanon as part of the Multinational Force.

August 8, 1983—Dispatch of AWACS and F-15 aircraft to Sudan for use in coordination with the government of Chad.

August 30, 1983—Further report on the American forces in Lebanon, including the death of two U.S. Marines.

October 25, 1983—Deployment of American military personnel to Grenada.

March 26, 1986—U.S. use of missiles against Libyan forces after an attack in the Gulf of Sidra.

CHRONOLOGY 8.1

The War Powers Resolution and Presidential Reports to Congress (continued)

April 16, 1986—U.S. air and naval strikes upon Libya in response to terrorist activities against Americans.
September 23, 1987—U.S. helicopter attack on an Iranian landing craft after it was seen laying mines in the Persian Gulf.
October 10, 1987—U.S. helicopter attack on Iranian naval vessels after being fired upon.
October 20, 1987—U.S. attack upon an Iranian offshore oil platform in the Persian Gulf after an Iranian silkworm missile attack against a U.S.-flagged tanker.
April 19, 1988—U.S. destruction of two Iranian offshore oil platforms and an attack on Iranian vessels in the Persian Gulf after the USS *Samuel B. Roberts* had hit a mine laid by Iran.
July 4, 1988—After the USS *Vincennes* and USS *Elmer Montgomery* fired upon two Iranian vessels in the Persian Gulf, and the *Vincennes* shot down an Iranian airliner, believing it to be a military aircraft.
July 14, 1988—Following the firing upon two Iranian vessels in the Persian Gulf by American helicopters after an attack.

Bush Administration (1989–1993)
December 2, 1989—The use of American combat air patrols in the Philippines to assist the government of Corazon Aquino in restoring order and protecting American lives.
December 21, 1989—The deployment of 11,000 U.S. forces to Panama for the purpose of protecting American lives, defending democracy, apprehending Manuel Noriega, and maintaining the Panama Canal Treaties.
August 6, 1990—The deployment of a reinforced rifle company and helicopter teams to Liberia for the purpose of evacuating American citizens from that country.
August 9, 1990—The deployment of American forces to Saudi Arabia to protect that nation after Iraq had seized Kuwait.
November 16, 1990—The enlargement of the U.S. deployment in the Persian Gulf region to secure "an adequate offensive military option" against Iraq.
January 18, 1991—The commencement of combat operations against Iraqi forces in both Kuwait and Iraq.
December 10, 1992—The deployment of American forces into Somalia on a humanitarian mission pursuant to a UN Security Council resolution.

Clinton Administration (1993–)
April 13, 1993—American forces taking part in NATO air operations over Bosnia to enforce the United Nations "no-fly zone."
June 10, 1993—The American Quick Reaction Force used in Somalia to respond to attacks upon U.N. forces in that country.
June 28, 1993—Launching of American naval vessels missile attacks against the Iraqi Intelligence headquarters in retaliation over its attempt to assassinate President Bush earlier in 1993.
July 9, 1993—The deployment of 350 American armed forces to Macedonia in the former Yugoslavia to assist in the maintenance of stability in the area.
October 18, 1993—A second report to the April 13, 1993 communication on U.S. activities in Bosnia.
October 20, 1993—Action taken by American ships to enforce the embargo imposed by the United Nations against Haiti.
January 8, 1994—A second report to the July 9, 1993 communication on U.S. involvement in Macedonia.

continued on next page

CHRONOLOGY 8.1

The War Powers Resolution and Presidential Reports to Congress (continued)

February 17, 1994—Expanded participation by the United States in the efforts by the United Nations and NATO to find a peaceful settlement in the former Yugoslavia with sixty American aircraft now committed to NATO operations.

March 1, 1994—Four Serbian planes shot down by American aircraft as part of American activity to enforce the "no-fly zone" in the former Yugoslavia.

April 12, 1994—Bosnian Serb forces shelled by American aircraft in the city of Gorazde in Bosnia-Herzegovina.

April 12, 1994—American combat-equipped forces sent to Burundi in southern Africa to assist in possible evaluation efforts of Americans and others fleeing the ethnic fighting in Rwanda.

April 19, 1994—An additional American contingent numbering 200 personnel sent to Macedonia in the former Yugoslavia.

April 20, 1994—American naval forces around Haiti continued to enforce the UN embargo and had boarded 712 vessels.

August 22, 1994—American planes under NATO command had attacked Serbian heavy weapons in the negotiated exclusion zone around Sarajevo.

September 21, 1994—The United States deployed 1500 American military personnel to Haiti in an effort to restore democracy.

November 22, 1994—American planes attacked bases used by Serbs around the city of Bihac in northwest Bosnia-Herzegovina.

December 22, 1994—The American soldiers presently in Macedonia to be replaced shortly by about 500 soldiers from an American contingent in Germany.

March 1, 1995—The deployment of 1,800 combat-equipped American forces into Somalia to aid in the withdrawal of UN personnel from Somalia.

March 21, 1995—A follow-up report to the one on September 21, 1994, concerning American military forces in Haiti.

May 24, 1995—A follow-up report to the ones on November 22, 1994, and December 22, 1994, regarding the use of American forces in Bosnia and Macedonia in the former Yugoslavia.

Continuing Controversies

Despite these reports, Congress has been dissatisfied with the level and depth of executive notification. Since the passage of the resolution, none of the six presidents has fully complied with it, and each president has viewed the resolution as unconstitutional. Further, several controversies continue to surround its operation.

Failing to Comply Fully. Executive reservations about the resolution are evident by the fact that presidents carefully phrase their congressional reports and do not fully comply with the resolution's requirements. In virtually every report that the six presidents have sent forward, they have used the same language. They are providing the report "in accordance with my desire that Congress be fully informed on this matter, and consistent with the War Powers Resolution."[30] In none of the reports, however, do the presidents acknowledge that they were *complying* with the War Powers Resolution. Indeed, only in his report on the *Mayaquez* incident in 1975 did President Ford cite the operative section [section 4 (a)(1)] of the resolution

CHRONOLOGY 8.1

The War Powers Resolution and Presidential Reports to Congress (continued)

September 1, 1995—American aircraft in support of UN and NATO operations in Bosnia launched a series of air strikes against Bosnian Serb forces around Sarajevo, Tuzla, Gorazde, and Mostar in Bosnia.
September 21, 1995—The United States now has 2,400 military personnel deployed in Haiti as part of the UN Mission in Haiti (UNMIH). The U.S. Support Group Haiti has an additional 260 American military personnel.
December 6, 1995—The Clinton administration notified Congress that "1,500 U.S. military personnel" had been deployed "to Bosnia and Herzegovina and Croatia as part of a NATO 'enabling force' to lay the groundwork for the prompt and safe deployment of the NATO-led Implementation Force (IFOR)." Another 3,000 American military personnel had been deployed to Hungary, Italy, and Croatia to assist in creating appropriate infrastructure for these forces.
December 21, 1995—The Clinton administration reported that about 20,000 American military personnel had been deployed to Bosnia-Herzegovina as part of IFOR, and that about 5,000 additional forces had been deployed elsewhere in the former Yugoslavia, mainly in Croatia. Another 7,000 U.S. military personnel would be sent to Hungary, Italy, and Croatia and other states in the region to support the IFOR operation.
March 21, 1996—The Clinton administration reported a "phased reduction" in American military personnel who where part of the United Nations Mission in Haiti (UNMIH). The remaining number of military (309), however, were "equipped for combat."

Sources: Compiled by the author from reports in "War Powers Resolution," *Hearings,* Committee on Foreign Relations, United States Senate, 95th Cong., July 13–15, 1977, 332–337; *The War Powers Resolution: Relevant Documents, Correspondence, Reports,* Subcommittee on International Security and Scientific Affairs of the House Committee on Foreign Affairs, December, 1983, 40–66, 84–85; Ellen C. Collier, "War Powers Resolution: Presidential Compliance," Congressional Research Service Issue Brief, April 25, 1989, and February 16, 1990; Ellen C. Collier, *The War Powers Resolution: Twenty Years of Experience* (Washington, DC: Congressional Research Service, the Library of Congress, January 11, 1994); Richard F. Grimmett, "War Powers Resolution: Presidential Compliance," Congressional Research Service Issue Brief, July 11, 1995, and June 12, 1996, update; and *Weekly Compilation of Presidential Documents,* Volume 25, December 25, 1989, 1984–1985, Vol. 26, August 13, 1990, 1225–1226, Vol. 31, March 6, 1995, 338, March 27, 1995, 452–453, May 29, 1995, 898–900, and September 11, 1995, 1473–1474.

(and, hence, acknowledge the authority of the resolution), although he did so only after the military conflict had ceased. In another case, President Reagan cited "section 4 (a) (2) of the War Powers Resolution," in reporting on the deployment of American military personnel sent into the Sinai Desert for peacekeeping purposes between Israel and Egypt, but that section of the resolution does not require limiting the deployment to only sixty days.[31] Further, in a few presidential reports to Congress (e.g., President Bush's report on sending a reinforced rifle company to Liberia, and President Clinton's report on the use of American air power against Bosnian Serb forces in August 1994), no specific reference was actually made to the War Powers Resolution.

Failing to Report. Beyond the kind of reporting by presidents, the failure to report some instances at all has also weakened the impact of the resolution. Critics charged, for instance, that President Richard Nixon failed to report to Congress when U.S. forces were used to evacuate Americans from Cyprus during the ethnic conflict on that island nation in 1974. President Jimmy Carter raised the ire of Representative Paul Findley for his failure to report to Congress after placing some American forces on alert and for sending U.S. transport aircraft to Zaire (now Congo) during secessionist activities in that country in May 1978.[32]

In the early 1980s, President Reagan became embroiled in controversy with Congress over the applicability of the War Powers Resolution in two different areas of the world: Central America and the Middle East. After President Reagan indicated in early 1981 that he was going to increase the number of American military advisors in El Salvador, questions were raised over whether the War Powers procedures needed to be invoked. Congressman Clement Zablocki, chairman of the House Foreign Affairs Committee at the time, sought clarification from Secretary of State Alexander Haig.[33]The executive's position was that these U.S. military personnel were not being introduced into hostilities, nor were they in a situation where "imminent hostilities might occur," as the War Powers Resolution required. Until such circumstances prevailed, the resolution did not apply.[34]

A similar situation arose over the applicability of the War Powers Resolution to American involvement in Lebanon. President Reagan's position had been that American forces, first dispatched there in 1982, were on a "peacekeeping mission" at the request of the Lebanese government and that they were neither involved in hostilities nor in any immediate danger. By the fall of 1983, however, Congress was unwilling to accept that position, especially after two Marines were killed on August 29, 1983. Instead, Congress sought to start the sixty-day clock under the War Powers Resolution. To head off this time limit on American forces in Lebanon, President Reagan proceeded to work out a compromise agreement over the United States military presence in Lebanon. The resulting legislation, the Multinational Force in Lebanon Resolution (October 1983), authorized the president to use American forces in Lebanon for eighteen months. For the first time, however, Congress had specifically imposed the requirements of the War Powers Resolution upon the president (as of August 29, 1983).

In President Reagan's second term and President Bush's single term, some episodes that appeared to be covered by the War Powers Resolution were also not reported to Congress. The Reagan administration, for instance, did not report to Congress on the United States Navy's interception of an Egyptian airliner carrying the hijackers of the *Achille Lauro* in 1985 or on the sending of American Army assistance to the Bolivian government in antidrug efforts in 1986. President Bush failed to report to Congress on sending American military advisors in the Andean countries of Colombia, Bolivia, and Peru as part of a new antidrug strategy and did not report the American efforts to convey Belgian troops into Zaire during September 1991.[35]

Although President Clinton has reported more frequently than other presidents since the passage of the War Powers Resolution, he has also been embroiled in considerable debate over the introduction of American forces in several different ways—UN peacekeeping operations generally, and Somalia, Haiti, and Bosnia, in particular. Both the Democratic-controlled Congress in 1993–1994 (the 103rd) and the Republican-controlled Congress in 1995–1996 (the 104th) have sought to restrict the use of American forces in UN operations through legislative initiatives. For the most part, these initiatives did not succeed, but, in October 1993, Congress passed legislation ending America's involvement in Somalia by March 31, 1994. In turn, this action (and the events in Somalia) pressured the Clinton administration to issue a new executive directive (Presidential Directive 25), restricting American involvement in such missions in the future (see Chapter 6). Throughout 1993 and 1994, though, Congress sought through various measures (amendments to legislation and sense of the House or Senate resolutions) to stop the deployment of American troops to Haiti or Bosnia, or at least to require prior congressional approval.[36] While the Clinton administration undoubtedly provided greater reporting in response to these congressional pressures, it continued to resist any limits on its perceived constitutional authority.

Failing to Consult. The "prior consultation" requirement has caused even greater difficulty between Congress and the executive branch. Members of Congress have generally held that the president has not really "consulted" with them before using American military forces, but that he has often merely "informed" them of his intended action.[37] The executive branch, on the other hand, has insisted that it has generally consulted with Congress and has kept Congress informed of its action.

The evidence is, at best, mixed based upon the limited instances available. President Ford, for example, "advised" members of the congressional leadership on his plans for the evacuation from Southeast Asia in 1975; President Reagan held a meeting with congressional leaders before the actual invasion of Grenada in 1983, but after he had signed the order; and President Reagan also met with congressional leaders after ordering the air strike against Libya in 1986, although, again, after he had directed it to be carried out; and President Bush met with congressional leaders seven hours before the invasion of Panama was to begin and informed them of his decision.[38]

In other instances, when presidents have chosen not to consult with Congress, they have defended their actions by pointing to the need for secrecy in carrying out the operation, the limited time available for consultation, and the inherent presidential power to act. When President Jimmy Carter, for instance, was confronted by Congress over his failure to consult prior to the Iran rescue mission in 1980, his legal counsel offered this staunch defense of presidential authority:

> His inherent constitutional power to conduct this kind of rescue operation, which depends on total surprise, includes the power to act before consulting Congress, if the President concludes, as he did in this case, that to do so would unreasonably endanger the success of the operation and the safety of those to be rescued.[39]

In 1989, when President Bush failed to consult Congress over his use of American aircraft to assist Corazon Aquino's government in the Philippines in avoiding an insurrection, his national security advisor, Brent Scowcroft, defended his action by stating:

> ...I can assure you that the President is committed to consultations with Congress prior to deployments of U.S. Forces into actual or imminent hostilities in all instances where such consultations are possible. In this instance, the nature of the rapidly evolving situation required an extremely rapid decision very late at night and consultation was simply not an option.[40]

Inadequate prior consultation has also characterized the Clinton administration. Although President Clinton has acknowledged that he has "a big responsibility to try to appropriately consult with members of Congress in both parties in a wide way whenever we are in the process of making a decision which might lead to the use of force," he also asserted that "I think that, clearly, the Constitution leaves to the President, for good and sufficient reasons, the ultimate decision-making authority."[41]

With the intervention into Haiti in September 1994, for example, the Clinton administration did little to consult with Congress prior to this action and subsequently acknowledged that it adopted a strategy that was not likely to allow congressional action. Instead, the strategy, according to one executive branch official, was "to get as much positive impact as we could without opening a debate that would be harmful, not helpful."[42] As if to highlight the lack of prior consultation, moreover, Congress passed a joint resolution in October 1994, stating that the President should have sought Congress's approval before deploying American troops in Haiti.[43]

With the air action over Bosnia by American forces, too, the Clinton administration generally acted and then informed Congress. In early April 1993, for example, the first American action in Bosnia was promptly reported to Congress, but consultation with "about two dozen congressional leaders on potential future action" took another two weeks for the administration.[44] By the fall of 1993, Congress was threatening to limit further American deployment in the former Yugoslavia without the prior approval of Congress. The administration sought to stop this action by promising to consult with Congress, although the extent of consultation was never made clear.[45] In August and September 1995 as the United States used its air power against the Bosnian Serbs to prod them toward the peace table, Congress was not consulted. Overall, then, the consultation on the use of American military power has remained haphazard or has been lacking by the Clinton administration.

In addition to the problem of eliciting presidential cooperation in the consultative process, several questions remain about the process itself. Three, in particular, are crucial.[46] First, when should consultation take place? That is, what kind of situations require discussions with Congress? Since the War Powers Resolution does not spell out all such circumstances, ambiguity remains. Second, what actions by the executive constitute consultation? Is informing or meeting with members of Congress on a presidential decision sufficient? Or does the course of action still need to be in doubt to justify full consultation? Third, with whom should the executive branch consult? Is consultation (in whatever meaning) with the congressional leadership sufficient? Or should only certain foreign policy committees be involved in the process? Congress and the executive have differing views on these items, and they have yet to be resolved.

Recent Events and the War Powers Resolution

While the War Powers Resolution has hardly been without controversy since its passage, several recent foreign policy episodes have sharply rekindled the debate over its utility and practicality for managing congressional–executive relations in this area. The first, the Persian Gulf War during the Bush administration, seemingly enhanced the standing of Congress when President Bush sought congressional approval to use American forces against Iraq over its invasion of Kuwait. Three other events—the use of American forces in Somalia, Haiti and Bosnia—did not advance the congressional role; they actually contributed to an unsuccessful effort in the United States House of Representatives simply to repeal the resolution.

The Gulf War. Although President Bush reported to Congress regarding his August 1990 decision to send American forces to Saudi Arabia to protect that country from possible Iraqi aggression after the seizure of Kuwait, he failed to acknowledge compliance with the War Powers Resolution or even its applicability to the situation. Initially, members of Congress did not object and did not take any action to start the sixty-day clock under the War Powers Resolution.

In November 1990, however, when President Bush announced that he was enlarging the American presence in the Persian Gulf to include an "offensive capability" against Iraq, congressional clamor began. Several members of Congress complained that the president needed to seek congressional authorization if he contemplated going to war. Calls were heard from both Republicans and Democrats that Congress should come back into a special session after the election to take up this issue. The president denied that any authorization was necessary and insisted that he had the necessary presidential powers. Indeed, some congressional leaders were willing to wait for a presidential request and until the new Congress was seated.[47]

The clamor did not stop, however. Opinion pieces appeared in elite newspapers challenging the president's interpretation of his powers. Public opinion polls indicated that the president ought to seek congressional support. Eventually, fifty-four members of Congress filed a suit in district court claiming that the president needed congressional authorization to use force, and hearings were held in the House and Senate Armed Services Committee, the Senate Foreign Relations Committee, and the House Foreign Affairs Committee, debating the wisdom of continuing sanctions against Iraq or going to war.

Adding further fuel to the issue between Congress and the president was the fact that the Bush administration had asked—and received—authorization from the United Nations Security Council to use force against Iraq, if necessary. UN Security Council Resolution 678, passed on November 29, 1990, authorized member states "to use all necessary means to uphold and implement" the previously passed resolutions calling for Iraq to leave Kuwait after January 15, 1991.[48] By contrast, no such request was made of Congress.

Finally, in early January 1991, President Bush changed his mind, after he sensed that his request would be successful in Congress, and sought legislative authorization.[49] After a soul-searching debate in both chambers, the House voted by a margin of 250-183 and the Senate by a margin of 52-47 to grant such authorization. More specifically, the "Authorization for Use of Military Force Against Iraq Resolution" endorsed the president's decision to use United States military forces to implement the UN Security Council resolutions regarding occupied Kuwait, if all diplomatic and peaceful means had been exhausted by the United States government. The measure made specific mention of the War Powers Resolution by noting that this Iraqi resolution constituted a specific statutory authorization as prescribed in the act and that it "supersedes any requirement of the War Powers Resolution."[50] The resolution required the president to report to Congress every sixty days on whether Iraq was complying with the applicable UN Security Council resolutions. While the resolution did not declare war explicitly, it was the functional equivalent because the president could use force if all the stipulations had been met.

To proponents of congressional prerogatives in foreign policy, then, the very act of the president's requesting congressional authorization was significant. It acknowledged the role of Congress in the use of force abroad, and it might establish a precedent for future American involvements. Further, the president's signing of this authorization, with the explicit references to the War Powers Resolution incorporated into it, was also significant. Since all presidents had denied its constitutionality,[51] President Bush's signing of the Iraqi resolution without challenging this section was a glimmer of hope that the War Powers Resolution may have come to assume some legitimacy.

Somalia, Haiti, and Bosnia. Any hopes that the War Powers Resolution had gained any new standing with the executive branch, however, were quickly dashed with American military involvement in Somalia, Haiti, and Bosnia. In each instance, Presidents Bush and Clinton reverted to a more familiar pattern since the resolution's passage in 1973. In the case of Somalia, when the United States (and United Nations) humanitarian and peacebuilding situation deteriorated in the summer and fall of 1993, Congress had to reassert its own prerogatives toward that country, since the Resolution had not served as a deterrent to sustained involvement. In this sense, the relative power of the resolution was diminished. As noted earlier, Congress did succeed, however, by adding an amendment to a defense appropriations bill, requiring the ending of American involvement in Somalia by March 31, 1994. While that amendment has been portrayed by one analyst as supporting the president's wishes on Somalia,[52] it also reflected Congress's resolve to more fully manage the sending of American forces abroad, even outside the War Powers Resolution.

In the case of Haiti in the fall of 1993 and 1994, Congress again attempted to restrict the Clinton administration's military options when the perception was that American forces were going to be sent there to restore democracy without prior congressional involvement. As one might expect, the White House strongly opposed such action. Yet the Senate passed a nonbinding resolution by a vote of 100–0 opposing the sending of United

States forces to Haiti and entertained stronger measures as well. Such an action seemingly had little effect, since the Clinton administration initially deployed some 2,000 American troops to Haiti in mid-September 1994 and the force was expected to grow to 15,000 from twenty-five nations shortly thereafter.[53] While reporting occurred under the War Powers Resolution, the report sent forward was informational ("informing the Congress" once again), and the consultation was minimal, as we noted earlier.

In the case of Bosnia, congressional frustration over the Resolution was heightened even further. During the summer of 1995, the Senate and the House passed a measure to lift the arms embargo, but the Senate also sought to restrict the conditions for the use of American forces in that troubled country to only assisting in extracting UN peacekeepers, and then only under particular circumstances.[54] President Clinton vetoed the measure, but then he later reversed his administration's policy somewhat by deciding to use American air power as part of a NATO response to an apparent Bosnian Serbs rocket attack on Sarajevo, the capital of Bosnia. Moreover, the NATO effort continued for several days and began to bring about some movement toward negotiations among the parties. By late 1995, as peace prospects brightened a bit, a new debate emerged between Congress and the president over sending American soldiers to enforce any peace settlement.

Once the Dayton peace accords were initialed in November and then formally signed in December 1995, the Clinton administration had fully committed American troops as part of that arrangement, despite congressional opposition. By then, Congress was unwilling to withdraw support from the military. As a result, the House and Senate could do little but pass a resolution supporting the troops, even as they opposed the overall Clinton administration policy. The episode illustrated once again the difficulty of making the War Powers Resolution operate effectively. Indeed, throughout the congressional debate on Bosnia, there was virtually little discussion of the resolution itself.

Reforming or Repealing the War Powers Resolution?

While such controversies continue to fuel the war powers debate into the 1990s, a larger, lingering question concerns the constitutionality of the resolution, in whole or part. In his veto message back in 1973, President Nixon questioned the constitutionality of that portion of the War Powers Resolution dealing with the withdrawal of troops prior to the sixty-day limitation through the use of a concurrent resolution and the imposition of a sixty-day limit on the use of such troops. In the *Chadha* decision (see Chapter 7), the Supreme Court seemingly resolved part of this question by invalidating the use of the concurrent resolution, or the "legislative veto," by Congress. Indeed, Congress acknowledged as much by passing legislation in late 1983 now requiring a joint resolution for any withdrawal of troops prior to the sixty-day period.[55] (A joint resolution differs from a concurrent resolution in that it requires the approval of a majority of both Houses of Congress *and* the president, while the concurrent resolution requires only majorities within Congress.) The constitutionality of the time limit, identified by the executive branch as a challenge to presidential powers in foreign affairs, has yet to be resolved by the Court or even to be directly challenged there. Yet, it remains a major reason why every president since Nixon has challenged the constitutionality of the entire resolution.[56]

Although some recommendations have been made to change the resolution to resolve these and other concerns, no effort has been successful. Numerous proposals were offered in 1988, for example, and extensive hearings were held in the House and the Senate, sparked by the use of American force in the Persian Gulf in 1987–1988. Some proposed the repeal of the resolution, others suggested strengthening the consultation procedures, and still others would have dropped the sixty-day limitation on the use of force and required an affirmative congressional vote on the use of force by the president.[57]

In June 1995, this frustration reached a peak when the House of Representatives voted on a repeal of the resolution. By a narrow margin (217-201), the House voted not to repeal the measure. Despite frustration over the resolution and the increasing belief of many members that the president should have a freer hand in the conduct of foreign policy, a sufficient number of representatives did not want to go quite that far. With the troubling situation in Bosnia still at hand, a conservative Republican member was reluctant to give the president a freer hand toward that problem ("The deepening crisis in the Balkans may lead us at some point to invoke the War Powers," he declared). Yet this member was also concerned about preserving congressional prerogatives, as weak as this measure had proved to be ("Every President finds Congress inconvenient. But we're a democracy, not a monarchy"). Another moderate Democratic member relied upon the constitutional argument more directly in defending the resolution: "The core principle behind War Powers is that sending troops abroad requires the sound collective judgment of the president and the Congress. I do not think that principle should be abandoned."[58] In sum, barring a real constitutional crisis in which the executive fails to comply in any fashion with the resolution over a sustained period of time, the prospects for significant reform or full repeal seem slim.

Yet, in a broader sense, and despite the unhappiness over presidential compliance, the War Powers Resolution seems to have served at least some of its original purposes: It has generally limited the executive branch's use of military force without involving Congress *in some fashion*; it has prevented long-term military involvements by the executive (such as the Vietnam War had been); and, perhaps more importantly, it probably has made the president more circumspect and cautious in his foreign military actions than before the resolution's enactment in 1973. Finally, although a counterfactual by definition cannot be demonstrated empirically, it has probably prevented the use of American ground forces by the president in some instances (e.g., in Central America during the 1980s).

CONTROLLING THE PURSE STRINGS

A third area of congressional response to executive power has been to use its funding power (the "purse strings") to reduce executive discretion and to increase congressional direction of American foreign policy. Legislative funding provisions were used in the 1970s and 1980s to achieve a variety of broad foreign policy objectives: (1) to reduce American military involvement abroad, (2) to cut off covert actions in the Third World, (3) to allow congressional review of the sale of weapons and the transference of nuclear fuels to other countries, (4) to specify the trading relations with other nations, and (5) to limit the transfer of American economic and military assistance to countries with gross violations of human rights, among other things. In several instances, specific countries were identified by Congress and restrictions imposed upon them as a means of shaping foreign policy. Specific human rights restrictions were applied to the transfer of military assistance to El Salvador, for example, and, for a time, Congress cut off all funding for the Nicaraguan Contras as a means of changing the Reagan administration's policy toward that country. "Earmarking" of foreign assistance funds, too, became a particularly popular mechanism as Congress has sought to affect foreign affairs.

Most of these measures, moreover, continue in use during the 1990s. And the power of the purse remained a potent one as long-time Democratic chairman of the Senate Appropriations Committee, Senator Robert Byrd (D-West Virginia) reminded the Clinton administration in October 1995 hearings over the prospect of sending American forces into Bosnia: "It's very important for the President to seek approval of Congress. The title of Commander in Chief is one thing. But the power of the purse is the greatest power in our Constitutional system."[59]

Cutting Off and Conditioning Funding

First of all, Congress has sometimes used (or tried to use) a blunt instrument to shape policy: The elimination of funds for foreign policy actions that it opposed. From 1966 to 1973, Congress cast ninety-four roll calls on questions relating to American involvement in Southeast Asia,[60] but only a few of these votes succeeded in changing American policy. Senator Frank Church (D-Idaho) was able to get a defense appropriation bill amended to bar the "introduction of U.S. ground combat troops into Laos or Thailand" in 1969, and he, along with Senator John Sherman Cooper (R-Kentucky), was also able to get an amendment passed to bar "U.S. military operations in Cambodia after July 1, 1970." Other congressional efforts to cut off funding during the height of the Vietnam War failed in either the House or the Senate or both bodies. By 1973, however, the situation had changed, and Congress succeeded in passing a sweeping measure that stopped funding as of August 15, 1973, for military activities "in or over or from off the shores of North Vietnam, South Vietnam, Laos, or Cambodia."[61] Later, in 1975, when President Ford asked Congress to approve new assistance to Vietnam shortly before its fall, Congress refused.[62]

Spurred by these efforts of using funding measures to shape policy in Vietnam, Congress enacted some other funding restrictions. In 1975, Congress cut off military and economic aid to Turkey because of its invasion of Cyprus earlier in that year.[63] (In that invasion, Turkey had used American-supplied weapons in violation of statutory requirements that they not be used for offensive purposes.) In 1976, Congress attached the Clark Amendment to the Arms Export Control Act.[64] This amendment prohibited American assistance to any group involved in the Angolan civil war.

In the 1980s, Congress continued to use the funding mechanism, but now with a more nuanced approach to policy: Congress placed restrictions or conditions on the use or continuance of funding. A few illustrations will make this point. In 1981, for example, Congress attached a human rights reporting requirement to the International Security and Development Cooperation Act of 1981 as a condition for continued military assistance to El Salvador.[65] Under the provisions of that law, every six months the executive was required to certify that progress was being made in that country toward improving human rights, continuing social and economic reform, and creating democratic political institutions. In 1983, Congress succeeded in placing one further restriction on military aid to El Salvador: Thirty percent of all military aid for fiscal 1984 (about $19.5 million) would be withheld until those accused of murdering four U.S. churchwomen, in December 1980, were brought to trial and a verdict rendered.[66]

In the other prominent attempt to guide American foreign policy in Central America during this period, Congress relied upon a combination of conditioning aid and cutting it off. From 1982 to 1986, Congress passed a series of Boland Amendments (named after Edward Boland [D-Massachusetts], chair of the House Intelligence Committee at the time) to first restrict and then prevent the Reagan administration from aiding the Nicaraguan Contras, who were fighting the Sandinista government at the time. Attached to defense appropriation bills and government "continuing resolutions," each of the three amendments became increasingly restrictive in specifying how funds could be used by the executive branch in assisting the Contras, eventually cutting off military aid entirely for a two-year time span before restoring it in 1986. As the Iran-Contra investigation was to reveal (see Chapters 5 and 10), however, violations of the Boland restrictions had already taken place during the two-year period (1984–1986) when no military assistance to the Contras was allowed.

In the 1990s, Congress had continued to use the funding mechanism to shape policy and the policy process. In recent authorization bills for foreign assistance and for the State Department, the House of Representatives has sought to reshape the foreign policy bureaucracies (e.g., by consolidating three former independent agencies, the Arms Control and Disarmament Agency, the United States Information Agency, and the Agency for International Development within the Department of State) and by making cuts in foreign assistance and by eliminating some programs.[67] More generally, the level of funding for the foreign policy account within the United States government budget has decreased dramatically and serves as an important measure of policy influence. Near the end of his time as secretary of state in October 1996, Warren Christopher bemoaned the fact that congressional support for international affairs spending had declined by 51 percent since 1984, after taking account of inflation, and that now such spending constituted only 1.2 percent of the federal budget.[68] Furthermore, since 1993, the support for diplomatic activities by the United States dropped about 16 percent.[69] By such funding decisions, Congress has indeed affected American foreign policy and indicated its policy disputes with the executive branch.

Earmarking of Funds

Congress may also shape foreign policy more specifically through earmarking for particular purposes. Legislation designating funds for specific regional or functional programs (e.g., African Development Foundation, refugee assistance programs) would qualify as earmarks, as would prohibition on the use of funds for particular countries (e.g., Zaire [now Congo] was excluded from Economic Support Fund moneys for fiscal year 1995, and Zaire, Sudan, Liberia, Guatemala, and Peru were prohibited from receiving military assistance funding under a provision of the Arms Export Control Act in the same year).[70] Yet, the more common use of the term refers to "specific amounts of foreign aid for individual countries."[71]

The data in Table 8.2 illustrate countries that received earmarked amounts of foreign assistance during fiscal year 1996. Israel and Egypt continue to be the principal beneficiaries of these earmarks, as they have for over a decade now, and two strategically important countries, Greece and Turkey, do as well. Interestingly, some former republics of the Soviet Union have now been earmarked for United States economic assistance, and other countries with political problems such as the former Yugoslavia, Burma, Cyprus, and Ireland also receive some designated aid, largely as part of incentives for maintaining or securing peace in those areas. While earmarks have their critics in that they restrict executive discretion and place a certain rigidity into the foreign assistance program, their defenders point to this

TABLE 8.2

Some Earmarked Foreign Assistance Funds by Country in Fiscal Year 1996

	Economic Aid	Military Aid
Israel	$1.2 billion	$1.8 billion
Egypt	$815 million	$1.3 billion
Turkey	$33.5 million	$320 million
Greece		$224 million
Former Yugoslavia	$40 million	
Ireland	$20 million	
Ukraine	$225 million	
Armenia	$85 million	
Cyprus	$15 million	
Burma	$2.38 million	

Source: Taken from P.L. 104-107, February 12, 1996.

mechanism as an important, and perhaps a principal, way for Congress to shape foreign policy.

Specifying Trade and Aid Requirements

By the 1970s and continuing into the 1980s, Congress sought other vehicles to ensure greater legislative participation in United States foreign policy. Trade and foreign aid legislation proved to be readily available mechanisms. Increasingly, Congress sought to add amendments to both kinds of legislation in order to work its will in foreign policy making. Amendments to important bills serve to illustrate this kind of action.

To the Trade Act of 1974, Congress added two important sections: the Jackson-Vanik and Stevenson amendments.[72] The Jackson-Vanik Amendment, named after Congressman Charles Vanik (D-Ohio) and Senator Henry Jackson (D-Washington), provided that the United States could grant most-favored-nation (MFN) status only to those countries that fostered a free emigration policy and did not impose "more than a nominal tax" on citizens wishing to emigrate. Without mentioning any country by name, the clear intent of the amendment was to prohibit the Soviet Union from gaining that status. The action proved successful, inasmuch as the Soviet Union rejected this provision as an intrusion on its national sovereignty. The Stevenson Amendment, sponsored by Senator Adlai Stevenson (D-Illinois), was a more direct affront to the Soviet Union. By limiting the amount of credit available to the Soviet Union from the United States to no more than $300 million this amendment effectively reduced the potential for expanded trade between the two countries. Once again, congressional restrictions were proving very important to shaping American policy, and particularly to the emerging detente relationship between the United States and the Soviet Union.

To the 1974 Foreign Assistance Act, Congress passed the Nelson-Bingham Amendment.[73] Under this amendment, introduced by Senator Gaylord Nelson (D-Wisconsin) and Congressman Jonathan Bingham (D-New York), Congress had the right to review for twenty days any intended arms sale of $25 million or more. Moreover, Congress reserved the right to reject such a sale by passing a concurrent resolution of disapproval. In the International Security Assistance and Arms Export Control Act of 1976, this provision was modified to allow congressional review of any offer to sell defense articles or services totaling $25 million or more, or any major defense equipment of $7 million or more.[74] The time limit for congressional review was extended from twenty to thirty days. The right of Congress to reject such a sale by concurrent resolution was maintained. By a "gentleman's agreement," in the words of *Congressional Quarterly Almanac*, the Ford administration agreed to an additional twenty-day period of "informal notification"—a policy that has been continued by the Carter, Reagan, Bush, and Clinton administrations.[75]

In the same security assistance legislation (and in earlier legislation on economic assistance), Congress added human rights considerations in dealing with other countries.[76] Neither security assistance nor economic assistance would be granted to those nations whose government "engages in a consistent pattern of gross violations if internationally recognized human rights." Similar provisions were added to United States funding for the multilateral banks, such as the World Bank, the Inter-American Development Bank, the African Development Fund, and the Asian Development Bank.[77]

Sometimes, too, new legislation sought to put a congressional stamp on these policy areas. In 1978, Congress passed the Nuclear Non-Proliferation Act to allow congressional input into this new and important area of trade policy. This act specified a number of important conditions for the transference of nuclear material to other nations: The safeguards established by the International Atomic Energy Agency (IAEA) must be applied to exported material, no exports could be used by the recipient nation to produce nuclear weapons, and the material could not be transferred to another nation without American approval. Furthermore, provisions were included that the United States must cease transference to a nation that exploded a nuclear bomb, that did not continue to adhere to IAEA safeguards, and that did not discourage a non-nuclear state from producing a nuclear bomb. In addition, Congress reserved the right to reject the transference of nuclear fuel supply to another nation by passing a concurrent resolution of disapproval.[78]

In 1988, Congress passed the Omnibus Trade and Competitiveness Act and incorporated a stringent trade retaliation provision in the bill known as "Super 301." (The name referred to the section of the trade bill that incorporated these measures.) This provision requires the U.S. Trade Representative to identify countries (with Japan as a principal target) that have employed "a consistent pattern of import barriers and market distorting practices" and to impose sanctions against them if negotiations to remove such practices fail over a year-and-a-half period.[79] Such a provision also indicates Congress's concern about the direction of United States trade policy and its increasing reluctance to leave so much discretion to the president, at least in this one critical area of trade policy. After its enactment, three countries, Japan, India, and Brazil, were publicly identified as violating Super 301. Subsequently, Japan and Brazil were dropped from the list of violators after some progress in negotiations.[80]

In the first half of the 1990s, congressional measures specifying foreign aid and trade requirements continued. In 1992, for example, Congress was instrumental in shaping the content of the Freedom Support Act, the principal initial effort by the United States to provide economic assistance to the former states of the Soviet Union. While the administration had requested broad spending discretion toward those states, Congress enacted limitations on aid levels and imposed conditionality on that aid. In addition, Congress passed legislation to assist the states of the former Soviet Union in dismantling their nuclear weapons in accordance with the START and START II treaties.[81] This legislation, popularly known as the Nunn-Lugar amendments, was an important initiative to deal with the newly emerging threat of "loose nukes" in the global arena.

Congress also initiated and passed the Horn of Africa Recovery and Food Security Act of 1992. This measure demonstrated Congress's ability to impose conditions placed upon foreign aid to countries in that region of the world: Under this law, prior to the granting of aid, "[t]he President must certify that the [recipient] government had begun to implement peace or national reconciliation agreements, demonstrated a commitment to human rights and democracy, and held or scheduled free or fair elections."[82]

In the trade area, Congress's record is more spotty, but some efforts were made. Perhaps the most celebrated effort centered around denying MFN trade status to China owing to its abysmal human rights records. Resolutions were introduced and, on occasion, passed by both Houses of Congress, only to be vetoed by the president. This pattern continued through the first year of the Clinton administration until the administration "de-linked" trade policy with China and human rights (see Chapter 6).

In another area, though, Congress did put its imprint on policy more firmly. It initiated, and passed, tougher sanctions against Cuba. The Cuban Democracy Act of 1992 directed that prohibitions be placed on United States subsidiaries in other countries from trading with Cuba.[83] While the measure was opposed by the administration, and some presidential flexibility was eventually incorporated into the legislation, it did reflect this continued congressional effort on trade policy. In 1996, after an anti-Castro plane was shot down in international waters off Cuba, Congress passed, and the president agreed to sign, a measure to tighten sanctions further. Under the Helms-Burton legislation, foreign individuals who traded with Cuba would be denied access to the United States, and foreign companies in Cuba who used property formerly belonging to Americans could be sued in American courts.

In sum, then, Congress increasingly uses the funding power and its commerce powers to affect American foreign policy. Moreover, these vehicles will likely remain important ones through the 1990s and their use will continue to take a variety of forms from cutting off funds, earmarking appropriations, or imposing some form of restrictions on spending.

CONGRESSIONAL OVERSIGHT

The fourth area of congressional resurgence is in the area of oversight. Oversight refers to Congress's reviewing and monitoring of executive branch action—in this case, of foreign policy actions. In general, oversight has expanded because Congress now has placed more and more reporting requirements on the executive branch, and congressional committees have increased their review activities as well. In particular, the resurgence in activity by key congressional committees—the International Relations (formerly, Foreign Affairs) and National Security (formerly, Armed Services) Committees in the House, the Foreign Relations and Armed Services Committees in the Senate—has been much more pronounced recently and has contributed to greater foreign policy oversight.[84]

Expansion of Reporting Requirements to Congress

The major mechanism of renewed congressional oversight of foreign policy has been the expansion of reporting requirements placed upon the executive branch. That is, the executive branch must file a written report on how a given aspect of American foreign policy was carried out. As we have noted, important pieces of foreign policy legislation already incorporate this kind of requirement (e.g., the Case-Zablocki Act or the War Powers Resolution), but the extent of such reporting requirements goes beyond these specific instances. By one estimate, in the late 1980s, approximately 600 foreign policy reporting requirements existed, a threefold increase from the early 1970s. Moreover, these reporting requirements are used "as a tool to oversee executive branch implementation of foreign policy" and "are [the] workhorses of congressional oversight."[85]

Three main types of reports are required of the executive branch: periodic or recurrent reports, notifications, and one-time reports. The periodic reporting requirement directs the executive branch to submit particular information to Congress every year, every six months, or even quarterly.[86] During the 1970s, for example, amendments were added to the Foreign Assistance Act that required an annual assessment of human rights conditions around the world. This report must be forwarded to Congress early in each new calendar year and becomes an important source of information on human rights globally. Similarly, the Arms Control and Disarmament Agency must submit an annual report to Congress on its activities in the previous year. This report "shall include a complete and analytical statement of arms control and disarmament goals, negotiations, and activities and an appraisal of the status and prospects of arms control negotiations and of arms control measures in effect."[87] Yet a third example of these annually required reports directs the executive branch to outline the foreign policies pursued by member countries of the United Nations. The aim of the report is to assess how the policies of those countries comport with the policies and interests of the United States. Finally, another annual report instructs the executive branch to prepare "a single, comprehensive and comparative analysis of the economic policies and trade practices of each country with which the United States has an economic or trade relationship."[88]

A second kind of report is a notification. These reports are by far the most frequent form of reporting and require the executive branch to inform the Congress that a particular foreign policy action is contemplated or has been undertaken. The notifications on executive agreements or on the use of military force fall into this category, but a series of notifications on arms sales, arms control measures, and foreign assistance constitute the bulk of these kinds of reports. Perhaps the most frequent notification occurs with changes in funding levels of foreign assistance toward particular countries. Under current law, the executive branch must notify Congress whenever it "reprograms" economic or military assistance funds from one program or project to another in a country. The number of these economic notifications have been extraordinarily large in recent years. In fiscal year 1984, some 718 notifications were sent to Congress; in fiscal year 1985, the number rose to 849; and in fiscal year 1986, the total was 744. By contrast, military reprogramming notifications are much less frequent, averaging only about ten per year. Part of the reason for the lesser number is simply the lesser amount of reprogramming in military aid. Another reason, however, is that reprogramming to several countries may be incorporated into one report.[89]

The third type of report is the one-time report, calling upon the executive branch to examine a particular issue or question. While these reports are probably the most infrequent, they can be very helpful in assisting Congress to understand an issue or in shaping future policy on the question. In the mid-1980s, with the passage of the Anti-Apartheid Act, for example, Congress called for ten one-time reports from the executive branch. Reports were sought on the degree to which the United States depended upon South Africa for minerals, the kind of programs available to help black South Africans, and the efforts that the United States undertook to obtain international cooperation to end apartheid.[90] In another piece of legislation enacted at about the same time, Congress required a different kind of one-time report. In this instance, the Secretary of Defense was directed to complete "a study of the functions and organization of the Office of the Secretary of Defense" and to submit a copy of that report to Congress within one year of enactment of the legislation.[91] In this way, Congress could keep track of the functioning of this executive branch.

In the 1990s, the one-time reports continued. In one recent appropriations measure for foreign assistance, for example, Congress required a one-time report on the extent to which developing countries were contributing to the "greenhouse effect" and what efforts would be most beneficial in reducing harmful emissions. In another, Congress required that the secretary of state report on the degree of support for the Khmer Rouge by the military of Thailand and on the Government of Thailand's effort to obstruct democracy in Burma.[92]

These differing kinds of reports are, of course, more than informational and more than record keeping on the part of Congress; they also can affect policy. The reports alert Congress to changes or potential changes in administration policy and may well set off "fire alarms" in some quarters of the House and the Senate. For instance, reports provided on proposed new arms sales to Arab states or to Israel may elicit reactions from different segments of Congress. Reports on new covert operations in various corners of the world may have a similar effect. As a result, such policy proposals may turn out to be stillborn or changed dramatically before enactment by Congress. On the other hand, even a one-time or yearly report can prove to be significant. Because the Department of State must report annually on global human rights conditions, members of Congress may be able to use that information to monitor the changing situation within a country and use the report in an attempt to impose new restrictions or to lift past ones. In numerous ways, then, these reports can prove beneficial to Congress and to the policy process.

Senate Foreign Relations Committee

In the first three decades after World War II, the Senate Foreign Relations Committee was quite active in the monitoring of the foreign policy actions of the president, but in more recent decades its influence has declined. Still, the committee can and does affect the foreign policy process from time-to-time, albeit not as regularly as in earlier decades.

Several reasons account for the committee's potential influence. First, the committee has constitutional and oversight responsibilities. Not only does the Senate Foreign Relations Committee have responsibility for monitoring foreign affairs activities, but it also is required to advise on and consent to treaties and presidential nominations for various diplomatic posts.[93] The committee also has been viewed as the most prestigious in the Senate (and perhaps in Congress) and provides a ready forum for those members seeking to shape foreign policy and national politics. Furthermore, the committee provides valuable foreign policy experience for those members who entertain presidential ambitions, for instance, and a number of committee members over the years have actively sought the presidential nomination of their party.

Second, the quality of the committee's leadership in the immediate post-World War II years contributed initially to its activism and influence. Particularly prominent among recent committee chairs was the late Senator J. William Fulbright (D-Arkansas). His penetrating hearings on American involvement in Vietnam contributed significantly to the national debate on this issue and to America's eventual withdrawal from Vietnam.[94] Further, his active involvement in the numerous reform efforts by Congress in the late 1960s and early 1970s assured the committee's prominence in the shaping of the nation's foreign policy.

The subsequent chairs in the 1970s and 1980s, however, did not gain the same stature as Fulbright, and the prestige and activism of the Senate Foreign Relations Committee began to wane.[95] Senators John Sparkman (D-Alabama) and Frank Church (D-Idaho) led the committee for only short periods in the 1970s, but it already demonstrated signs of a decline in the importance of its role from that of earlier decades. The committee, under the leadership of Senator Charles Percy (R-Illinois) from 1981 to 1984, continued in this same vein. Senator Percy was largely supportive of the policies of the Reagan administration as he led the committee, although he placed arms control higher on his list of priorities than the administration had. Yet he faced a committee deeply divided between left and right, and effective consensus and decision making became difficult.

Percy's successor, Senator Richard Lugar, a conservative Republican from Indiana, was a bit more effective. While Lugar initially supported the administration ("I think it is fair to say that I share the basic assumptions of the President and the Secretary of State in regard to foreign policy"[96]), he also led the committee "by charting a course and sticking with it, working behind the scenes to build consensus through compromise and patient prodding."[97] As a consequence, the committee was able to exert influence on several issues, including passage of South African sanctions and the ouster of Marcos in the Philippines, during his tenure.

When Senator Claiborne Pell (D-Rhode Island) moved up to the chairmanship after the 1986 elections, the influence of the committee languished once again. Although a competent and respected member of the Senate, Pell was not particularly outspoken or assertive in running the Committee. As a result, the visibility of the Senate Foreign Relations Committee declined under his leadership and, by one analysis, it was "even beginning to suffer by comparison with the House Foreign Affairs [International Relations] Committee."[98]

In January 1995, with the Republicans now in control of the Senate, Senator Jesse Helms (R-North Carolina) was appointed chair, and he came to the committee with a reputation for a strong ideological view of both foreign and domestic policy questions. Initially, Helms seemed to veer away from that inclination, as evidenced by his dropping his opposition to the START II treaty and tempering his initial hostility to the North Korean-United States nuclear agreement negotiated in October 1994.[99] By the middle of 1995, however, Helms was locked into a battle with the Clinton administration over the restructuring of the United States foreign affairs bureaucracy.

In particular, Helms wanted to restructure the Department of State in a way that would effectively eliminate three semiautonomous bureaucracies, the Agency for International Development (AID), the Arms Control and Disarmament Agency (ACDA), and the United States Information Agency (USIA). The result would have been a considerable downsizing of the foreign affairs bureaucracy, and, to critics, a severe downsizing of the American assistance program, too. In its place, Helms wanted to install a nongovernmental foundation to manage United States assistance abroad.[100]

When the Senate Democrats threatened to filibuster his reform bill on the Senate floor (and a cloture motion failed), Helms employed his power as chair of the Senate Foreign Relations Committee to hold up committee and Senate action on State Department promotions, some thirty ambassadorial appointments, and several important treaties, including the START II treaty and the Chemical Weapons Convention.[101] This impasse was finally broken when the Clinton administration yielded and agreed to have Senate Democrats work with Senate Republicans to come up with legislation acceptable to both sides for reshaping the foreign affairs bureaucracy.[102] In turn, Senator Helms compromised as well, finally allowing the administration some discretion in its bureaucratic restructuring, and the Clinton administration eventually ordered in April 1997 the development of a plan to integrate ACDA and AID into the Department of State and AID to report to the secretary of state (see Chapter 9).[103] Still, the case demonstrates the ability of one committee—and, indeed, one pivotal member of a committee—to affect the operation of foreign policy, at least for a time. Furthermore, the episode also illustrates that the Senate Foreign Relations Committee can play a pivotal role in the oversight of foreign policy making if it chooses to do so.

International Relations Committee

Unlike the Senate Foreign Relations Committee, the Committee on International Relations (called the Committee on Foreign Affairs throughout most of the post–World War II period) was seen as less prestigious than the Senate Foreign Relations Committee and some other committees in the House.[104] Unlike the other House committees, too, International Relations was less likely to assist the constituency or biennial reelection goals of a member of the House directly. It was also less useful than the Senate Foreign

Relations Committee as a springboard to national prominence on foreign policy matters. Furthermore, the House Committee had a more limited agenda, confined mainly to the preparation of the foreign assistance bill, and lacked the wide sweep of responsibilities that the Senate Foreign Relations Committee had.[105]

By the 1970s, however, the House Foreign Affairs Committee underwent a series of changes that produced a considerable resurgence of activity in this committee. The oversight function increased rather sharply as a result. As congressional analyst Fred Kaiser reports, in a 1973 survey ranking committees by the number of oversight hearings and meetings, the House Foreign Affairs Committee ranked third behind Appropriations and Government Operations; the House Foreign Affairs Committee was more than three times as active in oversight as the average of all committees in the lower chamber. Further, an analyst with the Congressional Research Service (CRS) is quoted by Kaiser as saying that "International Relations [Foreign Affairs] and Foreign Relations use the Foreign Affairs Division significantly more than any other committees use any other CRS Division."[106] This view was also confirmed in a Congressional Research Report that demonstrated that the total amount of research time spent by CRS for the House Foreign Affairs Committee was greater than for any other committee in Congress. Finally, Kaiser documents the increase in the use of field investigations, the General Accounting Office, and what he calls "Extra-Committee Oversight Activities" by the House Foreign Affairs Committee.[107]

This newfound zeal for oversight derives from the changing composition of the committee, the structural changes in the committee system within the House of Representatives, and a resurgent interest in foreign policy matters.[108] In the 1970s, the committee increasingly was composed of younger, more liberal members of the House, who viewed foreign policy matters as an important part of their legislative activities. Often elected in opposition to the Vietnam War, these new members were more determined than ever to make American foreign policy accountable to the House. Moreover, this trend of the committee being more liberal than the House as a whole continues to the 1990s.[109]

Structural reforms within the House have also assisted the oversight process. In an effort to open up the congressional process, limitations were placed on the authority of the committee chairs in the appointment of subcommittee chairs (they were now elected by the committee caucus) and in the number of subcommittees that any member could chair (the number was limited to one).[110] As a result, more liberal members of the committee emerged as subcommittee chairs. In addition, because of some jurisdictional changes, the House Foreign Affairs Committee (and consequently its subcommittees) gained more review power over international economic issues.[111] One result of this enlarged agenda was a change in subcommittee organization, from primarily regional subcommittees to new functional ones. Although the committee eventually settled on a combination of functional and regional subcommittees, the pattern of increased responsibility was set in motion.[112]

Yet another congressional reform of the 1970s also aided the House International Relations Committee. The committee and subcommittee staffs were enlarged and placed formally under the chairs of the particular committees or subcommittees. While these changes regarding the subcommittee chair's control of his or her staff were already in place on this committee, the rule changes in the House formalized them and staff grew.[113] One important consequence of these changes has been the significant increase in committee and subcommittee hearings by Foreign Affairs. While these hearings are both oversight and legislative in nature, the sheer volume increase conveys the increase in attentiveness by this committee to it foreign policy responsibilities. As Table 8.3 shows, the number of hearings by the International Relations Committee has grown dramatically since the 94th Congress, reaching over 700 meetings of the Committee and its subcommittees in the late 1970s and early 1980s, and remained at over 600 meetings until the 104th Congress, when the number fell back to under 500.

In short, the International Relations Committee has played a larger role in both the formulation and review of American foreign policy since the 1970s. Moreover, that role is likely to continue, as evidenced by committee action over the years. Some of its members at the time, such as Lee Hamilton (D-Indiana), Sam Gejdenson (D-Connecticut), Michael Barnes (D-Maryland), and Stephen Solarz (D-New York), were outspoken in criticizing the Reagan administration's defense and Central American policies, proved to be key players in the Iran-Contra investigation, and played a key role in monitoring Middle East policy development as well. Under the Bush administration, the role of the committee did not abate under the more active committee leadership of Dante Fascell (D-Florida), although the House leadership and other committees did seek to have an enhanced role.[114] During the first two years of the Clinton administration, this role and activism of the committee generally continued under the chairmanship of Lee Hamilton (D-Indiana).

With the Republicans in control of the committee after the 1994 elections, its assertiveness and legislative oversight appeared to have changed very little. The committee quickly proceeded to change its name from Foreign Affairs to International Relations, reduced the number of subcommittees, and took decisive action on its principal legislative measure, the foreign aid bill. With rather remarkable speed, and under the somewhat reluctant leadership of Benjamin Gilman (R-New York), who had long supported foreign assistance legislation, the committee passed a pared down foreign aid bill by mid-1995. Like the Senate measure discussed above, this bill abolished three foreign affairs agencies—AID, ACDA, and USIA—and it called for sharp cuts in total foreign assistance.[115]

While some of the committee action was no doubt directed by the new Republican House leadership, and hence beyond the committee itself, the rapidity with which the action was taken and its comprehensiveness reflect the sustained committee involvement. Importantly, though, Representative Gilman announced, upon assuming the chair of the committee, that his priorities would be foreign aid reform, a closer scrutiny of the American military role abroad, including its peacekeeping role, and a clear identification of American interests in the decision to send forces abroad.

In general, and across party control of the committee, the International Relations Committee and its subcommittees continue to be active partic-

TABLE 8.3

Committee and Subcommittee Hearings of the House International Relations Committee, 80th–103rd Congresses

Congress	Committee	Subcommittee	Total
80th (1947–1948)	218	45	263
81st (1949–1950)	250	46	296
82nd (1951–1952)	160	100	260
83rd (1953–1954)	159	122	281
84th (1955–1956)	164	60	224
85th (1957–1958)	158	123	281
86th (1959–1960)	141	170	311
87th (1961–1962)	151	139	290
88th (1963–1964)	135	187	322
89th (1965–1966)	120	243	363
90th (1967–1968)	127	191	318
91st (1969–1970)	91	267	358
92nd (1971–1972)	76	251	327
93rd (1973–1974)	97	198	295
94th (1975–1976)	143	355	498
95th (1977–1978)	218	560	778
96th (1979–1980)	240	531	771
97th (1981–1982)	240	462	702
98th (1983–1984)	210	398	608
99th (1985–1986)	241	377	618
100th (1987–1988)	345	308	653
101st (1989–1990)	198	493	691
102nd (1991–1992)	180	430	610
103rd (1993–1994)	292	315	607
104th (1995–1996)	288	164	452

Sources: Committee on Foreign Affairs, *Survey of Activities*, 97th Cong. (Washington, DC: U.S. Government Printing Office, 1983), pp. 263–264; Committee on Foreign Affairs, *Survey of Activities*, 99th Cong. (Washington, DC: U.S. Government Printing Office, 1987), p. 253; and Committee on International Relations, *Legislative Review Activities of the Committee on International Relations. One Hundred Fourth Congress* (Washington, DC: U.S. Government Printing Office, 1997), p. 123.

ipants in the oversight and legislative process, matching and perhaps even surpassing its Senate counterpart as noted earlier. In this sense, the House International Relations Committee continues to exercise a more independent and influential role in the monitoring and shaping of foreign policy than at any time during its postwar history.

Armed Services Committees in the House and Senate

The House National Security Committee (formerly Armed Services) and Senate Armed Services Committee have also enjoyed a bit of a renaissance in their foreign policy oversight activities in recent years. Throughout the 1950s and 1960s, both committees were often regarded as committees largely supportive of the Pentagon's point of view on policy matters. One study, focusing on data to 1970, found that these committees relied upon the Department of Defense for its information about military matters and "usually ratified administration proposals." Another analysis described its role up to the early 1970s as both an "advocate" and as an "overseer," with the House Armed Services Committee less of an overseer and more of an advocate than the Senate Armed Services Committee.[116] Yet, a recent analysis claims that the "stylized image" of the two committees as protector of a strong national defense and of local military bases and defense contractors remains, but that two changes—a move toward yearly military authorization procedures and an innovative approach to handling military base closings—have begun to alter this image.[117]

More generally, the changes in rules in Congress and in congressional procedures during the 1970s—coupled with changes in leadership—have enabled the armed services committees to match or approach what we described as happening with the House International Relations Committee. While the extent of legislative oversight of defense policy changed modestly at first, by the 1980s, the activities increased even more with the emergence of what one political scientist has called the "outside game" in defense policy making.[118] Because Congress as a whole was increasingly more interested in scrutinizing defense policy, the committees, too, had to examine legislative policy more carefully as well if they were to retain any legitimacy. While this did happen, one concern was that the committee's responsibilities will be eroded with continued Congress-wide involvement.

Both armed services committees have also benefited from more assertive leadership over the 1980s and into the 1990s. In the House, Les Aspin (D-Wisconsin) gained the chairmanship of the Armed Services Committee by leaping over other members with greater seniority and by offering a policy posture that tended to be more critical of Pentagon requests than previous leaders. Aspin's successor, Ron Dellums (D-California) headed the committee for only a two-year period, and, although traditionally an outspoken critic of the military establishment, he appeared to manage it in a more moderate, middle-of-the-road, manner than might have been initially expected.

Dellum's Republican successor after the 1994 election was Floyd Spence (R-South Carolina). The renamed House National Security Committee, under Spence's leadership, sought to implement the Republican "Contract with America" pledge for strengthening American military capabilities through the emphasis on greater readiness of United States military personnel and through greater defense spending levels as well. Indeed, he (and others) proposed "their own multiyear, hundred billion dollar plans to increase military spending and shift defense priorities" shortly after the beginning of the 104th Congress.[119] Indeed, by the end of this Congress, the Committee—and the House and Senate as a whole—had passed a defense spending bill surpassing what the Clinton administration had proposed.

In the Senate, Sam Nunn of Georgia, chair of Armed Services from 1987 to 1995, did not automatically prove to be a supporter of the military. Instead, he, too, demonstrated a willingness to challenge the Department of Defense and the administration in office with his own defense plans.[120] At the same time, Nunn sought to improve America's armed forces by increasing efficiency within the Pentagon and enhancing the conditions of military personnel. Moreover, he also evidenced a streak of independence over military affairs by continuing to support economic sanctions rather than military actions prior to the Persian Gulf War and by vigorously opposing the Clinton administration's effort to overturn existing policy on gays in the military. Finally, Nunn's Republican successor, Strom Thurmond (R-South Carolina), brought altered priorities to the Senate Armed Services Committee, ones more in line with its earlier tradition of being receptive to the Pentagon's wishes. In particular, Thurmond sought to increase military spending as a means of enhancing United States force readiness.

Despite these recent changes toward more directly advancing the interests of the Department of Defense, three different examples reveal the enhanced oversight (and policy-making) role of the Armed Services [National Security] Committees and their chairs in the United States Congress—especially in comparison to the foreign policy committees in both chambers. The first centered on the debate over the interpretation of the ABM Treaty during the funding for the Strategic Defense Initiative ("Star Wars") in 1987. Even though the Foreign Relations Committee held hearings on this matter, it was Senator Sam Nunn who proved particularly prominent in challenging the Reagan administration's new interpretation of the treaty. Under that interpretation, tests would be allowed for "space-based antimissile weapons without violating the treaty."[121] In a series of dramatic speeches on the Senate floor in March 1987, however, Senator Nunn successfully challenged that view and succeeded in convincing Congress to limit the testing of SDI in a way consistent with the traditional interpretation of the ABM Treaty.

The second prominent episode was over Operation Desert Shield, the Bush administration's policy to protect Saudi Arabia and other Gulf states from Iraq, in late 1990 and early 1991. In a series of probing hearings in November 1990, the Senate Armed Services Committee challenged administration policy on proceeding too quickly to war. Moreover, a number of prominent former governmental officials called for the continuance of economic sanctions rather than moving toward using the military option. While the Senate Foreign Relations Committee also held hearings, its work paled in significance to that of the Senate Armed Services Committee. In the House, too, the Armed Services Committee, led by Congressman Aspin, had more sustained hearings on this operation than did its counterpart, the House Foreign Affairs Committee. In this House committee, though, the sentiment of the committee appeared more supportive of the administration's policy than in the Senate chamber.

A third example focuses upon the increased use of committee-produced studies to guide future United States defense strategy and defense budgeting.

After the opening of the Berlin Wall, the Senate Armed Services Committee launched "a new defense strategy to guide U.S. force restructuring," and Senator Nunn challenged the Bush administration's approach to defense policy as well. In the House Armed Services Committee, at least three studies on future defense planning were developed and became, in part, the basis for defense budgeting in recent years. In all, these studies convey the degree to which defense strategy is now a staple of committee work in both the House and the Senate.[122]

In short, as these policy episodes illustrate and with the end of the Cold War, the two armed services committees will increasingly play a more active role in attempting to shape defense policy. They no longer can be expected to be merely reflective of the Pentagon's wishes. They now "seek a voice on major defense issues," and they will use "congressional strategizing" as "a new way of doing business" on defense matters.[123]

MECHANISMS OF CONGRESSIONAL INFLUENCE

A useful way to summarize the congressional role in the foreign policy process that we have been describing so far is to use some categories of influence that prominent political scientists have developed.[124] In the broadest sense, we can categorize congressional actions on foreign policy as either legislative and nonlegislative. Within the legislative category, Congress can pass substantive legislation on foreign policy or impose procedural legislation on the executive branch. Within the nonlegislative category, we can subdivide those mechanisms into institutional actions (i.e., action by Congress to express its view) and individual actions (i.e., action by members to convey their policy prescriptions).

Legislation: Substantive and Procedural

While Congress has the ability to legislate foreign policy with a particular bill or act (e.g., cutting off aid to the Nicaraguan Contras, imposing sanctions on South Africa, or lifting the arms embargo against Bosnia), those substantive pieces of legislation are relatively rare in terms of all of the activities that Congress undertakes. Political scientist Barbara Hinckley reports that, on average, only about seven to eight substantive pieces of foreign policy legislation have been approved by the House of Representatives per administration since the Kennedy years. In the Senate, the average of substantive foreign policy legislation is even lower, averaging five per administration. While Hinckley notes that foreign-policy related resolutions, primarily of a symbolic nature, have increased, the substantive amount of foreign policy legislation has remained markedly stable and small over the years.[125]

Procedural legislation, however, has grown dramatically, as our earlier discussion sought to convey. In such diverse areas as war powers, commitments abroad, covert operations, foreign aid, and trade, Congress has developed a wide array of procedures for discerning executive action and, in some instances, seeking to play a more direct role in changing or altering executive policy. In addition, as political scientist James Lindsay has pointed out, these procedural measures include the reporting and monitoring of policy and the creations of new bureaucracies and new offices within bureaucracies to allow greater congressional insight and involvement in the process.[126] The U.S. Trade Representative, for example, was a creation of Congress and has now been given increased powers over trade policy. Accompanying these enhanced powers in fact has been a requirement that five House members be designated as advisors to the USTR on trade policy issues.

Nonlegislative Actions: Institutional and Individual Actions

Nonlegislative actions by Congress have also assumed an increasingly larger role in congressional efforts to influence foreign policy.[127] Nonlegislative institutional actions by Congress range from holding hearings by standing committees, such as the Senate Foreign Relations Committee, over the sending of American forces to Bosnia as a peacekeeping force, to the use of select committees, such as the Iran-Contra committees, to investigate that issue. While these hearings may not and, in most instances, will not lead directly to legislation, they do serve to convey to the executive branch and to the public at large the congressional view on these matters. A second nonlegislative institutional action is the formal executive-congressional consultation that is called for in the War Power Resolution or the formal and informal notification procedures in the selling of arms abroad. Yet a third, and popular, nonlegislative institutional mechanism is the passing of various kinds of nonbinding resolutions (e.g., a concurrent or two-house resolution or a single ["sense of the House" or "sense of the Senate"] resolution) on a current foreign policy issue. In the Department of Defense Appropriations Act for 1994, Congress included two "sense of the Congress" resolutions that asserted that no funds could be used to deploy American forces "in the implementation of a peace settlement in Bosnia-Herzegovina, unless previously authorized by the Congress," and that no funds should be used for sending forces into Haiti unless one or more conditions, including prior congressional authorization, were met.[128] As these resolutions suggest, such nonbinding actions are not always followed, but they do put the executive on notice about the interest and intention of Congress on particular issues.

A final nonlegislative way for Congress to express its views on foreign policy activities is through individual actions. These ways are myriad, but a few illustrations will demonstrate how legislators in the 1990s can attempt to affect the foreign policy process. Some members have used newsletters and policy analyses to convey their views on foreign policy issues. Others have written individual letters directly to the president or an executive branch office, or they have joined with their colleagues in sending such letters. Still others have used the floor of the House and Senate, either during regular debate or at the beginning or end of the legislative day when time has been set aside for individual members to speak. Finally, too, members of Congress have increasingly used network media programs (morning, evening, or weekend interview shows) to make their cases about foreign policy issues.

Two other intriguing and more potent nonlegislative mechanisms have also been used by individual members: (a) dealing directly with foreign governments and (b) filing court challenges to the executive's foreign policy actions. In the case of the former, two recent examples will illustrate this phenomenon. Former House Speaker Jim Wright (D-Texas) prepared a peace plan for ending the conflict in Central America between the Contras and the Sandinista government in Nicaragua and then provided his plan to regional governmental representatives and to the State Department. While his plan was not ultimately adopted, his actions got the attention of the White House and stimulated some progress toward peace within the region. More recently, Senator Sam Nunn (D-Georgia), albeit at the behest of President Clinton in this instance, joined with former President Jimmy Carter and former chairman of the Joint Chiefs of Staff, General Colin Powell, to seek to remove the Haitian junta who had overthrown the democratically elected government of Jean-Bertrand Aristide.

In the case of court challenges, numerous lawsuits have been filed by individual members or groups of members of Congress to thwart actions taken by the president in foreign policy. These range from Senator Barry Goldwater's effort to stop President Carter from breaking the defense treaty with Taiwan without Senate approval (*Goldwater et al. v. Carter,* 1979) to Representative Ron Dellums (D-California) filing a suit to stop the Bush administration from going to war in the Persian Gulf in 1990 (*Dellums v. Bush,* 1990). Several other lawsuits (as also described in Chapter 7) have been filed by members of Congress, primarily to stop the use of force without congressional authorization. While these measures have gained considerable attention and notoriety for the members of Congress, they have largely failed to affect policy outcomes.

CONGRESSIONAL CHANGE AND FUTURE FOREIGN POLICY MAKING

Have all of these congressional changes, largely begun in the 1970s, permanently altered the foreign policy relationships between Congress and the executive that had evolved in the immediate post–World War II period? Alternate views abound from within and outside the executive and legislative branches and from analysts as well.

The Degree of Change

Congressional-executive scholars Thomas Franck, Edward Weisband, and I. M. Destler believe so.[129] They point to the structural and procedural arrangements that Congress now has put in place for dealing with foreign policy; the various pieces of legislation giving Congress more political clout; the larger foreign policy staffs on Capitol Hill and constituencies among the American public; and the adjustments that the president has made in his relationship with Congress (albeit, perhaps, grudgingly).

In a similar vein, analyst Jeremy Rosner points to a "the new tug-of-war," between the branches, largely as a result of the end of the Cold War. In this new environment, Rosner argues that the relationship between the two branches will vary by issue, with the president's approach to Congress and the issue being crucial. On some issues, such as those resembling Cold War concerns and suggesting a promise of domestic economic benefit (e.g., aid to Russia), the president will likely prevail if he takes an early and determined stance. On other issues, such as those not directly involving security (e.g., peacekeeping) and those dealing with nontraditional foreign policy concerns (e.g., human rights), Congress will likely dominate, especially if the president does not push these issues. Since more issues are likely to reflect the latter than the former in the years ahead, Congress will be "more assertive relative to the executive branch than during the late years of the Cold War."[130]

Constitutional lawyer Harold Hongju Koh and political scientist Barbara Hinckley, however, raise doubts about whether the changes over the years have been very significant or important to the policy process. Koh argues that the Congress ultimately has assented to presidential wishes because the reforms undertaken have been inadequate and the political will has been insufficient to stop the executive. Koh summarizes his position in this way: "Congress has usually complied with or acquiesced in what the president has done, through legislative myopia, inadequate drafting [of legislation], ineffective legislative tools, or sheer lack of political will."[131] In essence, there has been "much ado about nothing."

Hinckley is as skeptical, or perhaps more so, than Koh about the impact of this presumed congressional activism. She argues that conflict between the two branches is "in large part an illusion." There has been "no shift from a conventional to a reform pattern of policy making, as some popular wisdom leads us to expect. Congressional activity does not appear to be a response to the reforms of the 1970s or any post-Vietnam and post-Watergate malaise."[132] Indeed, the level of activity and the degree of foreign policy legislation has changed very little since the 1960s, in her judgment, and Congress has largely continued to defer to the executive in the foreign policy realm.

Yet, considerable other evidence from the 1970s through the early 1990s seems to provide at least some support for the earlier view. The Reagan administration, for example, was locked in heated policy battles with Congress on several foreign policy fronts during its time in office. Most prominent, of course, was the six-year struggle with Congress over the funding of the Nicaraguan Contras. Indeed, the Iran-Contra affair was a direct result of the policy restrictions imposed by Congress. The Reagan administration also fought with Congress over it reinterpretation of the Anti-Ballistic Missile (ABM) Treaty as it sought to proceed with the Strategic Defense Initiative ("Star Wars" program), the reflagging of Kuwaiti vessels in the Persian Gulf and congressional war powers, the imposition of economic sanctions on South Africa over its apartheid policy, and the congressional initiatives on international trade policy, among others.[133] These debates were substantive in content, with Congress concerned over the precise policy the executive was proposing, but they were also procedural, with Congress concerned about the manner in which policy was being formulated.

The Bush administration also sparred with Congress over both substance and procedure in foreign policy making. President Bush used his veto power four times in his first year to alter foreign policy legislation with which he did not agree—an extraordinarily high usage of the veto on foreign policy legislation in such a short time. He vetoed a bill that placed trade restrictions on the joint development of a jet fighter with the Japanese, foreign aid legislation with funding for a UN family-planning agency, a State Department authorization bill that included an amendment imposing criminal penalties on administration officials who sought to support, even indirectly, foreign policy goals inconsistent with United States law, and legislation that would have enabled Chinese students to remain in the country after their visas had expired.[134] In all instances, President Bush was successful, but this rancor indicated the continuing intensity of the congressional-executive rivalry in foreign affairs.

President Clinton experienced the same tumult with Congress over foreign policy making as did previous administrations. The debacle in Somalia in mid-to-late 1993, and the congressional response to end American involvement there formally by the end of March 1994, were early examples. More recently, congressional efforts to lift the arms embargo against the Bosnian Muslims in the summer of 1995 and then the extended debate over the sending of American forces into Bosnia as part of a peace plan for that country convey this same kind of struggle. Even on foreign policy battles that the Clinton administration has won, such as the passage of NAFTA and GATT, they required the use of considerable political capital and deal making by the president.

Such conflict has been lamented by a number of high officials, as they point to the difficulties of conducting foreign policy with a Congress constantly intruding on, or at least limiting, the president's freedom of action. A principal complaint, for instance, is that coherent foreign policy cannot result with this continuous struggle between Congress and the president. This view was most forcefully expressed, not by a member of the executive branch, but by a former member of the Senate, the late John Tower of Texas: "Five hundred and thirty-five Congressmen with different philosophies, regional interests and objectives in mind cannot forge a unified foreign policy that reflects the interests of the United States as a whole."[135] A former member of the House Foreign Affairs Committee, Charles Whalen of Ohio, has expressed similar reservations about the new assertiveness of Congress, and particularly, the House. He argues that the legislative branch may have gone too far in its zeal for reform.[136]

President Clinton has, like other presidents before him,[137] criticized these efforts at congressional micromanagement of foreign policy. His frustration with congressional foreign policy involvement was especially evident in 1995 when, after the Senate voted to lift the arms embargo against Bosnia unilaterally, he pointedly declared, "I do not believe that a unilateral lift of the arms embargo is the right way to go."[138] Later, as members of Congress, were challenging his effort to send American forces to Bosnia to enforce a possible peace agreement, he once again vowed that "we will not fail" in Bosnia and that "if the United States does not lead, the job will not be done."[139] While President Clinton declared previously that he would seek the support of Congress, he would not yield his powers as commander in chief to do what was necessary.

Congressional Reform and Policy Impact

A key question, of course, is how much effect these reforms have had on American foreign policy. For several different reasons, the substantive impact of the various reforms on American foreign policy have been much less widespread than might be anticipated by only examining the original legislation and thus lend support to those analysts who are skeptical about the degree of congressional activism.

First, the measures have been used relatively infrequently. Despite the arms sales review procedures, for instance, no arms deal has actually been denied to the executive branch since 1974, although the composition and timing of other deals may have been altered. The one arms deal that came closest to rejection was the AWACS sale to Saudi Arabia in October 1981. After an overwhelming vote disapproving the sale in the House (301–111), the Senate failed to disapprove the sale by a close vote (48–52).[140] The human rights requirements did not markedly change the economic or security assistance policies of the subsequent administrations, although they did result in the cutting off of aid to a few nations (e.g., Argentina, Chile) and the rejection of aid by some others (e.g., Brazil). When necessary, legislative loopholes were often found for strategically important states. In the 1970s, for example, exceptions were made for Iran, South Korea, and the Philippines. In the 1980s, El Salvador and Pakistan, for example, continued to receive large amounts of aid, despite sordid human rights records. Finally, Congress has not used certain powers granted to it under the Nuclear Non-Proliferation Act. In 1980, for example, it had the opportunity to stop the transference of nuclear fuel to a country (India) that had exploded a nuclear device, but it failed to do so. The House passed a resolution disapproving this sale by a vote of 298 to 98, but the Senate failed to pass the disapproval resolution by a vote of 46 to 48.[141]

The apparent weak public record should not be pushed too far, however. Some significant actions have been taken by Congress to stop executive action, and some administrations have been dissuaded from pursuing some policy options because of evident congressional opposition. In the first category, the Jackson-Vanik and Stevenson amendments and the cutoff in military aid to the Nicaraguan Contras stand out. Both amendments had an impact on trade and detente relations with the Soviet Union, and the Jackson-Vanik amendment continued to be a source of discussion until the end of the Soviet Union and beyond. The cutoff of Contra aid was not done through any new authority granted to Congress; rather it was done through the regular appropriation processes. Nonetheless, it is reasonable to argue that Congress was emboldened to challenge the executive more vigorously because of the new executive-legislative environment. In the second category, proposed arms deals with Jordan in the period from 1983 to 1985 had to be withdrawn because of congressional opposition, and apparently some covert operations were abandoned because of votes of opposition within the congressional intelligence committees.[142] In this sense, the presence of new procedures, even if Congress did not formally stop an action, had a tangible effect on policy.

A second factor that weakens congressional authority in foreign affairs is that much of this legislation has "escape clauses" for the president. If, for example, the president certifies that an arms sale must go forward for national security reasons despite a congressional rejection, he may proceed. In 1984, this waiver procedure was invoked—even though Congress had not acted—for the purpose of sending 400 "Stinger" antiaircraft missiles to Saudi Arabia during the escalating war between Iran and Iraq.[143] The most favored nation requirement in the Trade Act of 1974 also has an escape clause allowing the president the right to grant such a status if he so wishes. Indeed, this clause has been used since 1980 to grant such status to the People's Republic of China. The human rights requirements in the economic assistance legislation also can be waived, if the executive branch certifies that the aid will reach "needy people" in the recipient nation "and if either house of Congress didn't disapprove the waiver within thirty days."[144] In 1988, the Omnibus Trade Act allowed the president to waive retaliation against trading partners engaging in unfair practices by citing national security or national economic conditions, although obstacles exist to using such a waiver.[145] In 1995, too, the congressional effort to lift the arms embargo in Bosnia contained a presidential waiver provision. Under the legislation, the United States would end the embargo only after a United Nations withdrawal of forces "or 12 weeks from the date of a request by the Bosnian Government for a pullout of forces." Yet, the legislation also granted the president "the right to ask for unlimited thirty-day waivers if he certified that they were necessary for a safe withdrawal."[146] In effect, the lifting of the Bosnian arms ban would still be at the president's discretion.

A third reason for the limited impact of these congressional reforms focuses on the legislative veto, declared unconstitutional by the Supreme Court in *Immigration and Naturalization Service v. Chadha*.[147] Several of the important congressional reforms in foreign policy making—the War Powers Resolution, the arms sales amendment, and the Nuclear Non-Proliferation Act—incorporate this veto provision. While the removal of this veto power does not wholly paralyze congressional participation in any of these areas, it does make it more difficult to halt presidential action quickly. The president would still be restricted to sixty days for sending troops abroad, for example, but, as noted earlier, Congress could now not remove them before this time period without a joint resolution, instead of through the use of concurrent resolution provision. In effect, then, this kind of legislation would require a two-thirds majority to override an expected presidential veto, not just a simple majority under the concurrent resolution procedure.

While the elimination of the legislative veto has meant a weakening of the foreign policy capability of Congress, its impact should not be pushed too far, since the reporting and review mechanisms continue. In addition, the use and development of other instruments of congressional action have been developed. In two important areas (e.g., the enforcement of the

Jackson-Vanik amendment and approval of trade agreements), the absence of the legislative veto has actually opened up new avenues of congressional activity and oversight. Now the Congress has sought to employ "conditions bills," tougher measures specifying the actions of the president on trade policy beyond what the legislative veto will allow, and to use its informal consultations to threaten congressional action on trade agreements not submitted to it.[148] In addition, informal arrangements have evolved between the legislative and executive branches since *Chadha,* much like the "Good Friday Accords" over providing aid to the Nicaraguan Contras during the Bush administration. Under this accord, a political, but not a legal, "understanding" was worked out between the two institutions, allowing the Congress to in effect "veto" presidential action on future aid.[149] Finally, members of Congress, and particularly members of the Senate, can place "holds" on measures, temporarily stopping action on foreign policy items that they do not want to take up until they obtain some concession from the executive branch.

Yet a fourth factor reduces the substantive effect of the congressional reforms of the 1970s and 1980s. Despite the desire of members of Congress to assert their role in foreign affairs, they still perceive limits as to how far they should go in restricting the executive. Many members of Congress still rely upon the president for the initiation and the execution of foreign policy. Recall two statements by prominent members of Congress that we referenced in Chapter 7.

In late 1993, the chair of the House Foreign Affairs Committee at the time, Lee H. Hamilton (D-Indiana), perhaps best summarized the prevailing congressional perspective to a forum at the Department of State: "I do not fool myself about the role of Congress on foreign policy. It is an important actor, but presidential leadership is by far the most important ingredient in a successful foreign policy. Only the president can lead...We in the Congress...can help and support him."[150] In 1995, Speaker of the House Newt Gingrich echoed similar sentiments about the president's role in the foreign policy process and why, at the time, he wanted to repeal the War Powers Resolution: "...I want to strengthen the current Democratic President because he's the President of the United States, and the President of the United States on a bipartisan basis deserves to be strengthened in foreign affairs and strengthened in national security. He does not deserve to be undermined and cluttered and weakened."[151]

In short, what Congress seeks is to be involved in the formulation of policy, in conjunction with the president, but the implementation of policy is left to the executive branch. While members of Congress are unlikely to turn back to an earlier era of congressional acquiescence, they appear equally unlikely to pass many new restrictions on presidential power.[152] Instead, members of Congress will remain alert to exercise their prerogatives in foreign affairs, without seeking to direct American policy unilaterally.

Concluding Comments

As Chapters 7 and 8 have emphasized, Congress and the president share foreign policy making powers under the Constitution, and hence foreign policy is likely to remain a "contest" between them for the foreseeable future. Neither side is likely to yield its foreign policy prerogatives, nor is any structural change ultimately going to alter the inherent constitutional dilemma between these two branches. Instead, as Arthur Schlesinger, Jr., correctly noted some years ago, the problem is "primarily political,"[153] and will undoubtedly require efforts at cooperative solutions in procedural, rather than legislative, remedies. Greater consultation and institutional respect for the role of the other seem the best prescription for dealing with the continuing debate between the president and Congress. Indeed, one proposal for a "new compact" between the branches emphasizes both of these dimensions, rather than any new legislation, and it likely remains the most workable solution.[154]

While these two institutions are the preeminent actors in foreign policy making, they are not the only ones involved in the process. Within the executive branch in particular, diverse and important foreign policy bureaucracies—the Department of State, the Department of Defense, the National Security Council, the intelligence community, and several economic bureaucracies—can and do affect the formulation of American foreign policy. The next two chapters analyze these key bureaucracies and begin to offer a more complete picture of the foreign policy process.

Notes

1. See Natalie Hevener Kaufman, *Human Rights Treaties and the Senate* (Chapel Hill and London: The University of North Carolina Press, 1990). For other discussions of the Bricker Amendment, see Stephen A. Garrett, "Foreign Policy and the American Constitution: The Bricker Amendment in Contemporary Perspective," *International Studies Quarterly* 16 (June 1972): 187–220; and Duane Tananbaum, *The Bricker Amendment Controversy: A Test of Eisenhower's Political Leadership* (Ithaca and London: Cornell University Press, 1988).
2. See Michael Nelson, ed., *Congressional Quarterly's Guide to the Presidency* (Washington, DC: Congressional Quarterly, Inc., 1989), pp. 512–513; and *Congressional Quarterly's Guide To Congress*, 3rd ed. (Washington, DC: Congressional Quarterly, Inc., 1982), pp. 303–304.
3. See "Security Agreements and Commitments Abroad," Report to the Committee on Foreign Relations of the United States Senate by the Subcommittee on Security Agreements and Commitments Abroad, December 21, 1970.
4. The text of the resolution can be found in the *Congressional Record*, 91st Cong., 1st sess., June 25, 1969, 17245.
5. The text of the amended resolution can be found in "Agreements with Portugal and Bahrain," Senate Report No. 92-632, 92nd Cong., 2d sess., February 17, 1972, 1.
6. See P.L. 92-403.
7. See section 5 of P.L. 95-45 for the text of the amendment offered by Senator Clifford Case.
8. The data are from Report of the Comptroller General of the United States, "Reporting of U.S. International Agreements by Executive Agencies Has Improved," Report ID-78-57, October 31, 1978, p. 22.
9. The late reporting by agencies in 1977 is given in ibid., p. 23, while the data for 1981 were derived from "International Agreements," Communication from The President of the United States, February 24, 1982, House Document 97-148, 97th Cong., 2nd sess., 1–12. This report was furnished by the executive in accordance with the requirements of the Foreign Relations Authorization Act, Fiscal Year 1979. The information for 1988 was taken from *Report on International Agreements Transmitted to the Congress After*

Expiration of the Sixty-Day Period Specified in the Case-Zablocki Act which was provided by the House Foreign Affairs Committee.

10. Committee on Foreign Relations, United States Senate. *Treaties and Other International Agreements: The Role of the United States Senate.* A Study Prepared for the Committee on Foreign Relations, United States Senate, by the Congressional Research Service (Washington, DC: U.S. Government Printing Office, November 1993), p. 188.
11. On these matters, see ibid., pp. 190–193. The quoted material is from p. 190.
12. For a brief review of the Ervin bill, see Marjorie Ann Browne, *Executive Agreements and the Congress*, Issue Brief Number 1B75035 (Washington, DC: Congressional Research Service, The Library of Congress, 1981), p. 7. The Glenn bill was S. 1251, 94th Cong., 1st sess., and was introduced on March 20, 1975.
13. See H.R. 4439, 94th Cong., 1st sess., introduced on March 6, 1975.
14. The section of the Treaty Powers Resolution (S. Res. 434) quoted is from the *Congressional Record*, 94th Cong., 2nd sess., April 14, 1976, 10967. Also see a later version of the Treaty Powers Resolution (5. Res. 24), in the *Congressional Record*, 95th Cong., 1st sess., January 10, 1977, 696.
15. See "Foreign Relations Authorization Act, Fiscal Year 1979," Senate Report 95-842, 95th Cong., 2nd sess., May 15, 1978, 50–55. The Committee vote is discussed at p. 3. For action on the floor, see *Congressional Quarterly Almanac 1978* (Washington, DC: Congressional Quarterly, Inc., 1979), p. 413.
16. See Section 708 of P.L. 95-426, October 7, 1978.
17. Ibid. These reforms are also summarized in "Reporting of U.S. International Agreements by Executive Agencies Has Improved," p. 8.
18. The letters are reproduced in "International Agreements Consultation Resolution," Senate Report 95-1171, August 25, 1978, 2–3. These letters are also cited in Thomas M. Franck and Edward Weisband, *Foreign Policy by Congress* (New York: Oxford University press, 1979), p. 151, and notes 110–111.
19. The *Congressional Record*, 95th Cong., 1st sess., Vol. 124, Part 21, September 8, 1978, 28545.
20. *Treaties and Other International Agreements: The Role of the United States Senate*, pp. 193–194. The first passage quoted is at p. 193; the others are at p. 194.
21. P.L. 91-672. For the executive claim of not needing the Gulf of Tonkin Resolution to continue the war, see *Congress and the Nation* Volume III 1969–1972 (Washington, DC: Congressional Quarterly Inc., 1973), p. 947.
22. The entire text of the resolution can be found in the *New York Times*, November 8, 1973, p. 20, or in a variety of recent congressional reports. See, for instance, *The War Powers Resolution: Relevant Documents, Correspondence, Reports*, Subcommittee on International Security and Scientific Affairs, House Committee on Foreign Affairs, December 1983, pp. 1–6.
23. The following analysis is based upon the text of the War Powers Resolution (P.L. 93-148). A section-by-section analysis of the Resolution is provided in Robert A. Katzmann, "War Powers: Toward A New Accommodation," in Thomas E. Mann, ed., *A Question of Balance* (Washington, DC: The Brookings Institution, 1990), pp. 46–49.
24. Ibid., pp. 50 and 58, on this point.
25. The cases of presidential reports to the Congress under the War Powers Resolution were taken from "War Powers Resolution," hearings before the Committee on Foreign Relations, 95th Cong., July 13, 14, and 15, 1977, 332–337; and from *The War Powers Resolution: Relevant Documents, Correspondence, Reports*, pp. 40–66, 84–85.
26. The reporting by the Reagan administration in the 1986–1988 period is taken from Ellen C. Collier," War Powers Resolution: Presidential Compliance," Congressional Research Service Issue Brief 81050, February 16, 1990.
27. This report did not mention the War Powers Resolution, but it is included in a listing compiled by the Congressional Research Service, used here to update the listing through the Clinton administration. See Ellen C. Collier, *The War Powers Resolution: Twenty Years of Experience* (Washington, DC: Congressional Research Service, January 11, 1994), p. 48.

28. For reporting during the Bush administration, see ibid., and the *Weekly Compilation of Presidential Documents* 26 (August 13, 1990): 1225–1226.
29. Two of this total were "follow-up reports"—one in October 1993 from an earlier April 1993 report regarding American air actions over Bosnia-Herzegovina, the other in January 1994 as a follow-up to the July 1993 report deploying American forces in Macedonia in the former Yugoslavia. See Richard F. Grimmett, *War Powers Resolution: Presidential Compliance* (Washington, DC: Congressional Research Service, February 9, 1995), p. 13, on this point. The complete listing of Clinton administration reporting is taken from this source as well (pp. 13–14) and from updates of this report on July 11, 1995, and June 12, 1996.
30. This language is taken from President Bush's report on the Panama invasion, which is printed in *Weekly Compilation of Presidential Documents* 25 (December 25, 1989): 1985.
31. See Katzmann, "War Powers: Toward A New Accommodation," p. 65, for the *Mayaquez* reporting, and Collier, *The War Powers Resolution: Twenty Years of Experience*, p. 45, for the Reagan reporting over Sinai.
32. Jeffrey Frank, "Vietnam, Watergate Bred War Powers Act...Controversy Still Surrounds Law's Effects," *Congressional Quarterly Weekly Report*, October 1, 1983, 2019.
33. Zablocki's letter is reprinted in *The War Powers Resolution: Relevant Documents, Correspondence, Reports*, p. 51.
34. See the reply to Zablocki by Richard Fairbanks, former assistant secretary of state for congressional relations, in ibid., pp. 52–54.
35. Collier, "War Powers Resolution: Presidential Compliance," pp. 6 and 14, and Collier, *The War Powers Resolution: Twenty Years of Experience*, p. 51.
36. For some cataloguing of these congressional initiatives, see Grimmett, *War Powers Resolution: Presidential Compliance*, pp. 2–8. A "sense of the House" or "sense of the Senate" resolution is simply a statement made by the chamber of its opinion; it does not have the force of law.
37. Katzmann, "War Powers: Toward A New Accommodation," p. 61.
38. Ellen C. Collier, "The War Powers Resolution: Fifteen Years of Experience," Congressional Research Service, August 3, 1988, pp. 29–31; and Collier, "War Powers Resolution: Presidential Compliance," p. 3.
39. "Legal Opinion of May 9, 1980, by Lloyd Cutler, counsel to Former President Carter, on War Powers Consultation Relative to the Iran Rescue Mission," reprinted in *The War Powers Resolution: Relevant Documents, Correspondence, Reports*, p. 50.
40. Collier, "War Powers Resolution: Presidential Compliance," p. 5.
41. President Clinton is quoted in Thomas L. Friedman, "Clinton Vows to Fight Congress On His Power to Use the Military," *New York Times*, October 19, 1993, A18.
42. The official is quoted in Elaine Sciolino, "On the Brink of War, a Tense Battle of Wills," *New York Times*, September 20, 1994, A13, and the White House strategy for moving toward intervention is also set forth there.
43. Grimmett, *War Powers Resolution: Presidential Compliance*, p. 5.
44. Collier, "War Powers Resolution: Presidential Compliance," p. 49.
45. Grimmett, *War Powers Resolution: Presidential Compliance*, p. 7.
46. Collier, "The War Powers Resolution: Fifteen Years of Experience," pp. 27–29.
47. Adam Clymer, "Congress in Step," *New York Times*, January 14, 1991, A11.
48. UN Security Council Resolution 678 (1990), reprinted in Marjorie Ann Browne, *Iraq-Kuwait: U.N. Security Council Resolutions—Texts and Votes* (Washington, DC: Congressional Research Service, The Library of Congress, December 4, 1990).
49. Clymer, "Congress in Step," p. A11.
50. "Text of Congressional Resolution on the Gulf," *New York Times*, January 14, 1991, A11.
51. For a dissenting view on this conclusion, see Michael J. Glennon, *Constitutional Diplomacy* (Princeton, NJ: Princeton University Press, 1990), p. 93. He argues that only Nixon and Reagan viewed the withdrawal of troops requirements in the War Powers Resolution as unconstitutional.

52. Barbara Hinckley, *Less Than Meets the Eye* (Chicago and London: The University of Chicago Press, 1994), pp. 195–196.

53. For a discussion of the Senate vote on nonbinding resolutions, see Louis Fisher, *Presidential War Power* (Lawrence: University Press of Kansas, 1995), p. 156; also see Larry Rohter, "2,000 U.S. Troops Land Without Opposition and Take Over Haiti's Ports and Airfields," *New York Times*, September 20, 1994, A1.

54. See Donna Cassata, "Congress Bucks White House, Devises Its Own Bosnia Plan," *Congressional Quarterly Weekly Report*, June 10, 1995, 1653.

55. Collier, "The War Powers Resolution: Fifteen Years of Experience," pp. 9–11.

56. See Glennon, *Constitutional Diplomacy*, p. 93, for a dissenting view as discussed in footnote 51.

57. Katzmann, "War Powers: Toward A New Accommodation," pp. 66–69; Committee on Foreign Affairs, *Congress and Foreign Policy 1988* (Washington, DC: U.S. Government Printing Office, 1989), p. 9; and Collier, "The War Powers Resolution: Fifteen Years of Experience," pp. 45–50.

58. See Carroll J. Doherty, "House Approves Overhaul of Agencies, Polices," *Congressional Quarterly Weekly Report*, June 10, 1995, 1655–1656; and Katharine Q. Seelye, "House Defeats Bid to Repeal 'War Powers,' " *New York Times*, June 8, 1995, A5. The first two quoted passages are by Toby Roth (R-Wisconsin). The first one can be found in the former source at p. 1656, while the second one can be found in the latter source, p. A5. The last quoted passage is by Lee Hamilton (D-Indiana) and can be found in the second source at pp. 1655–1656.

59. Quoted in Eric Schmitt, "Senators Query U.S. Role in Bosnia," *New York Times*, October 18, 1995, A12.

60. The analysis of voting during the 1966–1972 period is drawn from "Congress Took 94 Roll-Call Votes On War 1966–72," *Congress and the Nation*, Volume III, 1966–1972 (Washington, DC: Congressional Quarterly Service, 1973), pp. 944–945. The quoted passages are from this source, too.

61. See P.L. 93-126 of October 18, 1973.

62. *Congressional Quarterly Almanac 1975* (Washington, DC: Congressional Quarterly Inc., 1976), pp. 306–315.

63. See Keith R. Legg, "Congress as Trojan Horses? The Turkish Embargo Problem, 1974–1978," in John Spanier and Joseph Nogee, eds., *Congress, The Presidency, and American Foreign Policy* (New York: Pergamon Press, 1981), pp. 107–131, and especially the chronology of events at pp. 108–109 for the passage of the arms embargo.

64. See Section 404 of P.L. 94-329. 90 Stat. 757.

65. See Section 728 of P.L. 97-113.

66. See P.L. 98-151. A description of the law is provided by John Felton, "Omnibus Bill Includes Foreign Aid Programs," *Congressional Quarterly Weekly Report*, November 19, 1983, 2435–2436.

67. See Doherty, "House Approves Overhaul of Agencies, Policies," p. 1655, and Carroll J. Doherty, "Bill Slashing Overseas Aid Gets Bipartisan Support," *Congressional Quarterly Weekly Report*, June 10, 1995, 1658.

68. "Force, Diplomacy and the Resources We Need for American Leadership," address by U.S. Secretary of State Warren Christopher, U.S. Military Academy, West Point, New York, October 25, 1996, available through the Internet. In inflation-adjusted spending, the international affairs budget (spending by the Department of State, the U.S. Information Agency, the Arms Control and Disarmament Agency, and the Agency for International Development) had declined from $37.5 billion in 1984 to $18.6 billion for 1996. See Thomas W. Lippman, "The Decline of U.S. Diplomacy," *The Washington Post National Weekly Edition*, July 22–29, 1996, for a State Department table showing the yearly changes in this budget from 1984 to 1996.

69. Briefing by Acting Secretary of State Strobe Talbott and Ambassador Craig Johnstone, "FY 1997 International Affairs Budget Request," Department of State, Washington, DC, March 20, 1996, available through the Internet.

70. These examples are taken from "Foreign Assistance Appropriations, 1995," which is Public Law 103-306. This law is reprinted in Committee on Foreign Relations and Committee on International Relations, *Legislation on Foreign Relations Through 1994* Volume I-A (Washington, DC: U.S. Government Printing Office, June, 1995), pp. 581 and 588.

71. "Most Aid Earmarked," *Congressional Quarterly Weekly Report*, January 20, 1990, 198. For some recent controversy over earmarking, see John Felton, "Dole Takes on Israeli Lobby, Proposes Cutting U.S. Aid," *Congressional Quarterly Weekly Report*, January 20, 1990, 196, 198.

72. See sections 402 and 613 of the Trade Act of 1974 (P.L. 93-618).

73. See Section 36 of P.L. 93-559.

74. See Section 36h of P.L. 94-329. The dollar totals were subsequently raised to $50 million and $14 million, respectively. See John Felton, "Hill Weighs Foreign Policy Impact of Ruling," *Congressional Quarterly Weekly Report*, July 2, 1983, 1330.

75. See *Congressional Quarterly Almanac 1981* (Washington, DC: Congress Quarterly, Inc., 1982), p. 132.

76. The economic aid legislation was the International Development and Food Assistance Act of 1975 (P.L. 94-161). The human rights provision can be found at Section 116. In the International Security and Arms Report Control Act, the human rights provision is Section 502b.

77. See P.L. 95-118, Section 701, and P.L. 94-302, Section 28. Also see the discussion of this human rights legislation in Lars Schoultz, "Politics, Economics, and U.S. Participation in Multilateral Development Banks," *International Organization* 36 (Summer 1982): 537–574.

78. These and other provisions of the act are summarized in *Congressional Quarterly Almanac 1978* (Washington, DC: Congressional Quarterly, Inc., 1979), pp. 350–356. Also see P.L. 95-242.

79. Quoted from the bill's conference report in Pietro S. Nivola, "Trade Policy: Refereeing the Playing Field," in Thomas E. Mann, ed., *A Question of Balance* (Washington, DC: The Brookings Institution, 1990), p. 238.

80. Clyde H. Farnsworth, "U.S. Drops Japan from Target List," *New York Times*, April 28, 1990, 17 and 19.

81. These examples are taken from Ellen C. Collier, "Congress and Foreign Policy 1992: Introduction" in Committee on Foreign Affairs, *Congress and Foreign Policy 1992* (Washington, DC: U.S. Government Printing Office, 1993), pp. 1–21; and U.S. Congress, Office of Technology Assessment, *Dismantling the Bomb and Managing the Nuclear Materials*. OTA-O-572 (Washington, DC: U.S. Government Printing Office, September, 1993), p. 130.

82. Collier, "Congress and Foreign Policy 1992: Introduction," p. 6.

83. Ibid., p. 11.

84. We do not mean to imply that other committees are not involved with foreign policy issues, but rather that these are the principal foreign policy authorizing committees. Other committees in the House and the Senate that deal with foreign policy would include Appropriations, Governmental Affairs (Senate), Government Reform and Oversight (House), Judiciary, and Select Intelligence, among others. It is important to note that the Foreign Operations Subcommittee of the House and Senate Appropriations Committees are extraordinarily important in appropriating foreign policy funding. Indeed, some would contend that they do more today to shape policy than the authorizing committees.

85. Ellen C. Collier, "Foreign Policy by Reporting Requirement," *The Washington Quarterly* 11 (Winter 1988): 81 and 77. This article is the source for the subsequent discussion as well.

86. The types of reports and the description of each are taken from ibid.

87. Committee on Foreign Affairs and Committee on Foreign Relations, *Legislation on Foreign Relations Through 1985* (Washington, DC: U.S. Government Printing Office, April, 1986), p. 907. The requirement for a report on member countries of the United Nations can be found at p. 956.

88. *Country Reports on Economic Policy and Trade Practices*, Report to the Committee on Foreign Relations and Committee on Finance of the U.S. Senate and Committee on Foreign Affairs and Committee on Ways and Means of the U.S. House of Representatives (Washington, DC: U.S. Government Printing Office, February, 1994).

89. The data on reprogramming reports were obtained from staff members of the House Committee on Foreign Affairs. A more complete description of reprogramming reporting is available in James M. McCormick, "A Review of the Foreign Assistance Program," memo prepared for the Office of the Honorable Lee Hamilton.

90. Collier, "Foreign Policy by Reporting Requirement," p. 80.

91. See P.L. 99-433, enacted on October 1, 1986.

92. These three examples of required reporting are taken from the Committee on Foreign Relations and Committee on International Relations, *Legislation on Foreign Relations Through 1994,* Volume I-A (Washington, DC: U.S. Government Printing Office, June, 1995), pp. 658 and 587, respectively.

93. A good source to get some idea of the range of activities of the Senate Foreign Relations Committee is the legislative activities reports. See, for example, the *Legislative Activities Report of the Committee on Foreign Relations*, United States Senate, 170th Anniversary 1816–1986 (Washington, DC: U.S. Government Printing Office, January 1986). For a more complete discussion of the changing role of the Senate Foreign Relations Committee and its oversight responsibilities, see James M. McCormick, "Decision Making in the Foreign Affairs and Foreign Relations Committees," in Randall B. Ripley and James M. Lindsay, eds., *Congress Resurgent: Foreign and Defense Policy on Capitol Hill* (Ann Arbor: University of Michigan, 1993), pp. 115–153.

94. *Congressional Quarterly's Guide To Congress*, p. 289.

95. Ibid., p. 289. On the problems of the committee and the difficulties faced by Percy as chair, see Richard Whittle, "Foreign Relations Committee Searches for Renewed Glory," *Congressional Quarterly Weekly Report*, March 14, 1981, 477–479.

96. Bernard Gwertzman, "Senator Planning Sweeping Hearing on Foreign Policy," *New York Times*, December 9, 1984, 20.

97. Helen Dewar, "Senate Foreign Relations Panel Founders," *Washington Post*, October 10, 1989, A12.

98. Ibid.

99. Dick Kirschten, "Where's the Bite?" *National Journal*, March 25, 1995, 739–742.

100. Ibid.

101. Elaine Sciolino, "Awaiting Call, Helms Puts Foreign Policy on Hold," *New York Times*, September 24, 1995, 1.

102. Elaine Sciolino, "Helms to Allow Action in Senate on Clinton Diplomatic Nominees," *New York Times*, September 30, 1995, 1.

103. See "Fact Sheet: Reinventing State, ACDA, USIA, and AID" (Washington, DC: Office of the Press Secretary, The White House, April 18, 1997), via the Internet; and Stephen Barr and Thomas W. Lippman, "Turf Diplomacy at State Department," *Washington Post*, May 28, 1997, A17.

104. Foreign Affairs is not ranked as the most popular committee in the House; it still ranks behind Ways and Means and Appropriations as a desirable committee assignment. See Fenno, *Congressman in Committees*, pp. 16–20. For a different ranking, see Randall B. Ripley, *Congress: Process and Policy*, 2nd ed. (New York: W. W. Norton and Company, 1978), p. 166.

105. See Fenno, *Congressman in Committees*, pp. 15–151, on the importance of the Senate Foreign Relations Committee. On the limited responsibilities of the House Foreign Affairs agenda, see ibid., pp. 213–215.

106. See Fred Kaiser, "Oversight of Foreign Policy: The U.S. House Committee on International Relations," *Legislative Studies Quarterly* 2 (August 1977): 259.

107. Fred M. Kaiser, "The Changing Nature and Extent of Oversight: The House Committee on Foreign Affairs in the 1970s," paper presented at the 1975 Annual Meeting of the Midwest Political Science Association, Chicago, Illinois.

108. Fred M. Kaiser, "Structural Change and Policy Development: The House Committee on International Relations," paper presented at the 1976 Annual Meeting of the Midwest Political Science Association; and Fred M. Kaiser, "Structural and Policy Change: The House Committee on International Relations," *Political Studies Journal* 5 (Summer 1977): 443–451.

109. Interviews with majority and minority staff in June 1982, reveal that they view the committee as more liberal than the House as a whole. Also see James M. McCormick, "The Changing Role of the House Foreign Affairs Committee in the 1970s and 1980s." *Congress & The Presidency* 12 (Spring 1985): 1–20; and James M. McCormick "Decision Making in the Foreign Affairs and Foreign Relations Committees," pp. 132–137.

110. *Origins and Development of Congress* (Washington, DC: Congressional Quarterly, Inc., 1976), p. 159.

111. Kaiser, "Structural and Policy Change: The House Committee on International Relations," p. 446.

112. For a recent listing of the subcommittees and for a brief history of the House Foreign Affairs Committee, see *Survey of Activities, 99th Congress* (Washington, DC: Government Printing Office, 1987).

113. Kaiser, in "Structural Change and Policy Development," pp. 21–22.

114. For a more complete discussion of the changing role of the House Foreign Affairs Committee and its oversight responsibilities, see McCormick, "Decision Making in the Foreign Affairs and Foreign Relations Committees," pp. 115–153.

115. Carroll J. Doherty, "Republicans Poised to Slash International Programs," *Congressional Quarterly Weekly Report*, May 13, 1995, 1334–1336; and Carroll J. Doherty, "Gilman Under Pressure," *Congressional Quarterly Weekly Report*, May 13, 1995, 1335.

116. The first study is one by Carol Goss cited in Edward J. Laurance, "The Congressional Role in Defense Policy: The Evolution of the Literature," *Armed Forces & Society*, 6 (Spring 1980): 437; the second is "Armed Services Committees: Advocates or Overseers?" *Congressional Quarterly Weekly Report*, March 25, 1972, 673–677.

117. Christopher J. Deering, "Decision Making in the Armed Services Committees," in Randall B. Ripley and James M. Lindsay, eds., *Congress Resurgent: Foreign and Defense Policy on Capitol Hill* (Ann Arbor: University of Michigan, 1993), pp. 155–182.

118. James M. Lindsay, "Congress and Defense Policy: 1961 to 1986," *Armed Forces & Society* 13 (Spring 1987): 371–401, for a discussion of these committees in the 1970s and 1980s. As he correctly notes, the Defense subcommittees on the House and Senate Appropriations Committee are equally important—or even more important—players on defense policy issues.

119. Cited in Paul Stockton, "Beyond Micromanagement: Congressional Budgeting for a Post-Cold War Military," *Political Science Quarterly* 110 (Summer 1995): 239.

120. Ibid. for mention of Nunn's and Aspin's effort. For a fuller discussion, see Paul N. Stockton, "Congress and U.S. Military Policy Beyond the Cold War," in Randall B. Ripley and James M. Lindsay, eds., *Congress Resurgent: Foreign and Defense Policy on Capitol Hill* (Ann Arbor: University of Michigan, 1993), pp. 235–259.

121. "Congress Reinforces Strings on SDI Program," *Congressional Quarterly Almanac 1987* (Washington, DC: Congressional Quarterly, Inc., 1988), p. 196. Also see pp. 195–199. The speeches by Senator Nunn on the Senate floor can be found in *Congressional Record*, March 11, 1987, S2967–2986; *Congressional Record,* March 12, 1987, S3090–3095; and *Congressional Record,* March 13, 1987, S3171–3173.

122. See Stockton, "Beyond Micromanagement: Congressional Budgeting for a Post–Cold War Military," p. 245, for the quotation and pp. 239, 245–247.

123. The first quote is from Deering, "Decision Making in the Armed Services Committee," p. 182, while the last two quoted passages are from Stockton, "Beyond Micromanagement: Congressional Budgeting for a Post–Cold War Military," p. 259.

124. The subsequent discussion here draws upon the insightful analyses by Eileen Burgin, "Congress and Foreign Policy: The Misperceptions," in Lawrence C. Dodd and Bruce I. Oppenheimer, eds., *Congress Reconsidered* (Washington, DC: CQ Press, 1993), pp.

333–363; and James M. Lindsay, "Congress and Foreign Policy: Avenues of Influence," in Eugene R. Wittkopf, *The Domestic Sources of American Foreign Policy: Insights and Evidence*, 2nd ed. (New York: St. Martin's Press, 1994), pp. 191–207.

125. See Barbara Hinckley, *Less Than Meets the Eye* (Chicago and London: The University of Chicago Press, 1994), pp. 26–29, esp. Tables 2.1 and 2.2. Given Hinckley's definition of what to include and exclude as legislation (see p. 25), the congressional role might be somewhat understated. Also, it is not clear which legislation is initiated by Congress and which is initiated by the president.

126. See Lindsay, "Congress and Foreign Policy: Avenues of Influence," pp. 198–201. Also see his "Congress, Foreign Policy, and the New Institutionalism," *International Studies Quarterly* 38 (June 1994): 281–304.

127. See Burgin, "Congress and Foreign Policy: The Misperceptions," for the types of non-legislative actions upon which we draw throughout this section and for more examples of these activities.

128. See Sections 8146 and 8147 of P.L. 103-139. These sections are reprinted in Subcommittees on International Security, International Organizations and Human Rights of the Committee on Foreign Affairs, U.S. House of Representatives, *The War Resolution: Relevant Documents, Reports, and Correspondence* (Washington, DC: U.S. Government Printing Office, May 1994 edition), pp. 254, 264, and 265.

129. Franck and Weisband, *Foreign Policy by Congress*, pp. 6–9; and I. M. Destler, "Dateline Washington: Congress as Boss?" *Foreign Policy* 42 (Spring 1981): 167–180.

130. Jeremy D. Rosner, *The New Tug-of-War: Congress, the Executive Branch and National Security* (Washington, DC: Carnegie Endowment for International Peace, 1995). The first quote is taken from the title and the second quote is at p. 3.

131. Harold Hongju Koh, *The National Security Constitution* (New Haven and London: Yale University Press, 1990), p. 117.

132. Hinckley, *Less Than Meets the Eye*, pp. 5 and 47, respectively.

133. Committee on Foreign Affairs, *Congress and Foreign Policy, 1988*, and Committee on Foreign Affairs, *Congress and Foreign Policy 1987* (Washington, DC: U.S. Government Printing Office, 1989).

134. "Bush's Dozen Vetoes," *New York Times*, June 16, 1990, 8; and "State Department Bill Clears, But Faces Bush's Veto," *Congressional Quarterly Weekly Report*, November 18, 1989, 3189.

135. John G. Tower, "Congress Versus The President: The Formulation and Implementation of American Foreign Policy," *Foreign Affairs* 60 (Winter 1981/82): 233.

136. Charles W. Whalen, Jr., *The House and Foreign Policy: The Irony of Congressional Reform* (Chapel Hill: The University of North Carolina Press, 1982).

137. President Reagan, for example, complained bitterly about the micromanagement of U.S. foreign policy through the use of "the blunt instrument of legislation." He criticized the trade policy that Congress enacted, its passage of restrictions on intelligence activities, its earmarking of foreign assistance, and its efforts to regulate arms sales abroad. In essence, Congress had gone beyond its appropriate role and had reduced the president's flexibility in the conduct of U.S. foreign policy. The occasion of President Reagan's remarks was a speech at the University of Virginia on December 16, 1988, as summarized and quoted in *Congress and Foreign Policy 1988*, p. 9.

138. Elaine Sciolino, "Defiant Senators Vote to Override Bosnian Arms Ban," *New York Times*, July 27, 1995, A1.

139. The last quotation is from Todd S. Purdum, "Clinton Cautions Against a Retreat into Isolationism," *New York Times*, October 7, 1995, 5.

140. *Congressional Quarterly Almanac 1981*, Volume 37 (Washington, DC: Congressional Quarterly, Inc., 1982), pp. 136, 138.

141. See "Congress and Nuclear Nonproliferation Policy," in *Congress and Foreign Policy—1980* (Washington, DC: Government Printing Office, 1981), pp. 89, 98. On human rights and foreign aid, see James M. McCormick and Neil J. Mitchell, "Human Rights and Foreign Assistance: An Update," *Social Science Quarterly* 70 (December 1989): 969–979.

142. On the halting of arms sales, see Bruce W. Jentleson, "American Diplomacy: Around the World and Along Pennsylvania Avenue," in Thomas E. Mann, ed., *A Question of Balance* (Washington, DC: The Brookings Institution, 1990), p. 161; and on the stopping of covert operations, see Gregory F. Treverton, "Intelligence: Welcome to the American Government," in Thomas E. Mann, ed., *A Question of Balance* (Washington, DC: The Brookings Institution, 1990), p. 91.

143. See Section 361 of P.L. 94-329. For the Saudi exception, see "U.S. To Send Saudi Arabia 400 Missiles," *Des Moines Register*, May 28, 1984, 1A, 11A.

144. Norman J. Ornstein and David W. Rohde, "Shifting Forces, Changing Rules, and Political Outcomes: The Impact of Congressional Change on Four House Committees," in Robert L. Peabody and Nelson W. Polsby, eds., *New Perspectives on the House of Representatives*, 3rd ed. (Chicago: Rand McNally, 1977), p. 259. This description, however, was before the *Chadha* decision.

145. Nivola, "Trade Policy: Refereeing the Playing Field," p. 238.

146. Sciolino, "Defiant Senators Vote to Override Bosnian Arms Ban," p. A8.

147. See Felton, "Hill Weighs Foreign Policy Impact of Ruling," pp. 1329–1330, for an assessment of the Supreme Court ruling on the legislative veto for foreign policy, and 462 U.S. 919 (1983).

148. Jessica Korn, *The Power of Separation* (Princeton, NJ: Princeton University Press, 1996), pp. 99–110, 116–119.

149. Michael J. Glennon, "The Good Friday Accords: Legislative Veto by Another Name?" *The American Journal of International Law* 83 (September 1989): 544–546.

150. Lee H. Hamilton, "American Foreign Policy: A Congressional Perspective," speech at the Department of State, Washington, DC, December 14, 1993, p. 8.

151. Quoted in Katharine Q. Seelye, "House Defeats Bid to Repeal 'War Powers,'" *New York Times*, June 8, 1995, A5.

152. These views are based on interviews with staff of the House Foreign Affairs Committee (June 1982), officials of the Department of State who deal with congressional relations (October 1981), and some participant observation in the House of Representatives in 1986 and 1987.

153. Schlesinger, "Congress and the Making of American Foreign Policy," *Foreign Affairs* 51 (October 1972): 106.

154. On a proposal for a foreign policy "compact" between the two branches, see Warren Christopher, "Ceasefire Between the Branches: A Compact in Foreign Affairs," *Foreign Affairs* 60 (Summer 1982): 989–1005.

CHAPTER 9

THE DIPLOMATIC AND ECONOMIC BUREAUCRACIES: DUPLICATION OR SPECIALIZATION?

The end of sharp distinctions between domestic and overseas interests underscores the need for one foreign policy process, run by and responsive to the White House.... [We] recommend that the National Security Council (NSC) be the catalyst and the point of coordination for this new, single foreign policy process.

State 2000: A New Model for Managing Foreign Affairs
December 1992

Trade is central to our foreign policy. It's the connecting tissue between countries. We must compete and win in the global economy.

Mickey Kantor, U.S. Trade Representative,
later Secretary of Commerce
March 23, 1995

Although the president may dominate the Congress's role in the foreign policy process, he cannot act alone. The president needs information and advice from his assistants and the various foreign affairs bureaucracies within the executive branch to formulate policy. The president also needs the aid of the executive branch to implement any foreign policy decision. Thus, while the president may ultimately choose a foreign policy option, such as economic sanctions or the use of force in Bosnia or Haiti, for example, the bureaucratic environment in which he operates greatly influences the decision process and the implementation of his choices.

The variety of agencies with an interest in foreign policy may be surprising. While the Department of Agriculture may seem primarily concerned with domestic farm issues, it also promotes the granting of foreign trade credits to countries such as Russia or Poland to promote American farm exports. While the Department of Treasury may monitor the money supply at home, it also advises the president on the need for a shift in the value of the United States dollar against the German mark or the Japanese yen to aid American trade abroad. While the Justice Department may be interested in controlling the use of illegal drugs at home, it also has an interest in drug production in other countries as well. One of the Justice Department's divisions, the Immigration and Naturalization Service (INS), is responsible for monitoring America's borders, but it is also interested in monitoring unrest in other countries that could lead to more refugees to the United States (e.g., political and economic unrest in Haiti or Mexico). In short, the principal foreign policy bureaucracies that we often think of (and even ones we may not immediately think of) compete to get the "president's ear" on international issues and to shape an outcome favorable to its bureaucracy. With the growth of global issues and the growth of the foreign affairs bureaucracy, comprehending the process of domestic bureaucratic politics has become critically important to understanding American foreign policy.

BUREAUCRATIC POLITICS AND FOREIGN POLICY MAKING

The "bureaucratic politics" approach to foreign policy making stands in contrast to the earlier discussions in which we emphasized the values and beliefs of American society as a whole, the values of particular presidents and administrations, or even the effects of institutions like Congress and the presidency on United States foreign policy. This approach views the emergence of policy from the interactions among the various bureaucracies, competing to shape the nation's actions. Policy thus becomes less the result of the values and beliefs of an individual political actor in the process (although each can surely have an effect) and more the result of the interaction process between and among several bureaucracies. Put differently, policy making is the result of the "pulling" and "hauling" among competing institutions.[1] Compromise within bureaucracies and coalition building across them become important ways in which policy ultimately emerges.

In this sense, the *process* of policy making becomes an important mechanism to arrive at the *substance* of policy.

While the bureaucratic politics model has long been used to study domestic policy, its sustained application in foreign policy dates from the early 1970s and the imaginative work by political scientist Graham Allison on the Cuban Missile Crisis, as well as to a more general work by political analyst Morton Halperin.[2] These two pioneering analyses sparked a more general interest in this approach, and it has now become a standard mode of foreign policy analysis.

A recent study analyzed "the sale of dual-use technology to Iraq" by the United States during the 1980s and early 1990s through the bureaucratic politics lens and provides an illustrative example of how this approach may be applied to understanding American foreign policy.[3] According to proponents of the bureaucratic politics model, "where you stand depends on where you sit." That is, the policy priority of a particular bureaucracy would likely predict its position in any decision situation.[4] In the case of arms sales to Iraq the aphorism seemed to work especially well.

On the one hand, the Department of Defense continuously argued against the sales of technology to Iraq because it potentially could be used for military purpose. On the other hand, the Department of Commerce argued that the promotion of such sales were a part of its mission and they aided America's trade balance. Interestingly, the Department of State joined the Department of Commerce in promoting export sales for its own reason: These sales served as a means of improving political–military ties with Iraq, an important nation in the Persian Gulf and the Middle East. The decision and implementation processes took on an even greater bureaucratic cast because policy making over controlling export policy was so dispersed within the United States government. As a result of these various factors, "the Pentagon never had a chance," according to this analyst. In short, by this account, bureaucratic politics, as contrasted to other explanations, largely accounted for Saddam Hussein's ability to secure American technology from 1984 through August 1990, right up to his invasion of Kuwait.

This same bureaucratic approach can be applied in order to understand the Clinton administration's policy toward Bosnia, in its earliest months. Some sharp divisions developed between different bureaucracies and their principal spokespersons concerning the use of American force versus the use of diplomacy to address that bitter dispute. On the one side, an alliance of sorts developed between Secretary of State Warren Christopher, representing that bureaucracy, and, somewhat ironically, the chairman of the Joint Chiefs of Staff at the time, General Colin Powell, representing the military. They tended to support a diplomacy solution and were doubtful that a military bombing strategy would work. On the other side, another informal alliance developed between National Security Advisor Anthony Lake, representing the White House staff view, and Secretary of Defense Les Aspin, representing the civilian decision making within the Pentagon. This side was more inclined toward the use of American force to stop the killing in Bosnia. (Note, in this instance, how bureaucratic position does not necessarily predict policy position, an approach applied in other cases and a source of criticism of this approach.[5]) Because of this policy stalemate among advisors and because of President Clinton's indecision as well, policy making toward Bosnia was stalled for a time, and bureaucratic stalemate contributed to policy inaction.[6]

The bureaucratic politics approach thus allows us to apply another perspective in order to interpret and understand American foreign policy. To apply this perspective, however, we must examine the key foreign policy bureaucracies within the executive branch, describe each one's role in the policy process, and assess their relative policy influence. In this way, we begin to evaluate the relative success of some bureaucracies in the shaping of foreign policy on particular issues as compared to others.

In particular, we analyze four central foreign policy bureaucracies in detail: the Department of State, the National Security Council, the Department of Defense, and the intelligence community. We will also survey the increasing role of several other bureaucracies (e.g., the Department of Commerce, Department of the Treasury, the Office of the United States Trade Representative, and the Department of Agriculture) and their role in shaping the foreign economic policy of the United States. In the last part of Chapter 10, we try to bring this discussion together by showing how these individual foreign policy bureaucracies coordinate with one another through the process of forming interagency groups (IGs). Throughout both chapters, we discuss a crucial question of the bureaucratic politics approach: How are foreign policy choices the result of both efforts at interdepartmental coordination and interdepartmental rivalries?

THE DEPARTMENT OF STATE

The oldest cabinet post and the original foreign policy bureaucracy in the American government is the Department of State. The department was established originally in 1781 under the Articles of Confederation as the Department of Foreign Affairs and became the Department of State in 1789 with the election of George Washington.[7] Over its 200-year history, the department has evolved into a large and complex bureaucracy with a variety of functions. Among those key functions are assisting the president in policy formulation on all international issues and implementing America's foreign relations abroad. In this way, the Department of State coordinates the United States overseas programs that emanate from Washington, D.C.[8] At the same time, the Department has had its influence weakened by internal and external problems over the years.

The Structure of State at Home

While the Department of State has always been arranged in a complex and hierarchical fashion, the Clinton administration undertook several organizational changes in an effort to rationalize the organizational structure and obtain greater efficiency in operation for the post–Cold War world.[9] Stimulated by Vice President Gore's National Performance Review (NPR) initiative, the Department's Strategic Management Initiative (SMI), Secretary of State Warren Christopher's directive on reorganization, and budget-cutting pressures of the Congress, the Department has sought to streamline its internal structure through reorganization and restructuring of decision-making responsibilities and has downsized its foreign operations (about forty embassies and consulates were scheduled to be closed during the Clinton administration).

Office of the Secretary. Figure 9.1 displays the internal organizational structure of the Department of State. This chart reflects some important changes from only a few years earlier. At the top of the structure, the Clinton administration formally established the Office of the Secretary to aid the decision making of the secretary of state and the deputy secretary of state, who are housed there, and to assist those two officials "establish an operational agenda for Under Secretaries, Assistant Secretaries, and other senior officials."[10] Now, too, several different departmental individuals, bureaus, and activities report directly to this Office. These range from the Policy Planning Staff, the Bureaus of Public Affairs and Legislative Affairs and the Bureau of Intelligence and Research to the activities of numerous ambassador-at-large, counselors, and coordinators of policy toward particular countries or regions (e.g., the Middle East Peace Process, counterterrorist activities, North Korea, and Russia, among others). The overall aim is to have a more sharply focused decision process among the principal policy formulators within the Department.

The Role of Under Secretaries. A second important change has been "to strengthen the role of the Under Secretaries" and to have them serve as "the principal foreign policy advisors to the Secretary."[11] These officials (and their divisions) are now responsible for managing and coordinating the principal activities under their aegis and serving as a "corporate board" to the secretary of state. The under secretary for political affairs now oversees the six regional bureaus (Bureau of African Affairs, Bureau of East Asian and Pacific Affairs, European and Canadian Affairs, Inter-American Affairs, Near Eastern Affairs, and South Asian Affairs) and the Bureau of International Organization Affairs. The under secretary for economic, business, and agricultural affairs is responsible for the Bureau of Economic and Business Affairs. More importantly, within this Undersecretariat, an Office of the Coordinator for Business Affairs has been established. This office emerged from Secretary of State Warren Christopher's commitment to establish an "America's Desk" within the Department and is primarily responsible for aiding United States business interests in dealing with other countries and for coordinating activities with other government departments in facilitating American business activities abroad. The under secretary for arms control and international security affairs has primary oversight of a wide range of security and defense questions through the Bureau of Political–Military Affairs which now answers directly to this Undersecretariat. The under secretary for global affairs, a newly created position at Secretary Christopher's directive, manages a number of functional bureaus dealing with several different policy questions: human rights and democracy, international narcotics, environmental affairs, and population, refugees,

FIGURE 9.1

The U.S. Department of State: Organization at a Glance

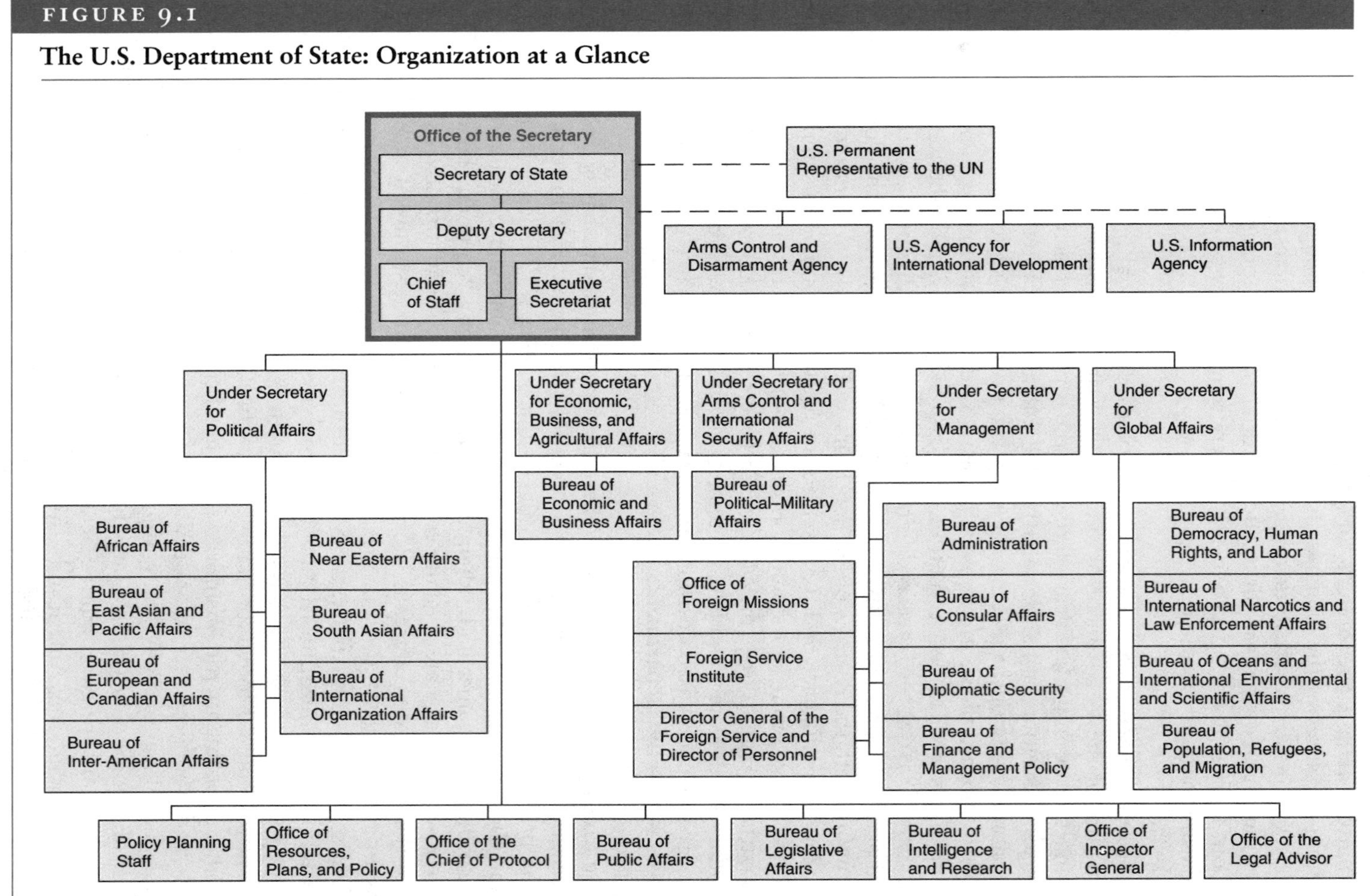

Source: U.S. Department of State *Dispatch Supplement* 6 (May 1995): 9.

and migration. Finally, the under secretary for management oversees many of the common internal administrative activities of the Department, ranging from operating the Foreign Service Institute, which provides language, political, cultural, and now business-promotion training for American governmental personnel assigned abroad, and managing the Department's Personnel Office. This Secretariat also manages the Bureaus of Administration, Consular Affairs, Diplomatic Security, and Finance and Management Policy.

An assistant secretary of state (some nineteen in all at present) heads each of the bureaus within the Department's structure and answers to either the Office of the Secretary or to the appropriate under secretary.[12] Because the recent reorganization has emphasized the need for the under secretaries to concentrate on broad overviews of policy, the assistant secretaries possess considerably greater latitude in policy formulation and decision making. As a result, these officials are likely to represent their bureaus within interagency groups consisting of other foreign affairs bureaucracies, in testimony before congressional committees or subcommittees, and perhaps with the secretary of state directly (although the chain of command goes through the appropriate under secretary).

Further, several functional activities were combined into new or consolidated bureaus, and the number of deputy assistant secretaries was scheduled for reduction in efforts to reduce the bureaucratic layering so evident in the State Department structure. On the one hand, several offices dealing with nuclear issues were consolidated into the Bureau of Political–Military Affairs. On the other hand, several international business activities were consolidated in the Bureau of Economic and Business Affairs.

Semiautonomous Agencies. In addition, four other agencies, attached to the Department of State in a semiautonomous fashion, complete the diplomatic apparatus of the United States government: the Office of the U.S. Permanent Representative to the United Nations, the Arms Control and Disarmament Agency, the U.S. Information Agency, and the U.S. Agency for International Development. The independent or semi-independent status of the last three remains quite precarious, especially with recent efforts to reorganize American foreign policy machinery by both executive and congressional officials. In 1993, for example, Secretary of State Warren Christopher proposed some rethinking of the independence of these agencies. Since the 1994 election, when Republicans gained control of the Congress and pursued the implementation of the "Contract with America," these offices have come under closer scrutiny, including calls for reorganization and elimination. Senator Jesse Helms, chair of the Senate Foreign Relations Committee, has called for the incorporation of many responsibilities of these agencies within the Department of State itself. Indeed, in April 1997, President Clinton directed that a plan for the reorganization of the U.S. Information Agency, Arms Control and Disarmament Agency, and the Agency for International Development be developed by September 1997. Under the proposed initiative, the Arms Control and Disarmament Agency would be incorporated into the Department of State within one year and the U.S. Information Agency within two years. The Agency for

International Development would remain a separate agency, but the secretary of state would have greater control over its activities.[13] The ultimate shape of these agencies, however, will still require congressional action. In this sense, the future status of three of the four semiautonomous agencies remains uncertain; still we can outline the specialized foreign policy responsibilities which each one pursued in the past.

The establishment of an Office for the U.S. Permanent Representative to the United Nations in the Department of State, an innovation undertaken by the Clinton administration, aims to allow America's UN ambassador to coordinate activities more directly with the Department of State and the Bureau of International Organization Affairs within the Department. Further, since the Clinton administration had placed the U.S. permanent representative on the Principals Committee of the National Security Council, an office in the Department of State provides a ready mechanism for greater coordination among the key policy makers.

The Arms Control and Disarmament Agency (ACDA) dates back to its establishment by Congress in 1961. Its responsibilities involve fostering global arms restraint, seeking arms control agreements with other states, and monitoring compliance with agreements in effect. Although its origins were initially tied to seeking nuclear weapons restraint, its efforts now include restraining conventional arms and weapons of mass destruction within developed nations and between developed and developing nations. This agency, for instance, has been deeply involved in the Strategic Arms Limitation Talks (SALT) of the 1970s, the Strategic Arms Reduction Talks (START) of the 1980s and 1990s, the Intermediate Nuclear Forces (INF) Treaty of 1987, and the Conventional Forces in Europe (CFE) discussions of the 1990s. The impact of this agency on arms control policy is dependent upon how much confidence the president and his key advisors place in this bureaucracy. During the Carter administration, for example, ACDA began to have a greater role to play in policy formulation.[14] For the Reagan administration, however, the White House assumed more direction in arms control policy, leaving less for this agency. For the Bush administration, the reliance upon the White House and the National Security staff for arms control policy implied a lesser dependence on ACDA. The Clinton administration committed itself "to strengthen and to revitalize ACDA in order for it to play an active role in meeting the arms control and nonproliferation challenges of the post–Cold War era.[15] ACDA Director John Holum testified before Congress in 1994 that the agency had been given a larger role: "Thus far, I have represented ACDA's perspective at principals' committee meetings [of the National Security Council] about once every 10 days, which I am told is dramatically more often than in the past."[16] Furthermore, ACDA played a useful role in securing an indefinite extension of the Nuclear Nonproliferation Treaty (NPT) in 1995.[17]

Created in 1953 in the early years of the Cold War, the third semiautonomous agency associated with the Department of State, the United States Information Agency (USIA), has evolved into an agency with several different responsibilities today. One of its missions is to explain "the official policies of the United States, its people, values and institutions," to other countries, another is to build "lasting relationships and mutual understandings" with nations and peoples abroad, and a third mission is to advise the American government on "foreign attitudes and their implications for U.S. policies."[18] To achieve these goals, USIA now broadcasts 900 hours weekly in forty-seven different languages through the Voice of America (VOA), operates Radio Marti, TV Marti, and WORLDNET, a satellite television network, and oversees the operations of Radio Free Europe/Radio Liberty and Radio Free Asia. USIA also distributes some of its news and information programming through the Internet in sixteen different languages. It publishes, in five languages, the Wireless File, daily news and information summaries and transcripts of selected speeches and statements of American governmental officials. This agency also operates 160 libraries in 110 countries as well as support libraries in 100 binational centers in 20 different countries. USIA sponsors an extensive series of educational and cultural exchange programs, including new initiatives for the newly independent states of the former Soviet Union and Eastern Europe, more traditional Fulbright scholar exchanges, and the International Visitor program. Through all of these activities, the United States Information Agency attempts to provide an accurate picture of the United States to other nations and peoples.

Despite what still appears as a very large set of diverse activities, USIA has actually undergone considerable downsizing in recent years. This trend seems likely to continue for the foreseeable future, as efforts are under way to control spending and to reshape America's foreign policy machinery after the Cold War. USIA's budget request for fiscal year 1996 ($1.3 billion), for instance, was $121 million lower than for fiscal year 1995, and its actual fiscal year 1997 budget was lower still ($1.1 billion).[19] It also initiated an 11 percent reduction in personnel (with more than 1,000 jobs scheduled for elimination) over the 1994–1996 period.

USIA has eliminated some entire areas of activities. Until recently, the agency published five magazines for distribution abroad, but these have fallen victims to budgetary constraints. Similarly, the United States Information Service (as the USIA is known abroad) has scheduled twelve libraries or outposts to be closed by the end of 1996, and it has altered service in others. One USIA library is restricting access to researchers only (thus eliminating public access in this foreign country), reducing staff, and employing new technology (e.g., CD-ROM and Internet facilities) at the expense of providing new books.[20] In addition to these changes, the ongoing debate over reintegrating the agency within the Department of State keeps the future of USIA in a most precarious state.

The United States Agency for International Development (USAID), another semiautonomous bureaucracy within the Department of State structure created by Congress in 1961, seeks to move United States foreign aid away from providing security assistance to greater considerations of economic need and development goals. The agency is an integral part of the International Development Cooperation Agency, an umbrella organization that coordinates the activities of several development units, including the Overseas Private Investment Corporation, the Trade and Development Program, the Development Coordination Committee, the Food for Peace Program, and United States participation in multilateral development banks and other international organizations and programs. The director of USAID also heads the International Development Cooperation Agency and thus serves as the president's and the secretary of state's principal advisor on international development activities.[21]

The current mission of USAID is to promote "sustainable development" worldwide by supporting programs on population and health, economic growth, the environment, and democratic development. Organizationally, USAID seeks to achieve these goals through a series of regional and functional bureaus and through its various AID missions or posts located in countries throughout the developing world. Its budget is quite small, at approximately one half of one percent of the United States federal budget (e.g., in fiscal year 1993, $7 billion, and in fiscal year 1997, $6 billion),[22] but, by combining its efforts with and through nongovernmental organizations (NGOs) working around the world, USAID points to numerous successes such as the eradication of smallpox, the immunization of millions of children worldwide, and assistance to small entrepreneurs.

This bureaucracy is undergoing the same kind of review and scrutiny as the two previous ones.[23] As with the other two agencies, USAID has been targeted for budgetary cut and possible incorporation into the Department of State. In an effort to stave off such actions, USAID has undertaken several actions to rationalize and downsize its operation. By the end of 1996, for example, twenty-one overseas missions were slated to be closed, staff reductions of over 1,200 had already occurred, and numerous internal reforms had been put into place. Still, calls have been made for a 50 percent reduction in the foreign aid budget and for USAID's functions to be taken up by various bureaus within the Department of State. Whatever the ultimate shape of the reorganization efforts, the implication for USAID is much the same as for ACDA and USIA: It is likely to play a less important foreign policy role than during the Cold War years.

The Structure of State Abroad

The State Department also has the responsibility to represent America abroad through United States missions, usually located in the capital city and with consulates in other major cities of host countries. As of March 1996, the United States operated about 260 embassies, missions, consular agencies, consulates general, and other offices abroad.[24] It also had ten missions at the headquarters of various intergovernmental organizations (e.g., the United Nations, the European Union, Organization of American States, and the International Civil Aviation Organization). In all, the United States conducts diplomatic relations with over 180 nations; there are only a few nations with whom the United States does not presently have diplomatic relations: Bhutan, Cuba, Iran, Iraq, and North Korea. In one of the newest diplomatic openings, relations with Vietnam were reestablished in 1995, and Palau, a former trust territory, was given full diplomatic recognition by the United States.

The United States embassy is headed by a chief of mission, usually an ambassador, who is the personal representative of the president and who is authorized to conduct United States foreign relations toward that country. The ambassador is assisted by the deputy chief of mission (DCM), who is largely responsible for conducting the day-to-day operation of the embassy staff. While political, economic, consular, and administrative foreign service officers from the Department of State serve the embassy, it also has representatives from several other executive departments housed within it. The composition of the "country team" of the United States mission in Venezuela illustrates this diversity (Figure 9.2).[25] The country team consists of an agricultural counselor from the Department of Agriculture, a public affairs counselor from USIA, a commercial counselor from the Department of Commerce, a defense attaché from the Department of Defense, and a military advisory group from the Department of Defense as well. Other agency representatives are also present, ranging from the Drug Enforcement Agency to the Internal Revenue Service. In addition, officials from the Central Intelligence Agency—using a cover of some other position—are often represented in the country team. In all, numerous departments and agencies serve within a single United States mission abroad. The actual size of the mission will be a function primarily of the size of the nation where the United States mission is located and the perceived political and strategic importance of that nation. In the Venezuelan mission, in June 1985, 108 Americans were employed in the United States mission in Caracas and the consulate in Maracaibo. By contrast, the United States Embassy staff totaled 266 in London and only 21 in Brazzaville, the People's Republic of the Congo at the time.[26] More recently (1994 data), the sizes of American missions abroad range even more widely than these examples, with about 1,100 United States direct hires in Germany (and an additional 800 foreign nationals) to a one-person mission in the Former Yugoslav Republic of Macedonia. Today, the median size of a United States mission abroad is roughly 100—equally divided between Americans and foreign nationals.[27]

As this overview indicates, the structure of the Department of State (and its affiliated agencies) appears to be quite large and complex. Yet, in reality, the Department itself is one of the smallest bureaucracies within the executive branch. In 1995, the State Department had about 25,000 employees with 8,800 in the United States and 16,000 abroad (including about 10,000 foreign nationals). (By contrast, the Department of Defense had about 850,000 civilian employees at the same time.[28]) It is smaller in size than all but four other cabinet departments (Department of Energy, Department of Labor, Department of Housing and Urban Development, and Department of Education).[29] Furthermore, the budget of the Department of State is one of the smallest within the government, at about $2.2 billion, and especially small when compared with other foreign affairs sectors of the government, such as the Department of Defense or the Central Intelligence Agency.[30]

The Weakened Influence of State

Despite its role as the principal foreign policy bureaucracy, and as the one that will usually offer the nonmilitary option for conducting foreign policy, the Department of State has been criticized for its effectiveness in both policy formulation and policy implementation.[31] As a consequence, the

FIGURE 9.2

The Structure of a U.S. Mission Abroad—Venezuela

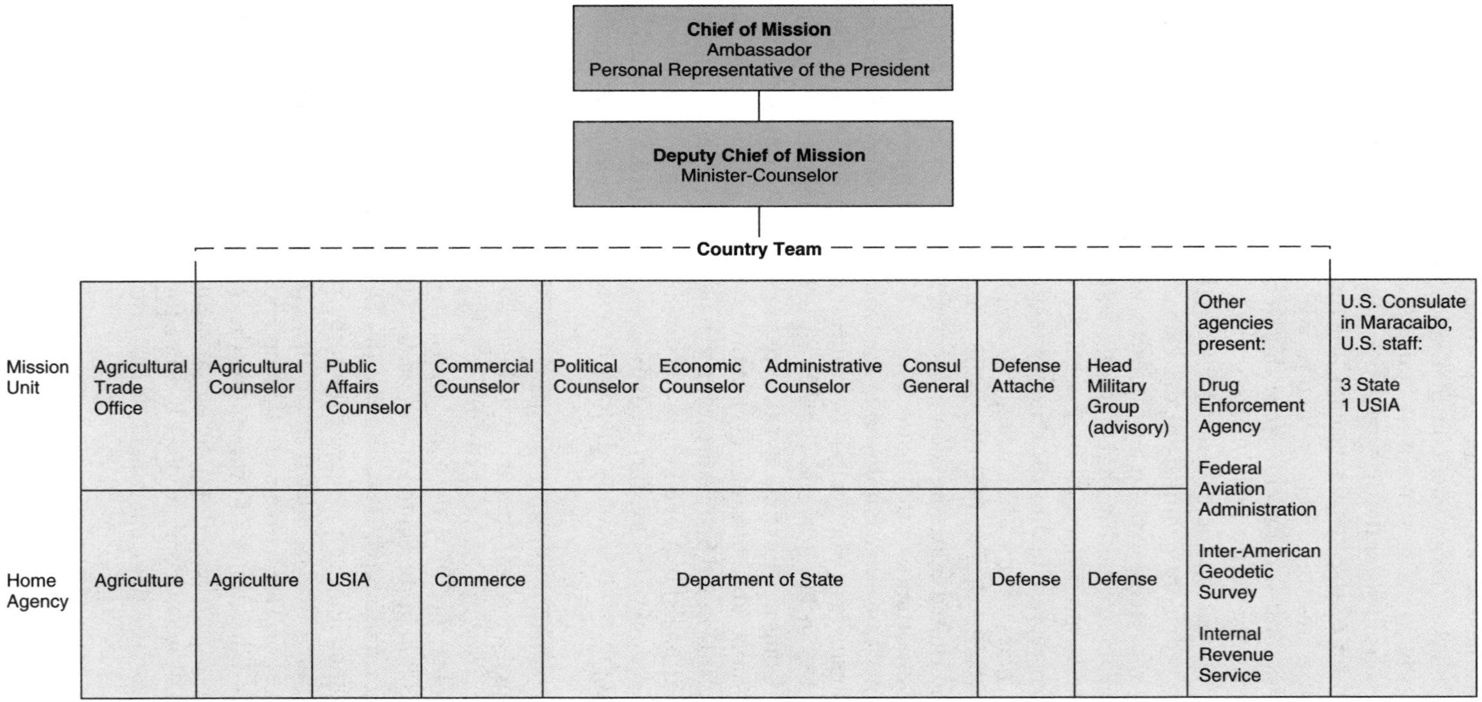

Chief of Mission
Ambassador
Personal Representative of the President

Deputy Chief of Mission
Minister-Counselor

Country Team

Mission Unit	Agricultural Trade Office	Agricultural Counselor	Public Affairs Counselor	Commercial Counselor	Political Counselor	Economic Counselor	Administrative Counselor	Consul General	Defense Attache	Head Military Group (advisory)	Other agencies present: Drug Enforcement Agency Federal Aviation Administration Inter-American Geodetic Survey Internal Revenue Service	U.S. Consulate in Maracaibo, U.S. staff: 3 State 1 USIA
Home Agency	Agriculture	Agriculture	USIA	Commerce	Department of State				Defense	Defense		

Source: U.S. Department of State, "Foreign Relations Machinery," *Atlas of U.S. Foreign Relations* (Washington, DC: Bureau of Public Affairs, October 1982), p. 6.

Department of State has not played the dominant role in recent administrations that its central diplomatic position might imply. Indeed, a recent departmental report has now formally acknowledged that the Department of State should not be the focus point for coordinating foreign policy. Instead, the *State 2000* report asserted "that the National Security Council (NSC) [should] be the catalyst and the point of coordination for this new, single foreign policy process."[32]

In this sense, the *policy influence* of the Department of State is comparatively less than that of other foreign policy bureaucracies in the United States government. The factors that have reduced the policy influence of the State Department range from a series of *internal* problems, such as its increasing budget problems, its size, the kind of personnel within this bureaucracy, the "subculture" within the organization, and the relationship between the secretary of state and the Department to a series of *external* problems—such as the relationship between the president and secretary, the relationship between the president and the Department, and the perception of the public at large, as well as the growth of other foreign policy bureaucracies (e.g., the National Security Council and the Office of the U.S. Trade Representative). Let us examine several of these factors in more detail to give some sense of the weakened influence of the Department of State.

The Problem of Resources. The first problem that the Department of State faces in the competition to influence foreign affairs and to carry out its responsibilities is resources. The small operating budget of the Department has been a perennial problem over the last decade, with the Congress reluctant to fund all of its needs. By contrast, the funding for the Department of Defense and the intelligence community grew in the 1980s, although these departments, too, are suffering from budgetary pressures after the end of the Cold War (see Chapter 10).

To be sure, the Department of State's budget has increased from about $700 million in 1979 to about $2.2 billion currently, but the effects of inflation, congressional mandates for establishing new departmental bureaus, and the expansion of foreign affairs responsibilities worldwide have caused a real problem. Moreover, the Congress has not always been responsive to the Department's needs and, indeed, has sought to stop some activities with which it disagrees (e.g., several controversial foreign assistance programs). In February 1987, Secretary of State George Shultz became so frustrated that he commented that State's budget problems were "a tragedy." As a result, "America is hauling down the flag...We're withdrawing from the world." By November 1987, the Department began hinting that 1,200 jobs would have to be eliminated, and several embassies and consulates around the world would need to be closed because of these mounting budget problems.[33]

By the time of the Clinton administration, the closing of numerous foreign posts (i.e., consulates, embassies) had become a reality. By the end of 1994, for example, the United States government closed seventeen foreign posts, and another twenty to twenty-five posts were under discussion.[34] In July 1995, nineteen overseas posts were scheduled for closing by the end of 1996. To be sure, many of these closings were consulates in peripheral locations around the world (e.g., consulates in Brisbane, Australia; Cebu, the Philippines; Udorn, Thailand; Bilbao, Spain; and Matamoros, Mexico) and represented efforts to consolidate operations within a country. A few, however, were embassies (e.g., Equatorial Guinea, Western Samoa, and the Seychelles).[35] Nonetheless, all of these closings reduce American presence globally and increase the workload for other posts.

At the same time, reductions in State Department staff have occurred as well. In May 1995, Secretary of State Warren Christopher indicated that 500 State Department positions would be eliminated to save money, streamline the policy process, and forestall even greater reductions by the Republican-controlled Congress. Six months later, the Department of State reported that over 1,100 jobs had been trimmed.[36] Furthermore, budgetary pressures remain as domestic efforts continued to balance the federal budget by 2002.

In the views of those at the Department of State, serious policy implications accompany these funding problems. First, State Department personnel are not adequately compensated or supported under such circumstances. Salaries are relatively low (compared to similar positions in the private sector), and salary increases are small. As a result, top-quality staff becomes more difficult to keep and less easy to recruit. While concerns have been expressed that the quality of the new recruits does not match that of earlier years, regular recruiting has been forestalled. The foreign service exam, the principal mechanism to screen new foreign service officers, was not even offered in two recent years (1994 and 1995). Second, budget restraints also mean that individuals are asked to carry greater and greater workloads, and, inevitably, the quality of their work suffers. Third, morale also suffers as officials are asked to do more with less and, sometimes, even to work without pay. Finally, America's foreign policy representation around the world potentially pays a price in this kind of environment. Both the collection of information and implementation of policy by the departmental personnel are unlikely to be as complete under such circumstances. All in all, then, from the Department of State's view, the continuing budget problem reduces both the incentives and the capacities of the Department for competing with other bureaucracies in shaping United States foreign policy.

The Problem of Size. A second problem of the Department of State, as it attempts to compete with other bureaucracies, focuses on its size. It is, at once, too large and too small. It is too large in the sense that there are "layers and layers" of bureaucracy through which policy reviews and recommendations must progress. At the present time, for example, there are six geographical and fourteen functional bureaus involved in policy making. In most instances, policy recommendations must go through the appropriate regional and functional bureaus before they can reach the "seventh floor," where the executive offices of the department are located.

As Bush's Secretary of State James Baker quickly found out, and reported in his memoir, getting things done at State can be a challenge: "Different floors of 'the building' [the State Department] had their own unique views on events: 'The seventh floor [where the Secretary and under secretaries are located] won't want it that way.' 'The sixth floor [where the assistant secretaries are] wants to reclama on that'....'EUR [the Bureau of European and Canadian Affairs] is out of control.'"[37] In this sense, the structure of State's bureaucracy hinders its overall effectiveness and reduces efficiency in developing policy.

At the same time, the Department has been criticized as too small, because it is dwarfed by the other bureaucracies in terms of political representation in the National Security Council interagency process (see Chapter 10). Furthermore, staff does not often carry the same domestic political clout as other large bureaucracies. Consider the lobbying power of the Department of Defense, the Department of Commerce, Department of Treasury, or even the Department of Agriculture; all these agencies have large and vocal constituencies to argue their policy position with the American people, the Congress, and, ultimately, the president. By contrast, the Department of State lacks a ready constituency within the American public to offer support and political lobbying within the Congress.[38] The State Department must therefore lobby by itself through the testimony of its officials during congressional hearings, through its informal contacts with congressional staff through the implementation of legislative action programs (LAPs), and through the interagency process. Suffice it to say, these avenues do not always yield political success for the Department of State.

The Personnel Problem. A third problem of the Department of State focuses on its personnel and the environment in which they operate. Foreign service officers, reserve foreign service officers, and civil service personnel from the United States Foreign Service comprise the principal officials of the department. Primary policy responsibility, however, rests with the approximately 7,300 foreign service officers (FSOs) in the department.[39] These officers have sometimes been depicted in the past as an "Eastern elite," out of touch with the country and determined to shape policy in line with their own foreign policy views. According to this line of criticism, many of these foreign service officers share the same educational background (e.g., Princeton, Harvard, Yale, Johns Hopkins, Fletcher School of Law and Diplomacy), overrepresent the Eastern establishment, and adopt a rather inflexible attitude toward global politics. However, several careful analyses of the foreign service officer corps challenge some of these stereotypes, and mid-career ("lateral entry") and minority recruitment efforts were undertaken to address them as well.[40] Nonetheless, this elitist image persists, as more recent assessments confirm, and it reduces the effectiveness of the Department of State.[41]

At least two additional personnel problems are perceived among members of Congress, the foreign affairs bureaucracy, and the public at large. One is the charge of "clientelism," or "clientitis."[42] That is, in an FSO's zeal to foster good relations with the country in which he or she is serving, the officer becomes too closely identified with the interests of that state, sometimes at the expense of American interests and the requirements of American domestic politics. While the criticism is largely overdrawn, it becomes an important staple of members of Congress or the executive branch who want to avoid relying too closely on the recommendations of the State Department.

A second problem is the level of expertise the State Department personnel and FSOs possess on increasingly specialized issues. While these individuals are undoubtedly capable generalists, the level of specific knowledge on technical subjects—and some reluctance to recruit outside experts—foster the charge that the quality of work is inadequate:

> Critics complain the State Department studies are long and too descriptive and often unsatisfactory. Based heavily on intuition, and almost never conceptual, many of the analyses are unaccompanied by reliable sources and information, or reflect the FSO's lack of adequate training and expertise; papers are so cautious and vague as to be of little use to policymakers who long ago concluded that such "waffling" constitutes the quintessential character of the "Fudge Factory at Foggy Bottom."[43]

The other side of this personnel complaint is exactly the reverse: "The tendency to assume that others do not understand foreign affairs as well as the Foreign Service."[44] With the emergence of sound academic programs, research institutes, and Washington think tanks on many specialized issues, and with political appointees in and out of government on a regular basis, State Department FSOs should be more willing to look to these individuals for policy advice as well.

The Subculture Problem. Accompanying this kind of personnel problem is a related one. Even if the individuals themselves are not the source of the problem for the Department of State, the *environment* of the department creates a personnel problem. A bureaucratic "subculture" has developed in the State Department that emphasizes the importance of "trying to *be* something rather than...trying to *do* something."[45] "Don't rock the boat" is the dominant bureaucratic refrain. Because of these institutional norms, obtaining regular promotions and ensuring career advancements become more important than creating sound, innovative policy: "Subcultural norms discourage vigorous policy debate within the Department....The Department is not inclined toward vigorous exploration of policy options and it is not inclined to let anyone else do the job for it."[46] Another analyst describes the subculture in this way: "The prudent course is the cautious course. 'Fitting in' has a higher value than 'standing out.'"[47]

More recently, former Secretary of State James Baker confirmed the persistence of this State Department subculture. In his experience, Baker noted, "the State Department has the most unique bureaucratic culture I've ever encountered."[48] While Baker acknowledged the skills of most foreign service officers, he also found that "some of them tend to avoid risk-taking or creative thinking" because of the bureaucratic environment.[49] As a result, he found that sole reliance on State Department officials in policy making was not possible.

The President and the Secretary of State. A fifth problem of the Department of State focuses on its relationship with the president and the secretary of state.[50] Postwar presidents and secretaries of state have often not made extensive use of the Department for policy formulation. Instead, presidents have tried to be their own "secretary of state" or have relied on key advisors instead of the appointed secretary of state for foreign policy advice. For these reasons, the power of the secretary of state in policy making may be more apparent than real. Even when the secretary of state enjoys the confidence of the president for formulating policy, he sometimes chooses not to involve the department widely and instead relies on a few key aides. Because of these patterns, the State Department's role has once again been diminished.

President John Kennedy, for example, initially sought to use the Department of State for foreign policy, but he ultimately came to rely upon his formal and informal advisors within the bureaucracy and the White House.[51] His secretary of state, Dean Rusk, did not enjoy a central role in the formulation of policy. President Kennedy's successor, Lyndon Johnson, made more use of Secretary Rusk than did Kennedy, but he, too, depended upon his national security advisor, first McGeorge Bundy, then Walt Rostow, for key foreign policy advice.[52]

Recent presidents have followed a similar pattern. President Richard Nixon did not view Secretary of State William Rogers as his key foreign policy advisor; instead, National Security Advisor Henry Kissinger was the primary architect of foreign policy during those years. President Carter initially tried to create a balance in policy making between Secretary of State Cyrus Vance and National Security Advisor Zbigniew Brzezinski, but he depended more on Brzezinski for shaping his response to global politics. In fact, Vance resigned in April 1980, after losing a policy dispute over the wisdom of attempting to rescue the American hostages in Iran. President Reagan came to office committed to granting more control of foreign policy to the secretary of state—first to Alexander Haig and then to George Shultz—but here, too, recent evidence suggests that at least three of Reagan's national security advisors, William Clark, Robert McFarlane, and John Poindexter, were quite influential in policy making at the expense of the secretary of state.[53] Indeed, Secretary Shultz testified to the Congress that on one of the major foreign policy initiatives he was generally kept in the dark. He knew little about the Iran arms deal—and opposed what he knew—and was not aware of the diversion of funds to the Nicaraguan Contras. After the Iran-Contra affair became public, Shultz gained more control of foreign policy than had previous secretaries of state in some time. Nonetheless, he continued to engage in protracted bureaucratic battles to put his stamp on policy.

Even the two postwar presidents who have relied on the secretary of state for policy formulation did not often go beyond him to enlist the full involvement of the department itself. Dean Acheson and George Marshall, secretaries of state under President Harry Truman, were primarily responsible for making their own foreign policy without much input on the part of the department.[54] Similarly, John Foster Dulles, secretary of state under President Dwight Eisenhower, was given wide latitude in the formulation of foreign policy.

The Bush and Clinton administrations tried to combine these various policy patterns. President Bush viewed foreign policy as an area of his own expertise since he had served as United States ambassador to the United Nations, director of the CIA, and the American representative to the People's

Republic of China. As such, he assumed a large role in policy formulation, but relied on both his close friend and secretary of state, James Baker, and his national security advisor, Brent Scowcroft. By contrast, during his first term, President Clinton eschewed the importance of foreign policy and largely left its oversight to Anthony Lake, his national security advisor, and Warren Christopher, his secretary of state. In his second term, he is more directly involved, but his national security advisor, Samuel Berger, and his secretary of state, Madeleine Albright, remain key formulators of policy.

More formally, then, both Bush and Clinton placed the national security advisor and his staff at the center of foreign policy making, as we shall discuss below, but both sought to include their secretaries of state in the foreign policy process.[55] Clinton's first secretary of state, Warren Christopher, for example, was the more public figure of President Clinton's foreign policy advisors (e.g., traveling to Europe to promote a new Bosnian effort or traveling to Asia to improve relations in that region). In the policy areas, too, Christopher played a key role, emphasizing the importance of economics as an American priority in foreign policy, the importance of Asia to America's future, the need for progress in the Middle East and reform in Russia, the dangers of nuclear proliferation, and the need to promote human rights. Given his lawyerly background, Christopher generally sought diplomatic and negotiated routes for these pressing foreign policy issues.[56]

Clinton's second secretary of state, Madeleine Albright, follows in these traditions. While she will continue to be the public spokesperson for American diplomacy, she is likely to be a more assertive policy formulator than was Christopher within the administration. Yet, she is unlikely to achieve any kind of independent policy-making role such as characterized some earlier secretaries in the post–World War II years, since the national security council system and the influence of the national security advisor militate against such independence (see Chapter 10). In sum, the secretary of state in the Clinton administration, like other recent administrations, will continue to be prominent, but will not dominate, policy formulation; instead, policy making will increasingly be a shared responsibility.

In sum, under any of the arrangements for the past five decades—where the secretary of state was primarily responsible for foreign policy, where the president relied upon other advisors for policy making, or where the president tried to be his own secretary of state—the Department of State's role in the formulation of foreign affairs has been reduced in comparison with other executive institutions or key individuals.

The President and the Department. Yet another aspect of the problem between the Department of State and the president was summarized by a former foreign service officer, Jack Perry, in this way: "...the Foreign Service does not enjoy the confidence of our presidents." Too often, foreign service officers are perceived as potentially "disloyal" to the president. Instead, they are seen as being loyal "either to the opposition party or else to the diplomat's own view of what foreign policy should be."[57]

The percentage of ambassadorships that go to political friends—mainly large campaign contributors with limited foreign policy experience—reflects this degree of suspicion between the president and State. These appointments

FIGURE 9.3

Career and Noncareer Appointments As Ambassadors, Kennedy Administration Through the Clinton Administration

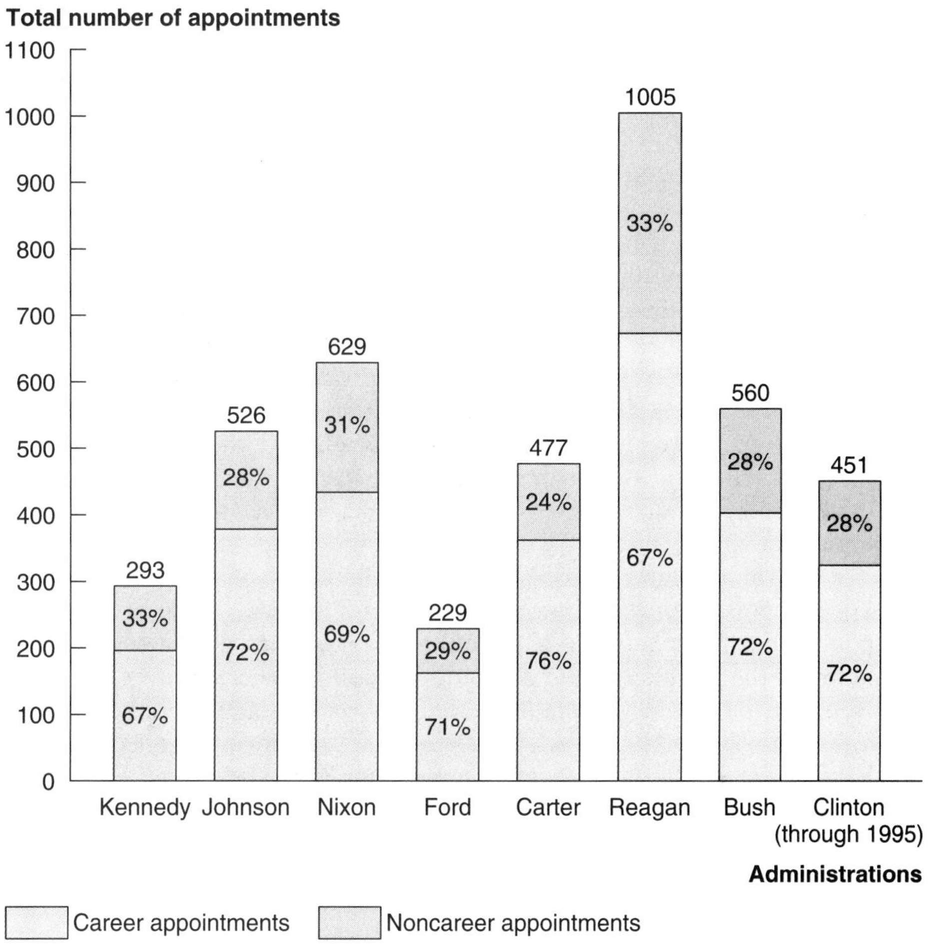

Source: The yearly data were generously provided by the American Foreign Service Association, based upon Department of State compilations, and the author calculated totals for each administration. The Kennedy total includes all of 1963, even though Johnson served in late November and December 1963, and the Nixon total includes all of 1974, even though Ford served from August 1974. From the Bush administration to the present, the data include appointments to multilateral ambassadorship (e.g., United Nations, NATO, and Organization for Economic Cooperation and Development).

reduce the opportunities available for career foreign service officers, whose aspirations may be to gain ambassadorships to cap their long service to the Department of State. While some analyses focusing on only the first year or so of an administration found somewhat higher percentage of appointments going to political friends as opposed to career diplomats,[58] the entire record of ambassadorial appointment by presidents from Kennedy through Clinton reveals that slightly less than one-third went to political friends and campaign contributors. The percentage of such appointments ranged from 24 percent for Carter to 33 percent for Kennedy and Reagan (see Figure 9.3).

While these percentages have remained relatively stable over the past eight administrations, what these numbers fail to reveal are that some key and prestigious ambassadorships in several administrations have not gone to presumably the most skilled foreign policy officials; instead, they have gone to large campaign contributors and political allies. President Clinton, for example, appointed the late Pamela Harriman, who had contributed $132,000 to Democrats in recent years, to be ambassador to France, and a successful hotel operator in California, M. Larry Lawrence, who donated $196,000 to the Democratic party, as ambassador to Switzerland. Other large contributors received ambassadorial appointments to the Netherlands, Austria, and Barbados.[59]

Aside from the influence of money in politics, critics see serious problems with such appointments from a policy point of view. They reduce the role of the Department of State in the foreign policy process, and the political appointees' inexperience may be damaging to the conduct of United States foreign policy. Furthermore, these ambassadors may feel much freer to circumvent the State Department in shaping policy and use "backchannels" to the White House. In doing so, they alienate the career personnel within an embassy and further weaken an orderly foreign policy process. One senator described such appointments starkly: They are "ticking time bombs moving all over the world."[60]

The United States ambassador to a small Asia-Pacific nation, and a political appointee of the Clinton administration, defends these kinds of appointments.[61] The political appointee as ambassador, he argues, has better access to the president than nonpolitical appointees. Furthermore, the president may be more willing to listen to his or her personal appointee than to a career diplomat. In this way, these kinds of appointments may actually enhance American diplomacy by better serving both the United States and the host country.

The use of political appointees within the Department of State and the weighing of political loyalties in appointing foreign service officers as ambassadors also exemplify this suspicion between State and the president. One tactic, for instance, has been to engage in a "purge" of bureaus and personnel that were perceived as not fully committed to the administration's policy. The Bureau of Inter-American Affairs suffered this fate early in the Reagan administration because it was not fully in tune with the priorities of the White House. The assistant secretary of state of this bureau was replaced with a career diplomat perceived as more loyal to the administration's goal, albeit lacking in Latin American experience. When the diplomat began to waver on policy, he was ultimately replaced by a political appointee who was a staunch conservative and wholly committed to the policy of aiding the Nicaraguan Contras. Ambassadors to several Central American countries (El Salvador, Nicaragua, and Honduras) from the Carter administration were fired or transferred because they were not viewed as fully committed to a marked change in policy to the region. In turn, they were replaced by "foreign service officers with reputations as good generalists willing to follow orders and not raise troubling questions."[62]

The Bush administration employed a number of political appointees, particularly at the top of the State Department bureaucracy. The four key political operatives for Secretary of State James Baker came from outside the Department, and one of them was responsible for screening all papers that reached the secretary. By one account, the Department's attitude "evolved from deep hostility to ambivalence" toward Baker and these appointees. The career foreign service people "felt altogether shut out for a time, and to some extent they still are."[63] They were, however, pleased that Secretary Baker was personally close to the president because, if they could break through to the leadership, they could play a greater role in policy making.

For the Clinton administration, the most notable political appointment within the Department of State was President Clinton's long-time friend and one-time roommate during their days at Oxford, and a former journalist, Strobe Talbott.[64] Talbott was initially appointed as an ambassador at large with special responsibilities to the Secretary of State regarding policy toward the former Soviet Union. By the end of President Clinton's first year in office, however, Talbott was appointed as deputy secretary of state, with numerous career officers being passed over. With his new title, Talbott largely continued his work on policy toward Russia, and his policy importance was manifest in that "only Talbott was in the room for Clinton's one-on-one with Yeltsin," during a Moscow summit in 1994.[65] In addition, he also began to assume a more consequential role across the policy agenda and in internal State Department operations.

Other critical Clinton appointments also went to key political allies and campaign activists, and the ranks of the foreign service were bypassed once again. The under secretaries for International Security Affairs and for Economic and Agricultural Affairs, for example, were outsiders as were the initial assistant secretary for European and Canadian Affairs and the director of USAID.[66] While these kinds of political appointments are not particularly new with the Clinton administration, they do reflect the eroding reliance on personnel within the Department itself.

As with other recent administrations, too, the policy direction of the Clinton administration, especially over Bosnia, caused grumbling within the State Department ranks because their advice was not heeded. By early 1994, five State Department officials resigned and others protested to the secretary.[67] While some were surely unhappy over the failure to heed the views of the foreign policy analysts within the Department and over policy changes by the administration, morale still remained "level," according to one close observer.[68]

Overall, though, the role of the career officials at the Department of State continued to erode, with increasing numbers of political appointees, both as ambassadors and as key departmental leaders. In a slightly different context, one former foreign service officer perhaps said it best more than a dozen years ago: "Creeping politicization has corrupted foreign service professionalism." In turn, this former FSO added, politicization "has hindered American diplomacy."[69]

The Public's View. A final reason for the Department of State's weakened influence derives from the whole domestic setting: The department has never really enjoyed a sound reputation among the American public. Beyond the view that the State Department is out of step with the nation as a whole, members of Congress and the executive branch have called for making the Department more efficient and effective. While the negative public image has perhaps waned over the decades, it, along with the other restraints evident within the Department, has produced a certain caution in policy choices advanced by State Department personnel.

THE NATIONAL SECURITY COUNCIL

The National Security Council (NSC) and its staff remains the bureaucracy that has enlarged its role in the foreign policy process over the last four decades. The NSC has grown from a relatively small agency with solely a policy-coordinating function to one with a separate bureaucratic structure and major policy-making function. Its head, now designated as the assistant to the president for national security affairs (or the national security advisor), is viewed as a major formulator of United States foreign policy, often surpassing the influence of the secretary of state and the secretary of defense.

Because of this evolution, an important distinction ought to be kept in mind as we discuss two different, but related, bureaucratic arrangements operating under the "National Security Council" label. One bureaucratic arrangement refers to the "NSC system" and focuses on the departmental memberships on the National Security Council itself and the subsequent interagency working groups established by presidents to coordinate policy making across the existing bureaucracies. That coordination process remains intact and is the focus of the last portion of Chapter 10. The other bureaucratic arrangement, and one that has become more commonly discussed lately, refers to the "NSC staff" (or simply "the NSC"), the separate bureaucracy that has developed over the years and which has increasingly played an independent role in United States foreign policymaking.[70] The following discussion focuses on the growth of that bureaucracy and its policy-making role and leaves the former to the next chapter.

The Development of the NSC Bureaucracy

As originally constituted under the National Security Act of 1947, the National Security Council was to be a mechanism for coordinating policy options among the various foreign affairs bureaucracies. By statute, members were to be limited to the president, the vice president, secretary of state, and secretary of defense, with the director of central intelligence and the chairman of the joint chiefs of staff as advisors; these members, along with others that the president might choose to invite, met to consider policy options at the discretion of the president.[71] Over time, the NSC system has evolved with a set of interdepartmental committees to support the National Security Council itself.

Table 9.1 portrays the composition of the National Security Council under the Clinton administration. The composition includes those required

TABLE 9.1

Composition of the National Security Council

Statutory Members of the NSC
- President
- Vice President
- Secretary of State
- Secretary of Defense

Statutory Advisors to the NSC
- Director of Central Intelligence
- Chair, Joint Chiefs of Staff

Other Attendees
- Chief of Staff to the President
- Assistant to the President for National Security Affairs
- U.S. Representative to the United Nations
- Secretary of Treasury*
- Assistant to the President for Economic Policy*
- Attorney General (for meetings dealing with her jurisdiction)
- Others as invited

*By executive order, the Clinton administration has designated these two appointees as members of the National Security Council.

Source: Presidential Decision Directive 2, The White House, Washington, DC, January 20, 1993.

by statute, but in 1993 some important additions were made to the regular attendees at such meetings. Most notably, by executive order, the secretary of treasury and the head of the National Economic Council were designated as members of the National Security Council as well.[72]

Under the original legislative mandate for the National Security Council, the assumption was that the *staff* of the NSC was to be small and its responsibilities focused largely on facilitating the coordination of activities among the various foreign affairs departments. Indeed, the NSC staff originally had only three major components: "(a) the Office of the Executive Secretary; (b) a Secretariat...and (c) a unit simply called 'the staff.'" The executive secretary and the secretariat were the permanent employees and generally undertook the actual coordinating activities of the Council. The staff "initially consisted wholly of officials detailed on a full-time basis by the departments and agencies represented on the Council" and was assisted by a full-time support group as well.[73] Their responsibilities focused on preparing studies on various regional and functional questions. Nonetheless, the staff members continued to maintain and coordinate their work with the respective departments from which they were drawn. Coordination across departments appeared to be more important than an independent assessment that they might undertake.

Presidents Truman and Eisenhower used the NSC as a coordinating body, too. Because President Truman had relatively strong secretaries of state, and because he tended to employ them for policy advice, he used the

National Security Council meetings primarily as an arena for the exchange of ideas (often not attending the meetings himself until the outbreak of the Korean War). President Eisenhower, by contrast, met with the National Security Council on almost a weekly basis and relied upon it for decision-making discussions. (By one account, Eisenhower attended 306 out of 338 NSC meetings during his presidency.) Actual policy decisions, however, seemed to have been made outside this forum, especially as Secretary of State John Foster Dulles gained decision-making influence.[74] For neither of these presidents, though, was the NSC staff the independent policy influencer that it was to become.

Under Eisenhower, however, the structure and staff of the National Security Council bureaucracy began to change and gain some greater definition. Eisenhower, for instance, created the post of special assistant to the president for national security affairs for Robert Cutler and named him the "principal executive officer" of the NSC.[75] The staff structure was also revamped and enlarged, and the mandate and duties of the NSC itself expanded. Most notably, President Eisenhower stated that members of the NSC were "a corporate body composed of individuals advising the President in their own right, rather than as representatives of their respective departments and agencies." In a later revision, however, he did indicate that "the views of their respective departments and agencies" ought to be stated as well.[76] While Cutler and the NSC staff continued to perform their coordinating role, President Eisenhower's statements were the first hints of a more independent policy role for the NSC bureaucracy and its staff. Moreover, such a view of the NSC bureaucracy would eventually become a reality during the succeeding administrations.

The Rise of the National Security Advisor

By the time of the Kennedy administration, the role of the National Security Council began to change, and a more prominent role for the national security advisor ("special assistant for national security affairs") emerged. Now more reliance was placed on key ad hoc advisors, including the national security advisor, but not on the NSC as such by the president. In fact, few meetings of the Council were held during the Kennedy years. Instead, the national security advisor began to emerge as a source of policy making, rather than as only a policy coordinator. As a result of Kennedy's reorganization of the NSC staff, the national security advisor had a number of previous staff responsibilities consolidated into his office. As a consequence, McGeorge Bundy became the first national security advisor to serve in a policy-formulating and policy-coordinating capacity.[77]

The role of national security advisor was enhanced even more during the administration of President Lyndon Johnson. Walt W. Rostow, successor to Bundy during much of President Johnson's term, and a small group of advisors (the "Tuesday Lunch" group) played an increasingly large role in the formulation of American foreign policy, and especially Vietnam policy.[78] As during the Kennedy years, the national security advisor gained influence, but the National Security Council, as a decision or discussion forum, actually declined in importance.

The full implication of this changed decision-making style became most apparent during the administration of President Richard Nixon.[79] In particular, the appointment of Henry A. Kissinger as national security advisor further transformed the use of the national security advisor in foreign policy making. Henry Kissinger, an academic and consultant to previous administrations, was familiar with, and critical of, the bureaucratic machinery of government. In large measure, he saw the bureaucracy as being an impediment to effective policy making and as hindering the job of the "statesman."[80] Through his considerable personal skill, Kissinger was able to reorganize the decision-making apparatus of the foreign policy bureaucracies so that he was able to dominate all the principal decision machinery, and the National Security Council and staff were to become the focal point of all policy analyses.

Kissinger accomplished this transformation through the development of a series of interdepartmental committees flowing from the National Security Council system. These committees included representatives from the other principal foreign policy bureaucracies, but, at the same time, they excluded those institutions from ultimate authority for making policy recommendations. In fact, Kissinger set up a senior review group, which he himself chaired, for examining all policy recommendations before they were sent to the National Security Council and the president.[81] Even when Kissinger became secretary of state (as well as national security advisor) in September 1973, and when Gerald Ford became president in August, 1974, this pattern of National Security Council staff dominance continued.

The National Security Advisor: The Carter and Reagan Administrations

Under President Jimmy Carter, the initial impulse was to reduce the role of the national security advisor and his staff (partly in reaction to the role that Henry Kissinger had played in the previous eight years) and to place more responsibility for foreign policy in the hands of the secretary of state. More accurately, President Carter's goal was to balance the advice coming to the president from the secretary of state and from the national security advisor. The elaborate NSC committee system developed during the Kissinger years was initially pared back to only two.[82] Ultimately, however, the national security advisor, Zbigniew Brzezinski, was able to play a more dominant role in the shaping of foreign policy and to work his will in the policy process due to the force of his personality, his strong foreign policy views, and the challenge of global events (e.g., the seizure of American diplomats in Iran in November 1979 and the Soviet invasion of Afghanistan in December 1979).[83] This development only continued the pattern of moving away from the Department of State and toward the national security advisor in the formulation of American foreign policy.

Under the Reagan administration, a return to the earlier pattern of collegial policy making was once again attempted. President Reagan's first secretary of state, Alexander Haig, came to office determined to restore the dominance of the Department of State (and especially the office of secretary) and to make himself the "vicar" of foreign affairs. In part to facilitate this reversion to the earlier model of policy making, a relatively inexperienced foreign policy analyst, Richard Allen, was appointed by President Reagan to be the national security advisor. In this environment, it seemed possible that the secretary of state could reassert his authority as the dominant force in the shaping of policy.

Although Secretary of State Haig achieved some initial success in shaping the foreign policy of the Reagan administration, he failed to dominate the process. Ultimately, he was forced to resign when policy frictions developed among the White House staff and the secretaries of state and defense and when a new national security advisor, William Clark, who was closer to President Reagan, was appointed. Power seemed to be shifting more perceptibly back to the White House and the national security advisor.

George Shultz, Haig's successor as secretary of state, initially appeared to be given some latitude in policy making, but National Security Advisor William Clark soon eclipsed his role. A series of events reflected this shift in decision making. Whether over arms control policy (e.g., the Strategic Defense Initiative), Central American policy (the removal of the ambassador to El Salvador and the firing of the assistant secretary of state for Inter-American affairs), or Middle Eastern policy (e.g., a change in the President's personal representative), the decisions once again illustrated the shift in policy dominance toward the NSC and away from the Department of State.[84] Indeed, by one assessment, Clark "became the most influential foreign policy figure in Reagan's entourage" in a very short time.[85] The shift was so perceptible that Shultz reportedly complained directly to the president that he could not do his job effectively if foreign policy decisions were made without his participation.[86]

Only under Clark's successor as NSC advisor, Robert McFarlane, and after the disclosure of the Iran-Contra affair did Shultz gain policy dominance. Because McFarlane was not personally close to President Reagan and because he felt constrained by the president's insistence on "cabinet-style" government, the pattern began to change somewhat. Still, crucial national security decision directives were issued by McFarlane's office, often without prior departmental clearance.[87] After November 1986 and the domestic political fall-out from the Iran-Contra affair, things changed more perceptibly.

While the Iran-Contra affair in one sense demonstrated the extent to which the NSC had dominated policy making (after all, the episode seemed to be directed entirely by individuals within the NSC), it also showed the dangers of such a procedure. Both investigations of this affair—the presidential inquiry, known as the Tower Commission, and the report of the two congressional committees—cited the dangers of allowing the National Security Council staff to run covert operations without presidential accountability, faulted the poor operation of the NSC system under the Reagan administration, and recommended reforms in the decision-making system itself.[88] After the firing of John Poindexter as national security advisor, Poindexter's two successors—first, Frank Carlucci and then, Colin Powell—were much more inclined to serve as policy coordinators than as policy formulators. As a result, Secretary of State George Shultz increasingly dominated the policy process.

The National Security Advisor: The Bush and Clinton Administrations

At least by formal design, the Bush administration returned to a more familiar pattern of NSC dominance of foreign policy making. In National Security Directive 1 (NSD-1), President Bush placed his national security advisor, Brent Scowcroft, and his deputy at the head of the foreign policy-making machinery by appointing them as chairs of the two key coordinating committees of the NSC system—the NSC/Principals Committee and the NSC/Deputies Committee (see Chapter 10 for details on these committees).[89] As heads of these two committees, the NSC and its staff were in a strong position to dominate the Departments of State and Defense in the shaping of policy. Further, the national security advisor, albeit in consultation with the secretaries of state and defense, was given responsibilities for establishing appropriate interagency groups to develop policy options, as the need arose.

With James Baker as Secretary of State and with Baker's close personal ties to President Bush, some raised doubts about Scowcroft's ability to dominate the process. However, with his previous experience as national security advisor under President Ford and with his background in bureaucratic politics, Scowcroft fared quite well. He did not seek the limelight, he put together a staff that was generally applauded, and he quickly undertook a broad review of American policy. Content to allow Baker to do more of the public relations side of foreign policy (e.g., congressional relations and trips abroad), Scowcroft ultimately was identified as the principal molder and the real "mover and shaker" of American foreign policy within the foreign policy hierarchy.[90]

Clinton's first national security advisor, Anthony Lake, was cut from the same cloth as Scowcroft and was less like, say, a Kissinger or Brzezinski in carrying out this foreign policy assignment. Lake did not seek the limelight and rarely got it. By one assessment, he was "surely the only national security advisor ever to stand beside the President in a New York Times photograph and be described as an 'unidentified' man."[91] While that comment surely understated his importance, it conveyed his style of influence: a quiet, behind-the-scenes approach.

Lake's influence derived from his geographical closeness to the president and Clinton's limited foreign policy experience and foreign policy interest. He saw the president every day to brief him on global development and served as the arbiter among the conflicting bureaucracies whether State, Defense, or the intelligence community. While Lake said that he was careful "that the President is getting all points of view," he also offered his own views. As he gained more confidence in his role, Lake assumed a more assertive posture in the policy debate. He was more likely to assert his own position sooner in the process "because it helps move issues to a resolution."[92] Despite a self-effacing personal style, Lake, after the president and vice president, was perhaps "the most powerful influence on foreign affairs."[93]

Lake's successor was his former deputy, Samuel (Sandy) Berger, appointed in December 1996. As with Lake, he appears likely to enjoy considerable policy influence, based upon his knowledge of foreign affairs and

FIGURE 9.4

The Structure of the National Security Council Staff Under President Clinton

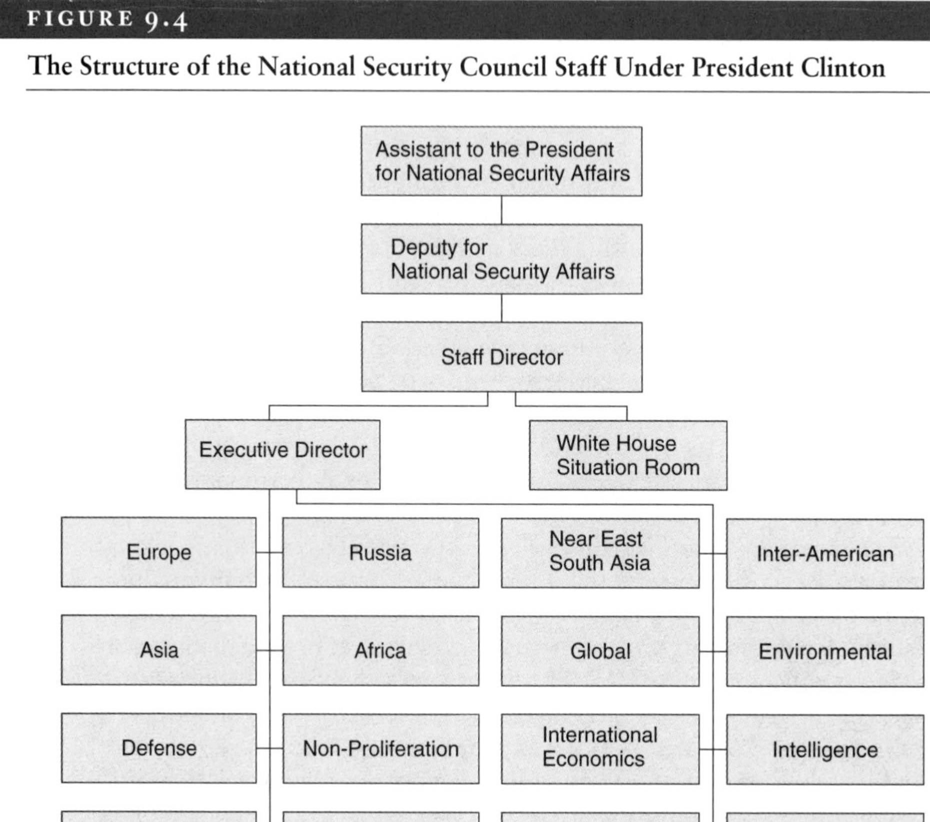

his close ties with the president. He had previously worked for Lake in the Department of State during the Carter administration and, in turn, worked for four years as Lake's top aide on the National Security Council during Clinton's first term. In addition, he has a long personal relationship with President Clinton, beginning with their involvement in the McGovern campaign for president in 1972.[94]

With a new foreign policy team in place for Clinton's second term, Berger's immediate challenge is to meld those new officials into a smoothly working team. With George Tenet (who formerly worked on the National Security Council Staff) heading the CIA, Berger will have a familiar face (and perhaps an ally) in any bureaucratic debates over policy that may develop with new secretaries at the Department of State and the Department of Defense. Yet, with his close ties to the president, Berger ought to be in a good position to continue as the most influential foreign policy maker, much as the assistants to the president for national security affairs have been over the past several decades.

Another important reason why Berger will likely possess such influence (as have other national security advisors) is the elaborate bureaucratic structure for the National Security Council and the national security advisor that has evolved over the last four decades. Figure 9.4 shows the present structure of the National Security Council staff. The NSC bureaucracy now has regional (e.g., Asian Affairs, African Affairs) and functional (e.g., International Economic Affairs, Defense) directorates and several important leadership positions. These positions start with the assistant to the president for national security affairs and his deputy, but they also include an executive secretary, a legal advisor, a legislative affairs advisor, and a counselor. As the NSC organizational structure imitates that of the Department of State, it is a direct and often successful competitor with that bureaucracy. Compare Figures 9.1 and 9.4 and note the similarity in the structures of the two organizations.

The increasing importance of the NSC staff in foreign policy making also reveals itself in the significance attached to the individuals appointed to its key positions. Indeed, an important gauge of the direction of American foreign policy can be gleaned from the kind of staff people appointed to the various divisions within the NSC organization and the foreign policy views that they possess. Moreover, these positions now rival and even surpass the importance of similar positions at the Department of State or the Department of Defense.

WHY TWO DEPARTMENTS OF STATE?

With the National Security Council and the Department of State competing for influence, the foreign policy apparatus of the United States has actually evolved into what political scientist Bert Rockman calls two Departments of State.[95] There are now "regular" channels (through the Department of State) and "irregular" channels (through the National Security Council) for foreign policy making. Yet, even this simple division is too narrowly drawn in reality; instead, the division ought to be stated more boldly. The division is really between the irregular channels, epitomized by the National Security Council, and the regular channels—including the Department of State and all the other foreign policy bureaucracies with foreign policy responsibilities. After all, the NSC controls the interagency process within the government (as we shall discuss in Chapter 10). Still, it is important to consider why these irregular processes have been in ascendancy and have actually come to dominate the foreign policy process, and why the regular channels have lost ground as a result.

Rockman offers several insightful reasons for the prominence of the irregular channels.[96] System overload is the first one. Overload refers to the tremendous amount of information and policy analyses available to the president from the various regular bureaucracies. Thus, the national security staff provides a ready arena for coordinating and distilling such a volume of material for the president—something that a single formal bureaucracy would not likely be able to do. As Rockman acknowledges, however, while overload might account for the coordination of policy within the NSC, it does not actually explain the decision-making growth of the NSC system. For this explanation, he looks to institutional and organizational arrangements within the foreign policy bureaucracies and the political culture within Washington.

Because the bureaucracies have their own parochial interests to protect, political advantage is often sought by one institution over another. A favorite tactic is the use of the press leak to undermine some unfavorable policy or position, especially in politically conscious Washington. This approach, moreover, is particularly endemic to the personnel in the regular channels, who believe that they are being left out of the decision process or who have, inevitably, divided loyalties—to the president on the one hand, and to their institutions on the other. Individuals in the irregular channels, however, would be less prone than disgruntled departmental officials to "go public" over a policy dispute, bound as they are to the president by appointment and ideology. Therefore, to protect his policy options, the president would prefer the confidentiality of his White House staff and the NSC system.

Along with the political rivalries, the regular channels (i.e., the Department of State) have institutional norms and bureaucratic subcultures that would be more prone to deflect (or "bury") innovative policy ideas that diverge too greatly from the status quo. By contrast once again, the irregular channels, presumably more committed to innovation and more committed to translating the president's views into policy, would be receptive to new ideas and might well be the catalyst of policy change themselves. In this way, too, the president's preferred position can be put into effect more quickly. Yet, as the Iran-Contra affair showed us, this zealotry has a price. After all, the "irregular" channels of John Poindexter and Oliver North from the National Security Council system carried out this activity because, they contended, they were doing what they perceived as the president's will.

Finally, the political culture of Washington only exacerbates these bureaucratic tendencies. Because the nation's capital operates on "bureaucratic politics" (the competition between departments), the president is constantly in danger of becoming only an arbitrator between agencies, rather than a policy maker, if he cannot control this infighting. Since the ties between the White House and the departments are never as strong as between the White House and its immediate staff, there is a tendency for a "we versus them" relationship to develop between these two groupings, with an attempt to isolate the departments. In short, numerous incentives exist for the executive to feel more confident making foreign policy through his staff rather than through regular departments, including the Department of State.

BUREAUCRACIES AND FOREIGN ECONOMIC POLICY MAKING

So far, our discussion in this chapter has focused on two key foreign affairs bureaucracies that deal primarily with the political aspects of policy making. In the next chapter, we focus on two bureaucracies that deal with military or quasi-military (covert operations) aspects of policy making. Yet a third aspect of the foreign policy making bureaucracy, however, addresses economic questions. While those bureaucracies are often avoided or given cursory treatment in books on foreign policy, they are increasingly crucial to the actions of the United States abroad.[97] As more international policy questions address issues of international economics and finance such as trade, debt policy, and investment, American foreign policy making becomes, more than ever, economic policy making. Indeed, the high priority that the Clinton administration has given to economic security (see Chapter 6) as a foreign policy goal reinforces this point.

Several bureaucracies that are often viewed as dealing only with domestic policy have actually emerged over the last four decades to assume important roles in shaping America's foreign economic policy. To illustrate both the breadth and growth of these bureaucracies, we identify several of them, describe the principal ways in which they contribute to foreign policy making, and discuss some issues with which they have been associated recently. We shall first discuss the newest economic bureaucracy, the Office of the U.S. Trade Representative, then turn to discuss the role of the Departments of State and Defense in economic issues, and finally describe the responsibilities of the Department of Treasury, Department of Commerce, and Department of Agriculture in the area of foreign economic policy. Some of these bureaucracies are more pivotal than others, and we shall try to specify the importance of each one.

Before we proceed, however, we ought to note several important characteristics of policy formulation in the foreign economic area, especially as it relates to trade policy.[98] First, only in the twentieth century (and usually dating from the passage of the Reciprocal Trade Agreements Act of 1934) has the executive branch assumed a lead role in the trade policy area, even though Congress still retains the constitutional prerogative to regulate foreign commerce. Second, trade policy formulation is quite diffuse within the executive branch. Some decisions are made wholly within a particular bureaucracy (e.g., at the deputy assistant secretary level in one of the relevant departments), others are made at the interagency group level (coordination among the bureaucracies), and still others are ultimately resolved by the president. Third, various bureaucracies are more likely to deal with different aspects of trade policy (e.g., import policy or export policy), and such dispersion reinforces the decentralized nature of foreign economic policy. The principal consequence of these various characteristics is that, like other foreign policy making areas, the process is highly subject to the vagaries of bureaucratic politics.

Office of the United States Trade Representative

In recent decades, the Office of the U.S. Trade Representative is the "primus inter pares" (first among equals) within the executive branch "for developing and coordinating United States trade, commodity, and direct investment policy" and for "leading and directing negotiations with other countries."[99] The U.S. Trade Representative has cabinet-level status and acts as "the principal trade advisor, negotiator, and spokesperson for the President on trade and related investment matters." Further, the USTR, both the agency and the individual heading the office, has wide-ranging responsibilities for coordinating the interagency process within the United States government, leading trade delegations abroad, and preparing policy questions for presidential decision making. As a result, the USTR has been at the center of such negotiations as the North American Free Trade Agreement (NAFTA), the General Agreements on Tariffs and Trade (GATT) [now the World Trade Organization (WTO)], and the new initiatives among Asia-Pacific Economic Cooperation (APEC) countries and countries of Latin America (the "Summit of the Americas").

The creation of the Office of the USTR is relatively new, and the growth in its power over trade policy is even more recent. The USTR, congressionally mandated by the Trade Expansion Act of 1962, was formally established by an executive order in 1963.[100] Only in the 1970s and 1980s, however, were its powers and responsibilities enhanced. In the Trade Act of 1974, USTR gained cabinet-level status and assumed responsibility for coordinating policy on trade matters. By an executive reorganization plan in 1980, its responsibilities expanded even further when its head was designated as the "chief trade negotiator" and as America's official representative to the major trade organizations. In addition, the staff of the office doubled in size to about eighty. More recently, the passage of the Omnibus Trade and Competitiveness Act of 1988 reaffirmed the powers of the Office of the USTR, and designated the head of the office (the USTR) as having primary responsibility for undertaking trade retaliation actions against unfair trading partners of the United States (section 301 of the act).

The Office of the USTR also represents the convergence of trade policy making in two other ways: It serves as a focal point for congressional involvement in affecting trade policy making and serves as the formal contact point for a series of private-sector advisory groups on trade-related policy questions. Beginning with the Trade Act of 1974, and through expansion in subsequent legislation (e.g., the Trade Acts of 1979 and 1988), five members of the House and the Senate serve as official advisors to the USTR. Similarly, the private sector has an elaborate system of advisory groups to the USTR to aid in shaping America's negotiating posture and general trade policy abroad. The Advisory Committee on Trade Policy and Negotiations, the Agricultural Technical Advisory Subcommittee, the Industry Sector Advisory Committee, and the Labor Sector Advisory Subcommittees, among others, give a sense of the variety of technical and functional area committees that interact on a regular basis with the USTR. In short, the Office of the USTR, with these myriad ties and responsibilities, is the "lead agency" for all international trade negotiations, and the USTR himself or herself generally is "the designated chair" of the interagency groups on trade matters.[101]

Besides the USTR, however, political analysts Stephen Cohen, Joel Paul, and Robert Blecker make clear that other "players" at the White House level considerably affect foreign economic policy making. While the cabinet-level economic coordinating bodies, such as the National Economic Council, play a crucial role in ultimately finalizing and ratifying policy formulation (see Chapter 10), other White House offices, such as the economic officials on the National Security Council (NSC), the Council of Economic Advisors (CEA), and the Office of Management and Budget (OMB), play a more secondary and advisory role in policy formulation. As budgetary considerations arise, however, the latter agency would necessarily weigh in as well.[102]

Departments of State and Defense

The two bureaucracies, which are normally thought of as political–military ones, do play important roles in foreign economic policy making. As our earlier discussion implies, the Department of State retains an especially important role, since its aim has been to coordinate security and economic policy toward the rest of the world and toward particular countries. Indeed, by one assessment, State's role was dominant on economic policy making questions up until World War II. During the Cold War, however, as political and security concerns came to dominate assessments at State, the Department lost some of its clout in the economic arena. By the mid-1970s, the Department of State's economic role had eroded to the extent that it "had become more of a major participant than a recognized leader" in economic questions. While State has largely stayed in that position, it has regained some clout as "economics consciousness-raising" occurred within the Department, and especially recently when the Clinton administration sought to place so much emphasis on foreign economic policy. As a consequence, the Department of State remains "sufficiently powerful ...to be in a position to veto intragovernmental agreement on virtually any international economic issue."[103]

By contrast, the other political–military bureaucracy, the Department of Defense, plays a less pivotal role in foreign economic policy than the Department of State, but it still can affect America's economic actions abroad, especially in advising on sensitive exports and the transfer of American technology.[104] Defense's role can be especially crucial when considering a sale of "dual-use" technology—technology with potential military and nonmilitary applications—to an unfriendly, or potentially unfriendly, country. During the Cold War years, the monitoring of such exports by the Department of Defense (and Commerce) was often pivotal. The United States developed an extensive list of restricted or prohibited trade items, and it cooperated with the efforts of other Western nations through the Coordinating Committee on Multilateral Export Controls (COCOM) to stop the transfer of sensitive technologies to Communist states. In both arenas, Defense played a key role in assessing the interests of the United States and the impact of any transfers on national security.[105]

As the Cold War waned and finally ended in the early 1990s, both the unilateral and multilateral export control lists have been sharply revised; consequently, the Department's role in the export process has lessened. In the mid- to late 1980s, for example, the Department of Defense was not very successful in stopping exports to Iraq, despite objections that the dual-use technology being considered for export had "the high likelihood of military end use."[106] In 1992, the Department was invited to assess the implications of selling of new technology (e.g., a new supercomputer) to China and to weigh into the policy debate over whether the licensing of this sale should go forward. While it opposed such a sale to China, the Departments of State and Commerce were on the other side for business and political reasons, and Defense's view was not persuasive.[107] Part of the reason that the Department of Defense does not possess more clout in this process is that its role is consultative rather than statutory. Furthermore, unlike the Department of Commerce, Defense lacks a public constituency that might aid it in the inevitable bureaucratic clashes over the promotion of such sales abroad. Finally, and with particular reference to export policy, the Department of Commerce retains the final authority on issuing export licenses.[108]

Department of the Treasury

The Department of Treasury today enjoys increased policy making clout, especially in international financial matters. Unlike the Department of State, which has had an historical role in foreign economic matters, Treasury's rise in influence has been more recent, primarily dating from the end of World War II. Indeed, the department has been described as the "enfant terrible of U.S. international economic policymaking," but as the one that now often dominates the rest of the bureaucracy on foreign economic questions.

The growth of the Department of the Treasury in policy influence has been attributed by one leading analyst to a variety of factors: the relative decline of American economic power globally, the increased recognition that external economic policies affect us at home, a renewed interest by policy makers in achieving economic goals by the United States, legislation granting the Treasury Department a greater global economic policy responsibility, and the enhanced role of the secretary of the treasury in economic policy making, among others. Furthermore, "the Treasury Department has undisputed control of U.S. international monetary policy…, international financial policy…, and international tax policy." Only the Department of State is equally as interested in the range of foreign economic policy.[109]

While Treasury has an elaborate bureaucratic structure in which various divisions could potentially have an impact on foreign economic policy making, the center of its activity are the offices and bureaus directed by the under secretary for international affairs. In particular, the under secretary has policy responsibility for running the Office of International Affairs, which monitors the whole array of foreign economic issues, including international monetary policy, trade and investment, global debt, and America's role in international financial institutions (e.g., International Monetary Fund and the World Bank). In addition, the under secretary has a pivotal role in coordinating policy with the other major market democracies (G-7 countries) and in preparing the United States position for the annual meetings of these countries.[110]

Four recent initiatives in the foreign economic area illustrate Treasury's policy making importance: the "Plaza Pact" of 1985, a five-nation agreement to lower the value of the dollar; the 1985 Baker Plan on international debt reform; the Brady Plan of 1989, another proposal on international debt; and the Mexican bailout plan of 1995. The first initiative, the Plaza Pact, sought to reduce the value of the dollar against other leading currencies as a means of helping the United States and world economies. The Pact took its name from the Plaza Hotel in New York, where representatives of the United States, Japan, West Germany, France, and Great Britain met. These representatives agreed that "further orderly appreciation of the main non-dollar currencies against the dollar is desirable" and that their governments would encourage this kind of an outcome.[111] Because the dollar had risen in value against other currencies during the 1980s, the value of American goods increased, making them more expensive for other nations to buy. One result was that America's trade deficit increased dramatically. As a consequence, the United States soon became interested in obtaining a decline in the value of the dollar. This effort was almost entirely a Treasury operation and challenged the prevailing Reagan administration policy, which opposed United States government intervention in the market.[112] The effort, moreover, quickly succeeded.

The Baker Plan, a proposal offered by the United States secretary of the treasury to the 1985 annual meeting of the World Bank and the International Monetary Fund, aimed to address the burgeoning international debt crisis. It called for commercial banks to assist fifteen particularly indebted nations (e.g., Mexico, Argentina, and Brazil in Latin America; Nigeria and Morocco in Africa; and the Philippines in Asia) by pledging to provide $20 billion in new loans through 1988, and for international lending institutions (e.g., the World Bank, and the Inter-American Development Bank) to provide $9 billion more. In exchange, the debtor nations would be asked to follow "anti-inflationary fiscal and monetary policies."[113] They would also be asked "to strengthen their private sectors, mobilize more domestic savings, facilitate investment, liberalize trade and pursue market-oriented approaches to currencies, interest rates, and prices."[114] Once again, this kind of proposal represented a departure from past Reagan administration policy, and it demonstrated, too, that the Treasury Department was taking the lead on foreign economic policy.

The third example of the Treasury Department's policy making is the Brady Plan of 1989, a plan named after President Bush's Treasury secretary, Nicholas Brady (although devised within the Department by an under secretary).[115] Unlike the Baker Plan, which proposed that poor countries grow their way out of debt, the Brady proposal was a debt-reduction proposal. Under this design, the commercial banks in rich countries would be encouraged to write off a portion of debt owed by Third World countries under a variety of schemes. One idea was to have international monetary institutions (e.g., the World Bank or the IMF) provide funding to poor countries which, in turn, would buy back a portion of their debt from commercial banks at a reduced price. Another would offer international guarantees to commercial banks for a portion of the debt owed by a country if those banks would write off a portion as well. Still a third idea, advanced before the Brady proposal, was for some form of "debt-equity swaps" in which commercial banks get some property or asset within a country or are repaid in local currency for debt owed in dollars.

The last example is the Department of Treasury's role in the Mexican bailout of 1995. In December 1994, the value of the Mexican peso had declined dramatically, from about 3.5 pesos to the United States dollar to more than 5.5 pesos by the end of that month, and eventually to almost 6.5 pesos to the dollar by early February 1995. The reason for this sharp drop in the value of the peso was the weakening Mexican economy. Over the previous several years, the Mexican government, banks, and businesses had borrowed heavily—in the billions of dollars—to fuel the rapid expansion of the economy. When investor confidence began to erode in 1993 and 1994, however, the Mexican government was forced to use its revenue to protect the value of the peso in the face of increasing pressure to devalue the currency. By the end of 1994, that effort had largely failed, and the value of the peso plummeted.[116]

This sharp decline in the peso's value foreshadowed a dramatic decline in Mexico's living standard, but it also had important implications for the United States. First, a weak Mexican economy would have direct and immediate consequences for the health of the American economy.[117] Since a significant portion of Mexican debt was held by American banks, mutual funds, and insurance companies, the inability of Mexico to pay its debts in a timely fashion would hurt the American economy, United States pension plans with Mexican investments, and American workers producing goods for export there. Second, a weak Mexican economy would have profound consequences for the success of the recently implemented North American Free Trade Agreement (NAFTA) among the United States, Canada, and Mexico. Third, a weak Mexican economy would have political and economic consequences within Mexico itself. Largely at the behest of the United States, Mexico had undertaken a series of market and political reforms to make its economy more open and its political system more democratic. Both kinds of reforms would be in jeopardy as a result of a serious downturn or collapse of the Mexican economy. Fourth, a weak Mexican economy would likely spark increased illegal immigration to the north, creating social and political dislocations in the United States. Finally, the collapse of the Mexican economy would likely lead to reverberations throughout the international global economy. As a Clinton administration official said at the time: "If Mexico had tumbled, there would have been more tumbling."[118]

As a consequence, the Clinton administration moved quickly to devise an assistance plan for Mexico, with the Department of Treasury taking the lead in developing and promoting such a plan.[119] The original plan developed by the Clinton administration provided for $40 billion in new loan guarantees by the United States to Mexico and about $13 billion in loans from the International Monetary Fund. The $40 billion guarantees would be exercised only if the Mexican government defaulted on its outstanding loan, but Mexican oil revenues would be used as collateral for this American assistance.[120] The plan, however, required congressional action, and opposition quickly developed in both the House and the Senate.

After several weeks of sparring with Congress, President Clinton abandoned this approach and adopted an alternative strategy. Under this new plan, emanating from the Department of Treasury as well, the United States decided to provide $20 billion to forestall a default by Mexico, to ask the International Monetary Fund to provide $17.5 billion in assistance and the Bank for International Settlements to add $10 billion, and to invite Canada and Latin American countries to contribute $2 billion more.[121]

The new American-devised $50 billion rescue plan provided an immediate shot-in-the-arm to the Mexican economy. The Mexican stock market responded quickly, and the peso strengthened. Mexico had a trade surplus by 1995, and exports and export earnings were higher as well. At the same time, however, Mexico's standard of living continued to suffer with such austerity measures, and political unrest occurred within the country as well.[122] Still, by mid-1996, a Mexican government bond offering was well received in the investment community, indicating that some confidence in the Mexican economy was returning.[123] Importantly, too, Mexico continued to meet its repayment deadlines to the United States, an action pleasing to the Clinton administration and its Department of the Treasury, and actually repaid the entire debt two years early in January 1997.[124]

Department of Commerce

The fifth key department in the foreign economic policy area is the Department of Commerce. Like the Office of the USTR, Commerce benefited from the 1980 executive reorganization act by gaining a wider mandate in formulating and implementing United States trade policy. It now has the principal responsibility for administering all import-export programs of the United States.[125] Two of the six major divisions within the department are directly involved in these tasks. They are the International Trade Administration and the Bureau of Export Administration, with each headed by an under secretary of commerce.[126]

The International Trade Administration has the responsibility for all United States trade policy (except agricultural products) and for assisting the U.S. Trade Representative in all trade negotiations. These activities range from formulating and implementing foreign economic policy, shaping all import policies, and promoting and developing American markets around the world. Although the USTR would likely take the lead role, ITA can provide valuable assistance.

Importantly, the ITA also has the responsibility for operating the U.S. and Foreign Commercial Service (US & FCS), the primary agency that aids American businesses seeking to export nonagricultural products. Through some forty-seven district and branch offices within the United States and through 132 posts in sixty-eight countries, this agency conducts a variety of activities to showcase American products and works with other government agencies and foreign organizations to aid American business.[127] In particular, US & FCS provides information on new markets to businesses, counsels and arranges contact between American companies and local businesses abroad, and holds trade shows and "trade events" to demonstrate the range of American products, especially those from small and medium-sized companies. Recently, too, the Department of Commerce has gone to more focused marketing by concentrating on ten "big emerging markets"—markets with large populations and great demand for products from abroad. In 1994, for example, the focus of attention was Argentina, Brazil, Indonesia, China, Hong Kong, Mexico, Poland, South Africa, South Korea, Taiwan and Turkey.[128]

Another important new function for the Department of Commerce is on the import side of the trade equation: the enforcement of antidumping and countervailing trade statutes to protect American businesses from unfair trade practices from abroad. (Prior to 1980, these responsibilities rested with the Department of the Treasury.) Antidumping statutes deal with monitoring imports from other countries to make certain that goods being sold in the United States are not below "fair market value," while countervailing statutes focus on whether production costs have been subsidized in a foreign country, hence making imported goods less costly within the American market.[129] In either instance, if such a determination were made, the Department could recommend retaliation, and import duties, for example, could be added to the products in question.[130] With the rise of the American trade deficit to $170 billion or more in the mid-1980s, with its continuance in the 1990s (over $150 billion in 1994), and with the rising tide of protectionism in various markets, such monitoring of imports and the recommending of appropriate action become crucial aspects of foreign economic policy for the United States.[131] With the completion of several new trade agreements to lower tariffs and eliminate nontariff barriers—such as the North American Free Trade Agreement (NAFTA) and the Uruguay Round of the General Agreements on Tariffs and Trade (GATT)—these monitoring activities now take on even more significance.

The Department of Commerce has thus gained some bureaucratic influence recently and has been working to open foreign markets to American products. The actions of the Commerce Department, particularly during the Clinton administration, illustrate its prominence. Under the leadership of the late Ron Brown, secretary of commerce from 1993 until he was tragically killed in a plane crash in Croatia in April 1996, the Department of Commerce had, arguably, a greater impact on American foreign policy than at any time since the Department shaped a trade policy with the Soviet Union during the Nixon administration.[132] Commerce was able to obtain this influence by organizing numerous promotional trips for American corporate executives to potentially new United States markets, ranging from South Africa and Northern Ireland to China and the Middle East. (Indeed, at the time of the plane crash in April 1996, Secretary Brown was leading a delegation of a dozen or more corporate executives to assist with reconstruction in Bosnia.[133]) Furthermore, the Department was able to tie these economic development efforts to domestic policy, as a means of promoting greater prosperity for the American economy at home, and to foreign policy, as a means of promoting peace and democracy abroad through economic development. In this way, too, the Department was able to stave off efforts to eliminate it as a cabinet-level department, as originally proposed by the Republican-controlled Congress in 1995.

Yet Commerce's overall role in the trade area still remains "more an operational than a policymaking" one.[134] Recent United States trade policy toward Japan, for example, demonstrates the limitations of Commerce's influence. Along with the Office of the USTR, the Department of Commerce has long been working to pry open the Japanese market. Both bureaucracies have taken a strong stand to pressure that country to make changes. This approach, however, has met resistance not only from the Japanese, but from other bureaucracies within the executive branch as well. The Department of the Treasury, a seeming natural ally on economic policy, takes a more cautious approach. As one Treasury official said: "We take a very broad macroeconomics view of U.S.–Japan relations. We don't worry much about specific products and industries." Another said: "We rely importantly on Japanese investment capital to help finance our trade and current account deficits."[135] More recently, even as strong an advocate of free trade as Clinton's under secretary of the treasury, Lawrence H. Summers, acknowledged the complicated nature of the relationship: "Not all the judgments you make when you think about how the United States should approach its trade relations with Japan are explicitly economic.... In that sense, I step aside from the role of being a pure economic scientist. There are different spheres for what are different kinds of activity."[136]

Resistance has also come from other foreign affairs bureaucracies that examine the Japanese relationship from a political–military perspective. The State and Defense Departments, which both look at the political–military implications of pressuring Japan too much, are reluctant to endorse the stronger position of the USTR and the Department of Commerce. Perhaps indicative of the prominence of the political–military considerations over the economic concerns in United States–Japanese relations were the renegotiation and the reaffirmation of the security treaty between the two countries in April 1996, even in the midst of ongoing trade disputes. In essence, the newly signed treaty was "an acknowledgment that diplomacy is something larger than trade," and that treaty sought to alter the perception that policy toward Japan had been "subcontracted" to the United States Trade Representative.[137] In short, then, the Department of Commerce remains a "subordinate power in U.S. government councils on...foreign economic policy formulation."[138]

Department of Agriculture

A sixth important economic bureaucracy with direct foreign policy responsibilities is the United States Department of Agriculture (USDA). This Department enters into the foreign policy arena through its involvement with agricultural trade and agricultural aid. Under several pieces of legislation, the USDA has the responsibility to monitor agricultural imports (and to suggest quotas if necessary) and to promote the export of American agricultural products. Under Public Law 480 (P.L.-480), the Agricultural Trade Development and Assistance Act, the USDA has primary responsibility for providing food aid to needy countries throughout the world.[139]

The Foreign Agricultural Service (FAS), the principal agency for formulating and implementing both agricultural trade and aid policy, is located in the Farm and Foreign Agricultural Services division of the Department of Agriculture. As the primary promoter of United States agricultural sales abroad, FAS does so in several different ways. First and foremost, it relies upon FAS attachés, who are posted at about seventy-five American embassies abroad and supported through an extensive support staff of agricultural experts in Washington. These individuals have a wide array of duties, which include observing the agricultural policies of host countries abroad, monitoring agricultural imports at home and making recommendations for quotas when necessary, analyzing agricultural trading patterns and trading prospects worldwide, and promoting American agricultural exports at home and abroad.

Second, over a decade ago, the FAS opened Agricultural Trade Offices (ATOs) abroad as yet another mechanism to promote American agricultural exports. In mid-1996, for example, twelve offices were operating in key foreign markets, with two new offices scheduled to open by the end of that year in Jakarta, Indonesia, and Miami. Through these ATOs, the Foreign Agricultural Service is involved in sponsoring trade exhibitions to showcase the variety and quality of American agricultural products.[140]

Third, FAS operates, in conjunction with the Commodity Credit Corporation (CCC) in USDA, the CCC's Export Credit Guarantee program, the Export Enhancement Program (EEP), the Dairy Export Incentive Program (DEIP), and the sale of surplus commodities. These various programs are further efforts to build markets abroad.[141] The DEIP, for instance, provides support to dairy exporters in an effort to broaden American markets abroad, sometimes leading to market clashes with other dairy exporters (e.g., Australia and New Zealand).

Finally, the Market Promotion program, authorized by Congress in 1990, furnishes cash or commodity assistance to American organizations seeking markets abroad. This kind of assistance goes primarily to those producers and exporters who may be encountering unfair trade competition in foreign markets.[142]

On the aid side, the FAS plays a central role in managing the Public Law 480 (P.L.-480) program, a program that provides both loans and grants in the form of food assistance and offers various incentives to help developing countries expand their agricultural sectors. The United States food aid effort totaled $1.1 billion in FY1996, a figure representing just under 10 percent of the total United States foreign assistance budget.

In particular, FAS has responsibility for managing the food loans (Title I) of P.L.-480, while the Agency for International Development (AID) has responsibility for food grants for emergency humanitarian and relief efforts (Title II) and for food aid that fosters food security and market reforms (Title III).[143] In addition, the Department of Agriculture provides food assistance through the Food for Progress (FFP) program, a program aiding countries that are expanding market principles in their agricultural sectors. The USDA also operates another program (the 416 [b] program) in which the United States donates surplus American commodities to needy countries. Finally, FAS's International Cooperation and Development program, in collaboration with the Agency for International Development, works to share United States agricultural and scientific knowledge with other countries and to foster global cooperation in these crucial areas.[144]

According to a recent analysis, the policy impact of the USDA on international agricultural trade is mixed. On the one hand, the Foreign Agricultural Service has a "major input when agricultural trade matters are concerned" in the policy-making process and its clout has increased "as U.S. agricultural trade has expanded."[145] President Bush's appointment of Clayton Yeutter as secretary of agriculture added further clout to the USDA in shaping agricultural trade policy. Yeutter had a sustained interest in trade policy (as a former U.S. Trade Representative) and was a strong believer in free trade in agriculture.[146] Indeed, the American position in the Uruguay Round of the General Agreements on Tariffs and Trade (GATT) negotiations, calling for dramatically lower agricultural subsidies and the elimination of trade barriers worldwide, reflected Yeutter's approach.

President Clinton's appointments of first Mike Espy and then Dan Glickman as his secretary of agriculture did not emphasize the international trade side within USDA as fully as had Yeutter's appointment. In fact, Glickman had actually voted against the final GATT agreement in Congress prior to his leaving that body in 1994 to become secretary of agriculture.[147] Yet, both secretaries quickly became advocates of free-trade policies as a way to strengthen American agriculture, with Espy strongly endorsing NAFTA for example, and Glickman eventually endorsing the opening of international markets.[148]

The principal mechanism for USDA to affect overall trade policy, however, is less through the secretary and more through the committee structures established under the Trade Act of 1974. Under the formula emerging from that legislation, USDA and the private sector participate in the agricultural advisory committees for trade and through the five agricultural technical advisory committees for trade. These committees make policy recommendations to the Secretary of USDA and to the United States Trade Representative. Moreover, these mechanisms have worked quite well in past negotiations and serve as a ready means of incorporating the public and private agricultural sectors into international trade negotiations.[149]

On the other hand, the Department of Agriculture hardly works its will in agricultural trade or sales abroad, as the ironic case of agricultural credits for Iraq illustrates. In the late 1980s and early 1990s, the USDA's Commodity Credit Corporation (CCC) was providing substantial credits to Iraq for purchasing American agricultural products.[150] Despite some growing concerns over Saddam Hussein's Iraq and its creditworthiness in the late 1980s, the CCC still allocated $30 million in additional loan guarantees in September 1988, just prior to a new fiscal 1989 credit of $1 billion and after having provided credits totaling $3.4 billion since FY1983. A year later, USDA's CCC again recommended $1 billion in credits for Iraq. By then, however, there were serious concerns in the Federal Reserve and the Department of Treasury regarding Iraq's financial standing. In a compromise, USDA agreed to lower its recommendation to $400 million. Shortly thereafter, USDA investigators found diversion of previous credits for purchasing arms, "criminal complicity" to defraud a bank, kickbacks to officials, and efforts to defraud the Department itself, and suspended its recommendation for any further credit. Yet USDA's decision was not the last word.

At that juncture, the State Department—particularly Secretary of State James Baker—and the White House engaged in a flurry of activities to get the original policy back on course, and they eventually carried the day.[151] Through considerable bureaucratic maneuvering and substantial political pressure, the original $1 billion proposal was reborn and put into effect as policy.[152] This decision was consistent with the national security policy of the time, which sought to employ "economic and political incentives for Iraq to moderate its behavior and to increase our [United States] influence with Iraq."

As this brief description illustrates, security interests ultimately continued to govern policy decisions, even, ironically, as USDA and its constituents were benefiting as a result of this reinstatement of policy orchestrated by the

Department of State and the White House. More generally, albeit in another context, some analysts have argued that the Department of State, the Department of Commerce, the Office of Budget and Management, and the National Security Council have increased their interest and expertise in agricultural trade policy and, in this way, are in a position to challenge the role of the Department of Agriculture.[153]

Concluding Comments

As this review of the Department of State, the National Security Council, and several economic bureaucracies demonstrates, the process of foreign policy making is much more complex than is often realized, and more actors are involved in the process than we immediately think. Although the Department of State may often be identified as the center of United States foreign diplomacy, the National Security Council has increasingly assumed a larger role in the shaping of American foreign policy. Similarly, while political and military issues are also often assumed as the pivotal ones in the foreign policy arena, economic issues are increasingly claiming more attention. Hence, the role of economic bureaucracies has been enlarged, with the Office of the United States Trade Representative and the Department of Treasury particularly prominent in shaping America's foreign economic policy.

Although the foreign policy bureaucracies discussed so far are important to policy making, other bureaucracies cannot be left out of this discussion. In the next chapter, therefore, we complete this survey of the foreign affairs bureaucracies by looking at the Department of Defense and the several bureaucracies known as the intelligence community. In that chapter, too, we shall take a closer look at the structural and procedural arrangements used by the two most recent presidents to coordinate the policy making process among these various bureaucracies within the executive branch.

Notes

1. Graham Allison, *Essence of Decision: Explaining the Cuban Missile Crisis* (Boston: Little, Brown, 1971), p. 144. It is also at p. 158, where Allison quotes from Roger Hilsman's *To Move a Nation* (Garden City, NY: Doubleday Publishing, 1964), p. 6.
2. Allison, *Essence of Decision: Explaining the Cuban Missile Crisis* and Morton H. Halperin with the assistance of Priscilla Clapp and Arnold Kanter, *Bureaucratic Politics and Foreign Policy* (Washington, DC: The Brookings Institution, 1974).
3. Christopher M. Jones, "American Prewar Technology Sales to Iraq: A Bureaucratic Politics Explanation," in Eugene R. Wittkopf, ed., *The Domestic Sources of American Foreign Policy: Insights and Evidence*, 2nd ed. (New York: St. Martin's Press, 1994), pp. 279–296. The quoted passages for the Iraqi case are at pp. 280 and 293, respectively, in this paragraph and the next one.
4. Note, however, that Allison, *Essence of Decision*, pp. 164–165, identifies not only bureaucracies as determinants of policy position. Instead, he refers to the variety of "players" in the process. Kim Richard Nossal, "Bureaucratic Politics and the Westminster Model," in Robert O. Matthews, Arthur G. Rubinoff, and Janice Gross Stein, eds., *International Conflict and Conflict Management: Readings in World Politics* (Scarborough, Ontario: Prentice-Hall of Canada, Inc., 1984), p. 125, makes this point from which we draw.
5. An earlier proponent of this model actually illustrates the lack of direct correspondence between bureaucratic position and policy stance in explaining the decision and the im-

portance of intrabureaucracy divisions as an explanation of foreign policy decisions as well. See Morton H. Halperin, "The Decision to Deploy the ABM: Bureaucratic and Domestic Politics in the Johnson Administration," *World Politics* 25 (October 1972): 62–95. For classic criticisms of the bureaucratic politics approach, see Stephen D. Krasner, "Are Bureaucracies Important? (Or Allison Wonderland)," *Foreign Policy* 7 (Summer 1972): 159–179; Robert J. Art, "Bureaucratic Politics and American Foreign Policy: A Critique," *Policy Sciences* 4 (1973): 467–490; and Nossal, "Bureaucratic Politics and the Westminster Model," pp. 120–127.

6. Elizabeth Drew, *On the Edge: The Clinton Presidency* (New York: Simon & Schuster, 1994), pp. 138–163.
7. *Department of State Completes 200 Years* (Washington, DC: United States Department of State, Bureau of Public Affairs, 1982), p. 1.
8. Report of the U.S. Department of State Management Task Force, *State 2000: A New Model for Managing Foreign Affairs* (Washington, DC: U.S. Department of State Publication 10029, January 1993).
9. Much of the discussion of the organizational and structural details of the Department of State during the Clinton Administration is drawn from "The United States Department of State: Structure and Organization," *Dispatch Supplement* 6 (May 1995), Supplement No. 3, 1–8. Also see Warren Christopher, "Department of State Reorganization," *Dispatch* 4 (February 8, 1993): 69–73. Many of the changes outlined in the next few pages were advanced in this Christopher directive.
10. Christopher, "Department of State Reorganization," p. 71.
11. Ibid., p. 69.
12. As former Secretary of State James Baker notes in his memoirs, the organization whereby the under secretaries report to the secretary and the assistant secretaries to the under secretaries was actually started during his time at the Department during the Bush administration. See James A. Baker III with Thomas M. DeFrank, *The Politics of Diplomacy: Revolution, War and Peace, 1989–1992* (New York: G. P. Putnam's Sons, 1995), pp. 35–36.
13. "Fact Sheet: Reinventing State, ACDA, USIA, and AID" (Washington, DC: Office of the Press Secretary, The White House, April 18, 1997), via the Internet; and Stephen Barr and Thomas W. Lippman, "Turf Diplomacy at State Department," *Washington Post,* May 28, 1997, A17.
14. See Duncan L. Clarke, *Politics of Arms Control: The Role and Effectiveness of the U.S. Arms Control and Disarmament Agency* (New York: The Free Press, 1979) on his assessment of ACDA under Paul Warnke during the Carter administration at pp. 4, 223, and 232. Particularly on the latter page, Clarke characterizes Warnke as "ACDA's most effective Director in executive branch deliberations."
15. See President Clinton's letter to Congress of March 28, 1994, which is reprinted in "A Revitalized ACDA in the Post–Cold War World," a joint hearing before the Subcommittee on International Security, International Organizations and Human Rights and International Operations of the Committee on Foreign Affairs, House of Representatives, 103rd Cong., 2nd sess., June 23, 1994, p. 44.
16. Ibid., p. 5.
17. On the role of the ACDA in arms control issues, see, for example, its recent annual report to Congress, U.S. Arms Control and Disarmament Agency, *Threat Control Through Arms Control: Report to Congress, 1994* (Washington, DC: U.S. Government Printing Office, July 13, 1995).
18. The information here is drawn from that provided in various components of USIA's worldwide web site, an information source readily available to all, with updates and more details on the various components of USIA activities, as identified here.
19. The last budget datum is from "The Agencies in Transition," *Washington Post,* May 28, 1977, A17. The first two budgets and the library budget data in the next paragraph are based upon Dick Kirschten, "Restive Relic," *National Journal*, April 22, 1995, 977.
20. Author Interview with USIS librarian in a country in Southern Europe.
21. *U.S. Government Manual 1994/1995*, July 1, 1994, 749–754.

22. See Office of the Vice President, *Creating a Government That Works and Costs Less, Agency for International Development* (Washington, DC: U.S. Government Printing Office, September 1993), p. 1.
23. The following pieces of information on USAID are drawn from various items on the worldwide web site for the Agency for International Development.
24. See *State Department: Actions Needed to Improve Embassy Management*, General Accounting Office Report (GAO/NSIAD–96–1, March 12, 1996): 1; "The United States Department of State: Structure and Organization," p. 1; and "The Agencies in Transition," p. A17.
25. For a brief and interesting description of the working of an embassy and the responsibilities of political officers, see Robert Hopkins Miller, *Inside an Embassy: The Political Role of Diplomats Abroad* (Washington, DC: Congressional Quarterly, Inc., 1992).
26. *Atlas of United States Foreign Relations* (Washington, DC: United States Department of State, Bureau of Public Affairs, December 1985), pp. 8–14.
27. *Overseas Presence: Staffing at U.S. Diplomatic Posts*, General Accounting Office Report (GAO/NSIAD–95–50FS, December 28, 1994): 33.
28. These data are taken from *The World Almanac and Book of Facts 1996* (Mahwah, NJ: World Almanac Books, 1995), p. 151. The estimate of foreign nationals employed by the Department of State is taken from *State Department: Survey of Administrative Issues Affecting Embassies*, General Accounting Office Report (GAO/NSIAD–93–218, July 12, 1993): 1. For a lower total of 7,168 "U.S. Direct Hires Overseas" for 1994, see *Overseas Presence: Staffing at U.S. Diplomatic Posts*, p. 15, but also see the discussion at p. 10 on the limitation of these data.
29. Bureau of Public Affairs, Department of State, "The International Affairs Budget—A Sound Investment in Global Leadership: Questions and Answers," October 1, 1995, via the Internet.
30. *Appendix, Budget of the United States Government Fiscal 1996* (Washington, DC: United States Government Printing Office, 1995), p. 689, shows the actual budget for fiscal year 1994 and the estimates for fiscal years 1995 and 1996. All of these budget figures indicate about $2.2 billion.
31. Among some readings that criticize the effectiveness of the Department of State are the following: I. M. Destler, *Presidents, Bureaucrats, and Foreign Policy* (Princeton, NJ: Princeton University Press, 1974), pp. 154–190; John Franklin Campbell, "The Disorganization of State," in Martin B. Hickman, ed., *Problems of American Foreign Policy*, 2nd ed. (Beverly Hills: Glencoe Press, 1975), pp. 151–170; Robert Pringle, "Creeping Irrelevance at Foggy Bottom," *Foreign Policy* 29 (Winter 1977–78): 128–139; Andrew M. Scott, "The Department of State: Formal Organization and Informal Culture," *International Studies Quarterly* 13 (March 1969): 1–18; and Andrew M. Scott, "The Problem of the State Department," in Martin B. Hickman, ed., *Problems of American Foreign Policy*, pp. 143–151.
32. *State 2000: A New Model for Managing Foreign Affairs*, p. 4.
33. Elaine Sciolino, "Austerity at State Dept. and Fear of Diplomacy," *New York Times*, November 15, 1987, 1 and 8; and John M. Goshko, "State Dept. Budget Faces New Cuts," *The Washington Post*, April 27, 1987, A6. The quoted passages are from the latter. On the continuing budget concerns, see Ronald I. Spiers, "The 'Budget Crunch' and the Foreign Service" (Washington, DC: United States Department of State, Bureau of Public Affairs, May 1988); and James Baker, "U.S. Foreign Policy Priorities and FY 1991 Budget Request" (Washington, DC: United States Department of State, Bureau of Public Affairs, February 1990).
34. "The United States Department of State: Structure and Organization," p. 1. For a listing of sixteen of seventeen posts closed in 1993 and 1994, see *State Department: Overseas Staffing Process Not Linked to Policy Priorities*, General Accounting Office Report (GAO/NSIAD 94-228, September 20, 1994): 18–19.
35. These data on the July 1995 announcement are from U.S. State Department Daily Press Briefing, July 18, 1995.
36. See Steven Greenhouse, "Christopher to Cut Jobs at State Dept.," *New York Times*, May 7, 1995, 4; and "The International Affairs Budget—A Sound Investment in Global Leadership: Questions and Answers."

37. Baker with DeFrank, *The Politics of Diplomacy: Revolution, War and Peace, 1989–1992*, p. 28.

38. On this point, see Henry T. Nash, *American Foreign Policy: Changing Perspectives on National Security* (Homewood, IL: The Dorsey Press, 1978), p. 139. Also, see Nash's excellent discussion on the problems of State, from which our overall discussion benefited.

39. See *State Department: Actions Needed to Improve Embassy Management*, p. 1. Also see "The International Affairs Budget—A Sound Investment in Global Leadership: Questions and Answers," which places the number at "about 4,000 diplomatic and consular service officers."

40. David Garnham, in particular, has looked at some of these stereotypes about the Department of State. While he finds that the background characteristics of FSOs differ from the general population, he reports that the FSOs do not differ from other groups in American society on psychological flexibility. Overall, he judges that this elitism has not negatively affected the conduct of U.S. foreign policy. See his "State Department Rigidity: Testing a Psychological Hypothesis," *International Studies Quarterly* 18 (March 1974): 31–39; and "Foreign Service Elitism and U.S. Foreign Affairs," *Public Administration Review* 35 (January/February 1975): 44–51.

41. Duncan L. Clarke, "Why State Can't Lead," *Foreign Policy* 66 (Spring 1987): 135; and Baker with DeFrank, *The Politics of Diplomacy: Revolution, War, and Peace, 1989–1992*, p. 28.

42. Clarke, "Why State Can't Lead," p. 134. Also, see Baker with DeFrank, *The Politics of Diplomacy: Revolution, War and Peace, 1989–1992*, p. 29.

43. Ibid., p. 133–134. "Foggy Bottom" refers to the area of Washington, D.C., where the Department of State and several executive agencies are located. Indeed, it is so familiar to Washington residents that it has its own subway stop named "Foggy Bottom."

44. Baker with DeFrank, *The Politics of Diplomacy: Revolution, War and Peace, 1989–1992*, p. 29.

45. Scott, "The Problem of the State Department," p. 146. Emphasis in original.

46. Scott, "The Department of State: Formal Organization and Informal Culture," p. 6.

47. Clarke, "Why State Can't Lead," p. 136.

48. Baker with DeFrank, *The Politics of Diplomacy: Revolution, War and Peace, 1989–1992*, p. 28.

49. Ibid., p. 31.

50. Nash, *American Foreign Policy: Changing Perspectives*, p. 139.

51. See I. M. Destler, "National Security Advice to U.S. Presidents: Some Lessons from Thirty Years," *World Politics* 24 (January 1977): 148–149, 153–154, 156–157. Also see I. M. Destler, *Presidents, Bureaucrats, and Foreign Policy*, pp. 96–99, for some differing views on how much President Kennedy wanted to rely upon the Department of State for foreign policy formulation.

52. Ibid., pp. 157–158, for a discussion of the extent of Rostow's duties and for a sense of how the secretaries of state and defense were involved in the process.

53. Hedrick Smith, *The Power Game: How Washington Works* (New York: Ballantine Books, 1988), pp. 558–562; and Theodore C. Sorensen, "The President and the Secretary of State," *Foreign Affairs* 66 (Winter 1987/1988): 231–248. But also see Leslie H. Gelb, "McFarlane Carving His Niche," *New York Times*, March 28, 1984, B10.

54. Nash, *American Foreign Policy: Changing Perspectives*, p. 100.

55. For a detailed assessment of the relationship between President Bush and Secretary of State James Baker, see Maureen Dowd and Thomas L. Friedman, "The Fabulous Bush and Baker Boys," *The New York Times Magazine*, May 6, 1990, 36. Other analyses available to assess the close ties between Bush and Baker and the enhanced role of the national security advisor under Bush can be found in John Newhouse, "Profiles (James Baker)," *The New Yorker*, May 7, 1990, 50–82; and Bernard Weinraub, "Bush Backs Plan to Enhance Role of Security Staff," *New York Times*, February 2, 1989, 1 and 6.

56. This assessment draws upon Barry Schweid, "Warren's World," *Foreign Policy* 94 (Spring 1994), 137–147; "The Flint Beneath the Suit," *The Economist*, February 13, 1993, 30; and "The Tortoise of Foggy Bottom," *The Economist*, January 8, 1994, 34.

57. Jack Perry, "The Foreign Service in Real Trouble, But It Can Be Saved," *Washington Post National Weekly Edition*, January 16, 1984, 21.

58. See, for John M. Goshko, "Appointing Loyalists as Envoys," *Washington Post*, April 28, 1987, A16, who reports that during the Reagan administration just under 40 percent of all ambassadors went to political appointments; and Elaine Sciolino, "Friends as Ambassadors: How Many Is Too Many?" *New York Times*, November 7, 1989, A1 and A8, who reports higher figures for Kennedy through Bush when focusing only on the first few months.

59. Steven Greenhouse, "Clinton Is Faulted on Political Choices for Envoy Posts," *New York Times*, April 13, 1994, A16.

60. Sciolino, "Friends as Ambassadors: How Many Is Too Many?" p. A8.

61. Author's conversation with the U.S. Ambassador of a small Asia-Pacific nation, July 1995.

62. John M. Goshko, "Clout and Morale Decline," *Washington Post*, April 26, 1987, A12.

63. Newhouse, "Profiles (James Baker)," p. 76.

64. "The State Roster," *Congressional Quarterly Weekly Report*, January 23, 1995, 185.

65. Schweid, "Warren's World," p. 144.

66. "The State Roster," p. 185.

67. See the commentary by two former Balkan specialists in the State Department who resigned in 1993 to protest Clinton administration policy: Marshall Freeman Harris and Stephen W. Walker, "America's Sellout of the Bosnians," *New York Times*, August 23, 1995, A15.

68. Schweid, "Warren's World," p. 143.

69. Perry, "The Foreign Service in Real Trouble, But It Can Be Saved," p. 21.

70. I am grateful to *Smith, The Power Game: How Washington Works*, p. 589, for drawing this distinction between the two. "The NSC" is his term.

71. Membership on the National Security Council has varied slightly by statute over time, but these are the ones that have remained continuously on the Council.

72. Stephen D. Cohen, *The Making of United States International Economic Policy*, 4th ed. (Westport, CT: Praeger, 1994), p. 79; and Charles W. Kegley, Jr., and Eugene R. Wittkopf, *American Foreign Policy: Pattern and Process*, 5th ed. (New York: St. Martin's Press, 1996), p. 363.

73. James S. Lay, Jr. and Robert H. Johnson, "Organizational History of the National Security Council during the Truman and Eisenhower Administrations," Report prepared for the Subcommittee on National Policy Machinery, August 11, 1960, p. 8.

74. Destler, "National Security Advice to U.S. Presidents: Some Lessons from Thirty Years," pp. 148–151, 153–159. Also see Nash, *American Foreign Policy: Changing Perspectives*, pp. 140, 172–174. On Truman's and Eisenhower's attendance of NSC meetings, see Lay and Johnson, "Organizational History of the National Security Council during the Truman and Eisenhower Administrations," pp. 5 and 24.

75. Ibid., p. 26. The characterization of Cutler as "the principal executive officer" is Lay and Johnson's.

76. Ibid., p. 30, and footnote 61.

77. For a discussion of how President Kennedy transformed the role of the national security advisor with Bundy, see I. M. Destler, "National Security Management: What Presidents Have Wrought," *Political Science Quarterly* 95 (Winter 1980–1981): 578–580; and Bromley K. Smith, "Organizational History of the National Security Council During the Kennedy and Johnson Administrations," monograph written for the National Security Council, February 1987.

78. Townsend Hoopes, *The Limits of Intervention* (New York: David McKay, 1968) for a discussion of the important influence of Rostow on LBJ, especially at pp. 20–22 and 59–62. For the identity, and critique, of the "Tuesday Lunch" group, see Irving Janis, *Groupthink* (Boston: Houghton Mifflin Company, 1972), pp. 101–135.

79. Destler, "National Security Management: What Presidents Have Wrought," p. 580.

80. Henry A. Kissinger, "Domestic Structure and Foreign Policy," in James N. Rosenau, ed., *International Politics and Foreign Policy*, rev. ed. (New York: Free Press, 1969), pp. 261–275, especially pp. 263–267.

81. See the diagram of the "Kissinger National Security Council System," in Nash, *American Foreign Policy: Changing Perspectives*, p. 197.

82. Elizabeth Drew, "A Reporter At Large: Brzezinski," *The New Yorker* (May 1, 1978), 94, reports that the initial National Security Council under Brzezinski consisted of only two committees: the Policy Review Committee and the Special Coordination Committee.

83. See the discussion of Brzezinski's role in Chapter 4. Also see Zbigniew Brzezinski, *Power and Principle: Memoirs of the National Security Advisor, 1977–1981* (New York: Farrar, Straus & Giroux, 1983).

84. On the disputes that precipitated Haig's firing, see Steven R. Weisman, "Aides List Clashes," *New York Times*, June 26, 1982, 1, 5; Leslie H. Gelb, "A Year in Office, Shultz Still Mapping His Way Through Diplomacy's Thicket," *Milwaukee Journal*, August 7, 1983, Accent on the News section, p. 2; also "Disappearing Act at Foggy Bottom," *Time*, August 8, 1983, 28.

85. Smith, *The Power Game: How Washington Works*, p. 593. The characterization of Clark's role in pushing the Strategic Defense Initiative is from pp. 594–599.

86. See "Shultz: No More Mr. Nice Guy?" *Newsweek*, August 22, 1983, 17; and "Shultz Peeved, Magazine Says," *Des Moines Register*, August 15, 1983, 8A. For Secretary of State Shultz's denial of the report, see "Aide Denies Shultz Losing His Influence," *Des Moines Register*, August 16, 1983, 1A, 2A.

87. Leslie H. Gelb, "McFarlane Carving His Niche," *New York Times*, March 28, 1984, B10.

88. *Report of the President's Special Review Board (Tower Commission Report)* (Washington, DC: U.S. Government Printing Office, February 26, 1987); and *Report of the Congressional Committees Investigating the Iran-Contra Affair* (Washington, DC: U.S. Government Printing Office, November 1987).

89. Weinraub, "Bush Backs Plan to Enhance Role of Security Staff," pp. 1 and 6, and National Security Council statement, "National Security Council Organization," mimeo, April 17, 1989, 3 pp.

90. John Barry with Margaret Garrard Warner, "Mr. Inside, Mr. Outside," *Newsweek*, February 27, 1989, 28; and R.W. Apple, Jr., "A Mover and Shaker Behind Bush Foreign Policy," *New York Times*, February 6, 1989, 3.

91. Jason DeParle, "The Man Inside Bill Clinton's Foreign Policy," *New York Times Magazine*, August 20, 1995, 34.

92. Lake is quoted in ibid. at p. 37.

93. Ibid., p. 34.

94. "Clinton Chooses a Foreign Policy Team," *New York Times*, December 23, 1992, A13; and James Bennet, "A Trusted Adviser, and a Friend," *New York Times*, December 6, 1996, A16. On the appointment of George Tenet, see Tim Weiner, "Clinton Proposes Acting C.I.A. Chief as Agency Leader," *New York Times*, March 20, 1997, A1, A14; and Tim Weiner, "For 'the Ultimate Staff Guy,' a Time to Reap the Rewards of Being Loyal," *New York Times*, March 20, 1997, A14.

95. Bert A. Rockman, "America's Departments of State: Irregular and Regular Syndromes of Policy Making," *The American Political Science Review* 75 (December 1981): 911–927.

96. Ibid., pp. 914–918. While this section draws upon Rockman's explanations, some of my own interpretations are added to his insights.

97. Two books that both address these economic bureaucracies and influenced the following discussion are Kegley and Wittkopf, *American Foreign Policy: Pattern and Process*, 5th ed. (New York: St. Martin's Press, 1996); and Howard J. Wiarda, *Foreign Policy Without Illusion* (Glenview, IL: Scott, Foresman, Little Brown Higher Education, 1990).

98. The following principles are drawn from the discussion in Stephen D. Cohen, Joel R. Paul, and Robert A. Blecker, *Fundamentals of U.S. Foreign Trade Policy* (Boulder, Co: Westview Press, 1996), pp. 105–108.

99. The first quote is from ibid., p. 109, while the last two are from the mission statement of the Office of the U.S. Trade Representative's home page on the World Wide Web.

100. The discussion is drawn from Cohen, *The Making of United States International Economic Policy*, pp. 57–59, and from Cohen, Paul, and Blecker, *Fundamentals of U.S. Foreign Trade Policy*, pp. 109, 153–154.

101. See Cohen, *The Making of United States Economic Policy*, pp. 59 and 57, for the two quotes.

102. Cohen, Paul, and Blecker, *Fundamentals of U.S. Foreign Trade Policy*, pp. 109–110.

103. Cohen, *The Making of United States International Economic Policy*, pp. 47–51. The quotes are at p. 50 for the first and p. 51 for the next two.

104. Ibid., p. 61.

105. Cohen, Paul, and Blecker, *Fundamentals of U.S. Foreign Trade Policy*, p. 47.

106. Quoted in Jones, "American Prewar Technology Sales to Iraq: A Bureaucratic Politics Explanation," p. 286.

107. Cohen, *The Making of United States International Economic Policy*, p. 182.

108. Jones, "American Prewar Technology Sales to Iraq: A Bureaucratic Politics Explanation," p. 286.

109. The quoted passages and the set of factors to explain Treasury's growth in influence are from Cohen, *The Making of United States International Economic Policy*, pp. 51–53.

110. Ibid., pp. 53–56, and *U.S. Government Manual 1995/1996*, July 1, 1995, pp. 459 and 461.

111. The quote is from Robert D. Hormats, "The World Economy Under Stress," in William G. Hyland, ed., *America and the World 1985* (New York: Pergamon Press, 1986), p. 469. Another source used here was Congressman Lee Hamilton, "The Decline of the Dollar," *Washington Report*, February 25, 1987.

112. The estimate of Treasury involvement is from Cohen, *The Making of United States International Economic Policy*, p. 239, in which he cites an unattributed interview with a Treasury Department official (note 14, p. 244).

113. S. Karene Witcher, "Baker's Plan to Relieve Debt Crisis May Spur Future Ills, Critics Say," *The Wall Street Journal*, November 15, 1985, 1.

114. Hormats, "The World Economy Under Stress," p. 474.

115. It was devised by Under Secretary David C. Mulford. See John R. Cranford, "Members Press for Details on Brady Proposal," *Congressional Quarterly Weekly Report*, March 18, 1989, 572, for this point and some examples of how the plan would work; and John R. Cranford, "Brady Signals Shift in Policy Toward Debt Reduction," *Congressional Quarterly Weekly Report*, March 11, 1989, 510–513, for an earlier discussion of the plan.

116. Peter Passell, "2 Views of the Peso: Wall St. vs. Main St.," *New York Times*, February 2, 1995, A6.

117. Patrick J. Lyons, "Mexico's Ripple Effects: Subtle Risks for Americans," *New York Times*, February 1, 1995, A11.

118. Bruce Stokes, "Tottering Markets," *National Journal*, February 18, 1995, 424. The official quoted is Treasury Undersecretary Lawrence H. Summers.

119. The central role of the Department of Treasury in devising this plan can be gleaned from the active involvement of the secretary of the treasury in seeking congressional support (see, for example, David E. Sanger, "U.S. Seeks Mexican Steps in Bid to Aid Bailout Plan," *New York Times*, January 26, 1995, A14) and from the importance of the under secretary of the treasury, Lawrence Summers, in securing the agreements on the final package (see, for example Douglas Jehl, "Slow-Building Despair Led to Decision on Aid," *New York Times*, February 1, 1995, A10).

120. David E. Sanger, "Clinton Offers $20 Billion to Mexico for Peso Rescue; Action Sidesteps Congress," *New York Times*, February 1, 1995, A1.

121. Ibid.

122. Bradford De Long, Christopher De Long, and Sherman Robinson, "The Case for Mexico's Rescue," *Foreign Affairs* 75 (May/June 1996): 8–14, especially at 12.

123. Julia Preston, "Mexico Happy with Response to New Bonds," *New York Times*, May 2, 1996, C1 and C6.

124. White House Press Release, "Remarks By the President at Signing of U.S.-Mexico Loan Agreement Protocol," January 15, 1997, via the Internet.

125. Cohen, *The Making of United States International Economic Policy*, p. 62.

126. *U.S. Government Manual 1995/1996*, July 1, 1995, p. 154.

127. Ibid., p. 161–162; and *International Trade: Coordination of U.S. Export Promotion Activities in Pacific Rim Countries*. General Accounting Office Report (GAO/GGD-94-192, August 29, 1994): 5.

128. Ibid., pp. 5–6. The quoted market phrase is in this source at p. 6.

129. Cohen, *The Making of United States International Economic Policy*, p. 62; and Kegley and Wittkopf, *American Foreign Policy: Pattern and Process*, p. 418.

130. The procedures for these countervailing duties and antidumping actions are spelled out in *Summary of Statutory Provisions Related to Import Relief* (Washington, DC: United States International Trade Commission, July 1993).

131. See *The World Almanac and Book of Facts 1996*, p. 206, for the 1994 trade deficit total.

132. Richard W. Stevenson, "A Role as Nation's Chief Salesman Abroad," *New York Times*, April 4, 1996, A7.

133. Leslie Eaton, "A Dozen Companies Await Word," *New York Times*, April 4, 1996, A7.

134. Cohen, *The Making of United States International Economic Policy*, p. 63.

135. These officials are quoted in Robert Pear, "Confusion Is Operative Word in U.S. Policy Toward Japan," *New York Times*, March 20, 1989, 6.

136. Quoted in Bruce Stokes, "Sharp Operator," *National Journal*, February 26, 1994, 468.

137. Steven Erlanger, "As Clinton Visits Changing Asia, Military Concerns Gain Urgency," *New York Times*, April 15, 1996, A1 and A6. The last quote is actually from Gregory Treverton, of the Rand Corporation, who was critiquing the Clinton administration's foreign policy and was quoted in this story.

138. Cohen, *The Making of United States International Economic Policy*, p. 63.

139. The discussion and what follows mainly draws upon *U.S. Government Manual 1995/1996*, July 1, 1995, pp. 113, 128–135, supplemented with Cohen, *The Making of United States International Economic Policy*, p. 63–64. I am also indebted to my colleague, Ross B. Talbot, for sharing his insight on agricultural policy making.

140. The number of current ATOs was based upon an interview with a knowledgeable official in the Department of Agriculture, June 1996. For an earlier critical assessment of ATOs, see *International Trade: Agricultural Trade Offices' Role in Promoting U.S. Exports Is Unclear*. General Accounting Office Report (GAO/GGD-92-65, January 16, 1992).

141. *U.S. Government Manual 1995/ 1996*, July 1, 1995, p. 134.

142. Ibid., p. 135.

143. Jonathan E. Sanford, with the assistance of Pamela D. Richardson, *Foreign Assistance: An Overview of U.S. Aid Agencies and Programs*. CRS Report for Congress (Washington, DC: Congressional Research Service, April 18, 1995), pp. 4 and 6; and Larry Q. Nowels, *Foreign Aid Budget and Policy Issues for the 104th Congress*, CRS Issue Brief (Washington, DC: Congressional Research Service, April 3, 1996), p. 7.

144. "The Foreign Agricultural Service—Mission Statement," U.S. Department of Agriculture, Foreign Agricultural Service, June 1996, pp. 4–5.

145. H. Wayne Moyer and Timothy E. Josling, *Agricultural Policy Reform: Politics and Process in the EC and the USA* (New York: Harvester Wheatsheaf, 1990), pp. 124 (note 6) and 120.

146. George Athan, "Yeutter Likely to Push for Free Trade, Exports," *Des Moines Register*, December 15, 1988, 1A and 11A.

147. Douglas Jehl, "Top Farm Job Likely to Go to Lawmaker from Kansas," *New York Times*, December 22, 1994, B12.

148. See Dan Looker, "The Politics of NAFTA Heat Up," *Successful Farming* 91 (September, 1993): 8; and Dan Glickman, "U.S. Opportunities" [Landon Lecture, Kansas State University] *Vital Speeches* (October 15, 1995): 5–10.

149. "Agricultural Advisory Committees for Trade," U.S. Department of Agriculture, Foreign Agricultural Service, July 1995, pp. 1.

150. The details of the Iraqi case here are drawn from Bruce W. Jentleson, *With Friends Like These* (New York and London: W. W. Norton and Company, 1994), pp. 83, 128–132.

151. Ibid., pp. 132–138.

152. The quoted passage is from National Security Directive 26 (NSD-26) and is taken from ibid., p. 94.

153. See Raymond F. Hopkins and Donald J. Puchala, *Global Food Interdependence: Challenge to American Foreign Policy* (New York: Columbia University Press, 1980), pp. 110–115, for a discussion of tensions between the Department of State and the USDA and the expansion of agricultural capacities in other bureaucracies in the 1970s.

CHAPTER

IO

THE MILITARY AND INTELLIGENCE BUREAUCRACIES: PERVASIVE OR ACCOUNTABLE?

The time has come to step into the future, to look at the world ahead and ask, what will America's role be? What type of military do we need for the 21st Century?

Secretary of Defense William S. Cohen
on the issuance of the Quadrennial Defense Review
May 1997

[T]he post Cold War threats to our national security are significant and complex. Intelligence—properly collected, analyzed, and distributed—can play a vital role in meeting these threats.... Both our human assets and our highly capable technical intelligence systems can provide vital information to our senior policy makers about what our potential enemies are doing.

CIA Director John M. Deutch
April 1995

This chapter continues the discussion of bureaucracies and foreign policy by examining the Department of Defense and the intelligence community. These bureaucracies increased their foreign and national security influence over the post–World War II years, but both now have come under closer scrutiny as the post–Cold War years have set in. Our discussion highlights those changes in influence over time and assesses each bureaucracy's relative position at the end of the century. In addition, this chapter explains the mechanism that the executive branch uses to coordinate policy making across the different bureaucracies discussed in the last two chapters. While individual bureaucracies may impact foreign policy making directly, the combined effect of several bureaucracies—or the success of one bureaucracy over another—occurs most often through the interagency or interdepartmental coordination process that all recent presidents have used.

THE DEPARTMENT OF DEFENSE

The Department of Defense may well be perceived as a bureaucracy that only implements policy, but, in fact, the Department of Defense contributes substantially to the formulation of foreign policy decisions. Its overall power has grown significantly over the past fifty years, but its role in foreign policy formulation remains a source of debate. Some would contend that it is but one bureaucracy within the foreign policy apparatus, albeit a powerful one.[1] Others would argue that it has a pervasive effect on American foreign policy making—often surpassing the competing bureaucracies within the executive branch.[2] Still others would suggest that it is the beginning point for the "military-industrial complex," a structure woven into American society (see Chapter 11).[3] Yet another view, and one especially prevalent today, claims that the military and its role ought to be changed substantially with the collapse of the Soviet Union and the advent of the post–Cold War era. Whichever view the reader adopts, there can be little doubt that the Department of Defense has increased its foreign policy making influence over the years and that, even in the face of changes in the 1990s, that influence is likely to remain for the foreseeable future.

The Structure of the Pentagon

The perceived influence of the Department of Defense begins with its considerable size and presence in the foreign policy decision-making apparatus of the government. As Figure 10.1 shows, the Pentagon (located across the Potomac River from the nation's capital in Arlington, Virginia, and named for the shape of the Department of Defense's headquarters) is a large and complex bureaucracy organized into key major divisions. These major divisions are further subdivided into a variety of departments, agencies, and offices that potentially affect many areas of American life.

The Department of Defense impacts the American public through the awarding of defense contracts, through domestic and foreign jobs created for United States corporations, and through the number of men and women

FIGURE 10.1

Department of Defense

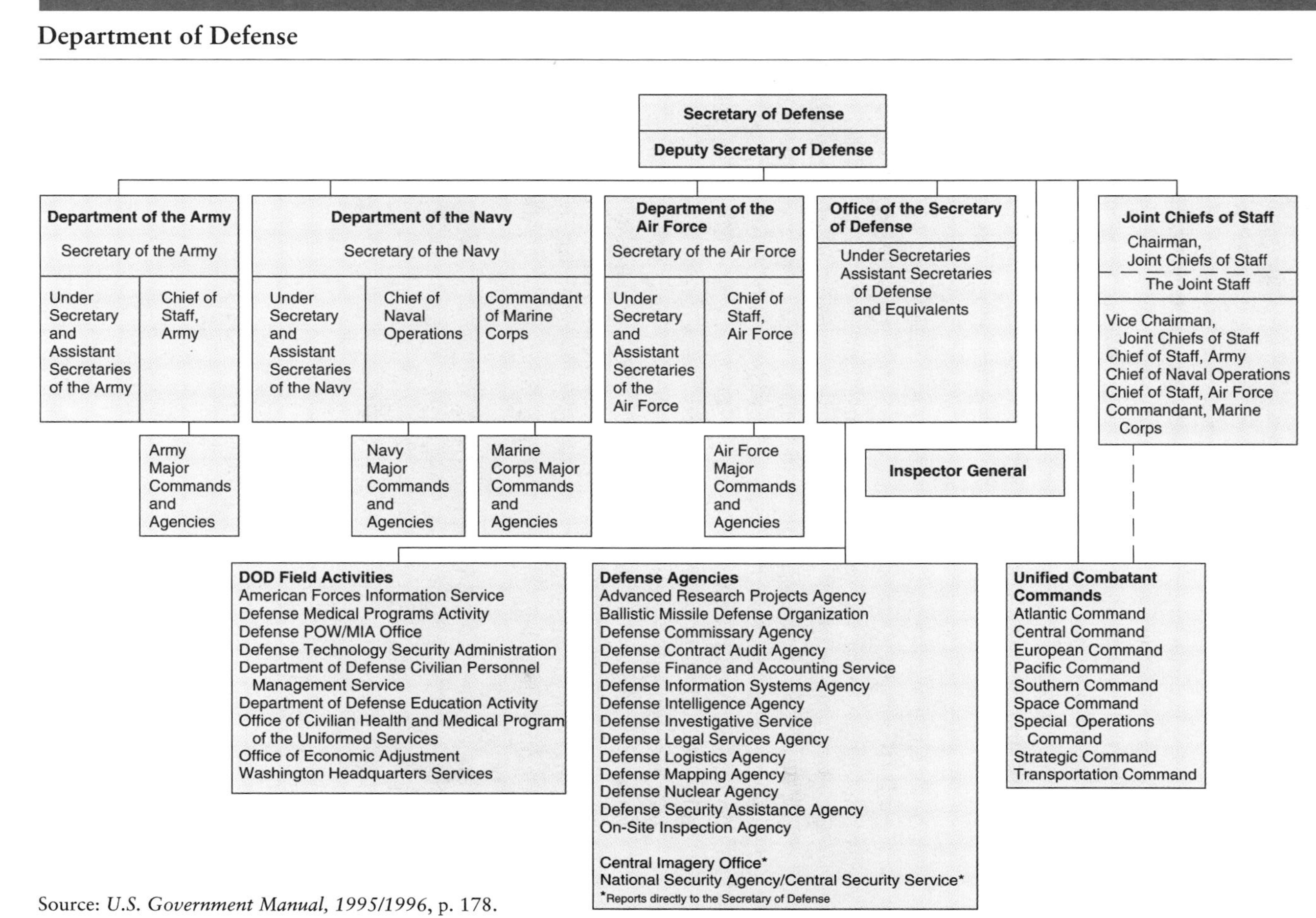

Source: *U.S. Government Manual, 1995/1996*, p. 178.

serving in the military services. In fiscal year 1995, for example, over $109 million in prime defense contracts was awarded within the United States, with every state and the District of Columbia sharing in those awards and the thousands of jobs they create.[4] Through September 30, 1995, the Department of Defense employed about 768,000 civilians, 1.1 million active-duty military personnel, and 1.7 million reserve and national guard personnel. The national defense outlays for fiscal year 1996 were estimated at about $266 billion.[5] In short, even with cuts in the defense budget over the past several years (and now some projected increases into the new century),[6] the impact of the Department of Defense expenditures on American society remain pronounced, fueled by concerns over the spread of weapons of mass destruction (e.g., biological, chemical, and nuclear), new instances of ethnic and religious conflicts (e.g., Bosnia, Rwanda, and Somalia), and the persistence of terrorism (e.g., the 1996 bombing in Saudi Arabia).

In terms of foreign policy formulation, three sectors of the Department of Defense are pivotal: (1) the secretary of defense; (2) the Joint Chiefs of Staff (JCS); and (3) the Office of the Secretary of Defense (OSD). The last, the Office of the Secretary of Defense, is the newest, and potentially the greatest, source of influence in affecting foreign policy formulation. OSD, the staff arm of the secretary of defense, consists of a variety of offices and agencies that deal with managing the department and developing foreign policy recommendations. Among OSD's mandated duties are the responsibility to "conduct analyses, develop policies, provide advice, make recommendations, and issue guidance on Defense plans and programs." It also has the responsibility to "develop systems and standards for the administration and management of approved plans and programs."[7] As the Office of the Secretary of Defense has grown over the years, it has become the principal focus for policy development and administration within the Department of Defense.

The policy division, headed by an under secretary of defense for policy, illustrates the crucial policy-formulating function within OSD. Within this division, for instance, several important policy offices operate: International Security Affairs; International Security Policy; Strategy, Requirements and Assessments; Special Operations and Low-Intensity Conflict; and Net Assessment. Each office, headed by an assistant secretary of defense, has an important stake in policy development.

Two of the middle-level offices within OSD illustrate the increased policy formulation role of the Department of Defense over the years: the Office of International Security Affairs (ISA) and the Office of International Security Policy. The former, in particular, gained prominence during the Vietnam War period when it was instrumental in offering policy advice.[8] Moreover, its responsibilities today cover such issues as security assistance, military assistance advisory groups and missions abroad, international economic and energy activities, and the monitoring of agreements with other nations, excluding the NATO countries.[9] ISA has gained such prominence in policy making that it has been labeled the "little State Department," because it provides a political component to the military analysis at the Pentagon. The ISA, however, declined in influence from Nixon to Carter, through some structural and procedural realignments.[10]

During the Reagan administration, the Office of International Security Policy assumed a larger role within the Department of Defense for policy influence. Its responsibilities encompassed policy development on NATO and European affairs, including nuclear and conventional forces, strategic and theater arms negotiations, nuclear proliferation questions, and oversight of existing agreements.[11] During those years, the assistant secretary of defense for international security policy was particularly prominent in speaking out on arms policy. Richard Perle often took the lead in shaping policy on the question of deploying intermediate-range nuclear missiles in Europe in the early 1980s and in developing the United States bargaining position on both intermediate-range and long-range nuclear forces at the arms control talks in Geneva. Indeed, his role in these negotiations, and in policy development generally, was so substantial that it has been chronicled in great detail by a political analyst, a rarity for a middle-level official in the foreign policy bureaucracy.[12]

Although these offices did not gain the same recognition in the Bush administration, their status returned during the Clinton years. Two assistant secretaries heading these offices were prominent policy analysts on leave from Harvard University: Joseph Nye, a leading scholar of international relations and foreign policy, headed the Office of International Affairs for a time; and Ashton Carter, a leading thinker and analyst in the nuclear weapons area, headed the Office of International Security Policy. Both sought to put an imprint on policy, and Nye, in particular, was deeply involved in shaping United States policy toward Asia.[13] Nonetheless, the importance of these two offices—and any other in the Department of Defense—will ultimately be a function of how the secretary of defense or even the president wants to use them to shape foreign policy.

The Joint Chiefs of Staff

The Joint Chiefs of Staff (JCS) is a second set of important policy advisors within the Department of Defense. The JCS, composed of the chief of staff of the Army, the Chief of Naval Operations, the chief of staff of the Air Force, the commandant of the Marine Corps, and the chairman of the Joint Chiefs, has been described as "the hinge between the most senior civilian leadership and the professional military."[14] The responsibility of the JCS is to provide the president and the secretary of defense with strategic planning and to coordinate the integration of the armed forces for use if necessary. In addition, the JCS recommends to the president and the secretary of defense the military requirements of the United States and how they are to be accomplished. Finally, the chairman of the Joint Chiefs, appointed by the president with the advice and consent of the Senate, is the primary military advisor to the secretary of defense, the National Security Council, and the president.[15]

Policy-making Constraints. Despite its statutory foreign policy duties, the Joints Chiefs of Staff probably has been less effective in shaping American policy since World War II than the civilian side of the Pentagon—for at least two reasons.

First, the Joint Chiefs has enjoyed only mixed favor with both presidents and secretaries of defense since 1947.[16] In fact, some presidents and secretaries have been at odds with the JCS and have tried to reduce its policy impact. President Eisenhower, for instance, was determined to "balance the budget and restrict military spending"—something the JCS did not favor.[17] With his own vast military experience in World War II, Eisenhower did not see the need to rely upon the JCS for advice and assistance, especially after it had publicly criticized his policy. Under President Kennedy, the situation for the JCS only worsened, as Secretary of Defense Robert McNamara attempted to streamline and modernize the management and operation of the Pentagon. Any initial confidence that President Kennedy might have placed in the JCS was quickly eroded as a result of what he perceived as bad policy advice on the Bay of Pigs invasion in April 1961.[18]

Relations between the JCS and the president improved from Johnson through Ford. During the Johnson administration, relations warmed a bit—especially after the disaffection and ultimately the resignation of Secretary of Defense McNamara in 1967—when the president increasingly became dependent upon the JCS for policy advice on the Vietnam War. Even before this occurrence, however, there is some evidence of President Johnson's more favorable tilt toward the Department of Defense, if not directly to the Joint Chiefs, in foreign policy making.[19] Under Presidents Nixon and Ford and when Melvin Laird was secretary of defense, the Joint Chiefs was clearly in the ascendancy in terms of influence, even though it did not apparently shape the critical policy positions during those years.[20]

Under the Carter and Reagan administrations, the situation changed once again and reliance on the JCS fluctuated. Carter's major policy decisions on troop withdrawals from Korea and the scrapping of the B-1 bomber were adopted with minimal JCS involvement.[21] By contrast, the Reagan administration appeared initially to be more receptive to the views of the JCS. At one point in his administration, President Reagan reportedly sent written praise to the Joint Chiefs for its policy advice.[22] Despite such praise, policy making for the Reagan administration was largely located elsewhere within the executive branch and the Department of Defense.

Second, each Joint Chief's commitment to his own service has reduced combined policy impact.[23] That is, each JCS member has the responsibility of managing his own military service as well as advising the president and the secretary of defense through the Joint Chiefs structure. In the estimate of one defense analyst, this individual service responsibility consumes an important portion of Joint Chiefs' time and diminishes their combined foreign policy formulation role. The divided loyalties among JCS members also produces policy differences within the Joint Chiefs themselves, and, in turn, policy recommendations reflect a compromise position among them which may not be vigorously supported by all members.[24]

Indeed, criticisms of the Joint Chiefs' recommendations have been particularly harsh. President Jimmy Carter's secretary of defense, Harold Brown, for instance, characterized the advice from the JCS as "worse than nothing." Another former high-ranking Pentagon official labeled it as "a laughingstock." Yet a third official—a former aide to Brown—said the advice was like a "bowl of oatmeal." Despite President Reagan's praise of the

JCS, Secretary of Defense Caspar Weinberger rejected or ignored the advice of the Joint Chiefs on such major issues as the basing mode for the MX and on the requirements of the Rapid Deployment Force.[25] Perhaps even more telling regarding the weakened influence of the JCS was President Reagan's failure to even remember the name of the chairman of the Joint Chiefs during a major portion of his administration. When testifying during the Iran-Contra trial of John Poindexter, President Reagan was asked if he recognized the name of John Vessey, chairman of the Joint Chiefs during much of his term in office. While he said that the name sounded "very familiar," he could not be certain as to who he was.[26]

Policy-making Reforms. In the Defense Reorganization Act of 1986 (also known as the Goldwater-Nichols Reorganization Act, after its congressional sponsors), Congress changed the power and authority of the Joint Chiefs of Staff to address these problems. In effect, the changes reduced the clout of the individual services in policy recommendations and increased the impact of the JCS as a whole.

One key change was to give more power to the chairman in policy formulation and recommendation. The chairman (and not the Joint Chiefs as such) was designated as the president's primary military advisor, and he was responsible for providing the executive with the range of military advice on any matter requested. Thus the chairman would not have to "water down" his recommendation to accommodate his JCS colleagues. The chairman also assumed statutory responsibility for preparing strategic military plans, future military contingency plans, and budget coordination within the military itself. Finally, the Joint Staff reported directly to the chairman, as did a newly appointed vice chairman.[27]

A second key change was in the command structure. The unified commanders, those responsible for coordinating the four different services operating in a particular region of the world, gained much greater authority. Under the previous arrangement, the individual services retained substantial authority in directing forces, but, under the reorganization, new authority now rested with those directing multiservice operations, greatly increasing the integration of forces across the branches.

In fact, the Goldwater-Nichols legislation has been characterized as "the most important piece of military legislation...in the last forty years...[and] the most dangerous."[28] In this view, the reorganization was important because it enhanced the power of the JCS chairman, but it was dangerous because it challenged civilian control of the military. This concern was seemingly given support with the appointment of General Colin Powell as chairman of the Joint Chiefs of Staff during the Bush administration.

Described as a "military intellectual," who took a "pragmatic and collegial approach" to policy making, General Powell was well versed in all aspects of national security policy.[29] Aided by the legal basis for policy influence offered by the Goldwater-Nichols Act, Powell was thus in a position to "become the most influential JCS chairman in U.S. history."[30] Indeed, Powell was soon appointed to a new executive defense committee established by the secretary of defense and became a key influence on policy formulation. Significantly, of course, he played a central role in designing the

American response to Iraq's intervention into Kuwait, including the resulting American buildup in Saudi Arabia and the Persian Gulf. By one assessment, moreover, Powell was "responsible for shaping the U.S. military response in the gulf," and his strategy of deploying "maximum force" was fully endorsed by President Bush.[31]

When Powell continued in office during the Clinton administration, policy analyst Richard Kohn argued that Powell was in a strong position to defy "a young, incoming president with extraordinarily weak authority in military affairs" in policy making, as he initially did over Bosnia. Further, he would be in a position to invite "resistance all down the line."[32] In this way, traditional civil-military relations might be transformed with greater military influence. Yet as Powell pointed out after his retirement from the JCS chairmanship, any perceived crises in civil-military relations simply did not exist: "[T]hings were not out of control...Presidents Bush and Clinton, and Secretaries Cheney and Aspin, exercised solid, unmistakable control over the Armed Forces and especially me."[33] Nonetheless, the JCS chairman's power and influence increased with the passage of Goldwater-Nichols.

Powell's successor during the first term of the Clinton administration, General John Shalikashvili, also benefited from Goldwater-Nichols. Although Shalikashvili lacked the significant political background of Powell in Washington (although he served as an aide to Powell in 1991 and 1992 and acted as a representative to the Department of State for Powell on occasions[34]), he had directed two politically sensitive military operations successfully before he assumed the chairmanship: one in aiding the Kurds in northern Iraq after the Gulf War, the other in planning possible airstrikes in Bosnia in 1992 and 1993 as NATO commander. Importantly, both operations put him in good stead with an administration weak on political–military background and interested in solidifying its policy in Europe and the Middle East. As such, Shalikashvili soon proved to be an important policy participant in the Clinton administration's policy making over Haiti and Bosnia in 1994 and 1995 and an articulate spokesperson for the administration on Capitol Hill. In short, the chairman of the Joint Chiefs had begun to play a more central role in policy making, even for an administration whose first secretary of defense (Les Aspin) sought to rely more on civilian leadership within the Pentagon.[35] Increased military involvement "has even strayed into the legitimate territory of the Office of Secretary of Defense (OSD)" and will likely continue for the foreseeable future, moreover, especially when adequate civilian strategists and civilian leaders do not exist.[36]

The Secretary of Defense

After the Office of the Secretary of Defense and the Joint Chiefs of Staff, the third policy advisor within the Department of Defense is the secretary himself. Over the postwar years, the secretary's role in policy making has been enhanced considerably. As the secretary's control of the department increased through the reform acts of 1953 and 1958, and as the confidence of presidents in their secretaries of defense rose, the influence of the office in foreign policy making expanded.[37] Two analyses challenge this view and contend that the powers of the secretary of defense are less than the responsibilities of the office and that the relative influence of the secretary can be easily overstated.[38] While noting the cautionary signs that have been raised over the power of the secretary of defense, a good case can still be made that the secretaries of defense on particular issues, and in recent administrations, have often commanded as much influence as the secretary of state. A brief survey of the most important occupants of this post seems to support this view.

Past Influential Secretaries. The most influential of the eighteen secretaries of defense since 1947 has been Robert McNamara, who was secretary of defense throughout President Kennedy's years in office and for most of President Lyndon Johnson's term. With his close ties to both presidents, McNamara, more than any other cabinet officer, exercised policy influence.[39] Given a wide mandate to modernize the Pentagon, McNamara was also allowed substantial latitude in shaping America's strategic nuclear policy. Moreover, he was the spokesperson who announced the change in strategic doctrine in two important areas: (1) the nuclear strategy toward the Soviet Union and (2) the defense strategy for NATO. In the former area, McNamara moved the United States nuclear strategy from one of "massive retaliation," in which the United States reserved the right of engaging in an all-out nuclear attack for an act of aggression by the Soviet Union, to one of "mutual assured destruction" (MAD). In the latter area, McNamara was instrumental in developing the strategy of flexible response for the United States and its European allies. This strategy called for the use of both conventional and nuclear forces to respond to any Soviet or Warsaw Pact aggression in Central Europe. Once again, the notion behind this strategy was to move away from simply a reliance upon an all-out nuclear response and instead to use conventional (i.e., non-nuclear) forces and short-, intermediate-, and long-range nuclear weapons in maintaining stability in Central Europe. Like MAD, this strategy remained a core element of America's defense posture throughout the Cold War.

Harold Brown, who served during the Carter administration, continued a pattern of secretaries of defense who were increasingly influential on foreign and defense policy making. Originally one of the "whiz kids" in the Department of Defense under Robert McNamara, Brown was able to shape Pentagon policy toward his own views and toward those of the president. On such controversial issues as the B-1 bomber, the Panama Canal treaties, and SALT II, Secretary Brown was quite successful in getting the military to follow his lead.[40] In turn, he was able to work well with the White House on several contentious policy questions. Furthermore, Brown enjoyed good relations with Zbigniew Brzezinski, the national security advisor to the president, who came to dominate policy during much of the Carter administration.[41]

Caspar Weinberger, secretary of defense until the last year of the Reagan administration, was an equally influential participant in the foreign policy process, particularly in bolstering defense expenditures. Aided by strong support from President Reagan, Weinberger achieved virtually all his requests for a conventional and strategic military buildup. Only by 1983 were the requests of the secretary and the Department of Defense for defense spending compromised.[42] Still, by fiscal year 1985, the Department of Defense's budget authority reached the highest in real terms for any period in the 1980s, a total of $295 billion. In subsequent years, however, Weinberger was not as successful, with the budget declining about 3.5 percent a year from fiscal year 1986 through fiscal year 1988. Nonetheless, Weinberger had been able to move the defense budget from less than $200 billion per year to nearly $300 billion per year in a very brief period of time.[43] Moreover, Weinberger's political influence lay in his close ties with President Reagan and with the president's second national security advisor, William Clark.[44]

President Bush's secretary of defense, Richard Cheney, was hailed by friends and adversaries as "bright, articulate, fair, unflappable, and eminently likable."[45] While Cheney's policy making clout did not seem to match that of his immediate predecessors, he proved to be a competent manager of the department, where he quickly put together a plan to reduce the size of the United States military for the post–Cold War era, and an articulate spokesman for the military on Capitol Hill, where he previously served as Wyoming's representative in the United States House for six terms. He also enjoyed the support of the public. In fact, during the crisis immediately after Iraq's intervention into Kuwait and then during the conduct of the Gulf War itself, Cheney's stature rose appreciably.[46] Along with General Colin Powell, he had primary responsibility for negotiating the initial commitment of United States forces to Saudi Arabia in August 1990, consulting with Congress over more arms sales to Saudi Arabia, and developing the shape of United States foreign policy in the region.

Clinton's Secretaries. Clinton's first two secretaries of defense have more mixed records in terms of policy influence. His first, Les Aspin, a congressman from Wisconsin and chairman of the House Armed Services Committee at the time of his move to the Pentagon, proved to be a better strategic thinker than a manager of the Department of Defense. Indeed, he was forced to resign by the end of the first year of the Clinton administration.[47] Clinton's second secretary of defense, William Perry, was Aspin's deputy secretary. He turned out to be a much better manager of the Pentagon than his predecessor, and he also sought to weigh in on some important policy matters as well.

Despite Aspin's short tenure at the Department of Defense, he was instrumental in leaving his imprint on American security policy in the incipient years after the Cold War's end. A recognized expert on military matters who served in Congress for more than twenty years, Aspin changed from being a bit of a gadfly attacking Pentagon waste and issuing a weekly news release on defense topics to often challenging the dominant view on defense within his own Democratic party.[48] For example, he supported the building of the MX missile by the Reagan administration during the 1980s and the use of force against Kuwait by the Bush administration during the 1990s. From his House committee chairmanship, too, he argued for more modest reductions in defense spending after the Cold War (even as he called for a restructuring of forces and strategy) and supported the selective use of American military forces.

Aspin was thus well equipped as a strategic thinker to serve as secretary of defense and as a policy formulator within the Department of Defense. He did, in fact, initiate three important evaluations of America's defense posture for the post–Cold War years during his brief tenure. His most important accomplishment was the completion of the "Bottom-Up Review," the study that outlined United States defense strategy after the Cold War and set forth the restructuring of the military to meet the threats of the new era (see Chapter 6). In addition, he announced and set into motion the Counterproliferation Initiative—to use both prevention and protection to counteract the emerging threats from weapons of mass destruction around the world. His third major endeavor, a review of United States nuclear posture after the Cold War, was not completed until after he had left office.

Despite these major initiatives in rethinking and restructuring American security policy, Aspin resigned under fire at the end of 1993. Several factors shaped his early departure. First, his personal style and managerial ability did not endear him to the military establishment ("The high brass found his friendly, schmoozy, arm-around-the-shoulder style too casual").[49] If Aspin's disheveled appearance and his informal personal style did not sit well with the military establishment, his tendency to treat the Pentagon as a "think tank," rather than a large organization to be managed, also created suspicion. Second, he did not prove to be a skilled spokesperson for the Department. According to critics, he went on too long in trying to explain policy to Congress and the public, often confusing rather than clarifying policy and leaving the impression of being inarticulate. His explanation on Capitol Hill for failing to authorize reinforcements in Somalia prior to the loss of American lives in October 1993 produced criticism from both the executive branch and Congress. As one executive aid noted: "A couple of very important Members of Congress gave the President a very strong report. It was clear that Aspin would never have the respect on the Hill necessary for a Secretary of Defense."[50] Third, he had important policy differences with the president and with the military. On the issue of gays in the military, Aspin sought to follow Clinton's position, but it cost him support in the defense establishment. Further, he differed with the president on Bosnia and tried to correct publicly a presidential statement on North Korea.[51] In short, he was not always perceived as a team player by the White House.

William Perry, a mathematician and former under secretary of defense for research and engineering during the Carter administration, succeeded Aspin.[52] In contrast to Aspin, Perry looked the part of the secretary of defense. More reserved and more formal, he had earned his credentials as a Pentagon bureaucrat and enjoyed the respect of the defense brass and Congress alike. Moreover, he apparently had the bureaucratic skills to manage what has been described as "the largest corporate entity in the world."[53] On the other hand, his political and policy making skills were suspect, and he had little background as a public spokesperson on security issues.[54]

In all these areas, however, Perry proved to be more successful than initially predicted. In the management of the Pentagon, Perry did quite well. He tightened up the running of meetings at the Defense Department, "pushed for reforms in the Pentagon's byzantine procurement system," sought to enhance the industrial base undergirding U.S. defense policy, and reaffirmed an emphasis on new technology to bolster America's defense.[55] In shaping policy, Perry worked to implement the "Bottom-Up Review" (albeit in modified form), proposed an easing in American "dual-use" technology exports to aid American businesses, and sought to develop a new concept—preventive defense— to guide future security policy. In particular, preventive defense would now be "the first line of defense of America, with deterrence the second line of defense, and with military conflict the third and last resort." In other words, the United States would not only develop programs, for example, to prevent the proliferation of weapons of mass destruction, but it would now be involved with other nations and their military organizations to promote democracy and foster understanding among nations.[56]

As a public spokesperson, Perry emerged as more credible and effective than some had guessed.[57] While deliberately not as visible as the Secretary of State Warren Christopher, Perry's testimony on Capitol Hill generally won respect for his grasp of issues and clarity of presentation. Because Perry had not cut nearly as high a profile as his predecessor, he also did not garner the public reaction that Aspin did. Still, he received some criticism, including at least one call for his resignation, over the security at the Saudi Arabian military base in which nineteen American military personnel were killed by a terrorist bomb in June 1996. In particular, his handling of a defense intelligence report prior to the attack that raised security concerns produced congressional and public inquiry.[58]

Perry's successor in the second term of the Clinton administration, former Republican Senator William Cohen, brings a bipartisan cast to national security policy. A veteran member of the Senate Armed Services Committee and an acknowledged expert on defense issues, Cohen faces formidable challenges ahead. He must implement a new defense structure for the post–Cold War world, identify more fully the criteria for the use of American forces abroad, and build support from a skeptical Congress on the defense policy of the Clinton administration.[59] The issuance of the Quadrennial Defense Review (see Chapter 6) is the beginning of this process.

In short, then, the debate over the size and composition of the defense budget after the Cold War continues apace. While both the Bush and Clinton administrations proposed five-year plans to reduce the size of the United States military in the face of the Soviet collapse, global events and domestic pressure often worked against those plans. While some contend that more defense cuts can be made in order to fund domestic programs and balance the budget, others warn of new and unforeseen dangers in global politics and, hence, the need for a stronger and more credible defense posture. Although this debate will undoubtedly continue for some time, one thing seems certain: The Department of Defense and the secretary of defense will continue to shape and influence American foreign policy formulation in this area.

THE INTELLIGENCE AGENCIES

The last important structure within the foreign affairs bureaucracy that we shall discuss is the intelligence community. Although the growth of America's intelligence apparatus owes much to the Cold War, the role of intelligence has hardly diminished in the post–Cold War era. Indeed, in an increasingly complex and interdependent world, the ability of policy makers to evaluate effectively the global political, economic, and social conditions may be more important than ever. With continued incidents of global terrorism (e.g., the bombing of the American housing complex at a Saudi Arabian military base), the rise of states with aggressive arms (e.g., Iraq and Iran), and the occurrence of potential ecological disasters worldwide (e.g., the destruction of the rainforests in Brazil), sound intelligence work remains as necessary—maybe even more so—than at the height of the Cold War.

While the intelligence community is often associated with the Central Intelligence Agency (CIA), it is really much more comprehensive than that single agency. There are intelligence units within the Department of Defense, the Department of Energy, the Department of the Treasury, the Federal Bureau of Investigation, and the Department of State. Each of these intelligence units concentrates on various aspects of information gathering and intelligence analysis. Within the Defense Department, for example, the Defense Intelligence Agency (DIA) operates services as do the intelligence agencies within each branch of the military.[60]

The Department of Defense also has three other intelligence agencies under its organizational structure. First, the National Security Agency (NSA) has responsibility for gathering signal intelligence from a variety of electronic and nonelectronic sources from foreign countries, breaking transmission codes of these sources, and developing secure transmission codes for several American government agencies.[61] Second, the National Reconnaissance Office also operates under auspices of the Department of Defense and "manages satellite reconnaissance programs for the entire U.S. intelligence community" and collects photographic, signal, and ocean surveillance intelligence.[62] Finally, a newly created intelligence structure is the Central Imagery Office, established by the Department of Defense and CIA directives in May 1992. This office produces maps, topography, and further imagery support for the Department of Defense, the CIA, and other governmental agencies, as needed, and works closely with the Department of Defense and CIA personnel employed in similar areas. Figure 10.2 portrays some of the important components of this extensive intelligence community.

The exact size and budget of the intelligence community is difficult to estimate, shrouded as it is in secrecy within Department of Defense funding, but some estimates are available. In the early 1970s, the intelligence community consisted of about 150,000 individuals, with a budget in excess of $6 billion annually, and by 1980, the total budget grew to over $10 billion. During the Reagan administration, spending on intelligence reportedly "sharply increased...for the CIA and other intelligence activities."[63] Indeed, the budget of the 1990s had increased threefold from the 1980s: The

FIGURE 10.2

The Intelligence Community

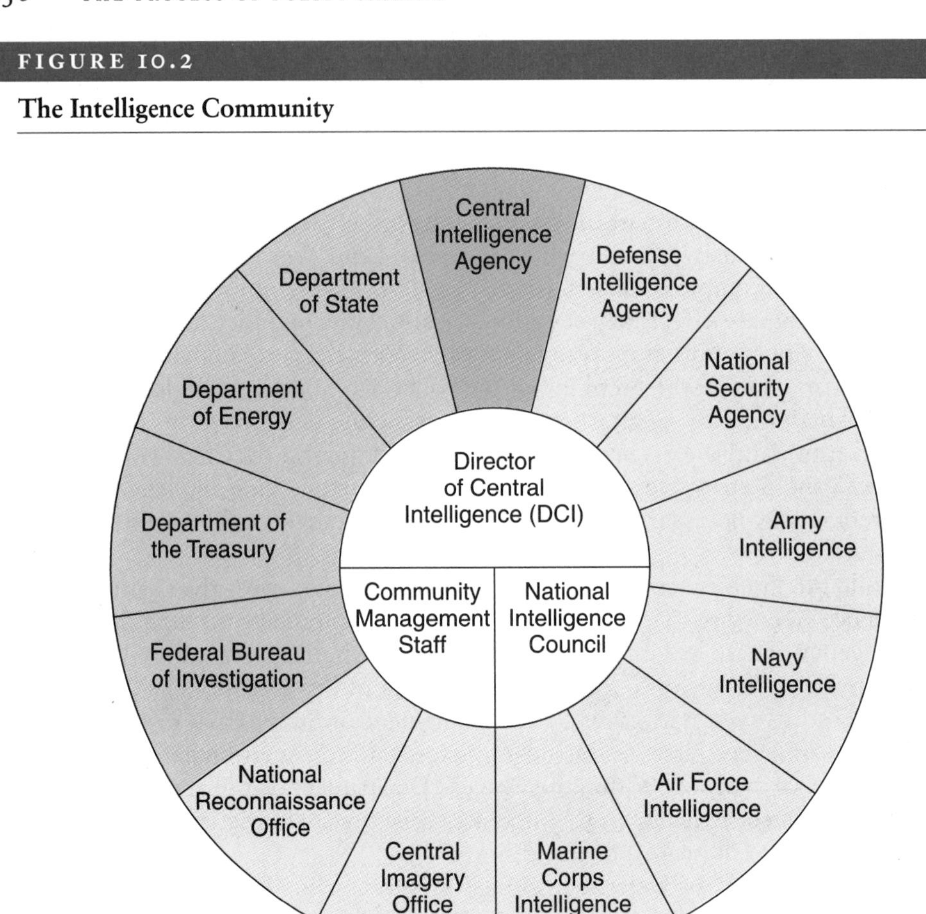

Source: *Factbook on Intelligence* (Washington, DC: Central Intelligence Agency, n.d.), p. 17.

Bush administration reportedly asked Congress for $30 billion in funding for intelligence activities during fiscal year 1991, and that figure represented only a "moderate increase" from 1990.[64] In mid-1994, Congress inadvertently published the current budget figure for the intelligence community (about $28 billion) in a declassified transcript of a Senate hearing, and, later, a House committee reported a budget breakdown for major intelligence components—with about $3.1 billion to the CIA, $13.2 billion to NSA, DIA, and the National Reconnaissance Office, and $10.4 billion to the intelligence units of the military branches.[65] By comparison, the intelligence community's budget amounts to 10 to 15 times as much as the budget for the Department of State.

As Figure 10.2 illustrates, the director of central intelligence (DCI) stands at the center of the intelligence community. The exact responsibility of the DCI and each agency within the intelligence community was spelled out in an executive order issued by President Reagan in December 1981 and remains in effect under the Clinton administration.[66] This order established that the DCI was responsible for developing the intelligence program and its budget and for directing the collection of all intelligence throughout the various agencies. In general, the DCI was given much greater control over intelligence matters than in the original National Security Act of 1947 or the Central Intelligence Act of 1949.

Under this order, too, the director of central intelligence was specifically designated the primary advisor to the president and the National Security Council for intelligence matters. The order also provided that the National Security Council could establish "such committees as may be necessary to carry out its functions and responsibilities under this Order."[67] Recent presidents have used different mechanisms for implementing this order.

The Reagan administration formed the Senior Interagency Group, Intelligence (SIG-I), to advise the NSC on intelligence matters. The membership on the committee varied from time to time, but it was mainly composed of the following: the director of central intelligence, the national security advisor, the deputy secretary of state, the deputy secretary of defense, the chairman of the Joint Chiefs, the deputy attorney general, the director of the FBI, and the director of the National Security Agency. This committee, under the leadership of the director of central intelligence, was to be the principal intelligence group within the United States government and was to oversee the collection of intelligence and the implementation of any intelligence decisions by the National Security Council. Later in the Reagan administration, the National Security Planning Group, a smaller and more select group of the National Security Council, assumed responsibility for monitoring covert intelligence activities.[68]

The Bush administration established a different arrangement. It relied upon the NSC Deputies Committee and a NSC Policy Coordination Committee on intelligence for monitoring intelligence activities. The latter interagency committee has initial responsibility over intelligence activities and is chaired by an individual appointed by the Director of the CIA, while the Deputies Committee, headed by the deputy national security advisor, has been given particular responsibility in the area of covert operations within the national security system. President Bush's directive on the organization of the National Security Council system explicitly called for "a representative of the Attorney General" to be in attendance when this committee discussed covert actions.[69]

The Clinton administration seems to have followed the arrangements developed by President Bush. Presidential Decision Directive 2, an order that established the membership on the National Security Council committees, is silent on the actual responsibility for reviewing and authorizing covert operations, but it does specify an additional member to the Deputies Committee of the NSC when considering intelligence operations: "When meeting on sensitive intelligence activities, including covert actions, the attendees shall include the appropriate senior representative of the Attorney General."[70] Since the congressional changes in intelligence accountability have placed increased emphasis on the legal basis for covert activities, the presence of a member of the attorney general's office is highly significant. In this connection, then, the Deputies Committee would seem to have primary responsibility over reviewing covert operations anticipated by the intelligence community.

Relative Influence in Policy Making

The policy-making impact of the CIA, and of the intelligence community more generally, stems from a central role in providing information about international issues and in evaluating different foreign policy options. Several different types of intelligence products developed by the intelligence community as a whole and by its components (i.e., CIA,. DIA, etc.) enable the community to affect the policy formulation process. By one estimate, the community produces at least fifteen different intelligence products for policymakers.[71] On a daily basis, for example, the intelligence community produces the *President's Daily Brief* and the *National Intelligence Daily*. These reports deal with immediate issues, using both open and classified sources for the reports. On an annual basis, the intelligence community produces its more familiar, and more comprehensive, intelligence products: the National Intelligence Estimates (NIEs) and the Special National Intelligence Estimates (SNIEs). NIEs are in-depth analyses of a particular country, region, or issue. The number of these reports completed each year varies by administration, but they range from several dozen to close to 100.[72] The SNIEs, as their name implies, are special intelligence reports in response to current developments around the world. Their exact number varies from year to year, depending upon the changing global events and the tasking from the intelligence leadership. In addition to these estimates, each of the major intelligence agencies produces a variety of separate intelligence reports for use and reference by policy makers and analysts.[73]

The National Intelligence Council (NIC) oversees and authorizes the production of the intelligence estimates for the community as a whole (also see Figure 10.2). It is composed of CIA intelligence officers, representatives from other departments with intelligence responsibilities (e.g., State, Defense), and civilians from universities and nonprofit organizations, and is the central decision-making body on intelligence production and analysis. In turn, the National Foreign Intelligence Board—the heads of the principal components of the intelligence community as outlined in Figure 10.2—"review[s] and approve[s] each estimate before it is published and sent to the president and other top officials."[74]

Despite these numerous reports and analyses, the intelligence community's effectiveness in the policy process remains difficult to gauge because of the secrecy surrounding its role and its activities. Since policy makers are heavily dependent upon the intelligence community for information about policy options, a reasonable inference is that its influence is quite substantial. Yet assessments of the intelligence community's analytic capabilities vary widely.

Acclaim for Its Policy Assessments. Marchetti and Marks, two severe critics of the CIA generally, nevertheless hint at the quality of its intelligence estimates. While CIA estimates on relative U.S.–USSR strength during the Cold War were not always successful in shaping policy and were subject to abuse on occasion, they argue, these estimates often served as a counterweight to the influence of the military planners in debates between the president and Congress. These analysts also point to the success of the agency in gathering intelligence leading to the showdown with the Soviet Union over missiles in Cuba in 1962.[75]

Others also point to the utility of the CIA's analytic assessments as well. One analyst points to the accuracy of its estimates during the early policy making on Southeast Asia—although the CIA's recommendations were not always followed by presidents and their advisors.[76] The CIA also reportedly assessed the situation in the Middle East correctly just prior to the outbreak of the Six-Day War in 1967. Policy makers, however, were unable to take effective action to prevent the war's occurrence.[77] Furthermore, the intelligence community painted a grim picture of the Soviet economy near the end of the country's existence, characterizing it as in a "near crisis," and pointed out that some modest decline in Soviet military spending had occurred.[78] Such estimates undoubtedly assisted policy makers in deciding on the degree of United States support to provide for *perestroika* in the USSR.

Other threads of evidence also have emerged that point more directly to the policy influence of the CIA in different regions of the world. Prior to the fall of the Shah of Iran in 1979, for example, the CIA reportedly exercised considerable influence over United States relations with Iran. Because the CIA assisted in establishing the Nicaraguan Contras, the forces opposed to the Sandinista regime, and because those forces were a key element in American policy toward Nicaragua throughout much of the 1980s, the intelligence community enjoyed a leading role in the formulation of policy in the area. Indeed, both the Department of State and the Department of Defense deferred to the intelligence community on this issue for a time, leaving policy largely to the CIA and to key White House allies.[79] Even after Congress cut all American military assistance to the Contras in October 1984, we now know, in light of the Iran-Contra investigation, that the CIA and National Security Council operatives, such as Admiral John Poindexter and Oliver North, remained active in supporting the Contras. Yet a third area where the intelligence community played a pivotal role in policy was aiding Afghanistan after the Soviet invasion in late 1979. The CIA ran an arms smuggling operation there for several years until the Soviets finally abandoned their effort in that country.[80]

Criticisms for Its Policy Assessments. At the same time, the intelligence community has been the object of severe criticism by presidents and others both for the quality of its intelligence and for its efforts to shape foreign policy. President Kennedy, in particular, lost confidence in the CIA over its policy recommendations that led to the ill-fated Bay of Pigs invasion.[81] As a result, Kennedy was later reluctant to accept fully the agency's intelligence advice and options on Southeast Asia or the Cuban Missile Crisis. Instead, he sought advice from other agencies and individuals to assist him in policy making. Later in the 1960s, the CIA was criticized over the loss of the intelligence ship, USS *Liberty*, during the Six-Day War in the Middle East, and the capture of the Navy spy ship, the *Pueblo*, by the North Koreans in 1968.[82] In the early 1970s, the intelligence community again came under attack for its failure to evaluate accurately the likelihood of the Yom Kippur War between Israel and its neighbors in October 1973.[83]

In the late 1970s, too, the quality of American intelligence came in for criticism yet again. At the time that the Shah of Iran was losing power in 1978, President Carter was moved to send off a sharply worded memo to his key advisors: "I am not satisfied with the quality of political intelligence. Assess our assets and as soon as possible give me a report concerning our abilities in the most important areas of the world. Make a joint recommendation on what we should do to improve your ability to give me political information and advice."[84] Indeed, an "Iran Postmortem" report on intelligence lapses over the Iranian revolution of 1979 noted myriad problems in assessing the internal situation of that country and in arriving at sound intelligence estimates: lack of intelligence sources near the Shah or in all the opposition groups; little discussion of CIA intelligence estimates within the bureaucracy or the airing of disagreements on those estimates; the inadequate use of publicly available sources; and conflicting meanings drawn from the words and phrases used in the intelligence estimates.[85] Furthermore, doubts were also raised about the failure of the intelligence community to assess more accurately the Soviet military buildup of the 1970s and the strength of the Soviet economy in the 1980s.[86]

In the 1980s and as the Cold War ended, the criticisms continued. Questionable intelligence estimates recommended the use of a grain embargo against the Soviet Union over that country's invasion of Afghanistan but failed to predict the bombing of the marine barracks in Lebanon in October 1983, which killed 241 Americans. Intelligence lapses over the changing events in Eastern Europe—whether it was over the opening of the Berlin Wall in November 1989, the sudden, violent fall of Nicolae Ceausescu in Romania in December 1989, or the initial reforms within the Soviet Union throughout 1989 and 1990—raised anew doubts about the CIA's analytic abilities. Even the successes during the Persian Gulf War of 1991 did not come without some intelligence failures: United States intelligence estimates placed the number of Iraqi forces in the Kuwait theater at 540,000, when the number was really closer to 250,000; they placed the number of mobile Scud launchers at 35, when the number totaled nearly 200; and they reported that Iraq had many chemical weapons in the Kuwaiti theater although none were found.[87]

More dramatic was the failure of the intelligence community to predict the collapse of the Soviet Union in 1991. To be sure, the intelligence community did predict an economic slowdown in the Soviet Union, but it was not successful in predicting the economy's collapse. Nor was it successful in pointing to the political demise of the Soviet Union itself (although, in fairness, few others did so either). Still, this shortcoming, coupled with other failures, led one senator to call for the CIA's functions to be turned over to the Department of State.[88]

Some Reasons for Intelligence Problems. Several reasons seem to account for these intelligence and policy failures. One focuses on the quality of intelligence produced by CIA analysts. As one of President Bush's advisors put it with reference to the changes in Eastern Europe, the CIA is "good at analyzing trends," and "poor at predicting the timing of events in the collapse of Eastern Europe." Testifying before Congress after the bombing of the American military complex in Saudi Arabia in the summer of 1996, Secretary of Defense William Perry pointed to another limitation in intelligence analyses: "The intelligence was not useful at a tactical level. It didn't specify the nature of the threat or the timing of the threat, and therefore it was not what we might call actionable intelligence in terms of doing our planning."[89] Another former CIA official raised questions about the adequacy of "fact-checking" by CIA analysts and the possible problem of exaggeration with the use of increasingly popular oral briefings of policymakers.[90] More generally, a former Defense official in the Reagan administration put the concern more bluntly: "The CIA's analysts 'collect a lot of facts and organize them very nicely. But their predictions are wrong.'"[91]

A second reason focuses on excessive reliance upon technology for intelligence assessments at the expense of human intelligence and analysis. With the increasing use of satellites and electronic interceptions of messages, for example, less reliance has been placed on agents in the field. Even those analysts who are at work are criticized as either too timid in their assessments, more interested in protecting their reputation than in taking risks, or overzealous—too often driven by ideological bias. Further, some intelligence analysts lack the necessary skills. While political analysts are plentiful, sometimes analysts with sociological and anthropological backgrounds are needed to assess more fully the changes occurring in a foreign society.[92] Evaluating the determination of Iraq's Saddam Hussein and his Revolutionary Council to keep Kuwait as well as estimating the loss of morale on the part of the Iraqi military from the United States air war of January and February 1991 require more than electronic intelligence.

A third reason for the failure of intelligence is competition among the various bureaucracies. As one official noted: "In intelligence, what you foresee is often affected by where you work."[93] The Defense Intelligence Agency (DIA), for example, often gives different intelligence estimates than the CIA. During the Cold War, the DIA tended to be more hawkish on Soviet intentions than the CIA, and the two agencies also sparred over estimates in particular regions (e.g., the likelihood of Soviet success in Afghanistan) or particular weapons systems (e.g., the capabilities of Soviet air defenses) in the past.[94] Such competing estimates will occur more frequently today, when more diverse actors and issues complicate global politics than they did during the Cold War. Under these circumstances, intelligence estimates sent to policy makers may simply become "compromises" between or among several intelligence bureaucracies.

Yet a fourth reason is the structure of leadership within the intelligence community. The director of CIA is also the head of the intelligence community, which cuts across many different foreign policy bureaucracies. Therefore, the degree to which the director can be an honest broker among these bureaus has been called into question, whether in distilling intelligence estimates or in assigning areas of responsibility. Indeed, the need for separating these two roles has been recommended as an important necessary reform,[95] although recent pressures seem to call for more centralization of control by the director. Nevertheless, the result of all these organizational concerns has been that the intelligence community's "product" has not always been as useful as it might be.

The Aldrich Ames Case and Pressures for Reform

Despite these internal analytic problems, the event that most startled the intelligence community came with the 1994 public revelations that a Soviet/Russian mole was operating in the Central Intelligence Agency. Aldrich "Rick" Ames, a Soviet counterintelligence agent in the CIA, was arrested in February 1994, plea-bargained for life imprisonment for himself (but a lesser sentence for his wife), and was quickly convicted of spying for the Soviet Union during the previous nine years. In the course of his lengthy espionage, however, Ames had shared literally hundreds of highly classified documents with the Soviet Union and identified a number of individuals from the Soviet and its allies who were working for the CIA. Ten of those identified were subsequently executed by the Soviets, and dozens of others were imprisoned.[96]

Both immediate and long-term damage flowed from this case for the intelligence community. First, Ames's lengthy espionage contributed to a flawed perception of the Soviet Union by the American intelligence community during the crucial years at the end of the Cold War. After the Soviet agents working for the United States were executed, for instance, the Soviet Union was able to use a series of double agents to feed false and misleading information to the United States about Soviet military strength. By one estimate, at least ninety-five American intelligence reports, derived in part from the false information, were sent to the highest governmental officials without warning them of their possible flawed sources. In the words of John Deutch, director of Central Intelligence, the false intelligence reports could have "influence[d] U.S. military research and development and procurement programs costing billions of dollars."[97]

Second, the amount of intelligence damage to United States interests may never be known. Ames provided an enormous amount of intelligence to the Soviet Union—"by far the worst breach of security in the intelligence agency's history"—and investigators have still not been able to piece together the extent of the damage. While Ames was required by his plea-bargain agreement to cooperate fully with intelligence officials, under subsequent questioning, he claimed that he could not remember everything that he revealed because he was always drunk when he met with his Soviet handlers. Yet, almost every time he took a lie-detector test after his conviction, he failed to pass it.[98]

Third, the Ames case shook the foundations of the internal workings of the intelligence community and raised the question over whether the intelligence community "culture" went too far to protect its members. As the subsequent investigations revealed, Ames had long had a serious drinking problem, received poor performance ratings, violated intelligence procedures (e.g., meeting with Soviet agents and not reporting the incidents, leaving his safe open at CIA headquarters), and appeared to be living beyond his government salary (e.g., paying cash for a half-million-dollar home and driving a Jaguar). While some of Ames's failings were recognized, little was done to address them.[99]

Fourth, while Congress had already sought to reform the intelligence analysis operations at the end of the Cold War and to address some of the problems discussed earlier, the Ames spy case produced a firestorm reaction from Congress and fueled anew calls for intelligence reform. Indeed, members of the House and Senate intelligence committees criticized the operation of the intelligence community and called for a substantial overhaul of its operation.[100] Importantly, in passing the intelligence authorization bill for fiscal year 1995, Congress set up a bipartisan Commission on the Roles and Capabilities of the United States Intelligence Community to examine the future of the intelligence community.[101]

Finally, the Ames case sparked several internal intelligence community investigations and led eventually to the resignation of James Woolsey as CIA director. Woolsey undertook three different kinds of investigations within the CIA—one to improve security procedures, a second to evaluate the damage that Ames had done, and a third to assess the quality of the operational supervision of Ames over his career as well as the merit of the investigation prior to his capture. Virtually all the reports turned out to be unflattering to the operation of the CIA. Spurred by these internal reports, Woolsey outlined a series of steps to begin overhauling security operations as early as July 1994, only a few months after Ames's arrest. In particular, he recommended improving personnel security by greater sharing of information among various subunits, so that suspicious behavior would not fall through the cracks, and working to change the organizational "culture" within the intelligence community that often seeks to protect members from suspicion or investigation.[102] However, when Woolsey subsequently announced that only letters of reprimand would be issued to eleven CIA officers over the Ames affair, the criticisms in Congress and within the CIA erupted.[103] By the end of 1994, Woolsey quietly resigned, and John Deutch, a former Pentagon official, took office as his successor in 1995, with the promise, once again, to reform the intelligence community. A similar task now faces Clinton's latest appointee as CIA director, George J. Tenet.[104]

CIA "SPECIAL ACTIVITIES" AND POLICY INFLUENCE

While the analysis side is a crucial component of the intelligence community, it is not the only one. The other "side" of the intelligence community consists of covert operations. This side of the intelligence community, too, has been increasingly criticized for its lack of accountability and control and for its considerable influence on the direction of American foreign policy. As a post–Cold War approach has emerged, critics have more frequently called for the elimination of these operations, on both policy and ethical grounds. These activities are not effective, and they are inconsistent with the ethical standards of the American people.[105]

American covert intelligence operations, or "special activities" as they are euphemistically called, are far more numerous than we often think, and they form important aspects of foreign policy making. These activities have included propaganda campaigns, secret electoral campaign assistance, sabotage, assisting in the overthrow of unfriendly governments, and, apparently, even assassination attempts on foreign officials. Clandestine military forces sent into Iraq to hunt down mobile Scud missile launchers during the Persian Gulf War illustrate one recent type of covert action, while funneling campaign money by the United States to the Nicaraguan opposition in its 1990 electoral battle with the Sandinistas represents another.

Many times, too, these covert activities involve counterintelligence activities, activities "concerned with protecting the government's secrets."[106] Part of this work involves such mundane efforts as classifying sensitive documents to keep them out of the public domain and providing adequate physical security for American secrets. Yet, part of counterintelligence also involves infiltrating the intelligence services of foreign governments, subverting and blackmailing agents through unethical means (e.g., creating compromising situations for foreign agents), and using measures to thwart the techniques that are being used against the United States.

Such covert (and not so covert) operations immediately raise questions about their compatibility with democratic values and how accountable the agents are for their actions. The public has often been divided on the wisdom of such activities and has expressed this uneasiness in public opinion polls. In 1995, for example, 48 percent of the public thought these activities were acceptable but 40 percent did not.[107] For most administrations in the post–World War II years, however, such ambivalence has apparently not mattered. Covert activities have been widely used and, as we shall see, have stirred serious concerns about their accountability to policy makers and the American people.

Origins and Usage of Covert Operations

Under the National Security Act of 1947, the CIA was not only authorized to collect intelligence, but it was also authorized "to perform such other functions and duties related to intelligence...as the National Security Council may from time to time direct."[108] By successive directives from the NSC and succeeding presidents, it has continued to hold that imperative. In President Reagan's 1981 executive order (and still the one operating during the Clinton administration), these covert operations were defined as "those activities conducted in support of national foreign policy objectives which are planned and executed so that the role of the United States government is not apparent or acknowledged publicly, and functions in support of such activities, but which are not intended to influence United States political process, public opinion, policies, or media, and do not include diplomatic activities or the collection and production of intelligence or related support functions."[109] As this directive suggests, the mandate is broad and open-ended.

The appeal of these measures to various presidents has been unmistakable: "Clandestine operations can appear to the President as a panacea, as a way of pulling the chestnuts out of the fire without going through all the effort and aggravation of tortuous diplomatic negotiations. And if the CIA is somehow caught in the act, the deniability of these operations, in theory, saves a President from taking any responsibility—or blame."[110] These activities, then, are not designed to be traceable to the White House.

The use of these activities has indeed been substantial during the postwar years, even if the exact number is not readily available. In its final report in 1977, the Senate Select Committee on Intelligence Activities (the Church Committee, named after its chair, Senator Frank Church of Idaho), which investigated the covert activities of the CIA over the postwar period, hints at the broad usage of these activities over the years and provided some figures as well:

> ...covert actions operations have not been an exceptional instrument used only in rare instances.... On the contrary, presidents and administrations have made excessive, and at times self-defeating, use of covert action. In addition, covert action has become a routine program with a bureaucratic momentum of its own.[111]

Between the years 1949 and 1952, the Church Committee reported that some 81 projects were approved by the director of central intelligence. In the Eisenhower administration, 104 covert operations were approved; in the Kennedy administration, 163; and in the Johnson administration, 142.[112]

Yet the exact totals go well beyond these numbers, as evidenced by a 1967 CIA memorandum that noted that only 16 percent of the covert operations received approval from a special committee to monitor them. By yet another estimate, several thousand covert actions were undertaken from 1961 on, with only a small percentage (14 percent) receiving review by the National Security Council or its committees.[113] Along with the number of activities, the justifications for undertaking covert operations have greatly expanded, "from containing International (and presumably monolithic) Communism in the early 1950s, to merely serving as an adjunct to American foreign policy in the 1970s."[114]

Covert operations, moreover, was an important instrument of foreign policy for the Reagan administration and remained so for the Bush and Clinton administrations. As former National Security Advisor Robert McFarlane has noted, the United States must have an option between going to war and taking no action when a friendly nation is threatened. In McFarlane's view, there must be something available between "total peace" and "total war" in conducting foreign policy.[115] Covert activity seemed to fit that middle category for a number of American administrations, including the Bush and Clinton administrations. Since President Bush served for a time as the director of the CIA in the 1970s, he was particularly attuned to the role that covert operations can play in providing another foreign policy alternative for the United States. Brent Scowcroft publicly endorsed covert actions several years before serving as Bush's national security advisor: "In many cases, covert action is the most effective, easiest way to accomplish foreign policy objectives. It is only effective if it remains covert."[116] There is little evidence to suggest that this view does not continue during the Clinton administration, as Congress in 1995 approved a contingency fund for covert operations generally and another fund solely for use against Iran eventually was established as well.[117]

Accountability and Covert Actions

The Church Committee Report and several other investigations questioned the degree of political accountability for these covert operations. Because the lines of accountability were not always operating, and because the CIA often carried on special activities without the full approval of the rest of the government, and particularly the White House, the agency's influence on policy was substantial. In effect, the agency could seemingly shape foreign policy.

These discretionary powers were in operation from the beginning of the agency. In the initial 1947 NSC directive for covert operations (NSC-4), no formal guidelines were established to approve or coordinate these activities. The only requirement was that the director of central intelligence would be certain, "through liaison with State and Defense, that the resulting operations were consistent with American policy." Up to 1955, for instance, there were still no clear procedures for approval of CIA covert operations. At best, the National Security Council required that consultation take place with the Department of State and the Department of Defense, although formal consultation with the president or his representative was not required. In fact, during the period from 1949 to 1952, the director of central intelligence apparently granted approval for covert operations without assistance.[118]

Even when clear NSC directives were issued for committee approval of covert operations (beginning in 1955), the procedures were not without some loopholes. As a CIA memorandum in 1967 reports:

> The procedures to be followed in determining which CA [covert action] operations required approval by the Special Group or by the Department of State and the other arms of the U.S. government were, during the period 1955 to March, 1963, somewhat cloudy, and thus can probably best be described as having been based on value judgments by the DCI [Director of Central Intelligence].[119]

Although new directives were issued in 1963 and 1970, slippage in accountability remained. Not all covert actions were discussed and approved by the new NSC committee, the Forty Committee (a committee established to review and monitor covert operations). Nor were the covert action proposals always coordinated with the Departments of State and Defense.[120]

Coupled with this weakness in executive branch accountability for CIA activities was the lack of any greater accountability by Congress during the bulk of the post–World War II years. Although in principle the Armed Services and the Appropriation Committees in the House and the Senate had oversight responsibility (and the CIA argued that it reported fully to the appropriate subcommittees), in practice, the CIA was under only "nominal legislative surveillance" throughout much of the Cold War period.[121] Chairs of these committees did not want to know of, or did not make concerted efforts to monitor, CIA activities. Further, Congress, as a whole, seemed reluctant to inquire significantly into intelligence activities.

One analysis has dubbed this inaction on the part of Congress a result of the "buddy system," a cozy relationship between top CIA officials and the several "congressional barons," usually key committee chairs or ranking minority members in the House and Senate Armed Services and Appropriations Committees.[122] Such members as Senators Richard Russell (D-

Georgia) and Leverett Saltonstall (R-Massachusetts) and Congressmen Carl Hayden (D-Arizona), Mendel Rivers (D-South Carolina), and Carl Vinson (D-Georgia) did not always want to know about all CIA activities or, at least if they did, they were able to squelch any attempts to let knowledge of these activities get beyond a small group. As a result, CIA covert activities were at best shared with a small congressional constituency whose inclination was not to challenge or disrupt any "necessary" CIA activity.

What such procedures allowed was that the CIA could by itself begin to *shape*, although perhaps not *direct*, American foreign policy. Without adequate accountability or control, the CIA could take actions that might be outside the basic lines of American policy or, at the very least, might create difficulties for the overt foreign policy of the United States. This latter problem in particular arose once covert actions were revealed. In this sense, the foreign policy influence of the intelligence community through the use of its covert side could be quite substantial. The exact significance of the CIA's influence cannot be fully determined, owing once again to the secrecy surrounding its operation.

The Hughes-Ryan Amendment

By the early 1970s, several key events weakened this congressional acquiescence to CIA covert operations and ultimately produced more congressional oversight. First, the Bay of Pigs attack against Castro's Cuba in 1961, almost solely a CIA-designed operation, proved to be a fiasco. As a result, President Kennedy became increasingly suspicious of reliance on that organization in policy formation. Second, the Vietnam War produced a large increase in CIA covert operations which, in turn, stimulated more congressional interest in these kinds of activities. Third, investigations over America's involvement in destabilizing the government of Salvador Allende raised questions about CIA activity abroad, too. And finally, the "Watergate atmosphere" of 1972–1974 emboldened Congress to challenge executive power across a wide spectrum, including intelligence activities.[123]

The first result of this new congressional interest was the Hughes-Ryan Amendment. Sponsored by Senator Harold Hughes (D-Iowa) and Representative Leo Ryan (D-California), this amendment to the 1974 Foreign Assistance Act began to impose some control on the initiation and use of covert activities. Its key passage is worth quoting in full:

> No funds appropriated under the authority of this or any other Act may be expended by or on behalf of the Central Intelligence Agency for operations in foreign countries, other than activities intended solely for obtaining necessary intelligence, unless and until the President finds that each such operation is important to the national security of the United States and reports, in a timely fashion, a description and scope of such operation to the appropriate committees of the Congress.[124]

Thus this amendment required that the president be informed about covert operations (hence eliminating the "plausible denial" argument for the executive) and that he must certify that each operation is "important to the national security of the United States." Further, the amendment directed the president to report, "in a timely fashion," any operation to the "appropriate" committees of the United States Congress. Under this provision, eight committees needed to be informed: the Committees on Armed Services and Appropriation in the House and the Senate, the Senate Foreign Relations Committee, the House Foreign Affairs (now, International Relations) Committee, and, later, the Senate and House intelligence committees established in 1976 and 1977, respectively.

In addition to these new reporting requirements under the Hughes-Ryan amendment, two separate investigations by the executive and legislative branches recommended several other changes in the monitoring of intelligence operations. An executive-ordered inquiry into intelligence activities in 1975 (the Rockefeller Commission) and a legislative inquiry by the Senate in 1975 and 1976 (the Church Committee) recommended several substantive and procedural changes in the operation of the Central Intelligence Agency, especially regarding covert operations. New legislative acts were proposed for gaining greater oversight of the CIA through joint or separate intelligence committees in Congress, through the establishment of an intelligence community charter by Congress, and through more stringent control over covert actions. The investigations also recommended consideration of a more open budgeting process, a limitation on the term of the directorship of the CIA, and the consideration of appointing a director from outside the organization.[125]

Aside from the establishment of intelligence committees in each house of Congress, few of these recommendations actually became law; some reforms, however, were incorporated in executive orders issued by Presidents Ford and Carter. President Ford issued an executive order in February 1976, in which the lines of authority over covert operations were spelled out and which expressly prohibited political assassination as an instrument of American policy. Two years later in January 1978, President Carter issued another executive order on the reorganization of the intelligence community, which included some recommended reforms, too.[126] Even though few reforms were translated into statutes, the various reform proposals did have the effect of calling attention to the accountability problem of the intelligence community as a whole, and especially to its covert side. As a result, the reforms did serve to lessen the influence of the intelligence community in foreign policy making.

Furthermore, Stansfield Turner, CIA director during the Carter administration, proceeded to undertake an organizational reshuffling to increase the powers of the director and to focus more on analytic intelligence than on covert operations. Turner also initiated a reduction in personnel within the CIA's Directorate of Operations, the bureau that handles clandestine operations. Veteran intelligence officers were dismissed from the intelligence service; by one account, over 800 members of the intelligence community were forced out by the end of 1977.[127] Not surprisingly, both of these actions were said to have hurt morale within the agency, and especially within the clandestine services.

Intelligence Oversight Act of 1980

Despite these efforts at greater control, the intelligence community and its allies were successful in stopping any further legislative restrictions. Most notably, proposed legislation to establish an intelligence community charter never became law. In fact, by 1980, the intelligence community was able to persuade Congress to repeal the Hughes-Ryan Amendment and its reporting requirements and to pass legislation that was deemed more workable.

This act, the Intelligence Oversight Act of 1980, retained the Hughes-Ryan provision that the president must issue a "finding" for each covert operation, but it modified the reporting requirements of that earlier act. (An intelligence finding is a statement, later required to be a written statement, in which a covert operation is defined and in which the president has certified that the operation is "important to the national security of the United States.") Now, the executive branch (either the director of central intelligence or the appropriate agency head) was required to report only to the Select Committee on Intelligence in the Senate and the Permanent Select Committee on Intelligence in the House.[128] Prior notification of all covert operations, however, was now specified in the law and not simply "in a timely fashion," as required under the Hughes-Ryan language. Further, the act also required that the executive branch report to the committees any intelligence failures, any illegal intelligence activities, and any measures undertaken to correct such illegal activities.

Some reporting discretion was also afforded to the president by two exemptions that were included in the statute. First, if the president deems that a covert operation is vital to national security, he may limit prior notification to a smaller group (the "Gang of Eight," as they came to be called) listed in the statute: the chairs and the ranking minority members of the House and Senate intelligence committees, the Speaker and minority leader of the House, and the majority and minority leaders of the Senate. Even in these exceptional instances, though, the president must ultimately inform the entire intelligence committees "in a timely fashion." Second, a more oblique, and potentially more troubling, exemption was also incorporated. The statute specifies that reporting of covert operations was to be followed "to the extent consistent with all applicable authorities and duties, including those conferred by the Constitution upon the executive and legislative branches of the Government." While the meaning of this passage is purposefully vague, it invites the executive branch to claim constitutional prerogatives on what information it will share with the legislative branch. (And, indeed, the Reagan administration apparently invoked this exemption to defend its delay in disclosing covert operations surrounding the Iran-Contra affair.)

By this legislation, a balance seemed to have been struck between the requirements of secrecy, as demanded by the intelligence community and the executive branch, and public accountability, as sought by the United States Congress and the public. The intelligence community gained the repeal of the Hughes-Ryan legislation, which it disliked, and Congress was able to gain knowledge of covert actions prior to their occurring, except in rare instances.

The initial application of even these requirements was not without controversy, however. When it was publicly revealed, in April 1984, that the CIA was involved in the mining of Nicaraguan harbors, the Senate Intelligence Committee reacted strongly in the belief that it had not been properly informed. (In fact, Senator Daniel Patrick Moynihan, vice chair of the Senate panel, resigned in protest for a time, although he later withdrew his resignation when CIA Director William Casey apologized for not keeping the committee fully informed.) Subsequent evidence indicated that, in fact, the CIA had informed the House and Senate committees, although the briefing on the Senate side was not as complete as it might have been. As a result of this episode, the CIA pledged to notify the Senate and the committee in advance of "any significant anticipated intelligence activity."[129] On balance, then, this incident demonstrates that the congressional intelligence committees seemed determined to preserve accountability on covert operations ordered by the executive branch.

THE IRAN-CONTRA AFFAIR: A CASE OF FAILED ACCOUNTABILITY

Only two years later, however, the revelations surrounding the Iran-Contra affair once again raised questions about how well congressional prerogatives regarding covert operations were respected. After Congress had cut off CIA funds to the Contras with the Boland amendment in October 1984 (see Chapter 8) and after the seizure of several American hostages in Lebanon beginning in the early 1980s, including the torture and killing of the CIA station chief in Beirut, members of the Reagan administration initiated covert operations to assist the Nicaraguan Contras in their struggle against the Sandinistas and to sell arms to Iran for that nation's help in freeing the American hostages in Lebanon. In turn, and without President Reagan's knowledge (according to his testimony), these two operations were linked when a portion of the Iran arms sales profits were funneled to the Contras. These covert actions unfolded from 1984 to 1986 without any congressional accountability or knowledge. Indeed, the House and Senate intelligence committees were kept in the dark about all of these activities until CIA Director William Casey testified before the committees on November 21, 1986. This testimony occurred nearly three weeks after the arms sales was revealed in a Lebanese newspaper, after it had been admitted by President Reagan, and after extensive reporting by the media.

A Failure to Comply with Existing Statutes?

Critics charged that the Iran-Contra episode was an example of the executive branch's failure to comply with the requirements of the Boland amendment and the Intelligence Oversight Act. House and Senate select committees investigated this episode, and their final joint report outlined numerous specific violations of the legislative statutes and agreed-upon congressional-legislative procedures. Three general violations will serve to illustrate the difficulty of congressional oversight of covert operations.[130]

First, contrary to the prohibitions in the Boland amendment, CIA and NSC staff of the Reagan administration sought a private organization (called "the Enterprise") "to engage in covert activities on behalf of the

United States." This organization became involved in both the arms sales to Iran and in aiding the Nicaraguan Contras, used "private and non-appropriated money" to carry on these activities, and received support from CIA personnel around the world. Beyond the specific prohibition of the Boland amendment, this covert operation violated the Intelligence Oversight Act. Neither was a finding prepared and approved by the president for this activity, nor was Congress informed of the existence of this operation. Indeed, when the press reported that this operation was under way in August 1985, the president "assured the public that the law was being followed," and in letters and appearances before Congress, National Security Advisor Robert C. McFarlane testified that "the letter and spirit" of the law were being obeyed with regard to aiding the Contras. (In March 1988, McFarlane pleaded guilty to charges that he misled Congress with such testimony.)

Second, the covert arms sales to Iran were carried out in a manner inconsistent with the Intelligence Oversight Act. Intelligence findings were neither properly prepared and approved by the president in all instances, nor were they reported to Congress "in a timely fashion." The first arms sale to Iran in August–September 1985 was completed only through an oral finding. By his testimony, however, President Reagan could not remember exactly when he approved this sale. A retroactive finding was prepared to cover the CIA's involvement in the second arms sale to Iran in November 1985, but this finding was ultimately destroyed by National Security Advisor John Poindexter in February 1986. Finally, a finding on arms sales to Iran was signed and approved by the president on January 17, 1986, but this finding was never shared with the intelligence committees of Congress or even the smaller Gang of Eight, as allowed under the Intelligence Oversight Act, until the episode was publicly revealed in November 1986.

Third, the transfer to the Nicaraguan Contras of a portion of the funds from the arms sales to Iran was inconsistent with government policy. It not only violated the Boland Amendment regarding military aid to the Contras, but it was done largely outside the established channels of government and represented a significant privatization of United States covert operations. At the very least, proper executive-legislative procedures involving covert operations were not followed, since these private individuals were not subjected to the same accountability procedures as public servants.

Recommendations of the Investigating Committees

In light of these and other violations, the congressional investigating committees concluded their investigation with several recommendations for improving the monitoring of covert operations. Although they acknowledged that the episode "resulted from the failure of individuals to observe the law, not from deficiencies in existing law or in our system of governance," in that spirit they proposed that "the principal recommendations...are not for new laws but for a renewal of the commitment to the constitutional government and sound processes of decisionmaking." Still, the committees did suggest that "some changes in law, particularly relating to oversight of covert operations" may be helpful. Their recommendations may be grouped into three general areas.

The first set of recommendations focused on improving the preparation and dissemination of presidential "findings" on covert operations. Findings should be in writing and reported in that form to Congress "prior to the commencement of a covert action except in rare instances and in no event later than 48 hours after a Finding is approved." They should include the names of all United States agencies involved in such operations but should restrict National Security Council members from participating in covert operations. Findings also should be limited to one-year duration (before possible recertification). All National Security Council members should be informed of such findings. And finally, no finding should recommend actions that are presently illegal under existing law.

The second set of recommendations called for a series of executive branch changes in monitoring the participation of private individuals used in covert operations, in preserving executive documents of such operations, and in strengthening treaties regarding foreign bank records of United States individuals so that the executive and congressional branches can gain access to them. In addition, Congress called for improved legal review of covert operations.

The third set of recommendations focused on steps that Congress could take to improve its oversight capacity by reviewing the adequacy of contempt statutes currently on the books, the effectiveness of several laws dealing with arms sales and arms transfers, and congressional procedures for safeguarding classified information.

Executive/Legislative Changes in Conducting and Monitoring Covert Operations

Prior to the final report of the two investigating committees, however, President Reagan issued a new directive for conducting and monitoring covert operations and for notifying Congress of these activities.[131] Several of the changes conform with the final recommendations that the committees made, but at least one did not.

President Reagan ordered changes concerning those who should conduct covert operations and those who should be informed about them within the government. Members of the National Security Council were barred from conducting covert operations. All executive branch agencies (and private individuals) participating in these operations were ordered to report in the same manner as currently required of the Central Intelligence Agency. An intelligence finding for a covert operation must be in writing and completed before the operation begins, except when an "extreme emergency" arises. Oral and retroactive findings were no longer to be permitted. All findings must be available to members of the National Security Council, thus ensuring that the secretary of state and the secretary of defense will be informed of such operations, which apparently had not occurred in the Iran-Contra case. And finally, all findings must be limited in duration and periodically reviewed.

Concerning the notification of Congress, however, President Reagan's directive did not necessarily represent a tightening of reporting requirements; instead, it opened up the possibility of even more delay. In his directive, Reagan pledged that his administration would notify Congress within two working days *after* a covert operation had begun, "in all but the most exceptional circumstances." Thus, a real possibility existed that the reporting of more and more covert operations would be delayed until after they have begun and, in some instances, perhaps very long after they had begun. Congress subsequently initiated legislation to tighten the Intelligence Oversight Act and to eliminate this loophole. While this legislation passed the Senate by 1988, it failed to pass the House.

When President Bush took office, and in a gesture of bipartisanship by Congress to the new president, the Speaker of the House decided not to take up this legislation for consideration by the full House.[132] As a result, the only wide-ranging legislative initiative to result from the Iran-Contra investigation failed to become law, and the only real change in the executive-legislative procedures for handling covert operations was President Reagan's 1987 directive. This directive, moreover, remained the policy of the Bush administration as well.[133]

Still, Congress did adopt several limited legislative remedies in 1988 and 1989 growing directly out of the Iran-Contra affair. The first legislation dealt with "third parties" transferring American supplies to another country. It specifically required the president to allow Congress thirty days to pass legislation to block such transfers from taking place. In the case of the Iran-Contra affair, as was noted earlier, Israel had transferred American-made antiaircraft missiles to Iran. Under this amendment, Congress would now have the right to stop such action within thirty days of being notified of it, if Congress were inclined to do so. A second legislative measure strengthened prohibitions on the sales of arms to countries supporting global terrorism. The third required the president to appoint an independent inspector general for the Central Intelligence Agency as one mechanism for closer monitoring of covert actions. And finally, a provision was added to a foreign aid appropriations bill that prohibits the use of such aid to be used as a lever to gain support for some foreign policy activity (e.g., aiding the Contras).[134]

In the intelligence authorization bill for fiscal year 1991, Congress took further action by enacting new legal procedures to govern covert operations. The law, in effect, finally put into statute some of the changes that were originally part of President Reagan's 1987 executive order, albeit in a more flexible way. The law, for the first time, provided a legal definition for a covert operation, required that the president approve, in writing, all covert activity by any executive agency, and outlawed all retroactive finding of covert actions. The bill, however, does allow some executive discretion on the use of third parties in carrying out such operations and allows the president "within a few days" to notify Congress of the initiation of such activities. The bill, however, did authorize the Department of Defense to develop proprietaries, or clandestine companies owned by the government, to facilitate the collection of intelligence information until the end of 1995.[135] Finally, the law continues to affirm the president's prerogative to assert "his constitutional authority to withhold information for more than a few days."[136]

THE INTELLIGENCE COMMUNITY: AFTER THE COLD WAR AND THE AMES CASE

With the end of the Cold War and the alarming disclosures from the Aldrich Ames case,[137] the intelligence community remains under increasing pressures to make significant reforms as we approach the twenty-first century. Both the Clinton administration and Congress have recently sought to reorganize and streamline the intelligence community, and analysts, both inside and outside government, have called for significant restructuring, and even some wholesale elimination. So far, however, the amount of change in the intelligence community has been incremental, but this foreign policy bureaucracy remains a serious target for reform in the years ahead.

New Executive/Legislative Actions

Driven by budget consideration and the new post–Cold War era, the Clinton administration directed budget and personnel staff cuts for the Central Intelligence Agency. Vice President Al Gore's National Performance Review (NPR), for example, initially sought a 12 percent personnel reduction in the CIA, but CIA Director James Woolsey, responding to continuing congressional budget pressures, announced even more severe cuts than the NPR required. Under Woolsey's plan, each of the four divisions or directorates within the CIA would be affected: The Directorate of Operations (the covert division within the CIA) would be cut by 700 by 1997; the Directorate of Intelligence by 1,000; the Directorate of Science and Technology by 26 percent by 1999; and Directorate of Administration administrative staff would be cut by 1,700 by the end of the decade.[138] Woolsey's successor, John Deutch, outlined a series of changes at his Senate confirmation hearings including replacing the top managers at the CIA, scrutinizing the Directorate of Operations, and turning over to the FBI some of the antiterrorism and drug trafficking responsibilities.[139] Shortly after Deutch took office, part of these changes were put into effect with the appointment of five new CIA officials.[140]

A more immediate restructuring of the intelligence community had occurred after the arrest of Aldrich Ames. President Clinton called for a reexamination of the government's counterintelligence operation and quickly issued Presidential Decision Directive 24 to do so. The directive abolished an existing counterintelligence facility and established a new National Counterintelligence Policy Board that would report to the president through the national security advisor. Senior representatives from the National Security Council, CIA, FBI, the Department of Defense, Department of State, Department of Justice, and a military service with a counterintelligence unit would lead this board. The directive also created a National Counterintelligence Center, consisting of members from the FBI, CIA, the Department of Defense, and the military services, whose task is to coordinate counterintelligence activities within the government. These new structures also directed closer collaboration between the FBI and the CIA in addressing counterintelligence problems.[141] Such failure to cooperate during the Ames investigation had, at the very least, lengthened that inquiry. All of these changes had the effect of weakening the dominance of the Central Intelligence Agency in conducting counterintelligence activities.

On the congressional level, too, the intelligence community has come under continuing review, but the actions to date have been modest. In the fiscal year 1995 intelligence authorization bill, as noted earlier, Congress had called for a Commission on the Roles and Capabilities of the U.S. Intelligence Community to report by March 1996. The report, however, rejected wholesale changes and proposed only a few modest changes: (1) a new deputy for the director of the CIA to assist with overall coordination of the intelligence community; (2) the consolidation of the imagery and mapping operations within the community; (3) increased coordination between intelligence actions and law enforcement to deal with proliferation threats, terrorism, drug trafficking, and organized crime; and (4) an open budget for the intelligence community. At the same time, the commission rejected the establishment of a new intelligence czar to coordinate overall activities and opposed the use of the intelligence community to engage in industrial spying, apparently a task routinely done by other governments against the United States.[142]

Even prior to the commission's report, however, Congress changed some elements of intelligence operations. In the intelligence authorization bill for fiscal year 1996, for example, the intelligence community's budget was trimmed to below the $28 billion figure, previously revealed publicly. Furthermore, the legislation established a new conditional fund for covert operations generally, provided funds specifically for a covert operation against Iran, pushed for buying new and small spy satellites to improve analytic capabilities and to save resources, and slowed efforts to consolidate agencies within the intelligence community. Finally, and specifically in light of the Ames case, the legislation allowed the CIA greater latitude in checking the credit records of individuals during counterintelligence operations.[143]

A Need for More Fundamental Reform?

While Congress and the president have taken some action, proposals for intelligence reform from inside and outside government have often been both much more disparate and more fundamental. Two illustrations suggest the range of these ideas. On the one hand, a former intelligence official argues that the intelligence community needs to undergo a major overhaul to meet the needs of the new information age effectively. Analyst Bruce Berkowitz contends that the Clinton administration's emphasis on "improving efficiency and responsiveness" and "setting roles, missions, and priorities" is not enough to improve the intelligence community for the twenty-first century. Instead, the intelligence community needs to define the information needed for the years ahead, design a system to meet those needs, and structure it in a way that will be adaptable. Such a restructuring may involve the dispersal of analysts throughout the policy-making community (rather than having them housed in a central organization as at present), the maintenance of competing analyses to reduce politicization of estimates, and perhaps allowing various analysts to devise their own intelligence-gathering instruments.[144]

On the other hand, another veteran government official, Roger Hilsman, calls for a more fundamental overhaul of the mission of the CIA: "The United States should get out of the business of both espionage and covert political action."[145] The contribution of espionage, he judges, "to wise decisions in foreign policy and defense is minimal. But the cost in lives, treasure, and intangibles is high." Similarly, he contends, that "covert action has been overused as an instrument of foreign policy," and it has tarnished the image of the United States. "While one action, taken in isolation, might seem worth the cost of slightly tarnishing the national image, the cumulative effect of several hundred blots has been to blacken it entirely, thus corroding one of America's major political assets—a belief abroad in American intentions and integrity." In short, the CIA's role should be only as "an independent research and analysis organization," and other intelligence operations in the rest of the government should be transferred to it.

A Democratic and Ethical Challenge

Hilsman's argument compels us to conclude this discussion with continuing vexing questions about intelligence operations. First, how consistent are intelligence activities with American democracy? And, second, what about the ethical standards that such actions portend for the United States in conducting its foreign policy? A free and democratic society surely seems at odds with the kinds of intelligence activities that we have described. Moreover, they stand in sharp contrast to the openness and public discussion of issues that Americans demand and promote at home. Similarly, do not some of these activities (e.g., entrapping and enticing foreign agents to engage in unethical conduct) affront the ethical standards of the society? Do they not place the United States in the awkward position of endorsing "the ends justifying the means" proposition with virtually any (unethical) behavior acceptable in pursuing foreign policy ends? During the Cold War, these kinds of questions may not have been confronted very directly or very often, since the rationale of fighting international communism was so easily offered. In the post–Cold War era, however, these and related questions need to be raised and addressed anew in deciding on the structure and operation of the intelligence community.

POLICY COORDINATION AMONG COMPETING BUREAUCRACIES

For the sake of convenience and clarity, we have described the role of the various executive bureaucracies in the foreign policy process separately. While each department, and groups within departments, may have an impact on policy, the formulation process is also coordinated across the various bureaucracies and policy makers. In the last section of this chapter, we briefly discuss how this coordination is achieved and how "bureaucratic politics" is played out among the foreign policy departments.

The National Security Coordinating System

Beginning in 1966, and initially as a means of placing the Department of State more fully at the center of the foreign policy process, a series of Interdepartmental Regional Groups (IRG) were established to coordinate policy recommendations. Each of these IRGs was headed by the appropriate assistant secretary of state.[146] An IRG, for instance, might consist of representatives from Defense, AID, the National Security Council, the Joint Chiefs of Staff, or whatever departments were appropriate for a particular region or issue. The principal aim in seeking widespread representation was to gain policy advice from various bureaucracies throughout the government. While these groups became a source of bureaucratic coordination, they also became a source of competition. Above the IRGs in the hierarchy, a Senior Interdepartmental Group (SIG), composed of higher-level representatives from the foreign policy bureaucracies and headed by the undersecretary of state, coordinated the activities of the IRGs. The SIG, in turn, were accountable to the NSC or the various departmental secretaries.

These kinds of working groups were the principal means of carrying the policy process across departments and became the model for subsequent administrations. Although succeeding presidents changed the IRGs to interdepartmental or interagency groups (IGs) or policy coordinating committees (PCC), their use as the principal mechanism for coordinating policy options continued. Even in the extremely hierarchical arrangements of the national security system during the Kissinger years, the use of IGs was not wholly abandoned, although it was altered. Over the years, however, these groups have undergone an important change; they have shifted from dominance by the Department of State toward greater control and direction by the National Security Council and its staff. A description of the interagency process during the three recent administrations (Reagan, Bush, and Clinton) provides a fuller sense of how these groups facilitate both coordination and competition among the various bureaucracies and how the National Security Council increasingly directs their operation.

The Reagan and Bush Administrations and the NSC System

The Reagan administration initially followed the same design as had earlier presidents, with a system of SIGs and IGs, but with a clear division of responsibility among the secretary of state, secretary of defense, and the director of central intelligence for different aspects of policy.[147] Specifically, the Reagan administration established four SIGs, which reflected the four major areas of national security issues—foreign policy, defense policy, intelligence policy, and international economic policy—with each headed by a representative from the Department of State, Department of Defense, the CIA, and the Department of Treasury, respectively. Under this arrangement, each SIG created its own IGs for development and review of policy options. These IGs, however, included representatives from other appropriate bureaus and agencies.

By the Reagan administration's second term, several changes emerged. The intelligence SIG was eventually supplanted by the National Security

Planning Group (NSPG) in monitoring covert operations. The Crisis Pre-planning Group and the Strategic Arms Control Group largely assumed the functions of the SIGs on foreign and defense policy, while the international economic SIG was transferred to the Economic Policy Council.[148] By early 1987, the system was changed once again with the establishment of the Policy Review Group (PRG), a body chaired by the deputy national security advisor and composed of other sub-cabinet officials from various foreign policy bureaucracies. Along with the NSPG, these groups became the key forums for policy coordination in the last two years of the Reagan administration, meeting over 170 times and coordinating policy on a wide range of activities.[149]

The Bush administration sought to streamline the policy coordination system across the various bureaucracies and to give even greater control to the national security advisor and his staff in shaping policy. As a result, a relatively simple three-tier hierarchical system of committees was established leading to the National Security Council itself. The most important committee below the NSC itself for policy coordination was the NSC Principals Committee (NSC/PC).[150] It was the senior interagency group for the consideration of all national security questions and was comprised of key cabinet-level officials with foreign policy responsibilities. The national security advisor chaired this committee and had responsibility for calling its meetings, setting its agenda, and preparing the appropriate policy papers. The second ranking committee in this process was the NSC Deputies Committee (NSC/DC). This committee reviewed the initial work of the interagency groups or the NSC Policy Coordinating Committees (NSC/PCC)—discussed below—and made its recommendations on policy as well. It was composed of sub-cabinet-level officials from the various foreign policy bureaucracies, and the deputy assistant to the president for national security affairs chaired it. By presidential directive, it had the responsibility to "ensure that all papers to be discussed by the NSC or the NSC/PC fully analyze the issues, fairly and adequately set out the facts, consider a full range of views and options, and satisfactorily assess the prospects, risks, and implications of each." The last set of committees in the policy coordination hierarchy was the NSC Policy Coordinating Committees (NSC/PCC). These committees, comparable to the interagency groups (the IGs) used by other administrations, were the ones that initially developed and prepared the policy options across departments for the administration. The NSC/PCC were both regional, covering all areas of the world, and functional, covering particular issues that were current.

The Clinton Administration and the NSC System

The NSC system for the Clinton administration largely followed the design of the Bush administration, although with its own refinements. Figure 10.3 portrays the overall structure of the process for both the development and implementation of foreign policy. Policy development ordinarily begins with a presidential review directive (PRD), which is sent up through the various layers of bureaucratic structure, and policy implementation of decisions made by the president and his national security council is put into effect

FIGURE 10.3

The National Security Council System for Policy Development and Implementation During the Clinton Administration

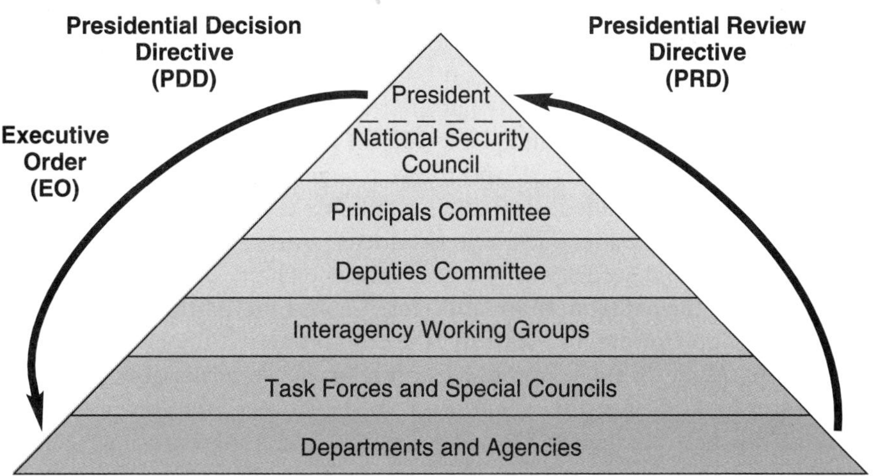

Source: Taken from the National Security Chart entitled "Policy Development and Implementation," National Security Council, Washington, DC.

through presidential decision directives (PDDs) or executive orders (EOs) sent from the president downward. In this structure, the departments, agencies, task forces, and special councils are at the bottom of this hierarchy for both policy development and implementation, while the basic components of the NSC system (interagency working groups, the deputies committee, and the principals committee) are nearer to the top of the hierarchy. At the top of this pyramid, of course, the National Security Council and the president ultimately make the foreign policy and defense decisions.

As with the Bush administration, the Clinton administration uses a three-tiered set of committees. Two of the three committees have the same names as during the Bush administration, NSC Principals Committee (NSC/PC) and the NSC Deputies Committee (NSC/DC), while the third one was renamed the NSC Interagency Working Groups (NSC/IWGs), a name more closely aligned to that used by earlier presidents for committees at this level of policy making. In function, the three committees vary only slightly from the Bush administration, and a brief description of each one will make these comparisons clear.

The most important difference between the Principals Committee in the two administrations is its membership.[151] While the Clinton administration has retained the secretaries of state and defense, the national security advisor, the director of central intelligence, and the chairman of the Joint Chiefs of Staff, it has added the United States ambassador to the United Nations and the assistant to the president for economic policy. In addition, the presidential directive on the creation of this committee states that the secretary of the treasury, the attorney general, and other department heads or agency heads may be invited to these meetings as well. The aim is clearly to provide a more global perspective and to focus beyond political–military issues only. Importantly, though, and in keeping with policies of the Bush administration, the national security advisor chairs these meetings and is responsible for their functioning.

The NSC Deputies Committee has both an expanded membership and an increased workload under the Clinton administration. Much of the membership remains the same (deputy national security advisor, under secretary of state for political affairs, under secretary of defense for policy, the deputy director of central intelligence, and the vice chairman of the JCS), but two members have been added: deputy assistant for economic policy and the national security advisor to the vice president. At the same time, however, the deputy national security advisor remains the chair, albeit that he must consult with officials from State and Defense and the National Economic Council, as appropriate, in operating the committee.

The workload of this committee is quite broad, in terms of both policy formulation and policy implementation. In the former area, it reviews the work of all the Interagency Working Groups, and apparently has special responsibilities in the area of intelligence activities as implied (albeit not spelled out) in the presidential directive. In a unique feature, too, the Deputies Committee has another policy-formulation responsibility. It shall be redesigned as the Deputies Committee/CM when it is dealing with crisis management issues. Under this arrangement, the national security advisor, or any national security council member who is on the principals or deputies committee, may ask for a meeting to deal with a crisis situation. Further, this committee shall initiate measures to prevent crisis situations from developing. In the implementation area, the NSC/DC has the central responsibility for evaluating the effectiveness of administration initiatives and for considering whether various policy directives "should be revamped or rescinded."

The last structure of the NSC system is really a set of committees, rather than an individual committee like the others. The series of Interagency Working Groups (NSC/IWGs) are committees established by the Deputies Committee. They may be either permanent or ad hoc, and, as in the Bush administration, they may deal with regional issues (e.g., an IWG on the Middle East) and functional issues (e.g., an IWG on counterterrorism), as shown in Figure 10.4. The Deputies Committee appoints the chairs of each IWG, but the chairs are usually assigned according to the department or agency that normally deals with particular issues. IWGs dealing with foreign and defense issues, for example, are generally chaired by an assistant secretary from the Departments of Defense or State, while IWGs dealing with international economic issues are normally chaired by an official from the Treasury Department or the National Economic Council. Finally, IWGs dealing with intelligence, arms control, nonproliferation, and crisis issues are likely to be chaired by an official from the National Security Council staff. While the IWGs may meet regularly, they shall do so as determined by the Deputies Committee. In this way, too, the Deputies Committee plays a crucial role in policy coordination and in directing the work of the IWGs.

Overall, then, the NSC system, especially through the coordinated work of the Deputies Committee and the Interagency Working Groups, may

FIGURE 10.4

National Security Council Policy Coordination Committees in the Clinton Administration

National Security Council

NSC Principals Committee (NSC/PC)

Members:
Secretary of State
Secretary of Defense
National Security Advisor (Chair)
Director of Central Intelligence
Chairman, Joint Chiefs of Staff
Economic Policy Advisor
United Nations Ambassador

NSC Deputies Committee (NSC/DC)

Members:
Deputy National Security Advisor (Chair)
Under Secretary of State for Political Affairs
Under Secretary of Defense for Policy
Deputy Director of Central Intelligence
Vice Chairman, Joint Chiefs of Staff
Deputy Assistant for Economic Policy
National Security Advisor to the Vice President

NSC Interagency Working Groups (NSC/IWGs)

Regional IWGs	*Functional IWGs*
Europe	Arms Control
Russia	Defense
Latin America	Intelligence
East Asia	Economics
Africa	Counterterrorism
Middle East	

IWGs are established at the discretion of the Deputies Committee, which also appoints the chair of each one. Normally, IWGs dealing with foreign and defense policy will be chaired by an assistant secretary from the Departments of Defense or State; IWGs dealing with international economic policy will be chaired by an official from the Treasury Department or the National Economic Council; and IWGs dealing with intelligence, arms control, nonproliferation, and crisis issues will be chaired by an official from the National Security Council staff.

Source: National Security Council organization charts, Washington, DC; and Presidential Decision Directive 2, January 20, 1993.

effectively manage both foreign policy formulation and foreign policy implementation. Furthermore, this system, if competently administered, serves as a ready mechanism for coordinating policy and managing conflicts between departments and bureaus.

Concluding Comments

The diplomatic, economic, military, and intelligence bureaucracies that we have discussed over the last two chapters all contribute to the shaping of the foreign policy of the United States. The influence of some has increased, while impact of others has declined in recent years. The National Security Council (and especially the NSC staff and the national security advisor), the Department of Defense, and key economic bureaucracies, such as the Department of Treasury and the United States Office of the Trade Representative, have gained influence in the shaping of policy. By contrast, the Department of State and the intelligence community have been beset by various problems and have probably lost influence over the post–World War II years. Still, the precise contribution of the bureaucracies in an administration is heavily dependent upon how the president chooses to use them and on the individuals within them. Just as the president is dependent upon the bureaucracy for policy advice, the standing of a bureaucracy within the policy process is dependent upon how the president decides to employ its advice.

In the next two chapters, we expand our analysis of the foreign policy-making process by examining those participants outside of the formal governmental structure. Political parties and interest groups are the focus of attention in the next chapter. Our aim is to assess how America's two major political parties have shaped foreign policy and to determine which interest groups, and under what conditions, play a role in policy making on international issues.

Notes

1. See Stanley Lieberson, "An Empirical Study of Military-Industrial Linkages," *American Journal of Sociology* 76 (January 1971): 562–584.
2. See, for example, Adam Yarmolinsky, *The Military Establishment: Its Impacts on American Society* (New York: Harper and Row, 1971).
3. See the chapter entitled, "Is There a Military–Industrial Complex Which Prevents Peace?" in Marc Pilisuk, with the assistance of Mehrene Larudee, *International Conflict and Social Policy* (Englewood Cliffs, NJ: Prentice-Hall, Inc., 1972), pp. 108–141.
4. Directorate for Information Operations and Reports, Department of Defense Prime Contract Awards by Region and State, Fiscal Years 1995, 1994, and 1993 (Washington, DC: U.S. Government Printing Office, n.d.), pp. 2, 6–7.
5. The latest available data on employees were provided by the Office of Public Affairs, Department of Defense in a phone interview (January 2, 1997). The estimated fiscal 1996 spending is from the U.S. Bureau of the Census, *Statistical Abstract of the United States: 1996*, 116th ed. (Washington, DC, 1996), p. 351.
6. Pat Towell, "Retrench Warfare Flares Anew Over Clinton's Budget," *Congressional Quarterly Weekly Report*, March 9, 1996, 626–631.
7. Directorate for Organizational and Management Planning, Office of the Secretary of Defense, *Organization and Functions Guidebook* (Washington, DC: Department of

Defense, August 1988), p. 9. This is only a partial listing of the "mission of the OSD." A more complete statement is contained on pp. 9 and 10.

8. See Hoopes, *The Limits of Intervention* (New York: David McKay, 1968), pp. 33–34, for a statement of ISA's role during the Kennedy-Johnson period.
9. *U.S. Government Manual 1989/1990*, July 1, 1989, p. 186.
10. See Henry T. Nash, *American Foreign Policy* (Homewood, IL: Dorsey, 1985), p. 94. By contrast, the Bureau of Politico-Military Affairs in the Department of State might be labeled the "little Defense Department" because of the military considerations in policy examined by this bureau. Further, there tend to be regular personnel exchanges between this bureau and the Pentagon that facilitate this military analysis. The "little Defense Department" was particularly important during the tenure of Secretary Alexander Haig because of the close working relationship between its director, Richard Burt, and Secretary Haig. On the changes in the role of ISA in the policy process, see Geoffrey Piller, "DOD's Office of International Security Affairs: The Brief Ascendancy of an Advisory System," *Political Science Quarterly* 98 (Spring 1983): 59–78.
11. *U.S. Government Manual 1989/1990*, p. 186.
12. See Strobe Talbott, *Deadly Gambits* (New York: Vintage Books, 1985) for a discussion of the key role of Assistant Secretary of Defense Richard Perle in arms control policy.
13. See, for example, Joseph S. Nye, Jr., "The Case for Deep Engagement," *Foreign Affairs*, 74 (July/August 1995): 90–102, which he published while at ISA. He returned to Harvard at the end of 1995.
14. Amos A. Jordan, William J. Taylor, Jr., and Lawrence J. Korb, *American National Security: Policy and Process*, 4th ed. (Baltimore and London: The Johns Hopkins University Press, 1993), p. 178. On the responsibilities of the JCS, also see Lawrence J. Korb, *The Fall and Rise of the Pentagon: American Defense Policies in the 1970s* (Westport, CT: Greenwood Press, 1979), p. 112; Korb's *The Joint Chiefs of Staff: The First Twenty-Five Years* (Bloomington: Indiana University Press, 1976), p. 7; and *U.S. Government Manual* 1995/1996, July 1, 1995, pp. 180–181.
15. Ibid.
16. Jordan, Taylor, and Korb, *American National Security: Policy and Process*, p. 178–180; and Korb, *The Fall and Rise of the Pentagon*, pp. 112–137.
17. Jordan, Taylor, and Korb, *American National Security: Policy and Process*, p. 178.
18. Korb, *The Fall and Rise of the Pentagon*, p. 115.
19. See the discussion in Neil Sheehan, Hedrick Smith, E. W. Kenworthy, and Fox Butterfield, *The Pentagon Papers: The New York Times* edition (New York: Bantam Books, Inc., 1971), pp. 234–270, on the bombing of North Vietnam and on the acceptance of the domino theory. Although the Department of Defense and its advisors did not get all they proposed, its influence in these decisions is still evident.
20. Jordan, Taylor, and Korb, *American National Security: Policy and Process*, p. 179.
21. Ibid.
22. David C. Martin and Michael A. Lerner, "Why the Generals Can't Command," *Newsweek*, February 14, 1983, 22.
23. Lawrence J. Korb, "The Joint Chiefs of Staff: Access and Impact in Foreign Policy," *Policies Studies Journal* 3 (Winter 1974): 171.
24. Ibid., pp. 171–173.
25. Martin and Lerner, "Why the Generals Can't Command," p. 22.
26. Excerpts from Reagan's Testimony on the Iran-Contra Affair," *New York Times*, February 23, 1990, A18.
27. This discussion of the Goldwater-Nichols Reorganization Act is taken from *Congressional Quarterly Almanac 1986* (Washington, DC: Congressional Quarterly, Inc., 1987), pp. 455–457.
28. Robert Previdi, *Civilian Control versus Military Rule* (New York: Hippocrene, 1988), p. 8, as cited in Douglas Johnson and Steven Metz, "American Civil-Military Relations: A Review of the Recent Literature," in Don M. Snider and Miranda A. Carlton-Carew,

eds., *U.S. Civil-Military Relations: In Crisis or Transitions?* (Washington, DC: The Center for Strategic & International Studies, 1995), p. 209.

29. Richard Halloran, "Bush Plans to Name Colin Powell to Head Joint Chiefs, Aides Say," *New York Times*, August 10, 1989, 1 and 10.
30. Johnson and Metz, "American Civil-Military Relations," p. 210.
31. Eleanor Clift and Thomas M. DeFrank, "Bush's General: Maximum Force," *Newsweek*, September 3, 1990, 36.
32. Richard H. Kohn, "Out of Control: The Crisis in Civil-Military Relations," *National Interest* 35 (Spring 1994): 13–14, as cited in Johnson and Metz, "American Civil-Military Relations," p. 210.
33. Colin L. Powell, John Lehman, William Odom, Samuel Huntington, and Richard H. Kohn, "Exchange on Civil-Military Relations," *National Interest* 36 (Summer 1994), 23, as cited in Johnson and Metz, "American Civil-Military Relations," p. 211.
34. Pat Towell with Matthew Phillips, "Shalikashvili Wins Praise as Joint Chiefs Nominee," *Congressional Quarterly Weekly Report*, August 14, 1993, 2238.
35. Ibid.
36. The quoted passage is from Eliot A. Cohen, "Are U.S. Forces Overstretched? Civil-Military Relations," *Orbis* 41 (Spring 1997): 181; and the last part is from Johnson and Metz, "American Civil-Military Relations," p. 212. They cite, for example, prominent analyst of civil-military relations, Samuel Huntington, to make this point.
37. The reform acts strengthening the secretary's role within the Department of Defense are "Reorganization Plan No. 6 of 1953," 67 Stat. 638–639, and the "Department of Defense Reorganization Act of 1958," P.L. 85-599, 72 Stat. 514–523.
38. See James Schlesinger, "The Role of the Secretary of Defense," in Robert J. Art, Vincent Davis, and Samuel P. Huntington, eds., *Reorganizing America's Defense: Leadership in War and Peace* (Washington, DC: Pergamon-Brassey's, 1985), p. 261; and Laurence E. Lynn, Jr., and Richard I. Smith, "Can the Secretary of Defense Make a Difference?" *International Security* 7 (Summer 1982): 45–69. The former discusses the role of the secretary of defense more generally, while the latter looks at the role of the secretary in the weapons development and acquisition process and the impact of the bureaucracy within the Pentagon in shaping outcomes.
39. Korb, *The Fall and Rise of the Pentagon*, p. 85.
40. Bernard Weinraub, "Browning of the Pentagon," *New York Times Magazine*, January 29, 1978, 44.
41. Brzezinski, *Power and Principle*, pp. 44–47.
42. Theodore H. White, "Weinberger on the Ramparts," *New York Times Magazine*, February 6, 1983, 18; Alice C. Maroni, *The Fiscal Year 1984 Defense Budget Request: Data Summary* (Washington, DC: Congressional Research Service, February 1, 1983); and Ellen C. Collier, "Arms Control Negotiations At Home: Legislative-Executive Relations," paper presented at the Annual Meeting of the International Studies Association, March 1984, p. 8.
43. The data reported here were calculated from Table IX in Alice C. Maroni, "The Fiscal Year 1989 Defense Budget Request Data Summary, " Congressional Research Service, No. 88–182F. The data are for the National Defense function category that included the Department of Defense and defense-related programs carried out by other agencies. If only the Department of Defense budget is used, the average increase from 1981–1985 is 9.1 percent, while the average decline in 1986–1988 is 2.0 percent.
44. White, "Weinberger on the Ramparts," p. 18.
45. John M. Broder and Melissa Healy, "Likeable Dick Cheney Can Get Mad When He Has To," *Los Angeles Times*, March 16, 1989, 20.
46. Andrew Rosenthal, "Cheney Steps to Center of the Lineup," *New York Times*, August 24, 1990, A7.
47. Pat Towell, "Aspin's Career A Balance of the Highs and Lows," *Congressional Quarterly Weekly Report*, May 27, 1995, 1484.

48. Michael R. Gordon, "Pathfinders of the Middle Ground: Leslie Aspin, Jr.," *New York Times*, December 23, 1992, A1 and A13.
49. Elizabeth Drew, *On the Edge: The Clinton Presidency* (New York: Simon & Schuster, 1994), p. 357.
50. Drew, *On the Edge: The Clinton Presidency*, p. 358.
51. For discussion of these issues, see ibid., pp. 357, 138–163, 364.
52. Charles Lane, "Perry's Parry," *The New Republic* 26 (June 27, 1994): 21–25.
53. Drew, *On the Edge: The Clinton Presidency*, p. 356.
54. Ibid., p. 373.
55. Lane, "Perry's Parry," p. 22.
56. "Remarks as Prepared for Delivery by William J. Perry, Secretary of Defense," John F. Kennedy School of Government, Harvard University, May 13, 1966, via the Internet.
57. Lane, "Perry's Parry," p. 22.
58. Philip Shenon, "GI's in Saudi Arabia Put On Highest Alert," *New York Times*, July 12, 1996, A6.
59. Adam Clymer, "A Career Bipartisan: William Sebastian Cohen," *New York Times*, December 6, 1996, A1 and A16.
60. *Intelligence: The Acme of Skill* (Washington, DC: Central Intelligence Agency, Public Affairs, n.d.), pp. 12–13.
61. Jeffrey T. Richelson, *The U.S. Intelligence Community* (Boulder, CO: Westview Press, 1995), pp. 25–26.
62. Ibid., pp. 29–32. The quote is from p. 29.
63. Victor Marchetti and John D. Marks, *The CIA and the Cult of Intelligence* (New York: Dell, 1974), p. 95, provides a breakdown of spending in the intelligence community for 1974 totaling $6.2 billion. Charles W. Kegley and Eugene R. Wittkopf report that for fiscal 1980 the budget for the intelligence community was thought to be $10 billion, based on *Congressional Quarterly* reports. See their *American Foreign Policy: Pattern and Process* (New York: St. Martin's Press, 1982), p. 373. The quoted passage is from "Reagan Puts Bombing Blame on Democrats: Carter-Era Intelligence Cuts Cited," *Des Moines Register*, September 27, 1984, 13A.
64. "Intelligence Budget Calls For a Record $30 Billion," *Des Moines Sunday Register*, April 8, 1990, 2A; and Robin Wright, "'91 Intelligence Budget Still Targets East Bloc," *Los Angeles Times*, April 8, 1990, A1.
65. The aggregate budget figure was first reported by a Senate committee. See Tim Weiner, "The Worst-Kept Secret in the Capital," *New York Times*, July 21, 1994, A11. A more detailed breakdown was reported in Tim Weiner, "$28 Billion Spying Budget Is Made Public by Mistake," *New York Times*, November 5, 1994, 54, as cited in Roger Hilsman, "Does the CIA Still Have A Role?" *Foreign Affairs* 74 (September/October 1995): 105.
66. See Executive Order 12333, "United States Intelligence Activities," December 4, 1981. This executive order can be found in *Code of Federal Regulations* (Washington, DC: Office of the Federal Register, National Archives and Records Service, 1982), pp. 200–216. Richelson, *The U.S. Intelligence Community*, p. 13 notes that it remains in effect.
67. Ibid., p. 201.
68. The interagency membership listing is from *Central Intelligence Agency Factbook* (Washington, DC: Central Intelligence Agency, Public Affairs, July 1982), p. 12. The reference to the National Security Planning draws upon the discussion in the unclassified extract from National Security Decision Directive (NSDD) 286, released on December 12, 1987, by the National Security Council.
69. See the memo from the National Security Council on "National Security Council Organization," dated April 17, 1989.
70. Presidential Decision Directive 2, "Organization of the National Security Council," January 20, 1993, p. 3.
71. Richelson, *The U.S. Intelligence Community*, p. 299.
72. Ibid., pp. 301–304.

73. Ibid., pp. 304–320.
74. Joseph S. Nye, Jr., "Peering into the Future," *Foreign Affairs* 73 (July/August 1994): 83. Nye was chairman of the NIC at the time that he published this article.
75. Marchetti and Marks, *The CIA and the Cult of Intelligence*, pp. 291–296.
76. See Chester L. Cooper, "The CIA and Decisionmaking," *Foreign Affairs* 50 (January, 1972): 221–236.
77. John H. Esterline and Robert B. Black, *Inside Foreign Policy: The Department of State Political System and Its Subsystems* (Palo Alto, CA: Mayfield Publishing Company, 1975), p. 35.
78. David E. Rosenbaum, "U.S. Sees Threats to Soviet Economy," *New York Times*, April 21, 1990, 4.
79. Philip Taubman, "CIA Taking Control of Nicaraguan Policy," *Des Moines Register*, April 20, 1984, 1A.
80. Tim Weiner, David Johnston, and Neil A. Lewis, *Betrayal: The Story of Aldrich Ames, An American Spy* (New York: Random House, 1995), p. 287.
81. See Irving Janis, *Victims of Groupthink* (Boston: Houghton Mifflin Company, 1972), pp. 14–49, for a discussion of the decision making on the Bay of Pigs invasion and the crucial involvement of the CIA. Also see Marchetti and Marks, *The CIA and the Cult of Intelligence*, p. 294, for how dissatisfied President Kennedy was over CIA action in the Bay of Pigs and how this might have affected his view of intelligence estimates during the Cuban Missile Crisis.
82. Esterline and Black, *Inside Foreign Policy*, p. 35.
83. Harry Howe Ransom, *The Intelligence Establishment* (Cambridge, MA: Harvard University Press, 1970), p. 240.
84. The note is quoted from Stansfield Turner, *Secrecy and Democracy: The CIA in Transition* (Boston: Houghton Mifflin Company, 1985), p. 113.
85. The "Iran Postmortem" report is discussed in Bob Woodward, *Veil: The Secret Wars of the CIA, 1981–1987* (New York: Pocket Books, 1987), pp. 106–108.
86. Robert F. Ellsworth and Kenneth L. Adelman, "Foolish Intelligence," *Foreign Policy* 36 (Fall 1979): 147–159. President Carter is quoted here at p. 148. Michael Wines, "C.I.A. Faulted on Rating Soviet Economy," *New York Times*, July 23, 1990, A5.
87. Several sources report some of these intelligence failures. See, for example, John Barry, "Failures of Intelligence?" *Newsweek*, May 14, 1990, 20–21; "NBC Nightly News," June 9, 1990; and Wines, "C.I.A. Faulted on Rating Soviet Economy," p. A5. On the Persian Gulf War failures, see "Intelligence Goofs," *Newsweek*, March 18, 1991, 38.
88. Nye, "Peering into the Future," pp. 84–85.
89. Philip Shenon, "Saudi Bombers Got Outside Support, Perry Tells Panel, *New York Times*, July 10, 1996, A4.
90. Allan E. Goodman, "Testimony: Fact-Checking at the CIA," *Foreign Policy* 102 (Spring 1996): 180–182.
91. Quoted in Barry, "Failures of Intelligence?" p. 20. The first quotation in this paragraph is from this article and at this page.
92. Turner, *Secrecy and Democracy: The CIA in Transition*, pp. 113–127, especially at p. 125. For a more recent assessment of the analytic difficulties of the CIA, see Tim Weiner, "House Panel Says C.I.A. Lacks Expertise to Carry Out Its Duties," *New York Times*, June 19, 1997, A13.
93. Nye, "Peering into the Future," p. 85.
94. Barry, "Failures of Intelligence?" pp. 20–21.
95. Turner, *Secrecy and Democracy: The CIA in Transition*, pp. 273–274.
96. Two recent books that catalogue Aldrich Ames's activities are David Wise, *Nightmover: How Aldrich Ames Sold the CIA to the KGB for $4.6 Million* (New York: Harper Collins, 1995) and Weiner, Johnston, and Lewis, *Betrayal: The Story of Aldrich Ames, An American Spy*. Information on the case here and in the subsequent section is taken from these sources.

97. Tim Weiner, "CIA's Chief Says Russians Duped the U.S.," *New York Times*, December 9, 1995, 1 and 5. The passage by Deutch is quoted at p. 5.

98. Tim Weiner, "CIA Remains in Darkness on Extent of Spy's Damage," *New York Times*, August 25, 1995, A1 and A8. The quote is from p. A1.

99. See Weiner, Johnston, and Lewis, *Betrayal: The Story of Aldrich Ames, An American Spy*. Only after an associate reported his apparent extravagant living was an initial inquiry begun. See pp. 144–145. The CIA did not start a full investigation apparently until late 1990. See p. 158.

100. Ibid., pp. 264–269.

101. Ibid., pp. 262–269. Also, see Mark T, Kehoe, "Brown Commission Shies Away From Radical Suggestions," *Congressional Quarterly Weekly Report*, March 2, 1996, 567, on the establishment of the commission.

102. Address by R. James Woolsey, "National Security and the Future Direction of the Central Intelligence Agency," at the Center for Strategic and International Studies, July 18, 1994.

103. Weiner, Johnston, and Lewis, *Betrayal: The Story of Aldrich Ames, An American Spy*, pp. 285–287.

104. Donna Cassata, "Deutch Promises Bold Steps to Overhaul the CIA," *Congressional Quarterly Weekly Report*, April 29, 1995, 1193.

105. See, for example, Hilsman, "Does the CIA Still Have a Role?"

106. Pat Holt, *Secret Intelligence and Public Policy* (Washington, DC: CQ Press, 1995), p. 109.

107. John E. Rielly, ed., *American Public Opinion and U.S. Foreign Policy 1995* (Chicago: Chicago Council on Foreign Relations, 1995), p. 37.

108. P.L. 253 in *United States Statutes at Large*, Volume 61, Part 1, 80th Cong., 1st sess., p. 498.

109. See Executive Order 12333, "United States Intelligence Activities," p. 215. See Marchetti and Marks, *The CIA and the Cult of Intelligence* and the *Church Committee Report* (note 81) for a discussion of types of covert operations.

110. Marchetti and Marks, *The CIA and the Cult of Intelligence*, pp. 281–282.

111. Foreign and Military Intelligence," Book 1, Final Report of the Select Committee to Study Governmental Operations with respect to Intelligence Activities, United States Senate, April 26, 1976, p. 425 (hereafter, the *Church Committee Report*, after chairman of the Committee, Senator Frank Church).

112. Ibid., p. 56.

113. Ibid., pp. 56–57.

114. Ibid., p. 57.

115. Bernard Gwertzman, "Top Reagan Aide Supports the Use of Covert Action," *New York Times*, May 14, 1984, 1 and 6.

116. Scowcroft made this statement during his appearance in "President Vs. Congress: War Powers and Covert Action," in the Public Broadcasting Series entitled *The Constitution: That Delicate Balance*, 1984.

117. Donna Cassata, "Spy Budget Cleared for Clinton; Plan for New Agency Curbed," *Congressional Quarterly Weekly Report*, December 23, 1995, 3894.

118. *Church Committee Report*, pp. 49–50.

119. Ibid., pp. 51–52.

120. Ibid., p. 54.

121. Ransom, *The Military Establishment*, p. 162.

122. Gregory F. Treverton, "Intelligence: Welcome to the American Government," in Thomas E. Mann, ed., *A Question of Balance* (Washington, DC: The Brookings Institution, 1990), pp. 72–76.

123. Ibid., pp. 74–75.

124. See P.L. 93-559, 88 Stat. 1804. The quoted passage is from section 32.

125. See *Church Committee Report*, note 68, and *Report to the President by the Commission on CIA Activities Within the United States* (Washington, DC: Government Printing Office, June, 1975), note 76, for a complete listing of the recommendations. The latter was named the Rockefeller Commission, after its chairman, Vice President Nelson Rockefeller.

126. On this point, see Harry Howe Ransom, "Strategic Intelligence and Intermestic Politics," p. 313. President Ford's Executive Order 11905 can be found in *Weekly Compilation of Presidential Documents* 12 (February 23, 1976): 234–243.

127. "Controversy Over 'Czar' for Intelligence," *U.S. News and World Report*, February 6, 1978, 50–52.

128. "Intelligence Authorization Act for Fiscal Year 1981," P.L. 96-450, 94 Stat. 1981–1982. This section and the following one draw upon earlier work reported in James M. McCormick and Steven S. Smith, "The Iran Arms Sale and the Intelligence Oversight Act of 1980," *PS* 20 (Winter 1987): 29–37.

129. The passage is quoted in Philip Taubman, "Moynihan to Keep Intelligence Post," *New York Times*, April 27, 1984, 7. On the extent to which the intelligence committees were informed, see Philip Taubman, "House Unit Says Report on Mines Arrived Jan. 31," *New York Times*, April 14, 1984, 1, 6; and his "How Congress Was Informed of Mining of Nicaragua Ports,"*New York Times*, April 16, 1984, 1, 4.

130. The following examples draw upon the "Executive Summary" in *Report of the Congressional Committees Investigating the Iran-Contra Affair* (Washington, DC: U.S. Government Printing Office, 1987), pp. 3–21. The quoted phrases are from this report as well.

131. Unclassified extract from National Security Decision Directive (NSDD) 286, and "Text of Letter on Covert Operations," by President Reagan to Senator David Boren in *New York Times*, August 8, 1987, 5. See also James M. McCormick, "Prior Notification of Covert Actions," *Chicago Tribune*, September 8, 1987, 11.

132. See Michael Oreskes, "Wright, in Gesture to Bush, Shelves Bill on Covert Acts," *New York Times*, February 1, 1989, 8.

133. Personal communication from the National Security Council, August 15, 1990.

134. *Congressional Quarterly Almanac 1988* (Washington, DC: Congressional Quarterly, Inc., 1989), pp. 498–499; and *Congressional Quarterly Almana 1989* (Washington, DC: Congressional Quarterly, Inc., 1990), p. 541.

135. Holt, *Secret Intelligence and Public Policy*, pp. 138–139.

136. Elaine Sciolino, "Conferees Agree to Curb President on Covert Action," *New York Times*, July 27, 1991, 1 and 8; and *Congressional Record*, July 25, 1991, H5898–H5907. The first quote in this paragraph is from the conference report in the *Congressional Record* at p. H5905 and also quoted in the *New York Times*, at p. 8, while the second quote in the paragraph is from the *New York Times* at p. 8.

137. Further impetus for CIA reform was the November 1996 arrest and charging of another CIA official with spying for Russia for the previous two years. He was described as the "highest-ranking CIA employee ever to be charged," and was providing information to Moscow at the very time that the Ames case became public. This official's alleged espionage was characterized "as far less damaging" than the Ames's activities, but it still revealed the problems within the intelligence community. See David Johnston, "U.S. Case Sets Out 2-Year Betrayal by C.I.A. Official," *New York Times*, November 19, 1996, A1 and A12. The quoted passages are from those two pages, respectively.

138. Woolsey, "National Security and the Future Direction of the Central Intelligence Agency," pp. 16, 19, 21, 23, and 24.

139. Cassata, "Deutch Promises Bold Steps to Overhaul the CIA," p. 1193. Also see Bruce D. Berkowitz, "Information Age Intelligence," *Foreign Policy* 103 (Summer 1996): 35.

140. Donna Cassata, "New CIA Staff Chosen to Ease Strained Relations with Hill," *Congressional Quarterly Weekly Report*, May 20, 1995, 1441.

141. "U.S. Counterintelligence Effectiveness," Statement by the Press Secretary, the White House, May 3, 1994, and "Fact Sheet: U.S. Counterintelligence Effectiveness," White House/NSC Press Office, July 19, 1994.

142. This summary of the commission's report is drawn from Kehoe, "Brown Commission Shies Away From Radical Suggestions," p. 567.

143. Cassata, "Spy Budget Cleared for Clinton; Plan for New Agency Curbed," pp. 3894–3895.

144. Berkowitz, "Information Age Intelligence," pp. 35–50.

145. Hilsman, "Does the CIA Still Have a Role?" The quoted passages are at pp. 110, 112, and 116, respectively.

146. Esterline and Black, *Inside Foreign Policy*, p. 23. On the Kissinger reorganization, see pp. 24–26.

147. The following discussion of SIGs and IGs in the Reagan administration is based upon the Statement of the President, "National Security Council Structure," January 12, 1982, reprinted in Robert E. Hunter, *Presidential Control of Foreign Policy: Management or Mishap?* The Washington Papers/91 (New York: Praeger, 1982), pp. 109–115 (additionally, see Hunter's discussion of this system, pp. 96–102, upon which we also relied); and Colin Campbell, *Managing the Presidency: Carter, Reagan, and the Search for Executive Harmony* (Pittsburgh: University of Pittsburgh Press, 1986), p. 43. In the original directive, only the first three SIGs were established. The international economic SIG was added later.

148. Ibid. The reference to the NSPG draws upon the unclassified extract from National Security Decision Directive (NSDD) 286.

149. The discussion of the changes since the Tower Commission Report is based upon Paul Schoot Stevens, "The National Security Council: Past and Prologue," *Strategic Review* 17 (Winter 1989): 61.

150. The description of the Bush administration's NSC policy coordination process is based upon material provided by the U.S. Army War College, Carlisle Barracks, Pennsylvania, December 1989, and a memo from the National Security Council on "National Security Council Organization," April 17, 1989.

151. The descriptions of the NSC committees and quotation about their activities during the Clinton administration are taken from Presidential Decision 2, January 20, 1993.

CHAPTER

II

POLITICAL PARTIES, BIPARTISANSHIP, AND INTEREST GROUPS

So let us find inspiration in the great tradition of Harry Truman and Arthur Vandenburg—a tradition that builds bridges of cooperation, not walls of isolation; that opens the arms of Americans to change instead of throwing up our hands in despair; that casts aside partisanship and brings together Republicans and Democrats for the good of the American people and the world.

President William Clinton
May 22, 1995

...ethnic politics, carried as they often have been to excess, have proven harmful to the national interest.... Ethnic advocacy represents neither a lack of patriotism nor a desire to place foreign interests ahead of American interests; more often it represents a sincere belief that the two coincide.

Former Senator Charles McC. Mathias, Jr.
"Ethnic Groups and Foreign Policy"
Foreign Affairs, Summer 1981

Beyond the president, Congress, and the bureaucracies, other participants also influence the American foreign policy process. Two additional key participants are political parties and interest groups. While these groups probably have less direct impact upon policy than the other participants discussed so far, they are increasingly viewed as important to the foreign policy process. By political parties we mean those organized groups who pursue their goals by contesting elections and perhaps controlling political offices.[1] These political organizations can influence foreign policy decisions directly by controlling elective offices, but they can also affect the policy content of others who control executive and legislative offices through criticism and debate. By interest groups we mean those portions of the population who are organized and seek political goals that they are unable to provide on their own.[2] These groups seek their political goals through the use of various lobbying techniques, ranging from making campaign contributions to a political candidate to face-to-face discussions with policy makers.

In the first half of this chapter, we examine the contribution of America's two principal political parties to the foreign policy process over the last four decades. We begin by focusing on the concept of bipartisanship in foreign affairs—a notion often invoked by policy makers to dampen partisan divisions over United States foreign policy—and assess its overall success. Next we turn to examine how the Vietnam War, and the events surrounding it, weakened any bipartisanship that may have existed. Finally, we summarize some recent evidence challenging the notion that bipartisanship ever existed and which instead points to the consistency in partisan differences in foreign affairs. In the second half of the chapter, we discuss several traditional foreign policy interest groups, identify some newer ones that have emerged in the foreign policy arena, and assess the relative impact of these various groups on the decision making process. To illustrate the increased importance of foreign policy interest groups generally, we focus on two types, economic and ethnic ones, which often have been viewed as particularly important in shaping United States foreign policy.

POLITICAL PARTIES AND THE BIPARTISAN TRADITION

America's two political parties do not, as a rule, differ in their programmatic or ideological positions on many domestic and foreign issues. Both the Democratic and Republican parties are more often seen as pragmatic organizations that adopt policy positions on such issues as taxation, bank reform, and health care to attract as many adherents as possible. While this description of the two major parties can be overstated and tends to apply more to party followers than to party leaders, it generally represents an accurate portrait of U.S. political parties, especially when compared to their European counterparts.[3]

This depiction of America's two major parties, moreover, has been applied particularly to the foreign policy arena. Despite the fact that the Republican party more often controlled the White House, and the Democratic party Congress, since World War II, bipartisanship has frequently been used to describe the nature of America's approach to foreign affairs. The origins of bipartisanship usually are attributed to the circumstances that the United States faced in the late 1940s and early 1950s. Because the international environment was so threatening during that period, a united approach seemed to be required for United States national security. In the words of one prominent politician of the time, "partisan politics...stopped at the water's edge."[4] In this approach, the United States national interest would necessarily supplant any partisan interest in foreign policy, and bipartisan cooperation between Congress and the president would supplant both institutional and partisan differences as well.

The exact meaning of bipartisanship, however, was not always clear, but it seemed to require at least two different, albeit complementary, kinds of cooperation between the legislative and executive branches.[5] One kind focused on achieving "unity in foreign affairs," and referred to the degree to which "policies [are] supported by majorities within each political party" in Congress. The other kind referred to a set of "practices and procedures designed to bring about the desired unity."[6] Put differently, Congress and the president would develop procedures in which each would participate in and consult with one another in the formulation of foreign policy and, in turn, a majority of congressional members from both parties would support the policy developed. These two kinds of cooperation implied that bipartisanship would involve collaboration in both the *process* of foreign policy making and its *outcome*.

The Cold War Years and Bipartisanship

The beginning of this bipartisan effort is usually attributed to the foreign policy cooperation that developed between Democratic President Harry Truman and the Republican chairman of the Senate Foreign Relations Committee, Senator Arthur Vandenberg of Michigan, in the immediate post–World War II years. After Senator Vandenberg had altered his isolationist stance and after President Truman committed himself to global involvement for the United States, the two leaders consciously sought to build a bipartisan foreign policy against Communist expansionism. To a large extent, they were successful in doing so. Indeed, the major foreign policy initiatives of the late 1940s were accomplished with substantial support across political parties. The passage of the Bretton Woods agreement, the United Nations Charter, the Greek-Turkish aid program, and the Marshall Plan, among others, garnered support from both parties and passed Congress with over 83 percent support, on average.[7]

The acceptance of the Cold War consensus by the major political parties and the public at large seemingly continued this bipartisan tradition in foreign policy through the Eisenhower and Kennedy administrations and into the Johnson one as well. Despite some party divisions over the attacks by Senator Joseph McCarthy upon "Communists" within the United States government, the "loss" of China, and the Korean war, the essential foreign policy unity of the two parties remained.[8] Even with the so-called "missile gap" of the late 1950s that was eventually carried into the 1960 presidential campaign, the parties continued to display markedly similar foreign policy orientations. Both parties in their 1956 party platforms expressed a desire for a bipartisan foreign policy, and the Republicans expressed this sentiment again in 1960.[9]

Both Democrats and Republicans came to stand for a similar posture toward world affairs: a strong national defense, an active global involvement by the United States, and staunch anticommunism. To be sure, some divisions existed within the two parties. The Republicans had to contend with a wing that still cherished isolationism, and the Democrats had to contend with a wing that was initially suspicious of the confrontational approach toward the Soviet Union. Further, the Democrats had to live with popular perceptions that portrayed them as the party associated with war (but also with prosperity), while the Republicans probably enjoyed the label as the party associated with peace (but not the one associating them with recession).[10] Democratic presidents—such as Franklin Delano Roosevelt with his role in leading the United States into World War II and Harry Truman with the outbreak of the Korean War—often convey the former perception, while Republican presidents—such as Herbert Hoover in the interwar years and Dwight Eisenhower after the Korean War—convey the latter.

Despite these different party factions and popular labels, the members of the two parties tended to stand for the same general principles in foreign policy. As political scientist Herbert McClosky and his associates report from their 1957–1958 survey data on party leaders and followers, the foreign policy differences between the parties were indeed small. In fact, the average difference between Democratic and Republican leaders was smaller for foreign policy than for any of the four domestic policy areas that McClosky examined. Democratic and Republican followers demonstrated the same pattern generally.[11]

This bipartisanship was also reflected in the policy "planks" that each party placed into its national platforms during the Cold War years. In a systematic analysis of the platforms of the Democrats and the Republicans from 1944 to 1964, political scientist Gerald Pomper reports that 47 percent of the party pledges on foreign policy were essentially the same in each and only 6 percent were in conflict.[12] Defense policy pledges were also quite similar: Seventy-three percent were the same and only 2 percent were in conflict. Such a level of bipartisanship on foreign policy was second only to civil rights among eight different policy categories analyzed, while the level of bipartisanship on defense policy was tied for third position with labor and agricultural issues. Finally, the percentages of conflicting pledges across the parties were equally low in comparison with the other policy categories.

The important consequence of this bipartisanship tradition is that separate party influence, as such, seemingly did not have a strong effect on the general strategies of American foreign policy. Instead, policy influence was mainly confined to the executive branch because the president could generally count on congressional and public support across political parties. Recall the high level of presidential success in foreign policy that we discussed in Chapter 7.

THE LIMITS OF BIPARTISANSHIP THROUGH THE VIETNAM ERA

Although bipartisanship was indeed the preeminent way to describe the roles of the two political parties during the Cold War years and beyond, some analysts recently (and even some at the time) have argued that the degree of partisan unity on foreign affairs was often overstated. I. M. Destler, Anthony Lake, and Leslie Gelb best capture this alternate view in describing the first fifteen years of the Cold War:

> These were said to be the halcyon days of bipartisanship or nonpartisanship, of Democrats and Republicans putting national interests above party interests. But such a description has always been more myth than reality. Conservatives and liberals were at one another's throat constantly. There was never a time when Truman was not besieged.... [Adlai E.] Stevenson tried to make foreign policy a key issue in the 1956 [presidential] campaign, and Mr. Kennedy succeeded in doing so in 1960.[13]

Destler, Lake, and Gelb do acknowledge, however, that part of the reason for the apparent unity in policy is explained by the fact that politicians would primarily "rally around the President's flag in East-West confrontations." But on "second-order issues," the parties "would squabble" regularly.[14]

Two decades earlier, a prominent foreign policy analyst, Cecil Crabb, reached a similar conclusion in characterizing the magnitude of bipartisanship from the late 1940s to the late 1950s.[15] In reviewing several cases of foreign policy and bipartisanship in that period, Crabb concluded that "there have been relatively few genuinely bipartisan undertakings in American postwar relations." While a bipartisan approach may provide stability and continuity in policy, he noted, it may also weaken the level of executive leadership, reduce the vigor of opposition party debate, and even weaken the party system. Such disadvantages, of course, could ultimately be harmful to the quality of United States foreign policy. In short, the characterization of the period as a bipartisan one was not wholly accurate, nor was the attempt to achieve such a policy approach necessarily a wise one.

Partisan/Ideological Differences and Foreign Policy Issues

A closer examination of several foreign policy issues during those years lends credence to the more limited view of bipartisanship that Destler and others and Crabb suggest. On foreign aid, military aid, defense expenditures, and trade issues, for example, a rather continuous degree of partisan division has been evident, even at the height of presumed bipartisan cooperation. Often, too, the Democrats were split on these issues between their northern wing (traditionally more liberal in orientation) and their southern wing (traditionally more conservative in orientation). Still, even when one of these wings joined forces temporarily with the Republicans, there were sufficient fluctuations between issues to limit the degree of bipartisanship and to produce partisan and ideological divisions.

On foreign economic assistance, for instance, northern Democrats and Republicans in the 1950s joined together ideologically to support these programs, while southern Democrats opposed them. In the 1960s through the early 1970s, northern Democrats generally continued their support and southern Democrats their opposition. Republicans, on the other hand, fluctuated from opposition in the early 1960s to support late in that decade and into the 1970s.[16]

On the issue of military assistance, in the Senate, northern Democrats generally supported the increase or maintenance of the same levels of funding until the early 1960s. By contrast, southern Democrats fluctuated in their support of military aid during the height of the Cold War, but they became more supportive during the Vietnam period. Republicans increasingly have come to support such assistance over the course of the postwar period, albeit starting with some initial reluctance in the early 1950s. In the House, the voting trends on military assistance have tended to be much more irregular across party lines, but the general direction for the parties is about the same as in the Senate.

On defense expenditures, too, partisan differences existed. Northern Democrats in the Senate, but less so in the House, supported increasing, or at least maintaining, defense expenditures in the 1950s, but northern Democrats in both houses began to oppose such expenditures in the 1960s and 1970s. Republicans, on the other hand, opposed such expenditures in the 1950s more than Democrats, but they tended to be much more supportive from 1960 onward when compared to the Democrats. Southern Democrats exhibited less variation in their behavior and continued to support defense expenditures.

On trade policy, too, some partisan differences in congressional behavior existed. Democrats generally were more supportive of a free trading system in the 1950s, while the Republicans were generally more protectionist in their orientation. By the middle of the 1960s, however, these trends had reversed, with Democrats becoming more protectionist, and the Republicans becoming more free-trade oriented.

The upshot of these analyses suggests that party influence—even at the height of bipartisanship—had an impact on specific details of foreign policy. To the extent that bipartisan foreign policy occurred, it necessarily had to operate within the confines of party differences. In this sense, partisan politics assisted in shaping United States foreign policy behavior to a greater extent than some might wish to acknowledge. Nevertheless, as political scientist Barry Hughes and others have reminded us, the position and party of the president still played an important role in these congressional voting results.[17]

The Effects of Vietnam

Although Destler, Gelb, and Lake acknowledge that some bipartisanship (or more accurately, "majorityship") existed from the 1940s to the 1960s, they go on to argue that "Vietnam changed all this."[18] As more Americans were drafted and sent abroad following the escalation of the Vietnam War in 1965, and as the conflict became a regular feature on the evening news,

President Johnson found himself facing a domestic political problem every bit as challenging as the war itself. The effects of this war were profound on domestic harmony and on any great semblance of cooperation across party lines. As Destler, Gelb, and Lake note, "The conceptual basis of American foreign policy was now shaken, and the politics of foreign policy became more complicated."

Zbigniew Brzezinski has aptly summarized the effect of Vietnam on any domestic unity in foreign policy in yet another way:

> Our foreign policy became increasingly the object of contestation, of sharp cleavage, and even of some reversal of traditional political commitments. The Democratic Party, the party of internationalism, became increasingly prone to the appeal of neo-isolationism. And the Republican Party, the party of isolationism, became increasingly prone to the appeal of militant interventionism. And both parties increasingly found their center of gravity shifting to the extreme, thereby further polarizing our public opinion."[19]

These changes in bipartisanship became evident in the support patterns for the Vietnam War within Congress. President Lyndon Johnson now had to rely upon Republicans and conservative (largely southern) Democrats for much of his support on Southeast Asian policy.[20] Opposition now began to come from liberals within his party and from a few Republicans. Party and ideological lines began to be drawn; strong support across party lines on a major foreign policy initiative was beginning to erode. As contentious as this issue was, Congress, controlled by Democratic majorities in the House and the Senate, was never successful in defeating Presidents Johnson or Nixon (through 1972) on a major funding bill for the Vietnam War.[21] In this sense, the essence of both party loyalty and bipartisanship remained, although both forces were drawn taut by the Vietnam involvement.

Toward the end of the Vietnam War, bipartisanship began to wear even thinner. With a Republican president in the White House and a Congress controlled by the Democrats, the consequence was the series of foreign policy reforms discussed in Chapter 8. While both parties supported a number of these reforms, Democrats, and particularly liberal Democrats, were generally more favorable to placing limits on the foreign policy powers of the executive than were the Republicans. Moreover, the major foreign policy reforms enacted by Congress occurred when Republican presidents were in office and the Democrats controlled both the Senate and the House.

In yet another barometer of changing foreign policy bipartisanship in the Vietnam period, we find increasing evidence of foreign policy partisanship, especially when compared to the Cold War years. The party platforms for 1968, 1972, and 1976 showed a marked decrease in bipartisanship.[22] Only 24 percent of the foreign policy pledges for these platforms were the same for Republicans and Democrats, while only 11 percent of the defense policy pledges were bipartisan. (Recall that the bipartisan pledges were about twice to three times those figures during the Cold War.) The two parties seemed to be moving in different directions in that the preponderance of pledges on foreign and defense policy were unique to each party. At the same time, the degree of foreign policy conflict on pledges remained low (at about 6 percent) for each policy area. In short, then, while bipartisanship was declining, outright partisan conflict had still not emerged.

By the 1980s, however, the level of partisan division on foreign policy increased even more. Key foreign policy issues like Central America, the Middle East, and national defense policy elicited clashes along party and ideological lines.[23] Congressional voting on covert aid to Nicaraguan rebels, for example, often saw Democrats pitted against the Republicans in Congress. On key defense votes, such as the development of the MX missile, the B-1 bomber, and the Strategic Defense Initiative ("Star Wars"), the pattern was much the same.[24] In this sense, there has been clear movement away from the bipartisan tradition of the past, especially on crucial defense and foreign policy issues.

BIPARTISANSHIP AND CONGRESSIONAL FOREIGN POLICY VOTING

Indeed, recent research raises some questions about the extent to which this tradition ever actually operated in terms of one aspect of bipartisanship, policy outcome. Recall that one component of bipartisanship implied unified policy outcome across the two branches and the parties. That is, a majority of congressional members of both parties supported the president's position on foreign policy. Research by McCormick and Wittkopf suggests that such bipartisanship, when defined by congressional voting on foreign policy issues, was less frequent than the popular view.[25] In several analyses of congressional foreign policy voting from the late 1940s to the late 1980s, they have argued that partisan and ideological conflict was more often the norm in foreign policy making than was any bipartisan harmony. In the analyses of over 2,400 congressional foreign policy votes on which the president took a position, they found that bipartisan policy unity was as often fantasy as fact.

Figure 11.1 portrays the results obtained by McCormick and Wittkopf for the extent of bipartisan voting in the House and Senate from 1947 to 1988 for eight different American administrations. With few exceptions, bipartisan voting has been more infrequent than conventional wisdom suggests. Only during the Eisenhower administration did bipartisan support (defined as the majority of both parties supporting the president) exist across the House and Senate on more than 50 percent of the foreign policy votes. While bipartisan support was greater in the Senate than in the House across these administrations, the level of bipartisanship was especially low in the latter chamber. If the Eisenhower administration were excluded, no more than 50 percent of the votes in any other administration obtained bipartisan support in the House. These results hardly support the view that bipartisanship was the norm for any extended period in the post–World War II years.

By contrast, Figure 11.2 illustrates the substantial degree of partisan divisions in these administrations since World War II. While the partisan gaps are greater in the House than in the Senate across these administrations, the divisions between the parties are still quite substantial. On average, the difference between parties in each chamber is about 20 percentage

FIGURE 11.1

Bipartisan Foreign Policy Voting in Congress, 1947–1988

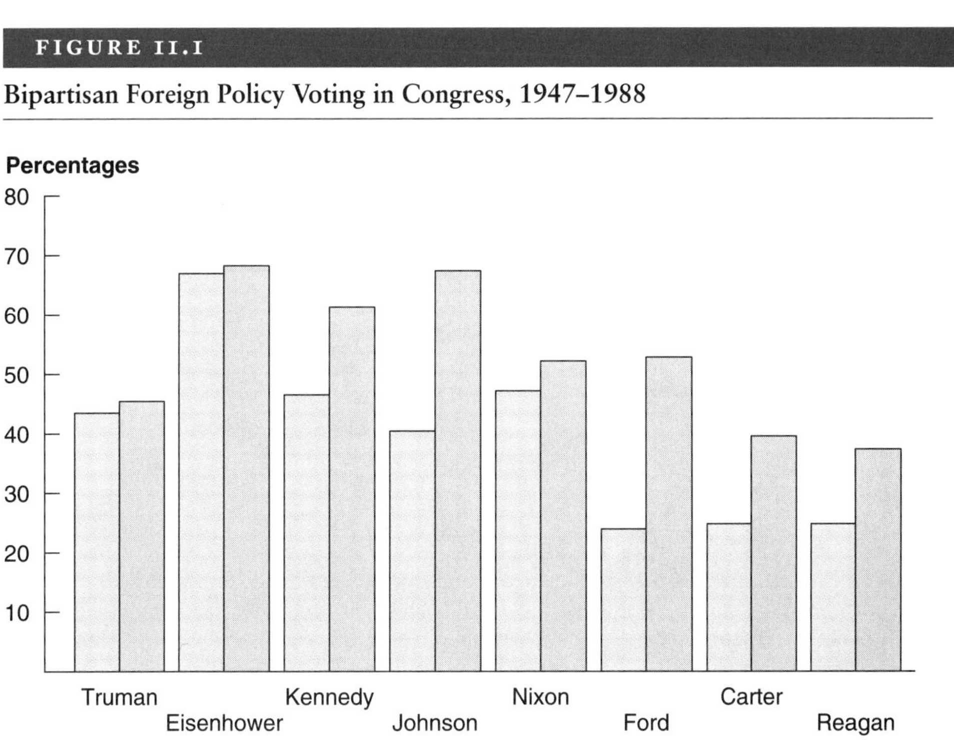

Note: Each bar represents the proportion of foreign policy votes on which a majority of both parties supported the president's position.

Source: James M. McCormick and Eugene R. Wittkopf, "Bipartisanship, Partisanship, and Ideology in Congressional-Executive Foreign Relations, 1947–1988," *The Journal of Politics* 52 (November 1990): 1085. Reprinted by permission of the University of Texas Press, publisher of *The Journal of Politics*.

points, with only the Eisenhower administration (in both the House and the Senate) and the Johnson administration (in the Senate) obtaining a noticeably smaller gap.

These partisan gaps have held across different foreign policy issues considered by Congress as well. Figure 11.3 shows the average congressional support for the president's party and the opposition party averaged across the eight administrations for foreign aid, foreign relations, national security, and trade votes. As the figure makes clear, the partisan differences are pronounced across all of them. In short, these results suggest that congressional voting on foreign policy issues has always been more partisan and less bipartisan than often portrayed.

When the Vietnam War was factored into these analyses, it did not change the overall conclusions. While partisan divisions increased somewhat in the post-Vietnam period, the impact of the war could generally not be separated from the effects of other factors. Only on national security voting did the pre- and post-Vietnam periods show some marked differences. Overall, though, the Vietnam War appeared not to be "a watershed

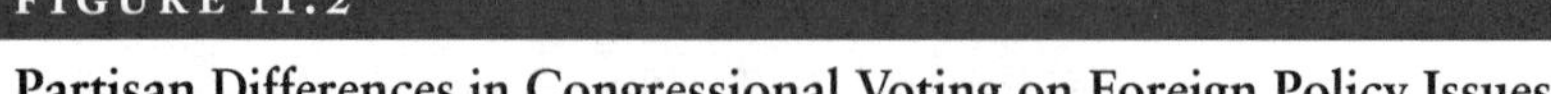

FIGURE 11.2

Partisan Differences in Congressional Voting on Foreign Policy Issues

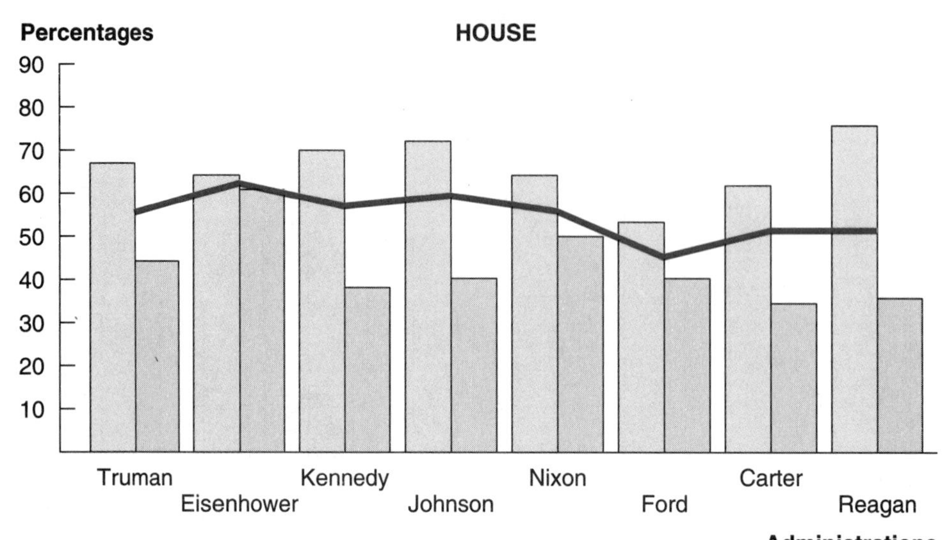

Percentages
SENATE
90
80
70
60
50
40
30
20
10
Truman
Eisenhower
Kennedy
Johnson
Nixon
Ford
Carter
Reagan
Administrations

Overall President's party Opposition party

Note: Each bar represents for each party the average percentage of support by members of Congress for the president's position on foreign policy votes. The overall line measures the average level of support for the president regardless of party.

Source: James M. McCormick and Eugene R. Wittkopf, "Bipartisanship, Partisanship, and Ideology in Congressional-Executive Foreign Relations, 1947–1988," *The Journal of Politics* 52 (November 1990): 1090. Reprinted by permission of the University of Texas Press, publisher of *The Journal of Politics*.

FIGURE 11.3

Partisan Support in Congressional Voting on Four Foreign Policy Issues, 1947–1988

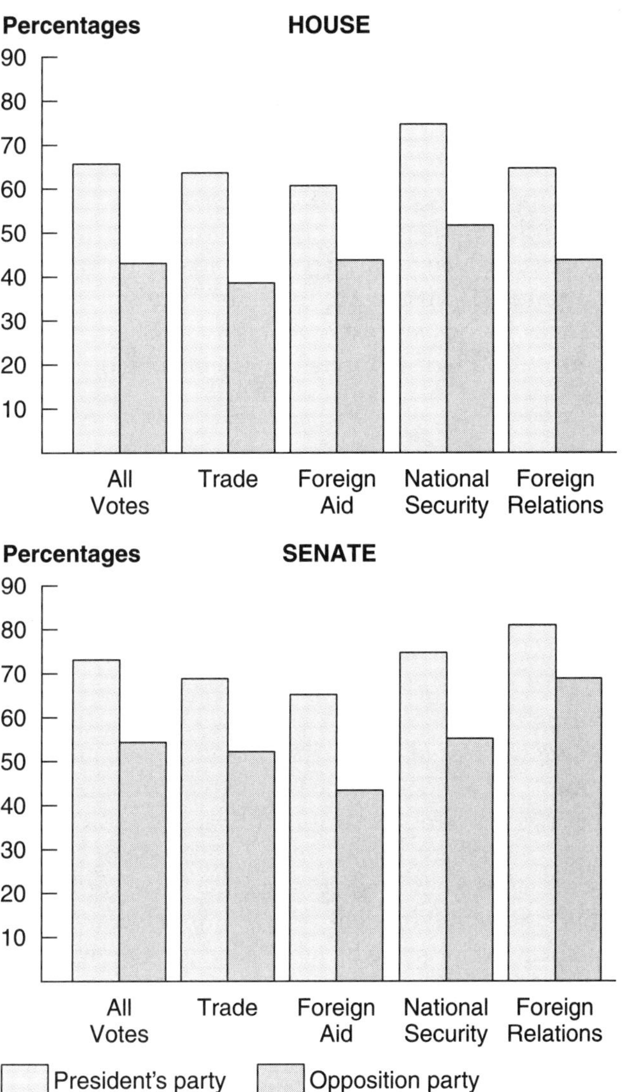

Note: Each bar represents the average percentage of party support on that issue across the eight administrations.

Source: James M. McCormick and Eugene R. Wittkopf, "At the Water's Edge: The Effects of Party, Ideology, and Issues on Congressional Foreign Policy Voting, 1947–1988," *American Politics Quarterly* 20 (January 1992): 42.

in postwar American bipartisanship."[26] Only in combination with other changes at home and in Congress did Vietnam produce an increase in partisan and ideological divisions.

While these results thus appear to raise doubts about the degree of bipartisanship, at least as measured through formal congressional voting, some caution needs to be exercised in interpreting the figures and pushing them beyond what they can demonstrate about bipartisanship in American foreign policy generally. These analyses, for instance, do not consider the other component of bipartisanship—the process side or the degree of informal consultations between the branches. That is, collaborative arrangements may have been developed and used between the branches, but these arrangements are not (and cannot) be reflected in the formal voting analyses. Further, these analyses do not weigh the importance of particular issues to the president, even though these are issues on which he has indicated a position. Thus, bipartisan outcomes may have operated on highly selective issues—salient to the president and the Congress—but that bipartisan cooperation may be imbedded in this larger set of votes on which the president still stated a position. Despite these necessary cautions, the congressional voting analyses do alert us against applying too quickly and too easily the "bipartisan" label to American foreign policy making during the Cold War years and after.

PARTISAN DIVISIONS TODAY: FROM REAGAN TO CLINTON

In short, while the debate continues over whether bipartisanship ever existed and over how much it has declined, partisan acrimony on foreign policy issues persists. The party differences in the foreign policy arena became so substantial during the first term of the Reagan administration that he felt compelled to undertake at least two important steps in an effort to rebuild bipartisan support. First, he appointed bipartisan presidential commissions to garner support for the modernization of America's strategic nuclear arsenal and for his Central American policy.[27] The task of both commissions was to diffuse the partisan bickering over these issues and to build support across party lines. Second, President Reagan also felt compelled to deliver a major foreign policy address in which he called for a return to an earlier era of executive–legislative cooperation:

> We must restore bipartisan consensus in support of U.S. foreign policy. We must restore America's honorable tradition of partisan politics stopping at the water's edge, Republicans and Democrats standing united in patriotism and speaking with one voice....[28]

Despite this appeal, party differences in Reagan's second term actually accelerated on foreign policy, fueled largely by the controversy surrounding the Iran-Contra affair (see Chapters 5 and 10).

When President Bush took office, partisan accord was so low that he felt it necessary to appeal for bipartisanship in foreign policy in his inaugural address. Two key passages summarize his view:

> We need a new engagement...between the Executive and the Congress.... There's grown a certain divisiveness.... And our great parties have too often been far apart and untrusting of each other.
>
> It's been this way since Vietnam. That war cleaves us still.... A new breeze is blowing—and the old bipartisanship must be made new again.[29]

Despite some initial efforts by both Republicans and Democrats and an important initial bipartisan Contra aid package early in 1989, Bush still faced partisan divisions over his foreign policy actions. Spirited debates occurred over defense expenditures in the post–Cold War era, the amount of assistance to the newly independent Eastern Europe, and the response to the Chinese crackdown in Tiananmen Square. The fractious argument in January 1991 over whether to continue with sanctions against Saddam Hussein's Iraq after his seizure of Kuwait or to go to war against Iraq continued this partisan and ideological debate.

To be sure, there were important exceptions to partisan discord (e.g., over the American intervention and the seizure of Manuel Noriega of Panama in 1989 and the initial bipartisan support over Iraq's seizure of Kuwait), but the level of bipartisanship in the Bush administration generally remained low. In fact, only one in five foreign policy votes in the House and less than one in three votes in the Senate received bipartisan support (see Figure 11.4). Partisan divisions remained as wide as during the Reagan administration, with gaps of 34 percent and 35 percent between Republicans and Democrats in the House and Senate, respectively (Figure 11.5).[30]

President Clinton, too, made an appeal for bipartisan support, although his appeal was now directed toward staving off the American impulse toward isolationism, seemingly revived with the end of the Cold War: "The

FIGURE 11.4

Bipartisan Foreign Policy Voting in the House and Senate, Bush and Clinton Administrations, 1989–1996

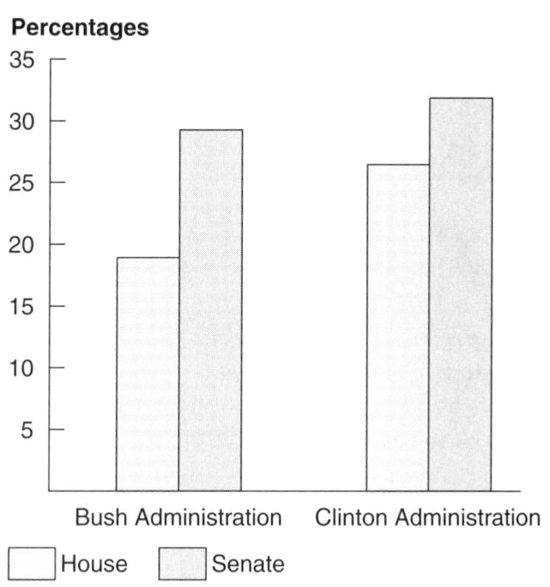

Source: James M. McCormick, Eugene R. Wittkopf, and David M. Danna, "Politics and Bipartisanship at the Water's Edge: A Note on Bush and Clinton," *Polity* 30 (Fall 1997, forthcoming).

FIGURE 11.5

Partisan Gap in the House and Senate, Bush and Clinton Administrations, 1989–1996

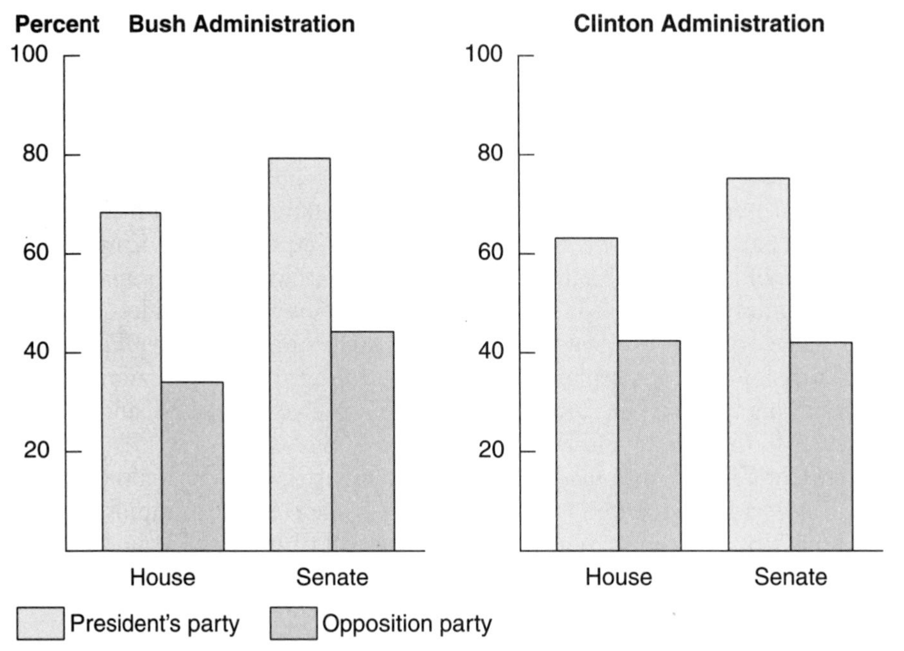

Source: James M. McCormick, Eugene R. Wittkopf, and David M. Danna, "Politics and Bipartisanship at the Water's Edge: A Note on Bush and Clinton," *Polity* 30 (Fall 1997, forthcoming).

new isolationists both on the left and the right would radically revise the fundamentals of our foreign policy that have earned bipartisan support since the end of World War II." Invoking the name of the father of bipartisanship, Senator Arthur Vandenberg, Clinton noted that America's past foreign policy "successes would not have been possible without a strong, bipartisan commitment to American's [*sic*] leadership." "Today," he continued, "it is Vandenburg's [*sic*] spirit that should drive our foreign policy and our politics."[31]

Still, the bipartisan decline and the partisan gaps continued unabated for the Clinton administration, the first after the Cold War. During its first term, the Clinton administration enjoyed bipartisan support only on about one in four foreign policy votes in the House of Representatives, and only about one in three in the Senate on which the president took a position (see Figure 11.4). This level of support was roughly in line with the relatively low level of bipartisan support received by the Bush and Reagan administrations. In terms of partisan differences, the levels for the Clinton administration were somewhat narrower in the House than in the Senate, the partisan gap for Clinton is about the same as it was for the Bush administration in the Senate, but it is somewhat smaller than Bush's in the House (see Figure 11.5).

For the Clinton administration, the partisan and ideological differences were quite sharp in several key foreign policy areas. On the use of American forces abroad, whether in Somalia, Bosnia, or Haiti, partisan differences were often sharply drawn in Congress, with Republicans less supportive of the use of force than Democrats. On defense issues, both partisan and ideological differences arose during the Clinton administration, with conservatives and liberals of both parties divided on spending on defense. Trade, too, produced sharp partisan differences, with the Clinton administration ultimately relying on Republican support to gain approval of the North American Free Trade agreement (NAFTA). Indeed, in one attempt to lessen partisan discord on foreign policy in his second term, President Clinton appointed William Cohen, a former Republican senator and a frequent critic of the Clinton administration's foreign policy, as his secretary of defense.

PARTISAN POLITICS AND THE FUTURE

Despite some notable exceptions, the long-term prospect for a restoration of bipartisanship (to the extent that it ever really existed) does not appear bright; instead, the more likely outcome is that partisan divisions will continue for the foreseeable future. Several reasons make this projection likely. First, divided government at the national level supports a continuation and intensification of partisan conflicts, not a diminution of their levels. Republicans won five of the last eight presidential elections between 1968 and 1996, and Democrats won control of both chambers of Congress in eighteen of the last twenty-four congressional elections between 1950 and 1996. During a majority of time, then, one party often controlled the White House and the other party Congress. In such a setting, partisanship is more likely and bipartisanship less likely.

Second, partisan and ideological cleavages have deepened between the major political parties over the past several decades, eroding further the prospect for bipartisan accommodation. Conservative Republicans are now replacing conservative Democrats in the South; conservative Democrats are switching parties, and their ideological preferences and party affiliations are more closely aligned; and moderates are fewer in both parties, as contentious issues further divide them. Without the cross-pressures between ideology and party in Congress, bipartisanship remains elusive.

Third, the end of the Cold War—the collapse of the Berlin Wall and the reunification of Germany, the end of communism in Central Europe, and the implosion of the Soviet Union—has seemingly jarred the foundation of American foreign policy making. The anti-Communist, anti-Soviet prism that had long served as the guide to policy in East-West and North-South relations and dampened domestic debate no longer exists. With its end, members of Congress and the executive branch now enjoy a wider latitude in considering foreign policy options, including the more careful consideration of domestic politics. As political analyst Michael Mandelbaum succinctly put it: "In the post–Cold War era, without an overarching principle to guide the nation's foreign relations...the promotion of domestic interests is the default strategy of American foreign policy."[32]

Fourth, the proliferation of new issues portend more, not fewer, partisan divisions as well. While security issues, virtually by definition, dominated the foreign policy agenda of the United States during the Cold War, other submerged or new foreign policy issues—dealing with economics, the environment, and social-cultural concerns—now crowd the political agenda. These issues, unlike security issues during the Cold War, do not always lend themselves to a common domestic position. Even to the extent that security issues remain on the agenda (e.g., the dangers posed by the spread of weapons of mass destruction or the emergence of territorial, ethnic, and religious conflicts), they do not easily evoke a common domestic response when compared to the Cold War era. To what extent, for instance, have territorial, ethnic, and religious disputes among the former republics of the Soviet Union or in Bosnia-Herzegovina produced a unified response among the American policy makers (or the public), especially when compared to Soviet action over Hungary or Czechoslovakia during the height of the Cold War?

Trade and environmental issues, for example, are likely to assume a larger role in foreign policy and are likely to exacerbate political divisions. As these kinds of economic issues are increasingly viewed as both foreign and domestic policy questions, and as Americans are affected differentially by these policy choices, partisan debate will intensify. Even if scientific agreement can be reached on the dimensions of such ecological challenges as acid rain, nuclear waste disposal, and global warming, common political actions to address these global issues will remain elusive and the setting will continue ripe for partisan discord. Since virtually any political decision on these issues is likely to affect the public differentially, more, not less, dissensus will result.

Finally, analyst Jeremy Rosner argues that the issues at stake and the degree of presidential involvement will likely be pivotal in determining executive–legislative relations on foreign policy after the Cold War, although partisan differences may exacerbate these factors. On some issues, for example, presidential dominance will likely continue: With traditional security issues that resemble Cold War concerns, that are tied to a national security threat, and that convey promise of some domestic economic benefit (e.g., aid to Russia), the president will be successful if he takes an early and determined stance, even in the face of partisan differences between the White House and the Congress. On other issues, Congress will likely hold greater sway: With nonsecurity and nontraditional issues that lack a tie to the Cold War, that are not a security threat, and that are not pushed by the president (e.g., United States involvement in peacekeeping missions), Congress will be successful if it remains determined. Overall, though, Rosner argues that, since more issues are likely to reflect the latter than the former in the years ahead, Congress will be "more assertive relative to the executive branch than it was during the late years of the Cold War."[33]

On balance, then, the influence of partisan politics on the direction of United States foreign policy is likely to become more identifiable than it has been in the past. And it is likely to intensify in the future.

INTEREST GROUPS AND THE FOREIGN POLICY PROCESS

Another participant in foreign affairs whose role has increased in importance is that of interest groups. The number of interest groups participating in the American political process in Washington is astounding, estimated at over 11,000 firms or groups and 15,000 individuals, in one recent assessment.[34] The interest groups concerned either with foreign policy exclusively, or with foreign and domestic policy in combination, are less than those totals, but their overall magnitude is still conveyed by those numbers. These foreign policy interest groups range from the oldest—the economic interest groups—to the newest—foreign lobbying groups. Within and between these two types of organizations, we may identify several other categories of foreign policy interest groups: labor unions, agricultural organizations, religious groups, ethnic groups, veterans organizations, single-issue interests, academic think tanks, and ideological groups, among others.

Interest groups primarily target Congress with their influence efforts. They seek to influence members of Congress and policy making through the use of professional lobbyists (e.g., lawyers or public relations firms) or their own staff personnel located or assigned to Washington. Yet a considerable portion of interest-group activities may also focus on influencing key foreign policy bureaucracies. The Department of Defense and the Department of State, for example, are important targets for these various pressure groups. Sometimes, too, these bureaucracies (and others discussed over the last two chapters) lobby Congress as well. In fact, a recent count listed 153 government bureaucracies, agencies, and commissions involved in lobbying efforts, ranging from the Executive Office of the President, the Department of Agriculture, the Department of State, and Department of Defense to the Agency for International Development, the CIA, and the United States Information Agency.[35]

Types of Foreign Policy Interest Groups

In order to give some sense of the magnitude of nongovernmental interest groups (although without pretending to provide an exhaustive list) and some of their foreign policy concerns, we identify several examples of the different types of foreign policy interest groups that are operating today.

Business Groups. Economic interest groups probably comprise the largest number of foreign policy groups. Several umbrella economic organizations lobby for business interests. For example, the National Association of Manufacturers, the United States Chamber of Commerce (and its global affiliates), the Committee on Economic Development, and the Business Roundtable, among others, would fit into this category.[36] Beyond these umbrella groups, particular manufacturing, industrial, and commodity interests usually engage in separate lobbying activities. The American Petroleum Institute, the American Textile Manufacturers Institute, the American Footwear Manufacturers Association, the National Cotton Council, and the National Coal Association are all examples of such lobbying groups. In addition, virtually all major corporations actively lobby for their particular foreign policy interests. The major defense contractors (such as General Dynamics, Lockheed Martin, Boeing, United Technologies, and General Electric) lobby Congress and the Department of Defense in particular. In short, virtually every major corporation on the Fortune 500 list has some kind of representation in Washington, and a large percentage of them are involved in foreign policy lobbying, too. All of these business lobbies generally share similar foreign policy goals: They seek to increase foreign trade, to expand their own exports, and, in a number of instances, to promote a strong national defense policy.

Labor Unions. A second important economic interest group is the American labor movement. This movement actively lobbies Congress and the executive branch on foreign policy issues. Its main interests are policy decisions that would affect the job security of its workers or would increase the amount of foreign imports. The labor movement recently has worked to protect American workers from importation of cheaper goods and the export of jobs by American multinational firms that seek cheaper labor markets abroad. As might be expected, such policy positions are often directly opposed to those of the business groups on both foreign and domestic policy questions.

The most prominent labor unions that have extensive lobbying efforts are the American Federation of Labor and Congress of Industrial Organizations (the AFL-CIO) and the United Auto Workers of America (UAW). In addition, within the AFL-CIO umbrella organization, there are over 100 separate affiliate unions that also lobby to protect their interests.[37] In the early 1990s, during the debate over the North American Free Trade Agreement, the AFL-CIO weighed in heavily in opposition to the pact, fearing the loss of jobs to cheaper labor in Mexico. Earlier, in the 1980s, the United Steelworkers of America actively sought to limit the importation of foreign steel from Japan and Europe as a way of protecting the jobs of American steelworkers. Over the years, unions and other interest groups have fought to pass restrictions in trade legislation to protect American jobs at home.

Although labor unions, like the major industrial concerns, are primarily interested in economic issues, they also have adopted positions on other foreign policy questions. Under the longtime leadership of George Meany, the AFL-CIO was particularly known for its staunch anti-Communist stances and for its effort to assist the global trade union movement, which would foster these positions.[38] Lane Kirkland, Meany's successor as president of the AFL-CIO, continued that policy. Today, the concern of the new AFL-CIO president, John Sweeney, has turned more domestic and has sought to rejuvenate labor unions at home among American ethnic groups and the young.[39]

Nonetheless, some foreign policy involvement by labor unions continues. The National Endowment for Democracy (NED) program initiated during the Reagan administration afforded the AFL-CIO a way to become more involved in the foreign policy process. As a result of legislation in

1983, the NED provided the AFL-CIO with funds to promote democracy in foreign countries. Such funds were to be used to set up seminars for foreign labor leaders, bring them to the United States, and assist them in promoting free and democratic institutions within their own countries.[40] Today, the American Institute of Free Labor Development (AIFLD), a joint enterprise with American business, is also a mechanism for promoting union development in poor countries and in affecting foreign policy. The AIFLD also receives considerable funding from the United States government's foreign assistance program and also provides covert assistance to friendly groups within developing countries.[41]

Agricultural Groups. Agricultural interests also attempt to influence the foreign policy process. The principal lobbying groups in this area are the American Farm Bureau Federation, the National Farmers Union, and the National Farm Organization.[42] While these organizations vary in the degree to which they believe that the federal government should intervene in the market economy, they all support efforts to increase the exports of farm products. Once again, while these organizations are primarily concerned with promoting agricultural interests, they also take stands on a variety of other foreign policy issues. The American Farm Bureau Federation at its 1996 national convention adopted foreign policy positions on international trade, agricultural exports, foreign aid, immigration, the United Nations, the World Bank, and the European Union, among other issues.[43]

Religious Organizations. Yet another set of readily identifiable interest groups intending to affect foreign policy are religious organizations. The most prominent among these groups are the National Council of Churches (various Protestant churches), the American Friends Service Committee (Quakers), and the National Conference of Catholic Bishops. Major religious groups, including the Methodists, the Unitarians, the Presbyterians, and the Baptists, have also been involved in foreign policy lobbying.[44] In addition, numerous affiliates of these different religious movements have engaged in lobbying efforts. By one estimate, there are over thirty different religious lobbies in Washington, D.C., alone.[45]

"Peace and justice" and "social concern" committees have been established by various religions as a better means of informing and involving their memberships in both foreign and domestic policy matters. Indirectly, too, these efforts assist the members of these religious faiths in petitioning their representatives, if they choose to do so. The American Friends Service Committee (AFSC), for example, has long been involved in group discussions of current international issues, in aiding the various conflicting parties in the Middle East and elsewhere, for instance, and has offered suggestions for a resolution of the conflict between the Palestinians and the Israelis.[46] Similarly, the May 1983 pastoral letter by the National Conference of Catholic Bishops on the possession and use of nuclear weapons, *The Challenge of Peace*, signaled a major illustration of foreign policy activism by that organization.[47] Various religious groups were also active in opposition to the Reagan administration's policy in El Salvador and Nicaragua, largely led by members of the Catholic Church.[48] Finally, the

Christian Coalition, led by Pat Robertson and Ralph Reed, has been a recent addition to these religious lobbying efforts and has had an impact on the foreign and domestic arenas.

Ethnic Groups. Ethnic groups are another gathering of important interests active in the foreign policy arena. Traditionally, the most active American ethnic groups have been those of Jewish, Irish, and East European heritage. Greeks, Hispanics, and African-Americans have also sought to influence American foreign policy.[49] With the end of the Cold War, ethnics with Central and Eastern European roots (e.g., Armenian-Americans, Czech-Americans, Slovak-Americans, Hungarian-Americans, among others) have revived their foreign policy activities.[50]

For all of these ethnic groups, the dominant theme of their participation in foreign affairs focuses usually on American policy toward the particular country or region of their ancestors' origin, rather than on general foreign policy questions. On policy issues related to Israel, Ireland, Cyprus, Central America, South Africa, and Central and Eastern Europe, these groups have been most active and have made their voices heard. Ethnic groups, as a whole, have often been identified as an especially important source of American foreign policy, and we shall have more to say about their influence later in this chapter.

Veterans Groups. Veterans groups or associations are also active in trying to influence the foreign policy of the United States. Such organizations as the Veterans of Foreign Wars, the American Legion, and the American Veterans of World War II are the best known of these groups.[51] Near the end of the Vietnam War, the Vietnam Veterans Against the War also entered the political arena, seeking at first to end American involvement and, later, to petition for better treatment of returning Vietnam veterans. More recently, veterans from the Persian Gulf War raised their collective voice for the American government to seek the origin of the "Gulf War syndrome," which has afflicted scores of military personnel returning from that war. Perhaps as an indication of how effective the veterans groups have been over the years, Congress established a separate cabinet department in 1988 to serve these interests.

Ideological Groups. Ideological groups have long been involved in American politics. Although these groups are often identified with questions of domestic politics, some are also active on foreign policy issues. The most prominent ideological groups are the Americans for Democratic Action (ADA), the principal liberal interest group in Washington politics, and the American Conservative Union (ACU), the principal conservative interest group in the nation's capital. Both of these groups evaluate members of Congress on foreign and domestic policy from their particular perspectives and issue yearly voting "scores" for all senators and representatives. These groups also actively work to make known their positions on major foreign policy issues.

Many other ideological groups from both ends of the political spectrum participate in foreign affairs issues. Over the years, those with a conservative viewpoint include the American Security Council, the John Birch Society, and the National Conservative Political Action Committee (NCPAC), while those with a liberal viewpoint include the Coalition for a New Foreign and Military Policy, the Women's International League for Peace and Freedom, the World Peace Through Law Association, the World Federalists, and the World Policy Institute.[52]

Think Tanks. Yet another category that might not be immediately identified as interest groups are the numerous "think tanks" that are located primarily in Washington.[53] These are organizations funded by individuals, corporations, and foundations that focus on analyzing a particular problem or array of problems to offer policy advice. These organizations share their results with the congressional and executive branches through testimony on Capitol Hill, through the publication of scholarly books and articles, and through opinion pieces appearing in several key elite newspapers, such as the *Christian Science Monitor*, *Los Angeles Times*, *New York Times*, *Wall Street Journal*, or *Washington Post*. In these various ways, they seek to influence policy and have been relatively successful: "More so than in any other country," one recent analysis reported, American think tanks "have played an influential role in foreign policy making," largely owing to the open nature of the American political system.[54]

The number of think tank groups is quite large and diverse, even if we were to consider only those devoted exclusively to foreign policy issues. These groups may be categorized in a variety of ways: ideologically (e.g., as liberal, moderate, or conservative in orientation) or chronologically (as the "Old Guard," think tanks, the "Cold War" contemporaries, and the new "partisan institutes").[55] While space precludes an exhaustive survey of these think tanks, a brief word or two about the major ones will illustrate the range and policy orientations of these organizations.

The best-known conservative think tanks in Washington are the Heritage Foundation and the Cato Institute. The Heritage Foundation analyzes both domestic and foreign policy issues from a relatively hard-line conservative position. Its views are disseminated through a quarterly magazine entitled *Policy Review* and through a myriad of reports on current topics. The Heritage Foundation gained prominence particularly during the Reagan administration. Several Reagan officials were drawn from its ranks, or they went there after serving in government. Its prominence continues today, as the foundation hosts periodic lectures by political candidates (e.g., presidential candidate, Pat Buchanan) or political activists (e.g., Ralph Reed, former executive director of the Christian Coalition). The Cato Institute is much newer than the Heritage Foundation, and it generally favors a libertarian view on policy matters, including foreign policy. This view translates into policy recommendations that promote a more isolationist or noninterventionist approach on the part of the United States in global affairs.

Somewhat in the middle politically are such institutions as the American Enterprise Institute (AEI) and the Center for Strategic and International Studies (CSIS). As its annual report states, AEI's goal is "preserving and improving the institutions of a free society—open and competitive private enterprise, limited and public-spirited government, strong and well-managed defense and foreign policies, and vital cultural and political values."[56] This think tank began as a strong conservative voice on foreign policy issues. While AEI has retained that characteristic on most foreign policy matters, it has also begun to broaden its political perspectives in recent years. CSIS began as an institute affiliated with Georgetown University and, while generally a conservative institute, it has moved toward more moderation in its outlook, too. Since 1987, it has operated independently and now has begun to attract some distinguished names to its staff, including Zbigniew Brzezinski and Henry Kissinger. Like AEI and most other think tanks, CSIS publishes a foreign policy journal, *The Washington Quarterly*, holds periodical seminars, and publishes various foreign policy materials.

The best-known liberal-leaning think tank is the Brookings Institution. Brookings has several divisions, with one devoted exclusively to foreign policy studies. Its policy recommendations are usually moderate or liberal in orientation, and it sometimes has been referred to as the "Democratic government in exile," since it has often been staffed by officials from Democratic administrations. Its seminars, publications—including a wide array of foreign policy books annually—and conferences are highly regarded among those of all political stripes. Along with the other think tanks, its policy recommendations are often relied upon for policy innovations on Capitol Hill and in the executive branch.

Finally, two other think tanks—one of the oldest and one of the newest—deserve brief mention. The Council on Foreign Relations arose after World War I, with an expressed anti-isolationist sentiment. Because membership was restricted to those elected to participate, it became a rather exclusive group that reviewed and commented on foreign policy issues.[57] It has remained so to this day. Over the years, too, the Council has sponsored numerous studies and book projects on foreign policy matters, continues to publish numerous books each year, and reviews published works throughout the foreign policy and international relations field. Perhaps its most important vehicle for exercising influence is its flagship journal, *Foreign Affairs*. Without question the leading journal in the field, it first published numerous influential foreign policy articles (e.g., George Kennan on containment in 1947, Richard Nixon on China in 1967), and those articles quickly became the basis for future policy actions. While it is theoretically open to a wide array of contributors, policy makers and former policy makers are often afforded a ready venue in this influential journal. For an academic publication, *Foreign Affairs* has an extraordinarily large circulation and is widely read and quoted in official Washington.

An example of the new kind of think tank emerging in Washington is the International Institute of Economics (IIE), an institute with exclusive focus on a changing global economy. It is "the exemplar of this brand of think tank. It is tightly focused on international economic policy. Its economic theory is avowed liberal in normative and methodological orientation."[58] IIE publishes a large number of monographs and books on a yearly basis. These publications are addressed to the academic and policy making community and are populated by people from government, academe, the press, corporations, and trade organizations. IIE is a ready resource for policy makers because of its physical proximity to the executive branch and Congress.

Single-Issue Groups. The single-issue interest group represents somewhat of a residual category for different kinds of groups that seek to influence foreign policy because of members' deeply held views on a particular policy question. These groups range widely, from the United Nations Association of the United States, which seeks to enhance support for the UN, to the Union of Concerned Scientists and the Arms Control Association, which back efforts to achieve arms limitations, to the Friends of the Earth or Greenpeace, which support efforts to preserve the global environment.[59] Moreover, these single-issue groups probably dwarf in size any other categories that we might identify, since they can form, lobby, and disband rather quickly. They also may be an amalgam of other interest groups that join together to lobby on a new issue on the political agenda at a particular moment in time.

Perhaps the leading illustration of a single-issue foreign policy group in the postwar period was the anti–Vietnam War movement of the 1960s and early 1970s. This group (really a coalition of groups such as the National Mobilization to End the War, the Moratorium Movement, the War Registers League, and even the radical wing of the Students for a Democratic Society, the Weathermen) was highly successful in rallying support among the American public and, eventually, in altering the course of American policy in Southeast Asia. At the height of the detente period in the early 1970s, too, other single-issue groups arose. Supporters and opponents of detente with the Soviet Union vigorously lobbied for their point of view with Congress and the executive.

In the 1970s and early 1980s, the most prominent single-issue foreign policy groups were those supporting and opposing the development of more nuclear weapons. In the late 1970s, the Committee on the Present Danger, composed primarily of conservative ex-government officials, was most active in opposition to the ratification of the SALT II treaty signed by President Jimmy Carter. The nuclear freeze movement—a broadly based coalition of individuals from various walks of life—that arose in opposition to the nuclear arms buildup by the Reagan administration called for the enactment of a mutual and verifiable freeze on the production and development of all nuclear weapons.[60]

By the mid-1980s, the largest set of single-issue groups united around the question of American policy in Central America. A decade-long debate developed over whether to provide or withhold aid to the Nicaraguan Contras in their fight against the Sandinista government. One study identified about 100 interest groups that were involved in lobbying Congress and the president on that issue.[61] Some were formed exclusively to address Central America; others had a larger policy agenda but were still very involved in this issue.

In the 1990s, the single issue of whether Congress should give its approval to the North American Free Trade Agreement (NAFTA)—establishing a free trade zone among the United States, Mexico, and Canada—

sparked interest group activity across the political spectrum. Table 11.1 portrays several of the different groups that participated in this debate to show the diversity of organizations active on the issue, and others have compiled more comprehensive listings.[62] U.S.A.-Nafta was the umbrella organization for over 2000 business groups supporting the agreement, while Citizen's Trade Campaign was the umbrella organization for a variety of opposition groups, including Ralph Nader's Public Citizen and other liberal groups. Yet, notice how labor unions and agricultural, environmental, and ideological groups lined up on opposite sides of this debate.[63]

Such divergent issues as immigration and Bosnia, too, have stimulated the development of issue-group activity in the 1990s, sometimes creating unusual temporary coalitions from more traditional lobbies. Over the question of immigration reform, for example, labor and business as well as conservative and liberal religious groups curiously turned out to be on the same side.[64] After the Dayton Accords—agreements that sought to bring peace to a troubled Bosnia and which called for sending American troops there—were signed, a diverse coalition called the "Committee for American Leadership in Bosnia" quickly formed and placed a full-page advertisement in the *New York Times* to support the sending of American military forces to implement the accord.[65] This coalition of liberal and conservative former government officials and foreign policy activists quickly (and temporarily) joined forces, illustrating anew the role of single-issue interest groups on a key foreign policy issue.

Foreign Lobbies. The newest recognized lobby group on foreign policy have been foreign lobbies. About 160 nations from every corner of the world, both large and small, are represented by lobbyists in Washington for their countries' interests.[66] In the main, the lobbyists for these nations are often American citizens who have been hired to explain their policies and to try to persuade Congress to give them more favorable treatment. Prominent examples are the lobbying efforts undertaken by South Africa, El Salvador, Saudi Arabia, and other Third World nations. Saudi Arabia, for instance, was particularly active in its lobbying efforts on the AWACS aircraft sale in 1981 and enlisted the support of several large American corporations to back its position.[67]

Perhaps the best-known and the most often maligned foreign lobby today is that of the Japanese. Over the years, Japan has hired numerous former members of Congress (e.g., James Jones [D-Oklahoma] and Michael Barnes [D-Maryland]) and former administrative officials (e.g., Eliot Richardson, former attorney general during the Nixon administration, and Stuart Eizenstat, former domestic policy aide to President Carter) to serve as its lobbyists and to attempt to influence Congress and the executive branch on American-Japanese relations, especially trade policy. In addition, Japan has hired some of the best-known public relations firms in Washington to get its message out. Both of these tactics have made its lobbying effort formidable, and often successful.

But Japanese lobbying has also done more than this. It has provided research money for several Washington think tanks, such as Brookings Institution, AEI, and the Center for Strategic and International Studies, to

TABLE 11.1

Interest Group Activity Over NAFTA in the 1990s

Groups That Supported NAFTA	Groups That Opposed NAFTA
U.S.A.-NAFTA	Citizens Trade Campaign
National Association of Manufacturers	AFL-CIO
American Automobile Manufacturers Association	United Auto Workers
U.S. Chamber of Commerce	Friends of the Earth
Natural Resources Defense Council	Public Citizen
American Farm Bureau Federation	United We Stand America
Empower America	Sierra Club
American Conservative Union	National Farmers Union

Sources: Keith Bradsher, "Last Call to Arms on the Trade Pact," *New York Times*, August 23, 1993, D1 and D3; Elizabeth Kolbert, "A Trade Pact Byproduct: $10 Million in TV Ads," *New York Times*, November 13, 1993, 10; Peter T. Kilborn, "Little Voices Roar in the Chorus of Trade-Pact Foes," *New York Times*, November 13, 1993, 10; and Box 12.2 in Stephen D. Cohen, Joel R. Paul, and Robert A. Blecker, *Fundamentals of U.S. Foreign Policy* (Boulder, CO: Westview Press, 1996), pp. 254–255.

support various studies, conferences, and academic chairs. While no direct Japanese benefit is specified from such think tank support, it does at least raise the question of whether independent analysis can be undertaken with such arrangements. A similar problem, albeit a less direct one, occurs over the funding of Japanese studies programs at various universities. By one estimate, "Japan funds about three-quarters of university research about Japan."[68] All of these efforts allow Japan access in Washington, and they make its lobbying effort powerful, although "the Japan lobby rarely wins battles on its own."

The newest set of foreign lobbying interest groups are those emerging from the republics of the former Soviet Union. These countries are rapidly hiring Washington law and lobbying firms to promote their interests in the nation's capital. By one assessment, Azerbaiijan, Belarus, Kazakhstan, Kirghizstan, Latvia, Moldova, Russia, Ukraine, and Uzbekistan have hired one or more firms to represent them. In fact, Russia and Russian firms had contracted with nine different law and consulting companies by late 1993.[69]

Importantly, too, China has developed a very large set of representatives to argue its case, especially on trade matters. High-priced and high-powered lawyers and former American government officials representing United States business concerns are opening doors to Chinese officials, while other firms and individuals are representing Chinese businesses in the United States. Representatives include former members of Congress (e.g., Howard Baker and Gary Hart) and former officials in the executive branch (e.g., Carla Hills, Lawrence Eagleburger, and Alexander Haig), among others.[70]

Their access to Chinese and American officials on behalf of the two countries' companies make for a very potent political force for maintaining most-favored-nation (MFN) trade status for China and for expanding American investment in, and trade with, China.

These kinds of activities, by Japan, Russia, China, and many other foreign countries, reflect the "internationalization" of lobbying efforts that has taken place today, and how lobbying, and even foreign lobbying, has become yet another part of the American foreign policy process.

THE IMPACT OF INTEREST GROUPS

How successful are these interest groups in affecting foreign policy? Unlike the president, Congress, and the foreign affairs bureaucracies that have direct control over policy, interest groups have at best only an indirect effect. By definition, interest groups do not control policy; rather, they seek to influence it. In this connection, most analysts suggest that, on the whole, these foreign policy groups do not do very well at that task. Several reasons are given for this view.[71] First of all, American foreign policy tends to be made more in the executive branch than in the congressional branch, as we noted in Chapter 7. Access by interest groups to the executive branch is more difficult than is access to Congress, with its varied committee and subcommittee structures. While interest groups do lobby the foreign affairs bureaucracies, their efforts may actually end up serving the bureaucracies' interests more than the lobbyist's.[72] Second, foreign policy issues and decisions are usually quite remote from the lives of Americans, and rallying support or opposition by interest groups poses a significant challenge.[73] Third, important foreign policy decisions are often made under crisis conditions—short decision time, high threat, or surprise in the executive branch. Under such conditions, foreign policy making is likely to be even more elitist than normal—more confined to a few members of the executive branch and more restricted in the amount of congressional participation. In such situations, avenues of influence for interest groups are further limited. Fourth—and perhaps most pivotal—with the magnitude of interest groups operating, it is likely that "countervailing" groups will arise to balance off the impact of a given interest group and, therefore, allow the policy makers more freedom of action.[74] Competing interest groups on NAFTA, as illustrated in Table 11.1, or competing interest groups on trade or immigration give members of Congress or the executive branch officials some latitude in making their own decisions on a foreign policy question.

Despite such difficulties, interest groups still do affect policy on some key issues. The principal areas appear to be issues involving American long-range policy toward the international system and on budget issues related to defense and foreign economic policy.[75] The former issues might be labeled "strategic" policy questions because they "specif[y] the goals and tactics of defense and foreign policy." Policy guidelines for actions directed toward a particular region (e.g., East Asia), country (e.g., Bosnia), or issue (e.g., nuclear nonproliferation) would qualify as strategic policies.

The latter issues might be labeled as "structural" policy questions because they focus on "procuring, deploying, and organizing military personnel and material...[and deciding] which countries will receive aid, what rules will govern immigration...."[76] Policy guidelines on the number of bases, the size and composition of the defense budget, and the distribution of foreign assistance would qualify as structural issues. The president often takes the lead on both policy questions (and especially the former ones), but congressional approval and fine-tuning of actions in both areas are almost always necessary. Since Congress allows more avenues of access by interest groups, they are likely to be more successful on these two kinds of issues.

Two types of interest groups appear to be particularly influential on foreign policy, especially within Congress. One is those economic groups that can be loosely identified as the "military-industrial complex," the other is ethnic groups.[77] The impact of the former set of groups is based upon the extensive access and involvement by numerous corporations over economic and defense issues that so often arise in Congress. The impact of the latter set of groups is based upon the interest that many Americans have in United States policy toward the country of their origin or toward a country with which they identify, e.g., Israel.[78] Let us examine both of these types of interest groups in a little more detail to give some sense of their relative influence today.

Economic Interest Groups

Our earlier discussion highlights the extraordinary number of economic interest groups seeking to influence foreign policy. These groups come from within the society, and now come from foreign countries as well. For an industrial capitalist economy, such as the United States, the existence of these groups should not be surprising. Yet, for several decades now, the close ties between these groups and the government have raised concerns over whether this linkage so dominates the foreign policy process that American society and American democracy suffer as a result. The most often cited constellation of economic interest groups affecting, or perhaps even dominating, American foreign policy is labeled "the military-industrial complex (MIC)." The origins of this label, and the theory underpinning it, deserve mention before we assess the degree of influence of the MIC on foreign policy.

The Theory of the Military-Industrial Complex (MIC)

First introduced into the American political lexicon by President Dwight Eisenhower, a decorated World War II general, as he was leaving office, the "military-industrial complex" refers to the presumed symbiotic relationship between the major industrial firms in the United States and the American defense establishment.[79] According to this theory, these industries become dependent upon the Department of Defense for military defense contracts and often apply pressure for a policy of strong military preparedness or even global military involvement as a means of continuing their economic well-being. More broadly, the phrase "military-industrial complex" has also been used to describe the informal ties that have developed among the top corporate sectors of American society and the political–military sectors of the American government.[80]

The first assumption underlying the military-industrial complex theory is that there is a unified elite within American society that dominates all important national and foreign policy decisions. This elite is held together by a set of interlocking structural relationships and by psychological and social constraints among the occupants of the key institutions.[81] In other words, the elites share similar educational and social backgrounds and frequently interact with one another.

The second assumption implicit in this theory is that this single elite's domination of policy making produces a distinct kind of American foreign policy, consistent with its interests. Such a policy emphasizes high military spending, interventionism abroad, and the protection of private property.[82] By pursuing these policies, the private interests of the military-industrial complex are safeguarded, especially in a world of ideological tension that existed during the Cold War.

Are these assumptions accurate? Does this political elite really exist? And is it successful in shaping policy consistent with the predictions of the theory of the MIC? With the end of the Cold War and the dramatic global transformations in the late 1990s, will the MIC's influence (to the extent that it exists) now wane, or will it gain influence anew as defense priorities change to meet newly identified threats and dangers in the international arena? Definitive answers to these questions are not easy to obtain, even though numerous researchers have sought to address them over the years. In our review of the available evidence, we believe that more of a case can be made for identifying the existence of a policy elite than for supporting the foreign policy consequences that are presumed to follow from the influence of that elite.

Evidence of a Single, Interlocking Elite. Analyses identifying the similar backgrounds of personnel in governmental offices and documenting the interactions between the military and the governmental sectors provide substantial support to the first assumption of the MIC theory. One of the earliest studies in this area reported that from 1944 to 1960, 60 percent of some 234 officials, mainly in the foreign affairs bureaucracies (Department of Defense, Department of State, the Central Intelligence Agency, etc.) came from important business, investment, and law firms. A relatively small number of these individuals (84) held over 63 percent of the positions. Thus, according to this research, a few key individuals dominated the foreign policy bureaucracies and circulated in and out of the government from the mid-1940s to 1960.[83]

More recently, political scientist Thomas Dye documented the background of key foreign policy officials throughout much of the post–World War II era and reached a similar conclusion about the extensive business ties of these policy makers.[84] Various secretaries of defense, for example, have had extensive links to large American corporations. Charles E. Wilson (1953–1957) was the president and a member of the board of directors for General Motors; Thomas Gates (1960–1961) was chairman of the board and chief executive officer of Morgan Guaranty Trust and also served on the boards of directors of General Electric, Bethlehem Steel, Scott Paper Company, and Insurance Company of America, among others; Robert S. McNamara (1961–1967) was president and a member of the board of directors of the Ford Motor Company; and Caspar Weinberger (1981–1987) was a vice president and a corporate director for Bechtel Corporation, a major global contractor, and served on the board of directors of such companies as Pepsico and Quaker Oats.

The same pattern has held true for secretaries of state. John Foster Dulles (1953–1959) was a partner of Sullivan and Cromwell, a prominent Wall Street law firm, and was on the boards of directors for the Bank of New York, Fifth Avenue Bank, the American Cotton Oil Company, and the United Railroad of St. Louis, among others; Dean Rusk (1961–1968) was a former president of the Rockefeller Foundation; and William P. Rogers (1969–1973) was a senior partner in Royal, Koegal, Rogers, and Wall, another prominent Wall Street law firm. Alexander Haig (1981–1982), for instance, not only served as military attaché to Henry Kissinger and as supreme allied commander of NATO, but he also served as an executive with United Technologies—a leading defense contractor. Before his appointment as secretary of state, George Shultz (1982–1989) was a high-ranking official with the Bechtel Corporation, and also had served on the boards of directors for the Borg-Warner Corporation, General Motors, and Stein, Roe, and Farnham, a Chicago-based investment advisory firm.

In the Bush administration, the patterns remained the same for several foreign policy members of the cabinet. Bush himself came from an old-line patrician family in Connecticut, and his secretary of state, James Baker, came from a background of the law and wealth. (Baker's father owned the Texas Commerce bank, a leading bank in that state.) Bush's national security advisor, Brent Scowcroft, was educated at West Point and Columbia University, worked for Kissinger and Associates, a private global consulting firm, and served as director of a Washington, D.C., bank prior to his appointment. The secretary of the treasury, Nicholas Brady, during that administration was a former head of Dillon, Read & Co., an important global investment banking firm, and served on the board of directors for Purolator Company, NCR, and Georgia International. Only Bush's secretary of defense, Dick Cheney (although he served a long time in Congress), and the chairman of the Joint Chiefs of Staff, Army General Colin Powell, did not have a strong business background.

Although Dye characterized the Clinton administration's top posts as largely "filled by lawyers, lobbyists, politicians, and bureaucrats,"[85] elements of a political and economic elite continued. While Clinton's own beginnings were modest, he was quickly taken under the wing of Senator J. William Fulbright, the influential chairman of the Senate Foreign Relations Committee, during his undergraduate days at Georgetown University in Washington, D.C. Fulbright's support and encouragement aided Clinton in obtaining a prestigious Rhodes scholarship to Oxford and afforded him the opportunity to develop contacts with many future leaders there.[86] As president, in fact, he appointed several colleagues from those days to key positions in his administration: Strobe Talbott as deputy secretary of state,

Ira Magaziner as his health care "guru" for a time, and Robert Reich as secretary of labor.[87]

Moreover, the top jobs went to professional politicians, steeped in the ways of Washington. Clinton's first secretary of state, Warren Christopher, had been the deputy secretary of state to Jimmy Carter (although he also came from a prestigious law firm in California), and his second secretary of state, Madeleine Albright, previously worked in the Carter administration and had served as American ambassador to the United Nations in the first Clinton term. His first national security advisor, Anthony Lake, was previously a foreign service officer in Vietnam, had worked on the National Security Council staff under Henry Kissinger, and was director of policy planning at the Department of State during the Carter administration,[88] and his second national security advisor, Samuel Berger, had worked at the State Department in the Carter administration. His first defense secretary, Les Aspin, was a long-time member of Congress and professional politician, and his second secretary of defense, William Perry, had worked in the Clinton administration, spent some time in academe, and had been a highly successful entrepreneur. His third secretary of defense, William Cohen, had served twenty-four years in Congress, the last eighteen in the Senate.

Four other aides, however, had prominent business credentials. Clinton's first chief of staff, and later a counselor to the president, Thomas McLarty, was an executive with a major natural gas company in Arkansas, and his secretary of energy, Hazel O'Leary, was an executive of a Minnesota utility company. Both of Clinton's secretaries of treasury had pronounced business ties: Lloyd Bentsen was a long-time United States senator from Texas who chaired the Finance Committee, but he also had extensive wealth and business holdings in Texas; and Robert Rubin was a Wall Street financier prior to assuming the position as deputy secretary of treasury and then the secretary position itself.[89]

Evidence for DOD/Defense Contractor Links. While this kind of study seems to identify some linkage between the business and political community and to suggest a circulating set of policy makers, other evidence provides support for the linkage between the military and major defense contractors, the other key component of this interlocking elite argument. In an analysis of the late 1980s and early 1990s, for example, the "revolving door" phenomenon between DOD personnel and defense contractors continued to operate as it had in the past.[90] In fiscal year 1987, 328 senior DOD officials and 3,199 DOD military officers who left government service went to work for defense contractors, and in fiscal year 1993, 145 senior DOD officials and 1,164 DOD military officers who left government service took positions with defense contractors.[91] While the 1987 totals and the 1993 totals represent only about 13 and 4 percent, respectively, of those who left government service among those ranks, the top military retirees—over half of the generals and admirals in 1988 and a quarter of the generals and admirals in 1994—took jobs with defense contractors. In other words, the highest-ranking military officers continued to find ready positions with the defense industry. Importantly, as this analysis noted, "the true number of crossovers is understated because the methodology for identifying the revolving-door population only captures persons whose employment with a defense contractor required a security clearance.[92]

Other analyses document the close working relationship between former DOD personnel, their new employers, and the Department of Defense in other ways. In a 1986 survey of former DOD personnel, for instance, the General Accounting Office (GAO) reported that 73 percent had defense contractor responsibilities while at DOD and 26 percent had similar responsibilities for defense contractors for whom they subsequently worked. About 82 percent of the former DOD personnel reported that they continued to have "work-related" communications with DOD officials after they had left their positions. While legislation now restricts some former DOD officials from being employed by certain defense contractors for two years after leaving government service and now requires governmental reporting on such hirings, recent studies indicate that these reporting requirements have not been very effective and that, because of several loopholes in the law, "the legislation limited few DOD personnel from obtaining post-DOD employment with defense contractors."[93]

This symbiotic relationship between the DOD officials and defense contractors gains even more credence in light of the various criminal charges that have been brought against lobbyists for defense contractors and in light of the large number of revelations about cost overruns and overcharging by defense contractors themselves. Several lobbyists have been charged and convicted of bribing DOD procurement officers to obtain lucrative contracts, for example, and major defense contractors (e.g., General Electric and the Electric Boat division of General Dynamics) have been accused of dramatic cost overruns. Still others have been accused of charging exorbitant prices for commonplace supplies to the military. By one analysis, "the military paid $511 for light bulbs that cost ninety cents, $640 for toilet seats that cost $12, $7600 for coffee makers, and $900 for a plastic cap to place under the leg of a navigator's stool" in an airplane.[94]

On balance, these analyses provide considerable evidence for the linkage among the business, military, and political community in American society. What they cannot answer directly, however, is whether these common backgrounds and ties produced policy primarily meeting the interests of these elites. Presumably, shared backgrounds would lead policy makers to take into account these economic groups in any foreign policy decisions or, at the very least, to allow ready access to key economic groups in order to make their case. Yet, more direct evidence on the second assumption of the MIC theory—the policy consequences of elite dominance—is needed to draw any firm conclusions about the role of the military industrial complex in foreign policy. Several studies have been undertaken to evaluate just such policy implications of the MIC theory.

Unfortunately, the evidence on the policy implications of the MIC theory is disparate, often focusing on various policy components and then attempting to draw larger inferences from those results. Further, these policy studies have more often pointed to differing conclusions about the MIC's effect than have the studies identifying close elite ties. On the one hand, some case analyses of particular foreign policy decisions provide strong support for the MIC theory, and the evidence on the awarding of military contracts to a select number of defense contractors does as well. On the other hand, other analyses of defense contracting raise doubts about the grip that the MIC has on American society and economy, and extensive studies of defense spending (and its effect) raise more general doubts about the theory's accuracy. On balance, these various studies point to a more mixed policy influence of the MIC than its proponents contend. To provide a flavor of the differing findings on the policy effects of the military industrial complex, let us summarize some of the recent evidence.

Analyses Supporting the Influence of the MIC. First, several case analyses of American foreign policy, ranging from the Marshall Plan of 1948 to the decision not to intervene in Indochina in 1954, to the decision to cut back the bombing in Vietnam in 1968, provide some support for the MIC. Berkowitz, Bock, and Fuccillo contend that "it would be difficult to point to a single decision that directly contravenes the interests of the business elite within the presidential court."[95] While they quickly add that the business elite may not have been successful on every decision, "when major issues are at stake, or when its interests are clearly and incontrovertibly involved,... the business elite proceeds with absolute unity of purpose and action."[96] Thus, they contend that the business elite view of foreign policy making provides the best explanation for America's actions abroad.

Second, the pattern of defense contracting is often used to demonstrate the policy influence of the military-industrial complex. The prime military contractors often turn out to be among the largest industrial corporations, and they are often the same ones year in and year out. In an analysis of the largest defense contractors for fiscal year 1995, for instance, we found that fifteen of the top fifty and twenty-three of the top 100 defense contractors were also ranked among the 100 largest corporations in America, based on the Fortune 500 list.[97] In fact these totals represent somewhat of a decline from our earlier analyses: For fiscal 1982 and fiscal 1988, this same comparison found forty and thirty-five, respectively, of the 100 largest corporations among the top 100 defense contractors in those years. At the same time, it is worth keeping in mind that the spending concentration remained high, with the top ten defense contractors in fiscal year 1995 obtaining over a third of the total contracts and the top twenty-five contractors getting 44 percent of the total DOD contracts.

Political scientist James Kurth has pointed out, moreover, that other evidence of concentration and continuity in defense contracting is available. That is, the defense contractors have largely remained the same over the last three decades—mainly the aircraft industries, and more recently the electronics industries; they have maintained their same ties with particular military branches (e.g., Boeing and Rockwell International with the Air Force contracts and Grumman primarily with the Navy); and they have maintained the same "product specialties"—particular kinds of weapons systems for each manufacturer.[98] The merger of Lockheed and Martin Marietta, two major defense contractors, only reinforces the degree of

TABLE II.2

Top 100 U.S. Defense Contractors and Their Corporate Sales Rank for FY 1995

Defense Contract Rank	Company	Corporate Sales Rank
1	Lockheed Martin Corporation	29
2	McDonnell Douglas Corporation	74
3	Tenneco Inc.	**
4	General Motors Corporation	1
5	Northrop Grumman Corporation	**
6	Raytheon Company	**
7	General Electric Company	7
8	Loral Corporation	**
9	The Boeing Company	40
10	United Technologies Corporation	30
11	General Dynamic Corporation	**
12	Litton Industries Inc.	**
13	Westinghouse Electric Corporation	**
14	Rockwell International Corporation	90
15	Textron Inc.	**
16	Science Applications Intl Corp.	**
17	TRW Inc.	**
18	Computer Sciences Corporation	**
19	ITT Industries Inc.	**
20	GTE Corporation	38
21	Fulcrum II Limited Partnership	**
22	Texas Instruments Incorporated	89
23	Tracor Inc.	**
24	AlliedSignal Inc.	73
25	FMC Corporation	**
26	Alliant Techsystems Inc.	**
27	Exxon Corporation	3
28	Olin Corporation	**
29	Dyncorp	**
30	Stewart & Stevenson Svcs Inc.	**
31	Black & Decker Corporation	**
32	International Business Machines	6
33	AT & T Corporation	5
34	Unisys Corporation	**
35	Carlyle Partners Leveraged Cap	**

continued on next page

TABLE II.2

Top 100 U.S. Defense Contractors (continued)

Defense Contract Rank	Company	Corporate Sales Rank
36	Boeing Skrsky Comanche Team JV	**
37	Mitre Corporation	**
38	Rolls-Royce PLC	**
39	MIT	**
40	Chrysler Corporation	9
41	United Defense LP	**
42	Logicon Inc.	**
43	Federal Express Corporation	**
44	Honeywell Inc.	**
45	OHM Corporation	**
46	Motorola Inc.	24
47	Halliburton Company	**
48	Harris Corporation	**
49	Johns Hopkins University	**
50	Draper Charles Stark Lab Inc.	**
51	Johnson Controls Inc.	**
52	UNC Incorporated	**
53	Bell Atlantic Corporation	**
54	Aerospace Corporation	83
55	NV Kon, Nederlandse Petroleum	**
56	Centex Corporation	**
57	United States Dept. Of Energy	**
58	CFM International Inc.	**
59	T I/Martin Javelin Joint Venture	**
60	Teledyne Inc.	**
61	Booz Allen & Hamilton Inc.	**
62	International Technology Corp.	60
63	Bechtel Group Inc.	**
64	Chevron Corporation	18
65	Salomon Inc.	**
66	Federal Prison Industries	**
67	Mesc Holdings, Inc.	**
68	Coastal Corporation	**
69	The Procter & Gamble Company	17
70	CSX Corporation	**
71	Worldcorp, Inc.	**

TABLE 11.2

Top 100 U.S. Defense Contractors (continued)

Defense Contract Rank	Company	Corporate Sales Rank
72	WMX Technologies Inc.	**
73	Xerox Corporation	41
74	Bay Tankers Inc.	**
75	Maersk Inc.	**
76	Sequa Corporation	**
77	Kaman Corporation	**
78	The Sverdrup Corporation	**
79	The Philip Morris Companies	10
80	CAE Inc.	**
81	Blake Construction Co., Inc.	**
82	RJR Nabisco Holdings Corp.	64
83	Government Technology Svcs Inc.	**
84	Nassco Holdings Inc.	**
85	Clark Enterprises Inc.	**
86	International Shipholding Corp.	**
87	Cubic Corporation	**
88	Esco Electronics Corporation	**
89	Gencorp Inc.	**
90	EG & G Inc.	**
91	M.A. Mortenson Companies	**
92	Atlantic Richfield Company	54
93	Oshkosh Truck Corporation	**
94	The Renco Group Inc.	**
95	Ogden Corporation	**
96	The General Electric Co. PLC	**
97	Arinc Incorporated	**
98	Nichols Research Corporation	**
99	Trinity Industries Inc.	**
100	Eaton Corporation	**

**Indicates companies that were not listed in the top 100 companies in corporate sales.

Sources: Defense contract rankings were taken from *100 Companies Receiving the Largest Dollar Volume of Prime Contract Awards Fiscal Year 1995* (Washington, DC: Department of Defense, Directorate for Information Operations and Reports, n.d.), while the corporate sales rankings for 1995 were taken from "The 500 Largest U.S. Industrial Corporations," *Fortune*, April 29, 1996, F-1 and F-3.

concentration in these areas. Such continuity provides additional evidence on how and why certain defense systems are purchased, and why some manufacturers are advantaged over others as well.

Analyses Challenging the Influence of the MIC. Other studies, however, raise doubts about the success of the military-industrial complex to shape and influence foreign policy, especially on defense spending. First, until the dramatic increase in military expenditures during the Reagan administration, defense spending, measured either as a percentage of the gross national product or as a percentage of the national budget, had actually declined over time. For the former measure, defense spending dropped below the 6 percent level, and, for the latter measure, defense spending fell to less than 25 percent. While defense expenditures edged up during the Reagan years to about 6.6 as a percent of the GNP for 1986 and constituted 28 percent of the federal budget (fiscal year 1987), both measures dropped significantly during the Bush and Clinton administrations. In the mid-1990s, defense expenditures were just over 4 percent of GNP and just under 19 percent of the federal budget.[99] Even with some projected increases as we approach the new century, the aggregate clout of the military-industrial complex on shaping defense spending has hardly been as pronounced as some imply.

Second, political scientist Bruce Russett, long a student of American defense expenditures, has cast doubt on the explanation for high defense budgets as attributable to the military-industrial complex only. Most assuredly, the military-industrial complex contributes to continued defense spending, but other factors in combination (such as domestic bureaucratic politics, technological momentum, and international actions) better explain the overall defense levels. Russett is quick to acknowledge, however, that domestic factors tend to have somewhat greater weight in this explanation than do international factors alone.[100] Furthermore, Hartley and Russett found "strong evidence...that public opinion...influence[d] government policy" on military spending from 1965 to 1990, although they acknowledged that the "exigencies of the arms race and the budget deficit were equally or more influential."[101]

Third, have American industries really been as dependent on defense spending for their prosperity as some imply or as the analyses focusing only on defense contractors suggest? In the aggregate, as reported in a classic study by sociologist Stanley Lieberson, few of the 100 largest industrial corporations in 1968 depended on military contracts for the bulk of their sales; in fact, 78 of the top 100 had less than 10 percent of their sales from military contracts, and only five corporations made more than 50 percent of their sales by military contracts.[102] In addition, Lieberson demonstrated that corporate income over time has been less dependent on military spending by the federal government than on nonmilitary spending. Finally, he shows that defense spending cutbacks would seriously harm only certain sectors of the economy (aircraft, ordinance, research and development, electronics, and nonferrous metals) rather than the economy as a whole. In short, while Lieberson does not deny the existence of the military-industrial complex, his evidence suggests that its dominance is less than others might contend.

Bruce Russett's work, to which we already referred, finds that profits in the defense industries are not systematically higher than those in nondefense industries, and the economy as a whole does not suffer dramatically with defense cutbacks. Instead, as with others, Russett sees the impact of defense spending tied to particular industries, and specifically to the aircraft industry.[103] Furthermore, he argues that military spending has not come at the expense of health and educational spending over the years 1941–1979. Only for the early part of the Reagan administration did military spending come directly from major cuts in health and education.[104]

Fourth, political scientist Steve Chan has carefully surveyed and analyzed myriad studies on the relationship between the economy and military spending.[105] These studies, too, produce mixed and inconsistent results on the positive or negative effect of military spending overall. Even with the likelihood of a peace dividend after the Cold War, the impact of defense cuts may be much less direct and immediate (if there is an effect at all) in increasing domestic welfare benefits or the "productivity gain" for American society than proponents of the MIC might project. On the one hand, several studies suggest that military spending actually serves both as an "economic prop" and as a "political prop" within the American setting. It is an economic prop because it provides jobs and cushions economic downturns, while it is a political prop because it changes according "to the rhythms of electoral cycles."[106] On the other hand, several alternative studies failed to find—or found limited—effects of defense spending on economic growth within the American economy. More generally, as Chan noted, "there is no direct, simple link between defense spending and macroeconomic performance."[107]

In sum, these various studies over the past several decades suggest two conclusions with important ramifications for the theory of the MIC: Neither the dependence of the American economy on high defense spending nor its substantial negative effects across the entire American economy is easily demonstrable. Instead, the military-industrial complex is a convergence of defense-oriented organizations that are constantly pursuing their interests. It has hardly been as successful as the common view that is advanced; defense spending has not been as dramatic as sometimes implied and its negative effect on the American economy may be less than is often assumed. Further, the MIC has met public resistance and interest-group opposition and appears to be continuing to face such challenges to this day.

To be sure, such assertions are not likely to end the debate over the relative influence of the military-industrial complex in policy making. This amalgam of interests may continue to be viewed as a powerful foreign policy interest group, even with the end of the Cold War and with calls for a domestic "peace dividend." In fact, the real test of these interest groups' influence may be yet to come. Can these interest groups continue to affect policy and achieve their goals in an environment of a seeming decline in defense needs and in an environment of budget deficits? If they can, then perhaps the argument about the relative impact of the MIC will become clear. If they cannot, those who took a more differentiated view of the power of this interest group may be more accurate.

What should not be lost in this discussion of the military-industrial complex is the continuing size and impact of these concentrations of interests. No matter what one's judgment is about the degree of control of the MIC, it is fair to conclude that the military-industrial sector seems to occupy a potentially important position in the shaping of foreign policy decisions, especially when compared to other interest groups. Moreover, the use of many high-tech weapons in the 1991 Persian Gulf War (e.g., bombs sent down air shafts into Iraqi storage facilities and the accuracy of the cruise missiles in attacking Baghdad), the rise of terrorist activity against Americans and American installations (whether in New York or in Saudi Arabia), and the increased use of United States peacekeepers around the world (e.g., Bosnia) may well have provided a resurgence in political clout for the military-industrial complex on Capitol Hill.

Ethnic Groups

The second major type of interest group that has enjoyed some success in influencing American foreign policy is comprised of ethnic groups. The leading ethnic lobbies today are probably the Jewish and Greek communities, two relative newcomers to the American political process. The Jewish lobby has been able to obtain a remarkable level of economic and military assistance for Israel over the postwar years (currently at $3 billion per year) and has been able to assist in steering American policy toward supporting that state since 1948. Only in the past decade or so has this strong support for Israel begun to wane a bit. In a more limited way, the Greek lobby has also enjoyed some success, especially in the middle 1970s.[108] It was able to garner sufficient congressional support to impose an American arms embargo on Turkey during the middle 1970s, despite active opposition by the executive branch.

By contrast, the influence of the older ethnic lobbies—those Americans of Irish and Eastern European heritage—has generally declined over the past forty years. The Irish lobby enjoyed its greatest success prior to World War II, while the East Europeans seemed most influential in the early Cold War years.[109] A new variant of the latter lobby, however, appears to be undergoing some resurgence recently. The Central and East European Coalition, formed in 1993, comprises sixteen American ethnic associations representing Armenian-Americans, Ukrainian-Americans, Czech-Americans, Slovak-Americans, Polish-Americans, Hungarian-Americans, Latvian-Americans, and a host of others. Members of this coalition seek to steer American policy toward the more rapid expansion of NATO, provide more aid to the former Soviet republics and the nations of Eastern Europe, and place less emphasis on the "Russian-centered path" chosen by the Clinton administration. Although these ethnics constitute only 8.5 percent of the total American population, they are concentrated in several midwestern states—with significant electoral votes in any hotly contested national election. As a result, both political parties have been wooing these ethnics heavily, including a series of set speeches by President Clinton and changes in the national security legislation in the Republicans' Contract with America to meet their concerns.[110]

Two newer American ethnic groups—Hispanics and African-Americans—are beginning to exercise some influence in the foreign policy process as well. TransAfrica, an organization to promote the interests of African-Americans, especially in Africa and the Caribbean, was formed only in 1977, but it has already had a noticeable effect on American foreign policy.[111] This group lobbied to keep economic sanctions on Rhodesia in the late 1970s in an effort to complete that country's movement toward majority rule and the creation of the nation of Zimbabwe. TransAfrica's influence was probably most pronounced in the effort to pressure the Reagan administration to move away from its policy of constructive engagement toward South Africa. In conjunction with the "Free South Africa Movement," TransAfrica played an important role in prodding the Reagan administration to apply economic sanctions in 1985 and then pushing Congress to override the Reagan veto of the Anti-Apartheid Act of 1986, a bill imposing more extensive sanctions than the 1985 measure. More recently, this organization and its leader, Randall Robinson, were pivotal in keeping the Haitian issue on the foreign policy agenda during 1993 and 1994 and in pushing the Clinton administration for stronger action against the military rulers in that country. In particular, the hunger strike by Robinson had an important symbolic effect on American policy makers at a time when Clinton policy toward the restoration of democracy in Haiti appeared to be faltering.

With the increasingly large percentage of Hispanics located in the South and Southwest, this ethnic group mainly focuses its attention on American policy toward Central and South America and toward such issues as immigration and refugees. So far, however, the Cuban American National Foundation (CANF) is the best-known and most successful of the Hispanic lobbying groups. Its strong anti-Castro message has impacted both political parties over the past several decades. While this lobby has generally been more influential on Republican administrations than Democratic ones, the Clinton administration, too, has heard its voice—whether it is in acting to halt appointments to the State Department, challenging efforts to cut funding for Radio Marti (the anti-Castro station in south Florida), or in responding to Cuba's shoot-down of two unarmed "Brothers to the Rescue" planes over international waters. Its principal legislative success recently was getting Congress to pass, and President Clinton to sign, the 1996 Helms-Burton Act, a bill imposing tougher economic sanctions against Cuba and companies that deal with the Castro regime. One member of Congress indirectly verified the foundation's influence by claiming that the lobby "uses difficult, difficult tactics whenever you disagree with them."[112]

Another sizable Hispanic group, the Mexican-American community, has been less successful and less prominent than CANF. Until its recent activism over anti-immigration legislation and NAFTA, this community had neither the same interest nor the same effect on national policy, either toward Mexico, Central America, or elsewhere, especially when compared to the Cuban-American community. Indeed, according to one analysis, on many issues regarding Central America, Mexican-American attitudes were not much different than those of the rest of the American public.[113]

Still, why have some of these ethnic groups been so successful and others less so? How can only some six million Jewish-Americans, slightly more than one million Greek-Americans, or less than one million Cuban-Americans excise influence in a nation of over 260 million citizens?[114] While we suggested some of the possible reasons earlier, a brief examination of perhaps the most successful ethnic lobby, the Jewish lobby, is particularly instructive in gaining some insight in how interest group influence can occur.

The Jewish Lobby: Sources of Its Influence. First of all, the Jewish lobby appears to be very well organized and directs its energies primarily toward foreign policy issues related to a single state, Israel. By one estimate, over seventy-five organizations exist that support Israel, and most are Jewish. Furthermore, these groups have two umbrella organizations to coordinate and guide their activities, the Conference of Presidents of Major American Jewish Organizations and the American-Israel Public Affairs Committee (AIPAC).[115]

AIPAC, in particular, is pivotal in lobbying by the Jewish community. It now has a yearly budget totaling $15 million, a membership of about 55,000 and offices in nine different American cities, including Washington, D.C., and has experienced considerable growth even since the mid-1980s.[116] It has a well-organized operation to facilitate maximum legislative and executive impact. "Action Alerts" are sent to key leaders throughout the country to stimulate response over some strategic issues,[117] and members are now directly linked through the Internet. These mechanisms enable members to learn about key issues under discussion in Congress, access sample letters for writing campaigns, and learn the names and addresses of members of Congress to contact. Indeed, AIPAC's activism has been pronounced, claiming involvement "in more than 2,000 legislative initiatives affecting U.S.-Israel relations," since the organization's founding in the early 1950s.[118] In fact, the lobby's comprehensive organizational structure appears crucial to its overall effort, in the estimate of one close observer: "The multitiered structural pyramid that links individual Jews in local communities across the country to centralized national foreign policy leadership groups in Washington and New York is the primary organizational factor that can explain the ability of the pro-Israel movement to mobilize rapidly and in a coordinated fashion on a national scale when important foreign policy issues arise."[119]

Second, AIPAC has particularly good access to Capitol Hill, although perhaps less access to the executive branch. It "is the envy of other lobbies for its easy access to the highest levels of government."[120] Through its frequent contacts with members of Congress and congressional staff and through its providing trips to Israel for new members of Congress,[121] AIPAC has been able to garner remarkable levels of support for some pro-Israeli legislation and has been able to stop legislation viewed as harmful to Israel. On the one hand, for instance, the lobby was able to gain some seventy-six co-sponsors in the Senate for the Jackson Amendment to the Trade Act of 1974. This legislation prohibited the granting of most-favored-nation

(MFN) status to any state that did not have a free emigration policy (see Chapter 8). It was clearly directed at the Soviet Union and its policy on Jewish emigration. A few years later, an identical number of senators coauthored a letter to President Ford urging him to stand behind Israel in any search for peace in the Middle East.[122]

On the other hand, the lobby has largely been able to alter or stop legislation that it did not support. Over the years, for instance, arms sales to Arab countries have been difficult to obtain in Congress. When such sales were approved, they often required modification, consistent with AIPAC's concerns. In 1987, for example, the Reagan administration had to change the composition of a proposed arms sale to Saudi Arabia to satisfy objections raised by Israel's supporters in the Senate. In 1988, Saudi Arabia completed a $30 billion arms deal with Britain, rather than incur the potential problems within Congress. At about the same time, a prospective arms deal with Kuwait was altered to address concerns raised by AIPAC.[123] Finally, and perhaps most indicative of the strong support that the Jewish lobby can generate, one study from the early 1970s found that Senate support for Israel averaged 84 percent and that such support existed across party lines.[124]

Yet a third reason for the success of the Jewish lobby is tied to the degree of sympathy for Israel among the American public, for differing reasons. The American public is often sympathetic toward Israel for moral and ethical reasons. It represents a people who have suffered greatly through history and who are believed to deserve a homeland of their own. American support is also tied to political motivation. Israel represents a democratic and Western-oriented state in a region of the world that does not seem to have many such examples.[125] In short, this latent public sympathy and support for Israel allows Jewish interest groups to obtain considerable overt support within Congress.

Equally important is the support for Israel that can be generated for domestic electoral reasons. Although the Jewish community is quite a small percentage of the nation's population (less than 3 percent), it is concentrated in some key states, especially along the East Coast and in California, Illinois, and Ohio.[126] As a consequence, its support can be pivotal in those areas in the success of any potential congressional or presidential candidate. Furthermore, while AIPAC does not make direct contributions to political campaigns, it has "close communications with the eighty-plus PACs [political action committees] that favor the Israeli cause. Its interlocking connections and directors with these PACs provide readily available funds when necessary."[127] Moreover, AIPAC's funding and support (or opposition) were crucial in key House and Senate campaigns in the 1980s.[128] For example, this organization was apparently instrumental in the defeat of incumbent Senators Jepsen (R-Iowa) and Percy (R-Illinois), who failed to support its position on some key votes. Finally, because the Jewish population has traditionally been quite active politically, there is even more incentive for potential presidents, senators, and representatives to be sympathetic to its view on the question of Israel.

A fourth reason deals with the relative weakness of the pro-Arab lobby, the counterpart of the pro-Israeli lobby. While the National Association of Arab Americans (NAAA) has increased its visibility and its activism since the Arab oil embargo of 1973–1974, it remains much less potent than the supporters of Israel.[129] The American-Arab Anti-Discrimination Committee, a more recent Arab lobby, has faced similar difficulties. As its leader, former Senator James Abourezk, indicated, his committee faces a formidable task of obtaining money and organization: "To have influence in Congress you have to have money for candidates or control a lot of votes. We're trying to build a grass-roots network; it's difficult for us to raise money."[130] Furthermore, these Arab lobbies have to contend with the impression they are more anti-Israel than pro-Arab. It is a charge they deny, but one that continues to plague them. In addition, the Arab lobby is often divided. After all, it represents a variety of different Arab states with differing political traditions in each and with considerable rivalries among one another. For these reasons, the pro-Arab lobbies do not yet serve as a good countervailing group to the influence of the Jewish lobby.

The Jewish Lobby: Questions About Its Influence. Although the Jewish lobby is usually identified as the most successful ethnic organization, its overall influence still remains a hotly debated issue. Especially with the changing events in the Middle East in the 1980s and 1990s, new questions have been raised about its impact. To some observers, the lobby remains far from omnipotent over American policy toward Israel or the Middle East in general, as illustrated by several recent setbacks and conflicts with Congress and the president and within its own organization.

Prior to the late 1970s and the Camp David Accords on the Middle East, the Jewish lobby had generally been able to forestall the supplying of military supplies to the Arab states and had been able to gain large military assistance for Israel from the American Congress. By 1978, however, success in these areas began to wane a bit, as the United States sought to pursue a more even-handed policy. The Jewish lobby was unable to stop the supply of United States fighter aircraft to Saudi Arabia and Egypt, despite strong lobbying efforts. More significantly, perhaps, the sale of AWACS and other technologically advanced aircraft equipment to Saudi Arabia in October 1981 was approved by Congress, despite strong AIPAC lobbying. Indeed, this defeat actually motivated the organization to double its efforts for the future, but it also suggested its limitations.[131]

American presidents and their administrations have challenged and criticized the Israeli government, despite possible opposition from the Jewish lobby. One former Carter administration aide put it this way: "The president can take a position that Israel opposes if the American people as a whole are behind him....Then the Jewish community will support him also. That happened with Ike [President Eisenhower] and the Sinai and it is still true."[132] Indeed, Presidents Carter and Reagan publicly opposed the expansion of Israeli settlements in the occupied territories and called for Israeli support of "land for peace" in the region as well. Reagan, too, pursued his own extensive lobbying effort to counteract AIPAC's over the sale of arms to Saudi Arabia in 1981. In 1990, President Bush held up $10 billion loan guarantees to the Israeli government over the settlement issues for a time, despite considerable political pressure to do otherwise. More recently, President Clinton and his administration did not alter their position in Middle

East peace negotiations, despite the victory of Benjamin Netanyahu in the 1996 Israeli election.

Finally, internal discord within the American Jewish community has also weakened the unity of its lobbying effort. After the massacres at the Palestinian camps of Shabra and Shatilla outside Beirut in September 1982, and the repressive response of the Israeli government to the *intifada*—the Palestinian uprisings in Israeli-occupied territories on the West Bank and the Gaza Strip beginning in 1987—fissures developed within the Jewish community and undoubtedly weakened the overall impact of this group in the American policy process.[133] As the peace process between Israel, its Arab neighbors, and the Palestinians evolved in the 1990s, additional divisions developed within the American Jewish community. In 1993, for example, the officers of AIPAC fired its long-time pragmatic director and moved the group's policy position toward a more hard-line stance on making concessions in peace negotiations in the Middle East. In effect, it moved AIPAC's position away from the Israeli Labor government of Yitzhak Rabin and closer to the opposition forces within Israel. This action divided the American Jewish community and AIPAC's relations with the Israel government at that time, and it hurt AIPAC's ties with some members of Congress.[134] In 1995, too, Israeli Prime Minister Rabin publicly criticized the American Jewish community for lobbying against policies of the Israeli government: "Never before have we witnessed an attempt by U.S. Jews to pressure Congress against the policies of a legitimate, democratically elected government."[135] Whether these fissures will remain with a new hard-line Israeli prime minister elected in 1996 remains an open question, but some divisions within the American Jewish community will likely linger.

Although evidence cited suggest that the Jewish lobby does not always succeed and may have some incipient organizational fissures, it also shows how an ethnic group may enter the foreign policy process, and, more specifically, how a well-organized and committed interest group can sometimes alter the direction of American foreign policy. Increasingly, interest groups, like political parties, are exercising an independent effect on United States foreign policy making.

Concluding Comments

Both political parties and interest groups are playing a more important role in foreign policy making today. Despite the American tradition of bipartisanship in foreign affairs, partisan differences have always been a characteristic of policy making. In recent decades, moreover, partisan (and ideological) differences on foreign policy questions have actually intensified and are likely to remain part of the American political landscape, especially as the United States confronts the dramatic changes of the twenty-first century. Interest groups, too, have become more pervasive in the foreign policy process. Both a greater number and a wider array of interest groups now participate in foreign affairs activities. While economic and ethnic groups remain particularly effective, foreign interests are increasingly seeking to influence policy as well.

In the next chapter, we complete our analysis of the policy-making process by examining the role of the media and public opinion in the foreign policy process. These two forces usually generate different reactions among casual observers. Because the media have grown so dramatically and intrude on so many aspects of American life, their influence, even on foreign affairs, is often taken for granted. The public, on the other hand, is at such a distance from where foreign policy decisions are made that considerable skepticism and questions often accompany a discussion of its role. In the next chapter, in examining the role of the media and public opinion, we seek to identify more fully their relative impact on the making of American foreign policy.

Notes

1. On the various definitions of political parties, see Frank J. Sorauf, *Party Politics in America* (Boston: Little, Brown and Company, 1984), pp. 6–28.
2. L. Harmon Ziegler and G. Wayne Peak, *Interest Groups in American Society*, 2nd ed. (Englewood Cliffs, NJ: Prentice-Hall, Inc., 1972), p. 3.
3. Herbert McClosky, Paul J. Hoffmann, and Rosemary O'Hara, "Issue Conflict and Consensus Among Party Leaders and Followers," *American Political Science Review* 14 (June 1960): 408–427.
4. The quote is taken from a speech by Senator Arthur H. Vandenberg to the Cleveland Foreign Affairs Forum. See John Felton, "The Man Who Showed Politicians the Water's Edge," *Congressional Quarterly Weekly Report*, February 18, 1989, 336.
5. For a history of bipartisanship and its various meanings, see Ellen C. Collier (ed.), *Bipartisanship and the Making of Foreign Policy: A Historical Survey* (Boulder, CO: Westview Press, 1991).
6. Cecil V. Crabb, Jr., *Bipartisan Foreign Policy* (Evanston, IL: Row, Peterson and Company, 1957), p. 5.
7. Robert Dahl, *Congress and Foreign Policy* (New York: Harcourt, Brace and Company, 1950), p. 229.
8. See the Republican party platform of 1952, which strongly attacks the Democrats, reprinted in Donald Bruce Johnson and Kirk H. Porter, *National Party Platforms, 1840*–1972 (Urbana: University of Illinois Press, 1973), pp. 497–500.
9. See the 1956 party platforms in ibid., pp. 524, 556; and the 1960 Republican platform, p. 606.
10. These trends have shifted lately, with the Democrats more associated with peace and the Republicans with prosperity. Public opinion data on these questions of war and peace and prosperity and recession from 1951–1984 were recently summarized in George Gallup, "GOP Edges Democrats in Poll on Prosperity Helm," *Des Moines Sunday Register*, April 29, 1984, 4A.
11. See McClosky, Hoffman and O'Hara, "Issue Conflict and Consensus Among Party Leaders and Followers," Table I, p. 410. At the same time, they do argue against the view that the two parties "hold the same views" on foreign policy (p. 417). Some differences are detectable.
12. Gerald Pomper, *Elections in America: Control and Influence in Democratic Politics* (New York: Dodd, Mead & Company, 1965), p. 194.
13. I. M. Destler, Leslie H. Gelb, and Anthony Lake, *Our Own Worst Enemy: The Unmaking of American Foreign Policy* (New York: Simon & Schuster, 1984), p. 17.
14. Ibid., pp. 60–61.
15. Crabb, *Bipartisan Foreign Policy*, p. 256.
16. This discussion and the following on military assistance, defense, and trade policy are drawn from the data and discussion in Barry Hughes, *The Domestic Context of Amer-*

ican Foreign Policy (San Francisco: W. H. Freeman and Company, 1975), pp. 130–144. On foreign aid voting, also see Barbara Hinckley, *Stability and Change in Congress*, 3rd ed. (New York: Harper and Row, 1983), p. 272.

17. Ibid. Also see Aage R. Clausen, *How Congressmen Decide: A Policy Focus* (New York: St. Martin's Press, 1973), pp. 192–212.
18. Destler, Gelb, and Lake, *Our Own Worst Enemy*, p. 61.
19. Zbigniew Brzezinski, "The Three Requirements for a Bipartisan Foreign Policy," in *The Washington Quarterly White Paper* (Washington, DC: Center for Strategic and International Studies, Georgetown University), pp. 14–15.
20. Leslie H. Gelb with Richard K. Betts, *The Irony of Vietnam: The System Worked* (Washington, DC: The Brookings Institution, 1979), p. 216.
21. "Congress Took 94 Roll-Call Votes on War 1966–1972," *Congress and the Nation, 1969*–1972, vol. III (Washington, DC: Congressional Quarterly Service, 1973), p. 944.
22. The figures were computed for these years by the author from the data provided in Pomper, *Elections in America*; and Gerald M. Pomper with Susan S. Lederman, *Elections in America: Control and Influence in Democratic Politics*, 2nd ed. (New York: Longman, 1980), p. 169. The former volume covered 1944–1964 party platforms, while the latter covered 1944–1976 ones.
23. One recent explanation has suggested that personal ideology more than any other factor (including party) may explain congressional voting in the post-Vietnam period. See, for example, Robert A. Bernstein and William W. Anthony, "The ABM Issue in the Senate, 1968–1970: The Importance of Ideology," *The American Political Science Review*, 65 (September 1974): 1198–1206; Wayne Moyer, "House Voting on Defense: An Ideological Explanation," in Bruce M. Russett and Alfred Stepan, eds., *Military Force and American Society* (NewYork: Harper and Row, 1973), pp. 106–141; and James M. McCormick and Michael Black, "Ideology and Senate Voting on the Panama Canal Treaties," *Legislative Studies Quarterly* 8 (February 1983): 4563.
24. See, for example, "House Votes to Aid El Salvador, Denies Nicaragua's Rebels," *Des Moines Register*, May 25, 1984, 1A, 20A; and "House Curb's MX, Votes $284 Billion to Military," *Des Moines Register*, June 1, 1984, 1A, 12A. For a systematic analysis of partisan differences in congressional voting on the MX, B-1, and SDI in the 1970s and 1980s, see James M. Lindsay, "Parochialism, Policy, and Constituency Constraints: Congressional Voting on Strategic Weapons, Systems," *American Journal of Political Science* 34 (November 1990): 936–960.
25. The following sections draw upon these pieces of research by James M. McCormick and Eugene R. Wittkopf: "Bush and Bipartisanship: The Past as Prologue?" *Washington Quarterly* 13 (Winter 1990): 5–16; "Bipartisanship, Partisanship, and Ideology in Congressional–Executive Foreign Policy Relations, 1947–1988," *Journal of Politics* 52 (November 1990): 1077–1100; and "At the Water's Edge: The Effects of Party, Ideology and Issues on Congressional Foreign Policy Voting, 1947–1988," *American Politics Quarterly* 20 (January 1992): 26–53.
26. McCormick and Wittkopf, "Bipartisanship, Partisanship, and Ideology in Congressional–Executive Foreign Policy Relations, 1947–1988," p. 1097. For an alternate view on the impact of Vietnam, see James Meernik, "Presidential Support in Congress: Conflict and Consensus on Foreign and Defense Policy," *Journal of Politics* 55 (August 1993): 569–587.
27. See the Statement by the president, "President's Commission on Strategic Forces, *Weekly Compilation of Presidential Documents* 19 (January 10, 1983): 3; and see "Summary of Kissinger Commission Report," *Congressional Quarterly Weekly Report*, January 14, 1984, 64–66, on these commissions.
28. "Excerpts From President Reagan's Speech on Foreign Policy and Congress," *New York Times*, April 7, 1984, 5.
29. These passages are taken from the inaugural address by President Bush, January 20, 1989.
30. The data and discussion on the Bush and Clinton administrations are based upon the work by the author with Eugene R. Wittkopf and David M. Danna. See our "Politics and Bipartisanship at the Water's Edge: A Note on Bush and Clinton," *Polity* 30 (Fall 1997, forthcoming). The figures are taken from that work.

31. "Remarks by the President to the Nixon Center for Peace and Freedom Policy Conference," Washington, DC, March 1, 1995, obtained via the Internet.
32. Michael Mandelbaum, "Foreign Policy as Social Work." *Foreign Affairs* 75 (January/February 1996): 26.
33. Jeremy D. Rosner, *The New Tug-of-War: Congress, the Executive Branch, and National Security* (Washington, DC: A Carnegie Endowment Book, 1995), pp. 2–3.
34. Arthur C. Close, J. Valerie Steele, and Michael E. Buckner, eds., *Washington Representatives 1995*, 19th ed. (Washington, DC: Columbia Books, Inc., 1995), p. 2.
35. Count done by author from ibid., pp. 877–886. It should be noted not all of these government groups necessarily are engaged in foreign policy lobbying efforts, although many are.
36. Norman J. Ornstein and Shirley Elder, *Interest Groups, Lobbying and Policymaking* (Washington, DC: Congressional Quarterly Press, 1978), pp. 35–39. The discussion in this paragraph also draws upon the list of organizations in Thomas L. Brewer, *American Foreign Policy: A Contemporary Introduction* (Englewood Cliffs, NJ: Prentice-Hall, Inc., 1980), p. 85; and upon Hughes, *The Domestic Context of American Foreign Policy*, pp. 157–171, for the foreign policy goals of business, labor, and farm groups.
37. Ornstein and Elder, *Interest Groups, Lobbying, and Policymaking*, p. 24.
38. For an overview of the foreign policy of the labor movement, and especially the AFL-CIO, see Carl Gershman, *The Foreign Policy of American Labor, The Washington Papers*, vol. 3, no. 29 (Beverly Hills: Sage Publications, 1975).
39. "It's Hip to Be Union," *Newsweek*, July 8, 1996, 44–45.
40. "Program to Promote Democracy Passed...After Deleting Funds for Two Parties," *Congressional Quarterly Almanac 1983* (Washington, DC: Congressional Quarterly, Inc., 1984), pp. 148–149.
41. See Pat M. Holt, *Secret Intelligence and Public Policy* (Washington, DC: CQ Press, 1995), p. 146.
42. Hughes, *The Domestic Context of American Foreign Policy*, pp. 168–171.
43. See *Farm Bureau Policies for 1996*. Resolutions on National Issues Adopted by Elected Voting Delegates of the Member State Farm Bureaus to the 77th Annual Meeting of the American Farm Bureau Federation (Reno, Nevada, January 1996).
44. *The Washington Lobby*, 4th ed. (Washington, DC: Congressional Quarterly, Inc., 1982), pp. 150–151, includes a list of the religious groups active over United States policy toward El Salvador.
45. Close et al., *Washington Representatives 1995*, p. 6.
46. See, for instance, any of the myriad publications from the American Friends Service Committee. A notable book on the Middle East conflict is *Search for Peace in the Middle East*, rev. ed. (Greenwich, CT: Fawcett Publications, Inc., 1970).
47. See *The Challenge of Peace: God's Promise and Our Response* (Washington, DC: United States Catholic Conference, May 3, 1983).
48. *The Washington Lobby*, pp. 152–153.
49. For an excellent overview of the key American ethnic groups and their role in foreign policy, see Charles McC. Mathias, Jr., "Ethnic Groups and Foreign Policy," *Foreign Affairs* 59 (Summer 1981): 975–998. Also see Abdul Aziz Said, *Ethnicity and U.S. Foreign Policy*, rev. ed. (New York: Praeger, 1981).
50. Dick Kirschten, "Ethnics Resurging," *National Journal*, February 25, 1995, 484–486.
51. Hughes, *The Domestic Context of American Foreign Policy*, pp. 171–174.
52. For a discussion of the development of the conservative movement and its foreign policy goals, see Richard A. Viguerie, *The New Right: We're Ready to Lead* (Falls Church, VA: The Viguerie Company, 1981); for a listing of other liberal and conservative interest groups as well as other types, see Brewer, *American Foreign Policy*, pp. 85–86; and for a listing of recent ratings of members of Congress for some of these groups, see J. Michael Sharp (ed.), *Directory of Congressional Voting Scores and Interest Group Ratings*, vols. 1 and 2 (Washington, DC: Congressional Quarterly, Inc., 1997). Also see this source for the discussion of ADA and ACU upon which we draw (pp. ix–x).

53. This section draws upon the following sources: Close et al., *Washington Representatives 1990*, pp. 480, 513, 517, 518, and 520; the *1988–1989 Annual Report of the American Enterprise Institute for Public Policy Research* (Washington, DC: American Enterprise Institute, 1989); and Howard J. Wiarda, *Foreign Policy Without Illusion* (Glenview, IL: Scott, Foresman/Little, Brown Higher Education, 1990), pp. 162–168.
54. Richard Higgott and Diane Stone, "The Limits of Influence: Foreign Policy Think Tanks in Britain and the USA," *Review of International Studies* 20 (January 1994): 32.
55. Ibid., pp. 15–34.
56. *1988–1989 Annual Report of the American Enterprise Institute for Public Policy Research*, p. 1.
57. Higgott and Stone, "The Limits of Influence: Foreign Policy Think Tanks in Britain and the USA," pp. 18–19.
58. Ibid., pp. 23–24. The rest of the paragraph draws on this source, too.
59. For a compilation of different categories of foreign policy interest groups (partly upon which we draw in our discussion), see Brewer, *American Foreign Policy: A Contemporary Introduction*, pp. 85–86.
60. Indeed, the freeze movement was very broadly based, in terms of both the kinds of groups and the individuals who participated in it. See Fox Butterfield, "Anatomy of the Nuclear Protest," *New York Times Magazine*, July 11, 1982, 14–17ff, for a discussion of the nature of this movement. For more recent assessments of the nuclear freeze, see Pam Solo, *From Protest to Policy: The Origins and Future of the Freeze Movement* (Cambridge, MA: Ballinger Publishing, 1988); and Douglas C. Waller, *Congress and the Nuclear Freeze: An Inside Look at the Politics of a Mass Movement* (Amherst: University of Massachusetts Press, 1987).
61. See Cynthia J. Arnson and Philip Brenner, "The Limits of Lobbying: Interest Groups, Congress and Aid to the Contras," paper prepared for presentation at a conference on Public Opinion and Policy Toward Central America, Princeton University, May 4–5, 1990.
62. See Box 12.2 in Stephen D. Cohen, Joel R. Paul, and Robert A. Blecker, *Fundamentals of U.S. Foreign Policy* (Boulder, CO: Westview Press, 1996) at pp. 254–255.
63. See Keith Bradsher, "Last Call to Arms on the Trade Pact," *New York Times*, August 23, 1993, D1 and D3; Elizabeth Kolbert, "A Trade Pact Byproduct: $10 Million in TV Ads," *New York Times*, November 13, 1993, 10; and Peter T. Kilborn, "Little Voices Roar in the Chorus of Trade-Pact Foes," *New York Times*, November 13, 1993, 10.
64. Roy Beck, "The Pro-Immigration Lobby" *New York Times*, April 30, 1996, A11.
65. See *New York Times*, December 7, 1995, A11.
66. The total was calculated by the author from the listing in Close et al., *Washington Representatives 1995*, pp. 967–980.
67. "How U.S. Firms Lobbied for AWACS on Saudi Orders," *Des Moines Sunday Register*, March 14, 1982, 1C.
68. The section on Japanese lobbying is based on John B. Judis, "The Japanese Megaphone," *The New Republic*, January 22, 1990, 20–25. The quoted passages are at p. 22 and p. 24. For a more comprehensive and critical treatment of the lobbying efforts by Japan, see Pat Choate, *Agents of Influence* (New York: Alfred A. Knopf, 1990).
69. See the listing of countries and firms in Dick Kirschten, "Greetings, Comrades!" *National Journal*, October 2, 1993, at p. 2191.
70. Peter H. Stone, "China Connections," *National Journal*, March 26, 1994, pp. 708–712.
71. The most succinct argument for this limited influence of interest groups is in Hughes, *The Domestic Context of American Foreign Policy*, pp. 198–202, from which part of this argument is drawn. Also see, however, Bernard Cohen, *The Public's Impact on Foreign Policy* (Boston: Little, Brown and Company, 1973); and Robert H. Trice, "Domestic Interest Groups and the Arab-Israeli Conflict: A Behavioral Analysis," in Abdul Aziz Said, *Ethnicity and U.S. Foreign Policy*, pp. 128–129, on the problem of gaining access to Congress and the executive on some types of issues.

72. See Cohen, *The Public's Impact on Foreign Policy*, pp. 100–103, and his discussion of how interest groups can be used by the executive branch.
73. On this point, see Eric M. Uslaner, "All Politics Are Global: Interest Groups and the Making of Foreign Policy," in Allan J. Cigler and Burdett A. Loomis, *Interest Group Politics*, 4th ed. (Washington, DC: CQ Press, 1995), p. 370.
74. Brewer, *American Foreign Policy: A Contemporary Introduction*, p. 89.
75. On those points, see Hughes, *The Domestic Context of American Foreign Policy*, pp. 200–201, especially Table 7.1.
76. James M. Lindsay and Randall B. Ripley, "How Congress Influences Foreign and Defense Policy," in Randall B. Ripley and James M. Lindsay, eds., *Congress Resurgent: Foreign and Defense Policy on Capitol Hill* (Ann Arbor: The University of Michigan Press, 1993), p. 19.
77. Cohen, *The Public's Impact on Foreign Policy*, p. 96, asserts that economic and ethnic groups appear most prominently, although his analysis is based primarily on interviews with the executive branch.
78. For some reasons for the strength of ethnic influence, see Mathias, "Ethnic Groups and Foreign Policy," pp. 980–981, 996.
79. See Dwight D. Eisenhower, "The Military-Industrial Complex," in Richard Gillam, ed., *Power in Postwar America* (Boston: Little, Brown, 1971), p. 158. Emphasis added.
80. See C. Wright Mills, *The Power Elite* (New York: Oxford University Press, 1956); and Gabriel Kolko, *The Roots of American Foreign Policy* (Boston: Beacon Press, 1969).
81. For a good summary presentation of this argument, see Marc Pilisuk, with the assistance of Mehrene Larudee, *International Conflict and Social Policy* (Englewood Cliffs, NJ: Prentice-Hall, Inc., 1972), pp. 108–141.
82. Ibid., pp. 113–132, especially p. 129.
83. Kolko, *The Roots of American Foreign Policy*, pp. 17–23.
84. The following data on the key foreign officials are from Thomas R. Dye, *Who's Running America? Institutional Leadership in the United States* (Englewood Cliffs, NJ: Prentice-Hall, Inc., 1976), pp. 56–58; and from *Who's Running America? The Bush Era*, 5th ed. (Englewood Cliffs, NJ: Prentice-Hall, Inc., 1990), pp. 89–105. The dates of service for some individuals have been corrected from what Dye reports. For a complete description of the background of Reagan administration appointees, see the national security section of Ronald Brownstein and Nina Easton, *Reagan's Ruling Class* (Washington, DC: The Presidential Accountability Group, 1982).
85. Thomas R. Dye, *Who's Running America? The Clinton Years,* 6th ed. (Englewood Cliffs, NJ: Prentice-Hall, 1995), p. 84.
86. Ibid., p. 70–71.
87. Ibid., p. 93.
88. Ibid., pp. 89–90.
89. Ibid., pp. 84, 87, 90–91.
90. See William Proxmire, "The Community of Interests in Our Defense Contract Spending," in Richard Gilliam, ed., *Power in Postwar America.*
91. These data are taken from, and in one instance recalculated from, Mark J. Eitelberg and Roger D. Little, "Influential Elites and the American Military After the Cold War," in Don M. Snider and Miranda A. Carlton-Carew, eds., *U.S. Civil-Military Relations: In Crisis or Transition?* (Washington, DC: The Center for Strategic and International Studies, 1995), pp. 47 and p. 48 (Table 3.1).
92. Ibid., p. 47.
93. The sources for this paragraph are the following General Accounting Office Reports: "DOD Revolving Door: Relationships Between Work at DOD and Post-DOD Employment," July 1986; "DOD Revolving Door: Processes Have Improved but Post-DOD Employment Reporting Still Low," September 1989; and "DOD Revolving Door: Few Are Restricted From Post-DOD Employment and Reporting Has Some Gaps," February 1990. The quoted passage is from the last cited report at p. 2.

94. Michael Parenti, *Democracy for the Few*, 5th ed. (New York: St. Martin's Press, 1988), p. 88.

95. Morton Berkowitz, P. G. Bock, and Vincent J. Fuccillo, *The Politics of American Foreign Policy* (Englewood Cliffs, NJ: Prentice-Hall, Inc., 1977), p. 289.

96. Ibid.

97. These statistics were calculated from the list of the top 100 defense contractors for fiscal year 1995 and from "The Fortune 500 Largest U.S. Industrial Corporations," *Fortune* (April 29, 1996): F-1 and F-3. The statistics for fiscal year 1982 and fiscal year 1988 are taken from earlier editions of this book.

98. For the information on the continuity and concentration in defense contracting, see James R. Kurth, "The Military-Industrial Complex Revisited," in Joseph Kruzel, ed., *1989–1990 American Defense Annual* (Lexington, MA: Lexington Books, 1989), pp. 195–215, especially pp. 196–199. The "product specialties" notion is his at p. 198.

99. The data in this paragraph come from U.S. Bureau of the Census, *Statistical Abstract of the United States: 1995*, 115th ed. (Washington, DC, 1995), p. 336; U.S. Arms Control and Disarmament Agency, *World Military Expenditures and Arms Transfers 1985* (Washington, DC: U.S. Government Printing Office, April 1985), p. 99.

100. Bruce Russett, *The Prisoners of Insecurity* (San Francisco: W. H. Freeman and Company, 1983), pp. 77–96.

101. Thomas Hartley and Bruce Russett, "Public Opinion and the Common Defense: Who Governs Military Spending in the United States?" *American Political Science Review* 86 (December 1992): 905–915. The quote is at pp. 911–912. This study is cited in Steve Chan, "Grasping the Peace Dividend: Some Propositions on the Conversion of Swords into Plowshares," *Mershon International Studies Review* 39 (April 1995): 58, and which directed me to it.

102. Stanley Lieberson, "An Empirical Study of Military-Industrial Linkages," *American Journal of Sociology* 76 (January 1971), especially pp. 568–572, 575–581.

103. Russett, *The Prisoners of Insecurity*, pp. 77–96.

104. Bruce Russett, "Defense Expenditures and National Well-Being," *The American Political Science Review* 76 (December 1982): 767–777.

105. Ibid., pp. 53–95. The quoted phrase is Chan's.

106. Ibid., p. 62. As Chan discusses, there are empirical studies on both sides of these contentions, but he specifically challenges the notion that there is evidence for "a powerful military-industrial complex" to sustain high military expenditures (p. 63).

107. Ibid., p. 68. Chan's conclusion here is drawn from a study by Stephen J. Majeski, "Defense Spending, Fiscal Policy, and Economic Performance," in Alex Mintz (ed.,), *The Political Economy of Military Spending in the United States* (London: Routledge, 1992), pp. 217–237. Majeski's general conclusion is at p. 231. Other studies showing different results are included in the Chan analysis, but most of the evidence seems to point in the direction of the findings reported here.

108. For a study that judges the Greek lobby second behind the Jewish lobby in influence, see Mathias, "Ethnic Groups and Foreign Policy," p. 990. Also see, Morton Kondracke, "The Greek Lobby," *The New Republic*, April 29, 1978, 14–16. For two studies that raise doubts about the importance of the Greek lobby over the Turkish arms embargo issue, see Clifford Hackett, "Ethnic Politics in Congress: The Turkish Embargo Experience"; and Sallie M. Hicks and Theodore A. Couloumbis, "The 'Greek Lobby': Illusion or Reality?" in Abdul Aziz Said, ed., *Ethnicity and U.S. Foreign Policy*, pp. 33–96.

109. Mathias, "Ethnic Groups and Foreign Policy," pp. 982–987.

110. Kirschten, "Ethnics Resurging," pp. 484–486 with the quoted passage at p. 486.

111. Robert W. Walters, "African-American Influence on U.S. Foreign Policy Toward South Africa," in Mohammed E. Ahrari, ed., *Ethnic Groups and U.S. Foreign Policy* (New York: Greenwood Press, 1987), pp. 65–82.

112. Dick Kirschten, "From the K Street Corridor," *National Journal*, July 17, 1993, 1815.

113. See Damian J. Fernandez, "From Little Havana to Washington, DC: Cuban-Americans and U.S. Foreign Policy," and Rodolfo O. de la Garza, "U.S. Foreign Policy and the

Mexican-American Political Agenda," in Mohammed E. Ahrari, ed., *Ethnic Groups and U.S. Foreign Policy* (New York: Greenwood Press, 1987), pp. 115–134 and 101–114, respectively.

114. Estimates for these groups vary, of course. These data are taken from tables in U.S. Bureau of the Census, *Statistical Abstract of the United States: 1995*, 115th ed. (Washington, DC, 1995), at pp. 14, 53, and 69.

115. See Trice, "Domestic Interest Groups and the Arab-Israeli Conflict: A Behavioral Analysis," pp. 121 and 122.

116. Paul Findley, *Deliberate Deceptions: Facing the Facts about U.S.-Israeli Relationship* (New York: Lawrence Hill Books, 1995), p. 95; Peter Beinart and Hanna Rosin, "Aipac Unpacked," *The New Republic* (September 20 & 27, 1993), p. 22; Hedrick Smith, *The Power Game* (New York: Ballantine Books, 1988), p. 216; and information on AIPAC from the World Wide Web under http://www.aipac.org/.

117. George W. Ball and Douglas B. Ball, *The Passionate Attachment* (New York: W. W. Norton and Company, 1992), p. 209.

118. Ibid.

119. Trice, "Domestic Interest Groups and the Arab-Israeli Conflict: A Behavioral Analysis," p. 126.

120. Findley, *Deliberate Deception*, p. 95.

121. Jacob Weisberg, "The Lobby With a Lock on Congress," *Newsweek*, October 19, 1987, 46.

122. *The Middle East: U.S. Policy, Israel, Oil and the Arabs*, 3rd ed. (Washington, DC: Congressional Quarterly, 1977), p. 96.

123. Harry Anderson, "Forced into British Arms," *Newsweek*, July 25, 1988, 47.

124. Robert H. Trice, "Congress and the Arab-Israeli Conflict: Support for Israel in the U.S. Senate, 1970–1973," *Political Science Quarterly* 92 (Fall 1977): 443–463.

125. Some of these reasons are discussed and indirectly tested in ibid.

126. Ibid., p. 457.

127. Ball and Ball, *The Passionate Attachment*, p. 209.

128. Smith, *The Power Game*, pp. 228–229.

129. *The Middle East: U.S. Policy, Israel, Oil and the Arabs*, pp. 102–108.

130. Christopher Madison, "Arab-American Lobby Fights Rearguard Battle to Influence U.S. Mideast Policy," *National Journal*, August 31, 1985, 1936.

131. Ball and Ball, *The Passionate Attachment*, pp. 213–215, and Smith, *The Power Game*, pp. 218–221.

132. Quoted in Charlotte Saikowski, "America's Israeli Aid Budget Grows," *Christian Science Monitor*, November 30, 1983, 5. The reference is to President Eisenhower's decision to stand firm against Israel after it invaded the Sinai Peninsula and to demand its immediate withdrawal, despite a pending election.

133. For a discussion of some of the dilemmas that the Jewish community faces in its advocacy of American policy in the Middle East, see Stephen S. Rosenfeld, "Dateline Washington: Anti-Semitism and U.S. Foreign Policy," *Foreign Policy* 47 (Summer 1982): 172–183.

134. Beinart and Rosin, "AIPAC Unpacked," pp. 20–23.

135. Alison Mitchell, "Rabin Rebukes Jews in U.S. Who Lobbied Against Pact," *New York Times*, September 30, 1995, 1.

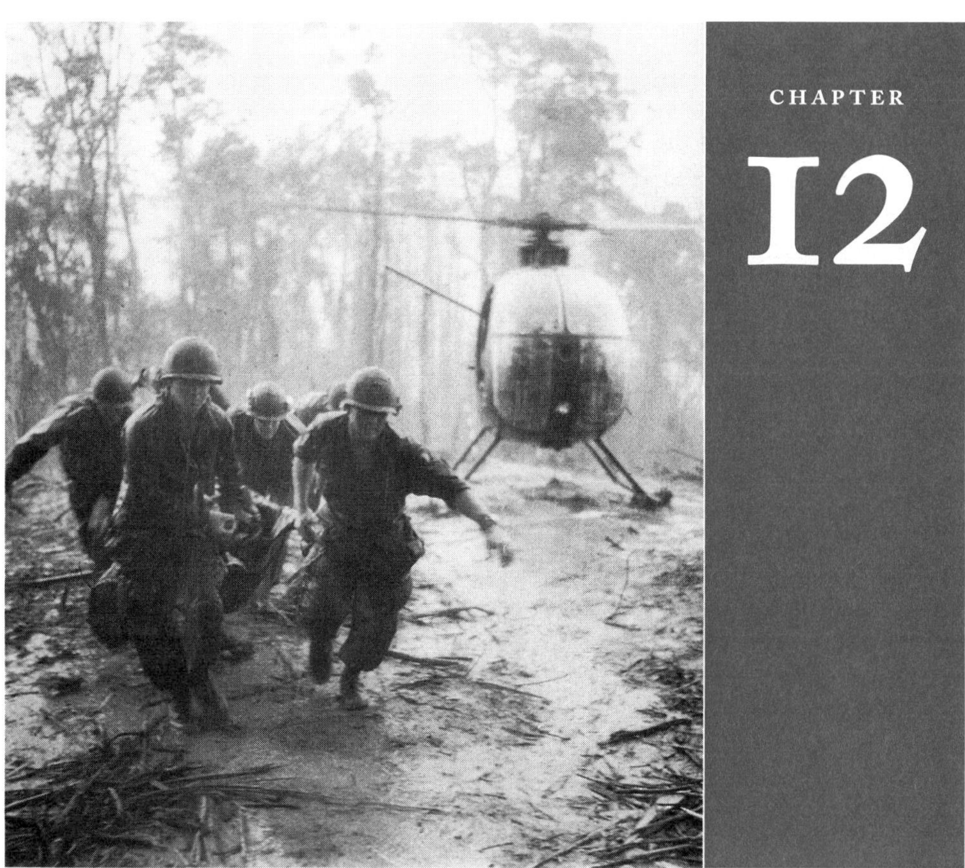

THE MEDIA, PUBLIC OPINION, AND THE FOREIGN POLICY PROCESS

...The debate on the relationship between foreign policy and the news media is often cast in one of two ways. The media either take foreign policy out of the hands of the elite and open the process to an ill-informed public or they are indentured servants of the foreign policy elite.

Bill Kovach, "Do the Media Make Foreign Policy?"
Foreign Policy, Spring 1996

Is public opinion a force for enlightenment...[or]...a barrier to thoughtful and coherent diplomacy, hindering efforts to promote national interests that transcend the moods and passions of the moment?

Ole R. Holsti, "Public Opinion and Foreign Policy: Challenges to the Almond-Lippman Consensus"
International Studies Quarterly, December 1992

The final two participants in the American foreign policy process that we shall discuss are the media and the public at large. Both the media and the public can and do affect the shape of United States foreign policy, albeit more indirectly than the other participants that we have described so far. The foreign policy issues that the media cover, and how they cover those issues, can affect the foreign policy process. The public's general views on foreign policy may be transmitted periodically through national polls, often conduced by the media, through contacts with their elected congressional officials at "town meetings," and through visits with executive branch officials as they travel across the country. Furthermore, elections at both the congressional and presidential levels are two periodic ways for the public to convey its sentiments on the direction of foreign as well as domestic policy. In all of these ways, the media and the public can share in the shaping of foreign policy.

In this chapter, we discuss the role and impact of these participants in the foreign policy process in some detail. In the earlier sections, we consider the expansion of the media in American political life and the different roles that analysts have suggested the media play in the foreign policy process. That is, are the media a separate actor and critic in the process (much like an interest group), or are they an accomplice of the government (often championing official policy positions)? Alternately, are the media some combination of these two roles? Further, how do the media affect the public and their views? In the later sections of the chapter, we consider the public's role in the foreign policy process and seek to answer several compelling questions about public opinion and foreign policy. Is the public largely uninformed about foreign policy? Are its views fickle and changeable, guided primarily by the wishes of the political leadership? Alternately, are the public's views more stable and consistent on foreign policy issues than some would suggest? Does, in fact, the public shape the directions of foreign policy at least over the long term, if not on every decision that occurs?

THE PERVASIVENESS OF THE MEDIA

We need to begin the discussion of the media in the foreign policy process by considering the media's magnitude (and growth) over the past few years and their place in American society. In general, Americans are increasingly bombarded by media outlets of all kinds, with the electronic media more pervasive than the print media. A caricature of this growth is the presumed "CNN-ization of the world," a reference to the highly successful Turner Broadcasting station that claims to be the "network of record" for breaking news events at home and around the world. Yet, the electronic explosion goes beyond CNN to include the growth in radio stations, changes in programming (such as the growth of talk radio and television news interview programs), and the rapid expansion of cable stations and cable systems seeking to rival CNN nationwide and worldwide (e.g., C-Span, MSNBC,

NBC SuperStation in Europe, and Britain's Sky TV broadcasting). More recently, the development of the Internet and the World Wide Web have added other avenues of instantaneous global communications. A few simple statistics will illustrate the kind of media transformation that has taken place over the past several decades.[1]

The Growth in Differing Media Outlets

In 1994, for example, 98 million Americans had access to radios, compared to 62 million just two and a half decades earlier. During that same time span, the number of radio stations grew by more than 50 percent, from 6,519 to 10,022. Television usage increased even more dramatically during that same time period, with 94 million sets in use in 1994 compared to 59 million sets in 1970. The number of television stations, however, increased at an even faster rate than the number of radio stations, growing from 862 to 1,512, an increase of 75 percent. Tied to this increase in television stations was the growth of cable television systems, spreading from 2,490 available systems in 1970 to 11,230 systems in 1994, an increase of 350 percent in twenty-five years.

By contrast, the print media has actually been contracting and consolidating. As of 1994, 1,714 daily newspapers were being published, a decline of 25 percent from just a year earlier.[2] Fewer and fewer companies (e.g., Gannett, Knight-Ridder, *Times-Mirror*, *New York Times*, and *Washington Post*) have gained an increasingly large foothold throughout the nation, by purchasing regional newspapers and nationalizing their circulations. The *New York Times* publishes regional editions that are readily available with your morning coffee in most major markets throughout the country; the *Wall Street Journal*, long available across the nation, has intensified its circulation effort on a national basis; the *Washington Post* publishes a national weekly edition with an established readership as well; and *USA Today* has emerged as a prime mass-circulation daily over the past two decades. Further, the Gannett chain (and publishers of *USA Today*), *Times-Mirror*, and the *New York Times* company now own newspapers (and television stations) across the country. Yet, these efforts at consolidation and increased national availability have not enhanced newspaper circulation or readership. Circulation, in fact, has declined from about 63 million readers in the late 1980s to about 60 million readers in 1994.

In addition to the traditional electronic and print media, newer electronic entries have propelled the worldwide communications explosion as well. The facsimile, or more popularly the fax machine, was instrumental in continuing the democracy movement in China in the late 1980s and has revolutionized communications to virtually every corner of the globe. The impact of computer technology has been even more profound via the Internet and the World Wide Web. Although instantaneous communications through electronic mail (E-mail) is commonplace to many under twenty-five today, the impact of E-mail in transforming global politics is indeed revolutionary. In short, the Internet and the World Wide Web have only accelerated the pervasiveness of electronic communication worldwide.

Old News Versus New News

The emergence of these different communications and media outlets (e.g., talk radio, cable TV, the Internet), or "new news" sources, has seemingly altered reliance on the traditional media outlets (e.g., network news and national newspapers), or the "old news" sources.[3] One indicator of this change is the precipitous drop in the viewership of the nightly network news broadcasts over the past two decades. In 1996, only 42 percent of American adult viewers regularly watched the nightly news on the three major networks. In 1993, this figure was 60 percent, while in the 1970s, it was about 80 percent. Furthermore, among young viewers (those under thirty), only 22 percent reported watching the television news broadcasts on a regular basis.[4] At the same time, the "old news" sources continue to have an important role in shaping the agenda and in stimulating discussion on the "new news" forums—talk radio or cyberspace.[5] In this sense, both traditional and new media sources continue to have a crucial role in political and social life.

The ultimate impact of this communication explosion on foreign policy is difficult to estimate. On the one hand, foreign policy coverage by the media is hardly immune to these dramatic changes in the communication arena. Indeed, these revolutionary changes are often viewed as having enhanced the American public's access to foreign affairs and, in turn, as having contributed to an enlarged role for the media in the foreign policy arena. Dramatic events worldwide bring dramatic and continuous coverage by the various media outlets. On the other hand, since coverage of foreign affairs by the American news media remains relatively small, with estimates of foreign policy coverage at about 11 to 16 percent in the print and national television networks[6] (and at only 2.6 percent in one study of ten leading newspapers[7]), the implications of these changes for foreign policy should not be exaggerated. Still, what events in the foreign policy arena are covered—and how they are covered—may have an important impact on the public debate over foreign policy. In this rapidly changing environment, then, the role of the media in the foreign policy process remains a topic of continued interest and discussion.

THE ROLE OF THE MEDIA IN THE FOREIGN POLICY PROCESS

More precise assessments of the media's role in American foreign policy immediately provoke a torrent of commentary and controversy. For purposes of our discussion, we can divide these assessments into three different categories.[8] One set of analyses focuses upon the media as largely a separate actor in the foreign policy process, sometimes seeking to advance their own views among the American people. Another set sees the media as largely an accomplice of the government policy and more often supportive, than critical, of official action. Yet, a third role portrays the media and the government in a "mutually exploitative" relationship in which each gains from the other. While all of these roles are often intermingled in discussions of the media and foreign policy, this last role appears to best represent the current relationship between the media and foreign policy makers. Before we discuss that third role, however, we first outline the two most frequently identified roles for the media in the foreign policy process and discuss some criticisms that question the accuracy of each one.

The Media As Actor

The argument is that in this role, the media in fact shape the foreign policy agenda for policy makers and the public. Since policy makers and the public depend upon the media for information about global events (and especially television, for instantaneous communication from around the world),[9] the media are a powerful force for determining the issues considered. Put somewhat differently, what the media decide to portray (or not portray) may have a powerful influence on the direction of American foreign policy. By extension, the media may exercise an independent effect on the foreign policy process. While evidence exists for this argument, other analysts caution against pushing this interpretation too far. Let us consider both kinds of evidence on this media role.

The Vietnam War. The emergence of this "media as actor" role usually dates from the Vietnam War. The media (and particularly television) provided vivid pictures of that conflict to the American public and policy makers, virtually on a nightly basis. The media portrayals of that war produced a lasting set of images for the American public and policy makers: The magnitude of killings and destruction on both sides often became nightly staples of the coverage; interviews with battlefield military officers and spokespersons often conveyed the difficulties of the war (including a particularly vivid interview in which a military officer declared that American forces had "to destroy the town to save it"[10]); and protests against the war at home became standard fare as well. These portrayals were often at odds with the upbeat assessments by American and South Vietnamese officials, who tended to laud the progress being made in the war. In short, the media often put policy makers on the defensive to explain their positions and to defend their policies. In this way, the media ultimately had a powerful effect on the direction of policy in the Vietnam War.

The so-called Tet offensive, countrywide attacks across South Vietnam by Viet Cong and North Vietnamese forces beginning in late January 1968, in particular illustrates the impact of the media on the conduct of the war and American foreign policy. Although these attacks ultimately proved to be a military failure, the amount of physical destruction, the number of casualties, and the widespread nature of the attacks, as portrayed by the media, conveyed another message. Indeed, the image created by the media implied a massive defeat for South Vietnamese and American forces. Despite efforts to explain the events in other ways, the media impression produced a "profound impact on American perceptions of the war at all levels," as one analyst noted, with a sharp decline in public optimism. In short, "the dramatic impact of the television coverage of the carnage, set against the official statements of optimism, had its effects."[11] (Years later, a detailed study documented the impact of the press coverage on this crucial foreign policy episode and the misleading way in which the Tet offensive was portrayed by the media.[12]) Indeed, in the immediate aftermath of this offensive, President Lyndon Johnson announced on March 31, 1968, that he would not be a candidate for president that fall. In short, the Tet offensive remains one of those events often described to convey the power of the media in affecting policy.

The Iran Hostage Crisis. In the late 1970s and early 1980s, the Iran Hostage Crisis, in which fifty-two Americans were held for 444 days in the United States embassy in Tehran, is another example used to portray the media's foreign policy role. In the first days of the hostage-taking, the ABC television network initiated a nightly program, "America Held Hostage," to outline the developments during the crisis. Each night, the title was augmented with the appropriate day (e.g., "America Held Hostage, Day 25").[13] As the crisis wore on, seemingly without resolution, the impact of these nightly episodes became clear: The American government appeared powerless to do much to intervene, and the ineptitude of the Carter administration became firmly planted in the minds of many Americans. Furthermore, with these continued portrayals, the impression created was that little else mattered on the world stage during those days. While the point is not to debate whether ABC and other media outlets were seeking this outcome, what is important is the fact that the media played a forceful role in conveying and creating a particular foreign policy image.

Ethiopia and Somalia. In the 1980s and 1990s, the media's portrayal of the death and starvation in Ethiopia and Somalia further demonstrates their power in the foreign policy arena. In the former case, journalist Peter Boyer summarized the media's impact in a 1984 NBC report on the widening Ethiopian famine:

> It was a jarring piece, movingly narrated by BBC correspondent Michael Buerk. "The faces of death in Africa," [Anchor Tom] Brokaw called it.
>
> The impact was immediate and overwhelming. The phones started ringing at NBC and at the Connecticut headquarters of Save the Children....The next night, NBC aired another BBC report and, again, the response was staggering. CBS and ABC a week later aired more reports on the famine—with even more response, more reports. The story had exploded.[14]

In 1991 and 1992, the media prodded the Bush administration to take more vigorous actions about the starvation and suffering in Somalia. Former Secretary of State Lawrence Eagleburger described the impact of television on policy making over Somalia in this way:

> I will tell you quite frankly television had a great deal to do with President Bush's decision to go in the first place, and, I will tell you equally frankly, I was one of those two or three that was strongly recommending he do it, and it was very much because of the television pictures of these starving kids, substantial pressures from the Congress that comes from the same source, and my honest belief that we could do this....[15]

Once again, the media's riveting portrayal of the suffering in that country ultimately led to the dispatch of American military forces to help with the distribution of food and needed supplies. Indeed, "among the most vivid scenes from that operation was the look of startled Navy seals in war paint hitting the beaches which had already been secured by television news crews to record the landing."[16] Such a scene was a dramatic and stark illustration of the power of the media in setting the foreign policy agenda and even in arranging a foreign policy action.

On occasion, too, individual members of the media can play an even more direct role in the foreign policy process—a role that media analyst, Doris Graber, has called "media diplomacy."[17] Three examples will suffice to illustrate this aspect of the media's foreign policy role.

The Missile Crisis. An ABC television reporter, John Scali, is often given considerable credit for aiding in the peaceful resolution of the nuclear standoff between the United States and the Soviet union during October 1962—the Cuban Missile Crisis. Scali was approached by a Soviet official and asked to transmit a proposal to the United States government for ending the crisis, a proposal that ultimately bore a resemblance to the final outcome.[18] To be sure, another American might have served as the channel for such information, but the fact that Scali, as a journalist, had contacts with Soviet officials reveals how members of the media may participate in the process.

Sadat and Begin. A second illustration of the role that individuals in the media can play involved the visit by Egypt's Anwar Sadat to Israel in November 1977.[19] During a CBS evening news broadcast anchored by Walter Cronkite a month or so earlier, Anwar Sadat and Israeli Prime Minister Menachem Begin were simultaneously interviewed from their home countries. During the course of the interview, Cronkite encouraged Begin to issue an invitation to Sadat to visit Israel. Begin did so, and Sadat's pathbreaking trip to Jerusalem was initiated. In a small, but important way, a member of the media became an actor in the foreign policy process.

The Persian Gulf War. A final illustration occurred during the Persian Gulf War. Peter Arnett was a reporter for CNN, who went to Baghdad, Iraq, prior to the outbreak of the war and stayed on during the conflict.[20] His actions gained him both notoriety and political attacks in the United States for his continued reporting from Iraq. As virtually the only Western source in Baghdad once the war broke out, Arnett became a lightning rod for critics of the media and foreign policy for seemingly taking at face value the Iraqi explanations of events during the war. He was also criticized by many "when he engaged Iraqi president Saddam Hussein in a long television interview," since this appeared to offer a ready "propaganda forum" for Hussein against his adversaries.[21]

Other Interpretations of the Role of the Media. Despite these examples and evidence that seem to support this first role, several analysts doubt the accuracy of describing the media as a foreign policy actor. Instead, they point to other explanations for the changing media coverage of foreign policy events. One leading media analyst, for example, disputes the accuracy of an "oppositional media" that presumably developed over Vietnam, and the

Tet offensive in particular.[22] While acknowledging that television references to Tet do reveal that the media coverage was more critical of policy after this offensive than before, this analyst contends that the reason was not that the media had changed its role, but rather that the domestic consensus on this foreign policy issue had evaporated, bringing more and more criticism of government policy.[23] As a result, the members of the media, relying on their norm of objective journalism, gave more and more coverage to this emerging controversy. Furthermore, as this analyst endeavors to show, the media continued to convey official government statements about the Vietnam War, provided about the same ratio of comments about anti-war supporters and supporters of the government after Tet, and offered little explicit independent commentary on the war.[24] Thus, this analyst challenges whether the media really was an actor in this case:

> The case of Vietnam suggests that whether the media tend to be supporting or critical of government policies depends on the degree of consensus those policies enjoy, particularly within the political establishment.... News content may not mirror the facts, but the media, as institutions, do reflect the prevailing pattern of political debate: when consensus is strong, they tend to stay within the limits of the political discussion it defines; when it begins to break down, coverage becomes increasingly critical and diverse in the viewpoints it represents, and increasingly difficult for officials to control.[25]

Contrary to the earlier argument, too, others would question that the media shaped the coverage of the Iran hostage crisis. Instead, they would point to the actions of the Carter administration itself for producing the significant media emphasis on this event.[26] Since President Carter proceeded to treat this issue as the most important problem facing the country and thus refused to leave Washington to campaign until it was resolved (the so-called "Rose Garden strategy"), the media necessarily provided more and more attention to the hostage crisis. While this argument surely has some attraction as an alternate explanation, it fails to explain the sustained coverage in Tehran by American media outlets.

Similarly, critics also would contend that the media have not always succeeded in shaping the foreign policy agenda. At least three recent cases suggest that significant media coverage does not always produce a foreign policy response by the United States. Consider the cases of Cambodia (Kampuchea), Bosnia, and Rwanda. Despite the "killing fields" in Cambodia in the late 1970s, and the media coverage of the 2 million who were being massacred by the Pol Pot regime there, American foreign policy changed very little toward that country or region during those years. Instead, the aftermath of the Vietnam War operated against a more aggressive stance toward that country by the United States. Similarly, despite dramatic television pictures from Bosnia revealing the killings in the markets of Sarajevo, the haunting figures of men held in prisoner of war camps, and wholesale killings and rapes in the name of ethnic cleansing, American policy makers were slow to change policy directions in the early 1990s. Once again, fear of a Vietnam-style quagmire prevailed for several years. Indeed, it was not until mid-1995 that the Clinton administration took a more determined stance. Finally, the ethnic slaughter of Tutsis in Rwanda in 1994 and its vivid portrayal by the media brought only a limited response by United

States policy makers. In this instance, too, the media had limited success in setting the foreign policy agenda. In contrast, and to make the point more fully about the limited effect of the media, consider instances when the United States acted without being prodded by television coverage. In humanitarian disasters, whether in Africa or Central Europe, American assistance often arrives before, or simultaneously with, the media.

Finally, the importance of media diplomacy should not be pushed too far, either. Despite the earlier examples, it is difficult to conclude that any of these media members ultimately shaped foreign policy. We now know, for example, that "backchannel" communications over resolving the Cuban Missile Crises were already under way between American and Soviet officials before John Scali became involved. Similarly, while Walter Cronkite may have aided the peace process in the Middle East, the Israeli and Egyptian officials ultimately had to take the bold steps to adjust their long-standing policies toward one another. Furthermore, despite the criticism of Peter Arnett's reporting in Iraq, no evidence exists that his actions changed American policy in any significant way during the Persian Gulf War. In sum, the role of the media as an actor appears overstated—or even inaccurate—to some critics.

The Liberal Media? Another aspect of this first role for the media focuses upon the ideological characteristics of the members themselves and the possible bias that they bring to their reporting. The American public often views the media as being elitist, as possessing a liberal political bias, and as trying to foist such views on policy. Several studies provide some support for these assertions. First, the media as a group is largely elitist in demographic characteristics and do not reflect the characteristics of the American public as a whole. In a survey of members of both print and television media, one major study reported that the media elite largely came from the northeast and north-central part of the country with urban and ethnic roots, were highly educated and from "mostly well off, highly educated members of the upper middle class," and had primarily "secular roots," with only half religious believers and less than 10 percent church-attenders.[27] Moreover, these demographic characteristics differed little between members of the print and electronic media surveyed. Second, members of the media were largely liberal in orientation, with 54 percent describing themselves as left of center and 17 percent as right of center. Another study of only the Washington press corps at about the same time found that 42 percent were liberal in orientation and 19 percent conservative.[28] Third, the partisan orientation of media members tended to be skewed in one direction as well. Over four-fifths of those surveyed supported Democratic presidential candidates Johnson, Humphrey, McGovern, and Carter in the elections immediately prior to the survey.[29]

More recent surveys in the mid-1980s and mid-1990s largely support this earlier media portrait. In 1985, the *Los Angeles Times* surveyed more than 2,700 print journalists and found that 56 percent had a liberal orientation, while only 18 percent had a conservative orientation. In 1996, in a survey of the heads of Washington bureaus for various media outlets and congressional correspondents, the Freedom Forum and the Roper Center found about the same breakdown—61 percent of these members of the media characterized themselves as "liberal" or "moderate to liberal," while only 9 percent viewed themselves as "conservative" or "moderate to conservative." Further, 89 percent of those surveyed said that they had voted for Clinton in 1992, while only 7 percent had voted for Bush.[30]

The important question is whether these personal characteristics mattered in what was reported or how it was reported. Many members of the media would argue that their journalistic training directs them to be fair and not to allow their personal beliefs and background affect their work. Thus, their social-political background or political leanings would not significantly alter their reporting on domestic or foreign policy matters. Moreover, some of these liberal members of the media work for conservative organizations whose principal goals are increasing their share of the market among American viewers and listeners and enhancing the corporations' profits. In such an environment, the reporters will be directed to follow a "good story," despite their political leanings, and will likely do so.

Others disagree strongly over claims that members of the media will not allow their personal views to intrude in their reporting. Indeed, one prominent political scientist and media analyst calls this argument "absurd." Instead, he argues that this liberal bias comes into play "more in the setting of the agenda than in the reporting of particular facts. What they choose to cover, what they think is important is the liberal agenda."[31]

In this sense, we are back to where we started this discussion: That is, the media are important in setting the foreign policy agenda. While how much the media set the agenda and how much they influence policy remain hotly debated questions, long-time media analyst Bernard Cohen, writing more than three decades ago about the press and foreign policy, still provides an apt summary of this first role of the media:

> ...the press is significantly more than a purveyor of information and opinion. It may not be successful much of the time in telling people what to think, but it is stunningly successful in telling its readers what to think *about*.[32]

The Media As Accomplice

A second role for the media might be stated most strongly as one wholly at variance with the first: The media, knowingly or not, acts as an accomplice of the government. Put differently, they become the "handmaidens" of the government in the portrayal of news and information.[33] At least three kinds of evidence support this view. First, the media are ultimately dependent upon the government for information and for providing sources of information on many foreign policy questions that arise. Second, the media elite and the political elite often share similar values and beliefs about foreign policy. As such, the media will give credence to the policy maker's positions on foreign policy. Third, government officials often seek to utilize the media for promotion of particular policies, and, increasingly, they are trained to do so.[34] In this environment, and in contrast to the first media role we discussed, members of the media have a difficult time being an independent actor in the process.

Media Dependency. The American interventions in Grenada (1983) and Panama (1989) as well as the Persian Gulf War illustrate the problems that the media have in playing an independent role and reveal how dependent they may become on the government for information. During the American intervention in Grenada in October 1983, and with the memory of the media's role in Vietnam in mind, the Reagan administration decided to exclude the media from joining the invading forces and sent home members who had reached the island nation on their own.[35] In this instance, information about American actions was tightly channeled so as to control the situation, leaving the media largely to report the official positions.

After this episode, a commission was established to arrange a new relationship between the media and the government (in this case, the Pentagon) over future American engagements abroad. This new system of a "pool," reporters representing both print and electronic media, would accompany future military actions.[36] The intervention in Panama in December 1989, was the first test of this arrangement. On the one hand, this procedure largely failed in the view of the media, since they remained under close scrutiny and control of Pentagon officials in Panama and were kept away from combat areas for long periods. On the other hand, the military and the government largely succeeded in conveying the media picture that they wanted.

The Persian Gulf crisis and war of 1990–1991 produced even greater governmental efforts to control and shape the information that emanated from that area of the world. Indeed, the Pentagon outlined detailed "ground rules" for reporting from the region.[37] Sizes of American or coalition units and their military components could not be disclosed, future operational plans were also forbidden, and exact locations of forces in Saudi Arabia, for example, could not be revealed. News "pool" operations were once again established, and "they became the essential mode of operation."[38] The daily military briefings on the Persian Gulf operations, generally carried live on CNN worldwide, were the primary sources of information for the many news organizations present in Saudi Arabia. Once again, the efforts to shape the story in a way that the government wanted proved to be largely successful.

Close Personal and Working Relationships. While these three illustrations are recent instances of the ability of the government to utilize the media in a way favorable to it, other mechanisms are available and have operated for some time. Often, members of the media and public officials form close personal and working relationships and can thus use one another to get a particular message across to the public and other policy makers. The leaking of information to particular reporters is the obvious and most direct way to achieve this end. Just as "sources" for the media develop in the government, foreign policy officials may use their media "contacts" to make their case to the American people. Some of these reporters, in either print or electronic media, become "Washington insiders," with easy contact and access to policy makers (although not always complying with the wishes of government officials).

While a pure example of such reporters is difficult to identify (since few media people would accept this characterization), the late James Reston, long-time columnist of the *New York Times*, fits this portrait, in part. A first-rate reporter and columnist on foreign and domestic issues, he was also closely tied with and highly trusted by Washington officials—"the quintessential Washington insider," in one commentator's judgment. In fact, in that analyst's view, he was too close to key officials: "Officials used him to test out new ideas on the public or to drop leaks for which they did not want to be held accountable. Because of his high position at the *Times* and his personal integrity, he was trusted both by those who provided the news and by those who read it."[39] Further, on at least one important occasion, Reston was willing to withhold a story after a presidential phone call. The story involved the emplacement of Soviet missiles in Cuba in 1962, at a time when the crisis had yet to become public. Yet, the Reston example is hardly a pure case because he also demonstrated journalistic independence at times, in particular with his support for the *Times's* publication of the *Pentagon Papers* in 1971. Moreover, he seemingly always judged the relationship between politicians and the press as a conflictual one.[40]

At a more general level, media representatives and public officials often have worked closely with one another to gain information and have relied on and trusted one another. The extent of this cooperation abroad is considerable, since the American embassy or consulate is the primary source of information for many reporters. This collaboration may extend to a reporter reading American embassy cable traffic on a regular basis in an African country, or another reporter holding back information about secret negotiations over Afghanistan at the request of an American ambassador.[41] At the very least, though, the collaboration often involves a regular and sustained exchange of information.

Government Use of the Media. Increasingly, the government has sought to establish ground rules for dealing with the media, not just in time of interventions or war as the Grenada or Persian Gulf cases suggest, but on a more ongoing basis. A former assistant secretary of state for Inter-American Affairs made the point bluntly about the need by government officials to shape the message emanating from the media: "We are not taught about the press as an instrument of foreign policy execution, and that is crucial.... You have to *use* the press, and when I say 'use,' I don't mean cynically, in the sense of hoodwinking. I mean use it in the sense that it's an instrument that is there for you."[42] As a result, in recent years, the Department of State has developed an extensive series of guidelines for dealing with the media and offered stern warnings about what to say and not say.[43] In short, governmental officials now receive both formal and informal training in managing media relations.

Much as with the role of the media as actor, critics would caution about relying too fully on this second role to summarize the relationship between the media and foreign policy makers. First, while acknowledging that members of the media are dependent upon the "golden triangle" (White House, Pentagon, and State Department) for gathering news (and hence the official government position often gets considerable attention), a "professional norm" exists that "discourages taking sides by looking to report different sides of a debate."[44] As we noted earlier, too, as the policy debate among officials emerges—whether between the Pentagon or State or between the White House and Congress—the media are able to play a more expansive role than just conveying the officially stated government position. Moreover, "when official conflict is sustained, the new gates tend to open to grassroots groups, interest groups, opinion polls, and broader social participation."[45] In this way, the media are increasingly successful in being more than an accomplice of the government.

Second, members of the media are fully aware of the effort by government officials to engage in "spinning"—the strategy of officials to convey a particular image or interpretation of foreign policy events and to try to get the media to convey that view.[46] As a result, members of the media would likely take precautions to guard against conveying only the official interpretation. Furthermore, as foreign policy issues become interestingly contentious and partisan, members of the media will seek out alternate sources in order to get their interpretation of events.

The Media and the Government: Mutually Exploitative?

As the criticism of the media as accomplice illustrates, an increasing tension has developed in the relationship between the media and the foreign policy community, suggesting a third possible relationship between these two organizations today. This third possibility actually strikes a middle ground between the two roles discussed so far. Neither the "media as actor" nor the "media as accomplice" best characterizes the relationship; instead, an intermediate role exists in which the media and the government seek to take advantage of the relationship with the other. This role has been aptly described as a "mutually exploitative" relationship between the media and foreign policy makers by one analyst:

> Both organizations [the United States foreign policy community and the media] promote their own version of reality around the world; the foreign policy apparatus does so to serve its own policy interests; the media do so because that is what they do. Both are adept at supporting, manipulating, or attacking the other. The relationship is sometimes competitive and sometimes cooperative, but that is only incidental to its central driving force: self-interest.[47]

In particular, recent foreign policy and media activities, most notably in connection with the Persian Gulf War, gave rise to this characterization of the relationship. In analyzing interview data from foreign and defense officials during the Gulf War and other interview data with journalists and officials regarding Soviet-American relations somewhat earlier, "the mutual exploitation theme quickly emerged," according to one media analyst. For large percentages of the policy officials, the media sources were often the only or "the fastest source of information."[48] Conversely, "the policymakers saw nothing unusual about using the media as a communications instrument to address other national leaders and populations."[49]

The success of the media versus the policy makers in this relationship varies by issue.[50] On issues dealing with the environment, human rights, and human-interest stories generally, sometimes called "low politics" issues, the media are more effective in impacting the policy process. Human rights violations of ethnic minorities and the struggle for freedom and independence by indigenous groups are often easily portrayed through the medium of television. The media can use compelling visual images to try to get such an issue on the foreign policy agenda. On issues dealing with arms control or the accuracy of weapons systems, sometimes called "high politics" issues, policy makers may have an advantage. Consider the media's difficulty of trying to convey the debate for and against arms control agreements without official arguments, or consider the media's ability to convey the accuracy of smart bombs or information on troop movements without reliance on the military. As a long-time foreign policy journalist noted recently: "Media technology is rarely as powerful in the hands of journalists as it is in the hands of political figures who can summon the talent to exploit the new invention."[51] In sum, then, both media and the foreign policy community may well feed off the skills of one another as both seek to promote their interests. In many ways, "mutually exploitative" may be a more accurate way to think about the relationship between these two organizations, rather than simply trying to characterize the media as always an independent actor or as always a government accomplice in the foreign policy process.

THE MEDIA´S IMPACT ON THE PUBLIC

The final topic to consider in their relationship is the media's effects upon the views and opinions of the public. While our next section will focus more directly on the nature of the public's view of foreign policy and its foreign policy role, the media obviously have some impact on the public's perceptions prior to those opinions. In a real sense, of course, the public is greatly subject to the kind and extent of information that the media provide it. As political scientists Benjamin Page and Robert Shapiro note: "Many events—especially distant happenings in foreign affairs—do not directly and immediately affect ordinary citizens, and therefore, do not speak for themselves." Instead, such events must be reported and "*interpreted.*"[52] In this sense, the media matters, but how much and to what degree?

In a study covering a fifteen-year period (1969–1983), Page and Shapiro have begun to sort out the media's role by assessing the impact of several different providers of news on television, such as "the president, members of his administration and fellow partisans, members of the opposing party, interest groups,...experts, network commentators or reporters...foreign nations or individuals, unfriendly states," and several others on the changes in the public's view of several foreign and domestic policies.[53] From their analyses, two important findings emerged. First, the public's views were relatively stable over time (only about 50 percent of the time over the years did they change), even in the context of a variety of different interpreters of television news. (We shall discuss more fully the stability of public opinion on foreign policy in the next section.) Second, when opinion change did occur in the short term, news commentators—more than any of the other providers of news—produced the most change of the public's opinion. In this sense, the media, and especially news commentators, mattered in affecting the public's view more than presidents, policy experts, and foreign nations.

Yet Shapiro and Page also seek to put these results in a larger context by noting that, while foreign policy views by the public are often interpreted through the media by elites, "people seem to have reacted directly to events themselves, sometimes going against elite interpretations."[54] Furthermore, they note that "gradual social and economic trends, and world and national events—which have some unmediated impact" combine with those reported through the mass media to affect opinion change.[55] In short, then, the evidence is quite strong that the public is not made up of mindless robots wholly swayed by the latest media pictures and portrayals, but that opinion change among the public comes from many sources and not exclusively from the media.[56]

PUBLIC OPINION AND FOREIGN POLICY: ALTERNATE VIEWS

With an understanding of the role of the media, we now turn to examine more directly the public's role in the foreign policy process. We divide our discussion and analysis into two differing perspectives about public opinion and foreign policy and evaluating the evidence for each of them. Finally, we conclude by judging which perspective seems more appropriate for the current period.

According to the first perspective about foreign policy opinion, the public is uninterested, ill-informed, and subject to considerable leadership from the top on foreign policy matters. In the strongest form of this position, public opinion is less a shaper of United States foreign policy and more likely to be shaped by it. As a consequence, public opinion plays little or no role in shaping American foreign policy. According to the second perspective, the public plays a somewhat larger, albeit still limited, role in the foreign policy process. While the public may not be fully informed on foreign policy and may lack sustained interest in such matters, its views are more structured and consistent over time than many have previously contended. As such, the public can affect foreign policy making, especially over the long haul. In the course of this discussion, too, we evaluate how much impact public opinion has on policy making—indirectly through presidential and congressional elections and directly through current policy actions—as a way to gain some insight into the utility of these two alternate perspectives.

FOREIGN POLICY OPINION: UNINFORMED AND MOODISH

Except for very rare occurrences, public opinion has limited impact on the foreign policy process. In this view, only during wars or international crises is the public sufficiently concerned about foreign policy to affect it directly. The principal reason for this limited impact is the public's lack of interest in, and knowledge about, foreign affairs. Even when specific foreign policy views of the public are expressed, they often prove susceptible to short-term shifts—produced, for example, by presidential leadership, the wording of questions in public opinion polls, or rapidly changing international events. In this context, public opinion serves as a relatively weak restraint on policy makers.

Public Interest and Knowledge of Foreign Affairs

Low levels of public understanding of and concern about foreign policy issues have existed throughout the post–World War II years. In a 1947 study of Cincinnati, Ohio, for instance, only 30 percent of the public was able to explain in a simple way what the United Nations did. In an analysis two years later, the public was equally uninformed. By this assessment, only 25 percent of the public was judged to possess reasonably developed opinions, 45 percent had only limited knowledge of world affairs, and 30 percent was classified as uninformed.[57]

Public opinion data from more recent decades are not much different. According to studies by Free and Cantril, only 26 percent of the American population was well informed on foreign policy issues during the 1960s, another 35 percent was moderately informed on foreign affairs, and 39 percent was simply uninformed. Somewhat indicative of this low level of knowledge was the public's information on the North Atlantic Treaty Organization (NATO), the center of America's containment efforts during the Cold War. According to this analysis, 28 percent of the public had never heard of NATO, only 58 percent knew that the United States belonged to that organization, and only 38 percent indicated that the Soviet Union was not a member of NATO.[58]

Throughout the past three decades, the level of interest in and knowledge of foreign affairs has not changed appreciably—even in the context of a more educated electorate. Based upon the six quadrennial surveys of the American public on foreign policy issues conducted by the Chicago Council on Foreign Relations from 1974 to 1994, local community news received the highest level of interest (between 55 percent and 65 percent over the years), while news about other countries was much lower (about 32 percent on average).[59] News about America's relations with other countries, however, ranked a bit higher, ranging from 44 percent to 53 percent across the surveys. Interestingly, news about United States relations with other countries stimulates more interest than simply news about other countries, but it still trails interest in local community affairs. Figure 12.1 shows a comparison of interest in different types of news over the six surveys.

Overall, four important findings emerge about the level of interest in foreign affairs from reviewing these six surveys: (1) interest in news about other countries never surpasses interest in news about national and community affairs; (2) interest in news about local affairs is on the rise, while interest in foreign news has declined lately; (3) the level of interest in foreign news is "partly a function of education," with the higher the level of edu-

FIGURE 12.1

Percent of the American Public Very Interested in Various Types of News, 1974–1994

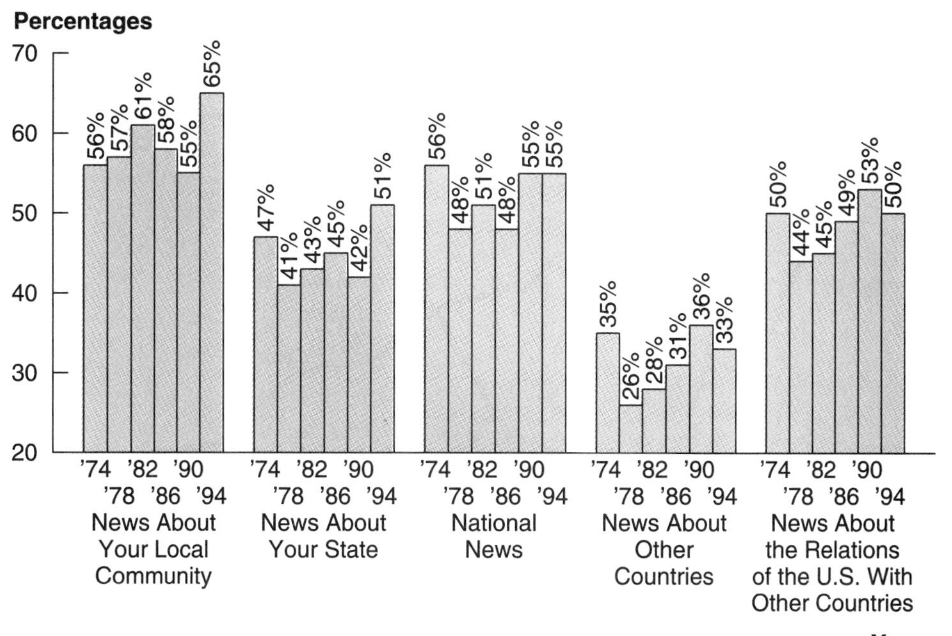

Sources: John E. Rielly, ed., *American Public Opinion and U.S. Foreign Policy 1987* (Chicago: The Chicago Council on Foreign Relations, 1987), p. 8; John E. Rielly, ed., *American Public Opinion and U.S. Foreign Policy 1991* (Chicago: The Chicago Council on Foreign Relations, 1991), p. 9; and John E. Rielly, ed., *American Public Opinion and U.S. Foreign Policy 1995* (Chicago: The Chicago Council on Foreign Relations, 1995), p. 9.

cation, the more interest; and (4) few Americans are capable of discussing major foreign policy problems in detail.[60]

If interest in foreign affairs is relatively low, it is hardly surprising to find that the knowledge about foreign affairs is equally limited. In fact, these surveys generally concluded that only about 21 to 23 percent of the American public is fully informed on foreign policy matters and constitutes what has been called the "attentive public." The results for 1990 are a little higher, with 29 percent of the public surveyed characterized as "high attentives," although the criteria for attentiveness are less demanding in this survey than in earlier ones.[61]

We can demonstrate the paucity of knowledge among the public on foreign affairs more concretely by considering the accuracy of the public's information about two major foreign policy activities. The first involved funding the Nicaraguan Contras in their battle against the Sandinista regime. This issue dominated the foreign policy landscape during the Reagan administration and even continued into the first year of the Bush administration, and, in many ways, it was the most divisive foreign policy question

FIGURE 12.2

Level of Knowledge Regarding Which Side the U.S. Government Supported in Nicaragua, 1983–1987

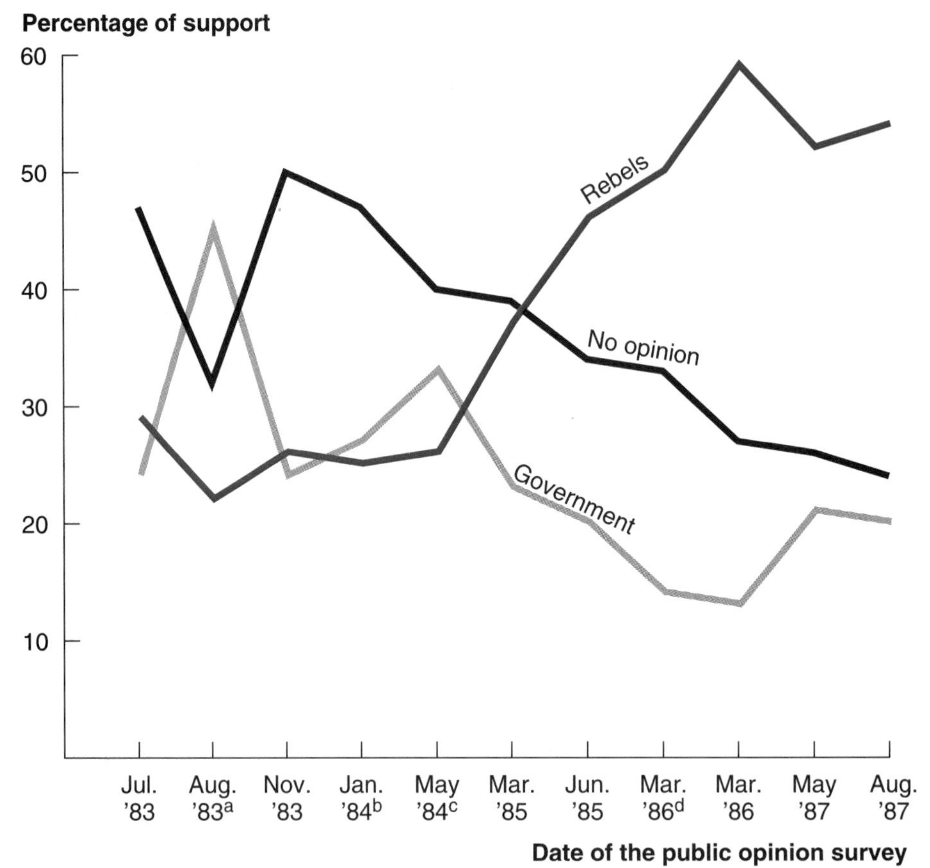

Source: Taken in part from the table in Richard Sobel, "Public Opinion About United States Intervention in El Salvador and Nicaragua." *Public Opinion Quarterly* 53 (Spring 1989): 120.

during that time. Yet, during a substantial portion of the 1980s, a majority of the public did not know, with certainty, which side the United States was backing: the Contra rebels or the Sandinista government.

Based upon a series of public opinion surveys by ABC/*Washington Post* from 1983 to 1987 (Figure 12.2), it was not until a June 1985 poll that a majority of the public correctly noted that the United States government was supporting the Contras. Even at that late date in American involvement, a third of the public still had "no opinion" when asked which side the United States was backing in Nicaragua. Indeed, throughout 1983, 1984, and part of 1985, "no opinion" was generally the most popular response when asked this kind of question.[62]

The second example deals with the amount of foreign aid that the United States transfers to other countries. While foreign aid is hardly a new item on the foreign policy agenda (foreign aid has been a staple of American foreign policy since the end of World War II), the public has a low level of knowledge about how much the United States actually provides to other countries. In a 1995 survey by the University of Maryland's Program on International Policy Attitudes, the public's median estimate of the amount of the federal budget spent on American foreign aid was 15 percent. In reality, it is about 1 percent and has been at that level for a long time. Similarly, four-fifths of the respondents thought that the United States spends "more" on foreign aid than do other highly developed countries.[63] In fact, in terms of relative percentage, the United States has ranked at or near the bottom among the industrial countries for decades. In fairness to the American public (and perhaps the reason for the confusion in responding to this question), the United States has always been the leading donor or second leading donor (after Japan) in terms of total dollar amount of foreign assistance. Yet this inability on the part of the American public to differentiate between the total amount of aid versus relative amount of effort still suggests some limitation on the level of knowledge about foreign aid.

Foreign Policy As an Important Issue

Despite the low level of knowledge and interest in international affairs generally, the public still has often viewed foreign policy as an important issue facing the country. During portions of the last five decades, for example, foreign policy has been identified as the most important issue facing the nation. Only more recently has foreign policy been replaced by economic concerns as the principal issue identified by the American people.

During the height of the Cold War and throughout America's involvement in Vietnam, for instance, national security issues usually were cited by 40 to 60 percent of the public as the most important problem.[64] In the early to middle 1980s, foreign policy issues (e.g., such as fear of war or international tensions) were occasionally listed as "the most important problem facing this country today" in the periodic polls taken by the Gallup organization.

In the immediate post-Vietnam years (e.g., 1973 through 1980) and in much of the 1980s and early 1990s, however, domestic issues, and particularly domestic economic issues, generally have outstripped any foreign policy issue as the most important concern of the public.[65] By one estimate, economic concerns from about 1975 through 1985 often captured "over 60 percent of the public. The level of [economic] concern rarely dropped below an absolute majority and typically fell below the 50 percent mark only when energy concerns periodically peaked at 10 percent or higher."[66]

During the early to mid-1990s, economic and social issues typically were identified as the most important problems. General concerns about the economy, issues of crime and violence, and, somewhat less so, health care ranked at or near the top of the list. Foreign policy issues or issues tied to international affairs received very few mentions in the identification of the most important problems during those years.[67]

Figure 12.3, which portrays the relative importance of foreign and domestic policy issues among the American public from the four most recent

FIGURE 12.3

The Relative Importance to the American Public of Foreign and Domestic Problems: 1982, 1986, 1990, and 1994

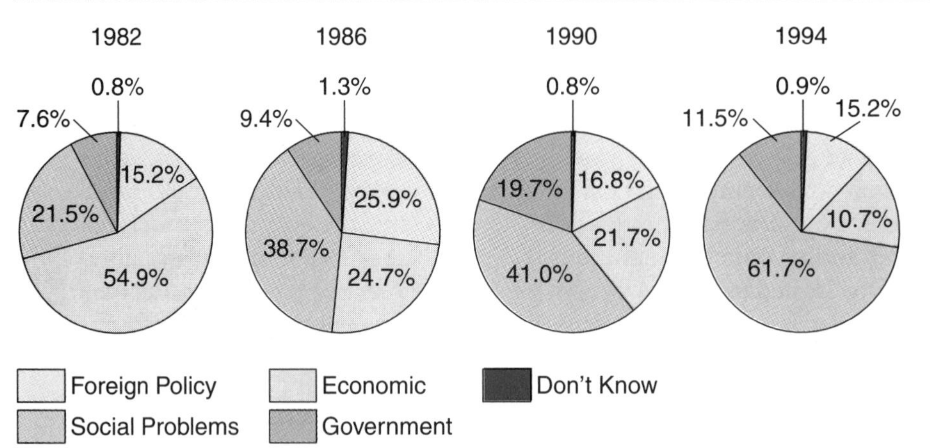

Sources: Taken from a portion of Table 1-2 in John E. Rielly, ed., *American Public Opinion and U.S. Foreign Policy 1991*, and from a portion of Figure 1-3 in John E. Rielly, ed., *American Public Opinion and U.S. Foreign Policy 1995*. Both are taken from p. 10 in these publications.

Chicago Council on Foreign Relations surveys discussed earlier, shows most strikingly the importance of economic and social issues to the American public over the past two decades. Note that these two issue areas generally outdistanced all other problems, except for foreign policy issues in 1986. In that year, foreign policy problems were slightly ahead of economic problems (25.9 percent and 24.7 percent of the total, respectively), while social issues were most pronounced, with 38.7 percent of the total. In the latest survey, however, perceived social problems were at record levels, and foreign policy concerns (11.5 percent) only slightly edged out governmental problems (10.7 percent).

Still, if foreign policy has captured a portion of the public's attention, why has the public not been more informed and more influential in shaping policy? Part of the explanation rests in the two earlier items we discussed: the low level of sustained interest in foreign policy and the low level of knowledge of foreign policy. Because the public concern has largely been episodic and tied to particular international events, and because the public's knowledge of foreign policy questions has remained relatively low, its ability to influence policy has remained relatively weak.

Presidential Leadership

Another important factor in why the public has not been more influential is related to the American public's susceptibility to presidential leadership. According to evidence provided by political scientist John Mueller, the president has often been the most admired person in the country.[68] As a consequence, because the public is not well informed on foreign policy issues, a tendency has developed to defer to the president's judgment on such matters. Several recent examples illustrate this phenomenon.

When President Lyndon Johnson changed his war policy during the Vietnam conflict, the public generally was willing to shift to support that policy—even if were a reversal of its earlier-expressed position. Prior to the bombing of oil depots around Hanoi and Haiphong, a majority of the public opposed such bombing. After the bombing policy was begun by the Johnson administration, however, 85 percent supported it. A similar shift, dictated by a presidential initiative, occurred later in that war. Before President Johnson initiated a bombing halt in 1968, 51 percent of the public supported the continuation of bombing. After President Johnson announced his decision for a partial bombing halt, a majority (64 percent) of the public favored this new policy option.[69] In both instances, then, the American public was very susceptible to presidential leadership.

A similar example occurred during President Nixon's handling of the war in Southeast Asia. Just prior to the American invasion of Cambodia in 1970, a Harris Poll was conducted that asked whether the public supported the commitment of the American forces to that country. Only 7 percent favored such a policy. Yet, after President Nixon went on national television to explain his decision to send American troops into Cambodia, another Harris Poll indicated that 50 percent of the American public supported the policy.[70] In other words, in a matter of three weeks, public opinion turned around rather dramatically, with only the president's speech as the important intervening event.

In the post-Vietnam and post–Cold War periods, such ready acceptance of presidential leadership might seem more difficult to obtain, but, in fact, it has continued. Prior to the seizure of American hostages in Iran in November 1979, President Jimmy Carter's approval rating was only 32 percent. By the end of December, his approval rating had jumped up to 61 percent. Furthermore, President Carter initially got high marks from the public over his handling of the Iranian situation, with 82 percent of the American people applauding his actions.[71] While this "rallying around the president" can be short-lived, as President Carter was about to find out, it nevertheless allows the executive considerable latitude to take foreign policy initiatives without suffering any immediate domestic repercussions.

President Reagan also influenced public opinion on foreign policy issues by exercising presidential leadership. Although he met resistance on several foreign policy issues—placing American forces in Lebanon in 1982, backing the Contras in Central America, and opposing the nuclear freeze issue—he was still able, by his actions, to increase support from the American public for his policy positions. After the terrorist bombing of the marine headquarters in Beirut, Lebanon, and the loss of 241 Americans, the level of the public's approval of United States troops stationed in that country increased from 36 percent in late September 1983 to 48 percent by late October 1983. Similarly, President Reagan's decision to send United States troops to Grenada won quick approval from the American public, with 55 percent supporting this action and 31 percent opposing it. Both of these levels of support for the president were accompanied by an increase in overall approval of his handling of the presidency.[72]

Despite consistent overall disapproval of his administration's policy toward Nicaragua, President Reagan's efforts on behalf of that policy had some noticeable, albeit modest, effect on public opinion. After he gave a speech to a joint session of Congress in April 1983, for instance, the public's support for his handling of Central America policy rose from 21 percent to 36 percent by November 1983. Yet, most other polls between April and November showed increases of only a few percentage points.[73] When Reagan engaged in a series of speeches to the public and Congress from March 1986 to June 1986, we find some increase in public approval for his "handling the situation in Nicaragua." In early March 1986, the approval rating was only 37 percent, but by April, it rose to 47 percent and remained at about that level (45 percent) through June 1986.[74]

President George Bush was also able to use his foreign policy actions to gain additional public support. In the first two years of his term, President Bush generally enjoyed strong support for his foreign policy actions. Yet his decisions to intervene into Panama in December 1989 to topple and seize Manuel Noriega, as well as to respond with military forces to Iraqi President Saddam Hussein's intervention into Kuwait in August 1990, won him even greater approval. After the United States assault on Panama, President Bush's approval rating went up to 80 percent in January 1990, and after his decision on August 8, 1990, to send American forces to support Saudi Arabia against Saddam Hussein, his approval rating shot up again, reaching 77 percent in mid-August 1990.[75] After Congress gave its approval to use force in the Gulf against the Iraqis in January 1991, and as first the air war and then the ground war began, President Bush's popularity shot up once again. Indeed, his popularity reached about 90 percent by the time of the cease-fire in March 1991.[76] Dramatic and decisive foreign policy actions have often tended to rally support for the president, and thus President Bush was no exception.

President Clinton, too, experienced the same phenomenon of "rallying around the flag" by the American people over his Haitian actions during the fall of 1994. As the military government in Haiti was steadfast in its resistance to restoring the democratically elected government, the Clinton administration increasingly hinted that military action would be required and gained UN authorization to do so if necessary. Yet the American public was skeptical of such action, with only a little more than a third supporting this option.[77] Overall approval "of the way Bill Clinton is handling the situation in Haiti" was equally low (27 percent) in early September 1994, and was only slightly higher (35 percent) on September 14, 1994, the day before President Clinton's nationwide address pledging to use American force to remove the military regime. After that speech, however, the poll results demonstrated the potency of presidential leadership. Clinton's approval for handling Haiti shot up to 53 percent and was still at 48 percent at the end of the month of September.[78] The "rally effect" helped President Clinton in the short run.

The question that inevitably accompanies this rise is how long it will be sustained. The general answer is that, as other events capture the public's attention, such support begins to erode. In short, though, the potency of the presidency as a shaper of foreign policy opinion continues, and it serves as an important restraint on the effectiveness of overall public sentiment in directing foreign policy making. Yet, it is not all-encompassing, as we shall show later in this chapter.

Gauging Public Opinion

Other difficulties also seemingly diminish the effectiveness of public opinion. Because the public's views are not always well developed or firmly held, question wording and even the terms used in public opinion polls can alter the public's view from survey to survey. As Rosenberg, Verba, and Converse hypothesize, the concepts used to describe American involvement in Vietnam could influence the level of public support or opposition to that war. If negative terms were used (such as "defeat" or "Communist take over"), the public would likely be more defensive and hawkish in its response. If other negative terms were use ("the increase in killings" or "the continued costs of the war"), the public might respond in a more dovish or conciliatory manner.[79]

A study of the various public opinion polls regarding aid to the Nicaraguan Contras in the 1980s confirmed the effects of question wording. When the public was asked about funding these opposition forces and specific references were made to "President Reagan," to "the Contras," or to the "Marxist government" in Nicaragua, the level of support for Contra aid was generally higher among the American public than when such references were left out. By contrast, when references to the amount of money involved in supporting the Contras was mentioned, or when the question format was more "balanced" in treating the competing parties involved in the conflict, the level of public support was lower than in polls without such characteristics. While the overall effect of question wording on support or opposition to Contra aid was relatively modest, it did have a discernible effect.[80]

Similarly, the number of options presented to a respondent can also be important in affecting the result. One analysis of public attitudes on the SALT treaty in the 1970s illustrated how different question wording produced different policy implications. Two sets of polls (a Harris Poll and an NBC-AP Poll) asked only the questions of support or opposition to the SALT treaty; another set of polls (Roper) provided information on the treaty and provided more options. The latter found only about 40 percent support for SALT, while the former found between 67 and 77 percent approval.[81] The explanation for such disparity in the results was tied to the kind of options and information provided to the respondents. While question wording is always a possible source of error in gauging public opinion, it is a particularly crucial one when the public's views are not well developed or deeply held.

Public opinion polls asking which side the United States was supporting in Nicaragua illustrate the same problems of how knowledge levels and question options can shape the results. As we noted earlier, the public generally was not able to identify correctly which side the United States was backing in Nicaragua until 1985 and 1986. Generally, those polls, however, used only two options in seeking to discern whom the United States was backing ("the rebels" or "the government"). Polls conducted by CBS/*New York Times*, however, used *three* options for ascertaining which side the United States was backing ("the current government," "the people fighting the government," or "haven't you been following this closely enough to say?"). In these polls, the last option obtained the highest percentage of responses at the same time that the other polls, with only two options, showed the American public more knowledgeable.[82]

More recent survey results about American involvement in Bosnia continue to demonstrate the role of question wording and the number of options in affecting opinion results. After the December 1995 signing of the Dayton Accords, which supported the placing of a NATO implementation force (IFOR) in Bosnia (a force that would include about 20,000 American military personnel), the American public disapproved of the presence of United States troops in that country by a 54 percent to a 41 percent margin. Moreover, Gallup reported a greater degree of intensity among those who disapproved ("43% strongly disapprove") than among those who approved ("only 24% strongly approve"). Yet, when a more detailed question about this deployment was asked using three options and including a reference to the president in each, the results differed: Thirty-six percent continued to disapprove and opposed Clinton's actions, 33 percent opted for supporting the deployment and the president's decision, and 27 percent contended that the United States should not deploy troops, but the president's decision as commander in chief should be supported. By this breakdown, and in the words of one assessment, "60% of the public can be counted as at least weak supporters of U.S. involvement in Bosnia."[83] Such results contrast sharply with those when only the approve/disapprove dimensions were used, and when no explicit reference to the president was made.

In short, in an environment of limited foreign policy knowledge and a variety of options, one may get different responses to the questions asked. Such results once again raise doubts about how much credence officials give to competing results and thus erode the impact of public opinion on foreign policy.

Public Opinion and Fluctuating Moods

Gabriel Almond, an early pioneer in the analysis of public attitudes on foreign policy, has aptly summarized the portrait of American public opinion that we have sketched so far. The American public view is essentially a "mood" toward foreign affairs that lacks "intellectual structure and factual content." This mood is largely "superficial and fluctuating," "permissive," and subject to the elite leadership influence "if they [the policy makers] demonstrate unity and resolution."[84]

With these fluctuating and permissive moods, the role of public opinion as a shaper of foreign policy is surely diminished. While the public can exercise some impact during periods of crises or war, in general it is more apt to follow the direction of the leadership. Similarly, while the fluctuation in moods may not be as great as it once was, as Almond later acknowledged, public opinion is still largely unstable and unstructured. Consequently, and as Almond put it, public opinion "cannot be viewed as standing in the way of foreign policy decisions by American governmental leaders."[85]

The influential American journalist and student of public opinion Walter Lippmann took an equally dim view of the role of public opinion and foreign policy, but he saw it as far more dangerous than did Almond. As one analyst put it, Lippmann saw "the mass public as not mrerely uninterested and uninformed, but as a powerful force that was so out of synch with reality as to constitute a massive and potentially fatal threat to effective government and policies."[86] As Lippmann himself wrote, "The people have impressed a critical veto upon the judgments of informed and responsible officials. They have compelled the government, which usually knew what would have been wiser, or was necessary, or what was more expedient, to be late with too little, or too long with too much, too pacifist in peace and too bellicose in war...."[87]

Some evidence by other scholars seems to allay Lippmann's fears.[88] One scholar, for example, found, as the earlier discussion implied, that the public's views were not consistent or "constrained." That is, an individual's views in one area did not correlate well with views in another. In other words, the American mass public seems to lack any underlying structures, at least with the 1950s and 1960s data. As a result, mass opinion, with such disparate and changeable views across individuals, could hardly serve as a restraining force on policy makers. A whole series of scholars, too, have questioned whether public opinion really affects foreign policy. Whether Congress or the executive was studied by these analysts, only the most tenuous link (or none at all) existed between opinion and policy. In short, in the perception of these early scholars, little compelling evidence could be summoned to suggest that public opinion mattered much in the conduct of foreign policy.

FOREIGN POLICY OPINION: STRUCTURED AND STABLE

Recent research reaches a less pessimistic conclusion about public opinion and its role in the foreign policy process. In this view, even in the context of a relatively uninformed mass public and one that is susceptible to elite or presidential leadership, foreign policy attitudes of the American public are not as irrelevant to policy making as others might suggest. At least two interrelated reasons are offered to support this view: (1) the public's attitudes are more structured and stable than has often been assumed; (2) the public mood is more identifiable and less shiftable and potentially more constraining on policy makers' actions than is sometimes suggested.

The Structure of Foreign Policy Opinions

How is it possible that opinions can be structured and stable if, as we demonstrated earlier, knowledge and interest in foreign affairs are so relatively low among the American public? Political scientists Jon Hurwitz and Mark Peffley have begun to untangle this apparent anomaly. They have argued that individuals utilize information shortcuts to make political judgments and to relate preferences toward specific foreign policy issues from general attitudes. Thus, paradoxically, ordinary citizens can hold coherent attitude structures, even though they lack detailed knowledge about foreign policy. As they write:

> Individuals organize information because such organization helps to simplify the world. Thus, a paucity of information does not *impede* structure and consistency; on the contrary, it *motivates* the development and employment of structure. Thus, we see individuals as attempting to cope with an extraordinarily confusing world (with limited resources to pay information costs) by structuring views about specific foreign policies according to their more general and abstract beliefs.[89]

Research by political scientists Benjamin Page, Robert Shapiro, and Eugene Wittkopf has begun to demonstrate more fully the accuracy of this position. In extensive analyses of public opinion surveys from the 1930s to the 1980s, Shapiro and Page demonstrated that public opinion has changed relatively slowly over time. "When it has changed, it has done so by responding in rational ways to international and domestic events...." In their view, public opinion does not tend to be "volatile or fluctuate wildly." Instead, they conclude that "collective opinion tends to be rather stable; it sometimes changes abruptly, but usually by only small amounts; and it rarely fluctuates."[90] In short, the public is markedly "rational" and stable in its foreign policy beliefs.

Through comprehensive analyses of Chicago Council on Foreign Relations surveys, Wittkopf determined the structure of American foreign policy opinion and demonstrated its stability over the past three decades.[91] His analyses reveal that the American people have not only been divided over *whether* the United States should be involved in foreign affairs (the traditional isolationism/internationalist dimension) but they also have been divided over *how* they should be involved (the cooperative/militant dimension). Yet these divisions over America's foreign policy role have remained remarkably consistent among the public over the years.

More specifically, the American public is divided along two continua: a continuum of *cooperative internationalism* and a continuum of *militant internationalism*. Where Americans fall on those continua are based upon attitudes and opinions "about how broad or narrow the range of U.S. foreign policy goals should be; about the particular countries in which the United States has vital interests; and about the use of force to protect others."[92] The intersection of those two continua produces four distinct belief systems and best describes the structure of American foreign policy opinion today. Figure 12.4 visually displays the structure of the belief systems across the four quadrants.

Wittkopf labeled the four segments of the public holding these belief systems as *internationalists*, *isolationists*, *accommodationists*, and *hardliners*.[93] Internationalists are those individuals who support both cooperative and militant approaches to global affairs and are largely reflective of American attitudes prior to the Vietnam War. Both the unilateral use of American

FIGURE 12.4

The Distribution of the Mass Public Among the Four Types of Foreign Policy Beliefs, 1974–1994

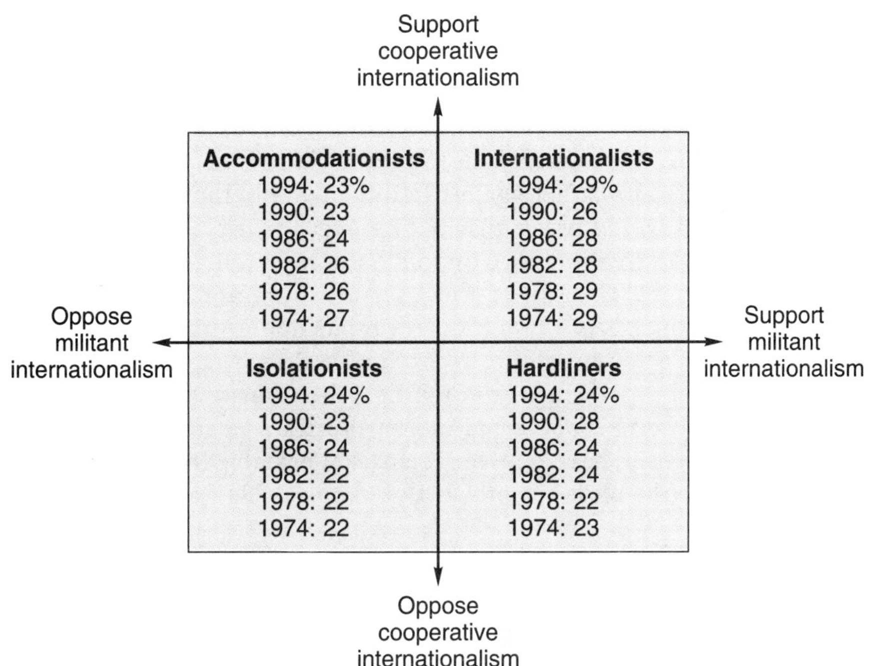

Sources: The source for the diagram and the data for the years 1974–1986 are from Eugene R. Wittkopf, *Faces of Internationalism: Public Opinion and American Foreign Policy*, p. 26. Copyright © 1990, Duke University Press. Reprinted by permission of the publisher. The more recent data are drawn from Eugene R. Wittkopf, "Faces of Internationalism in a Transitional Environment," *Journal of Conflict Resolution* 38 (September 1994): 383; and personal communication with Eugene R. Wittkopf.

force and cooperative efforts through the United Nations would find support among this segment of the public. In the Persian Gulf War, for example, internationalists likely supported both UN efforts to resolve the conflict over Kuwait, and then the use of American and coalition force to expel Iraq from Kuwait. In Bosnia, too, this segment would support American efforts at diplomatic resolution (e.g., through the Dayton Accords), but it would also back the deployment of American forces as part of a peacekeeping force.

Isolationists are those individuals who tend to reject both cooperative internationalism and militant internationalism and would favor a reduced role for the United States in global affairs. In the Gulf War, they would not have supported the use of force toward Iraq or even believed that a vital interest was at stake over the seizure of Kuwait. In Bosnia, isolationists would neither support American involvement nor would they believe that an American interest was at stake in that ethnic conflict.

Accommodationists are those individuals who favor cooperative internationalism but oppose militant internationalism. They would likely have supported the use of economic sanctions against Iraq over Kuwait, but they would not have supported the use of force. The same distinction toward American action in Bosnia would arise: support for the use of sanctions against Serbia and Bosnia, opposition to the use of force by the United States there.

Finally, and in contrast to accommodationists, hardliners are those individuals who favor militant internationalism and oppose cooperative internationalism. In the case of the Gulf War, hardliners would likely have wanted to use force earlier against Iraq than would the other segments of the public and would prefer that option over the use of diplomacy. They would have preferred the same option in the case of Bosnia as well.

By Wittkopf's assessment, these segments are almost evenly divided among the public.[94] As a result, the restraints upon American policy makers come from a variety of directions. Internationalists, for example, constitute about 28 percent of the public; isolationists about 23 percent; accommodationists 25 percent; and hardliners 24 percent.[95] These percentages, moreover, have remained remarkably stable from the initial survey in 1974 to the most recently analyzed one (1994), as Figure 12.4 also shows.

These underlying belief systems among the public are important for understanding the role of public opinion and foreign policy for several reasons. First, they are highly predictive of what policy these segments of the public will support. Over 80 percent of internationalists and over 60 percent of accommodationists are supporters of United States participation in peacekeeping operations, while isolationists and hardliners oppose such actions. Similarly, internationalists and accommodationists are strong supporters of continuing or increasing aid to Russia, while, once again, hardliners and isolationists strongly oppose it. In contemplating another kind of action in Europe—the use of American troops to defend that region—internationalists and hardliners are the strongest proponents of such action, while accommodationists and isolationists are the weakest. Similarly, an overwhelming majority of both internationalists and hardliners are strongly supportive of coming to the aid of Japan if it were invaded, but only a minority of accommodationists and isolationists are. Indeed, these two coalitions are evident across a wide array of issues that have been examined.[96]

Second, the different foreign policy belief systems are closely tied to a number of other sociopolitical characteristics of the American public. As such, these foreign policy divisions are deeply ingrained within the American political landscape. In particular, the political ideology of an individual and his or her level of education are good predictors where that individual falls among these belief systems.[97] Political "liberals," for instance, tend to be accommodationists, political "conservatives" tend to be hardliners, and political "moderates" tend to be internationalists. College-educated individuals tend to be both internationalists and accommodationists, those with a high school education tend to be both internationalists and hardliners, and those with less than a high school education tend to be hardliners. As

Wittkopf's analysis of the 1994 survey reveals, however, those respondents who "describe themselves as either very conservative or very liberal both reveal strong *isolationist* tendencies—the only political groups that do."[98]

The patterns of these belief systems are less clear-cut by region and party. The East is, by and large, composed of those individuals who are accommodationists; the Midwest and West fluctuate among three belief systems—the accommodationist, internationalist, and hardliner categories—during the four earlier surveys; and the South varies between the hardliner and internationalist camp over these analyses. Most interestingly, though, these belief systems are not closely tied to partisanship. While there was some tendency for those possessing hardline or internationalist belief systems to be Republicans and those possessing accommodationist and internationalist belief systems to be Democrats, the differences among these belief systems were sufficiently blurred across the parties to make accurate predictions quite difficult.

Third, because these divisions exist within the public and have been consistent over time, the leadership is now more constrained than some might argue. Foreign policy decision makers must now gauge which groups will support or oppose particular foreign policy actions and must calculate the acceptable limits of their foreign policy actions. In any earlier era, if previous research findings were accurate portrayals of the public, the president, for example, did not have to make such calculations; instead, he could rather routinely count on public support. With these persistent divisions, though, that possibility is less assured. In this sense, this kind of structure and consistency in belief, far from freeing the foreign policy leaders to pursue their own course, may actually constrain the actions of various administrations.

An Alternative View of the Public Mood

If we can take this initial conclusion one step further, we can begin to suggest a somewhat larger role for the "public mood" in the policy process as well. Two political scientists, Bernard Cohen and V. O. Key, writing shortly after Almond's initial work on the public "mood" and foreign policy, suggest as much with their concepts of "climate of opinion" and the "context of public opinion."

Bernard Cohen introduced the concept of "climate of opinion" to summarize the public's view on foreign policy actions. This notion refers to the foreign policy decision-making environment which, "by creating in the policymaker an impression of a public attitude or attitudes, or by becoming part of the environment and cultural milieu that help to shape his own thinking, may consciously affect his official behavior."[99] A few years later, V. O. Key expanded upon this notion by introducing what he called the "context of public opinion." This notion suggests how the public's overall views can affect governmental action, including the foreign policy arena. Key's description of this concept and how it operates is worth quoting at some length:

> That context is not a rigid matrix that fixes a precise form for government action. Nor is it unchangeable. It consists of opinion irregularly distributed among the people and of varying intensity, of attitudes of differing convertibility into votes, and

> of sentiments not always readily capable of appraisal. Yet that context, as it is perceived by those responsible for action, conditions many of the acts of those who must make what we may call "opinion-related decisions." The opinion context may affect the substance of action, the form of action, or the manner of action.[100]

These alternate views of the "public mood," suggest that the foreign policy opinions of the American people form a part of the political milieu—even in the foreign policy realm. In this way, foreign policy opinion might be thought of as setting the broad outlines of "acceptable" policy without necessarily dictating the day-to-day policy choices of decision makers. Thus, gauging the public mood, and acting within the constraints of that mood, becomes an important task for successful policy makers. A brief survey of the recent public moods or climates of opinion, gleaned from several sources, will illustrate their relationship to, and impact on, American foreign policy. Keep in mind, however, that policy makers will also try to alter or adjust that public mood to their liking, much as Almond and others have suggested.

The Cold War Mood. During the height of the Soviet-American Cold War period, for instance, the public expressed strong support for an active American role in global affairs. The level of support for global involvement was also quite predictive of public commitments to the Marshall Plan, NATO, and a willingness to stop communism through military action. In fact, after examining a number of public opinion polls for the late 1940s through the early 1960s, political scientist William Caspary concluded that the American public demonstrated a "*strong* and *stable* 'permissive mood' toward international involvements."[101] Further, another analyst saw the Cold War period as one in which "policymakers became imprisoned by popular anticommunism even though, in most cases, the policymakers were too sophisticated really to share the popular perspective."[102] Thus the values of the postwar consensus (see Chapters 2 and 3) were firmly embedded in the public and policy makers alike and largely shaped the policy choices.

The "Vietnam Syndrome." The "searing effects" of the Vietnam War on the beliefs of the American public toward international affairs have been widely analyzed.[103] In the immediate post-Vietnam period, for instance, there was a decided turn inward on several important dimensions of foreign and military involvement. In late 1974, roughly one-third of the American public favored a cutback in the defense budget, and over 50 percent believed that "we should build up our own defenses and let the world take care of itself."[104] In addition, there was considerable public aversion to sending United States troops to support friendly nations that were attacked or even to sending military and economic aid to such states. Only in the case of an attack upon Canada did a majority of the public (77 percent) support American military involvement. Attacks upon Western Europe or upon Israel gained support from only 39 percent of the public in the case of the former region and only 27 percent in the case of the latter state. Support for using military and economic aid to help friendly countries that were attacked was equally low. Only 37 percent of the public supported the American government's using these tactics. Finally, the American public also favored a cutback in military aid and opposed CIA political operations, presumably because each of these areas further involved the United States abroad.

While the public mood tended to reject an active military and political involvement in international affairs in the immediate post-Vietnam period, this view should not imply an abandonment of an "active role" for the United States in world affairs. In fact, 66 percent of the public still supported a continued global role for the United States, but this global role was to take a different form than that prescribed by the Cold War consensus. When asked to rank the importance of a variety of different goals for the United States, the public placed greatest importance on such aims as keeping the peace and promoting and defending America's security. Next, however, the public indicated that the United States should concentrate on a large number of domestic and global *economic* problems—such as securing adequate energy supplies, protecting American jobs, and solving global food, inflation, and energy problems. Most importantly, perhaps, the traditional goals of the Cold War period, such as containing communism, defending allies, and helping to spread democracy and capitalism abroad, were ranked relatively low by the public. In the words of one analyst at that time: "The cold war sense of urgent threat is gone from America's political consciousness."[105]

In essence, then, the public sought a *more limited political role, but a larger economic one.* Moreover, the public wanted the United States to emphasize *cooperation* with other nations in solving common problems. Finally, the public seemed to back away from acceptance of some of the crusading goals summarized under the Cold War consensus.

This mood, moreover, did seem to have a dampening effect on the actions of both the Ford and Carter administrations. The ability to use force and to intervene globally was sharply reduced. The Ford administration, for example, was unable to win any public (or congressional) support for last-minute aid to South Vietnam and Cambodia prior to their collapse in 1975. Nor was President Ford about to muster support for vigorous action on behalf of the National Front for the Liberation of Angola in their struggle with the Soviet-backed Popular Movement for the Liberation of Angola. An exception, however, was the popular response to the swift military action ordered by President Ford over the seizure of the American merchant vessel, the *Mayaguez*, by Cambodia in May 1975.

In the context of this foreign policy mood, the appeal of a Jimmy Carter presidential candidacy is quite understandable. With Carter's call for an emphasis upon global issues, downplaying of the East-West dispute, and calling for universal human rights, his candidacy was well within the limits of the public mood in the middle 1970s. In essence, the popular mood, summarized under the heading of the "Vietnam syndrome," was in place among the American public and was generally respected by the political leadership.

The "Self-Interest" Mood.[106] The public mood changed somewhat, however, by the late 1970s, especially as the relationship between the United States and the Soviet Union began to deteriorate during the second and third years of the Carter administration. Moreover, there was an increased perception of threat from the Soviet Union among the American public. By one analysis, concern with the power of the Soviet Union had replaced Vietnam as the "central preoccupation of American foreign policy."[107] As a result, the public mood began to move away, albeit slowly, from the limits of the "Vietnam syndrome."

In this context, the public was now more willing to increase defense expenditures, support American military actions abroad, and tolerate CIA activities in other nations.[108] Thirty-two percent of the public now said that the United States spent too little on defense (as compared to 13 percent in 1974) and only 16 percent said that the United States spent too much (as compared to 32 percent in 1974). A majority of the public now supported sending troops if Panama closed access to the Canal or if the Soviets invaded Western Europe. Furthermore, a plurality (48 percent of the public) favored the use of American troops if West Berlin were attacked, and 42 percent favored a United States response to a Soviet invasion of Japan. The public was now also more supportive of allowing the CIA to work inside other countries to support American interests. In 1978, 59 percent of the public supported such actions, compared to only 43 percent in 1974. While this interventionist sentiment still had its limits, it had increased from the 1974 period.[109]

At the same time, there was a certain amount of ambivalence about any rekindling of past crusading efforts on the part of the United States. Although some Cold War goals (such as protecting allies and containing communism) had increased in importance as foreign policy preferences from their 1974 levels, the domestic and foreign economic concerns remained most important for the American public (such as "keeping up the value of the dollar," "securing adequate supplies of energy," and "protecting the jobs of American workers").[110]

This ambivalence was especially demonstrated in the mixed reaction to the Soviet Union. Although 56 percent of the public believed that the United States was "falling behind the Soviet Union in power and influence," the public remained committed to greater cooperation in joint energy efforts, joint scholarly exchanges, and pursuing arms limitations.[111] In short, sentiment for maintaining détente seemed still in place, especially among the attentive public.[112]

In sum, then, by the late 1970s, the public mood was for a more "self-interested" and nationalistic foreign policy than in 1974, but one that continued to maintain elements of economic and political cooperation with other nations. Furthermore, the public continued to be "wary of direct involvement that characterized United States policy in the 1960s," but they still remained determined to defend important commitments in the world.[113] In this context, the success of the Reagan candidacy is explainable, especially as President Jimmy Carter was increasingly perceived as incapable of dealing effectively with foreign policy matters.

The Public Mood in the 1980s. The public mood in the 1980s changed little from that of the late 1970s. Yet the Reagan administration adopted some policies that were at variance with the public mood. In this situation, it is important to evaluate the ultimate effect of the public mood.

The foreign policy goals, as expressed by the public in two national polls conducted in late 1982 and late 1986, remained essentially the same as in 1978.[114] Global and domestic economic concerns continued to have the highest priority, while containing communism and defending allies retained their somewhat lower ranking. At the same time, the public expressed a slight increase in the level of support for interventionism than they did in the late 1970s. For instance, the public supported sending U.S. troops to Western Europe and Japan if they were attacked. No other country or region received over 45 percent approval for such action, but a third of the public favored using U.S. troops "if the Arabs cut off oil shipments to the U.S. or if Arab forces invade Israel."[115] The public thus seemed to be selective in choosing between vital and secondary interests that were necessary to protect. There was, for example, substantial opposition to sending American troops into El Salvador if the leftists were succeeding or into Taiwan if China invaded.[116]

On the question of the Soviet Union in 1982 and 1986, the public remained ambivalent, much as they had in 1978. While the Soviet Union ranked the lowest or second lowest of any nation (after Iran) when the public was asked to rank states on a "thermometer scale," the public remained committed to seeking better ties with the USSR: Seventy-seven percent (in 1982) and 82 percent (in 1986) favored arms control agreements, 64 percent in 1982 favored undertaking joint energy projects with the Soviets, and 70 percent (in 1982) and 76 percent (in 1986) favored the resumption of cultural and educational exchanges.[117]

As previously indicated, such a public mood generally clashed with the priorities of the Reagan administration, especially during its first term.[118] While President Reagan brought back some of the rhetoric and policies of the Cold War consensus, the public mood opposed several of these foreign policy priorities. The Reagan administration wanted to increase defense spending and engage in a defense buildup; the public was now content to keep the budget as it was and to seek arms control agreements instead. The Reagan administration wanted to engage in a more confrontational policy toward the Soviet Union; the public wanted to seek more cooperative exchanges with that nation. The Reagan administration wanted to increase military assistance; the public continued to oppose such aid by a wide margin.

Such disagreements between the public mood and public policy undoubtedly put some strain on what the Reagan administration could do in its foreign policy. In this sense, these disagreements contributed to a political climate that ultimately facilitated accommodation with the Soviet Union, on the one hand, and served as a restraint on the extent of the policy course pursued toward Nicaragua, on the other.

"Pragmatic Internationalism"—The Public Mood in the 1990s. With the repercussions from the dramatic events during 1989 through 1991—the fall of the Berlin Wall, the emergence of democracy in Eastern Europe, the unification of Germany, the Iraqi invasion of Kuwait, and the collapse of the Soviet Union—the public mood has now evolved to one described as "pragmatic internationalism."[119] While about two-thirds of citizens remained committed to an active role for the United States in global affairs, the public remains more concerned about domestic economic and social problems than foreign policy ones and appears less willing to intervene in the affairs of other states. While the American public does not reject global leadership, it seeks a greater sharing of that responsibility with multilateral organizations and wants the United States to be more selective in the actions it takes abroad.

Overall, however, foreign policy problems continue to rank low on the public's agenda, as the Chicago Council survey emphasizes: "Foreign policy–related problems now constitute the smallest number of overall problems since 1978 for the public."[120] To the extent that foreign policy concerns are identified as important goals for the United States, five of the top six most often mentioned as "very important" reflect domestic social and economic concerns tied to the international arena: "stopping the flow of illegal drugs into the U.S.," "protecting the jobs of American workers," "controlling and reducing illegal immigration," "securing adequate supplies of energy," and "reducing our trade deficit with foreign countries."[121] The only traditional security issue among the six is the goal of "preventing the spread of nuclear weapons."

While the level of perceived "national economic vulnerability" has declined somewhat from the 1990 Chicago survey,[122] the public's worry over Europe's and Japan's economic threat remains. In the 1994 survey, 71 percent of the public (the same as the 1990 survey) believes that Japan is unfair in its trade practices, and 35 percent (down from 40 percent in 1990) believes that Europe is unfair.[123] While this emphasis upon domestic and foreign economic issues continues a trend over the past two decades, its intensity and pervasiveness have increased.

What is perhaps better evidence of the public's present mood toward international affairs is where individuals believe that American interests lie. Interestingly, Russia continues to hold an important place, although the public still views that country with an admixture of friendliness and wariness. On the positive side, 20 percent of the American people in 1994 believed that the United States should increase foreign aid to Russia, and slightly more than a third believe that it should remain the same. Russia was also viewed as more friendly and in a more favorable light than in the past. Indeed, Russia was now tied for sixth at 54 degrees (with Israel and Brazil) out of twenty-three countries on a "thermometer" ranking of friendliness ranging from 0 to 100 degrees. It was surpassed only by Canada, Great Britain, Italy, Germany, Mexico, and France. Russian President Boris Yeltsin, too, was favorably ranked by the American public, following only Pope John Paul II, Henry Kissinger, Jimmy Carter, George Bush, Nelson Mandela, and Bill Clinton on a similar thermometer rating.[124]

Even as the public expresses these views, however, a substantial majority of the American public (81 percent) believes "that the military power of Russia represents either a critical or an important possible threat to the vital interests of the United States in the next 10 years."[125] Further, a majority of the public is willing to support the use of American force if Russia invades Western Europe and two-fifths of the public supports the expansion of NATO, which is often viewed as a way of deterring any future Russian expansionism. Nonetheless, the overall summary of these results stands in contrast to the 1986 survey by the Chicago Council on Foreign Relations, in which American-Soviet relations ranked at the top as a foreign policy problem and in which the Soviet Union was ranked near the bottom in this favorability index.[126]

In other ways, though, the new post–Cold War era evokes different priorities among the public. Now, Japan, Saudi Arabia, Kuwait, and Mexico are ranked as vital interests by the public. While Japan remains an important ally in a region of increasing problems, its economic competitiveness also continues to be a concern. Yet, as America's economic competitiveness has increased, the public's concern with Japan has diminished a bit.[127] Saudi Arabia and Kuwait rank as vital interests owing to their vast supply of oil, their proximity to troublesome states in the Middle East, Iran and Iraq, and questions about their domestic political stability. Mexico, too, has emerged as a vital interest for the United States. Not only does that country border on the United States, but, with the North American Free Trade Agreement now in effect, the fortunes of the two countries are linked as never before.

By mid-decade, too, China had emerged as one of the vital interests of the United States. Almost three-fifths of the public views China's emergence as a world power as a "critical" threat to the United States, and two-thirds of the public believes that China's role in ten years will be greater than it was in 1994.[128] More generally, the Asian region—whether the economic threat from Japan, the political–economic threat from China, and the possible nuclear threat from North Korea—has emerged as an area of considerable concern for the American public,[129] unlike Europe, where the variety of threats has diminished with the end of the Cold War.

Despite identifying some new states as vital foreign policy interests, several traditional security concerns continue. Indeed, on defense spending, the public's views have stabilized since the early 1990s. At that time, almost a third of the public favored cuts in the defense budget. Now, a half to two-thirds or more of the public (depending on the question wording) favors keeping the defense budget the same or even increasing it.[130] The same holds for views toward the NATO commitment. In the 1990 survey, while a majority of the public still supported that organization, it wanted a smaller commitment of American forces. In the 1994 survey, 56 percent of the public supports keeping the present commitment to NATO and 42 percent of the public supports the expansion of NATO to include Czech Republic, Hungary, and Poland.[131] Finally, public attitudes on the use of American force abroad convey this sense of pragmatic internationalism on the part of the public. Only in instances of a Russian invasion of Western Europe and an Iraqi invasion of Saudi Arabia are a majority of the American public willing to use American troops to defend these countries. In a series of other instances (e.g., an invasion of Israel by its Arab neighbors, a North Korean invasion of South Korea, or a Russian invasion of Poland), a majority of the public opposed the deployment of United States troops.[132] In short, the public remains cautious and selective of where it would support the use of American military force abroad.

Part of the reason for some enhanced concern with security issues may also be tied to the emergence of new "critical threats." Indeed, two-thirds of the public see the spread of nuclear weapons to unfriendly countries, the influx of immigrants and refugees to the United States, and international terrorism among these new threats. Majorities of the public also view "economic competition from Japan" and "the development of China as a world power" as other dangers.[133]

In sum, the overall portrait of the public mood suggests a continued, but limited, role for the United States in foreign affairs, with new actors and issues replacing the long-dominant Cold War focus. The rise of a more powerful China, both economically and militarily, or the ethnic conflicts rife in Bosnia, Somalia, and Rwanda, for example, are now likely to be the kind of concerns dominating the foreign policy agenda. New threats (e.g., the spread of nuclear weapons, terrorism, and drug trafficking) as well as the expanding global economic competition also continue to share the attention and priorities of the American public as we move to the next millennium.

Some Evidence of Stability and Consistency in Public Opinion

Although the public mood can change over time and seems to do so in reasonable and predictable ways, several researchers have found that American foreign policy opinion remains equally "coherent," "consistent," and "stable" when considering several salient issues. As we discussed earlier, Shapiro and Page are leading proponents of this view of public opinion, and their work is worth citing in some detail.

In a recent analysis, for example, these scholars report that, "the proportions of Americans thinking the United States should sell arms varied markedly from one country to another" from 1975 to 1985, yet they also contend that this variation always occurred in a coherent way.[134] While some countries (e.g., England and West Germany) received more support from the public for such sales than other countries (e.g., Greece, Turkey, and Iran), the patterns were markedly the same or consistent across the years. A similar consistency occurred regarding aid to El Salvador during the early to mid-1980s. The public consistently supported sending military advisors and assisting with training for the Salvadorian troops, but just as consistently opposed the introduction of American troops, over a series of surveys. Support and opposition for foreign aid generally, the building of the MX missile in the 1980s, free trade, and other foreign policy issues exhibit the same stability over differing time periods. Thus Shapiro and Page conclude in this way: "Stability is the rule for foreign as well as domestic issues. When opinion changes do occur, many do so quite gradually...."[135] In addition, they add that the public—even in the face of new information and new global conditions—"are regular, predictable, and generally sensible" in their opinions."[136]

In another context, political scientist Bruce Jentleson also illustrates the consistency and stability of public opinion on a highly salient issue—the use of American military force abroad. In a detailed analysis of public opinion polls on nine different uses of American force in the 1980s and early 1990s (including the Persian Gulf War of 1990 and 1991), Jentleson finds that public support or opposition is closely tied to the "*principal policy objective*" for using force. In instances of "*foreign policy restraint*"—the use of force to stop "aggressive actions against the United States or its interests"—public support is generally always higher than for instances of seeking "*internal political change*"—the use of force to support a friendly government in power or trying to overthrow an unfriendly regime. While those findings in themselves are of interest, the important implication for public opinion and foreign policy is that the public is not always swayed by presidential leadership and that the public is not "as boorish, overreactive, and generally the bane of those who would pursue an effective foreign policy." Instead, as Jentleson says, the public is "pretty prudent" and, we might add, pretty consistent in its foreign policy beliefs.[137]

Two other recent studies largely support Jentleson's main conclusion about the stability of public opinion. One study extends Jentleson's analysis back in time to include the entire Cold War period and also introduces a number of other factors that may account for his earlier results. Contrary to Jentleson's position that the consistency in public support or opposition was only a recent phenomenon, Oneal and his colleagues find that "Jentleson...is correct in believing that the American people discriminate among foreign policy objectives in evaluating the use of force" and have done so throughout the Cold War Years.[138] Put differently, the "pretty prudent" public is not a recent phenomenon.

The other study by Andrew Kohut and Robert Toth focused exclusively on the early to mid-1990s, including the Gulf War, Somalia, and Bosnia, and generally found that public opinion on the use of force was consistent as well. In particular, they report that the American public was willing to use force in only two situations: "[I]f it feels America's vital interests are at stake, and if American military force can provide humanitarian assistance without becoming engaged in a protracted conflict."[139] Once again, their analysis suggests that the policy objective is crucial (albeit a bit broader than what Jentleson found) in affecting the level of support and that the public does not blindly follow its leaders in any use of force (e.g., the expansion of the American involvement in Somalia in 1993). At the same time, they do point out that the ability of leaders (e.g., President Bush over the Persian Gulf) to explain their objectives to the American people was important in gaining support.[140] On balance, and in line with a more optimistic view of public opinion, support for the use of force was arrayed in consistent ways in these recent episodes.

THE IMPACT OF PUBLIC OPINION ON FOREIGN POLICY

One of the most difficult analytic tasks is to assess the overall effect of public opinion on foreign policy. Even if public opinion can be characterized as structured and stable, as we have suggested, a fundamental question remains: How much difference does public opinion really make in the foreign policy process? Are congressional and presidential elections mechanisms of popular control on foreign policy issues? Is Congress or the president really constrained in policy choices by what the public thinks? Some recent analyses provide partial answers to these questions, but the questions also remain important subjects of debate.

Foreign Policy Opinion and Presidential Elections

One way for public opinion to register an impact on foreign policy is through the electoral process, and especially through presidential elections every four years. In this way, the electorate can use their votes to punish political candidates with unpopular foreign policy views and reward those with whom they agree. Yet numerous analyses have raised doubts whether presidential elections are really referenda on foreign policy.

First, for example, presidential elections are rarely fought on foreign policy issues. Instead, domestic issues, and especially domestic economic issues, have dominated American presidential campaigns in the post–World War II years. By most assessments, only in the 1952 and 1972 presidential elections was foreign policy a central campaign issue between the candidates. Both of these elections, however, occurred in very special circumstances—United States involvement in two highly unpopular wars, Korea and Vietnam.

Second, even when foreign policy might be an issue in a presidential election, the stances of the candidates are not sufficiently different from one another for the public to distinguish between them. In the 1968 presidential campaign, for example, the Vietnam War was an issue, but the two candidates, Richard Nixon and Hubert Humphrey, were not perceived to be markedly different from one another in their positions on the war.[141] As a result, foreign policy did not turn out to be decisive in how the public voted in that campaign.

Third, even if foreign policy were viewed as salient by the public, its overall effect on the election outcome is viewed as quite small. In a classic analysis on this point, Warren Miller reports that the decline in support for the Republican candidate from the 1956 to the 1960 election based upon their respective foreign policy stances was minuscule—one half of one percent. Instead of the Republicans having a 2.5 percent vote advantage because of their foreign policy position in 1956, the advantage fell to 2.0 in the 1960 election.[142] Two decades later, in the 1980 contest between Jimmy Carter and Ronald Reagan, a similar small effect was reported. Despite the popular impression that the impact of the Iran hostage situation would severely hurt Carter's reelection prospects, a careful analysis of voting behavior in that election found otherwise. Ronald Reagan's issue position on foreign and domestic matters produced only about a 1 percent difference in the vote outcome. Instead, the voters' decisions were more fully related to the overall dissatisfaction with President Carter's performance in office and with doubts "about his competence as a political leader."[143]

Left unanswered by these and similar analyses, however, is whether even these small differences between the candidates in the aggregate did not affect the outcome in particular states, and hence the electoral votes of one presidential candidate over another. Especially in a close national election, such as the 1960 election between Kennedy and Nixon in which less than one percentage point separated the candidates, foreign policy opinion may have mattered. Put more precisely, in close state votes during such presidential elections, a swing of even a few percentage points could dramatically affect the national electoral vote count. To date, however, detailed state studies of presidential elections are not available to answer such questions.

Also left unanswered by these analyses is whether the activities in the foreign policy arena by incumbents contribute to creating an image of competence or incompetence that can also affect the outcome of elections. While specific foreign policy opinion may not be a central factor in voting decisions, presidential actions can convey a general impression of effectiveness in the global arena. On the face of it, this description seems to fit what happened in 1980, when President Carter's inability to manage foreign affairs probably hurt him at the polling booth with the public. In this (albeit indirect) way, foreign policy mattered. Conversely, President Clinton seemingly sought to be "Peacemaker in Chief" with his actions in Haiti, Bosnia, and Northern Ireland. By taking these actions, according to one analysis, the "president hopes to do well with voters by doing good on the international stage."[144] At the same time, too much emphasis by an incumbent president on foreign affairs may have an effect electorally. In 1992, the perceived excessive attention by President Bush on foreign affairs, and his perceived inattention to domestic policy, proved costly among voters.

Finally, one recent study has begun to reconceptualize the relationship between foreign policy opinion and recent presidential elections. This approach suggests that when candidate differences are large and foreign policy issues are salient, the public's views do affect the election outcomes. These conditions existed not only in 1952 and 1972, as has been noted, but they also were prevalent in the 1964, 1980, and 1984 presidential elections.[145] In such circumstances, public opinion on foreign policy matters probably made a difference in the election outcomes. Voters could see differences between the candidates, and these differences influenced voting decisions.

Foreign Policy Opinion and Congressional Elections

To even a greater degree than presidential elections, congressional elections are rarely depicted as referenda on foreign policy questions. Elections for the House of Representatives, in particular, are hardly ever fought on foreign policy questions. Foreign policy questions in United States Senate races are only occasionally salient. In both instances, the foreign policy positions of candidates are likely to be marginal to their campaigns.

Still, foreign policy may play a role in these elections in some negative and positive ways. On the one hand, if an incumbent is perceived as too involved in foreign affairs or spends too much time on foreign policy matters, he or she could be subject to electoral punishment by the public for neglecting the "folks back home." On the other hand, congressional candidates are often sure to be on the "right" side of particular issues related to foreign affairs in order to foreclose electoral punishment. Candidates from districts or states with substantial military spending are unlikely to oppose such activities; candidates with large Jewish constituencies are likely to be very supportive of Israel; and candidates from south Florida districts, for example, are likely to be strongly opposed to any compromise policy with Cuba's Fidel Castro. It is perhaps no accident that a Democratic congressman and senatorial candidate from New Jersey in 1996 was a leading proponent of a tougher policy toward Cuba, especially with a large Hispanic population in that state. On occasion then, a congressional candidate's foreign policy position may have considerable substantive impact, especially on a vocal and politically active minority within a member's district or state.

On occasion, too, foreign policy issues may take on an important *symbolic* importance in congressional races, even if their *substantive* importance is less clear. Political analyst Jeremy Rosner provides an interesting illustration of this phenomenon during a special congressional election in Oklahoma in May 1994.[146] The Democratic candidate in the race allowed as how he did not object to placing American troops under a UN commander in a peacekeeping operation. While it is unclear how important or salient this issue really was to Oklahoma congressional voters (although large percentages, when asked, said they opposed this position), the Republican candidate seized upon his opponent's stance to portray him as out of touch with Oklahomans. Indeed, the Republican candidate used a mailing to district voters outlining his opponent's position on the potential UN action and was able to spark interest and concern among some voters who responded. Furthermore, based upon polling data, he was able to target a particularly sensitive group (in this case, young Republicans) to stimulate its support over this foreign policy issue. In this way, a congressional candidate was able to have a foreign policy issue assume much greater importance than its substance implied, and he was able to paint his opponent as too closely tied to Washington and the Clinton administration, and not sufficiently tied to Oklahoma voters. In this sense, foreign policy opinion may matter to congressional candidates, although in a slightly different, and more irregular way than we might think.

Foreign Policy Opinion and Policy Choices

If it is difficult to argue that elections are regular referenda on foreign policy opinion, it is perhaps even more difficult to sustain the view that foreign policy opinion matters for particular policy choices. Only in rare instances, when the public has been mobilized, for example, by the president with a nationwide television address or by some interest groups over an upcoming vote in Congress, does public opinion seem to matter over an immediate foreign policy decision facing the country. In this sense, the effect of public opinion on individual policy decisions appears to be sporadic and exceptional.

Over the last two decades, we have witnessed examples of just these kinds of sporadic events, although the public's success level in controlling the outcomes has been mixed. In the late 1970s, public opinion, as expressed in various polls, was strongly opposed to the treaties calling for the transference of the Panama Canal back to the country of Panama by the year 2000. As a result, President Carter had a very difficult time gaining Senate approval. Despite his initial opposition to any changes in the treaties, he had to accept several understandings and amendments to make them more acceptable at home. Further, President Carter was forced to lobby hard for their passage with members of the United States Senate. Only then was he able to squeak out a narrow victory, 68–32. While public opinion did not ultimately stop these treaties, it affected the nature of the debate and their final provisions.

President Reagan had a similar experience over the issue of aid to the Nicaraguan Contras, as we have alluded to earlier in this chapter. He went on nationwide television several times to appeal for public support for his position. In this case, though, he was not always successful in obtaining increased support for the Contras. Indeed, in the aggregate, public opinion remained opposed, and Congress generally gave him much less than he wanted. In this particular case, then, public opinion, more than in the Panama Canal debate, ultimately contributed to a change in policy course by the Reagan administration and later by the Bush administration.

The latter case is especially instructive in another sense. The public's consistent opposition to aid to the Nicaraguan Contras made it much more difficult for the Reagan administration to pursue the more assertive course that it favored. Congress often reflected that public discontent, and military and economic funding for the Contras throughout the 1980s was a constant political problem. Further, if the public had been more supportive of the Reagan administration policy in Nicaragua, according to a former high-ranking official, the administration would have sought more money for the Contras and would have been more assertive about the American role in the area as well.[147] Such a statement does not imply that the public opinion in any real sense directed each and every United States foreign policy action toward Nicaragua, but it did serve a more important role than it is sometimes afforded.

Over the past two decades, several systematic studies provide more promising results on the relative effectiveness of public opinion in shaping foreign policy decisions. These studies have analyzed long-term trends in the relationship for particular issues (e.g., defense spending and arms control), and assessed the receptivity of foreign policy makers to public opinion. In general, the results suggest that public opinion (or the public mood) do serve as a guide to policy direction in the foreign policy area, although not as a guide to every individual foreign policy decision.

Political scientists Benjamin Page and Robert Shapiro, to whom we referred earlier, provide important results on the long-term trends in this relationship. In their massive analysis of the directional changes in public opinion and public policy over five decades (1935 to 1979), they sought to answer a key central question: When public opinion moved in one direction on an issue, did public policy follow that direction? What they found was that policy changes generally *did* follow the direction of opinion in both the domestic and foreign affairs arenas in the period of their analysis. For the foreign policy arena, in particular, they report that policy and opinion were congruent in 62 percent of the foreign policy cases examined. Further, policy really did seem to follow opinion, rather than the other way around. As they conclude, "it is reasonable in most of these cases to infer that opinion change was a *cause* of policy change, or at least a proximate or intervening factor leading to government action, if not the ultimate cause."[148] Nonetheless, they also indicate that their analysis could not and did not answer how much opinion was affected by the efforts of politicians and interest groups. While normatively optimistic about the effect of public opinion on policy formation, they caution that all the intervening linkages between opinion and policy are yet to be fully explored.

Examining the impact of public opinion and arms control, political scientist Thomas Graham has begun to specify these linkages. In particular, he identifies the importance of four factors for public opinion to affect foreign policy making at the executive and congressional level.[149] First, the magnitude of public opinion on a foreign policy issue must be substantial. He estimates that "public opinion must reach at least consensus levels (60 percent and higher) before it begins to have a discernible effect on decision making."[150] Second, public opinion can be most effective when it aids in getting an issue on the decision-making agenda (e.g., public support for arms control talks) and during the ratification process (e.g., support or opposition to arms control treaties). Third, the effectiveness of public opinion is also contingent on political elites evaluating and understanding the public's view. While modern polling techniques aid this process, the level of understanding of the public's view by post–World War II administrations varies considerably. In Graham's view, this level of understanding by the executive, not the public, poses a formidable barrier for policy impact. Fourth, the president or the political elites must be effective in translating the public's views into " articulate themes" that will reinforce or elicit public support. While these factors pose problems for the impact of public opinion, Graham still contends "that public opinion has had a significant impact on decision making for several decades, and it can be documented as far back as Franklin D. Roosevelt."[151]

In a similar vein, albeit for a shorter time span (1965–1990), Thomas Hartley and Bruce Russett demonstrate the potency of public opinion in affecting defense spending.[152] As they report, "with other influences held constant, we find that if the percentage of public opinion favoring increases in military spending rises, then the level of military spending will increase." The converse was also true: As public opinion opposing defense increases rises, "actual spending tends to come down." Furthermore, they undertook elaborate statistical tests to uncover the impact of the government on affecting public opinion. Importantly, they report that public opinion appears to be largely an independent outside factor in affecting defense spending.

Finally, two analyses by political scientist Philip Powlick demonstrate the new attention that foreign policy makers in Washington are giving to public opinion.[153] While National Security Council staffers and State Department officials generally have retained a skeptical view about the public's knowledge and sophistication in assessing foreign policy, at the same time, they are quite receptive to incorporating public opinion into the foreign policy process: "Among the foreign policy officials interviewed for this study," Powlick reports, "the notion that public support of policy is a sine qua non—and that it must therefore be a major factor in policy decisions—is so widespread as to suggest the existence of a 'norm' within the bureaucratic subculture."[154] Furthermore, this result stands in sharp contract to analyses of more than two decades earlier when public opinion seemed to matter little to these policy makers.[155] These officials, however, often rely upon Congress, the news media, interest groups, and other elites to gauge "public opinion," rather than "unmediated opinion" (e.g., public opinion polls) only. Thus while the amount of unmediated opinion transmitted to the policy makers appears to be greater than in earlier decades, and public opinion appears to be more important as well, the level of "filtered" opinion remains an obstacle for sustained public impact. As a result, foreign policy makers can "justify their policy decisions as having been made after taking public opinion into account, whether or not such decisions necessarily reflect the opinions of the mass public."[156]

Concluding Comments

The foreign policy opinions of the American people play a part in the foreign policy making process in the United States. What remains open to debate, however, is the magnitude of the impact of those opinions. One view sees those opinions as "moodish," relatively shiftable, and subject to leadership from the top; another view sees them as structured, relatively stable, and setting some limits on executive (or even congressional) action.

This debate over the public's impact on foreign policy, moreover, extends to other questions as well. Differing views exist on the overall influence of public opinion on specific foreign policy decisions and general policies adopted by the government. Even the impact of foreign policy opinion on presidential and congressional elections remains unclear. In short, then, while the precise impact of public opinion on foreign policy may still be debated, the fact remains that political leaders, or prospective ones, cannot (and do not) wholly ignore the public's views—even on seemingly distant foreign policy issues.

Notes

1. The data on the media reported here are taken from, and percentages calculated from, the U.S. Bureau of the Census, *Statistical Abstract of the United States: 1995*, 115th ed. (Washington, DC, 1995): pp. 570–571.
2. David D. Newsom, *The Public Dimension of Foreign Policy* (Bloomington and Indianapolis: Indiana University Press, 1996), pp. 45 and 240, note 3.
3. The title of the section and initial information draws from "Old News Ain't Beat Yet," *The Economist*, May 18, 1996, 32.
4. Ibid.
5. Ibid.
6. Doris A. Graber, *Mass Media and American Politics,* 3rd ed. (Washington, DC: CQ Press, 1989), p. 328.
7. Michael Emery, "An Endangered Species: The International Newshole," *Gannett Center Journal* 3 (Fall 1989): 151–164.
8. For an early analysis of different roles of the press in the foreign policy process, see Bernard Cohen, *The Press and Foreign Policy* (Princeton, NJ: Princeton University Press,

1963), pp. 4–5; and for a more recent one, see John T. Rourke, Ralph G. Carter, and Mark A. Boyer, *Making American Foreign Policy* (Guilford, CT: The Dushkin Publishing Group, Inc., 1994), pp. 338–354. Another recent study that identifies the first two roles and analyzes them for the *New York Times* can be found in Nicholas O. Berry, *Foreign Policy and the Press* (Westport, CT: Greenwood Press, 1990). Also see, Bill Kovach, "Do the News Media Make Foreign Policy?" *Foreign Policy* 102 (Spring 1996): 169–179. All of these studies aided our thinking about these roles.

9. It is not an accident that the Communications Center at the Department of State in Washington always has a television set available (and usually on), even as cables from American posts around the world are being sorted and distributed to the appropriate bureau, office, or desk within the Department.
10. Quoted in Leslie H. Gelb with Richard K. Betts, *The Irony of Vietnam: The System Worked* (Washington, DC: The Brookings Institution, 1979), p. 171.
11. Both quotes are from Timothy J. Lomperis, *The War Everyone Lost—and Won* (Washington, DC: CQ Press, 1993), p. 78.
12. See Peter Braestrup, *Big Story: How the American Press and Television Reported and Interpretated the Crisis of Tet 1968,* two volumes (Boulder, CO: Westview Press, 1977) as cited in ibid.
13. Interestingly, this program evolved into the late-night ABC program *Nightline* at the end of the crisis. This program continues to this day as a weeknight news and analysis forum.
14. Quoted in Newsom, *The Public Dimension of Foreign Policy*, pp. 47–48.
15. Quoted in Stephen Hess, *International News & Foreign Correspondents* (Washington, DC: The Brookings Institution, 1996), pp. 1–2. The passage originally came from the CNN program, "Reliable Sources," October 6, 1994.
16. W. Lance Bennett, "The News about Foreign Policy," in W. Lance Bennett and David L. Paletz, eds., *Taken by Storm: The Media, Public Opinion, and U.S. Foreign Policy in the Gulf War* (Chicago and London: The University of Chicago Press, 1994), p. 12.
17. Doris A. Graber, *Mass Media and American Politics*, 5th ed. (Washington, DC: CQ Press, 1997), p. 349.
18. Robert F. Kennedy, *Thirteen Days* (New York: W. W. Norton and Company, 1969), pp. 90–91. While Soviet withdrawal of missiles for an American pledge not to invade Cuba was the proposal, the ultimate settlement also involved the American withdrawal of missiles from Turkey. See Chapter 4 for more discussion of this point.
19. See Graber, *Mass Media and American Politics*, 5th ed., pp. 349–350, for a discussion of this episode.
20. See Peter Arnett's detailed description of his time in Baghdad in his *Live From the Battlefield* (New York: Simon & Schuster, 1994). Arnett's flight jacket from the war was put on display at CNN headquarters in Atlanta after his return to the United States.
21. Graber, *Mass Media and American Politics,* 5th ed., p. 351.
22. Daniel C. Hallin, *We Keep America on Top of the World: Television and the Public Sphere* (London and New York: Routledge, 1994), pp. 40–57.
23. Ibid., at pp. 44–48 and pp. 52–53.
24. Ibid., at pp. 48–50, 51, and 50, respectively.
25. Ibid., p. 55. For a similar conclusion on how the media "index" news coverage "to the intensity and duration of official conflicts," see W. Lance Bennett, "The Media and the Foreign Policy Process," in David A. Deese, ed., *The New Politics of American Foreign Policy* (New York: St. Martin's Press, 1994), pp. 168–188, especially at pp. 179–181.
26. I am grateful to James M. Lindsay for bringing this argument to my attention.
27. S. Robert Lichter, Stanley Rothman, and Linda S. Lichter, *The Media Elite* (Bethesda, MD: Adler & Adler, 1986), pp. 21–23. The quoted passages are at p. 23.
28. The first study reported is from ibid., p. 28, while the second is from a study by Stephen Hess of the Brookings Institution and quoted in ibid. at p. 40.
29. Ibid., p. 30.

30. The studies and the data in this paragraph are taken from James K. Glassman, "The Press: Obvious Bias..." *The Washington Post*, May 7, 1996, A19.
31. The media argument is taken form ibid., as is the quotation, which is from Larry Sabato.
32. Cohen, *The Press and Foreign Policy*, p. 13. Emphasis in original.
33. The term is from Patrick O'Heffernan, "A Mutual Exploitation Model of Media Influence in U.S. Foreign Policy," in W. Lance Bennett and David L. Paletz, eds., *Taken by Storm: The Media, Public Opinion, and U.S. Foreign Policy in the Gulf War* (Chicago and London: The University of Chicago Press, 1994), p. 231, in which he summarizes Bernard Cohen's conclusion of his 1963 book.
34. See, for example, David D. Pearce, *Wary Partners: Diplomats and the Media* (Washington, DC: Congressional Quarterly, Inc., 1995).
35. Newsom, *The Public Dimension of Foreign Policy*, p. 86. For a scathing account of the press's deference during the Reagan administration, see Mark Hertsgaard, *On Bended Knee: The Press and the Reagan Presidency* (New York: Farrar, Straus & Giroux, 1988).
36. Johanna Neuman, *Lights, Camera, War* (New York: St. Martin's Press, 1996), pp. 207–208. The "pool" term is quoted from Neuman at p. 207.
37. These are outlined in Pete Williams, "Ground Rules and Guidelines for Desert Shield," in Hedrick Smith, ed., *The Media and the Gulf War* (Washington, DC: Seven Locks Press, 1992), pp. 4–12.
38. Hedrick Smith, "Preface," in Hedrick Smith, ed., *The Media and the Gulf War*, p. xviii.
39. R.W. Apple, Jr., "James Reston, a Journalist Nonpareil, Dies at 86," *New York Times*, December 7, 1995, B19. The commentator quoted was Ronald Steel.
40. Ibid.
41. The examples are from Pearce, *Wary Partners: Diplomats and the Media*, pp. 1–3.
42. Ambassador Alexander Watson was quoted in ibid., p. 10.
43. See the various appendices in ibid., pp. 169–186.
44. Bennett, "The Media and the Foreign Policy Process," p. 179.
45. Ibid.
46. On the problems for the media in this connection, see ibid., pp. 180–181.
47. O'Heffernan, "A Mutual Exploitation Model of Media Influence in U.S. Foreign Policy," pp. 232–233.
48. Ibid., p. 236.
49. Ibid., p. 237.
50. The discussion of issues draws upon ibid., p. 240.
51. Journalist Johanna Neuman is quoted in Kovach, "Do the News Media Make Foreign Policy?" p. 171. The comment is originally from Neuman, *Lights, Camera, War*, p. 8.
52. Benjamin I. Page and Robert Y. Shapiro, *The Rational Public: Fifty Trends in Americans' Policy Preferences* (Chicago and London: The University of Chicago Press, 1992), p. 321. Emphasis in original.
53. Ibid., p. 342. The discussion of the findings is drawn from pp. 341–347.
54. Ibid., p. 354.
55. Ibid., p. 353.
56. Ibid., p. 354.
57. These data are from Gabriel A. Almond, *The American People and Foreign Policy* (New York: Praeger, 1960), p. 82.
58. These data are from Lloyd A. Free and Hadley Cantril, *The Political Beliefs of Americans: A Study of Public Opinion* (New York: Clarion Books, 1968), pp. 60–61.
59. See John E. Rielly, ed., *American Public Opinion and U.S. Foreign Policy 1987* (Chicago: The Chicago Council on Foreign Relations, 1987), p. 8; John E. Rielly, ed., *American Public Opinion and U.S. Foreign Policy 1991* (Chicago: The Chicago Council on Foreign Relations, 1991), p. 9; and John E. Rielly, ed., *American Public Opinion and U.S. Foreign Policy 1995* (Chicago: The Chicago Council on Foreign Relations, 1995), p. 9.

60. Ibid., pp. 6, 9, and 10. The quote is from p. 10.

61. Rielly, *American Public Opinion and U.S. Foreign Policy 1987*, p. 9; and John E. Rielly, ed. *American Public Opinion and U.S. Foreign Policy 1983* (Chicago: The Chicago Council on Foreign Relations, 1983), p. 9. The results for 1990 can be found at p. 9 in Rielly, *American Public Opinion and U.S. Foreign Policy 1991*. The 1995 survey did not indicate the size of the attentive public for the 1994 data. Given the modest changes overall in the latest survey, the percentage estimate from the early ones still appears to hold.

62. Richard Sobel, "Public Opinion About United States Intervention in El Salvador and Nicaragua," *Public Opinion Quarterly* 53 (Spring 1989): 120. Also see Richard Sobel, "Public Opinion About U.S. Intervention in Nicaragua: A Polling Addendum," in Richard Sobel, ed., *Public Opinion in U.S. Foreign Policy: The Controversy Over Contra Aid* (Lanham, MD: Rowman and Littlefield Publishers, Inc., 1993), pp. 59–70.

63. Steven Kull, "What the Public Knows That Washington Doesn't," *Foreign Policy* 101 (Winter 1995–96): 108–109.

64. On this point, see John E. Rielly, "American Opinion: Continuity, Not Reaganism," *Foreign Policy* 50 (Spring 1983): 88; and Bruce Russett and Donald R. Deluca, "'Don't Tread on Me': Public Opinion and Foreign Policy in the Eighties," *Political Science Quarterly* 96 (Fall 1981): 393–395.

65. See various years of *The Gallup Poll: Public Opinion* (New York: Random House, Annual); John E. Rielly, ed., *American Public Opinion and U.S. Foreign Policy 1975, 1979, 1983, 1987* (Chicago: The Chicago Council on Foreign Relations); and Tom W. Smith, "The Polls: America's Most Important Problems, Part I: National and International," *Public Opinion Quarterly* 49 (Summer 1985): 264–274.

66. Ibid., p. 266.

67. George Gallup, Jr., *The Gallup Poll: Public Opinion 1993* (Wilmington, DE: Scholarly Resources, Inc., 1994), pp. 168–169; George Gallup, Jr., *The Gallup Poll: Public Opinion 1994* (Wilmington, DE: Scholarly Resources, Inc., 1995), p. 28; and George Gallup, Jr., *The Gallup Poll: Public Opinion 1995* (Wilmington, DE: Scholarly Resources, Inc., 1996), pp. 13–14.

68. John E. Mueller, *War, Presidents and Public Opinion* (New York: John Wiley and Sons, Inc., 1973), Ch. 8.

69. Ibid., pp. 70–74.

70. Milton J. Rosenberg, Sidney Verba, and Philip E. Converse, *Vietnam and the Silent Majority* (New York: Harper and Row, 1970), pp. 26–28.

71. See "Opinion Roundup" *Public Opinion* (February/March 1980), pp. 27 and 29.

72. These *New York Times/CBS News Poll* results are reported in David Shribman, "Poll Shows Support for Presence of U.S. Troops in Lebanon and Grenada," *New York Times*, October 29, 1983, 9.

73. See Table 4-24 in Sobel, "Public Opinion About U.S. Intervention in Nicaragua: A Polling Addendum," p. 68. For an assessment that this presidential speech was not very successful, see William E. LeoGrande, "Did the Public Matter? The Impact of Opinion on Congressional Support for Ronald Reagan's Nicaragua Policy ," in Richard Sobel, ed., *Public Opinion in U.S. Foreign Policy: The Controversy Over Contra Aid* (Lanham, MD: Rowman and Littlefield Publishers, Inc., 1993), p. 173.

74. See Table 4-23 in Sobel, "Public Opinion About U.S. Intervention in Nicaragua: A Polling Addendum," p. 68.

75. These data are taken from Michael Oreskes, "Support for Bush Declines in Poll," *New York Times*, July 11, 1990, A8; and Andrew H. Malcom, "Opponents to U.S. Move Have Poverty in Common," *New York Times*, September 8, 1990, 6.

76. On the patterns in Presidents Bush's popularity, see Robin Toner, "Did Someone Say 'Domestic Policy'?" *New York Times*, March 3, 1991, 1E and 2E. A CNN (Cable News Network) poll and a *Newsweek* poll placed President Bush's popularity at about 90 percent at the immediate end of the Persian Gulf War. See Ann McDaniel and Evan Thomas with Howard Fineman, "The Rewards of Leadership," *Newsweek*, March 11, 1991, 30.

77. Andrew Kohut and Robert C. Toth, "Arms and the People," *Foreign Affairs* 73 (November/December 1994): 60.
78. Gallup, *The Gallup Poll: Public Opinion 1994*, pp. 141, 145, and 148.
79. Rosenberg, Verba, and Converse, *Vietnam and the Silent Majority*, pp. 24–25. The authors do not actually use poll data to make this point about question wording; instead, they rely upon these hypothetical examples to demonstrate the underlying argument.
80. Brad Lockerbie and Stephen A. Borrelli, "Question Wording and Public Support for Contra Aid, 1983–1986," *Public Opinion Quarterly* 54 (Summer 1990): 195–208.
81. David W. Moore, "The Public Is Uncertain," *Foreign Policy* 35 (Summer 1979): 68–70.
82. See Sobel, "Public Opinion About United States Intervention in El Salvador and Nicaragua," p. 120, where he reproduces these poll results. These concerns are also discussed in LeoGrande, "Did the Public Matter? The Impact of Opinion on Congressional Support for Ronald Reagan's Nicaragua Policy," pp. 175–177.
83. Gallup, *The Gallup Poll: Public Opinion 1995*, pp. 192–195. The quoted materials are from p. 195. For the approve/disapprove question, the public could respond along a continuum from strongly approve or approve to disapprove or strongly disapprove. See p. 192.
84. Gabriel A. Almond, *The American People and Foreign Policy* (New York: Frederick A. Praeger, 1960), pp. 53, 69, and 88. The original edition of this book was published in 1950 by Harcourt, Brace, and Company, Inc.
85. Ibid., p. xxii, from the new introduction to the 1960 edition.
86. Ole R. Holsti, "Public Opinion and Foreign Policy: Challenges to the Almond-Lippmann Consensus," *International Studies Quarterly* 36 (December 1992): 442.
87. Quoted in ibid.
88. Ibid., pp. 443–444. The studies referred to in this paragraph from Holsti are Philip E. Converse, "The Nature of Belief Systems in Mass Publics," in David E. Apter, ed., *Ideology and Discontent* (New York: Free Press, 1964), pp. 206–61; Bernard C. Cohen, *The Public's Impact on Foreign Policy* (Boston: Little, Brown, 1973); and Warren E. Miller and Donald E. Stokes, "Constituency Influence in Congress," *American Political Science Review* 57 (March 1963): 45–56.
89. Jon Hurwitz and Mark Peffley, "How Are Foreign Policy Attitudes Structured? A Hierarchical Model" *American Political Science Review* 81 (December 1987): 1114. Emphasis in original.
90. Robert Y. Shapiro and Benjamin I. Page, "Foreign Policy and the Rational Public," *Journal of Conflict Resolution* 32 (June 1988): 211 and 243. A more complete statement of their views can be found in their *The Rational Public: Fifty Trends in Americans' Policy Preferences*.
91. Eugene R. Wittkopf, *Faces of Internationalism: Public Opinion and American Foreign Policy* (Durham, NC: Duke University Press, 1990), pp. 25–33. Analyses of the more recent Chicago Council surveys by Wittkopf may be found in Eugene R. Wittkopf, "Faces of Internationalism in a Transitional Environment," *Journal of Conflict Resolution* 38 (September 1994): 376–401, for the 1990 survey; and Eugene R. Wittkopf, "What Americans Really Think About Foreign Policy," *The Washington Quarterly* 19 (Summer 1996): 91–106.
92. These are the items used for the analysis of the 1994 survey in ibid., p. 94. Slightly different ones were used for analyzing the 1990 survey; see Wittkopf, "Faces of Internationalism in a Transitional Environment," p. 381. For the 1974 through 1986 surveys, these underlying attitudes were largely tapped by questions about the use of American force abroad, communism, and American-Soviet relations. See *Faces of Internationalism: Public Opinion and American Foreign Policy*, p. 25. The end of the Cold War necessitated the use of different items, since the attitudes toward communism and American-Soviet relations were no longer appropriate.
93. Ibid., pp. 25–30. The application of Wittkopf's typology to the Persian Gulf War was aided by a personal communication with him.
94. The analytic technique of factor analysis contributes to the more even distribution among the four quadrants, although differences exist among the groupings.

95. Wittkopf, *Faces of Internationalism*, p. 26; Wittkopf, "Faces of Internationalism in a Transitional Environment," pp. 376–401, for the 1990 results; and personal communication with Eugene R. Wittkopf for the 1994 data. The numbers are rough averages within each quadrant across the surveys.

96. These examples are drawn from Wittkopf, "What Americans Really Think About Foreign Policy," pp. 95–99; and Wittkopf, *Faces of Internationalism,* pp. 27–32, especially the table at p. 28 and the discussion at p. 30.

97. Ibid., pp. 44–49.

98. Wittkopf, "What Americans Really Think About Foreign Policy," p. 103. His 1994 analysis of the other sociodemographic characteristics of the public for these belief systems (and reported at pp. 103–104) generally support the results from his earlier work.

99. Bernard Cohen, *The Political Process and Foreign Policy: The Making of the Japanese Peace Settlement* (Princeton, NJ: Princeton University Press, 1957), p. 29. We should note, however, that Cohen is relatively skeptical about the impact of public opinion overall. See note 32.

100. V. O. Key, Jr. *Public Opinion and American Democracy*. (New York: Alfred A. Knopf, 1961), p. 423.

101. William R. Caspary, "The 'Mood Theory': A Study of Public Opinion and Foreign Policy," *The American Political Science Review* 54 (June 1970): 546. Emphasis in original.

102. Bruce Russett, "The Americans' Retreat from World Power," *Political Science Quarterly* 90 (Spring 1975): 9.

103. The phrase is from ibid., p. 8. For other judgments of the Vietnam War and its impact on the foreign policy beliefs of the American public and its leaders, see, for instance, Eugene R. Wittkopf and Michael A. Maggiotto, "Elites and Masses: A Comparative Analysis of Attitudes Toward America's World Role," *The Journal of Politics* 45 (May 1983): 303–334; and Ole R. Holsti and James N. Rosenau, "Vietnam, Consensus, and the Belief Systems of American Leaders," *World Politics* 32 (October 1979): 1–56.

104. John E. Rielly, ed., *American Public Opinion and U.S. Foreign Policy 1975* (Chicago: Chicago Council on Foreign Relations, 1975), p. 12. The rest of the data in this section are from this report. The national sample survey was conducted in December 1974, by Harris and Associates for the Chicago Council on Foreign Relations.

105. Russett, "The Americans' Retreat from World Power," p. 8.

106. The title is from John E. Rielly, "The American Mood: A Policy of Self-Interest," *Foreign Policy* 34 (Spring 1979): 74–86.

107. John E. Rielly, ed., *American Public Opinion and U.S. Foreign Policy 1979* (Chicago: Chicago Council on Foreign Relations, 1979), p. 4.

108. The data cited here are from ibid.

109. A Harris survey in early 1980 showed majority public support for use of U.S. troops if the Soviets attacked the Persian Gulf area, Iran, or Pakistan. See "Use of U.S. Troops to Defend Invaded Countries Endorsed," *Houston Post*, February 26, 1980, 3C.

110. Rielly, *American Public Opinion and U.S. Foreign Policy 1979*, p. 12.

111. Ibid., p. 15.

112. Ibid., p. 12.

113. Ibid., p. 7. Also Rielly, "The American Mood: A Foreign Policy of Self-Interest."

114. Rielly, *American Public Opinion and U.S. Foreign Policy 1983*, p. 4.

115. Ibid., p. 6 and Rielly, *American Public Opinion and U.S. Foreign Policy 1987*, p. 32.

116. Rielly, *American Public Opinion and U.S. Foreign Policy 1983*, pp. 6 and 31; and Rielly, *American Public Opinion and U.S. Foreign Policy 1987*, p. 32.

117. These results are taken from Rielly, *American Public Opinion and U.S. Foreign Policy 1983*, p. 32; and Rielly, *American Public Opinion and U.S. Foreign Policy 1987*, p. 31.

118. See the tables in Rielly, *American Public Opinion and U.S. Foreign Policy 1983*, p. 35; and Rielly, *American Public Opinion and U.S. Foreign Policy 1987*, p. 35, which compare the public's views with those of the Reagan administration. Also, see p. 29 of the latter report for a discussion of public attitudes on military expenditures.

119. This summary of the current mood is based upon John E. Rielly, "The Public Mood at Mid-Decade," *Foreign Policy* 98 (Spring 1995): 76–93; and Rielly, *American Public Opinion and U.S. Foreign Policy 1995*.

120. Ibid., p. 6.

121. Rielly, *American Public Opinion and U.S. Foreign Policy 1995*, p. 15.

122. Rielly, "The Public's Mood at Mid-Decade," p. 81.

123. Rielly, *American Public Opinion and U.S. Foreign Policy 1995*, pp. 24–25.

124. See Figures III-3 in Rielly, *American Public Opinion and U.S. Foreign Policy 1995*, p. 22, and the discussion on p. 21.

125. Ibid. Also see the tables on the public's views toward Russia on pp. 24–25.

126. Rielly, *American Public Opinion and U.S. Foreign Policy 1991*, p. 6, provides a comparison with earlier assessments of the Soviet Union in 1986 and before.

127. Rielly, *American Public Opinion and U.S. Foreign Policy 1995*, p. 23.

128. Ibid., p. 25.

129. Rielly, "The Public Mood at Mid-Decade," p. 84.

130. Rielly, "Public Opinion: The Pulse of the '90s," pp. 83, 86, and 89; and Rielly, *American Public Opinion and U.S. Foreign Policy 1995*, p. 34.

131. Ibid., pp. 35–36.

132. Ibid., p. 35.

133. Ibid., p. 21.

134. Robert Y. Shapiro and Benjamin I. Page, "Foreign Policy and Public Opinion," in David A. Deese, ed., *The New Politics of American Foreign Policy* (New York: St. Martin's Press, 1994), pp. 216–235. The quote is from p. 218.

135. Ibid., p. 223.

136. Ibid., p. 226.

137. Bruce W. Jentleson, "The Pretty Prudent Public: Post Post-Vietnam American Opinion on the Use of Military Force," *International Studies Quarterly* 36 (March 1992): 49–74. The quoted passages are from pp. 50 and 71, respectively. Emphasis in the original.

138. John R. Oneal, Brad Lian, and James H. Joyner, "Are the American People 'Pretty Prudent'? Public Responses to U.S. Uses of Force, 1950–1988," *International Studies Quarterly* 40 (June 1996): 261–280. The quoted passage is at p. 273.

139. Kohut and Toth, "Arms and the People," p. 47.

140. Ibid., p. 50.

141. See John H. Aldrich, John L. Sullivan, and Eugene Borgida, "Foreign Affairs and Issue Voting: Do Presidential Candidates 'Waltz Before a Blind Audience'?" *American Political Science Review* 83 (March 1989): 136.

142. Warren E. Miller, "Voting and Foreign Policy," in James N. Rosenau, ed., *Domestic Sources of Foreign Policy* (New York: The Free Press, 1967), p. 226. Also, see LeoGrande, "Did the Public Matter? The Impact of Opinion on Congressional Support for Ronald Reagan's Nicaragua Policy," p. 6; and John Spanier and Eric M. Uslaner, *American Foreign Policy Making and the Domestic Dilemmas* (Pacific Grove, CA: Brooks/Cole Publishing Company, 1989), p. 216.

143. Gregory B. Markus, "Political Attitudes During an Election Year: A Report on the 1980 NES Panel Study," *American Political Science Review* 76 (September 1982): 558. This point is also discussed in Spanier and Uslaner, *American Foreign Policy Making and the Democratic Dilemmas*, p. 216, from which we draw.

144. R.W. Apple, "Clinton's Peace Strategy," *New York Times*, December 2, 1995, 1.

145. See the chart in Aldrich, Sullivan, and Borgida, "Foreign Affairs and Issue Voting: Do Presidential Candidates 'Waltz Before a Blind Audience'?" p. 136.

146. The discussion in this paragraph draws upon the description and analysis of the Oklahoma case provided in Jeremy Rosner, "The Know-Nothings Know Something," *Foreign Policy* 101 (Winter 1995–1996): 116–127.

147. See the commentary by Ronald Hinckley referring to an interview that he conducted with Eliot Abrams, the assistant secretary of state for Inter-American Affairs during the

Reagan administration, in "Public Diplomacy: Seeking Public Support for Contra Aid Policy," in Richard Sobel, ed., *Public Opinion in U.S. Foreign Policy: The Controversy over Contra Aid* (Lanham, MD: Rowman and Littlefield Publishers, Inc., 1993), p. 160.

148. Benjamin I. Page and Robert Y. Shapiro, "Effects of Public Opinion on Policy," *American Political Science Review* 77 (March 1983): 186. Emphasis in original. The discussion in this paragraph is drawn from this article. For the recent summary of their work on foreign policy, see Benjamin I. Page and Robert Y. Shapiro, *The Rational Public*, pp. 172–320.

149. Thomas Graham, "Public Opinion and U.S. Foreign Policy Decision Making," in David A. Deese, ed., *The New Politics of American Foreign Policy* (New York: St. Martin's Press, 1994), pp. 190–215.

150. Ibid., p. 196. These four factors are discussed at pp. 195–199, from which we draw.

151. Ibid., p. 195.

152. Thomas Hartley and Bruce Russett, "Public Opinion and the Common Defense: Who Governs Military Spending in the United States?" *American Political Science Review* 86 (December 1992): 905–915. The quoted passages are at p. 911.

153. Philip J. Powlick, "The Attitudinal Bases for Responsiveness to Public Opinion among American Foreign Policy Officials," *Journal of Conflict Resolution* 35 (December 1991): 611–641; and Philip J. Powlick, "The Sources of Public Opinion for American Foreign Policy Officials," *International Studies Quarterly* 39 (December 1995): 427–451.

154. Powlick, "The Attitudinal Bases for Responsiveness to Public Opinion among American Foreign Policy Officials," p. 634.

155. See Bernard C. Cohen, *The Public's Impact on Foreign Policy.*

156. Powlick, "The Sources of Public Opinion for American Foreign Policy Officials," p. 447.

3

CONCLUSION

In Part I, we suggested how the formulation of American foreign policy was marked by a considerable degree of value consensus prior to the Vietnam War and to a substantial degree of value shifts from one administration to the next, after that war and through the early years after the formal end of the Cold War. In Part II, a central message was how the various political institutions—the executive, the Congress, and the bureaucracies, for example—have become increasingly competitive in the shaping of American foreign policy in the post-Vietnam and post–Cold War periods. Indeed, the impetus for foreign policy change gained even more momentum with the collapse of the Berlin Wall, the unraveling of communism in Eastern Europe in 1989 and 1990, and the collapse of the Soviet Union in 1991. But a crucial problem remains for American foreign policy: Can a coherent foreign policy be developed without the emergence of a new foreign policy value consensus to replace the one first challenged by the Vietnam War and now eroded still further with the end of the Cold War? Can American policy long endure the constant shifts and changes in approach that have marked the last several decades and still play a major role in world affairs? Put more generally, should and will the United States remain active in global politics? And, if so, what should be the shape of that role and its rationale?

The concluding chapter examines both the need and prospects for a new consensus in U.S. foreign policy making. As we enter a new millennium, the need for such a consensus appears to be greater than ever before, but the task of building and sustaining one is formidable as well. Several alternate approaches to that new consensus have been offered in recent years. A summary of the different approaches will increase awareness of the various options available and will facilitate discussion and debate on the direction of American foreign policy in the twenty-first century.

AMERICAN FOREIGN POLICY VALUES AND THE FUTURE

"Vital questions of policy do not lend themselves to ad hoc, short-term approaches.... Predictability is essential if allies are going to count on us or if foes are to think twice before challenging American interests. Policymakers need bearings by which to judge international events."

Richard Haass
"Paradigm Lost"
Foreign Affairs, January/February 1995

I believe...that the distinction between interests and values is largely fallacious.... Among the reasons the opposition between interests and values is a sham are that a great power has an "interest" in world order that goes beyond strict national security concerns and that its definition of order is largely shaped by its values.

Stanley Hoffmann
"In Defense of Mother Teresa: Morality in Foreign Policy"
Foreign Affairs, March/April 1996

As we approach a new millennium, a consensus among the American people on the role of the United States in world affairs remains elusive. While the debate over the Vietnam War began the erosion of a foreign policy value consensus, the end of the Cold War has accelerated the process. For some, if American policy is to be more coherent and consistent as we approach the next century, however, policy makers and the public need to begin to identify the values and beliefs to guide American diplomacy and, if possible, to pursue a series of policies consistent with those principles. The constant shifts in policy emphasis from one administration to the next neither serve America's long-term interests nor provide much guidance to policy makers in the executive or legislative branches of government. For others, these shifts challenge whether any consensus can or should be pursued. Efforts to build a consensus are difficult and time-consuming, and any consensus may be incomplete or even dangerous in the post–Cold War world, characterized as it is with numerous and difficult problems.

In this last chapter, we discuss the issue of a new foreign policy consensus. We begin by identifying more fully the extent of underlying value conflicts among the leaders of American foreign policy in recent years. Then we turn to evaluating the problems of, and prospects for, developing a new foreign policy consensus at the dawn of a new century. Finally, we provide a brief sketch of the several alternate approaches that have been proposed in shaping the future role of the United States in the post–Cold War world.

A NATION DIVIDED

An abundance of evidence exists at both the mass and elite levels on the degree of value conflict over the current direction of foreign policy. As we have noted, the United States has witnessed discernible shifts in its foreign policy approach with the coming of each new administration over the last three decades. From the rejection of the values of the Cold War consensus, to the power politics of the Kissinger period, to the idealism of the Carter years, to the revival of containment of the Reagan years, to the modified realism of the Bush administration, and now to the liberal internationalism of the Clinton administration, the American approach to foreign policy has gone through substantial modification almost every four years. While some would argue for significant stability in American foreign policy goals and objectives over much of the past fifty years, this view fails to account fully for the changes in emphasis from one administration to the next.[1] Further, this view fails to capture the pervasive divisions in value orientation among the leadership (the foreign policy elites) and the American people, since the post-Vietnam era, and now continuing in the post–Cold War years.

Value Differences Within Elites

Political scientists Ole Holsti and James Rosenau's recent analyses provide compelling evidence of divisions among foreign policy leaders or elites that started after the Vietnam War and continue to the present day. Employing

FIGURE 13.1

The Distribution of Hardliners, Internationalists, Isolationists, and Accommodationists Among American Foreign Policy Leaders, 1976–1996

Militant Internationalism		Cooperative Internationalism: Oppose	Cooperative Internationalism: Support
	Support	**Hardliners** 1976 20% 1980 20% 1984 17% 1988 16% 1992 9% 1996 13%	**Internationalists** 1976 30% 1980 33% 1984 25% 1988 25% 1992 33% 1996 29%
	Oppose	**Isolationists** 1976 8% 1980 7% 1984 7% 1988 8% 1992 5% 1996 10%	**Accommodationists** 1976 42% 1980 41% 1984 51% 1988 52% 1992 53% 1996 48%

Source: Ole R. Holsti, "Continuity and Change in the Domestic and Foreign Policy Beliefs of American Opinion Leaders," a paper prepared for presentation at the American Political Science Association annual meeting, Washington, DC, August 27–31, 1997, Table 8. Used by permission of the author.

the fourfold analytic categories (isolationists, hardliners, accommodationists, and internationalists) that Wittkopf developed to assess public opinion (see Chapter 12), Holsti and Rosenau's evaluation of their six foreign policy leadership opinion surveys from 1976 through 1996 found significant elite divisions across those four categories as well. Moreover, the divisions were reasonably constant from one survey to the next, although the elites were more sharply divided recently.[2] Figure 13.1 shows the percentages of the foreign policy leaders in each of the four new categories for the six surveys.

Accommodationists and internationalists turn out to be the two largest components of those surveyed, with the former constituting 48 percent in 1996 and the latter 29 percent. Hardliners and isolationists, by contrast, form much smaller components of the foreign policy leadership with 13 percent and 10 percent, respectively.[3] With the exception of the hardliners, who have dropped by about 35 percent since the immediate post-Vietnam years, the divisions among the leaders have remained quite stable.

Consistent with the earlier analyses, too, Holsti and Rosenau report that "ideology, political party, and occupation are by far the strongest predictors of foreign policy orientations, whereas military service, age, foreign travel and gender are weakly related to attitudes."[4] More specifically, they found that hard-liners and accommodationists tended to be conservatives and Republicans, while accommodationists tended to be liberals and Democrats. Isolationists tended to be more conservative than liberal and more

Republicans or independents than Democrats.[5] Overall, though, the striking aspects of these results are the sustained differences within each survey, and the sustained similarities in structure of the results across each survey.[6] In this sense, consistency and coherence exist in shaping elite opinion into discernible foreign policy differences.

This lack of consensus within elites (and also among the mass public, as we indicated in Chapter 12) is complicated in yet another way: the failure of both elites and masses to share these policy orientations to the same degree. That is, despite the fact that attitudes of elites and masses are similarly structured into comparable belief systems, some of the different belief systems are not held in the same proportion by the foreign policy elites and the public. For instance, the American leadership tends to be much more *internationalist* (in both the militant and cooperative varieties) than is the mass public. By contrast, the mass public tends to favor more *hardline* (a more militant internationalism) and *isolationist* policies than do the elites.[7] Such disparities between elites and masses reduce the effectiveness of making foreign policy with widespread support.

These elite/mass issue differences are more directly portrayed in some data from the latest comprehensive foreign policy opinion survey published by the Chicago Council on Foreign Relations. Table 13.1 compares some responses to several foreign policy questions of a general public survey and a leadership survey (composed of knowledgeable Americans from government, business, communications, education, and foreign policy institutes). Both surveys were conducted in October and November 1994.

Attitudes toward the world and toward specific policies evidence sharp policy differences between the public and their leaders. The public, for instance, is less committed to an active world role than are leaders, but it is more committed to strengthening the United Nations than are the foreign policy elites. The leaders (or elites) are slightly more willing to cut defense spending, but slightly more committed to NATO than is the public as a whole.[8] The public, on the other hand, is generally much less willing to use force than the leaders, while it is also dramatically more skeptical of foreign aid than is the leadership. Finally, although the results are not fully revealed in Table 13.1, the public is much more supportive of efforts to protect the economic interests of Americans (e.g., protecting American jobs and seeing Japan as a critical threat) and to address social concerns with international connections (e.g., illegal immigration and drug trafficking) than are the leaders. In short, even as the shape of public opinion has changed, as we noted in Chapter 12, the gap between elites and masses on several foreign policy questions remains. Indeed, according to the most recent assessment, the magnitude of the differences between elites and masses has been "substantial and enduring" over the years of these foreign policy surveys.[9]

In sum, then, major analyses of post-Vietnam and post–Cold War opinion portray the same picture of America's leadership: a foreign policy elite divided over how the United States ought to act in the world. Further, the divisions between the elite and the masses on a number of important foreign policy questions remain as well. Whether the formal end of the Cold War will enable consensus to reemerge remains a question, but, given the signif-

TABLE 13.1

Differences Between the Leaders and the Public—1994

	Public	Leaders	Gap (Leaders minus Public)
Diplomatic and Involvement Abroad			
Best to take an active part in world affairs	69%	98%	+29%
Strengthening the United Nations a very important goal	53%	33%	+20%
Foreign Aid			
Favor economic aid to other nations	50%	88%	–38%
Cut back economic aid programs	62%	32%	+30%
Increase aid to Palestinians	9%	49%	–40%
Increase aid to E. Europe	26%	56%	–30%
Favor selling military equipment to other nations	16%	47%	–31%
Use of Force			
Favor use of U.S. troops if North Korea invaded South Korea	45%	84%	–39%
Favor using U.S. troops if Russia invaded Western Europe	61%	92%	–31%
Favor using U.S. troops if Iraq invaded Saudi Arabia	58%	86%	–28%
Trade			
Sympathize with eliminating tariffs	40%	79%	–39%
NAFTA mostly good for U.S.	62%	87%	–25%

Note: Percentages are of those holding an opinion.

Source: Taken in part from John E. Rielly, ed., *American Public Opinion and U.S. Foreign Policy 1995* (Chicago: Chicago Council on Foreign Relations, 1995), Figure VI-1 at p. 39.

icant divisions over the last three decades, the challenge remains a formidable one.

A NEW FOREIGN POLICY CONSENSUS?

Indeed, the shifts in policy from one president to another and the cleavages that have developed both among and between American leaders and the public seem to point to the need to develop a new foreign policy consensus. Such a consensus might engender widespread support among the American people and might lend coherence and direction to United States policy. Calls for a new foreign policy consensus are hardly new; since the end of the

Vietnam War, they have been frequent, and they have accelerated in the post–Cold War years.

Calls for a New Consensus

Sprinkled throughout the writings of foreign policy scholars and practitioners in the 1970s, for example, were calls for new approaches to replace the cold war consensus in guiding American foreign policy.[10] Prior to his becoming national security advisor in the Carter administration, Zbigniew Brzezinski argued that the Vietnam experience had shattered the WASP foreign policy elite and that Henry Kissinger's global design failed to replace the lost elite. Thus, he contended, there was a "need for national leadership that was capable of defining politically and morally compelling directions to which the public might then positively respond."[11] A little later, political scientist Stanley Hoffmann published a lengthy volume on this very topic.[12] Beginning with an extensive critique of what he called the "containment cycle" (1946 to 1968) and the "Kissinger cycle" (1969 to 1976) of United States policy, Hoffmann proceeded to suggest why a new approach was needed and why the time was right.

In the 1980s and 1990s, the debate continued. One scholar lamented that a foreign policy consensus had not emerged and that the United States was experiencing a foreign policy "crack-up."[13] As American leaders and the public became increasingly divided into those concerned with the "security culture" and those concerned with the "equity culture," foreign policy faltered badly in his judgment. Thus, a new foreign policy coalition was still needed to replace the working coalition of the Cold War years. With the demise of communism in Eastern Europe and the collapse of the Soviet Union, calls for a new consensus, or at least new approaches, were once again rampant.[14] Yet, such a consensus has not emerged and remains the most formidable challenge for American foreign policy. But are there any real prospects that it will come about in the near future?

At least three lingering and important questions remain over forming a new consensus: (1) Should it be developed? Will a new consensus be necessary or functional for American policy in the 1990s and beyond? (2) Can it be developed? That is, in the context of a divided leadership and a divided public, how is a new consensus going to be forged? (3) Most importantly, perhaps, what values should constitute this new consensus?

Some doubt that a foreign policy consensus can be constructed in the near future and believe that any short-term consensus that might emerge may be detrimental to sound foreign policy. One view, for example, is that the foreign policy interests of the United States today are too diverse to be summarized under a single rubric, as anticommunism did during the height of the Cold War. Furthermore, domestic interests are now often perceived to be closely linked to foreign policy (e.g., trade policy and domestic employment), so that foreign policy action might only reinforce existing domestic policy divisions. Yet, "...while a consensus may make a country easier to govern, it does not necessarily make for good policy."[15] As a result, foreign policy may have to be made piecemeal—on a case-by-case basis—and in the same manner as domestic policy, by building coalitions as issues come along. Indeed, the Clinton administration was often accused of following this very path during its first term.

Another approach—less demanding than an overarching consensus, but more than a case-by-case approach to policy—would be to identify and obtain agreement on dealing with key issues or key nations in the world.[16] For instance, a consensus might be built on the need to pursue arms control in today's nuclear world, regardless of policy occurrences in other issue areas. Similarly, it might be possible to gain some consensus among the American public and its leadership on how to conduct future relations with Russia or China as the traditional ideological division has ended or eroded. In short, this intermediate approach to consensus building would be less demanding and, in this sense, more achievable. In part, the Clinton administration appears to be adopting this approach, especially as it began its second term in office.

If a consensus were to emerge, however, dangers exist with it. If a premature consensus develops—i.e., one that is not firmly embedded in the elites and the public at large—it might simply be a set of simple moral slogans that would not reflect the complexity of policy needed for today's world.[17] For instance, both the Carter and Reagan administrations might have been accused of employing such a strategy—with the resultant consequence that neither's effort sufficed as a satisfactory consensus for the public as a whole. A consistent complaint about both the Bush and Clinton administrations was that they tended to make their foreign policy decisions more with an eye on the public opinion polls at home and less with an eye to the long-term interests of the United States.

Furthermore, a premature consensus could easily turn out to be a target for those opposed to a particular approach. The actions of the Clinton administration over Somalia illustrate this argument. Emboldened by some initial success in providing humanitarian relief in that war-torn country in early 1993, the Clinton administration moved to expand its efforts into "nation building," activities to restore a working government to Somalia by attempting to defeat a particularly troublesome clan and capture its leader in mid-1993. Such efforts quickly failed, American lives were lost, and opposition forces within Congress and the public turned against these expanded American actions.

The Clinton administration seemingly followed the same course in recommending American military actions toward Haiti and Bosnia. Although the public was extremely skeptical over using military force in both areas, the administration still proceeded to do so. Opposition domestic forces challenged these efforts, and the actions became rallying points against the Clinton approach. In both instances, though, the relative success of the operations succeeded in muting criticism, in contrast to the Somalia experience.

A related and more critical danger for any consensus has been aptly summarized by Gelb and Betts.[18] "Doctrine and consensus," they note, "are the midwives to necessity and the enemy of dissent and choice." Because the military containment belief system had been so firmly interwoven into the American policy process in the 1950s and 1960s, America's Vietnam policy became almost a certainty. Thus, once beliefs become so dominant in the policy process, movement away from them becomes extraordinarily difficult.

Nonetheless, Gelb and Betts acknowledge that some doctrinal consensus is necessary in foreign policy making ("It lends coherence and direction to policy; it puts particular challenges in perspective; it enables the bureaucracy to handle routine problems without constant and enervating debates; it translates values into objectives..."), but they call for one "with escape hatches."[19] A more pragmatic consensus that will be adaptive to changing circumstances is the key in their view. Given America's past, however, that task may be more difficult than it sounds. Somewhat ironically, they note, while Americans often pride themselves on pragmatism in domestic affairs, they have been much more prone to adopt ideological postures in foreign affairs. In their view, a new consensus must avoid this tendency.

Developing a New Consensus

Can a workable foreign policy consensus emerge that takes into account these possible dangers? The answer, of course, is still very much open to question, but one proponent argues: "There is no sensible alternative but to try."[20] At a minimum, the following requirements would seem to be necessary.

Political leadership will undoubtedly be the first requisite. This leadership, however, must not be one that yearns for some past glory; instead, it must accept the changed global reality—a world increasingly divided—and be willing to evoke change by pursuing a more differentiated foreign policy. The second requisite is that the leadership must be willing to educate the public continuously on foreign policy. A third, and crucial, requisite for this new consensus is that the public evaluate its beliefs and values on what the United States should stand for in the world, the extent to which domestic values should shape American policy, and the degree to which various political, economic, and military instruments are acceptable for implementing foreign policy.

None of these requisites will be easy to achieve. Political leaders often opt for domestically attractive foreign policy stances, and they find educating the public on foreign policy issues difficult. Similarly, the public has too often shown little interest in or knowledge about foreign affairs; traditional beliefs remain appealing. A coherent foreign policy, however, requires that such an effort be made by the leadership and the public. The leadership task is especially difficult today because the elite-mass value divisions are ideologically based and because these divisions are *within* generations rather than across them. Thus, simple appeals to only one segment of the American public will not suffice; instead, the leadership must be much more creative in identifying values and policies that will appeal across groups. Furthermore, with pressing international political problems—whether it be the potential spread of nuclear weapons, the continuing global debt crisis, or the effects of global warming—American political leadership probably does not have the luxury of waiting until dramatic international events help to forge a new value consensus (as the events of the late 1940s and early 1950s assisted in forging the Cold War consensus).[21]

Alternate Approaches to Building a Consensus

What, then, might be some of these overarching values that the political leadership could use to mold any new consensus? Several alternate approaches have been proposed recently, and they largely conform to the four different segments within the elites and the public that we discussed earlier. For simplicity's sake, let us group them under four general headings: (1) a neo-isolationist approach; (2) a more self-interested and unilateral approach to American involvement; (3) an approach emphasizing more completely democratic and ethical ideals in American foreign policy; and (4) an approach emphasizing greater international cooperation in American foreign policy. While we cannot do full justice to any of them in this short space, and some of the approaches are not as mutually exclusive as the four groupings suggest, we can give some sense of the range of options that are being suggested.

Neo-Isolationism. The first alternative might be labeled a "neo-isolationism" approach. In the immediate aftermath of the Vietnam War, for example, several calls arose for neo-isolationism as the most promising path for American foreign policy, and with the end of the Cold War, this general theme emerged once again. This approach is closely akin to the isolationist segment in the mass and elite opinion analyses that we reported earlier.

Writing prior to the breakup of the Soviet Union but as Eastern Europe was changing, a former government official perhaps most vigorously portrayed the view of those who yearn for a reduced or detached role for the United States in world affairs.[22] His approach would be less the result of a conscious policy decision on the part of the United States and more the result of changed international circumstances. Because the emerging international system will be more fragmented and regionalized, the United States should move toward greater" strategic independence" by seeking "to quarantine regional violence and compartmentalize regional instability." The best approach to achieve this outcome will be not "by active intervention" but by encouraging "regional balances of power, whether bipolar or multipolar."[23]

In this kind of an international system, the national security strategy of the United States would involve protecting only limited key values: "the lives and domestic property of citizens, the integrity of national territory, and the autonomy of political processes."[24] Promoting and protecting values beyond these will lose their relevance. Efforts to reshape the international system, for example, or to expand human rights globally would no longer be core United States values. As a consequence, defense plans could be scaled back; American commitments through extended deterrence would be substantially weakened; and United States actions would assume a more limited role in shaping global politics. On balance, the United States will be able to do nothing less because, in this view, the nation must "adjust to a world beyond order and control."[25]

After the end of the Cold War, Eric Nordlinger echoed this approach and called for a new national strategy based on "isolationism reconfigured."[26] The proposed strategy called for "an exceptionally narrow security perimeter, beyond which political–military activism is limited to a bare minimum."[27] In other words, the United States would work to protect key concerns, but it would take a very limited role in world affairs. Five reasons or assumptions underpinned the promotion of this nonengagement approach. First, the United States "enjoys a privileged position in being strategically immune"[28] from external threats, reducing the need for an expansive American role. Second, the intention of potential challengers cannot be determined with much confidence, and as a result, the United States should not pursue a more assertive international posture. Third, a strategy of nonengagement is at least as effective as a strategy of engagement for the United States "in warding off any and all unacceptable actions against the narrow core perimeter—be they economic competition and pressures, minor probes, deterrent challenges, coercive threats or outright attacks."[29] Fourth, the "challenger's intentions" in the international arena today are assumed to be largely benign, furthering support for nonengagement over engagement. Fifth, and finally, there are "ubiquitous possibilities of strategic mismanagement"[30] with a more complex approach than a national strategy based on limited engagement. In other words, the likelihood of policy-making mistakes increases with greater global involvement.

Furthermore, Nordlinger argues that this strategy has other advantages. It will still allow the United States to promote its "extrasecurity values"—such as promoting its liberal ideals and its domestic welfare—than a strategy of "strategic internationalism."[31] This national strategy is also more compatible with the various competing political cultures prevalent in American society.[32] In short, nonengagement, or isolationism reconfigured, is a viable approach for the United States after the Cold War.

A New Unilateralism. Others suggest a considerably different approach for the United States in the post–Cold War world—an approach based on greater American unilateralism in foreign policy. In this approach, the United States would remain engaged in the world, albeit in a more selective, self-interested way than it operated during the Cold War. The variants proposed under this general approach would be particularly appealing to those who identify with the hardliner/internationalist segments of the American public and its leaders.

In one variant of this unilateral approach, the goal for the United States would be to pursue more single-mindedly its global economic interests. In particular, economic nationalism would be adopted to replace anticommunism as the unifying force in American foreign policy and would be used as the means to restore America's competitiveness and global standing.[33] In effect, the United States would adopt more protectionist trade policy and take more selective and vigorous economic actions worldwide. The political/military emphasis in United States foreign policy would necessarily take a backseat in any such strategy. American public opinion continues to support this position, since, as we reported earlier, important foreign economic issues remain the dominant ones on the foreign policy agenda for most Americans.[34]

Two other recent variants within this approach would promote increasing degrees of United States leadership in world affairs, including the use of more and more American military capabilities. Richard Haass, a former official in the Bush administration, called for a policy built around the concept of "augmented realism," or "realism plus," and a policy grounded in American leadership in the post–Cold War era.[35] Although realism alone, with its emphasis primarily on promoting order among states (and with less emphasis on what goes on within states), will not be acceptable to the ethical traditions of most Americans, it should nonetheless be the beginning norm for American foreign policy. In particular, "America's principal focus should be on threats to interstate order...which pose the greatest danger to the full range of U.S. interests."[36] Beyond that norm, other actions, such as promoting trade to foster political pluralism in other states and promoting moderation in foreign policy actions by adversaries, should be pursued. The promotion of democracy and human rights, too, "ought not...be overlooked." Yet Haass adds an important caveat: "In times of crisis,...support for humanitarian and Wilsonian interests must depend on the severity of the problem, the simultaneous existence of overriding strategic interests, and America's ability to do something constructive at an affordable price."[37] In sum, American leadership is indispensable to achieving these goals: "Washington is first among unequals and should act accordingly."[38]

Kristol and Kagan largely follow Haass's reasoning in suggesting a new foreign policy direction, but they call for an even more assertive unilateral role for the United States in affecting global affairs.[39] Rather than acceding to a reduced role for the United States in world affairs after the Cold War, Kristol and Kagan actually call for the United States to pursue a "benevolent global hegemony,"[40] an approach in which American power and influence would be largely generous and unselfish in leading and promoting global order. A principal aim of this approach would be to preserve American predominance around the world through "strengthening America's security, supporting its friends, advancing its interests, and standing up for its principles."[41] As they see it, "American hegemony is the only reliable defense against a breakdown of peace and international order." To sustain and promote this global role, the United States must also pursue a policy of "military supremacy and moral confidence" by enhancing defense spending, increasing citizen awareness of America's international role, and pursuing actions abroad "based on the understanding that its moral goals and its fundamental national interests are almost always in harmony."[42]

Each of these first two approaches has problems and shortcomings as organizing schema for United States foreign policy. While we cannot delineate them in detail here, some indication of these potential difficulties merits brief mention. On the one hand, the neo-isolationist proposals inevitably bump up against a public that remains largely internationalist in focus, albeit less so on the political–military side than on the economic side. On the other hand, too much unilateral involvement and a sustained hegemonic role must confront a public increasingly weary of international responsibilities and more focused on domestic concerns. Finally, too stark an emphasis on realism—acting only to create order in global affairs—without a reliance on guiding moral principles runs two possible risks: increasing public cynicism about the short-term motivations of politicians, and affronting the ethical impulses toward foreign affairs still prevalent among the American people.

A Democratic Imperative. Yet a third alternative, first suggested almost two decades ago by George Quester, would involve a return to America's traditional emphasis upon its domestic values in dealing with the world.[43] That is, the United States would place greater reliance upon the principles of political democracy (e.g., "free contested elections with a free press") as the basis of our policy toward other nations. This alternative should be particularly appealing to those who identify with the internationalist/accommodationist segments of the American public and its leaders. That is, the United States would stand for its principles in the world, but the government would promote them cooperatively with other states and organizations in the international system.

According to Quester's original formulation, the consensus that really was lost by the Vietnam War was a sense of confidence in America's values and its sense of worth to the rest of the world. As a result, Americans subsequently applied a double standard in approaching the international system. While we are willing to apply the standards of political democracy in conducting foreign relations with Western Europe and Canada, for instance, we were unwilling to apply those same standards in dealing with states of the developing world.

This movement away from the "democratic ideal" had serious consequences for the United States in the immediate post-Vietnam years. To many Americans the United States no longer served as a model to the world. Instead, other states, without democratic values, assumed that position. Further, as these nations have moved away from traditional American beliefs, the "altruistic impulses" within the United States—its social and economic concern for other nations—declined. In fact, an isolationist sentiment has gained some credibility. In order to arrest such trends, a return to democratic values as a basis of policy remains crucial in Quester's view.

This democratic impulse has now gained renewed currency with the demise of communism in Eastern Europe and the Soviet Union. Democracy has the advantage of being an approach in which the United States supports "the good guys in the world, a Wilsonian foreign policy."[44] Such a policy has another attraction as well. By perfecting democratic institutions at home and then seeking to promote them abroad, "democracy promotion would forge a sense of community that would make both the internal and international purpose of the United States not just a 'government policy' but a source of national identity."[45]

The Clinton administration's emphasis on the "enlargement of democracy" around the world, coupled with its emphasis on free trade, seeks to capture elements of these Wilsonian and democratic traditions.[46] Furthermore, the key assumption of the Clinton administration, that "democracies do not fight one another," translates into building a more peaceful world as it builds a more democratic one. The emphasis upon democracy as the organizing scheme for foreign policy making, the emphasis upon promoting American values abroad, and the efforts to transform the global community to a more pacific one resonate well with the American public. Despite this appeal, however, this approach also faces serious challenges.

How does one go about building democracies? Does the United States have "the will and the wallet" to undertake such a task? Even if the democratic peace proposition is valid, as several recent studies suggest,[47] the transition from nondemocracies to democracies is destabilizing for the global community. That is, as states go through this process of democratization, the road is rocky for the global community. While the end condition of movement to a democratic world may be pacific, the process of building a democratic order and the movement toward "mature democracies" may not be.[48]

A New Internationalism. A fourth approach would focus upon building a world community—a rather dramatic break from the essentially bipolar arrangement of the Cold War or the unilateral or unipolar impulse of the United States after the Cold War. The approach should be particularly appealing to those who identify with the accommodationist segment of the American public and its leaders and want to work cooperatively with the world community.

About two decades ago, political scientist Stanley Hoffmann outlined something akin to this global community idea, and his insights are worth considering in contemplating the details of this new world order.[49] In his view, this kind of foreign policy would emphasize world order values as the dominant theme for American foreign policy and it would be based upon three strategic guidelines for implementing such a foreign policy. The first premise would be an emphasis upon building on the world order that presently exists—whether through international institutions (e.g., the United Nations), through formal ties (e.g., a new nuclear arms agreement among the superpowers), or through informal beliefs and standards (e.g., the increasing recognition of global interdependence). Second, the United States would have to adopt a much more pluralist approach to the world by showing greater willingness to adapt to changed global conditions and by demonstrating a strong commitment to negotiating differences between states. Third, according to Hoffmann, national security policy would also need to be turned "into an aspect of world order policy." In other words, the emphasis would not be on maximizing the national interest, but on seeking global accommodation.

The methods—or the "operational code—that Hoffmann suggests for putting these general guidelines into effect are also formidable. First, the United States should follow a consistent course in which international concerns must prevail over domestic concerns: Domestic political considerations should not be allowed to sidetrack efforts to build world order. Second, negotiations must be sought with all states, no matter the degree of commonality with them. Further, in bargaining situations, we must not be put off by new coalitions that might emerge—even if some of our presumed partners join them. Third, we must understand, even while searching for global order, that foreign policy is ultimately a political process among *states*.

To some extent, these global community efforts have made great strides. On the political level, for instance, the record is substantial: the dramatic increase in United Nations peacekeeping efforts since the end of the Cold War; the expansion of NATO activities "out of area" (e.g., in Bosnia); the expansion of NATO with the "Partnership for Peace" program, incorporating Eastern European states into the organization; the cooperation and support of a wide array of nations in the Middle East peace efforts; and the expansion of the Association of Southeast Asian Nations (ASEAN) to include a political forum—the ASEAN Regional Forum with members within and outside the region, including the United States.

On an economic level, for instance, the record of organizational cooperation is even more remarkable: the expansion and development of the European Union (EU); the completion of NAFTA and GATT; the beginning efforts with the "Summits of the Americas" and the Asia-Pacific Economic Cooperation (APEC) organization; and the incipient discussion of a transatlantic organization as well.

As with the other approaches, however, an international cooperative approach to foreign policy would likely spark concerns and challenges. While there is public support for an international role for the United States, there remains some skepticism about too much political cooperation at the international level. As we noted earlier, there is majority public support for expanding the activities of the United Nations, but the public sentiment generally is more toward a selective international involvement. Deep and sustained involvements in UN peacekeeping missions are often problematic, but efforts at "peacebuilding" and "peacemaking"—transforming the political landscape of other countries—as was attempted in Somalia often result in little public support.

On the economic level, international cooperation also raises some concerns, including the implications of pursuing worldwide and regionwide free trade agreements.[50] This approach grows out of the functionalist tradition within international politics—more cooperation in so-called "low politics" arenas will eventually yield cooperation in "high politics" arenas as well—but it also grows out of the controversial notion that states and societies are more interested in their own absolute gains than in their relative gains vis-à-vis their neighbors or trading partners.[51] That is, absolute gains by all participants in a cooperative venture (such as in a trading bloc) will be the driving force in sustained cooperative relations among states, not the relative gain arguments of the realists.

The evidence for this assertion is mixed. While the EU may be identified as a successful illustration of this argument, some regional trading bloc formed in the 1960s does not support it. Several dissolved or failed almost as quickly as they were formed—largely over political rivalries. The East African Common Market and the Central American Common Market easily come to mind. With the expanding number of these free trade areas, and potential free trade areas, the argument will surely be tested in the late 1990s and the early years of the twenty-first century. Furthermore, Americans are more likely to be differentially affected by international trade compacts and international environmental actions, yielding less, not more, support for this attempt at international cooperation. Finally, too, economic and environmental actions on a global scale will likely create more conflict, not less, between states and within states, since value differences will quickly emerge on such sensitive questions.

Concluding Comments

Which approach or combination of these approaches (if any) will emerge as the basis of a new foreign policy consensus in the years ahead? A greater emphasis on domestic values? A movement toward greater unilateralism? The development of greater international cooperation? A revival of isolationism? We obviously cannot say with any certainty, because the public and elite debate continues. Nevertheless, these contrasting approaches continue to highlight the fact that one important component of the historical American debate has largely been resolved, while the other continues. Most of these approaches generally agree upon the need for continued American engagement in world affairs, albeit in sharply different degrees, but the extent of domestic moral principle as the overarching guide to policy actions remains a source of debate. In this sense, the debate over the one key value that was closely associated with America's past has been changed dramatically, largely away from isolationism to some global participation, but the other key value—moral principle—continues as a source of argument as we enter the new century.

Such debate, however, does not have to be debilitating for American foreign policy. Instead, it can strengthen the unity and resolve of the nation to address its common foreign policy concerns, even as American society seeks to resolve what values it wants to promote in the global arena. Writing at the end of the Vietnam War, Richard Holbrooke, who most recently was America's principal negotiator in producing the Dayton Accords over Bosnia, captured the painful, yet hopeful, situation the United States faced then:

> We have been going through a relentless and grueling reexamination of ourselves, a period of self-revelation and public exposure that might have caused a revolution in a country less strong than ours....What is vitally important is that we learn from our mistakes and our past, but not give up our dreams and values as a nation.[52]

In large measure, the comments of Richard Holbrooke remain apt, as we debate the direction of American foreign policy after the Cold War and at the dawn of a new century.

Notes

1. See Charles W. Kegley and Eugene R. Wittkopf, *American Foreign Policy: Pattern and Process*, 4th ed. (New York: St. Martin's Press, 1991) for an argument along these lines.
2. Ole R. Holsti and James N. Rosenau, "The Structure of Foreign Policy Beliefs Among American Opinion Leaders—After the Cold War," *Millennium* 22 (Summer 1993): 235–278; and Ole R. Holsti, "Continuity and Change in the Domestic Foreign Policy Beliefs of American Opinion Leaders," paper presented for the American Political Science Association annual meeting, Washington, DC, August 27–31, 1997, and is the basis of Figure 13.1. I am most grateful to Professor Holsti for granting me permission to use these data from his paper.
3. Holsti and Rosenau, "The Structure of Foreign Policy Beliefs Among American Opinion Leaders—After the Cold War," p. 258.

4. Ibid., p. 248.
5. Ibid. Also see Ole R. Holsti and James N. Rosenau, "The Structure of Foreign Policy Attitudes Among American Leaders," *Journal of Politics* 52 (February 1990): 94–125, for another earlier analysis in this same vein.
6. Other post-Vietnam analyses of elite beliefs by Wittkopf have largely confirmed and more fully specified the foreign policy divisions that Holsti and Rosenau initially suggested. (See Eugene R. Wittkopf, *Faces of Internationalism: Public Opinion and American Foreign Policy* [Durham, NC: Duke University Press, 1990], pp. 107 –133.) By sophisticated statistical analyses of the leadership sample gathered by the Chicago Council on Foreign Relations in 1974, 1978, 1982, and 1986, Wittkopf found that elite beliefs, just as the public beliefs, can generally be divided into the fourfold categories of accommodationists, internationalists, isolationists, and hardliners—based upon the respondents' attitudes toward militant and cooperative internationalism. Only for the 1982 results does this fourfold categorization not hold.
7. See Eugene R. Wittkopf and Michael A. Maggiotto, "Elites and Masses: A Comparative Analysis of Attitudes Toward America's World Role," *The Journal of Politics* 45 (May 1983), especially pp. 312–323; Eugene R. Wittkopf, "Elites and Masses: Constancy and Change in Public Attitudes Toward America's World Role," a paper delivered at the annual meeting of the Southern Political Science Association, Birmingham, Alabama, November 1983; and Wittkopf, *Faces of Internationalism*, pp. 134–165.
8. John E. Rielly, ed., *American Public Opinion and U.S. Foreign Policy 1995* (Chicago: The Chicago Council on Foreign Relations, 1995), pp. 34–36.
9. The discussion is from ibid., pp. 38–40. The quoted passage is at p. 38.
10. For some Vietnam era calls for a new consensus, see, for example, Lincoln P. Bloomfield, "Foreign Policy for Disillusioned Liberals," *Foreign Policy* 9 (Winter 1972–73): 55–68; Thomas L. Hughes, "The Flight From Foreign Policy," *Foreign Policy* 10 (Spring 1973): 141–156; and Philip Windsor, "America's Moral Confusion: Separating the Should from the Good," *Foreign Policy* 13 (Winter 1973–74): 139–153. A survey of *Foreign Affairs*, the other leading journal on foreign policy, produced a number of commentaries on this breakdown of the old consensus and a need for another set of unifying values purposes. Interested readers should see, for example, John V. Lindsay, "For a New Policy Balance," *Foreign Affairs* 50 (October 1971): 1–14; Kingman Brewster, Jr., "Reflections on Our National Purpose," *Foreign Affairs* 50 (April 1972): 399–415; Zbigniew Brzezinski, "U.S. Foreign Policy: The Search for Focus," *Foreign Affairs* 51 (July 1973): 708–727; and Max Lerner, "America Agonistes," *Foreign Affairs* 52 (January 1974): 287–300.
11. Zbigniew Brzezinski, "America in a Hostile World," *Foreign Policy* 23 (Summer 1976): 89.
12. Stanley Hoffmann, *Primacy or World Order* (New York: McGraw-Hill, 1978).
13. Thomas L. Hughes, "The Crack-Up: The Price of Collective Irresponsibility," *Foreign Policy* 40 (Fall 1980): 33–60. Actually Hughes argues that the two "cultures" have always existed in the postwar period, even during the time of presumed consensus before Vietnam. At that time, however, there had been a "workable dissensus" (p. 52). This point raises the larger issue of the extent to which the Cold War consensus was a true consensus. Admittedly, the systematic empirical evidence for the present "dissensus" among the leadership and the public is more readily available than that for the consensus of the immediate postwar years.
14. See, for example, Graham Allison and Gregory F. Treverton, eds., *Rethinking America's Security: Beyond Cold War to New World Order* (New York: W. W. Norton, 1992); Terry L. Deibel, "Strategies Before Containment: Patterns for the Future," *International Security* 16 (Spring 1992): 79–108; John Lewis Gaddis, *The United States and the End of the Cold War: Implications, Reconsiderations, and Provocations* (New York: Oxford University Press, 1992); Zalmay Khalilzad, "Losing the Moment? The United States and the World After the Cold War," *The Washington Quarterly* 18 (Spring 1995); 87–107; Richard A. Melanson, *American Foreign Policy Since the Vietnam War: The Search for Consensus from Nixon to Clinton*, 2nd ed. (Armonk, NY: M. E. Sharpe, 1996); and Andrew Rosenthal, "Farewell, Red Menace," *New York Times*, September 1, 1991, 1 and 14, among many others, as well as the detailed examples discussed below.

15. James Chace, "Is a Foreign Policy Consensus Possible?" *Foreign Affairs* 57 (Fall 1978): 16. For Chace's latest view, including this quotation, see James Chace, "The Dangers of a Foreign Policy Consensus," *World Policy Journal* 13 (Winter 1996/97): 97.
16. I am indebted to Professor Ole Holsti of Duke University for suggesting this point about consensus on issues.
17. Chace, "Is a Foreign Policy Consensus Possible," p. 15. Actually, Chace quotes from Hoffmann's *Primacy and Order* to make this point.
18. Leslie H. Gelb with Richard K. Betts, *The Irony of Vietnam: The System Worked* (Washington, DC: The Brookings Institution, 1979), pp. 365–369.
19. Ibid., pp. 365 and 366.
20. Hughes, "The Crack-Up: The Price of Collective Irresponsibility," p. 59.
21. For the classic statement of the impact of international events on domestic images, see Karl W. Deutsch, "External Influences on the Internal Behavior of States," in R. Barry Farrell, ed., *Approaches to Comparative and International Politics* (Evanston, IL: Northwestern University Press, 1966), pp. 5–26.
22. Earl C. Ravenel, "The Case for Adjustment," *Foreign Policy* 81 (Winter 1990–1991): 3–19.
23. Ibid., pp. 3,4,6, and 8.
24. Ibid., p. 15, is the source of the quotation. The discussion of changed defense needs follows at pp. 16–17.
25. Ibid., p. 19.
26. Eric A. Nordlinger, *Isolationism Reconfigured: American Foreign Policy for a New Century* (Princeton, NJ: Princeton University Press, 1995).
27. Ibid., p. 31.
28. Ibid., p. 41.
29. Ibid., p. 43.
30. Ibid.
31. Ibid., p. 181.
32. Ibid., pp. 263–278.
33. Norman J. Ornstein and Mark Schmitt, "Dateline Campaign '92: Post–Cold War Politics," *Foreign Policy* 79 (Summer 1990): 176–182. For another recent unilateralist analysis, see Alan Tonelson, "What Is the National Interest?" *The Atlantic Monthly* (July 1991): 35ff.
34. See Rielly, *American Public Opinion and U.S. Foreign Policy 1995*, for this theme.
35. Richard Haass, "Paradigm Lost," *Foreign Affairs* 74 (January/February 1995): 43–58.
36. Ibid., p. 55.
37. Ibid., p. 56.
38. Ibid.
39. William Kristol and Robert Kagan, "Toward A Neo-Reaganite Foreign Policy," *Foreign Affairs* 75 (July/August 1996): 18–32.
40. Ibid., p. 20.
41. Ibid., p. 23.
42. Ibid., pp. 23 and 27.
43. This section relies upon Quester, "Consensus Lost," *Foreign Policy* 40 (Fall 1980): 18–32. The quoted phrases are at pp. 22, 29, and 31. A more complete analysis of his views is presented in George Quester, *American Foreign Policy: The Lost Consensus* (New York: Praeger, 1982).
44. The comment was by the late Congressman Les Aspin (D-Wisconsin), and he is quoted in Ornstein and Schmitt, "Dateline Campaign '92: Post–Cold War Politics," p. 184.
45. Ibid., p. 185.
46. The discussion in this and the next paragraph draws from my "Assessing Clinton's Foreign Policy at Midterm," *Current History* 94 (November 1995): 373.

47. Bruce M. Russett, *Grasping the Democratic Peace: Principles for a Post–Cold War World* (Princeton, NJ: Princeton University Press, 1993), p. 21; and Zeev Maoz and Bruce Russett, "Normative and Structural Causes of Democratic Peace, 1946–1986," *American Political Science Review* 87 (September 1993): 624–638. Also see David A. Lake, "Powerful Pacifists: Democratic States and War," *American Political Science Review* 86 (March 1992): 24–37.
48. Edward D. Mansfield and Jack Snyder, "Democratization and War," *Foreign Affairs* 74 (May/June 1995): 79–97.
49. This discussion is drawn from Hoffmann, *Primacy or World Order*, pp. 241–266.
50. The following draws upon my "Assessing Clinton's Foreign Policy at Midterm," pp. 373–374.
51. For an analysis of the "relative gain" versus the "absolute gain" argument, see Joseph M. Grieco, "Anarchy and the Limits of Cooperation: A Realist Critique of the Newest Liberal Institutionalism," in Charles W. Kegley, Jr., ed., *Controversies in International Relations Theory: Realism and the Neoliberalism Challenge* (New York: St. Martin's Press, 1995), pp. 151–171.
52. Richard Holbrooke, "A Sense of Drift, A Time for Calm," in Steven C. Spiegel, ed., *At Issue: Politics in the Global Arena* (New York: St. Martin's Press, 1977), p. 12.

A SELECTED BIBLIOGRAPHY

Acheson, Dean. *Present at the Creation.* New York: W. W. Norton & Company, Inc., 1969.

Adler, David Gray. "The Constitution and Presidential Warmaking: The Enduring Debate." *Political Science Quarterly* 103 (Spring 1988): 1–36.

Aldrich, John H., John L. Sullivan, and Eugene Borgida. "Foreign Affairs and Issue Voting: Do Presidential Candidates 'Waltz Before a Blind Audience'?" *American Political Science Review* 83 (March 1989): 123–141.

Allison, Graham. *Essence of Decision: Explaining the Cuban Missile Crisis.* Boston: Little, Brown and Company, 1971.

———, and Gregory F. Treverton, eds. *Rethinking America's Security: Beyond Cold War to New World Order.* New York: W. W. Norton & Company, 1992.

Almond, Gabriel A. *The American People and Foreign Policy.* New York: Praeger, 1960.

———, and Sidney Verba. *The Civic Culture.* Boston: Little, Brown and Company, 1963.

Alperovitz, Gar. *Atomic Diplomacy: Hiroshima and Potsdam.* New York: Ransom House, 1965.

Ambrose, Stephen E. *Rise to Globalism: American Foreign Policy 1938–1976.* New York: Penguin Books, 1976.

Arnett, Peter. *Live From the Battlefield.* New York: Simon & Schuster, 1994.

Aron, Raymond. "Ideology in Search of a Policy." In *America and the World 1981,* William P. Bundy, ed. New York: Pergamon Press, 1982.

Bailey, Thomas A. *A Diplomatic History of the American People.* New York: F. S. Crofts & Co., 1942.

———. *The Man on the Street: The Impact of American Public Opinion on Foreign Policy.* New York: Macmillan, Inc., 1948.

Baker, James A., III, with Thomas M. DeFrank. *The Politics of Diplomacy: Revolution, War and Peace, 1989*–1992. New York: G. P. Putnam's Sons, 1995.

Ball, George W., and Douglas B. Ball. *The Passionate Attachment.* New York: W. W. Norton & Company, 1992.

Bay, Christian. *The Structure of Freedom.* New York: Atheneum Publishers, 1965.

Bennet, Douglas J., Jr. "Congress in Foreign Policy: Who Needs It?" *Foreign Affairs* 57 (Fall 1978): 40–50.

Bennett, W. Lance. "The Media and the Foreign Policy Process." In *The New Politics of American Foreign Policy,* David A. Deese, ed. New York: St. Martin's Press, 1994.

———, and David L. Paletz, eds. *Taken by Storm: The Media Public Opinion, and U.S. Foreign Policy in the Gulf War.* Chicago and London: The University of Chicago Press, 1994.

Beres, Louis Rene. *People, States, and World Order.* Itasca, IL: F. E. Peacock Publishers, Inc., 1981.

Berkowitz, Bruce. "Information Age Intelligence." *Foreign Policy* 103 (Summer 1996): 35–50.

Berkowitz, Morton, P.G. Bock, and Vincent Fuccillo, eds. *The Politics of American Foreign Policy.* Englewood Cliffs, NJ: Prentice-Hall, Inc., 1977.

Bernstein, Robert A., and William W. Anthony. "The ABM Issue in the Senate, 1968–1970: The Importance of Ideology." *American Political Science Review* 68 (September 1974): 1198–1206.

Berry, Nicholas O., ed. *U.S. Foreign Policy Documents, 1933–1945: From Withdrawal to World Leadership.* Brunswick, OH: King's Court Communications, Inc., 1978.

———. *Foreign Policy and the Press.* Westport, CT: Greenwood Press, 1990.

Betts, Richard K. "Misadventure Revisited." In *A Reader in American Foreign Policy,* James M. McCormick, ed. Itasca, IL: F. E. Peacock Publishers, Inc., 1986.

Blechman, Barry M., and Stephen S. Kaplan. *Force Without War.* Washington, DC: The Brookings Institution, 1978.

Blight, James G., and David A. Welch. *On the Brink: Americans and Soviets Reexamine the Cuban Missile Crisis.* 2nd ed. New York: The Noonday Press, 1990.

Bliss, Howard, and M. Glen Johnson. *Beyond the Water's Edge: America's Foreign Policies.* Philadelphia: J. B. Lippincott Co., 1975.

———. *Consensus at the Crossroads: Dialogues in American Foreign Policy.* New York: Dodd, Mead & Co., Inc., 1972.

Bloomfield, Lincoln P. "Foreign Policy for Disillusioned Liberals?" *Foreign Policy* 9 (Winter 1972–73): 55–68.

———. "From Ideology to Program to Policy." *Journal of Policy Analysis and Management* 2 (Fall 1982): 1–12.

———. *In Search of American Foreign Policy.* New York: Oxford University Press, 1974.

Bond, Jon R., and Richard Fleisher. *The President in the Legislative Arena.* Chicago: The University of Chicago Press, 1990.

Boorstin, Daniel J. *America and the Image of Europe: Reflections on American Thought.* New York: Meridian Books, 1960.

Braestrup, Peter. *Big Story: How the American Press and Television Reported and Interpreted the Crisis of Tet 1968.* 2 vols. Boulder, CO: Westview Press, 1977.

Brewer, Thomas L. *American Foreign Policy: A Contemporary Introduction.* Englewood Cliffs, NJ: Prentice-Hall, Inc., 1980.

Brewster, Kingman, Jr. "Reflection on our National Purpose." *Foreign Affairs* 50 (April 1972): 339–415.

Brown, Seyom. *The Faces of Power: Constancy and Change in United States Foreign Policy From Truman to Reagan.* New York: Columbia University Press, 1983.

Browne, Marjorie Ann. *Executive Agreements and the Congress.* Issue Brief Number IB75035. Washington, DC: The Library of Congress, 1981.

Brownstein, Ronald, and Nina Easton. *Reagan's Ruling Class.* Washington, DC: The Presidential Accountability Group, 1982.

Brzezinski, Zbigniew. "America in a Hostile World." *Foreign Policy* 23 (Summer 1976): 65–96.

———. "How The Cold War Was Played." *Foreign Affairs* 51 (October 1972): 181–204.

———. *Power and Principle: Memoirs of the National Security Advisor, 1977–1981.* New York: Farrar, Straus & Giroux, 1983.

———. "U.S. Foreign Policy: The Search for Focus." *Foreign Affairs* 51 (July 1973): 708–727.

Buckley, William F., Jr. "Human Rights and Foreign Policy." *Foreign Affairs* 58 (Spring 1980): 775–796.

Bull, Hedley. "A View From Abroad: Consistency Under Pressure." In *America and the World 1978,* William P. Bundy, ed. New York: Pergamon Press, 1979.

Bundy, William P. "A Portentous Year." In *America and the World 1983,* William P. Bundy, ed. New York: Pergamon Press, 1984.

Burgin, Eileen. "Congress and Foreign Policy: The Misperceptions." In *Congress Reconsidered,* Lawrence C. Dodd and Bruce I. Oppenheimer, eds. Washington, DC: CQ Press, 1993.

Campbell, Colin. *Managing the Presidency: Carter, Reagan, and the Search for Executive Harmony.* Pittsburgh: University of Pittsburgh Press, 1986.

Campbell, John Franklin. "The Disorganization of State." In *Problems of American Foreign Policy.* 2nd ed., Martin B. Hickman, ed. Beverly Hills: Glencoe Press, 1975.

Carleton, David, and Michael Stohl. "The Foreign Policy of Human Rights: Rhetoric and Reality from Jimmy Carter to Ronald Reagan." *Human Rights Quarterly* 9 (May 1985): 205–229.

Carroll, Holbert N. *The House of Representatives and Foreign Affairs.* Pittsburgh: University of Pittsburgh Press, 1958.

Carter, Jimmy. *Keeping Faith.* New York: Bantam Books, 1982.

Caspary, William R. "The 'Mood Theory': A Study of Public Opinion and Foreign Policy." *American Political Science Review* 54 (June 1970): 536–547.

Chace, James. "The Dangers of a Foreign Policy Consensus." *World Policy Journal* 13 (Winter 1996/97): 97–99.

———. "Is a Foreign Policy Consensus Possible?" *Foreign Affairs* 57 (Fall 1978): 1–16.

The Challenge of Peace: God's Promise and Our Response. Washington, DC: The United States Catholic Conference, May 3, 1983.

Chan, Steve. "Grasping the Peace Dividend: Some Propositions on the Conversion of Swords into Plowshares." *Mershon International Studies Review* 39 (April 1995): 53–95.

Christopher, Warren. "Ceasefire Between the Branches: A Compact in Foreign Affairs." *Foreign Affairs* 60 (Summer 1982): 989–1005.

Choate, Pat. *Agents of Influence.* New York: Alfred A. Knopf, 1990.

Clarke, Duncan L. *Politics of Arms Control: The Role and Effectiveness of the U.S. Arms Control and Disarmament Agency.* New York: The Free Press, 1979.

———. "Why State Can't Lead." *Foreign Policy* 66 (Spring 1987): 128–142.

Clausen, Aage R. *How Congressmen Decide: A Policy Focus.* New York: St. Martin's Press, 1973.

Clausewitz, Carl von. *On War.* Ed. and trans. by Michael Howard and Peter Paret. Princeton, NJ: Princeton University Press, 1976.

Clinton, David. "Tocqueville's Challenge." *The Washington Quarterly* 11 (Winter 1988): 173–189.

Cohen, Bernard. *The Political Process and Foreign Policy: The Making of the Japanese Settlement.* Princeton, NJ: Princeton University Press, 1957.

———. *The Press and Foreign Policy.* Princeton, NJ: Princeton University Press, 1963.

———. *The Public's Impact on Foreign Policy.* Boston: Little, Brown and Company, 1973.

Cohen, Stephen D. *The Making of United States Economic Policy.* 3rd ed. New York: Praeger, 1988.

———. *The Making of United States International Economic Policy.* 4th ed. Westport, CT: Praeger, 1994.

———, Joel R. Paul, and Robert A. Blecker. *Fundamentals of U.S. Foreign Trade Policy.* Boulder, CO: Westview Press, 1996.

Coles, Harry L. *The War of 1812.* Chicago: The University of Chicago Press, 1965.

Collier, Ellen C. "Foreign Policy by Reporting Requirement." *The Washington Quarterly* 11 (Winter 1988): 75–84.

Congress and the Nation 1945–1964. Washington, DC: Congressional Quarterly Service, 1965.

Congressional Quarterly's Guide to Congress. 3rd ed. Washington, DC: Congressional Quarterly, Inc., 1982.

Cooke, Jacob E., ed. *The Federalist.* Middletown, CT: Wesleyan University Press, 1961.

Cooper, Chester L. "The CIA and Decisionmaking." *Foreign Affairs* 50 (January 1972): 221–236.

Cooper, Joseph, and Patricia A. Hurley. "The Legislative Veto: A Policy Analysis." *Congress & the Presidency* 10 (Spring 1983): 1–24.

Corwin, Edward S. *The President: Office and Powers 1787*–1957. New York: New York University Press, 1957.

Crabb, Cecil V., Jr. *Bipartisan Foreign Policy.* Evanston, IL: Row, Peterson and Company, 1957.

———. *The Elephants and the Grass: A Study of Nonalignment.* New York: Frederick A. Praeger, 1965.

———. *Policymakers and Critics: Conflicting Theories of American Foreign Policy.* New York: Frederick A. Praeger, Inc., 1976.

———, and Pat M. Holt. *Invitation to Struggle: Congress, the President, and Foreign Policy.* Washington, DC: Congressional Quarterly Press, 1980.

Craig, Gordon A., and George, Alexander L. *Force and Statecraft.* 3rd ed. New York and Oxford: Oxford University Press, 1995.

Cumings, Bruce. *The Origins of the Korean War. Volume II: The Roaring of the Cataract, 1947–1950.* Princeton, NJ: Princeton University Press, 1990.

Dahl, Robert A. *Congress and Foreign Policy.* New York: Harcourt, Brace and Company, 1950.

———. *Modern Political Analysis.* 2nd ed. Englewood Cliffs, NJ: Prentice-Hall, Inc., 1970.

Dallek, Robert. *The American Style of Foreign Policy.* New York: Alfred A. Knopf, 1983.

Deering, Christopher J. "Decision Making in the Armed Services Committees." In *Congress Resurgent: Foreign and Defense Policy on Capitol Hill,* Randall B. Ripley and James M. Lindsay, eds. Ann Arbor: The University of Michigan Press, 1993.

Deibel, Terry L. "Strategies Before Containment: Patterns for the Future." *International Security* 16 (Spring 1992): 79–108.

De la Garza, Rodolfo O. "U.S. Foreign Policy and the Mexican–American Political Agenda." In Mohammed E. Ahrari, ed., *Ethnic Groups and U.S. Foreign Policy.* New York: Greenwood Press, 1987.

De Long, Bradford, Christopher De Long, and Sherman Robinson. "The Case for Mexico's Rescue." *Foreign Affairs* 75 (May/June 1996): 8–14.

DeParle, Jason. "The Man Inside Bill Clinton's Foreign Policy." *New York Times Magazine,* August 20, 1995, 32–39, 46, 55, and 57.

Destler, I. M. *American Trade Politics.* Washington, DC: Institute of International Economics and New York: The Twentieth Century Fund, 1992.

———. "Dateline Washington: Congress as Boss?" *Foreign Policy* 42 (Spring 1981): 167–180.

———. "National Security Advice to U.S. Presidents: Some Lessons from Thirty Years." *World Politics* 24 (January 1977): 143–176.

———. "National Security Management: What Presidents Have Wrought." *Political Science Quarterly* 95 (Winter 1980–1981): 573–588.

———. *Presidents, Bureaucrats, and Foreign Policy.* Princeton, NJ: Princeton University Press, 1974.

———, Leslie H. Gleb, and Anthony Lake. *Our Own Worst Enemy: The Unmaking of American Foreign Policy.* New York: Simon & Schuster, 1984.

De Tocqueville, Alexis. *Democracy in America.* ed. and abridged by Richard D. Heffner. New York: New American Library, 1956.

Deutsch, Karl W. "External Influence on the Internal Behavior of States." In *Approaches to Comparative and International Politics,* R. Barry Farrell, ed. Evanston, IL: Northwestern University Press, 1966.

Devine, Donald J. *The Political Culture of the United States.* Boston: Little, Brown and Company, 1972.

Donovan, John C. *The Cold Warriors: A Policy-Making Elite.* Lexington, MA: D.C. Heath and Company, 1974.

Drew, Elizabeth. "A Reporter At Large: Brzezinski." *The New Yorker* (May 1, 1978): 90–130.

———. *On the Edge: The Clinton Presidency.* New York: Simon & Schuster, 1994.

Dye, Thomas R. *Who's Running America? The Bush Era.* Englewood Cliffs, NJ: Prentice-Hall, Inc., 1990.

———. *Who's Running America? The Clinton Years.* 6th ed. Englewood Cliffs, NJ: Prentice-Hall, Inc., 1995.

———. *Who's Running America? Institutional Leadership in the United States.* Englewood Cliffs, NJ: Prentice-Hall, Inc., 1976.

Easton, David. *The Political System.* New York: Alfred A. Knopf, Inc., 1953.

Eisenhower, Dwight D. "The Military-Industrial Complex." In *Power in Postwar America,* Richard Gillam, ed. Boston: Little, Brown and Company, 1971.

Emery, Michael. "An Endangered Species: The International Newshole." *Gannett Center Journal* 3 (Fall 1989): 151–164.

Esterline, John H., and Robert B. Black. *Inside Foreign Policy: The Department of State Political System and Its Subsystem.* Palo Alto, CA: Mayfield Publishing Company, 1975.

Etzold, Thomas H. "The Far East in American Strategy, 1948–1951." In *Aspects of Sino–American Relations Since 1784,* Thomas H. Etzold, ed. New York: New Viewpoints, 1978.

Executive Legislative Consultation on Foreign Policy: Strengthening Foreign Policy Information Sources for Congress. Washington, DC: Government Printing Office, February 1982.

Falk, Richard A. "What's Wrong with Henry Kissinger's Foreign Policy." *Alternatives* 1 (March 1975): 79–100.

Fenno, Richard F., Jr. *Congressmen in Committees.* Boston: Little, Brown and Company, 1973.

Fernandez, Damian J. "From Little Havana to Washington, D.C.: Cuban-Americans and U.S. Foreign Policy." In *Ethinic Groups and U.S. Foreign Policy,* Mohammed E. Ahrari, ed. New York: Greenwood Press, 1987.

Ferrell, Robert H. *American Diplomacy: A History.* New York: W. W. Norton & Company, Inc., 1975.

———. *American Diplomacy: The Twentieth Century.* New York: W. W. Norton & Company, 1988.

Findley, Paul. *Deliberate Deceptions: Facing the Facts about U.S.-Israeli Relationship.* New York: Lawrence Hill Books, 1995.

Fisher, Louis. *The President and Congress: Power and Policy.* New York: Free Press, 1972.

———. *Presidential War Power.* Lawrence: University Press of Kansas, 1995.

Fleisher, Richard. "Economic Benefit, Ideology, and Senate Voting on the B-1 Bomber." *American Politics Quarterly* 13 (April 1985): 200–211.

———, and Jon R. Bond. "Are There Two Presidencies? Yes, But Only for Republicans." *The Journal of Politics* 50 (August 1988): 747–767.

Fleming, D. F. *The Cold War and Its Origins, 1917–1960.* New York: Doubleday & Co., Inc., 1961.

Franck, Thomas M., and Edward Weisband. *Foreign Policy by Congress.* New York: Oxford University Press, 1979.

Free, Lloyd A., and Hadley Cantril, *The Political Beliefs of Americans: A Study of Public Opinion.* New York: Clarion Book, 1968.

Freedman, Lawrence. *The Evolution of Nuclear Strategy.* New York: St. Martin's Press, 1981.

Fulbright, J. William. *The Arrogance of Power.* New York: Vintage Books, 1966.

Furlong, William L. "Negotiations and Ratification of the Panama Canal Treaties." In *Congress, The Presidency, and American Foreign Policy,* John Spanier and Joseph Nogee, eds. New York: Pergamon Press, 1981.

Gaddis, John Lewis. "Containment: A Reassessment." *Foreign Affairs* 55 (July 1977): 873–887.

———. *The Soviet Union and the United States: An Interpretative History.* New York: John Wiley and Sons, Inc., 1978.

———. *Strategies of Containment.* New York: Oxford University Press, 1982.

———. *The United States and the End of the Cold War: Implications, Reconsiderations, and Provocations.* New York: Oxford University Press, 1992.

———. *The United States and the Origins of the Cold War 1941–1947.* New York and London: Colombia University Press, 1972.

———. "Was the Truman Doctrine A Real Turning Point?" *Foreign Affairs* 52 (January 1974): 386–402.

Garnham, David. "Foreign Service Elitism and U.S. Foreign Affairs." *Public Administration Review* 35 (January/February 1975): 44–51.

———. "State Department Rigidity: Testing a Psychological Hypotheses." *International Studies Quarterly* 18 (March 1974): 31–39.

Gelb, Leslie H. with Richard K. Betts. *The Irony of Vietnam: The System Worked.* Washington, DC: The Brookings Institution, 1979.

Gershman, Carl. *The Foreign Policy of American Labor.* The Washington Papers, 3, no. 29. Beverly Hills: Sage Publications, 1975.

Gibson, Martha Liebler. "Managing Conflict: The Role of the Legislative Veto in American Foreign Policy." *Polity* 26 (Spring 1994): 441–472.

———. *Weapons of Influence: The Legislative Veto, American Foreign Policy, and the Irony of Reform.* Boulder, CO: Westview Press, 1992.

Glennon, Michael. *Constitutional Diplomacy.* Princeton, NJ: Princeton University Press, 1990.

———. "The Good Friday Accords: Legislative Veto by Another Name?" *The American Journal of International Law* 83 (September 1989): 544–546.

Goldstein, Judith, and Robert O. Keohane, eds. *Ideas and Foreign Policy: Beliefs, Institutions, and Political Change.* Ithaca and London: Cornell University Press, 1993.

Goncharov, Sergei N., John W. Lewis, and Xue Litai. *Uncertain Partners: Stalin, Mao, and the Korean War.* Stanford, CA: Stanford University Press, 1993.

Goodman, Allan E. "Testimony: Fact-Checking at the CIA." *Foreign Policy* 102 (Spring 1996): 180–182.

Graber, Doris A. *Mass Media and American Politics.* 5th ed. Washington, DC: CQ Press, 1997.

Graham, Thomas. "Public Opinion and U.S. Foreign Policy Decision Making." In *The New Politics of American Foreign Policy,* David A. Deese, ed. New York: St. Martin's Press, 1994.

Grieco, Joseph M. "Anarchy and the Limits of Cooperation: A Realist Critique of the Newest Liberal Institutionalism." In *Controversies in International Relations Theory: Realism and the Neoliberalism Challenge.* Charles W. Kegley, Jr., ed. New York: St. Martin's Press, 1995.

Grosser, Alfred. *French Foreign Policy Under DeGaulle.* Boston: Little, Brown and Company, 1965.

Gulick, Edward V. *Europe's Classical Balance of Power.* Ithaca, NY: Cornell University Press, 1955.

Haass, Richard. "Paradigm Lost." *Foreign Affairs* 74 (January/February 1995): 43–58.

Hackett, Clifford. "Ethnic Politics in Congress: The Turkish Embargo Experience." *In Ethnicity and U.S. Foreign Policy,* Abdul Aziz Said, ed. New York: Praeger, 1981.

Haig, Alexander. *Opening Statement at Confirmation Hearings.* Washington, DC: Bureau of Public Affairs, Department of State, January 9, 1981.

———. *A Strategic Approach to American Foreign Policy.* Washington, DC: Bureau of Public Affairs, Department of State, August 11, 1981.

Hallin, Daniel C. *We Keep America on Top of the World: Television Journalism and the Public Sphere.* New York: Routledge, 1994.

Halperin, Morton H., with the assistance of Priscilla Clapp and Arnold Kanter. *Bureaucratic Politics and Foreign Policy.* Washington, DC: The Brookings Institution, 1974.

Hamilton, Lee H., and Michael H. Van Dusen. "Making the Separation of Powers Work." *Foreign Affairs* 57 (Fall 1978): 17–39.

Hansen, Roger D., Albert Fishlow, Robert Paarlberg, and John P. Lewis. *U.S. Foreign Policy and the Third World Agenda 1982.* New York: Praeger, 1982.

Hart, Albert Bushnell. *The Monroe Doctrine: An Interpretation.* Boston: Little, Brown and Company, 1916.

Hartley, Thomas, and Bruce Russett. "Public Opinion and the Common Defense: Who Governs Military Spending in the United States?" *American Political Science Review* 86 (December 1992): 905–915.

Henkin, Louis. "Foreign Affairs and the Constitution." *Foreign Affairs* 66 (Winter 1987/1988): 284–310.

———. *Foreign Affairs and the Constitution.* Mineola, NY: The Foundation Press, Inc. 1972.

Herring, George C. *America's Longest War: The United States and Vietnam 1950–1975.* 2nd ed. New York: Alfred A. Knopf, 1986.

———. *LBJ and Vietnam: A Different Kind of War.* Austin: University of Texas Press, 1994.

Hertsgaard, Mark. *On Bended Knee: The Press and the Reagan Presidency.* New York: Farrar, Strause & Giroux. 1988.

Hess, Stephen. *International News & Foreign Correspondents.* Washington, DC: The Brookings Institution, 1996.

Hicks, Sallie M., and Theodore A. Couloumbis. "The 'Greek Lobby': Illusion or Reality?" in *Ethnicity and U.S. Foreign Policy,* Abdul Aziz Said, ed. New York: Praeger, 1981.

Higgott, Richard, and Diane Stone. "The Limits of Influence: Foreign Policy Think Tanks in Britain and the USA." *Review of International Studies* 20 (January 1994): 15–34.

Hilsman, Roger. *To Move A Nation.* Garden City, NY: Doubleday Publishing, 1964.

———. "Does the CIA Still Have A Role?" *Foreign Affairs* 74 (September/October 1995): 104–116.

Hinckley, Barbara. *Less Than Meets the Eye.* Chicago and London: The University of Chicago Press, 1994.

———. *Stability and Change in Congress.* 3rd ed. New York: Harper and Row, 1983.

Hoffmann, Stanley. "Carter's Soviet Problem." *The New Republic* 79 (July 29, 1978): 20–23.

———. *Gulliver's Troubles, or the Setting of American Foreign Policy.* New York: McGraw-Hill, 1968.

———. *Primacy or World Order.* New York: McGraw-Hill, 1978.

———. "Requiem." *Foreign Policy* 42 (Spring 1981): 3–26.

———. "A View From At Home: The Perils of Incoherence." In *America and the World 1978,* William P. Bundy, ed. New York: Pergamon Press, 1979.

Holbrooke, Richard. "A Sense of Drift, A Time for Calm." In *At Issue: Politics in the Global Arena,* Steven C. Spiegel, ed. New York: St. Martin's Press, 1977.

Holloway, David. "Gorbachev's New Thinking." In *America and the World 1988/89,* William P. Bundy, ed. New York: Council on Foreign Relations, 1989.

Holsti, Ole R. "The Belief System and National Images: A Case Study." *The Journal of Conflict Resolution* 6 (September 1962): 244–252.

———. "Public Opinion and Foreign Policy: Challenges to the Almond-Lippmann Consensus." *International Studies Quarterly* 36 (December 1992): 439–466.

———. "The Three-Headed Eagle: The United States and System Change." *International Studies Quarterly* 23 (September 1979): 339–359.

———, and James N. Rosenau. *American Leadership in World Affairs.* Boston: Allen & Unwin, 1984.

———. "America's Foreign Policy Agenda: The Post-Vietnam Beliefs of American Leaders." In *Challenges to America: United States Foreign Policy in the 1980s,* Charles W. Kegley, Jr., and Patrick J. McGowan, eds. Beverly Hills: Sage Publications, 1979.

———. "Does Where You Stand Depend on When You Were Born? The Impact of Generation on Post-Vietnam Foreign Policy Beliefs." *Public Opinion Quarterly* 44 (Spring 1980): 1–22.

———. "A Leadership Divided: The Foreign Policy Beliefs of American Leaders, 1976–1980." In *Perspectives on American Foreign Policy,* Charles W. Kegley, Jr., and Eugene R. Wittkopf, eds. New York: St. Martin's Press, 1983.

———. "The Structure of Foreign Policy Attitudes Among Leaders." *Journal of Politics* 52 (February 1990): 94–125.

———. "The Structure of Foreign Policy Beliefs Among American Opinion Leaders—After the Cold War." *Millennium* 22 (Summer 1993): 235–278.

———. "Vietnam, Consensus, and the Belief Systems of American Leaders." *World Politics* 32 (October 1979): 1–56.

———, Richard A. Brody, and Robert C. North. "The Management of International Crisis: Affect and Action in American-Soviet Relations." In *Theory and Research on the Cause of War,* Dean G. Pruitt and Richard C. Snyder, eds. Englewood Cliffs, NJ: Prentice-Hall, Inc., 1969.

Holt, Pat. *Secret Intelligence and Public Policy.* Washington, DC: CQ Press, 1995.

Hoopes, Townsend. *The Limits of Intervention.* New York: David McKay, 1968.

Hopkins, Raymond F., and Donald J. Puchala. *Global Food Interdependence: Challenge to American Foreign Policy.* New York: Columbia University Press, 1980.

Hormat, Robert D. "The World Economy Under Stress." In *America and the World 1985,* William G. Hyland, ed. New York: Pergamon Press, 1986.

Hsiao, Gene T. ed. *Sino-American Detente and Its Policy Implications.* New York: Praeger Publishers, Inc., 1974.

Hughes, Barry B. *The Domestic Context of American Foreign Policy.* San Francisco: Freeman, 1978.

Hughes, Thomas L. "The Crack-Up: The Price of Collective Irresponsibility." *Foreign Policy* 40 (Fall 1980): 33–60.

———. "The Flight From Foreign Policy." *Foreign Policy* 10 (Spring 1973): 141–156.

Hunt, Michael H. *Ideology and U.S. Foreign Policy.* New Haven, CT: Yale University Press, 1987.

Hunter, Robert E. *Presidential Control of Foreign Policy: Management or Mishap?* The Washington Papers/91. New York: Praeger, 1982.

Hurwitz, Jon, and Mark Peffley. "How Are Foreign Policy Attitudes Structured? A Hierarchical Model." *American Political Science Review* 81 (December 1987): 1099–1120.

Hyland, William G. "U.S.-Soviet Relations: The Long Road Back." In *America and the World 1981,* William P. Bundy, ed. New York: Pergamon Press, 1982.

Isaacson, Walter. *Kissinger: A Biography.* New York: Simon & Schuster, 1992.

Janis, Irving. *Victims of Groupthink.* Boston: Houghton Mifflin Company, 1972.

Jensen, Kenneth M. ed. *Origins of the Cold War: The Novikov, Kennan, and Roberts' 'Long Telegrams' of 1946.* Washington, DC: United States Institute of Peace, 1991.

Jensen, Lloyd. *Explaining Foreign Policy.* Englewood Cliffs, NJ: Prentice-Hall, Inc., 1982.

Jentleson, Bruce W. "American Diplomacy: Around the World and Along Pennsylvania Avenue." In *A Question of Balance,* Thomas E. Mann, ed. Washington, DC: The Brookings Institution, 1990.

———. "The Pretty Prudent Public: Post Post-Vietnam American Opinion on the Use of Military Force." *International Studies Quarterly* 36 (March 1992): 49–74.

———. *With Friends Like These.* New York and London: W. W. Norton & Company, 1994.

Jervis, Robert. "The Impact of the Korean War on the Cold War." *The Journal of Conflict Resolution* 24 (December 1980): 563–592.

Joffe, Josef. "The Foreign Policy of the German Federal Republic." In *Foreign Policy in World Politics.* 5th ed., Roy C. Macridis, ed. Englewood Cliffs, NJ: Prentice-Hall, Inc., 1976.

Johnson, Loch, and James M. McCormick. "Foreign Policy by Executive Fiat." *Foreign Policy* 28 (Fall 1977): 117–138.

———. "The Making of International Agreements: A Reappraisal of Congressional Involvement." *The Journal of Politics* 40 (May 1978): 468–478.

Jones, Christopher M. "American Prewar Technology Sales to Iraq: A Bureaucratic Politics Explanation." In *The Domestic Sources of American Foreign Policy: Insights and Evidence.* 2nd ed., Eugene R. Wittkopf, ed. New York: St. Martin's Press, 1994.

Jones, Joseph M. *The Fifteen Weeks.* Chicago: Harcourt, Brace and World, Inc., 1955.

Jordan, Amos A., William J. Taylor, Jr., and Associates. *American National Security: Policy and Process.* Baltimore: The Johns Hopkins University Press, 1981.

———, and Lawrence J. Korb. *American National Security: Policy and Process.* 4th ed. Baltimore: The Johns Hopkins University Press, 1993.

Kaiser, Fred. "Congressional Control of Executive Actions in the Aftermath of the *Chadha* Decision." *Administrative Law Review* 36 (Summer 1984): 239–274.

———. "Oversight of Foreign Policy: The U.S. House Committee on International Relations." *Legislative Studies Quarterly* 2 (August 1977): 233–254.

———. "Structural and Policy Change: The House Committee on International Relations." *Policy Studies Journal* 5 (Summer 1977): 443–451.

Kaiser, Karl. "Germany's Unification." In *America and the World 1990/1991,* William P. Bundy, ed. New York: Council on Foreign Relations, Inc., 1991.

Kahler, Miles. "The United States and Western Europe: The Diplomatic Consequences of Mr. Reagan." In *Eagle Defiant: United States Foreign Policy in the 1980s,* Kenneth A. Oye, Robert J. Lieber, and Donald Rothchild, eds. Boston: Little, Brown and Company, 1983.

Karnow, Stanley. *Vietnam: A History.* New York: The Viking Press, 1983.

Katzmann, Robert A. "War Powers: Toward a New Accommodation," In *A Question of Balance,* Thomas E. Mann, ed. Washington, DC: The Brookings Institution, 1990.

Kaufman, Natalie Hevener. *Human Rights Treaties and the Senate.* Chapel Hill and London: The University of North Carolina Press, 1990.

Kavass, Ivor I., and Mark A. Michael. *United States Treaties and Other International Agreements Cumulative Index 1776–1949.* Buffalo, NY: William S. Hein and Company, Inc., 1975.

Kegley, Charles W. "The Bush Administration and the Future of American Foreign Policy: Pragmatism or Procrastination?" *Presidential Studies Quarterly* 19 (Fall 1989): 717–731.

———, ed. *Controversies in International Relations Theory.* New York: St. Martin's Press, 1995.

———, and Eugene R. Wittkopf. *American Foreign Policy: Pattern and Process.* 5th ed. New York: St. Martin's Press, 1991.

———. "Beyond Consensus: The Domestic Context of American Foreign Policy." *International Journal* 38 (Winter 1982–1983): 77–106.

Kellerman, Barbara, and Ryan J. Barilleaux. *The President as World Leader.* New York: St. Martin's Press, 1991.

Kennan, George. *American Diplomacy 1900–1950.* New York: Mentor Books, 1951.

———. "Containment Then and Now." *Foreign Affairs* 65 (Spring 1987): 885–890.

———. "Is Detente Worth Saving?" *Saturday Review* (March 6, 1976): 12–17.

———. *Memoirs 1925–1950.* Boston: Little, Brown and Company, Inc., 1967.

———. "The Sources of Soviet Conduct." *Foreign Affairs* 65 (Spring 1987): 852–868.

Kennedy, Robert F. *Thirteen Days.* New York: Signet Books, 1969.

Kihl, Young W. *Politics and Policies in Divided Korea: Regimes in Contest.* Boulder, CO: Westview Press, 1984.

Kirkpatrick, Jeane J. "Dictatorships and Double Standards." *Commentary* 68 (November 1979): 34–45.

Kissinger, Henry A. *American Foreign Policy.* 3rd ed. New York: W. W. Norton & Company, Inc., 1977.

———. *Diplomacy.* New York: Simon & Schuster, 1994.

———. "Domestic Structure and Foreign Policy." In *International Politics and Foreign Policy.* Rev. ed., James N. Rosenau, ed. New York: Free Press, 1969.

———. *A World Restored: Metternich, Castlereagh and Problems of Peace 1812–1822.* Boston: Houghton Mifflin Company, 1957.

Knight, Andrew. "Ronald Reagan's Watershed Year?" In *America and the World 1982,* William P. Bundy, ed. New York: Pergamon Press, 1983.

Koh, Harold Hongju. *The National Security Constitution.* New Haven, CT: Yale University Press, 1992.

Kohut, Andrew and Robert C. Toth. "Arms and the People." *Foreign Affairs* 73 (November/December 1994): 47–61.

Kolko, Gabriel. *The Roots of American Foreign Policy.* Boston: Beacon Press, 1969.

Kolodziej, Edward A. *French International Policy Under DeGaulle and Pompidou.* Ithaca, NY: Cornell University Press, 1974.

———. "Revolt and Revisionism in the Gaullist Global Vision: An Analysis of French Strategic Policy." *The Journal of Politics* 33 (May 1971): 448–477.

Kondracke, Morton. "The Greek Lobby." *The New Republic* (April 29, 1978): 14–16.

Korb, Lawrence J. *The Fall and Rise of the Pentagon: American Defense Policies in the 1970s.* Westport, CT: Greenwood Press, 1979.

———. "The Joint Chiefs of Staff: Access and Impact in Foreign Policy." *Policy Studies Journal* 3 (Winter 1974): 170–173.

———. *The Joint Chiefs of Staff: The First Twenty*–Five Years. Bloomington: Indiana University Press, 1976.

Korbel, Josef. *Detente in Europe: Real or Imaginary?* Princeton, NJ: Princeton University Press, 1972.

Korn, Jessica. *The Power of Separation.* Princeton, NJ: Princeton University Press, 1996.

Kovach, Bill. "Do the New Media Make Foreign Policy?" *Foreign Policy* 102 (Spring 1996): 169–179.

Krasner, Stephen D. "The Tokyo Round: Particularistic Interests and Prospects for Stability in the Global Trading System." *International Studies Quarterly* 23 (December 1979): 491–531.

Kristol, William, and Robert Kagan. "Toward a Neo–Reaganite Foreign Policy." *Foreign Affairs* 75 (July/August 1996): 18–32.

Kull, Steven. "What the Public Knows That Washington Doesn't," *Foreign Policy* 101 (Winter 1995–96): 102–115.

Kurth, James R. "The Military-Industrial Complex Revisited." In Joseph Kruzel, ed., *1989–1990 American Defense Annual.* Lexington, MA: Lexington Books, 1989.

Ladd, Everett C., Jr. "Traditional Values Regnant." *Public Opinion* 1 (March/April 1978): 45–49.

LaFeber, Walter. *America, Russia, and the Cold War 1945–1975.* New York: John Wiley & Sons, Inc., 1976.

———. *The American Age: United States Foreign Policy at Home and Abroad since 1750.* New York: W. W. Norton & Company, 1989.

———. *Inevitable Revolutions: The United States in Central America.* New York: W. W. Norton & Company, 1984.

Lake, David A. "Powerful Pacifists: Democratic States and War." *American Political Science Review* 86 (March 1992): 24–37.

Lane, Charles. "Perry's Parry." *The New Republic* 26 (June 27, 1994): 21–25.

Lasswell, Harold D. *Politics: Who Gets What, When, and How.* New York: Whittlesey, 1936.

Lawson, Ruth C. *International Regional Organizations: Constitutional Foundations.* New York: Praeger, 1962.

Leffler, Melvyn P., and David S. Painter, eds. *Origins of the Cold War: An International History.* London and New York: Routledge, 1994.

Legg, Keith R. "Congress as Trojan Horse? The Turkish Embargo Problem, 1974–1978." In *Congress, the Presidency, and American Foreign Policy,* John Spanier and Joseph Nogee, eds. New York: Pergamon Press, 1981.

Legum, Colin. "The African Crisis." In *America and the World 1978,* William P. Bundy, ed. New York: Pergamon Press, 1979.

LeLoup, Lance T., and Steven A. Shull. "Congress Versus the Executive: The 'Two Presidencies' Reconsidered." *Social Science Quarterly* 59 (March 1979): 704–719.

Lerche, Charles O., Jr., and Abdul A. Said. *Concepts of International Politics.* 3rd ed. Englewood Cliffs, NJ: Prentice-Hall, Inc., 1979.

Lerner, Max. "America Agonistes." *Foreign Affairs* 52 (January 1974): 287–300.

Levgold, Robert. "The Revolution in Soviet Foreign Policy." In *America and the World 1988/89,* William P. Bundy, ed. New York: Council on Foreign Relations, 1989.

Lichter, S. Robert, Stanley Rothman, and Linda S. Lichter, *The Media Elite.* Bethesda, MD: Adler & Adler, 1986.

Lieberson, Stanley. "An Empirical Study of Military-Industrial Linkages." *American Journal of Sociology* 76 (January 1971): 562–584.

Lieberthal, Kenneth. "A New China Strategy." *Foreign Affairs* 74 (November/December 1995): 35–49.

Lindsay, James M. "Congress and Defense Policy: 1961 to 1986." *Armed Forces and Society* 13 (Spring 1987): 371–401.

———. "Congress and Foreign Policy: Avenues of Influences." In *The Domestic Sources of American Foreign Policy: Insights and Evidence.* 2nd ed., Eugene R. Wittkopf, ed. New York: St. Martin's Press, 1994.

———. *Congress and the Politics of U.S. Foreign Policy.* Baltimore and London: The Johns Hopkins University, 1994.

———. "Parochialism, Policy, and Constituency Constraints: Congressional Voting on Strategic Weapons Systems." *American Journal of Political Science* 34 (November 1990): 936–960.

———, and Wayne M. Steger. "The 'Two Presidencies' in Future Research: Moving Beyond Roll-Call Analysis." *Congress & The Presidency* 20 (Autumn 1993): 103–117.

Lindsay, John V. "For a New Policy Balance." *Foreign Affairs* 50 (October 1971): 1–14.

Lipset, Seymour Martin. *The First New Nation.* Garden City, NY: Anchor Books, 1967.

Locke, John. *The Second Treatise of Government.* Oxford: Basil Blackwell 1966.

Lockerbie, Brad, and Stephen A. Borrelli. "Question Wording and Public Support for Contra Aid, 1983–1986." *Public Opinion Quarterly* 54 (Summer 1990): 195–208.

Lomperis, Timothy J. *The War Everyone Lost—and Won.* Washington, DC: CQ Press, 1984.

Lynn, Laurence E., Jr., and Richard I. Smith. "Can the Secretary of Defense Make a Difference?" *International Security* 7 (Summer 1982): 45–69.

Maggiotto, Michael, and Eugene R. Wittkopf. "American Public Attitudes Toward Foreign Policy." *International Studies Quarterly* 25 (December 1981): 601–632.

Maier, Charles S., ed. *The Origins of the Cold War and Contemporary Europe.* New York: New Viewpoints, 1978.

Majeski, Stephen J. "Defense Spending, Fiscal Policy, and Economic Performance." In *The Political Economy of Military Spending in the United States,* Alex Mintz, ed. London: Routledge, 1992.

Mandelbaum, Michael. "Foreign Policy as Social Work." *Foreign Affairs* 75 (January/February 1996): 16–32.

———. *The Nuclear Question: The United States and Nuclear Weapons 1946–1976.* Cambridge: Cambridge University Press, 1979.

Mansfield, Edward, and Jack Snyder. "Democratization and War." *Foreign Affairs* 74 (May/June 1995): 79–97.

Maoz, Zeev, and Bruce Russett. "Normative and Structural Causes of Democratic Peace, 1946–1986." *American Political Science Review* 87 (September 1993): 624–638.

Marantz, Paul. "Prelude to Detente: Doctrinal Change Under Khrushchev." *International Studies Quarterly* 19 (December 1975): 501–528.

Marchetti, Victor, and John D. Marks. *The CIA and the Cult of Intelligence.* New York: Dell, 1974.

Mark, Eduard. "The Questions of Containment: A Reply to John Lewis Gaddis." *Foreign Affairs* 56 (January 1978): 430–441.

Markus, Gregory B. "Political Attitudes During an Election Year: A Report on the 1980 NES Panel Study." *American Political Science Review* 76 (September 1982): 538–560.

Mathias, Charles McC., Jr. "Ethnic Groups and Foreign Policy." *Foreign Affairs* 59 (Summer 1981): 975–998.

May, Ernest R. *"Lessons" of the Past: The Use and Misuse of History in American Foreign Policy.* New York: Oxford University Press, 1973.

Mayne, Richard. *The Recovery of Europe 1945–1973.* Garden City. NY: Anchor, 1973.

Maynes, Charles W. "America Without the Cold War," *Foreign Policy* 78 (Spring 1990): 3–25.

———. "Who Pays for Foreign Policy?" *Foreign Policy* 15 (Summer 1974): 152–168.

McCain, John. "Imagery or Purpose? The Choice in November." *Foreign Policy* 103 (Summer 1996): 20–34.

McClosky, Herbert, Paul J. Hoffmann, and Rosemary O'Hara. "Issue Conflict and Consensus Among Party Leaders and Followers. *American Political Science Review* 14 (June 1960): 408–427.

McCormick, James M. "Assessing Clinton's Foreign Policy at Midterm." *Current History* 94 (November 1995): 370–374.

———. "The Changing Role of the House Foreign Affairs Committee in the 1970s and 1980s." *Congress & The Presidency* 12 (Spring 1985): 1–20.

———. "Congressional Voting on the Nuclear Freeze Resolutions," *American Politics Quarterly* 13 (January 1985): 122–136.

———. "Decision Making in the Foreign Affairs and Foreign Relations Committees." In *Congress Resurgent: Foreign and Defense Policy on Capitol Hill,* Randal B. Ripley and James M. Lindsay, eds. Ann Arbor: The University of Michigan Press, 1993.

———. "The NIEO and the Distribution of American Assistance." *The Western Political Quarterly* 37 (March 1984): 100–119.

———, ed. *A Reader in American Foreign Policy.* Itasca, IL: F. E. Peacock Publishers, Inc., 1986.

———, and Michael Black. "Ideology and Voting on the Panama Canal Treaties." *Legislative Studies Quarterly* 8 (February 1983): 45–63.

———, and Neil Mitchell. "Human Rights and Foreign Assistance: An Update." *Social Science Quarterly* 70 (December 1989): 969–979.

———, and Steven S. Smith. "The Iran Arms Sale and the Intelligence Oversight Act of 1980." *PS* 20 (Winter 1987): 29–37.

———, and Eugene R. Wittkopf. "At the Water's Edge: The Effects of Party, Ideology, and Issues on Congressional Foreign Policy Voting, 1947–1988." *American Politics Quarterly* 20 (January 1992): 26–53.

———. "Bipartisanship, Partisanship, and Ideology in Congressional-Executive Foreign Policy Relations, 1947–1988." *The Journal of Politics* 52 (November 1990): 1077–1100.

———, Eugene R. Wittkopf, and David M. Danna. "Politics and Bipartisanship at the Water's Edge: A Note on Bush and Clinton." *Polity* 30 (Fall 1997, forthcoming).

McElroy, Robert W. *Morality and American Foreign Policy: The Role of Ethics in International Affairs.* Princeton, NJ: Princeton University Press, 1992.

Mee, Charles L., Jr. *Meeting at Potsdam.* New York: M. Evan & Co., Inc., 1975.

Meernik, James. "Presidential Support in Congress: Conflict and Consensus on Foreign and Defense Policy." *Journal of Politics* 55 (August 1993): 569–587.

Melanson, Richard A. *American Foreign Policy Since the Vietnam War: The Search for Consensus from Nixon to Clinton.* 2nd ed. Armonk, NY: M. E. Sharpe, 1996.

Merrill, John. *Korea: The Peninsular Origins of the War.* Newark: University of Delaware, 1989.

The Middle East: U.S. Policy, Israel, Oil and the Arabs. 3rd ed. Washington, DC: Congressional Quarterly, 1977.

Miller, Hunter, ed. *Treaties and Other International Acts of the United States of America.* Vol. 2. Washington, DC: U.S. Government Printing Office, 1931.

Miller, Robert Hopkins. *Inside an Embassy: The Political Role of Diplomats Abroad.* Washington, DC: Congressional Quarterly, Inc., 1992.

Miller, Warren E., and Donald E. Stokes. "Constituency Influence in Congress." *American Political Science Review* 57 (March 1963).

Mills, C. Wright. *The Power Elite.* New York: Oxford University Press, 1956.

———. "The Structure of Power in American Society." In *Power in Postwar America,* Richard Gillam, ed. Boston: Little, Brown and Company, 1971.

Molineu, Harold. "Human Rights: Administrative Impact of a Symbolic Policy. "In *The Analysis of Policy Impact,* John G. Grumm and Stephen L. Wasby, eds. Lexington, MA: Lexington Books, D. C. Heath and Company, 1981.

Moore, David W. "The Public Is Uncertain." *Foreign Policy* 35 (Summer 1979): 68–73.

Morgenthau, Hans J. "The Mainsprings of American Foreign Policy." In *A Reader in American Foreign Policy,* James M. McCormick, ed. Itasca, IL: F. E. Peacock, Inc., 1986.

———. *Politics Among Nations: The Struggle for Power and Peace.* New York: Alfred A. Knopf, 1973.

Moyer, Wayne, "House Voting on Defense: An Ideological Explanation." In *Military Force and American Society,* Bruce M. Russett and Alfred Stepan, eds. New York: Harper and Row, 1973.

———, and Timothy E. Josling. *Agricultural Policy Reform: Politics and Process in the EC and the USA.* New York: Harvester Wheatsheaf, 1990.

Mueller, John E. *War, Presidents and Public Opinion.* New York: John Wiley and Sons, Inc., 1973.

Nash, Henry T. *American Foreign Policy: Changing Perspectives on National Security.* Homewood, IL: The Dorsey Press, 1978.

Nelson, Michael. ed. *Congressional Quarterly's Guide to the Presidency.* Washington, DC: Congressional Quarterly, Inc., 1989.

Neuman, Johanna. *Lights, Camera, War.* New York: St. Martin's Press, 1996.

Newhouse, John. "Profiles (James Baker)." *The New Yorker* (May 7, 1990): 50–82.

Newsom, David C. *The Public Dimension of Foreign Policy.* Bloomington and Indianapolis: Indiana University Press, 1996.

Nivola, Pietro S. "Trade Policy: Refereeing the Playing Field. In *A Question of Balance,* Thomas E. Mann, ed. Washington, DC: The Brookings Institution, 1990.

Nixon, Richard M. "Asia After Viet Nam." *Foreign Affairs* 46 (October 1967): 111–125.

———. *U.S. Policy for the 1970s: A New Strategy for Peace: A Report to the Congress.* Washington, DC: Government Printing Office, February 12, 1970.

Nordlinger, Eric A. *Isolationism Reconfigured: American Foreign Policy for a New Century.* Princeton, NJ: Princeton University Press, 1995.

North, Robert C. *The Foreign Relations of China.* 2nd ed. Encino and Belmont, CA: Dickenson Publishing Company, Inc., 1974.

Nye, Joseph S., Jr. "The Case for Deep Engagement." *Foreign Affairs* 74 (July/August 1995): 90–102.

———. *Nuclear Ethics.* New York: The Free Press, 1986.

———. "Peering into the Future." *Foreign Affairs* 73 (July/August 1994): 82–93.

Nye, Russel B. *This Almost Chosen People.* East Lansing: Michigan State University Press, 1966.

Oldfield, Duane M., and Aaron Wildavsky. "Reconsidering the Two Presidencies." *Society* 26 (July/August 1989): 54–59.

Ogley, Roderick, ed. *The Theory and Practice of Neutrality in the Twentieth Century.* New York: Barnes & Noble, Inc., 1970.

O'Halloran, Sharyn. "Congress and Foreign Trade Policy." In *Congress Resurgent: Foreign and Defense Policy on Capitol Hill,* Randall B. Ripley and James M. Lindsay, eds. Ann Arbor: The University of Michigan Press, 1993.

O'Heffernan, Patrick. "A Mutual Exploitation Model of Media Influence in U.S. Foreign Policy." In *Taken by Storm: The Media, Public Opinion, and U.S. Foreign Policy in the*

Gulf War, W. Lance Bennett and David L. Paletz, eds. Chicago and London: The University of Chicago Press, 1994.

Oneal, James R., Brad Lian, and James H. Joyner. "Are the American People 'Pretty Prudent'? Public Responses to U.S. Uses of Force, 1950–1988." *International Studies Quarterly* 40 (June 1996): 261–280.

Origins and Development of Congress. Washington, DC: Congressional Quarterly, Inc., 1976.

Organski, A. F. K. *World Politics.* New York: Alfred A. Knopf, Inc., 1968.

Ornstein, Norman J., and Shirley Elder. *Interest Groups, Lobbying and Policymaking.* Washington, DC: Congressional Quarterly Press, 1978.

———, and David W. Rohde. "Shifting Forces, Changing Rules, and Political Outcomes: The Impact of Congressional Change on Four House Committees." In *New Perspectives on the House of Representatives,* Robert L. Peabody and Nelson W. Polsby, eds. Chicago: Rand McNally, 1977.

———, and Mark Schmitt. "Dateline Campaign '92: Post–Cold War Politics." *Foreign Policy* 79 (Summer 1990): 169–186.

Osgood, Robert E. *Ideals and Self-Interest in America's Foreign Relations.* Chicago: The University of Chicago Press, 1953.

———. "The Revitalization of Containment." In *America and the World* 1981, William Bundy, ed. New York: Pergamon Books, 1982.

Page, Benjamin I., and Robert Y. Shapiro. "Effects of Public Opinion on Policy." *American Political Science Review* 77 (March 1983): 175–190.

———. *The Rational Public: Fifty Years of Trends in Americans' Policy Preferences.* Chicago: The University of Chicago Press, 1992.

Park, Richard L. "India's Foreign Policy." In *Foreign Policy in World Politics.* 5th ed., Roy C. Macridis, ed. Englewood Cliffs, NJ: Prentice-Hall, Inc., 1976.

Pastor, Robert. *Congress and the Politics of U.S. Foreign Economic Policy 1929–1976.* Berkeley: University of California Press, 1980.

Payne, James L. *The American Threat.* College Station, TX: Lytton Publishing Company, 1981.

Pearce, David C. *Wary Partners: Diplomats and the Media.* Washington, DC: Congressional Quarterly, Inc., 1995.

The Pentagon Papers (*New York Times* edition). New York: Bantam Books, Inc., 1971.

Percy, Charles H. "The Partisan Gap." *Foreign Policy* 45 (Winter 1981–82): 3–15.

Perkins, Dexter. *The American Approach to Foreign Policy.* Cambridge, MA: Harvard University Press, 1962.

———. *The Evolution of American Foreign Policy.* 2nd ed. New York: Oxford University Press, 1966.

———. *Hands-Off: A History of the Monroe Doctrine.* Boston: Little, Brown and Company, 1941.

Pierre, Andrew J. *The Global Politics of Arms Sales.* Princeton, NJ: Princeton University Press, 1982.

Pilisuk, Marc, with the assistance of Mehrene Larudee, *International Conflict and Social Policy.* Englewood Cliffs, NJ: Prentice-Hall, Inc., 1972.

Pomper, Gerald. *Elections in America: Control and Influence in Democratic Politics.* New York: Dodd, Mead & Company, 1968.

———, with Susan S. Lederman. *Election in America: Control and Influence in Democratic Politics.* 2nd ed. New York: Longman, 1980.

Powlick, Philip J. "The Attitudinal Bases for Responsiveness to Public Opinion Among American Foreign Policy Officials." *Journal of Conflict Resolution* 35 (December 1991): 611–641.

———. "The Sources of Public Opinion for American Foreign Policy Officials." *International Studies Quarterly* 39 (December 1995): 427–451.

Pringle, Robert. "Creeping Irrelevance at Foggy Bottom." *Foreign Policy* 29 (Winter 1977–78): 128–139.

Proxmire, William. "The Community of Interests in Our Defense Contract Spending." In *Power in Postwar America,* Richard Gillam, ed. Boston: Little, Brown and Company, 1971.

Quester, George. *American Foreign Policy: The Lost Consensus.* New York: Praeger, 1982.

Ransom, Harry Howe. *The Intelligence Establishment.* Cambridge, MA: Harvard University Press, 1970.

Ravenal, Earl C. "The Case for Adjustment," *Foreign Policy* 81 (Winter 1990–1991):3–19.

———, et al. "Who Pays for Foreign Policy? A Debate on Consensus." *Foreign Policy* 18 (Spring, 1975): 80–122.

Ray, James Lee. *Global Politics.* 2nd ed. Boston: Houghton Mifflin Company, 1983.

Report of the Congressional Committees Investigating the Iran-Contra Affair. Washington, DC: U.S. Government Printing Office, November 1987.

Report to the President by the Commission on CIA Activities Within the United States. Washington, DC: U.S. Government Printing Office, June 1975.

Report of the President's Special Review Board (Tower Commission Report). Washington, DC: U.S. Government Printing Office, February 26, 1987.

Richelson, Jeffrey T. *The U.S. Intelligence Community.* Boulder, CO: Westview Press, 1995.

Rielly, John E. "The American Mood: A Foreign Policy of Self Interest." *Foreign Policy* 34 (Spring 1979): 74–86.

———. "American Opinion: Continuity, Not Reaganism." *Foreign Policy* 50 (Spring 1983): 86–104.

———. "America's State of Mind." *Foreign Policy* 66 (Spring 1987): 39–56.

———. "The Public Mood at Mid-Decade." *Foreign Policy* 96 (Spring 1995): 76–93.

———. "Public Opinion: The Pulse of the '90s." *Foreign Policy* 82 (Spring 1991): 79–96.

———, ed. *American Public Opinion and U.S. Foreign Policy 1975.* Chicago: Chicago Council on Foreign Relations, 1975.

———, ed. *American Public Opinion and U.S. Foreign Policy 1979.* Chicago: Chicago Council on Foreign Relations, 1979.

———, ed. *American Public Opinion and U.S. Foreign Policy 1983.* Chicago: Chicago Council on Foreign Relations, 1983.

———, ed. *American Public Opinion and U.S. Foreign Policy 1987.* Chicago: Chicago Council on Foreign Relations, 1987.

———, ed. *American Public Opinion and U.S. Foreign Policy 1991.* Chicago: Chicago Council on Foreign Relations, 1991.

———, ed. *American Public Opinion and U.S. Foreign Policy 1995.* Chicago: Chicago Council on Foreign Relations, 1995.

Ripley, Randall B. *Congress: Process and Policy.* 2nd ed. New York: W. W. Norton & Company, 1978.

———, and James M. Lindsay, eds. *Congress Resurgent: Foreign and Defense Policy on Capitol Hill.* Ann Arbor: The University of Michigan Press, 1993.

Rizopoulous, Nicholas, ed. *Sea-Changes: American Foreign Policy in a World Transformed.* New York: Council on Foreign Relations Press, 1990.

Robinson, James A. *Congress and Foreign Policy-Making.* Rev. ed. Homewood, IL: The Dorsey Press, 1967.

Rockman, Bert A. "America's Departments of State: Irregular and Regular Syndromes of Policymaking." *American Political Science Review* 75 (December 1981): 911–927.

Rokeach, Milton. *Beliefs, Attitudes and Values.* San Francisco: Jossey-Bass, Inc., 1953.

Rosenberg, Milton J., Sidney Verba, and Philip E. Converse. *Vietnam and the Silent Majority.* New York: Harper and Row, 1970.

Rosenfeld, Stephen S. "Dateline Washington: Anti-Semitism and U.S. Foreign Policy." *Foreign Policy* 47 (Summer 1982): 172–183.

Rosner, Jeremy D. "The Know-Nothings Know Something." *Foreign Policy* 101 (Winter 1995–96): 116–129.

———. *The New Tug-of-War: Congress, the Executive Branch, and National Security.* Washington, DC: A Carnegie Endowment Book, 1995.

Russett, Bruce. "The Americans' Retreat from World Power." *Political Science Quarterly* 90 (Spring 1975): 1–22.

———. "Defense Expenditures and National Well-being." *American Political Science Review* 76 (December 1982): 767–777.

———. *Grasping the Democratic Peace: Principles for a Post–Cold War World.* Princeton, NJ: Princeton University Press, 1993.

———. *The Prisoners of Insecurity.* San Francisco: W. H. Freeman and Company, 1983.

———, and Donald R. Deluca. "'Don't Tread on Me': Public Opinion and Foreign Policy in the Eighties." *Political Science Quarterly* 96 (Fall 1981): 381–399.

———, and Elizabeth C. Hanson. *Interest and Ideology: The Foreign Policy Beliefs of American Businessmen.* San Francisco: W. H. Freeman, 1975.

Sagan, Scott. *The Limits of Safety: Organizations, Accidents, and Nuclear Weapons.* Princeton, NJ: Princeton University Press, 1993.

Said, Abdul Aziz. *Ethnicity and U.S. Foreign Policy.* Rev. ed. New York: Praeger, 1981.

Salisbury, Harrison E. *War Between China and Russia.* New York: W. W. Norton & Company, Inc., 1969.

Schlesinger, Arthur, Jr. "Congress and the Making of American Foreign Policy." *Foreign Affairs* 51 (October 1972): 78–113.

———. "Foreign Policy and the American Character." *Foreign Affairs* 62 (Fall 1983): 1–16.

———. "Human Rights and the American Tradition." *Foreign Affairs* 57 (Winter 1978/1979): 503–526.

———. *The Imperial Presidency.* Boston: Houghton Mifflin Company, 1973.

Schlesinger, James. "The Role of the Secretary of Defense." In *Reorganizing America's Defense: Leadership in War and Peace,* Robert J. Art, Vincent Davis, and Samuel P. Huntington, eds. Washington, DC: Pergamon-Brassey's, 1985.

Schoultz, Lars. "Politics, Economics, and U.S. Participation in Multilateral Development Banks." *International Organization* 36 (Summer 1982): 537–574.

Scott, Andrew M. "The Department of State: Formal Organization and Informal Culture." *International Studies Quarterly* 13 (March 1969): 1–18.

———. "The Problem of the State Department." *In Problems of American Foreign Policy.* 2nd ed., Martin B. Hickman, ed. Beverly Hills: Glencoe Press, 1975.

Scott, Len, and Steve Smith. "Political Scientists, Policy-Makers, and the Cuban Missile Crisis." *International Affairs* 70 (October 1994): 659–684.

Scudder, Evarts Seelye. *The Monroe Doctrine and World Peace.* Port Washington, NY: Kennikat Press, 1972.

Search for Peace in the Middle East. Rev. ed. Greenwich, CT: Fawcett Publications, Inc., 1970.

Sewell, John W. *The United States and World Development Agenda 1980.* New York: Praeger, 1980.

———, and John A. Mathieson. "North-South Relations." In *Setting National Priorities Agenda for the 1980s,* Joseph A. Pechman, ed. Washington, DC: The Brookings Institution, 1980.

Shapiro, Robert Y., and Benjamin I. Page. "Foreign Policy and the Rational Public." *Journal of Conflict Resolution* 32 (June 1988): 211–247.

———. "Foreign Policy and Public Opinion." In *The New Politics of American Foreign Policy,* David A Deese, ed. New York: St. Martin's Press, 1994.

Shull, Steven A., ed. *The Two Presidencies: A Quarter Century Assessment.* Chicago: Nelson/Hall Publishers, 1991.

Sigelman, Lee. "A Reassessment of the Two Presidencies Thesis." *The Journal of Politics* 41 (November 1979): 1195–1205.

Sigler, John H. "Descent From Olympus: The Search for a New Consensus." *International Journal* 38 (Winter 1982–83): 18–38.

Sigmund, Paul E. "Latin America: Change or Continuity?" In *America and the World 1981,* William P. Bundy, ed. New York: Pergamon Press, 1982.

Silverstein, Gordon. *Imbalance of Powers: Constitutional Interpretation and the Making of American Foreign Policy.* New York: Oxford University Press, 1997.

———. "Judicial Enhancement of Executive Power." In *The President, The Congress, and the Making of Foreign Policy,* Paul E. Peterson, ed. Norman and London: University of Oklahoma Press, 1994.

Smith, Hedrick. *The Media and the Gulf War.* Washington, DC: Seven Locks, 1992.

———. *The Power Game: How Washington Works.* New York: Ballantine Books, 1988.

Smith, Jean Edward. *The Constitution and American Foreign Policy.* St. Paul, MN: West Publishing Company, 1989.

Smith, Tom W. "The Polls: America's Most Important Problems, Part I: National and International." *Public Opinion Quarterly* 49 (Summer 1985): 264–274.

Snider, Don M., and Miranda A. Carlton-Carew, eds. *U.S. Civil-Military Relations: In Crisis or Transitions?* Washington, DC: The Center for Strategic & International Studies, 1995.

Sobel, Richard. "Public Opinion About United States Intervention in El Salvador and Nicaragua." *Public Opinion Quarterly* 53 (Spring 1989): 114–128.

———, ed. *Public Opinion in U.S. Foreign Policy.* Lanham, MD: Rowman and Littlefield Publishers, Inc., 1993.

Solo, Pam. *From Protest to Policy: The Origins and Future of the Freeze Movement.* Cambridge, MA: Ballinger Publishing, 1988.

Spanier, John. *American Foreign Policy Since World War II.* 9th ed. New York: Holt, Rinehart and Winston, 1982.

———. *The Truman-MacArthur Controversy and the Korean War.* New York: W. W. Norton & Company, 1965.

———, and Eric M. Uslaner. *American Foreign Policy Making and the Democratic Dilemmas.* 5th ed. New York: Holt, Rinehart and Winston, 1989.

Spero, Joan Edelman. *The Politics of International Economic Relations.* 2nd ed. New York: St. Martin's Press, 1981.

Steinbrunner, John D. "Nuclear Decapitation." *Foreign Policy* 45 (Winter 1981–82): 16–28.

Stilman, Edmund, and William Pfaff. *Power and Impotence: Tire Failure of America's Foreign Policy.* New York: Vintage Books, 1966.

Stockton, Paul. "Beyond Micromanagement: Congressional Budgeting for a Post–Cold War Military." *Political Science Quarterly* 110 (Summer 1995): 233–259.

———. "Congress and U.S. Military Policy Beyond the Cold War." In *Congress Resurgent: Foreign and Defense Policy on Capitol Hill,* Randall B. Ripley and James M. Lindsay, eds. Ann Arbor: The University of Michigan Press, 1993.

Stoessinger, John G. *Crusaders and Pragmatists.* 2nd ed. New York: W. W. Norton & Company, 1985.

———. *Henry Kissinger: The Anguish of Power.* New York: W. W. Norton & Company, Inc., 1976.

———. *Nations in Darkness: China, Russia, and America.* 3rd ed. New York: Random House, 1978.

———. *Why Nations Go To War.* 5th ed. New York: St. Martin's Press, 1990.

Story, Dale. "Trade Politics in the Third World: A Case Study of the Mexican GATT Decision." *International Organization* 36 (Autumn 1982): 767–794.

Stubbing, Richard A. with Richard A. Mendel. *The Defense Game: An Insider Explores the Astonishing Realities of America's Defense Establishment.* New York: Harper & Row, 1986.

Sundquist, James L. *The Decline and Resurgence of Congress.* Washington, DC: The Brookings Institution, 1981.

Talbott, Strobe. "Buildup and Breakdown." In *America and the World 1983*, William P. Bundy, ed. New York: Pergamon Press, 1984.

———. *Deadly Gambits: the Reagan Administration and the Stalemate in Nuclear Arms Control.* New York: Vintage Books, 1985.

Tananbaum, Duane. *The Bricker Amendment Controversy: A Test of Eisenhower's Political Leadership.* Ithaca and London: Cornell University Press, 1988.

Terhune, Kenneth W. "From National Character to National Behavior: A Reformulation." *Journal of Conflict Resolution* 14 (June 1970): 203–264.

Tower, John G. "Congress Versus the President: The Formulation and Implementation of American Foreign Policy." *Foreign Affairs* 60 (Winter 1981/82): 229–246.

Treverton, Gregory F. "Intelligence: Welcome to the American Government." In *A Question of Balance,* Thoman E. Mann, ed. Washington, DC: The Brookings Institution, 1990.

Trice, Robert H. "Congress and the Arab-Israeli Conflict: Support for Israel in the U.S. Senate, 1970–1973." *Political Science Quarterly* 92 (Fall 1977): 443–463.

———. "Domestic Interest Groups and the Arab-Israeli Conflict: A Behavioral Analysis." In *Ethnicity and U.S. Foreign Policy.* Rev. ed., Abdul Aziz Said, ed. New York: Praeger, 1981.

Trout, B. Thomas. "Rhetoric Revisited: Political Legitimation and the Cold War." *International Studies Quarterly* 19 (September 1975): 251–284.

Truman, Harry S. *Year of Decision.* New York: Doubleday & Co., Inc., 1955.

Tucker, Robert. "America in Decline: The Foreign Policy of 'Maturity.'" In *America and the World 1979,* William P. Bundy, ed. New York: Pergamon Press, 1980.

———, and David C. Hendrickson. "Thomas Jefferson and American Foreign Policy." *Foreign Affairs* 69 (Spring 1990): 135–156.

Turner, Stansfield. *Secrecy and Democracy: The CIA in Transition.* Boston: Houghton Mifflin Company, 1985.

United States Department of State. *State 2000: A New Model for Managing Foreign Affairs.* Washington, DC: U.S. Department of State, January 1993.

Uslaner, Eric. "All Politics Are Global: Interest Groups and the Making of Foreign Policy." In *Interest Group Politics.* Allan J. Cigler and Burdett A. Loomis, eds. Washington, DC: CQ Press, 1995.

Varg, Paul A. *Foreign Policies of the Founding Fathers.* East Lansing: Michigan State University, 1963.

Viguerie, Richard A. *The New Right: We're Ready to Lead.* Falls Church, VA: The Viguerie Company, 1981.

Waller, Douglas C. *Congress and the Nuclear Freeze: An Inside Look at the Politics of a Mass Movement.* Amherst: University of Massachusetts Press, 1987.

Walters, Robert W. "African-American Influence on U.S. Foreign Policy Toward South Africa." In *Ethnic Groups and U.S. Foreign Policy,* Mohammed E. Ahrari, ed. New York: Greenwood Press, 1987.

The Washington Lobby. 4th ed. Washington, DC: Congressional Quarterly, Inc., 1982.

Weiner, Tim, David Johnston, and Neil A. Lewis. *Betrayal: The Story of Aldrich Ames, An American Spy.* New York: Random House, 1995.

Westphal, Albert C. V. *The House Committee on Foreign Affairs.* New York: Columbia University Press, 1942.

Whalen, Charles W., Jr. *The House and Foreign Policy: The Irony of Congressional Reform.* Chapel Hill: The University of North Carolina Press, 1982.

Whiting, Allen S. *China Crosses the Yalu.* Stanford, CA: Stanford University Press, 1960.

Wiarda, Howard J. *Foreign Policy Without Illusion.* Glenview, IL: Scott, Foresman/Little, Brown Higher Education, 1990.

Wildavsky, Aaron. "The Two Presidencies." *Trans-action* 3 (December 1966): 7–14.

Willetts, Peter. *The Non-Aligned Movement: The Origins of a Third World Alliance.* London: Frances Pinter, Ltd. 1979.

Willrich, Mason, and John B. Rhinelander, eds. SALT: *The Moscow Agreements and Beyond.* New York: The Free Press, 1974.

Windsor, Philip. "America's Moral Confusions: Separating the Should from the Good." *Foreign Policy* 13 (Winter 1973–74): 139–153.

Winham, Gilbert. "Developing Theories of Foreign Policy Making: A Case Study for Foreign Aid." *The Journal of Politics* 32 (February 1970): 41–70.

Wise, David. *Nightmover: How Aldrich Ames Sold the CIA to the KGB for $4.6 Million.* New York: HarperCollins, 1995.

Wiseman, Henry, and Alastair M. Taylor. *From Rhodesia to Zimbabwe: The Politics of Transition.* New York: Pergamon Press, 1981.

Wittkopf, Eugene R. "Elites and Masses: Constancy and Change in Public Attitudes Toward America's World Role." Paper delivered at the Annual Meeting of the Southern Political Science Association, Birmingham, Alabama, November 3–5, 1983.

———. *Faces of Internationalism: Public Opinion and American Foreign Policy.* Durham, NC: Duke University Press, 1990.

———. "Faces of Internationalism in a Transitional Environment." *Journal of Conflict Resolution* 38 (September 1994): 376–401.

———. "Public Attitudes Toward American Foreign Policy in the Post-Vietnam Decade." Paper delivered at the Annual Meeting of the International Studies Association, March 27–31, 1984.

———. "What Americans Really Think About Foreign Policy." *The Washington Quarterly* 19 (Summer 1996): 91–106.

———, and Michael A Maggiotto. "Elites and Masses. A Comparative Analysis of Attitudes Toward America's World Role." *The Journal of Politics* 45 (May 1983): 303–334.

———, and James M. McCormick. "The Cold War Consensus: Did It Exist?" *Polity* 22 (Summer 1990): 627–653.

———. "The Domestic Politics of Contra Aid: Pubic Opinion, Congress, and the President." In *Public Opinion in U.S. Foreign Policy: The Controversy over Contra Aid,* Richard Sobel, ed. Lanham, MD: Rowman and Littlefield Publishers, Inc., 1993.

Woodward, Bob. *Veil: The Secret Wars of the CIA, 1981*–1987. New York: Pocket Books, 1987.

Wormuth, Francis D. "Presidential Wars: The Convenience of 'Precedent.'" In *Problems of American Foreign Policy.* 2nd ed., Martin B. Hickman, ed. Beverly Hills: Glencoe Press, 1975.

Yankelovich, Daniel. "Farewell to 'President Knows Best.'" In *America and the World 1978,* William P. Bundy, ed. New York: Pergamon Press, 1979.

Yarmolinsky, Adam. *The Military Establishment: Its Impact on American Society.* New York: Harper and Row, 1971.

Yergin, Daniel. *Shattered Peace. The Origins of the Cold War and the National Security State.* Boston: Houghton Mifflin Company, 1977.

Zagoria, Donald S. *The Sino-Soviet Conflict 1956*–1961. Princeton, NJ: Princeton University Press, 1962.

Zelikow, Philip D. "The United States and the Use of Force: A Historical Summary." In *Democracy, Strategy, and Vietnam,* George K. Osborn, Asa A. Clark IV, Daniel J. Kaufman, and Douglas E. Lute, eds. Lexington, MA: D. C. Heath and Company, 1987.

Ziegler, L. Harmon, and G. Wayne Peak. *Interest Groups in American Society.* 2nd ed. Englewood Cliffs, NJ: Prentice-Hall, Inc., 1972.

NAME INDEX

SUBJECT INDEX

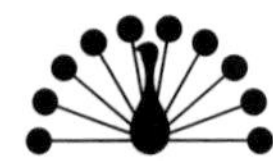

AMERICAN FOREIGN POLICY AND PROCESS
Third Edition
Edited by John Beasley
Picture research by Cheryl Kucharzak
Production supervision by Kim Vander Steen
Designed by Jeanne Calabrese Design, River Forest, Illinois
Composition by Point West, Inc., Carol Stream, Illinois
Paper, Finch Opaque
Printed and bound by Quebecor Printing, Kingsport, Tennessee